T0181520

Lecture Notes in Computer Science 12940

More information about this subseries at http://www.springer.com/series/7412

Ignacio Rojas · Daniel Castillo-Secilla ·
Luis Javier Herrera · Héctor Pomares (Eds.)

Bioengineering and Biomedical Signal and Image Processing

First International Conference, BIOMESIP 2021
Meloneras, Gran Canaria, Spain, July 19–21, 2021
Proceedings

 Springer

Editors
Ignacio Rojas (iD)
University of Granada
Granada, Spain

Daniel Castillo-Secilla (iD)
University of Granada
Granada, Spain

Luis Javier Herrera (iD)
University of Granada
Granada, Spain

Héctor Pomares (iD)
Universidad de Granada
Granada, Granada, Spain

ISSN 0302-9743   ISSN 1611-3349   (electronic)
Lecture Notes in Computer Science
ISBN 978-3-030-88162-7   ISBN 978-3-030-88163-4   (eBook)
https://doi.org/10.1007/978-3-030-88163-4

LNCS Sublibrary: SL6 – Image Processing, Computer Vision, Pattern Recognition, and Graphics

This Springer imprint is published by the registered company Springer Nature Switzerland AG
The registered company address is: Gewerbestrasse 11, 6330 Cham, Switzerland

Preface

We are proud to present the set of final accepted and selected papers for the first edition of the International Conference on Bioengineering, Biomedical Signal, and Image Processing (BIOMESIP), held during July 19–21, 2021 in Gran Canaria (Spain). The conference was organized by the University of Granada (https://biomesip.ugr.es/).

This edition of BIOMESIP, due to the state and situation of the COVID-19 pandemic, took place as a hybrid conference, where there were face-to-face presentations and online presentations. All the presentations were broadcast using the Zoom platform, so that all the speakers can interact and attend the different sessions.

BIOMESIP aims to bring together leading academic scientists, researchers, and research scholars to exchange and share their experiences and research results on all aspects of biomedical signal and image processing.

The objective of BIOMESIP 2021 was to create a friendly environment that could lead to the establishment or strengthening of scientific collaborations and exchanges among attendees, and therefore BIOMESIP 2021 solicited high-quality original research papers (including significant work-in-progress) on any aspect of biomedicine and biomedical engineering.

In addition, a special session (workshop/satellite conference) was organized in which different aspects, solutions, and technologies applicable to COVID-19 were analyzed.

The proceedings include a selection of the communications presented at the conference.

The list of topics in the Call for Papers for BIOMESIP 2021 were as follows:

1. Medical imaging: computer-aided diagnosis; physics of medical imaging; image processing; biomedical applications in molecular, structural, and functional imaging; computerized medical imaging and graphics; image guided radiation therapy; cardiovascular imaging; 2D/3D/4D imaging trends and techniques; and neuroimaging.
2. Biomedical signals: pattern recognition and machine learning for biosignal data; biomedical device engineering; acquisition and digitization of biosignals; biomedical signal and image filtering; biomedical signal measurement; acquisition and processing; wearable sensors and systems; biometrics; cardiovascular signals; real-time systems; and biosignal-based user interfaces.
3. Biomedicine: biomedical computing; personalized medicine; nanomedicine; medical education; collaborative medicine; biomedical signal analysis; biomedicine in industry and society; and electrotherapy and radiotherapy.
4. Biomedical engineering: computer-assisted surgery; therapeutic engineering; interactive 3D modeling; clinical engineering; telemedicine; biosensors and data acquisition; patient monitoring; biomedical robotics; bionanotechnology; and genetic engineering.

5. Healthcare and diseases: computational support for clinical decisions; image visualization and signal analysis; disease control and diagnosis; genome-phenome analysis; biomarker identification; drug design; and computational immunology.

6. E-health: technology and devices; information processing; telemedicine/e-health applications and services; medical Image processing; video techniques for medical images; integration of traditional medicine and e-health; and sport and biomedical sciences.

7. COVID-19: a special session analyzing different aspects, fields of application, and technologies for addressing COVID-19.

At the end of the submission process, and after a careful peer review and evaluation process (each submission was reviewed by at least 2, and on average 3.1, Program Committee members or additional reviewers), 46 contributions were accepted for publication in LNCS, according to the reviewers' recommendations.

In this edition of BIOMESIP 2021, we were honored to have the presence of the following invited speakers:

- Sivaramakrishnan Siva Rajaraman, National Library of Medicine, National Institutes of Health, Maryland, USA.
- Min Xu, Carnegie Mellon University, USA.
- Hamidreza Namazi, Monash University, Australia.
- Lucia Billeci, University of Pisa, Italy.
- Indrani Roy, University College London, UK.

It is important to note that, for the sake of consistency and readability of the book, the papers are not organized as they were presented in the BIOMESIP 2021 sessions but instead classified under twelve chapters (basically following the topics list included in the Call for Papers):

1. Biomedical Applications in Molecular, Structural, and Functional Imaging
2. Biomedical Computing
3. Biomedical Signal Measurement, Acquisition, and Processing
4. Computerized Medical Imaging and Graphics
5. Disease Control and Diagnosis
6. Neuroimaging
7. Pattern Recognition and Machine Learning for Biosignal Data
8. Personalized Medicine
9. COVID-19. Clinical
10. COVID-19. Disease
11. COVID-19. General
12. COVID-19. Health

We would like to express our gratitude to the members of the different committees for their support, collaboration, and good work. We specially thank our Program Committee, the Technical Assistant Committee, the reviewers, and the invited speakers. Finally, we want to thank Springer, and especially Ronan Nugent and Anna Kramer, for their continuous support and cooperation.

August 2021

Ignacio Rojas
Daniel Castillo
Luis Javier Herrera
Héctor Pomares

Organization

General Chairs

Ignacio Rojas
Daniel Castillo
Luis Javier Herrera
Hector Pomares

Technical Assistant Committee

Francisco Carrillo-Perez
Juan Carlos Morales
Olga Valenzuela
Oresti Banos
Fernando Rojas

Program Committee

Amir Abdoli	Jahrom University of Medical Sciences, Iran
Pranav Ajmera	Dr. D. Y. Patil Medical College, Hospital and Research Center, India
Mehmet Aksahin	Baskent University, Turkey
Raul Alcaraz Martínez	University of Castilla-La Mancha, Spain
Turki Alotaiby	King Abdulaziz City for Science and Technology, Saudi Arabia
Ali Mohammad Alqudah	Yarmouk University, Jordan
Lee Alvin	University College London, UK
Amine Amyar	Harvard Medical School - Beth Israel Deaconess Medical Center, USA
Theodoros Arvanitis	University of Warwick, UK
Oleg Aslanidi	King's College London, UK
Nilesh Bahadure	Sanjay Ghodawat University, India
Dragana Bajic	University of Novi Sad, Serbia
Michela Balconi	Catholic University of Milan, Italy
Fabio Baselice	Università Parthenope, Italy
Giuseppe Baselli	Politecnico di Milano, Italy
Vladimir Bashkirov	Loma Linda University, USA
Lucia Billeci	Institute of Clinical Physiology, National Research Council of Italy (IFC-CNR), Italy
Katarzyna Blinowska	University of Warsaw, Poland
Larbi Boubchir	University of Paris 8, France

Contents

Computerized Medical Imaging and Graphics

Disease Control and Diagnosis

Neuroimaging

Pattern Recognition and Machine Learning for Biosignal Data

Personalized Medicine

COVID-19. Disease

COVID-19. General

COVID-19. Health

Short Papers

Biomedical Applications in Molecular, Structural, and Functional Imaging

Image Motion Correction of GATE Simulation in Dedicated PET Scanner with Open Geometry

Héctor Espinós-Morató[1]($^{(\boxtimes)}$) (iD), David Cascales-Picó[1] (iD), Marina Vergara[1,2] (iD), and María José Rodríguez-Álvarez[1] (iD)

[1] Instituto de Instrumentación para Imagen Molecular (i3M), Universitat Politècnica de València (UPV) - Consejo Superior de Investigaciones Científicas (CSIC), 46022 Valencia, Spain
{hespinos,dcaspic}@i3m.upv.es
[2] Department of Imaging and Pathology, Division of Nuclear Medicine, KU Leuven, 3000 Leuven, Belgium

Abstract. Positron Emission Tomography (PET) images are considerably degraded by respiratory and involuntary motions of the patient inside the scanner, having a direct effect in a misdiagnosis. In this paper, a dedicated PET scanner with an open geometry is proposed. This PET configuration poses several challenges to image reconstruction, such as limited angles, motion correction and the sensitivity correction problem. The paper presents a GATE simulation study of image motion correction using XCAT phantom using a multi-frame algorithm called Enhance Multiple Acquisition Frames (EMAF) to correct rigid body and respiratory motion with list-mode data using time of flight (TOF) information and patient motion. This approach is implemented in three phases: frames cutting, image reconstruction and finally image registration. Additionally, the information provided by the TOF is used to improve the reconstruction due to the lack of angular information provided by the proposed open geometry system. Two performance tests are applied to validate the results, obtaining a remarkable resolution improvement after being processed. The peak signal noise ratio (PSNR) values for the corrected and uncorrected images are, respectively, 30 versus 28 dB, and for the image matching precision (IMP), 89% versus 78%. The obtained results show that the method improves the signal intensity over the background in comparison with other literature methods, maximizing the similarity between the ground-truth (static) image and the corrected image and minimizing the intra-frame motion.

Supported by the Spanish Government Grants TEC2016-79884-C2, PID2019-107790RB-C22, and PEJ2018-002230-A-AR; the Generalitat Valenciana GJIDI/2018/A/040l and the PTA2019-017113-1/AEI/10.13039/501100011033; the European Union through the European Regional Development Fund (ERDF); and the European Research Council (ERC) under the European Union's Horizon 2020 research and innovation program (Grant Agreement No. 695536).

I. Rojas et al. (Eds.): BIOMESIP 2021, LNCS 12940, pp. 3–12, 2021.
https://doi.org/10.1007/978-3-030-88163-4_1

Keywords: Frame-based algorithm · Time of flight · Respiratory motion correction · Non-rigid motion correction · GATE simulation · XCAT phantom · Spatio-temporal registration.

1   Introduction

Organ-dedicated PET systems [1] present some advantages in comparison with conventional or Whole-Body (WB) scanners, i.e., a better spatial resolution and contrast recovery, a higher sensitivity by placing the detectors closer to the organs and a lower cost. The doses of radio-tracer agents injected to the patient is reduced, this makes possible to minimize the radiation exposure, one critical aspect associated to Nuclear Medicine (NM).

In addition, PET scanner explorations tend to put stress on patients (especially those suffering from claustrophobia) [2], who must remain still during the entire scanning process. For these reasons, a dedicated specific open system with modular and optimized geometry that maximizes the angular coverage of the dedicated organ is highly desirable.

Some example of this type of system can be found, e.g. ClearPEM PET [3] or MAMMI PET [4] for breast cancer or ProsPET for prostate cancer [5]; yet, not very common. In this work we present an open PET geometry configuration for an organ-dedicated, where the patient has freedom of movement.

A motion correction strategy based in a framing method present some advantages when compared to other methods. Specifically, joint reconstruction and system matrix modelling present a high computational load in comparison to that of the frame-based methods. In other cases, the system matrix is not available, and the model cannot be applied. Lastly, event rebinning does not allow us to have non-deformable motions such as heartbeat or breathing.

However, despite frame-based motion correction methods presenting a considerable amount of advantages, they also have deficiencies. One of them is the presence of noise in the reconstructed images when motion occurs inside the time duration of a given frame (intra-frame motion). Another example is the image degradation as a consequence of low count statistics that some of the frames can present when the motion is sudden. These deficiencies can affect the clinical practice, where it is necessary to have frames with high statistics and low noise to improve lesion detectability.

In order to overcome the greatest deficiencies of the frame-based algorithms, a novel frame-based motion correction algorithm is proposed in this study. This method is called EMAF (enhanced multiple acquisition frames). The main differences from the original MAF algorithm (multiple acquisition frames developed by Piccard [13]) is that EMAF use of an adaptive threshold in order to divide the original dataset in frames when some prior knowledge of the size of the lesion is present, allowing one to reduce the dose administered to the patient while providing a good, motion-free estimation. It also allows for grouping motions that share similar features under the same frame, thereby increasing the statistics on each frame and reducing the intra-frame motion artefacts. Once the frames are defined, multilevel spatio-temporal registration is performed to ensure a good signal-to-noise ratio.

To summarize, the proposed open PET system poses several challenges to image reconstruction, including (1) a limited angle problem, (2) a motion correction problem, and (3) a sensitivity correction problem.

The paper presents a reconstruction and registration framework to correct rigid and respiratory motion by respiratory gating in list-mode data using time of flight (TOF) information based on a multi-frame algorithm approach based on EMAF algorithm.

2   Materials and Methods

2.1   PET System and GATE Simulation

The PET system was designed [6] with a modular geometry consisting of two panels of 32 × 530 × 353 millimetres with 180 centimetres of separation between them (see Fig. 1). Each panel was formed by 24 modules of 64 LYSO crystals. In order to cover enough angular information, the panels rotates 90 degrees in the longitudinal axis every 5 s.

A 20 s simulation was performed in GATE [7–9] with the XCAT voxelized image [10]. GATE simulation was done with back-to-back gamma particles using a 5 nanoseconds of coincidence window, 10% of blurring resolution and an 350–650 keV energy window.

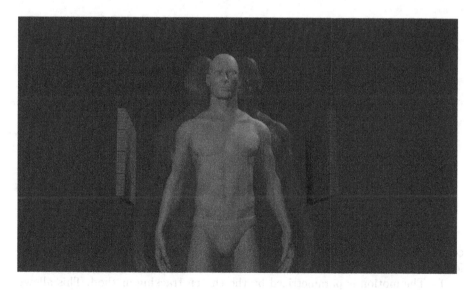

Fig. 1. PET system and a representation of the simulated motion

2.2   XCAT Phantom

XCAT phantom [10] was used to simulate a ^{18}F-FGD scan of a total-body of 1.75 m of height with 1.2 Bq/mm^3 organs activities concentration. The torso region was cropped afterwards. A lung lesion of 20 millimetres diameter was inserted in the upper lobe of the left lung. The proportion between the lesion to lung contrast was set 4.5:1.

2.3   EMAF Algorithm

Respiratory motion [11] was simulated with a magnitude of 12 millimetres in the anterior-posterior direction and 20 millimetres in the superior-inferior direction. Four cycles of five seconds were reproduced. Additionally, a oscillatory rigid torso-motion in the lateral axis (X) was simulated with the equation $x = A sin(2\pi f t)$ with amplitude (A) of 10 centimetres, and frequency (f) of 0.2 Hz (see Fig. 1).

The presented EMAF algorithm [12] (shown in Fig. 2) is an improved modification based on Picard's original Multiple Acquisition Frames (MAF) Algorithm [13] in order to overcome their most important limitations, such a prefixed number of frames and a short frames with low statistics.

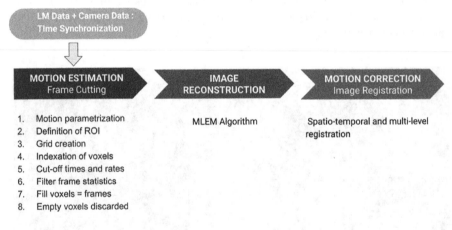

Fig. 2. Proposed algorithm workflow

This method described in detail in [14] consists of three phases. First, the coincidence data given by the PET scanner are divided into different frames following the next steps:

1.- The motion is parametrized by the chosen tracking method. This allows have a 3D motion parametrization in the three directions and angles.

2.- Starting from the previous step, a region of interest (ROI) around the source is defined. This region needs to be wide enough to fit any position recorded by the tracking method. This region will be the grid T.

3.- The ROI is rebinned into an equidistributed and equispaced grid in which the size of each bin (what it defines as voxel) is a free parameter.

4.- Each of the voxels that make up the grid is numbered with an index associated with a certain position in the 3D space. The source motion each moment is stored. This is achieved through two parameters, the time in which the source travels from one voxel to another (called cut-off time) and the index of the voxel (cut-off rates).

5.- In order to apply a time filter, the total time that the source spends in each voxel is calculated. These steps are only followed for those voxels with a total time higher than half the average total voxel time. In this way, using voxels with small statistics that can add noise to the final image is avoided.

6.- For every voxel that passes the aforementioned filter, a new list-mode file is created using the cut-off time and cut-off rate. Once the process has finished, voxels that are completely empty in the grid are discarded.

Coming up next (in the second part of the algorithm), each of those frames are reconstructed separately, and, finally, an spatio-temporal image registration method is performed to align and register the frames into the final reconstructed image.

The approach exposed has two clear advantages: (1) it allows one to group in the same frame motions occurring in the same spatial region, which increases the statistical information; (2) it does not need to prefix a priori the number of possible frames, which allows one to obtain a greater or lesser accuracy depending on the other voxel size of implementation being used.

2.4   Parameter Settings

Once the experimental design carried out has been shown and the steps that make up the movement correction algorithm have been explained, the parameters used in the experimental setting are detailed below.

The algorithm applied for the reconstruction was an iterative Maximum Likelihood expectation maximization [15] with ordered subsets (MLEM-OS).

All the images had a size of $256 \times 256 \times 120$ with pixel size of 1 mm. Five iterations with three subsets were employed for the reconstruction and no corrections were applied.

The motion correction registration EMAF step is a purpose- built subroutine written in C++ and based on the Insight Toolkit (ITK) architecture [16,17]. Spatio-temporal B-spline is applied in a multilevel registration [18], we used a mean square difference (MSD) as the cost function.

The cost function was minimized using gradient descent with 0.01 mm spatial resolution. The optimization is stopped when either a minimal incremental improvement of 0.05 root mean square error (RMSE) value in the cost function is achieved or upon completing 500 rigid iterations plus 300 affine iterations it has been realized (early stop criterion).

One of the points that is taken into account in the development of the registration part is the problem of tissue compression and the partial volume effect (PVE) since they lead to intensity modulations at the same points (pixels) of different reconstructed frames. This effect is usually more visible in thin structures.

In order to avoid image defects caused by intensity variation, we consider the mass preservation property of PET images.

We justify this, taking into account that, when the data are divided into frames, all of them are formed in the same time interval, that is, the entire acquisition time. In other words, in any frame, it is assumed that no radioactivity can be lost or added, apart from some minor changes to the edges of the field of view. For mass preservation, the variational algorithm for mass-preserving image registration (VAMPIRE) algorithm is used [19–23].

Finally, optimization of the multilevel registration algorithm is incorporated. Of first, the algorithm tries to solve discrete optimization at a very coarse level (with a small number of unknowns).

At the time, the approximation transformation is interpolated to the next finer level and used as an initial estimate for minimization of the next objective function.

The procedure is repeated until the transformation is of the desired resolution (user-selected threshold). Consequently, multiple versions of the original images are constructed by iterative downsampling and smoothing of the data.

This procedural scheme has several advantages. First, the likelihood of ending in a local minimum is reduced, as only the main characteristics are taken into account at a certain level. Second, numeric methods, such as that of Gauss–Newton, converge faster for an initial estimate close to the minimum. Third, solving the problems on the coarse grid is computationally more efficient, and, in most cases, only small corrections are required at finer levels.

2.5   Performance Metrics

To validate our corrections two quantitative metrics were used. On the one hand, the Peak Signal to Noise Ratio (PSNR) measured the power of corrupting noise that affects the fidelity of an image representation. Higher values represent a high- quality image.

On the other hand, an Intensity Matching Precision (IMP) test was applied. It measured how deviated the intensities of the moving and fixed images are. A higher IMP value implied a better image matching.

The two metrics have the following expressions:

$$PSNR_{X,F} = 20 log_{10} \left(\frac{f_{peak}}{RMSE_{X,F}} \right) \tag{1}$$

$$IMP_{X,F} = \left(1 - \frac{RMSE_{X,F}}{\sqrt{E[F^2]}} \right) \tag{2}$$

where X, F are the moving and fixed images respectively. f_{peak} is the maximum pixel value in the fixed image, and $E[F^2] = \frac{1}{2} \sum_{i=1}^{n} f_i^2$, is the second moment of the fixed image intensity distribution.

3   Results and Discussion

It is proposed a motion correction method of respiratory- gated PET images together with a non-limited patient motion in an open geometry PET system. The experimental results show that spatio-temporal registration has the potential to yield an accurate motion artefacts reduction.

Figure 3 clearly shows that the motion corrected image displays a higher spatial resolution than the uncorrected one. The uncorrected image appears totally blurred, while the lung lesion is conserved in the corrected image. Slight blurring defects were unavoidably found in the image due to lack of lateral information described to the design of our PET system.

The image quality is substantially improved after motion correction using our algorithm, compared to the uncorrected image. The values of PSNR were 30 dB versus 28 dB between static-corrected and static-uncorrected images respectively. The IMP test displayed the same behaviour, with 89% versus 78% between static-corrected and static-uncorrected.

Comparing different experimental designs performed by the proposed motion correction algorithm (EMAF) [14] in closed geometry in comparation with an open planar geometry as described in this manuscript, it can conclude that the results for the Cardio-PET system proposed are relatively good. The results of the EMAF algorithm carried out for closed geometry (ring) give us PSNR values between 37–40 dB, while for CardioPET system, the PSNR result is situated at 30 dB.

If it compared the values of the IMP metric, obviously the values obtained with the application of the motion correction algorithm EMAF are slightly higher for a closed PET geometry (about 90% on average) than for open geometry(89%), due in large part to the loss of angular information mentioned above that the planar PET system shown in the manuscript presents.

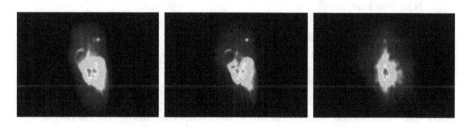

Fig. 3. Reconstruction of the torso-body image (torso with a spherical lesion in the lung). Left to right: static, corrected and uncorrected image. The view is exactly in the same body position of Fig. 1

4   Conclusions

The paper presents a novel motion correction algorithm composed of three phases (motion estimation, image reconstruction, and motion correction). The approach is based on image registration and frame acquisition of the data. Firstly, the list-mode data obtained from the scanner were sorted into quasi-static frames through a method of cutting into frames consisting of several steps (Fig. 2).

Secondly, each frame was reconstructed using a built in-house MLEM-OS algorithm. Finally, all of the reconstructed frames were registered in order to obtain a final reconstructed image, taking into account that the registration had to be hyperelastic, nonlinear multilevel and spatio-temporal.

Although the number of frames that EMAF produces is minimal, when large spatial motion ranges are present or the structures under study are very small, it produces a high number of frames, which leads to an increase in the computational load.

Despite this limitation, the EMAF algorithm is a robust enhancement that solves the major problems of the original frame-based algorithm and improves the performance of motion correction in a low-intensity range both in closed and opened PET systems.

5   Acronyms

The following acronyms are used in this manuscript displayed in alphabetical order:

EMAF	Enhanced Multiple Acquisition Frames
IMP	Intensity Matching Precision
MLEM-OS	Maximum Likelihood Expectation Maximization with Ordered Subsets
MSD	Mean Square Difference
MAF	Multiple Acquisition Frames
NM	Nuclear Medicine
PSNR	Peak Signal to Noise Ratio
PET	Positron Emission Tomography
RMSE	Root Mean Square Error
ROI	Region Of Interest
TOF	Time of flight
XCAT	4D Extended Cardiac-Torso Phantom
VAMPIRE	Variational Algorithm for Mass-Preserving Image REgistration
WB	Whole-Body

Acknowledgments. This research has been supported by the Spanish Government Grants TEC2016-79884-C2, PID2019-107790RB-C22, and PEJ2018-002230-A-AR; the Generalitat Valenciana GJIDI/2018/A/040l and the PTA2019-017113-1/AEI/10.13039/501100011033; the European Union through the European Regional Development Fund (ERDF); and the European Research Council (ERC) under the European Union's Horizon 2020 research and innovation program (Grant Agreement No. 695536).

Author contributions. Conceptualization: H.E-M. and M.J.R-Á.; methodology: H.E-M.; software: H.E-M., M.V., and D.C-P.; validation: H.E-M. and D.C-P.; formal analysis: H.E-M., D.C-P., and M.V.; investigation, H.E-M., D.C-P., M.V., and Á.H-M.; resources: H.E-M.; data curation, H.E-M., M.V., and D.C-P.; framing: D.C-P.; reconstruction: M.V.; registration: Á.H-M. and H.E-M.; writing—original draft preparation: H.E-M.; writing—review and editing: D.C-P., M.V., Á.H-M., and M.J.R-Á.; visualization: D.C-P. and H.E-M.; supervision: M.J.R-Á.; project administration: M.J.R-Á.; funding acquisition: M.J.R-Á.; J.M.B.B. All authors have read and agreed to the published version of the manuscript.

References

1. González, A.J., Sánchez, F., Benlloch, J.M.: Organ-dedicated molecular imaging systems. In: IEEE Transactions on Radiation and Plasma Medical Sciences, vol. 2, no. 5, pp. 388–403, September 2018. https://doi.org/10.1109/TRPMS.2018.2846745

2. Vaquero, J.J., Kinahan, P.: Positron emission tomography: current challenges and opportunities for technological advances in clinical and preclinical imaging systems. Ann. Rev. Biomed. Eng. **17**, 385–414 (2015). https://doi.org/10.1146/annurev-bioeng-071114-040723

3. Abreu, M.C., et al.: Design and evaluation of the clear-PEM scanner for positron emission mammography. IEEE Trans. Nucl. Sci. **53**(1), 71–77 (2006). https://doi.org/10.1109/TNS.2006.870173

4. Moliner, L., et al.: Design and evaluation of the MAMMI dedicated breast PET. Med. Phys. **39**(9), 5393–5404 (2012). https://doi.org/10.1118/1.4742850

5. Cañizares, G., Gonzalez-Montoro, A., Freire, M., et al.: Pilot performance of a dedicated prostate PET suitable for diagnosis and biopsy guidance. EJNMMI Phys. **7**, 38 (2020). https://doi.org/10.1186/s40658-020-00305-y

6. Oliver, S., Moliner, L., Ilisie, V., Benlloch, J.M., Rodríguez-Álvarez, M.J.: Simulation study for designing a dedicated cardiac TOF-PET system. Sens. (Basel, Switz.) **20**(5), 1311 (2020). https://doi.org/10.3390/s20051311

7. Jan, S., Santin, G., Strul, D., et al.: GATE: a simulation toolkit for PET and SPECT. Phys. Med. Biol. **49**(19), 4543–4561 (2004). https://doi.org/10.1088/0031-9155/49/19/007

8. Jan, S., Benoit, D., Becheva, E., et al.: GATE V6: a major enhancement of the GATE simulation platform enabling modelling of CT and radiotherapy. Phys. Med. Biol. **56**(4), 881–901 (2011). https://doi.org/10.1088/0031-9155/56/4/001

9. Sarrut, D., Bardiès, M., Boussion, N., et al.: A review of the use and potential of the GATE Monte Carlo simulation code for radiation therapy and dosimetry applications. Med. Phys. **41**(6), 064301 (2014). https://doi.org/10.1118/1.4871617

10. Segars, W.P., Sturgeon, G., Mendonca, S., Grimes, J., Tsui, B.M.: 4D XCAT phantom for multimodality imaging research. Med. Phys. **37**(9), 4902–4915 (2010). https://doi.org/10.1118/1.3480985

11. Chan, C., et al.: Non-rigid event-by-event continuous respiratory motion compensated list-mode reconstruction for PET. IEEE Trans. Med. Imaging **37**(2), 504–515 (2018). https://doi.org/10.1109/TMI.2017.2761756

12. Cañizares, G., et al.: Motion correction of multi-frame PET data. IEEE Nuclear Science Symposium and Medical Imaging Conference (NSS/MIC), pp. 1–4 (2019)

13. Picard, Y., Thompson, C.J.: Motion correction of PET images using multiple acqui-sition frames. IEEE Trans. Med. Imaging **16**, 137–144 (1997). https://doi.org/10.1109/NSS/MIC42101.2019.9059930.Picard
14. Espinós-Morató, H., Cascales-Picó, D., Vergara, M., Hernández-Martínez, Á., Ben-lloch Baviera, J.M., Rodríguez-Álvarez, M.J.: Simulation study of a frame-based motion correction algorithm for positron emission imaging. Sensors **21**(8), 2608 (2021). https://doi.org/10.3390/s21082608
15. Shepp, L.A., Vardi, Y.: Maximum likelihood reconstruction for emission tomog-raphy. IEEE Trans. Med. Imaging **1**(2), 113–122 (1982). https://doi.org/10.1109/TMI.1982.4307558
16. McCormick, M., Liu, X., Jomier, J., Marion, C., Ibanez, L.: ITK: enabling repro-ducible research and open science. Front. Neuroinf. **2014**(8), 13 (2002). https://doi.org/10.3389/fninf.2014.00013
17. Yoo, T.S., et al.: Engineering and algorithm design for an image processing API: a technical report on ITK – the insight toolkit. In: Westwood, J. (eds.) Proceedings of Medicine Meets Virtual Reality, pp. 586–592. IOS Press Amsterdam (2002)
18. Bai, W., Brady, S.M.: Spatio-temporal image registration for respiratory motion correction in pet imaging. In: Proceedings of the 2009 IEEE International Sympo-sium on Biomedical Imaging: from Nano to Macro, Boston, MA, USA, 28 June–1 July 2009; ISBI 2009, pp. 426–429. IEEE, New York, (2009)
19. Gigengack, F., Ruthotto, L., Burger, M., Wolters, C.H., Jiang, X., Schafers, K.P.: Motion correction in dual gated cardiac PET using mass-preserving image regis-tration. IEEE Trans. Med. Imaging **31**, 698–712 (2012)
20. Arsigny, V., Fillard, P., Pennec, X., Ayache, N.: Fast and simple calculus on tensors in the log-euclidean framework. In: Duncan, J.S., Gerig, G. (eds.) MICCAI 2005. LNCS, vol. 3749, pp. 115–122. Springer, Heidelberg (2005). https://doi.org/10.1007/11566465_15
21. Neumaier, A.: Solving ill-conditioned and singular linear systems: a tutorial on regularization. SIAM Rev. **40**, 636–666 (1998)
22. Burger, M., Modersitzki, J., Ruthotto, L.: A hyperelastic regularization energy for image registration. SIAM J. Sci. Comput. **35**, B132–B148 (2013)
23. Pennec, X.., Stefanescu, R.., Arsigny, V.., Fillard, P.., Ayache, N..: Riemannian elasticity: a statistical regularization framework for non-linear registration. In: Duncan, J.S., Gerig, G. (eds.) MICCAI 2005. LNCS, vol. 3750, pp. 943–950. Springer, Heidelberg (2005). https://doi.org/10.1007/11566489_116

Optimizing Photoacoustic Tomography: Lymphatic Drainage from the Brain in Pigmented Mice

Balal Mian[1], Vladislav Toronov[1,2(✉)], Xun Zhou[3], and Yeni H. Yucel[1,2,3,4]

[1] Ryerson University, 350 Victoria Street, Toronto, Ontario M5B 2K3, Canada
toronov@ryerson.ca
[2] Institute of Biomedical Engineering, Science and Technology (iBEST), Li Ka-Shing
Knowledge Institute, 7th Floor, LKS 735 209 Victoria Street, Toronto, Ontario M5B 1T8, Canada
[3] Keenan Research Centre for Biomedical Science of St. Michael's Hospital, 30 Bond St,
Toronto, Ontario M5B 1W8, Canada
[4] Ophthalmology and Vision Sciences and Laboratory Medicine and Pathobiology, Temerty
Faculty of Medicine, Medical Sciences Building, University of Toronto, 1 King's College Circle,
Toronto, Ontario M5S 18, Canada

Abstract. We report the development and results of an efficient optoacoustic tomography protocol based on a multispectral photoacoustic imaging system, novel contrast agent, and novel wavelength optimization technique to image the dynamics of the lymphatic drainage from the brain in pigmented mice.

Keywords: Photoacoustic · Multispectral · Contrast agent · Brain · Cerebrospinal fluid

1 Introduction

Although in recent years photoacoustic tomography (PAT) has become one of the standard in-vivo imaging techniques, new applications constantly require further improvements in image spatial and temporal resolution and functional specificity. An important new target for the application of PAT is the lymphatic drainage from the brain, where new details of the anatomy have been discovered only very recently [1]. Recently the lymphatic drainage from the brain has been potentially linked to neurodegenerative diseases, such as Parkinson's disease, Alzheimer's disease, and amyotrophic lateral sclerosis [2]. Also abnormalities in the lymphatic drainage from the brain can be related to glaucoma and the spaceflight-associated neuro-ocular syndrome (SANS). Since lymph dynamics are similar in mouse and man, the factors causing the neurological diseases can be efficiently studied by PAT using a mouse model provided that the resolution and specificity of the tomography are adequate to this fine target. In particular, SANS can be studied using NASA hindlimb unloading rodent model [3], which simulates microgravity by producing a headward CSF shift in animals whose hindlimbs are elevated.

© Springer Nature Switzerland AG 2021
I. Rojas et al. (Eds.): BIOMESIP 2021, LNCS 12940, pp. 13–24, 2021.
https://doi.org/10.1007/978-3-030-88163-4_2

The challenges of PAT imaging of lymphatic drainage in small animals include the need of the high spatial resolution including deep brain and neck regions, high temporal resolution to follow the dynamic processes of lymphatic drainage, transparency of the lymph, and the need to image mice pigmented with melanin. Earlier, the study of lymphatic drainage imaging by multi-wavelength PAT in albino mouse model was approached in [4]. However, many transgenic mouse models used as models of neurological diseases are on pigmented genetic backgrounds [5], and melanin, a particularly strong endogenous optical absorber with variation in distribution, may affect quantification of other endogenous and exogenous optical absorbers with PAT [6]. In order to overcome the above challenges, we use the multispectral optoacoustic tomography (MSOT) together with a novel photoacoustic tracer [7] and a novel wavelength optimization technique [8].

2 Methods

2.1 Animal Model

The study was performed after the institutional Animal Care Committee approval. The study included C57BL6/J (Jackson Laboratory, USA), a mouse strain with melanin pigmentation, a common strain used for transgenic mice [9]. Under general anesthesia animals were wrapped in waterproof plastic foil and placed into the imaging chamber filled with warmed water. Images in the area of the neck lymph nodes were first acquired without any contrast agents, then 5 µL of 1 mM QBB tracer were injected into the cerebrospinal fluid in the brain of the mouse, and next images were acquired 10, 20, 30, 40, 50, 60 and 90 min after the tracer was injected.

2.2 Contrast Agent

A novel hybrid photoacoustic-fluorescent contrast agent was prepared by conjugating albumin with a NIR non-fluorescent dye (QC-1) and a visible spectrum fluorescent dye, a BODIPY derivative [7]. The new hybrid tracer QC-1/BSA/BODIPY (QBB) had a low minimum detectable concentration (2.5 µM), a steep linear range (2.4–54.4 µM; slope 3.39 E-5), and high photostability.

2.3 Photoacoustic Imaging System

Images were acquired using a commercially available MSOT system (MSOT *inVision 128*, iThera Medical GmbH) equipped with a tunable optical parametric oscillator pumped by a 532 nm Nd:YAG laser, which provided the output pulses at the repetitions rate of 10 Hz, maximum pulse energy of 100 mJ, and at the optical wavelengths from 680 nm to 980 nm with 2 nm step. Based on the 10 Hz pulse repetition rate, and 10 frames required to make an averaged image, the image acquisition rate is 1 wavelength per second. Therefore, reducing the number of wavelengths required to separate the tracer from other chromophores directly results in increasing the image acquisition rate. The illumination wavelength selection was performed using the method based on minimizing the condition number of the extinction matrix [8].

2.4 Multispectral Unmixing of Chromophore Distributions

The pixel intensity of a photoacoustic image is proportional to the local optical absorption coefficient of the medium (tissue) $\mu(\lambda)$, which is the function of the optical wavelength λ [10]. On the other hand, according to the Beer-Lambert law, the absorption coefficient linearly depends on the concentrations of the chromophore at the pixel location as

$$\boldsymbol{\mu}(\lambda) = \mathbf{E}(\lambda)\boldsymbol{c}, \tag{1}$$

where $\mu(\lambda)$ is the measured vector of the absorption coefficient corresponding to different wavelengths, c is the vector of the concentrations to be determined, and $E(\lambda)$ is the known matrix of specific absorption (extinction) coefficients of chromophores at different wavelengths. In this study the multispectral unmixing of chrompophores was performed using the linear regression solution of Eq. (1) for the concentrations of oxy- and deoxy- hemoglobin, melanin, and QBB [11]. Since the measured pixel intensity was proportional to the optical absorption coefficient with some unknown constant coefficient, the concentrations of chromophores also could be determined up to this unknown constant factor. Since images were not calibrated, instead of the chromophore concentrations measured in mole/L our PAT method provided the chromophore abundance measured in arbitrary units.

The chromophore maps reconstructed using reduced number of wavelengths were quantitatively compared with the maps obtained using 151 wavelengths based on the peak signal to nose ratio and structural similarity index measure, which were introduced in [12] as the error sensitivity metrics and the structural similarity, respectively, of an image against a reference image. The peak signal to noise ratio (PSNR) measured in dB represents the human perception of image similarity:

$$PSNR = 10Log_{10}\frac{peakvalue^2}{MSE} \tag{2}$$

where *MSE* is the mean square error, *peakvalue* is the maximum possible pixel value of the image. The structural similarity index measure (SSIM) is a measure of the perceived quality calculated as

$$SSIM = \frac{(2\mu_x\mu_y + C_1)(2\sigma_{xy} + C_2)}{(\mu_x^2 + \mu_y^2 + C_1)(\sigma_x^2 + \sigma_y^2 + C_2)}, \tag{3}$$

where μ_x, μ_y, σ_x, σ_y, *and* σ_{xy} are the local means, standard deviations, and cross-covariance for the entire image or a window x, y, C_1 and C_2 are the variables to stabilize the division with weak denominator.

3   Results

Figure 1 shows maps of the chromophore distribution in the neck region obtained by the linear regression analysis using 151 wavelengths within 680–980 nm with 2 nm step, 11 empirical wavelengths, and four optimized wavelengths. The top row maps (a-c) show the distributions of oxy- and deoxyhemoglobin, and QBB. The bottom row maps (d-f) include QBB only. One can see that only four optimized wavelengths provide the chromophore map (c) much more similar to the one obtained using 151 wavelengths (a) than that obtained with 11 empirical wavelengths (b). However, in terms of only QBB mapping both the four wavelength set (f) and the 11- wavelength set (e) provide similar maps to the one obtained using 151 wavelengths (d).

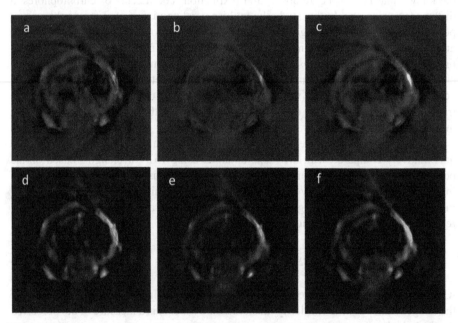

Fig. 1. A comparison of the maps of the chromophore distribution in the neck region obtained using 151 wavelengths within 680–980 nm with 2 nm step (a, d), 11 empirical wavelengths (b, e), and four optimized wavelengths (c, f). Red, blue, yellow, and green colors correspond to oxy-hemoglobin, deoxy-hemoglobin, melanin, and QBB, respectively (Color figure online).

This conclusion is also supported by the quantitative comparison of the chromophore distribution maps. Figure 2 shows PSNR and SSIM values comparing chromophore distribution maps obtained using 11 wavelengths and four wavelengths with the maps obtained using 151 wavelengths. One can see that PSNR values are higher for the 4-wavelength set than for the 11-wavelength set, while SSIM values for both sets are close to 1.

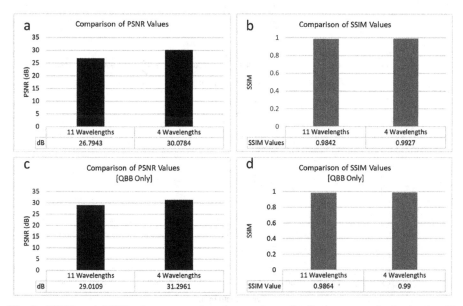

Fig. 2. PSNR and SSIM values comparing chromophore distribution maps obtained using 11 wavelengths and four wavelengths with the maps obtained using 151 wavelengths.

The thick curves in Fig. 3 show the absolute (measured) and differential spectra of the mean pixel intensity in the left and right cervical lymph nodes. The thin curves show the linear regression fits. The linear regression model for the absolute spectra included oxyhemoglobin, deoxyhemoglobin, QBB, and melanin. The differential spectra were obtained by subtracting the absolute spectra. For example, the thick blue curves in Fig. 3(b) were obtained by subtracting the absolute pre-scan spectra from the 20-min spectra in Fig. 3 (a). The linear regression model for the differential spectra included oxyhemoglobin, deoxyhemoglobin, and QBB. Since melanin was a constant chromophore, the melanin term was cancelled by subtraction in the linear regression for the differential spectra.

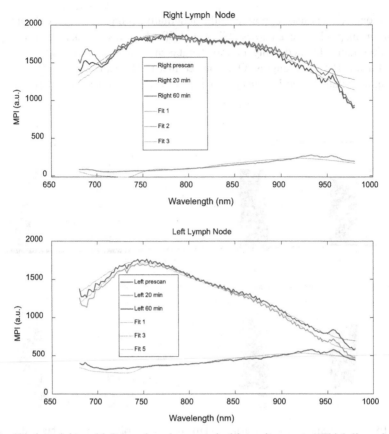

Fig. 3. Absolute right and left lymph node mean pixel intensity spectra: Thick lines show the experimental data and thin lines show the linear regression fitting results.

The values of QBB abundance resulting from the linear regression fittings shown in Figs. 3 and 4 are plotted in Fig. 5 (a) and (b). Figure 5 (c) and (d) show the slopes of the QBB temporal traces at 20 min and 60 min after the tracer injection.

The most accurate QBB traces in Fig. 5 (a) and (b) were the red curves obtained form the linear differential regressions using 151 wavelengths. These traces were most accurate because they were based on a maximum number of wavelengths and minimum number of predictors (chromophores). The large deviation of the blue curve in Fig. 5 (a) from the red curve indicated that the inclusion of melanin into the regression model in some cases resulted in significant errors in the estimation of the QBB amount changes in lymph nodes. In Fig. 5 (c) the large deviation of the blues bars from others indicated that the melanin related error also translated into the estimation of the MPI slopes, which were the main quantitative characteristics of the rate of lymph concentration changes in the nodes.

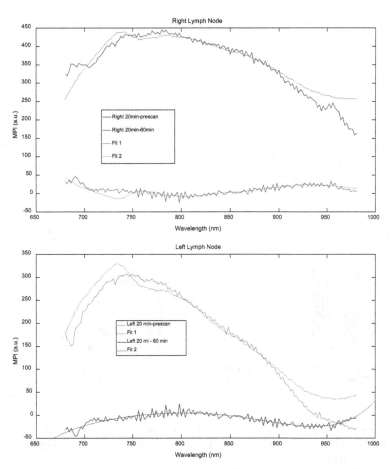

Fig. 4. Differential right and left lymph node mean pixel intensity spectra: Thick lines show the experimental data and thin lines show the linear regression fitting results.

From Fig. 5 one can also see that the 11-wavelength set provided better accuracy of the estimation of the MPI slopes than the 4-wavelength set in terms of the comparison with the values obtained using the differential spectra at 151 wavelengths. Therefore, the temporal tracking of the lymphatic drainage in a larger group of animals was performed using the 11-wavelength set.

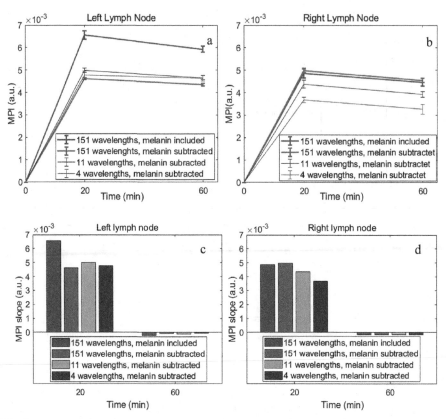

Fig. 5. Temporal changes (top row) and slopes (bottom row) of the QBB abundance in the lymph nodes measured using different wavelength sets and regression models (including or excluding melanin) (Color figure online).

Figure 6 shows the lymph node QBB traces obtained from six C57 mice using the 11-wavelength set. Panels (a) and (b) show the traces obtained using the absolute spectra and the regression model including HHb, HbO2, QBB and melanin; panels (c) and (d) show the traces obtained using the differential data and the regression model including HHb, HbO2, QBB and no melanin. The differential data were obtained by subtracting the MPI spectrum measured at 10 min from the spectra measured at 20 to 90 min. The pre-scan spectra were not used as the position of the animal in the imaging chamber could not be always maintained exactly the same before and after the injection. The slope of the QBB MPI traces in the lymph nodes at each time interval between successive measurements was used as the quantitative characteristics of the rate of lymphatic drainage.

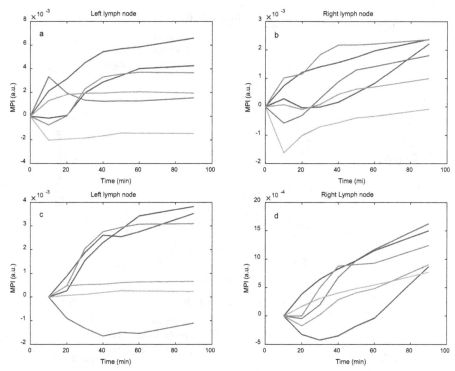

Fig. 6. Lymph node QBB MPI traces in six C57 mice obtained using the 11-wavelength set: (a) and (b) – using the regression model including HHb, HbO2, QBB and melanin; (c) and (d) using the differential regression model including HHb, HbO2, QBB and no melanin. Same curve colors correspond to the same animals. Zero time corresponds to the QBB injection moment.

Figure 7 shows the group average QBB MPI slopes at different intervals between measurements corresponding to the traces shown in Fig. 6, resulting from the absolute spectra and the regression model including melanin and from the differential spectra and the regression model without melanin. Figure 7 also shows the p-value from the paired t-test comparing slope samples resulting from the two data processing methods. In Fig. 7 one can see that the absolute spectra with melanin on average resulted in higher QBB slopes than the more accurate differential spectra without melanin. Although the size of the sample was small (only six animals), the difference between average slopes obtained by two methods was statistically significant ($p < 0.05$) at 30–40 min and 80–90 min for the left lymph node and at 40–50 min for the right node.

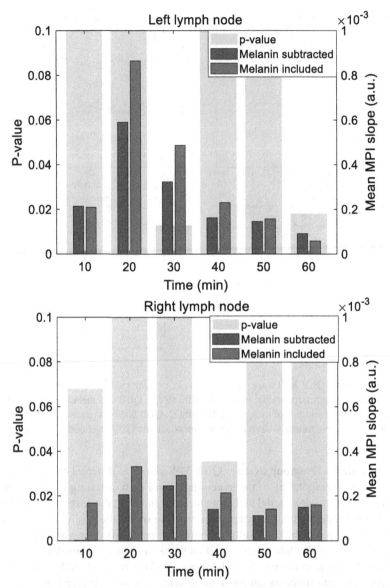

Fig. 7. Comparison of group average QBB MPI slopes corresponding to the traces shown in Fig. 5 the red color corresponds to trances shown in Fig. 6 (a) and (b) resulting from the absolute spectra and the regression model including melanin; the dark blue color corresponds to traces from Fig. 6 (c) and (d) resulting from the differential spectra and the regression model without melanin. The light blue shadow shows the p-value from the paired t-test comparing slope samples resulting from the two data processing methods (Color figure online)

4   Conclusion

We have shown that our optimized MSOT allows for the accurate dynamic imaging of the lymphatic drainage from the brain into neck lymph nodes with the temporal resolution of few seconds per image. The rate of lymphatic drainage at various locations in the body of a mouse can be quantified by an index based on the slope of the tracer's MSOT mean pixel intensity. A set of 11 wavelengths provides accurate maps of the hemoglobin and tracer with the temporal resolution of few seconds per image. In pigmented mice the effects of the melanin can be significantly reduced by using differential spectra. Since QBB tracer also worked as a fluorescent contrast agent, the in vivo MSOT results can be validated by post-mortem examination of lymph node sections using hyperspectral fluorescence microscopy [13]. Our next steps will also include applying our MSOT methods to the hindlimb unloading rodent model [3] to study possible relationship between SANS [14] and the disruption of the lymphatic drainage caused by microgravity.

Acknowledgement. We acknowledge the support of the Canadian Space Agency [19HLSRM02] and the Henry Farrugia Research Fund.

References

1. Mathieu, E., Gupta, N., Ahari, A., Zhou, X., Hanna, J., Yücel, Y.H.: Evidence for cerebrospinal fluid entry into the optic nerve via a glymphatic pathway. Invest. Ophthalmol. Vis. Sci. **58**, 4784–4791 (2017)
2. Neves, S.P.D., Delivanoglou, N., Mesquita, S.D.: CNS-Draining Meningeal Lymphatic Vasculature: Roles, Conundrums and Future Challenges. Frontiers in pharmacol. **12**, 655052 (2021)
3. Morey-Holton, E.R., Globus, R.K.: Hindlimb unloading rodent model: technical aspects. J. Appl. Physiol. **92**, 1367–1377 (2002)
4. Yücel, Y.H., et al.: Active lymphatic drainage from the eye measured by noninvasive photoacoustic imaging of near-infrared nanoparticles. Invest. Ophthalmol. Vis. Sci. **59**(7), 2699–2707 (2018)
5. Yoshiki, A., Moriwaki, K.: Mouse phenome research: implications of genetic background. ILAR J. **47**, 94–102 (2006)
6. Neuschmelting, V., Lockau, H., Ntziachristos, V., Grimm, J., Kircher, M.F.: Lymph node micrometastases and in-transit metastases from melanoma: in vivo detection with multispectral optoacoustic imaging in a mouse model. Radiology **280**, 137–150 (2016)
7. Cardinell, K., et al.: A novel photoacoustic-fluorescent contrast agent for quantitative imaging of lymphatic drainage. Photoacoustics **21**, 100239 (2021)
8. Xia, J., Junjie, Y., Wang, L.H.V.: Photoacoustic tomography: principles and advances. Electromagnetic Waves **147**, 1–22 (2014)
9. Tzoumas, S., Ntziachristos, V.: Spectral unmixing techniques for optoacoustic imaging of tissue pathophysiology. Philos. Trans. R. Soc. A: Math., Phys. Eng. Sci. **375**(2107), 20170262 (2017)
10. Nassif, I.A., Zhou, X., Yücel, Y.H., Toronov, V.: Wavelength optimization in the multispectral photoacoustic tomography of the lymphatic drainage in mice. Photoacoustics. **12**, 75–81 (2018)

11. Wang, Z., Bovik, A.C., Sheikh, H.R., Simoncelli, E.P.: Image quality assessment: from error visibility to structural similarity. IEEE Trans. Image Process. **13**, 600–612 (2004)
12. Pawlowski, M.E., Dwight, J.G., Nguyen, T.-U., Tkaczyk, T.S.: High performance image mapping spectrometer (IMS) for snapshot hyperspectral imaging applications. Opt. Express **27**, 1597–1612 (2019)
13. Bryant, C.D.: The blessings and curses of C57BL/6 substrains in mouse genetic studies. Ann. N Y Acad. Sci. **1245**, 31–33 (2011)
14. Martin Paez, Y., Mudie, L.I., Subramanian, P.S.: Spaceflight Associated Neuro-Ocular Syndrome (SANS): A Systematic Review and Future Directions. Eye Brain. **12**, 105–117 (2020)

Biomedical Computing

Relationships Between Vertical Jump and Composite Indices of Femoral Neck Strength in a Group of Young Women

Anthony Khawaja[1,2], Pierre Kamlé[1,3], Elie Maliha[1,4], Ghassan Maalouf[4], Hechmi Toumi[3], Antonio Pinti[5(✉)], and Rawad El Hage[1]

[1] Department of Physical Education, Division of Education, Faculty of Arts and Sciences, University of Balamand, El-Koura, Lebanon
[2] Faculty of Sport Sciences, Antonine University, Mejdlaya-Zgharta, Lebanon
[3] I3MTO, Université d'Orléans, E4708 Orléans, France
[4] Faculty of Medicine, Bellevue University Medical Center, Saint Joseph University, Mansourieh, Lebanon
[5] DeVisu, Design, Visuel, Urbain, UPHF, EA2445 Valenciennes, France
antonio.pinti@uphf.fr

Abstract. The purpose of this study was to investigate the relationships between vertical jump and composite indices of femoral neck strength (Compression strength index (CSI), bending strength index (BSI) and impact strength index (ISI)) in a group of young women. 206 young women (18 to 35 years) voluntarily participated in this study. Weight and height were measured, and body mass index (BMI) was calculated. Body composition, bone mineral content (BMC), bone mineral density (BMD) and trabecular bone score (TBS) were determined for each individual by Dual-energy X-ray absorptiometry (DXA). Composite indices of femoral neck strength (CSI, BSI and ISI) were calculated. Vertical jump was evaluated using a validated field test (Sargent test), and maximum power (P max, in watts) of the lower limbs was calculated accordingly. Vertical jump was positively correlated to CSI ($r = 0.36$; $p < 0.001$), BSI ($r = 0.30$; $p < 0.001$) and ISI ($r = 0.33$; $p < 0.001$). After adjusting for weight, vertical jump remained positively correlated to CSI ($p = 0.026$). The correlations between vertical jump and bone variables disappeared after adjusting for fat mass. The current study suggests that vertical jump is a positive determinant of composite indices of femoral neck strength in young women.

Keywords: Vertical jump · DXA · Peak bone mass · Osteoporosis

1 Introduction

Osteoporosis is a global public health problem, most common in postmenopausal women [1]. It is estimated that 15% of women suffer from osteoporosis around the age of 50; 30% around the age of 70; and 40% around the age of 80 [1]. Peak bone mass is a major determinant of bone mass and the risk of subsequent fracture [2]. A 10% increase in

© Springer Nature Switzerland AG 2021
I. Rojas et al. (Eds.): BIOMESIP 2021, LNCS 12940, pp. 27–38, 2021.
https://doi.org/10.1007/978-3-030-88163-4_3

peak bone mass can delay the onset of osteoporosis by 13 years [3. Increasing the BMD peak by 10% reduces the risk of fracture by 50% [3–5]. Several interconnected factors influence the build-up of bone mass during growth [6]. Physiological determinants of peak bone mass include heredity, vitamin D concentrations, calcium intake, protein intake, endocrine factors (sex steroids, IGF-1, 1.25(OH)2D) and mechanical stresses such as physical activity and body weight [6]. Physical activity has been considered an important factor in the prevention of osteoporosis [7]. Physical activity practice is considered the best preventive measurement against the decrease in BMD with age [7]. However, the mechanisms by which physical activity affects bone density are complex [7]. They are not yet fully understood, but they start with a mechanical stimulus which is relayed by the osteocytes [7]. It is recommended to practice regular physical activity throughout life [7]. Vigorous muscle exercise appears to be the most effective type of physical activity with a positive effect on BMD [7]. The regular practice of physical activities characterized by significant mechanical stress stimulates bone formation and improves BMD in the most solicited sites [8, 9]. In fact, according to the Frost theory [10] known as the mechanostat, the resistance of the bone adapts to the mechanical stresses applied to it. In addition, exercise that exerts high mechanical stresses on bone such as resistance training or structured jump-training, increases BMD in pre- and post-menopausal women [11]. Several studies have shown a significant correlation between BMD and the performances obtained in some physical tests used in current sports practice [12–15]. A recent study found that vertical jump, maximum power of the lower limbs, and 1-RM half-squat are positively correlated with bone variables in overweight and obese adult women [16]. Similarly, another recent study demonstrated a positive association between vertical jump, maximum power and bone variables in a group of young adults [17].

BMD measured by dual-energy X-ray absorptiometry (DXA) is considered as the reference standard to diagnose osteoporosis [18] and the best determinant of bone strength [19]. However, only 50–70% of bone strength can be explained by BMD [20]. Also, hip bone strength is also influenced by other factors such as femoral neck (FN) width and bending strength [21, 22]. Karlamangla et al. [22] have examined the prediction of incident hip fracture risk by composite indices of FN strength (compression strength index [CSI], bending strength index [BSI], and impact strength index [ISI]) constructed from DXA scans of the hip. These indices integrate FN size and body size with bone density [23]. CSI, BSI, and ISI reflect the ability of the FN to withstand axial compressive and bending forces and to absorb energy from an impact [23]. Furthermore, these indices have been shown to improve hip fracture risk and bone strength assessments in the elderly [22–24].

Many previous studies conducted on young adults have found that body weight, BMI and fat mass are negatively correlated to composite indices of femoral neck strength while physical activity levels are positive determinants of these bone indices [25–32]. In accordance with these results, two previous studies have shown positive associations between physical activity level and CSI, BSI and ISI [33, 34]. In the study conducted by Sardinha et al. [33] on prepubertal children, the results showed that vigorous physical activity is positively associated with CSI, BSI, and ISI values. Mori et al. [34] conducted a study on adult women, and the results demonstrated that a greater physical activity level is associated with higher composite indices of FN strength. Moreover, a recent study found that vertical jump is positively correlated with CSI and ISI in middle-aged men [32]. However, the relationship between vertical jump and composite indices of femoral neck strength in young women needs to be elucidated. The purpose of this study was to investigate the relationships between vertical jump and composite indices of femoral neck strength in a group of young women. We hypothesized that vertical jump would be significantly associated with composite indices of femoral neck strength in this population. The identification of new determinants of composite indices of femoral neck strength in young women would allow screening and early management of future cases of osteoporotic fractures.

2   Material and Methods

2.1   Subjects and Study Design

Two hundred and six young women whose ages ranged from 18 to 35 years voluntarily participated in the present study. All participants were non-smokers and had no history of major orthopedic problems or other disorders known to affect bone metabolism. Pregnant women, amenorrheic women, and those taking medications that may affect bone and calcium metabolism (corticosteroid or anticonvulsant therapy) were excluded from the study. All participants completed an interview about medical history including menstrual history and medication use. The work described has been carried out in accordance with the declaration of Helsinki (regarding human experimentation developed for the medical community by the World Medical Association). Other inclusion criteria included no diagnosis of comorbidities and no history of fracture. An informed written consent was obtained from the participants.

2.2   Anthropometrics

Height (in centimeters) was measured in the upright position to the nearest 1mm with a standard stadiometer. Body weight (in kilograms) was measured on a mechanic scale with a precision of 100 g. Subjects were weighed wearing only underclothes. Body mass index (BMI) was calculated as body weight divided by height squared (in kilogram per square meter) [35]. Body composition including lean mass (LM; Kg) and fat mass (FM; %, Kg) was evaluated by dual-energy X-ray absorptiometry (DXA; GE Healthcare, Madison, WI).

2.3   Bone Variables

BMC (in grams) and BMD (in grams per square centimeter) were determined for each individual by Dual-energy X-ray absorptiometry (DXA; GE Healthcare, Madison, WI) at the whole body (WB), lumbar spine (L1-L4), total hip (TH), and femoral neck (FN; GE Healthcare). L1-L4 TBS was also evaluated by DXA [36–38]. The TBS is derived from the texture of the DXA image and has been shown to be related to bone microarchitecture and fracture risk. The TBS score can assist the healthcare professional in assessing fracture risk [37, 38]. Composite indices of femoral neck strength (CSI, BSI, ISI) were calculated [22–24].

The ability of the femoral neck to withstand compressive and bending forces proportional to body weight can be approximated by the following indices: Compression strength index = (FN BMD * femoral neck width) / body weight, and Bending strength index = (FN BMD * femoral neck width^2) / (hip axis length * body weight). The ability of the femoral neck to absorb the energy of impact in a fall from standing height is given by: Impact strength index = (FN BMD * femoral neck width * hip axis length) / (body height * body weight). In our laboratory, the coefficients of variation were less than 1% for BMC and BMD [39–42]. The same certified technician performed all analyses using the same technique for all measurements.

2.4 Vertical Jump

The vertical jump was evaluated using a field test (Sargent test). Two main parameters were retained: vertical jump performance (cm) and power (w). The subjects performed three jumps with 2 min of recovery between jumps. The highest vertical jump was selected. Maximum power (P max, in watts) of the lower limbs was calculated [43].

P max (w) = $\sqrt{g/2}$ * body weight (kg) * $\sqrt{H}$ * 9.81; g is equal to 9.81 m/s^2 and H is vertical jump height in meters.

2.5 Statistical Analysis

The means and standard deviations were calculated for all clinical data and for the bone measurements. Associations between vertical jump and bone variables were given as Pearson correlation coefficients, and r values were reported. Multiple linear regression analysis models were used to test the relationships of vertical jump and FM with bone variables as well as the relationships of vertical jump and weight with bone variables, and r2 values were reported. Statistical analyses were performed using the SigmaStat 3.1 Program (Jandel Corp., San Rafael, CA). A level of significance of p < 0.05 was used.

3 Results

3.1 Clinical Characteristics and Bone Data of the Study Population

Age, weight, height, BMI, LM, FM, FM percentage, bone variables, vertical jump and maximum power are shown in Table 1.

Table 1. Clinical Characteristics of the Study Population.

Characteristics	Mean ± SD	Range
Age (yr)	24.0 ± 3.9	18 – 35
Weight (kg)	65.0 ± 14.0	43 – 114
Height (m)	1.61 ± 0.06	1.44 – 1.81
BMI (kg/m^2)	24.8 ± 5.0	16.8 – 42.4
Lean Mass (kg)	38.412 ± 6.399	28.219 – 67.674
Fat Mass (kg)	24.673 ± 9.159	5.667 – 53.932
Fat Mass %	36.6 ± 6.7	9.5 – 51.7
WB BMC (g)	2241 ± 325	1695 – 3982
WB BMD (g/cm^2)	1.086 ± 0.101	0.895 – 1.479
L1-L4 BMD (g/cm^2)	1.144 ± 0.127	0.817 – 1.522
L1-L4 TBS	1.425 ± 0.102	1.128 – 1.744
TH BMD (g/cm^2)	0.977 ± 0.130	0.695 – 1.457
FN BMD (g/cm^2)	0.956 ± 0.144	0.625 – 1.574
CSI (g/kg-m)	4.735 ± 0.918	2.345 – 8.589
BSI (g/kg-m)	1.471 ± 0.392	0.574 – 4.032
ISI (g/kg-m)	0.299 ± 0.055	0.145 – 0.468
Vertical jump (m)	0.166 ± 0.084	0.040 – 0.600
Maximum power (w)	547 ± 138	264 – 958

BMI, body mass index; WB, whole body; BMC, bone mineral content; BMD, bone mineral density; TBS, trabecular bone score; L1-L4, Lumbar spine; TH, total hip; FN, femoral neck; CSI, compression strength index; BSI, bending strength index; ISI, impact strength index; SD, standard deviation.

3.2   Correlations Between Clinical Characteristics and Bone Variables

Vertical jump was positively correlated to compression strength index (CSI) ($r = 0.36$; $p < 0.001$), bending strength index (BSI) ($r = 0.30$; $p < 0.001$) and impact strength index (ISI) ($r = 0.33$; $p < 0.001$). Maximum power was positively correlated to WB BMC ($r = 0.40$; $p < 0.001$), WB BMD ($r = 0.18$; $p < 0.05$), L1-L4 BMD ($r = 0.17$; $p < 0.05$), TH BMD ($r = 0.18$; $p < 0.05$) and FN BMD ($r = 0.26$; $p < 0.01$). LM was positively correlated to WB BMC ($r = 0.82$; $p < 0.001$), WB BMD ($r = 0.68$; $p < 0.001$), L1-L4 BMD ($r = 0.39$; $p < 0.001$), L1-L4 TBS ($r = 0.21$; $p < 0.01$), TH BMD ($r = 0.58$; $p < 0.001$) and FN BMD ($r = 0.60$; $p < 0.001$). LM was negatively correlated to CSI ($r = -0.38$; $p < 0.001$), BSI ($r = -0.33$; $p < 0.001$) and ISI ($r = -0.38$; $p < 0.001$). FM was positively correlated to WB BMC ($r = 0.41$; $p < 0.001$), WB BMD ($r = 0.42$; $p < 0.001$), L1-L4 BMD ($r = 0.23$; $p < 0.001$), L1-L4 TBS ($r = 0.22$; $p < 0.01$), TH BMD ($r = 0.33$; $p < 0.001$) and FN BMD ($r = 0.31$; $p < 0.001$). FM was negatively correlated to CSI ($r = -0.63$; $p < 0.001$), BSI ($r = -0.40$; $p < 0.001$) and ISI ($r = -0.59$; $p < 0.001$) (Table 2).

Table 2. Correlation Coefficients between Clinical Characteristics and bone variables.

	WB BMC (g)	WB BMD (g/cm^2)	L1-L4 BMD (g/cm^2)	L1-L4 TBS	TH BMD (g/cm^2)	FN BMD (g/cm^2)	CSI (g/kg-m)	BSI (g/kg-m)	ISI (g/kg-m)
Age (yr)	0.03	0.03	−0.01	−0.11	−0.11	−0.15*	−0.17*	−0.08	−0.19**
Weight(kg)	0.67***	0.62***	0.35***	0.29***	0.51***	0.52***	−0.53***	−0.40***	−0.54***
Height (m)	0.57***	0.27***	0.13	−0.15*	0.23***	0.33***	0.06	−0.05	−0.01**
BMI (kg/m^2)	0.47***	0.53***	0.32***	0.36***	0.44***	0.41***	−0.59***	−0.39***	−0.56***
FM (kg)	0.41***	0.42***	0.23***	0.22**	0.33***	0.31***	−0.63***	−0.40***	−0.59***
FM %	0.08	0.18**	0.11	0.18**	0.14*	0.11	−0.61***	−0.35***	−0.57***
LM (Kg)	0.82***	0.68***	0.39***	0.21**	0.58***	0.60***	−0.38***	−0.33***	−0.38***
Vertical jump (m)	−0.04	−0.13	−0.01	−0.15	−0.1	−0.05	0.36***	0.30***	0.33***
Maximum power (w)	0.40***	0.18*	0.17*	0.05	0.18*	0.26**	−0.05	−0.04	−0.05

BMI, body mass index; FM, fat mass; LM, lean mass; WB, whole body; BMC, bone mineral content; BMD, bone mineral density; TBS, trabecular bone score; L1-L4, Lumbar spine; TH, total hip; FN, femoral neck; CSI, compression strength index; BSI, bending strength index; ISI, impact strength index. *$p < 0.05$. **$p < 0.01$. ***$p < 0.001$.

3.3 Multiple Linear Regressions

After adjusting for weight, vertical jump remained positively correlated to CSI ($p = 0.026$). After adjusting for vertical jump, weight remained negatively correlated to CSI ($p < 0.001$), BSI ($p < 0.001$) and ISI ($p < 0.001$). Weight was a stronger determinant of CSI than vertical jump (Table 3). The correlations between vertical jump and bone variables disappeared after adjusting for FM. FM remained negatively correlated to CSI ($p < 0.001$), BSI ($p < 0.001$) and ISI ($p < 0.001$) after adjusting for vertical jump (Table 4).

Table 3. Multiple Linear Regression models with vertical jump and weight as independent variables

	Coefficient ± SE	t value	p value
Dependent variable: CSI ($r^2 = 0.617$)			
Constant	6.822 ± 0.398	17.153	< 0.001
Vertical Jump (w)	1.677 ± 0.748	2.244	0.026
Weight (kg)	-0.0380 ± 0.00505	-7.516	< 0.001
Dependent variable: BSI ($r^2 = 0.487$)			
Constant	2.078 ± 0.182	11.391	< 0.001
Vertical Jump (w)	0.553 ± 0.342	1.616	0.108
Weight (kg)	-0.0115 ± 0.00230	−5.024	< 0.001
Dependent variable: ISI ($r^2 = 0.591$)			
Constant	0.434 ± 0.0274	15.827	< 0.001
Vertical Jump (w)	0.0866 ± 0.0514	1.684	0.095
Weight (kg)	-0.00237 ± 0.000345	-6.864	< 0.001

CSI, compression strength index; BSI, bending strength index; ISI, impact strength index.

Table 4. Multiple linear regression models with vertical jump and fat mass as independent variables.

	Coefficient $\pm$ SE	t value	p value
Dependent variable: CSI ($r^2 = 0.643$)			
Constant	5.969 $\pm$ 0.271	22.025	< 0.001
Vertical Jump (w)	1.143 $\pm$ 0.747	1.529	0.128
Fat Mass (kg)	−0.0606 $\pm$ 0.00737	-8.223	< 0.001
Dependent variable: BSI ($r^2 = 0.469$)			
Constant	1.745 $\pm$ 0.129	13.497	< 0.001
Vertical Jump (w)	0.520 $\pm$ 0.353	1.474	0.143
Fat Mass (kg)	-0.0164 $\pm$ 0.00352	-4.662	< 0.001
Dependent variable: ISI ($r^2 = 0.610$)			
Constant	0.378 $\pm$ 0.0189	20.040	< 0.001
Vertical Jump (w)	0.0628 $\pm$ 0.0515	1.219	0.225
Fat Mass (kg)	-0.00376 $\pm$ 0.000514	-7.318	< 0.001

CSI, compression strength index; BSI, bending strength index; ISI, impact strength index.

4 Discussion

The current study conducted on a group of young women mainly shows that vertical jump is positively correlated to CSI, BSI and ISI. The strengths of the associations between vertical jump and composite indices of femoral neck strength were low to moderate in this population. These results highlight the positive influence of vertical jump performance of the lower limbs on composite indices of femoral neck strength in young women. After adjusting for weight, vertical jump remained positively correlated to CSI. Weight was a stronger determinant of CSI than vertical jump. The correlations between vertical jump and composite indices of femoral neck strength disappeared after adjusting for FM. Our results are in accordance with those of a previous recent study conducted on middle-aged men that found that vertical jump is positively correlated to CSI and ISI [32]. Accordingly, our results highlight the importance of increasing vertical jump performance of the lower limbs to prevent osteoporotic fractures later in life. The vertical jump test highlights the relative power. Accordingly, the relationships between vertical jump performance and composite indices of femoral neck strength may be influenced by the weight status of the studied population. Our study showed that maximum power is positively correlated to BMC and BMD values. In contrast, we did not find any association between maximum power and composite indices of femoral neck strength. The strengths of the associations between maximum power and bone variables were poor to moderate in our study. These results highlight the positive influence of maximum power of the lower limbs on BMC and BMD in young women. Hence, our results accentuate the importance of increasing maximum power of the lower limbs to prevent osteoporosis later in life. Our results are in line with those of many previous studies conducted on young adults [16, 17, 32, 44, 45]. A recent study has demonstrated a positive correlation between maximum power and BMC, BMD and geometric indices of hip bone strength (CSA, CSMI, and Z) in middle-aged men [32]. However, this study did not find any correlation between maximum power and composite indices of femoral neck strength [32]. A recent study has shown that maximum power is a positive determinant of many bone variables in a group of young overweight and obese women [16]. In line with these results, a recent study has found a positive correlation between maximum power and WB BMC, WB BMD, FN CSA and FN CSMI in young men [17]. This study also found a positive correlation between maximum power and WB BMC, WB BMD, TH BMD, FN BMD, FN CSA, FN CSMI and FN Z in young women [17]. After adjusting for LM, maximum power remained significantly correlated to WB BMC, L1-L4 BMC, TH BMC and FN CSMI in young men, whereas the correlation between maximum power and bone variables disappeared after adjusting for LM in young women [17]. A previous study has demonstrated a positive correlation between maximum power and BMD in both young women and men [44]. Another previous study has shown a positive correlation between maximum power and WB BMC, WB BMD, L1-L4 BMD, TH BMD, and FN Z in a group of young overweight and obese men [44]. However, these correlations disappeared after adjusting for LM [45]. Our results confirm the positive importance of LM on bone health in young adults. LM was positively correlated to WB BMC, BMD and L1-L4 TBS. On the other hand, LM was negatively correlated to CSI, BSI and ISI. Furthermore, LM appears to be a positive predictor of BMC, BMD and TBS in young women. For this reason, implementing strategies to increase LM is important for young women to avoid the occurrence of osteoporosis later in life. A recent study has shown that LM is a positive determinant of BMD, CSA, CSMI, Z and ISI in young overweight men [30]. Our results are consistent with those of many previous studies that have shown that LM is an important determinant of WB BMC, FN CSA and FN Z [45–52]. A cross-sectional study conducted on a group of 70 osteoporotic postmenopausal women has demonstrated a significant correlation between LM and bone variables such as BMC and BMD [53]. It has suggested that FN BMD and femur BMD were correlated to LM [53]. A previous study conducted on a group of young adults has shown that LM was positively correlated to WB BMC and WB BMD in both young men and women [44]. The present study shows that FM is positively correlated to WB BMC, BMD and L1-L4 TBS. It also shows that FM is negatively correlated to CSI, BSI and ISI. After adjusting for vertical jump, FM remained negatively correlated to CSI, BSI and ISI. Our results are in line with those of two studies [27, 54] which suggested that obesity is associated with lower CSI, BSI, and ISI values in young men and women. Accordingly, implementing strategies to reduce FM is important in women to avoid the occurrence of osteoporotic fractures later in life. A similar conclusion has been found in a study conducted on children [55]. In addition, a recent study [30] conducted on young overweight men has demonstrated a negative association between FM and CSI and BSI. Another recent study [31] conducted on the same population has found that FM is negatively associated with CSI, BSI and ISI. Similarly, a study [32] conducted on middle-aged men has shown that FM is negatively associated with CSI and ISI. Hence, fat mass seems to be a negative determinant of composite indices of femoral neck strength in both genders. Despite its originality, the present study had some limitations. First, the cross-sectional nature of the present study is a limitation because it cannot evaluate the confounding variables. The second limitation is the 2-dimensional nature of DXA [56, 57]. Finally, maximum power was not directly measured but indirectly calculated using a formula after performing a vertical jump test. However, to our knowledge, the present study is one of few studies that aimed at exploring the relationships between vertical jump and composite indices of femoral neck strength in young women. Vertical jump and maximum power are easily calculated when performing a simple physical test.

5   Conclusion

In conclusion, the current study suggests that vertical jump is a positive determinant of composite indices of femoral neck strength (CSI, BSI and ISI) in young women. Our study is one of very few studies that demonstrated positive correlations between vertical jump and composite indices of femoral neck strength in young women. Thus, implementing strategies to increase vertical jump performance of the lower limbs in young women may be useful for preventing osteoporotic fractures later in life. Finally, our study may be useful for the prevention and early detection of osteoporosis and osteopenia.

Acknowledgments. This study was supported by a grant from the research council of the University of Balamand.

Disclosure of Interest.   None of the authors reported a conflict of interest related to the study.

References

1. Shakil, A., Gimpel, N.E., Rizvi, H., et al.: Awareness and prevention of osteoporosis among south asian women. J. Community Health. **35**, 392–397 (2010)
2. Keen, R.W.: Pathophysiology of osteoporosis. In: Clunie, G., Keen, R.W. Osteoporosis, 2nd edn. Oxford Rheumatology Library. United Kingdom (2014)
3. Rizzoli, R., Bianchi, M.L., Garabédian, M., McKay, H.A., Moreno, L.A.: Maximizing bone mineral mass gain during growth for the prevention of fractures in the adolescents and the elderly. Bone **46**(2), 294–305 (2010)
4. Hernandez, C.J., Beaupré, G.S., Carter, D.R.: A theoretical analysis of the relative influences of peak BMD, age-related bone loss and menopause on the development of osteoporosis. Osteoporos. Int. **14**(10), 843–847 (2003)
5. Melton, L.J., Atkinson, E.J., Khosla, S., Oberg, A.L., Riggs, B.L.: Evaluation of a prediction model for long-term fracture risk. J. Bone Miner. Res. **20**(4), 551–556 (2005)
6. Bonjour, J.P., Chevalley, T., Ferrari, S., Rizzoli, R.: The importance and relevance of peak bone mass in the prevalence of osteoporosis. Salud Publica Mex. **51**(1), S5–S17 (2009)
7. Khawaji, M., Astermark, J., Akesson, K., Berntorp, E.: Physical activity for prevention of osteoporosis in patients. Haemophilia **16**, 495–501 (2010)
8. Ainsworth, B.E., Youmans, C.P.: Tools for physical activity counseling in medical practice. Obes. Res. **10**(1), 69S-75S (2002)

9. Nikander, R., Sievänen, H., Heinonen, A., Kannus, P.: Femoral neck structure in adult female athletes subjected to different loading modalities. J. Bone Miner. Res. **20**, 520–528 (2005)
10. Frost, H.M.: Bone's mechanostat: a 2003 update. Anat. Rec. A Discov. Mol. Cell. Evol. Biol. **275**, 1081–1101 (2003)
11. Giangregorio, L.M., et al.: Too Fit to Fracture: exercise recommendations for individuals with osteoporosis or osteoporotic vertebral fracture. Osteoporos. Int. **25**, 821–835 (2014)
12. Vicente-Rodriguez, G., Dorado, C., Perez-Gomez, J., Gonzalez-Henriquez, J.J., Calbet, J.A.: Enhanced bone mass and physical fitness in young female handball players. Bone **35**, 1208–1215 (2004)
13. Dixon, W.G., et al.: Low grip strength is associated with bone mineral density and vertebral fracture in women. Rheumatology (Oxford) **44**, 642–646 (2005)
14. Sirola, J., Rikkonen, T., Tuppurainen, M., Jurvelin, J.S., Alhava, E., Kröger, H.: Grip strength may facilitate fracture prediction in perimenopausal women with normal BMD: a 15-year population based study. Calcif. Tissue Int. **83**, 93–100 (2008)
15. Sherk, V.D., Palmer, I.J., Bemben, M.G., Bemben, D.A.: Relationships between body composition, muscular strength, and bone mineral density in estrogen-deficient postmenopausal women. J. Clin. Densitom. **12**, 292–298 (2009)
16. Berro, A.J., et al.: Physical performance variables and bone parameters in a group of young overweight and obese women. J. Clin. Densitom. **22**(2), 293–299 (2019)
17. Khawaja, A., et al.: Does muscular power predict bone mineral density in young adults? J. Clin. Densitom. **22**(3), 311–320 (2019)
18. Kanis, J.A., Kanis, J.A.: Assessment of fracture risk and its application to screening for postmenopausal osteoporosis: Synopsis of a WHO report. Osteoporosis Int 4, 368–381 (1994). https://doi.org/10.1007/BF01622200
19. Kanis, J.A., McCloskey, E.V., Johansson, H., Oden, A., Melton, L.J., Khaltaev, N.: A reference standard for the description of osteoporosis. Bone **42**(3), 467–475 (2008)
20. Stone, K.L., et al.: BMD at multiple sites and risk of fracture of multiple types: long-term results from the study of osteoporotic fractures. J. Bone Miner. Res. **18**, 1947–1954 (2003)
21. Black, D.M., et al.: Proximal femoral structure and the prediction of hip fracture in men: a large prospective study using QCT. J. Bone Miner. Res. **23**, 1326–1333 (2008)
22. Karlamangla, A.S., Barrett-Connor, E., Young, J., Greendale, G.A.: Hip fracture risk assessment using composite indices of femoral neck strength: the Rancho Bernardo study. Osteoporos. Int. **15**, 62–70 (2004). https://doi.org/10.1007/s00198-003-1513-1
23. Yu, N., et al.: Evaluation of compressive strength index of the femoral neck in Caucasians and Chinese. Calcif. Tissue Int. **87**, 324–332 (2010). https://doi.org/10.1007/s00223-010-9406-8
24. Ayoub, M.L., et al.: DXA-based variables and osteoporotic fractures in Lebanese postmenopausal women. Orthop. Traumatol. Surg. Res. **100**, 855–858 (2014)
25. El Hage, R.: Composite indices of femoral neck strength in adult female soccer players. J. Clin. Densitom. **17**, 212–213 (2014)
26. El Hage, R., Zakhem, E., Zunquin, G., Theunynck, D., Moussa, E., Maaloufet, G.: Does soccer practice influence compressive strength, bending strength, and impact strength indices of the femoral neck in young men? J. Clin. Densitom. **17**(1), 213–214 (2014)
27. Berro A, Fayad N, Pinti A, et al. 2017 Maximal oxygen consumption and composite indices of femoral neck strength in a group of young women. In: International Conference on Bioinformatics and Biomedical Engineering. Springer, Cham:369–75https://doi.org/10.1007/978-3-319-56148-6_32
28. Khoury, C.E.I., et al.: Decreased Composite Indices of Femoral Neck Strength in Young Obese Men. J. Clin. Densitom. **20**(2), 268–270 (2017)
29. Khoury, G.E., et al.: Maximal oxygen consumption and composite indices of femoral neck strength in a group of young overweight and obese men. J Clin Densitom **21**(2), 310–311 (2018)

30. Zakhem, E., et al.: Influence of physical activity level on composite indices of femoral neck strength in a group of young overweight. J. Clin. Densitom. **23**(4), 596–603 (2020)
31. Zakhem, E., Sabbagh, P., Khoury, C.A., Zunquin, G., Baquet, G., El Hage, R.: Positive correlations between physical activity level and composite indices of femoral neck strength in a group of young overweight and obese men. Sci. Sport **36**(3), 210–217 (2020)
32. Finianos, B., Zunquin, G., El Hage, R.: Composite indices of femoral neck strength in middle-aged inactive subjects vs former football players. J. Clin. Densitom. **24**(2), 214–224 (2021)
33. Sardinha, L.B., Baptista, F., Ekelund, U.: Objectively measured physical activity and bone strength in 9-year-old boys and girls. Pediatrics **122**(3), e728–e736 (2008)
34. Mori, T., et al.: Physical activity as determinant of femoral neck strength relative to load in adult women: findings from the hip strength across the men- opause transition study. Osteoporos. Int. **25**, 265–272 (2014). https://doi.org/10.1007/s00198-013-2429-z
35. World Health Organization: Obesity: Preventing and managing the global epidemic. WHO technical report series, Geneva (2000)
36. Beck, T.J., Ruff, C.B., Warden, K.E., LeBoff, M.S., Cauley, J.A., Chen, Z.: Predicting femoral neck strength from bone mineral data. A structural approach. Invest. Radiol. **25**(1), 6–18 (1990)
37. Silva, B.C., Broy, S.B., Boutroy, S., Schousboe, J.T., Shepherd, J.A., Leslie, W.D.: Fracture risk prediction by non-BMD DXA measures: the 2015 ISCD Official Positions Part 2: trabecular bone score. J. Clin. Densitom. **18**(3), 309–330 (2015)
38. Harvey, N.C., et al.: Trabecular bone score (TBS) as a new complementary approach for osteoporosis evaluation in clinical practice. Bone **78**, 216–224 (2015)
39. El Hage, R., et al.: Maximal oxygen consumption and bone mineral density in a group of young Lebanese adults. J. Clin. Densitom. **17**, 320–324 (2014)
40. El Hage, R., Bachour, F., Sebaalt, A., Issa, M., Zakhem, E., Maalouf, G.: The influence of weight status on radial bone mineral density in Lebanese women. Calcif. Tissue Int. **94**(4), 465–467 (2014)
41. El Hage, R., et al.: The influence of obesity and overweight on hip bone mineral density in Lebanese women. J. Clin. Densitom. **17**(1), 216–217 (2014)
42. Zakhem, E., et al.: Physical performance and trabecular bone score in a group of young Lebanese women. J. Clin. Densitom. **18**, 271–272 (2015)
43. Harman, E., Rosenstein, M., Frykman, P., Rosenstein, R., Kraemer, W.: Estimation of human power output from vertical jump. J. Strength Conditioning Res. **5**(3), 116–120 (1991)
44. Zakhem, E., et al.: Performance physique et densité minérale osseuse chez de jeunes adultes libanais. J. Med. Liban. **64**(4), 193–199 (2016)
45. Khoury, C.E., et al.: Physical performance variables and bone mineral density in a group of young overweight and obese men. J. Clin. Densitom. **21**(1), 41–47 (2018)
46. Petit, M.A., Beck, T.J., Hughes, J.M., Lin, H.M., Bentley, C., Lloyd, T.: Proximal femur mechanical adaptation to weight gain in late adolescence: a six-year longitudinal study. J. Bone Miner. Res. **23**, 180–188 (2008)
47. Shea, K.L., et al.: Loss of bone strength in response to exercise-induced weight loss in obese postmenopausal women: results from a pilot study. J. Musculoskelet. Neuronal. Interact. **14**, 229–238 (2014)
48. MacKelvie, K.J., McKay, H.A., Petit, M.A., Moran, O., Khan, K.M.: Bone mineral response to a 7-month randomized controlled, school-based jumping intervention in 121 prepubertal boys: associations with ethnicity and body mass index. J. Bone Miner. Res. **17**(5), 834–844 (2002)
49. Nikander, R., Sievänen, H., Heinonen, A., Kannus, P.: Femoral neck structure in adult female athletes subjected to different loading modalities. J. Bone Miner. Res. **20**(3), 520–528 (2005)

50. Lorentzon, M., Mellström, D., Ohlsson, C.: Association of amount of physical activity with cortical bone size and trabecular volumetric BMD in young adult men: the GOOD study. J. Bone Miner. Res. **20**(11), 1936–1943 (2005)
51. Bonjour, J.P., Chevalley, T., Rizzoli, R., Ferrari, S.: Gene environment interactions in the skeletal response to nutrition and exercise during growth. Med. Sport Sci. **51**, 64–80 (2007)
52. El Hage, R., et al.: Effects of 12 weeks of endurance training on bone mineral content and bone mineral density in obese, overweight and normal weight adolescent girls. Sci. Sports **24**(3–4), 210–213 (2009)
53. Genaro, P.S., Pereira, G.A., Pinheiro, M.M., Szejnfeld, V.L., Martini, L.A.: Influence of body composition on bone mass in postmenopausal osteoporotic women. Arch. Gerontol. Geriatr. **51**(3), 295–298 (2010)
54. Khoury, G.E., et al.: Bone variables in active overweight/obese men and sedentary overweight/obese men. J. Clin. Densitom. **20**, 239–246 (2017)
55. Rocher, E., El Hage, R., Chappard, C., Portier, H., Rochefort, G.Y., Benhamou, C.L.: Bone mineral density, hip bone geometry, and calcaneus trabecular bone texture in obese and normal-weight children. J. Clin. Densitom. **16**(2), 244–249 (2013)
56. Beck, T.J.: Measuring the structural strength of bones with dual-energy X-ray absorptiometry: principles, technical limitations, and future possibilities. Osteoporos. Int. **14**(5), S81–S88 (2003)
57. Beck, T.J.: Extending DXA beyond bone mineral density: understanding hip structure analysis. Curr. Osteoporos. Rep. **5**(2), 49–55 (2007)

Automatic Classification of Valve Diseases Through Natural Language Processing in Spanish and Active Learning

Pablo Pérez-Sánchez[1], Víctor Vicente-Palacios[1,3(✉)], Manuel Barreiro-Pérez[1,2],
Elena Díaz-Peláez[1,2], Antonio Sánchez-Puente[1,2], Jesús Sampedro-Gómez[1,2],
Alberto García-Galindo[1], P. Ignacio Dorado-Díaz[1,2], and Pedro L. Sánchez[1,2]

[1] Servicio de Cardiología, Hospital Universitario de Salamanca-IBSAL,
Salamanca, Spain
[2] CIBERCV, Instituto de Salud Carlos III, Madrid, Spain
[3] Philips Ibérica, Madrid, Spain
victor.vicente.palacios@philips.com

Abstract. A correct label classification of data allows improving healthcare processes and research. However, labeling is a difficult and expensive process, which limits its use and quality. We propose a proof of concept based on Natural Language Processing and active learning, in order to automatically structure information from a text in Spanish in the field of echocardiography.

Echocardiographic reports from a Health National System Cardiology Department were analyzed. Reports were divided into a training corpus (26,699 reports) and a validation corpus (2,881 reports). The design of the model was focused on the automatic labeling of aortic and mitral valve disease (stenosis/insufficiency) and their valve nature (native/prosthetic). The following steps were followed to build the models: data preparation, vectorization, and model fitting and validation. Results were compared with the manually labeled ground truth data from the physicians reporting the echocardiographic studies.

Four machine learning algorithms were compared: logistic regression, naïve bayes, random forest, and support vector machine; obtaining the last our best results with areas under the ROC curve of 0.92 and 0.93 for aortic and mitral stenosis, 0.87 and 0.89 for aortic and mitral insufficiency, and 0.97 and 0.96 for native aortic and mitral valve, respectively. Natural Language processing tools are useful to automatically structure and label echocardiographic information in Spanish text format. The developed models combined with active learning are capable of performing a correct prospective labeling.

Keywords: Machine learning · Valvular heart disease · Natural language processing

1 Introduction

Any care, management or research process requires a prior analysis of structured data on the field of interest, which must be of sufficient quality and classified

© Springer Nature Switzerland AG 2021
I. Rojas et al. (Eds.): BIOMESIP 2021, LNCS 12940, pp. 39–50, 2021.
https://doi.org/10.1007/978-3-030-88163-4_4

according to the main variables or categories for their correct interpretation. However, obtaining them is costly and tedious.

Taking echocardiographic imaging as an example, the quality of the data to be analysed depends closely on the prior work of the physician who has to categorise the data from the analysis of DICOM (Digital Imaging and Communication On Medicine) files, the measurements recorded and the associated reports in a single repository. A correct and complete registration of labels associated with the database of this repository facilitates patient follow-up and allows, on a sufficient volume of data, its interpretation and use for the correct distribution of resources and the eventual elaboration of predictive models.

However, much of the data contained in echocardiographic reports is unstructured and therefore not accessible for nimble analysis; and as a consequence, manual extraction of the information contained in free text involves a high cost in terms of both money and time [6]. Natural language processing (NLP) allows us, through artificial intelligence algorithms [5], to automatically extract and structure relevant clinical information from free text and semi-structured data sources [20]. Also, within artificial intelligence, there is a relatively new concept called active learning that allows for agile and high quality data labelling, suggesting labels to the user based on the activity they have previously performed [2].

In this work we develop and validate a natural language processing system in Spanish, based on active learning, which allows: firstly, to automatically identify and tag the text information of echocardiographic studies; and secondly, to offer labels to the operator to increase the volume and quality of the structured data collected prospectively.

2   Methods

2.1   Corpus

In the development of the system, two corpora from different databases belonging to a Cardiology Service of the Spanish National Health System were used: one to build the system and the other to validate it.

The training corpus used for model building was extracted from the database associated with the echocardiography digital image repository (IntelliSpace Cardiovascular, Philips Healthcare). From a total of 103,669 text reports of echocardiographic studies corresponding to the years 2007–2018, all those reports whose information had been structured and labeled by the physicians reporting the echocardiogram were used as training corpus; in total 26,969 reports. In doing so, it was possible to contrast the results of the automatic predictive algorithms with the manual labeling during clinical practice by physicians. The labels chosen for this proof of concept were: aortic stenosis, mitral stenosis, aortic insufficiency, mitral insufficiency, as well as the native or non-native (prosthetic) nature of the valve studied, aortic and/or mitral. The tricuspid and pulmonary valves were not considered in the development of the system, given the low casuistry for tricuspid and pulmonary stenosis found in our database. However, the incorporation of active learning techniques into the developed system allows new labels to be added and new predictive models to be incorporated progressively.

The corpus used for external validation of the models was extracted from the database associated with the electronic medical record (Mediconnect, Fleischhacker) implemented in January 2019 in the same department. This database hosts different workflows, all structured with tags, including the one corresponding to echocardiography. The validation corpus consists of 2,881 text reports of echocardiographic studies; all of them, as previously indicated, manually labelled at the time by the doctors who reported the echocardiogram.

The fact that the labelling system and architecture of the two databases are different is an added value as they are independent training and validation corpora.

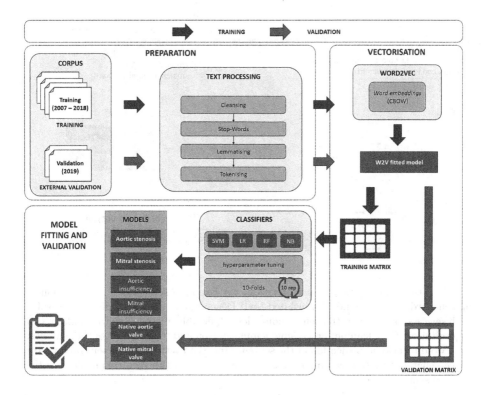

Fig. 1. Workflow diagram.

2.2 Development of the Natural Language Processing System

Figure 1 shows the workflow used in the development of the system in which the three steps carried out to build the system are identified: preparation of training and validation corpora, vectorisation, and model fitting and validation.

The training corpus and the second validation corpus go through each of the three aforementioned blocks independently.

Preparation. In this step we proceeded to clean, process and standardise training and validation corpora. To do so, we eliminated special and numeric characters, terms without syntactic value, as well as determiners, conjunctions, prepositions, punctuation marks, diacritics and stop-words (terms or words that do not provide a relevant meaning). The set of stop-words chosen is the one included in the Spanish module of the Python spacy library [8].

We then proceeded to lemmatise and tokenise all selected terms. By lemmatising we fixed the corresponding lemma of our word, thus reducing the influx of terms. Tokenising consisted of assigning each word a unique identity.

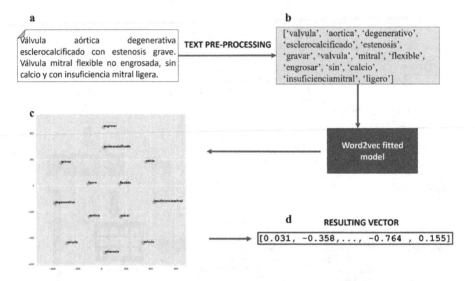

Fig. 2. Visual explanation of vectorisation. (a) Example sentence of a conclusion of an echocardiographic study. Translated text: Degenerative sclero-calcified aortic valve with severe stenosis. Non-thickened, non-calcified, flexible mitral valve with mild mitral regurgitation. (b) Cleaning, processing, lemmatisation and tokenisation of the sentence. (c) Two-dimensional projection of the sentence terms onto the multidimensional vector space generated by the training corpus. (d) Extraction of the vector equivalent to the original sentence.

Vectorisation. Although textual information cannot be used directly in most predictive models, it is possible to obtain a vector representation for each of the terms contained by means of techniques based on unsupervised neural networks, known as word embeddings. In particular, in our study we used the Continuous Bag of Words [1] technique, as shown in Fig. 2, previously defining a selection of 200 terms and a context delimited by the 8 words closest to the term to be vectorised.

As a result of the application of this technique, a vector representation was obtained for each of the terms in the training corpus, resulting in a matrix that stored the most relevant syntactic information.

Model Fitting and External Validation. The training corpus was used to adjust the 4 machine learning algorithms used: logistic regression, naive bayes, random forest, and support vector machine [5]; to which in turn an individual hyperparameter tuning [23] was applied. This hyperparameter tuning was performed with k-folds [21] cross-validation methodology; specifically using 10 repetitions of 10-folds [22].

Finally, an external validation of the performance of the models developed on the validation corpus was carried out.

2.3 Evaluation Metrics

After the development of the predictive models, they were evaluated on the validation corpus, comparing the decisions generated and the labels defined by the practitioners, resulting in confusion matrices on which the following metrics were calculated: sensitivity or True Positive Rate, Precision or Positive Predictive Value, Specificity or True Negative Rate, and the Area under the ROC curve.

2.4 Software and Open Source.

The programming language used in this article was Python and the libraries used for text processing and model fitting were spacy [8], gensim [25], luigi [16] and scikit-learn [18], umap-learn [14] and hdbscan [13].

All the developed code used to train and evaluate the NLP models, as well as an interactive visualisation of the vocabulary used, is openly available at https://github.com/IA-Cardiologia-husa/VHD_NLP. We have also incorporated an open demo of the active labelling application at https://valvularheartdisease. herokuapp.com/.

3 Results

3.1 Frequency of Valvulopathies in Echocardiographic Reports

Table 1 shows the relative frequency of each of the valve diseases and their prosthetic or native character for the 26,699 echocardiographic reports used as training corpus and the 2,881 echocardiographic reports used as validation corpus. The labels chosen in both databases, from which the frequency of each valvulopathy was obtained. The labels were, at the time, manually assigned by a total of 75 different physicians who interpreted and wrote the reports of the echocardiographic studies used in the development of the PLN model. In both datasets the most frequent valve disease was the presence of mitral regurgitation, followed by aortic regurgitation and aortic stenosis.

Table 1. Frequency of each of the valve diseases studied and their prosthetic or non-prosthetic nature for the training and validation corpora.

		Stenosis		Insufficiency		Prosthesis	
		Aortic	Mitral	Aortic	Mitral	Aortic	Mitral
Training corpus	Yes	3.169 (16,3%)	1.213 (6,8%)	7.947 (35,5%)	10.849 (45,8%)	2.060 (7,8%)	1.518 (5,8%)
	No	16.288 (83,7%)	16.489 (93,1%)	14.464 (64,5%)	12.852 (54,2%)	24.248 (92,2%)	24.790 (94,2%)
	Total	19457	17702	22411	23701	26308	26308
Validation corpus	Yes	256 (8,9%)	142 (4,9%)	673 (23,4%)	1.138 (39,5%)	385 (13,4%)	268 (9,3%)
	No	2.625 (91,1%)	2.739 (95,1%)	2.208 (76,6%)	1.743 (60,5%)	2.496 (86,6%)	2.613 (90,7%)
	Total	2881	2881	2881	2881	2881	2881
Total		29.191 (19,1%)	22.340 (14,6%)	20.585 (13,4%)	25.294 (16,5%)	26.584 (17,3%)	29.191 (19,1%)

3.2   Model Adjustment

To develop and fit the model we used the training dataset.

Table 2 shows the discriminatory capacity of the 4 machine learning classifiers used after fitting the models for each label analysed (aortic stenosis, mitral stenosis, aortic regurgitation, mitral regurgitation, native aortic valve, and native mitral valve) using the training corpus. As can be observed, the classifier with the best results was the support vector machine method. Therefore, it was the one chosen for the construction of the final model and the one evaluated on the validation corpus.

3.3   Model Performance (External Validation)

The performance of the model was evaluated using different data (external validation) to those used in its development. In our case, the validation corpus came from a second independent database, Mediconnect.

Figure 3 shows the resulting ROC curves for each type of valve disease analysed. All of them show values higher than 0.85, which guarantees the high performance of the models.

Compared to the manual labelling of the physicians who reported the echocardiographic studies at the time (Table 3), we achieved an accuracy of 93.9% for aortic stenosis, 96.0% for mitral stenosis, 82.4% for aortic regurgitation, 75.3% for mitral regurgitation, 94.7% for native aortic valve and 94.8% for native mitral valve. It is important to note that the performance of the model developed has the capacity to adjust depending on whether we are looking for a higher percentage of valve disease that we correctly label as such (sensitivity) or a higher percentage of non-valvulopathy that we correctly label as such (specificity).

Table 2. ROC area under the curve of the four classifiers used to fit the models in the training corpus.

	Model	Mean	Deviation
Aortic stenosis	Logistic regression	0.963	0.007
	Naive bayes	0.880	0.043
	Random forest	0.951	0.010
	Support vector machine	**0.967**	0.008
Mitral stenosis	Logistic regression	0.975	0.010
	Naive bayes	0.933	0.021
	Random forest	0.969	0.011
	Support vector machine	**0.980**	0.008
Aortic insufficiency	Logistic regression	0.896	0.013
	Naive bayes	0.800	0.024
	Random forest	0.863	0.013
	Support vector machine	**0.906**	0.015
Mitral insufficiency	logistic regression	0.880	0.010
	Naive bayes	0.784	0.017
	Random forest	0.869	0.013
	Support vector machine	**0.886**	0.007
Native aortic valve	Logistic regression	0.983	0.007
	Naive bayes	0.940	0.010
	Random forest	0.979	0.005
	Support vector machine	**0.986**	0.007
Native mitral valve	Logistic regression	0.989	0.005
	Naive bayes	0.953	0.021
	Random forest	0.983	0.006
	Support vector machine	**0.990**	0.004

Table 3. Model performance (%) resulting from testing our automatic predictive algorithms against the manual labelling performed by the physicians reporting the echocardiographic study. *TP = True positives; FP = False positives; TN = True negatives; FN = False negatives; SN = sensitivity; SP = Specificity*

	TP	FP	TN	FN	SN	SP	Accuracy
Aortic stenosis	4.5	1.7	89.4	4.4	50.8	98.2	93.9
Mitral stenosis	1.4	0.5	94.6	3.6	27.5	99.5	96.0
Aortic insufficiency	11.8	6.0	70.6	11.5	50.7	92.1	82.4
Mitral insufficiency	25.0	10.2	50.3	14.5	63.3	83.1	75.3
Native aortic valve	1.8	3.7	82.9	1.6	88.1	95.7	94.7
Native mitral valve	5.2	1.1	89.6	4.1	56.3	98.8	94.8

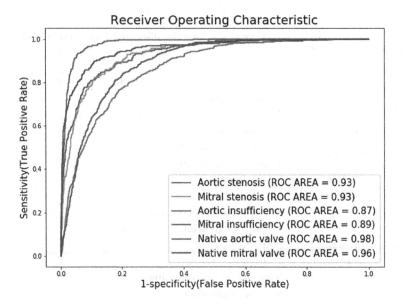

Fig. 3. ROC curves for final support vector machine models (external validation)

3.4 Deployment of the System in a Free Demo and Active Learning

In order to better understand the functioning of the developed NLP system, which incorporates the different support vector machine models we have built to automatically classify the labels aortic stenosis, mitral stenosis, aortic insufficiency, mitral insufficiency, native aortic valve, and native mitral valve, we have built an open demo (Fig. 4; https://valvularheartdisease.herokuapp.com/). Once the user writes the report and submits it, thanks to the active learning built into the NLP system, we can suggest labels to the technician or cardiologist; so that the technician or cardiologist only has to correct incorrect ones if they exist, and then confirm them. Thus, periodically the model is able to learn progressively and improve its efficiency. Moreover, active learning allows us to add new labels, whether they are different pathologies, the degree of valvulopathies or others, progressively being able to prospectively evaluate our algorithms and improve their performance. A cardiology service may perform between 100 and 200 echocardiograms per week. Therefore, a weekly periodicity to adapt the NLP models to the system and analyze errors would be sufficient. Semi-automation of this process would allow errors to be analyzed and parameters to be adjusted in a more optimized way.

App (Demo)

Conclusión Estudio Ecocardiográfico

El botón ejemplo genera ejemplos aleatorios de reportes ecocardiográficos.

Para que funcione correctamente la aplicación los textos escritos han de parecerse o ser reportes ecocardiográficos. La longitud del texto escrito puede influenciar (textos cortos pueden tener peor resultado).

| Ejemplo |

```
Resumen de la interpretación
Estudio de buena calidad realizo en fibrilacion auricular con FVM bien controlada.

Dispositivo bien posicionado sin trombos ni GAPs.

V alvula mitral con regurgitacion moderada (TA 120/70)
Valvula aortica con insuficiencia leve sin estenosis.
Ventyriculo izquieredo de tamaño y funcion sistolica global y segmentaria normales.
Auricula izquierda severamente dilatada.
```

| Submit |

Estenosis Aórtica	Estenosis Mitral	Insuficiencia Aórtica	Insuficiencia Mitral	Válvula Aórtica Nativa	Válvula Mitral Nativa
No ⌄	No ⌄	Si ⌄	Si ⌄	Si ⌄	Si ⌄

| Commit |

Fig. 4. Active Learning application demo (Spanish). In the text box, the physician enters the free text corresponding to the echocardiographic report in Spanish and then validates it (submit button). The natural language processing system suggests the labels, allowing them to be corrected in case of error; finally, once the practitioner is satisfied with them, he/she validates the labels (commit button) and the system stores the answers. These responses allow the system to periodically improve its performance and adapt to its users.

4   Discussion

The recommendations of the European Society of Cardiology for the standardisation of the performance, storage and reporting of echocardiographic studies estimate that the average time for the performance of a standard transthoracic echocardiography is between 30 and 40 min [7]. This time includes interpretation and reporting of the images obtained. In some cases, it may take even longer depending on the physician's experience, the complexity of the case or the use of dedicated analysis software for specific aspects (3D, myocardial deformation, etc.). Most of this time is spent on quantification and interpretation, making it difficult to dedicate time for regular labelling of information in daily practice. However, labelling carried out correctly and systematically facilitates patient follow-up and allows, on a sufficient volume of data, its interpretation and use for the correct distribution of resources and the eventual elaboration of predictive models.

It is in this healthcare scenario that artificial intelligence plays an increasingly important role, facilitating the development of medical applications that automate as far as possible healthcare, management or research processes [5]. Natural language processing is a major field of artificial intelligence that seeks to create computational algorithms capable of interpreting and interrelating with natural or human language [4]. In medical practice [12], natural language processing can be applied for different tasks such as automatic speech recognition [19], linguistic pattern recognition, text classification [10], to facilitate research [9] or for the automatic annotation of study reports [24].

In the case of cardiology, and more specifically echocardiography, there are applications of various kinds, from automatic reporting of echocardiographic studies [15], or the automatic extraction of left ventricular ejection fraction through regular expressions [11]. However, most applications have been developed in English; there are numerous opportunities in different languages, including Spanish, which, with more than 500 million Spanish speakers in the world, represents an important niche for the development of natural language processing tools applied to this field [17].

Our Spanish-language model involves an effort in the specific analysis of echocardiographic terms, specifically valvulopathies, and the tasks it incorporates could contribute to methodological advances for the clinical application of natural language processing. In this sense, and to the best of our knowledge, it is the first natural language processing model in Spanish applied to cardiology with structured and free publication guidelines, accessible from this publication; which means that it is completely transparent to researchers and that any of them can contribute improvements to the model. We have also incorporated an active learning system into the natural language processing model that prospectively suggests labels to the clinician based on the written echocardiographic report, which can be corrected if errors are found. Thanks to these corrections, the system is able to improve progressively.

As mentioned above, this paper describes the proof of concept of the creation, development and application of a natural language processing and active learning model in echocardiography. Valvulopathy labels were selected due to their clinical importance, their prevalence as a pathology, the diversity in their degree of affectation and the variety in their wording. As an example, note the good performance obtained by the model in the interpretation of reports written by a total of 75 different physicians, with different expressions and modes of wording; allowing the information to be summarised into closed variables that can be analysed and traced. Although the current model is limited to the labels described, this system is flexible, allowing the incorporation of new labels, fields and variables, within and even outside the field of echocardiography.

Another possible aspect is the development of decentralised models known as federated learning [3], in different hospitals of the National Health System, which would allow the construction of transversal models without the need for additional efforts in the active cooperation of doctors or the sharing of data between centres. This type of model, in addition to providing more objective results, has the advantage of generalising results in a more efficient way.

It is appropriate to highlight some possible improvements with respect to the presented model. First, text preprocessing (tokenization, lemmatization, stopwords) can be detrimental if relevant information for the analysis is lost. Second, the incorporation of simpler techniques such as regular expression analysis could help to improve the model. Finally, the style used in echocardiographic reports is reasonably similar, and thus an unsupervised study of similarities could be interesting for the creation of standard reports that could serve as reference.

Among the limitations of the present work is the fact that the model was adjusted only to valvulopathies and developed in a single centre; although two independent corpora were applied for its creation and subsequent validation.

5   Conclusions

The developed model demonstrates the usefulness of NLP for automatically structuring and tagging information in text format and Spanish language from a large medical repository. The adjusted models combined with active learning, allow to improve the results and facilitate the correct labelling in a prospective way. The present model is adjusted to valvular variables in echocardiographic studies, but it can be applicable to different medical fields.

References

1. Banerjee, I., Madhavan, S., Goldman, R.E., Rubin, D.L.: Intelligent word embeddings of free-text radiology reports. In: AMIA Annual Symposium Proceedings, pp. 411–420 (2017)
2. Bressan, R.S., Camargo, G., Bugatti, P.H., Saito, P.T.M.: Exploring active learning based on representativeness and uncertainty for biomedical data classification. IEEE J. Biomed. Health Inf. 23(6), 2238–2244 (2018)
3. Chen, J., Abbod, M., Shieh, J.S.: Integrations between autonomous systems and modern computing techniques: a mini review. Sensors 19(18), 3897 (2019)
4. Chen, P.H.: Essential elements of natural language processing: what the radiologist should know. Acad. Radiol. 27(1), 6–12 (2020)
5. Dorado-Díaz, P.I., Sampedro-Gómez, J., Vicente-Palacios, V., Sánchez, P.L.: Applications of artificial intelligence in cardiology. the future is already here. Rev. Esp. Cardiol. (Engl. Ed.) 72(12), 1065–1075 (2019)
6. Esteva, A., et al.: A guide to deep learning in healthcare. Nat. Med. 25(1), 24–29 (2019)
7. Evangelista, A., et al.: European association of echocardiography recommendations for standardization of performance, digital storage and reporting of echocardiographic studies. Eur. J. Echocardiogr. 9(4), 438–48 (2008)
8. Honnibal, M., Johnson, M.: An improved non-monotonic transition system for dependency parsing. In: Proceedings of the 2015 Conference on Empirical Methods in Natural Language Processing. Association for Computational Linguistics, Lisbon, September 2015
9. Hughes, K.S., Zhou, J., Bao, Y., Singh, P., Wang, J., Yin, K.: Natural language processing to facilitate breast cancer research and management. Breast J
10. Hughes, M., Li, I., Kotoulas, S., Suzumura, T.: Medical text classification using convolutional neural networks. Stud. Health Technol. Inform. 235, 246–250 (2017)
11. Kim, Y., et al.: Extraction of left ventricular ejection fraction information from various types of clinical reports. J. Biomed. Inf. 67, 42–48 (2017)
12. Kreimeyer, K., et al.: Natural language processing systems for capturing and standardizing unstructured clinical information: a systematic review. J. Biomed. Inf. 73, 14–29 (2017)
13. McInnes, L., Healy, J., Astels, S.: Hdbscan?: hierarchical density based clustering. J. Open Source Softw. 2(11), 205 (2017)
14. McInnes, L., Healy, J., Saul, N., Grossberger, L.: Umap: uniform manifold approximation and projection. J. Open Source Softw. 3(29), 861 (2018)
15. Nath, C., Albaghdadi, M.S., Jonnalagadda, S.R.: A natural language processing tool for large-scale data extraction from echocardiography reports. PLoS One 11(4), e0153749 (2017)

16. Nowotka, M.M., Gaulton, A., Mendez, D., Bento, A.P., Hersey, A., Leach, A.: Using chembl web services for building applications and data processing workflows relevant to drug discovery. Expert Opin. Drug Discov. **12**(8), 757–767 (2017)

17. Névéol, A., Dalianis, H., Velupillai, S., Savova, G., Zweigenbaum, P.: Clinical natural language processing in languages other than english: opportunities and challenges. J. Biomed. Seman. **9**(1), 12 (2018)

18. Pedregosa, F., et al.: Scikit-learn: machine learning in python. J. Mach. Learn. Res. **12**, 2825–2830 (2011)

19. Poder, T.G., Fisette, J.F., Déry, V.: Speech recognition for medical dictation: Overview in quebec and systematic review. J. Med. Syst. **42**(5), 89 (2018)

20. Pons, E., Braun, L.M., Hunink, M.G., Kors, J.A.: Natural language processing in radiology: a systematic review. Radiology **279**(2), 329–43 (2016)

21. Rodríguez, J.D., Pérez, A., Lozano, J.A.: Sensitivity analysis of kappa-fold cross validation in prediction error estimation. IEEE Trans. Pattern Anal. Mach. Intell. **32**(3), 569–75 (2009)

22. Sampedro-Gómez, J., et al.: Machine learning to predict stent restenosis based on daily demographic, clinical and angiographic characteristics. Can. J. Cardiol. **36**, 1624–1630 (2020)

23. Wong, J., Manderson, T., Abrahamowicz, M., Buckeridge, D.L., Tamblyn, R.: Can hyperparameter tuning improve the performance of a super learner?: a case study. Epidemiology **30**(4), 521–531 (2019)

24. Zech, J., et al.: Natural language-based machine learning models for the annotation of clinical radiology reports. Radiology **287**(2), 570–580 (2018)

25. Řehůřek, R., Sojka, P.: Software framework for topic modelling with large corpora. In: Proceedings of the LREC 2010 Workshop on New Challenges for NLP Frameworks. ELRA (2010)

Biomedical Signal Measurement, Acquisition and Processing

Automated Annotation of Valence and Arousal During Cognitive Activity

Valentina Markova$^{(\boxtimes)}$ (ID), Todor Ganchev (ID), and Miroslav Markov

Technical University of Varna, Studentska Street 1, 9010 Varna, Bulgaria
via@tu-varna.bg

Abstract. We present an automated annotation method, which infers emotional arousal and valence tags based on physiological signals. This is performed with the help of binary detectors trained to recognize high/low arousal or passive/negative valence. The arousal and valence detectors were created from representative datasets containing evoked emotional reactions to widely used audio-visual stimuli. Next, these detectors were used to annotate physiological signals collected during different types of cognitive activity in the context of acute stress scenarios. We show that the automatically generated tags are correlated with work efficiency during various cognitive activities. The availability of such an automated annotation method would facilitate future studies on the influence of individual differences concerning work performance and the ability to cope with acute stress and cognitive overload. Such functionality could be essential for creating adaptive human-machine interfaces that account for the person's current emotions, cognitive load, and acute stress level.

Keywords: Work efficiency · Cognitive workload · Emotions · EDA · PPG

1 Introduction

Human emotions play a significant role in our life. Often, they are the reason for successes in our careers or support important decisions that we make. Due to them, we fail in our activities or at least perform below our capabilities. On the other hand, widely used terms as stress (e.g., stress at work) and excitement also affect the human ability to perform particular tasks. Research questions such as how these factors interact and how they affect cognitive load, attention and performance are still not entirely answered, although extensive research results exist. Understanding the nature of emotional states is essential for various research areas – neurology, neurobiology, psychology and psychiatry, and artificial intelligence. The correct recognition and assessment of such states would provide opportunities for individual performance prediction, avoid undesirable outcomes from specific activities or the chance to influence these states in order to achieve positive outcomes.

Such knowledge could be of particular importance concerning the increasingly developing field of Human-Machine Interaction (HMI). For efficient collaboration between humans and machines, a machine would need to possess functionalities that allow it to

© Springer Nature Switzerland AG 2021
I. Rojas et al. (Eds.): BIOMESIP 2021, LNCS 12940, pp. 53–62, 2021.
https://doi.org/10.1007/978-3-030-88163-4_5

recognize correctly and respond adequately to different emotional states and the detected level of stress. Machines would also need functionality to detect mental fatigue and the degree of attention directly related to the cognitive load experienced by humans.

In brief, here we understand cognitive load (CL) as the cognitive resources required for specific task completion [1]. CL concerns various cognitive activities, and knowing the actual levels is crucial regarding the performance during specific activities. The mental effort that one needs to make to solve a specific task depends on the task difficulty, prior knowledge, motivation and current emotional state. Researchers in [2, 3] show that different cognitive activities require various cognitive demands (with adequate levels of emotional affect) for optimal performance. According to Yerkes Dodson law [4], stress and arousal could help cognitive processes, such as attention or problem solving, yet this relation becomes negative after a certain point.

Numerous studies have investigated the interaction between cognitive abilities and emotional states. The emotions, according to Russell's model, are presented in two-dimensional space by the factors: valence (ranging from negative to positive) and arousal (low to high) [5]. In [6], it was shown that positive emotion improves the understanding and processing of information. Their research suggested that moderate emotional intensity usually provokes a better understanding of both positive and negative texts. Furthermore, the influence of valence on work performance was demonstrated using an emotional Stroop test [7]. Besides, results presented in [8] showed that interference from emotional distractors increased when the cognitive load was high.

The traditional approach for affect state recognition is based on features computed from multiple physiological signals fed to a machine learning algorithm. Among these are physiological signals obtained from sources such as Electrocardiogram (ECG), Photoplethysmogram (PPG), Electrodermal Activity (EDA), respiration and Encephalogram, which are frequently used for model development in stress detection, emotion recognition and cognitive load assessment. This approach is based on the preselection of stimuli that evoke specific emotional or cognitive conditions and machine learning methods for automated recognition. Depending on the research perspective, there are various well-known and widely used experimental setups, based on pictures, audio-video clips, cognitive tasks with different difficulty levels, video games, evoking different emotions and work-related stress.

The abovementioned and many other studies investigating the possible relationships between cognitive workload, emotions, and variations of physiological signals observed certain correspondences; however, it remains unclear how these categories interact and their cumulative effect on work efficiency. In the current study, we investigate the applicability of an automated annotation process that helps for tagging portions of physiological signals captured during cognitive activities. The automated tagging process (Sect. 2) is based on the use of purposely-developed binary classifiers, which are trained to discriminate between high/low arousal and negative/positive valence labels. The corresponding arousal and valence models are developed using recordings of physiological signals captured during stimulation with pictures and music videos to evoke specific emotional arousal and valence reactions with different intensities. The use of task-specific classifiers for the automated extraction of information about emotional arousal and valence conditions during various cognitive tasks could become an essential instrument for the facilitation of future research on the relations between emotional and cognitive aspects of mental performance.

2 Method

In the present work, we propose a method for the automated annotation of physiological signals acquired during cognitive activities concerning emotional arousal and valence conditions. The tags obtained after annotation could help assess the current work efficiency of individuals or can be used to provide clues about the current mental state of humans for the needs of adaptive human-machine interfaces. The functionality provided by our method aims to facilitate the understanding of work performance in scenarios involving intense computer use, yet it will be helpful in other use cases which involve intense human-machine interactions. For instance, a use case involving intelligent human-machine interaction would require that the machine becomes aware of humans' momentous emotional arousal and valence. Such sensitivity would allow the machine to adapt the communication strategy and behaviour according to the human operator's current cognitive load, attention, and stress levels. Such adaptability is essential for developing human-friendly interfaces, but more importantly, for improving work efficiency and safety in human-robot collaboration setups.

In the following Sect. 2.1, we outline the overall concept of the proposed annotation method, and in Sect. 2.2, we describe the resources required to implement this concept. We demonstrate its feasibility in Sect. 2.3, where we provide a detailed description of one particular implementation. Experimental validation of the proposed concept and a qualitative assessment of the automated annotation accuracy for the current implementation are presented in Sect. 4.

2.1 Overall Concept

The overall concept of the proposed annotation process aiming at the automated tagging of emotional arousal or valence is shown in Fig. 1. The block diagram shown in the figure holds both for the arousal and valence annotation systems. The last is because the workflow is identical for the annotation of low/high emotional arousal and positive/negative valence, except that different metadata are needed to create and optimize the corresponding blocks. Therefore, in the following, we outline the process for both arousal and valence collectively.

As shown in Fig. 1, the proposed method relies on the availability of an annotated dataset, D_v, consisting of physiological recordings and the corresponding metadata for emotional arousal or valence. The *Train* and *Test* subsets of D_v are used to train and optimize the performance of the purposely-developed binary detectors. We also obtain a quantitative assessment of the annotation process performance and reliability based on the *Test* subset. The training and the optimization phases of detector development share identical signal processing and feature extraction steps; however, they operate on different subsets of D_v the *Train* and *Test* data correspondingly. Next, the optimized binary detectors are used for inferring the corresponding tags for untagged recordings, available in the dataset D_c. Depending on what metadata was used during model creation, the automated processing of D_c results in the generation of the required tags: {*low arousal, high arousal*} or {*positive valence, negative valence*}. The annotation process can be performed either on a frame level or an entire recording level, depending on the actual needs of the target application.

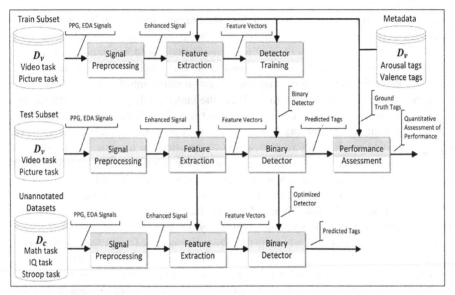

Fig. 1. The overall concept of the annotation process for high/low emotional arousal and positive/negative valence

2.2 Resources Required

Here, we focus on human-machine collaboration scenarios, and thus, the proposed process is meant to annotate physiological recordings acquired during various cognitive activities. In the current research, we consider annotation of emotional conditions occurring during cognitive activity associated with three tasks: solving simple Math problems, solving logical problems typically found in IQ tests, and colour recognition as implemented in the traditional Stroop test. In the implementation presented in Sect. 2.3, we consider that the physiological signals acquired during these three tasks constitute the D_c dataset. It is essential to mention that these three tasks correspond to different types of mental workload and, in the specific setup, are also designed to cause stress due to the limited time for response. This limited-time setup is purposely designed to obtain further understanding of the interrelationship between mental workload and emotions.

The development of reliable binary detectors of low/high emotional arousal and positive/negative valence tags depends on the quality of the dataset D_v. In general, it is expected that D_v would represent the emotional conditions of interest, and at the same time, it is avoid from other influences that might be due to physical or emotional stress, significant mental effort, or other sources of influence. For that purpose, the

Train and *Test* subsets of D_v were meant to represent the reactions to emotion-evoking stimuli which do not require significant cognitive effort. Because of that, we designed the dataset D_v entirely from recordings collected while the participants were watching musical video clips and pictures. The data collection procedure did not require any response, so the participants were expected to remain focused on what they watched. The musical audio-video clips and the pictures stimuli used to create D_v were carefully selected to elicit emotions in the four quadrants of the arousal-valence space. The specific choice of stimuli affects the metadata composition and the training data balance used for the detector development.

2.3 Implementation

Let us assume the availability of a representative dataset, D_v, consisting of physiological recordings that capture the spontaneous reactions of the peripheral nervous system to visual stimuli, which evoke emotional responses. According to a well-established methodology, the stimuli used to create D_v consist of tagged music video clips and emotion-evoking pictures [10]. As shown in Fig. 1, the PPG and EDA signals obtained from the dataset D_v are preprocessed, which involves segmentation, eliminating undesired variability, and suppressing artefacts. The enhanced PPG and EDA signals are next used to compute a large number of features. These signal preprocessing and feature extraction steps are standard for all data flows shown in Fig. 1. Afterwards, feature normalization and feature selection are applied to select a person-independent subset of relevant features. Finally, the feature vectors obtained for the training dataset are used in the detector training process. The feature vectors computed for the test and unannotated datasets are identical to those selected during the detector development process. The feature vectors computed from the test subset of D_v are used to finetune the accuracy of the binary detectors of high/low emotional arousal and positive/negative valence. Once the performance of the binary detectors is decided satisfactory, these are used to infer the corresponding tags on a frame-level or recording level for a dataset, D_c, which contains untagged physiological recordings acquired during various cognitive activities.

3 Experimental Setup

In the context of the current study, the CLAS (A database for cognitive load, affect and stress recognition dataset) [9] was preferred as a repository that combined visual stimuli evoking emotions in the four quadrants of the arousal-valence system with multi-task cognitive activities. The experimental setup aims to provoke people to concentrate, memorize, and decide problems using logic and prior knowledge. For this reason, we created a five-step procedure that includes three cognitive activities: a Math test, a Stoop test, and an IQ test, and two emotion elicitation tasks; 16 video clips and 16 pictures inducing different emotions according to the valence-arousal plane. The complexity, duration of stimuli, and time for reaction in each cognitive task were designed to cause stress. Thus, we assessed each participant's performance under stress caused by the short time allowed for task completion.

In brief, the CLAS dataset contains synchronized recordings of ECG, PPG, EDA and accelerometer data of 62 people. The data acquisition protocol includes a one-minute baseline record followed by {a Math test, recovery time, Stroop test, recovery time, IQ test, recovery time, Video clips, recovery time, Pictures set}. The Recovery stimuli between the tasks aimed to give time for people to relax a bit and recover their attention capacity.

The PPG and EDA recordings of 56 participants acquired during the abovementioned three cognitive tasks {Math, IQ, Stroop}, available in the CLAS database [9], were used to validate the proposed method. The overall procedure comprised signal preprocessing, feature extraction, feature vectors post-processing, and tags prediction based on the trained models for both modalities – arousal and valence. Here, we closely followed the signal processing and feature extraction procedures as in [10].

3.1 Feature Set

In the current study, we used the PPG and EDA recordings of the 56 participants from the CLAS dataset to validate the proposed automated annotation of physiological signals in terms of valence and arousal. For each user, there was data corresponding to a set of 16 emotionally tagged video clips and four blocks with four emotionally tagged pictures each. We experimented with pre-specified tags of visual stimuli retrieved from the DEAP database [11] and IAPS [12] to develop valence and arousal models. The overall process of signal preprocessing and the features extraction are described in [13]. In brief, the PPG and EDA signals were divided into blocks of 50 s with overlapping of 10 s, and next, we computed the same set of 39 features.

In total, six experiments were performed: detection of arousal and valence with video clips only (V), pictures only (P), and a common dataset containing both pictures and video dataset (VP). These differ in the amount of data, as the picture and video clips recordings have different durations, 80 and 60 s, respectively.

The binary detectors of valence and arousal were evaluated directly against the corresponding ground-true tags C_k assigned to the visual stimuli (video clips and pictures). The recognition performance was estimated as an average weighted classification accuracy as defined in Sect. 3.3. Throughout all trials, for each person-specific binary detector, we implemented a leave-one-out cross-validation algorithm.

For a better understanding of the influence of emotional state and worked-related stress on the cognitive load and work efficiency, we performed two kinds of experiments: firstly, we developed statistical models of arousal and valence based on the pre-specified tags of the audio-visual stimuli, which were evaluated for consistency of decisions. Then, we used the created models to generate tags. Finally, we analyzed the correlation between automatically generated tags for three kinds of cognitive activities.

3.2 Detection

Firstly, the person-specific detectors of valence and arousal for each user were trained. These detectors are built as purposely-developed classifiers based on the Support Vector Machine (SVM) with the polynomial kernel, trained with the Sequential Minimal Optimization (SMO) method. The class labels C_k were obtained based on the metadata, where the pre-specified tags for each audio-visual stimulus are available. In such a way, we created six automated detectors – a different one for each of the three datasets {V, P, VP}, for either high/low emotional arousal or positive/negative valence detection.

The adjustable parameters of the SVM classifier were finetuned through the leave-one-out approach and grid search. The search range was set as follows: *box constrain* $C \in [10e - 6, 10e + 0]$ with *step* $10e + 0.2$, *tolerance* $\varepsilon \in \{10e - 8, 10e - 7\}$, and *polynomial order* $p \in \{1, 2, 3\}$. The classifier fine tuning was carried out for each of the three datasets {V, P, VP}, outlined in Sect. 3.1, and separately for the arousal and valence cases.

3.3 Performance Metrics

We use the metric *classification accuracy* for the quantitative assessment of the actual implementation presented in Sect. 3. Specifically, the classification accuracy of the person-specific valence or arousal detectors was evaluated as the weighted sum of the class-specific accuracy attained for the two classes, $C_k = \{low\ arousal, high\ arousal\}$ or $C_k = \{positive\ valence, negative\ valence\}$:

$$A(n) = \frac{1}{2}\left(\frac{n_{cf}}{n_f} + \frac{n_{ct}}{n_t}\right), n = 1, \ldots N \tag{1}$$

where n_{cf} (true negative) is the number of correctly detected vectors related to the class $C_k = low\ arousal$ or *positive valence*, and n_{ct} is the number of correctly detected occurrences for the class $C_k = high\ arousal$ or *negative valence*, depending on the detector purpose.

Finally, in Sect. 4, we present the *average detection accuracy* computed for all participants in percentages. The average detection accuracy of the various experimental setups considered here provides information for the actual performance in each setup.

4 Results

4.1 Detection Performance Evaluation

At the initial stage, we evaluate the performance of the six statistical models for the automated generating of the high/low emotional arousal and positive/negative valence tags concerning their detection accuracy. During this evaluation, we followed the experimental protocol and procedures outlined in Sect. 3. The numerical results for the detection accuracy are shown in Table 1. Specifically, each cell in the table shows the average detection accuracy computed over all participants for each modality (emotional arousal or valence) and the corresponding dataset {V, P, VP}. In all experiments, we used vectors of 39 features.

Based on the numerical results shown in Table 1, we can conclude that the three cognitive tasks are characterized with significantly different results in terms of average detection accuracy. Specifically, the averaged detection accuracy for the arousal models based on the common dataset (video and pictures) is about 10% higher than those computed by the videos or picture datasets alone. The difference in the average detection accuracy for the case of valence annotation is even more significant. The detector built only from the video data has an average accuracy of 71.7%, and the one developed based on the video clips and pictures data has average detection accuracy of 85.8%. For the valence detectors, there was no significant difference between the average detection accuracy obtained when the detectors are built only from video (V) or only from the picture (P) datasets – the difference between these is only 2.5%.

Table 1. The average detection accuracy in percentages for the arousal and valence detectors built from different subsets of data {V, P, VP}

Detectors	rousal model	Valence model
	Average Accuracy	Average Accuracy
Video clips, V	71.6%	71.7%
Pictures, P	77.6%	74.2%
Video clips & Pictures, VP	82.5%	85.8%

Based on the observed experimental results, we can conclude that the valence and arousal models built from the videos and pictures (VP) dataset led to higher average detection accuracy.

4.2 Automatically Generated Tags

The valence and arousal detectors built from the dataset consisting of videos and pictures (VP), which was found advantageous in Sect. 4.1, was used to automatically generate the high/low emotional arousal and positive/negative valence tags for the physiological signals collected during cognitive activity in the context of acute stress scenarios.

Table 2 presents the correlations between the automatically generated arousal and valence tags and participants' physiological responses to different cognitive activities. The automatically generated valence tags showed the strongest correlations between participants' reactions to Stroop and Math tests. Despite the induced stress condition, for 44 participants, we have observed positive valence responses to all cognitive tasks. It turned out that the effect of valence is negative for 12.5% of participants. The emotional intensity induced by IQ, Math, and Stroop tests vary between the tasks and partici-pants. Approximately 20% of the participants were observed to experience high arousal during the cognitive tasks. The high arousal levels helped to about 36% - their overall performance scores exceeded the average.

Table 2. Correlation between arousal and valence and the performance scores

Cognitive Activity	Emotional Influence	
	Arousal	Valence
IQ and Math	71.4%	80.3%
Stroop and Math	85.7%	89%
Stroop and IQ	78.6%	84%
Math, Stroop and IQ	67.8%	78.6%

5 Conclusion

In the current study, we investigated the applicability of an automated annotation process that helps for tagging portions of physiological signals captured during cognitive activities with high/low arousal and negative/positive valence labels. The arousal and valence models were developed using recordings of physiological signals captured during stimulation with pictures and music videos to evoke specific emotional arousal and valence reactions with different intensities.

We demonstrated that the automatically generated tags are correlated with work efficiency during various cognitive activities. The availability of such an automated annotation method would facilitate future studies on the influence of individual differences concerning work performance and the ability to cope with acute stress and cognitive overload. Such functionality would also contribute towards obtaining a multi-faceted analysis on the dependence of work efficiency from personal treats and emotions.

Furthermore, based on the analysis of the individual performance results obtained during the Math, IQ, and Stroop tasks, we deem that one can use the proposed arousal and valence annotation method in studies on the interrelations between work efficiency and emotions. The automated arousal and valence annotation method could also provide essential evidence about the emotional state of the human operator, which could facilitate intelligent human-machine interfaces. These interfaces could be equipped with abilities for flexible adaptation of the machine behaviours according to the momentous mental state of the human.

Acknowledgements. This research was supported by the Bulgarian National Science Fund (BNSF), with grant agreement FNI № KP-06-PN37/18, entitled "Investigation on intelligent human-machine interaction interfaces, capable of recognising high-risk emotional and cognitive conditions".

References

1. Conway, D., Dick, I., Li, Z., Wang, Y., Chen, F.: The effect of stress on cognitive load measurement. In: Kotzé, P., Marsden, G., Lindgaard, G., Wesson, J., Winckler, M. (eds.) INTERACT 2013. LNCS, vol. 8120, pp. 659–666. Springer, Heidelberg (2013). https://doi.org/10.1007/978-3-642-40498-6_58

2. Wu, D., et al.: Optimal arousal identification and classification for affective computing using physiological signals: virtual reality Stroop task. IEEE Trans. Affect. Comput. **1**(2), 109–118 (2010)
3. Petrucci, M., Pecchinenda, A.: The role of cognitive control mechanisms in selective attention towards emotional stimuli. Cogn. Emot. **31**(7), 1480–1492 (2017)
4. Yerkes, R.M., Dodson, J.D.: The relation of strength of stimulus to rapidity of habit-formation. J. Comp. Neurol. Psychol. **18**(5), 459–482 (1908)
5. Russell, J.A.: A circumplex model of affect. J Pers Soc Psychol. **39**, 1161–1178 (1980)
6. Mukundan, C.R., Kacker, P.: Emotional Arousal - The Driving Force of Life. J. Psychol. Clin. Psychiatry **9**, 00505 (2018)
7. Megalakaki, O., Ballenghein, U., Baccino, T.: Effects of valence and emotional intensity on the comprehension and memorization of texts. Front. Psychol. **10**, 179–186 (2019)
8. Ben-Haim, M.S., Williams, P., Howard, Z., Mama, Y., Eidels, A., Algom, D.: The emotional Stroop task: assessing cognitive performance under exposure to emotional content. J. Vis. Exp. JoVE **112**, 53720 (2016)
9. Markova, V., Ganchev, T. Kalinkov, K.: CLAS: a database for cognitive load, affect and stress recognition. In: 2019 International Conference on Biomedical Innovations and Applications (BIA), Varna, Bulgaria, pp. 1–4 (2019)
10. Kalinkov, K., Markova, V., Ganchev, T.: Front-end processing of physiological signals for the automated detection of high-arousal negative valence conditions. In: 2019 X National Conference with International Participation (ELECTRONICA), Sofia, Bulgaria, pp. 1–4 (2019)
11. Koelstra, S., et al.: DEAP: a database for emotion analysis using physiological signals. IEEE Trans. Affect. Comput. **3**(1), 18–31 (2012)
12. Lang, P.J., Bradley, M.M., Cuthbert, B.N.: International affective picture system (IAPS): affective ratings of pictures and instruction manual. Technical Report A-8. University of Florida, Gainesville, FL. (2008)
13. Kalinkov, K., Ganchev, T., Markova, V.: Adaptive feature selection through fisher discriminant ratio. In: 2019 International Conference on Biomedical Innovations and Applications (BIA), Varna, Bulgaria, pp. 1–4 (2019)

Focal and Generalized Seizures Distinction by Rebalancing Class Data and Random Forest Classification

Lina Abou-Abbas[1,2]($\boxtimes$), Imene Jemal[2,3], Khadidja Henni[1,2], Amar Mitiche[2,3], and Neila Mezghani[1,2]

[1] Imaging and Orthopaedics Research Laboratory, The CHUM, Montreal, Canada
lina.abou-abbas.1@etsmtl.net
[2] Research Center LICEF, Teluq University, Montreal, Canada
[3] INRS - Centre Énergie, Matériaux Et Télécommunications, Montréal, Canada

Abstract. Epileptic seizures are caused by abnormal electrical activity of brain cells, frequently accompanied by a short-lived loss of control or awareness. Epileptic seizures differ depending on their origin in the brain. They can be categorized as either focal or generalized in onset. The identification of seizure category is essential in brain surgery and in selecting medications that could help bring seizures under control. It is not always feasible to find out exactly if the seizure was generalized or focal without a thorough analysis of the continuous prolonged electroencephalographic (EEG) waveforms. In this study, we propose an automatic classification method based on Hjorth parameters measured in EEG. 1497 EEG signals from the Temple University Hospital Seizure Corpus (v.1.5.1) are used. Hjorth parameters (activity, complexity, and mobility) are extracted from these EEG records. To address class imbalance, data was rebalanced by Synthetic Minority Over Sampling (SMOTE). We also investigated the impact of changing the window length on the random forest classifier. For comparison, cost-sensitive learning has been applied by providing more weight to the minority class (generalized seizure) directly in the classifier. The performance of the proposed method was compared using accuracy, recall, and precision measures. Our method achieved a highest accuracy rate of 92.3% with a recall of 92.7% and precision of 91.8% using Hjorth parameters extracted from 10 s windows and rebalanced using SMOTE. A slight variation in performance measures occurred according to window size.

Keywords: Generalized and focal seizures · EEG · Hjorth parameters · SMOTE · Weighted random forest classification

1 Introduction

Epileptic seizures are characterized by an intense sudden burst of electrical activity in the brain. They have various causes and treatments and can affect people of all ages [1]. Epileptic seizures can be classified into two main categories: generalized and focal. Generalized seizures occur when an abnormal electrical activity involves concurrently

© Springer Nature Switzerland AG 2021
I. Rojas et al. (Eds.): BIOMESIP 2021, LNCS 12940, pp. 63–70, 2021.
https://doi.org/10.1007/978-3-030-88163-4_6

both sides of the brain [1]. Focal seizures, instead, are characterized by excessive electrical discharge in areas of a single brain side [1]. Around seventy percent of seizures can be controlled by medications. Following recent advances in machine learning based solutions for seizure detection [2, 3], the next challenge is the classification of seizures into focal or generalized. Recognition of epileptic seizure localization is crucial for drugs selection and surgery procedures. EEG signal interpretation remains the most effective and simple way for the localization of seizure origin. Because EEG visual inspection and interpretation is laborious, time consuming, and requires a trained expert, efficient automatic methods are necessary.

There have been several studies of automatic classification of seizures to characterize focal versus non-focal seizures: Sharma et al. [4] used a wavelet EEG representation to classify focal versus non-focal EEG signals, and reported an accuracy of 94.25%, whereas Bhattacharyya et al. [5] used rhythms extracted from empirical wavelet transforms to obtain an accuracy of 90%. A novel method based on empirical mode decomposition and phase space reconstruction was proposed in [6], results showed an accuracy of 96% in classifying focal EEG signals. In [7] Saputro et al. combined Mel Frequency Cepstral Coefficients, Hjorth components, and independent component analysis, reaching 91.4% recognition using a support vector machine. In [8] Roy et al. utilized a features extraction step based on calculating the eigenvalues by magnitude of the Fast Fourier Transform across all EEG channels and showed that a classification of seizure type is possible with an accuracy of 90.1% using the k-NN classifier. Das et al. in [9] discriminates between focal and non-focal signals, by using log-energy entropy derived from the combined empirical mode decomposition and discrete wavelet domain and reported a maximum accuracy of 89.4% with k-NN.

The automated ability to differentiate seizure types such as focal vs. generalized remains a largely neglected topic due to both a lack of clinical datasets and annotations complexity. The TUH EEG corpus [10] has recently become the largest publicly available dataset to support epilepsy research, offering the opportunity to develop automatic prediction, detection and classification systems for epileptic seizures. To date, only a limited number of studies have used this challenging database for the task of seizure classification [7, 8]. While these previous works showed promising results in classifying seizure types by analyzing EEG signals in time and frequency domains, computing complexity remains a major issue.

The Hjorth descriptor is a set of nonlinear features providing spectral properties of the EEG signals in the time domain [11]. It consists of three parameters: activity, mobility, and complexity (see Table 1). The activity represents the mean power of the signal and mobility its mean frequency. Complexity is the estimate of the signal bandwidth [11]. Hjorth parameters can be computed fast, and implementation is straightforward because their calculation is based on the signal variance and its derivatives. The computational cost is generally considered low compared to other methods. The Hjorth descriptor was shown by several studies to be useful to analyze nonstationary EEG signals and was successfully used in different applications, such as emotion recognition, mental-task discrimination, epilepsy prediction, and focal EEG signals classification [7, 12, 13].

Over the last decade, Random forest classifier (RF) has received growing attention due to its robust performance across a wide range of medical applications such as early seizure detection, automated sleep stage identification and recognition of Alzheimer's disease [14, 15]. The RF classifier, an ensemble learning method, uses a bagging scheme where classification is determined by majority voting [16]. Since medical data is often subject to class imbalance, which means the different classification categories are not equally represented, classifiers generally tend to be biased in favor of the majority class when equal weights are assigned to classes. Therefore, two techniques were introduced to address data imbalance: (1) cost-sensitive learning (giving each class a mis-classification cost or weight according to its distribution in the whole training dataset) and, (2) data resampling (under-sampling or over-sampling). SMOTE is based on generating synthetic minority examples by interpolation to oversample the minority class in the original training set [17]. In this study, we propose and investigate a method based on Hjorth parameters representation and random forest classification to distinguish focal from generalized epileptic seizures. We study the effect of varying the processing EEG window size. To address class imbalance, which is due to the uneven representation of generalized and focal seizure classes, we implemented the weighted sampler function [18] into the classifier and compared its results to a conventional random forest classifier preceded with SMOTE [17]. We show that the latter method enhanced the overall performance of the classifier.

Table 1. Hjorth parameters - y(t) is the signal and y'(t) is its derivative and var is the variance

Parameter	Equation
Activity	$var(y(t))$
Mobility	$\sqrt{\dfrac{\text{var}(y'(t))}{\text{var}(y(t))}}$
Complexity	$\dfrac{mobility(y'(t))}{mobility(y(t))}$

2 Materials and Methods

2.1 Database

Data is from the TUH EEG Seizure Corpus (TUSZ) v1.5.1 [19]. It was recorded in a real-time clinical environment using the International standard 10/20 system with 24 to 36 channels. The standard 19 EEG channels were used in this study. EEG segments have been labeled by experts. All uninteresting portions of the data, including eye blinks, artifacts, and noise were eliminated from the EEG records. The seizure segments annotated as generalized and focal were considered by this study. The dataset consists of EEG signals collected from 115 patients of which 61 are females. The data contains 218 sessions that were broken to 1497 files, of which 1069 contain focal seizures. The sampling frequency varies between 250 and 500 Hz. Table 2 summarizes the database of this study. Figure 1 shows plots of generalized and focal seizure EEG records. More details about the dataset can be found in [10, 19].

Table 2. Overview of the subset of the tusz eeg corpus used in our study for seizure type classification

Description	Number
Patients (F)	115 (61)
Sessions	218
Files	1497
Focal Seizures	1069
Generalized Seizures	428
Duration of Focal Seizure in hrs	147.49
Total duration in hrs	287.79

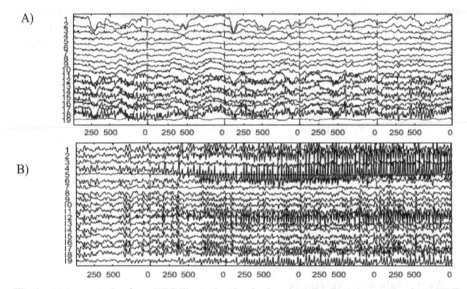

Fig. 1. A) An example of raw EEG illustrating focal seizure epochs. B) An example of raw EEG illustrating generalized seizure epochs

2.2 The Proposed Method

A bandpass filter with cutoff frequencies (0.5:75) Hz has been used, followed by a 60 Hz notch filter. The data has been re-referenced to the average of all electrodes, followed by re-sampling to 256 Hz. Window sizes of 5-, 10-, 15- and 20- s were considered. Hjorth activity, mobility, and complexity parameters were then extracted from each channel of the pre-processed EEG signals and for each window size separately. A feature vector of dimension 57 was considered at each run. The supervised classification was carried out using the RF Classifier. The classifier was chosen based on its successful use in previous works [14, 15, 20]. 10-fold cross validation was employed for training and testing to avoid over fitting and to ensure stable and reliable results, where EEG signals are partitioned randomly into 10 subsets, where nine are for training and the remainder for testing. In a first set of experiments, the weighted random forest classifier was considered to balance class weights. In a second set of experiments, data was rebalanced using the SMOTE prior to being used as input to classification. The performance of the classifier was evaluated using accuracy, recall and precision measures.

3 Experimental Results

The analysis described in this work was carried out using MATLAB R2020b and Python. The study explored the use of four window sizes. Results of classification of focal vs. generalized seizure EEG records are summarized in Tables 3 and 4. The performance of classification was calculated by averaging the accuracy, recall, and precision obtained using the test data in each of the 10 iterations. In both Tables 3 and 4, windows of 5, 10, 15, and 20 s, were compared. The first evaluation uses the weighted random forest classifier. Results in Table 3 show a maximum accuracy of 87.3% obtained using the 10s window with a recall of 58.9% and precision of 90.6%. The second evaluation uses SMOTE followed by a conventional random forest. Results in Table 4 show a maximum accuracy of 92.3% with a recall of 91.9%, and precision of 92.6%, obtained using the 10 s window size. An increase in window size corresponds to a slight decrease in performance.

Table 3. Classification performance of the weighted random forest classifier using four window sizes

	Window size in second			
	5 s	10 s	15 s	20 s
Accuracy	0.867	**0.873**	0.867	0.862
Recall	0.619	0.589	0.562	0.485
Precision	0.896	0.906	0.891	0.894

Performance was also investigated using the receiver operating characteristic (ROC) curve analysis and area under the curve (AUC) metric. The ROC curve represents the cut-off values between the true positive and false positive rates. Figure 2 displays ROC curves when weighted RF is used. Figure 3 displays ROC curves when SMOTE is used followed by a conventional RF. Figures 2 and 3 give the performance with 10-fold cross validation. AUC for each fold is shown in each figure, in addition to the mean of AUC.

Results indicate that performance is good for all folds, giving an average of AUC equal to 92% for weighted RF. A high value of 98% AUC is obtained with RF preceded with SMOTE. In summary, RF classification preceded by SMOTE yields the best performance for each of the 10-folds compared to weighted RF.

Table 4. Classification performance of the our approach using smote followed by random forest classifier

	Window size in second			
	5 s	10 s	15 s	20 s
Accuracy	0.918	**0.923**	0.922	0.921
Recall	0.903	0.919	0.927	0.928
Precision	0.931	0.926	0.918	0.916

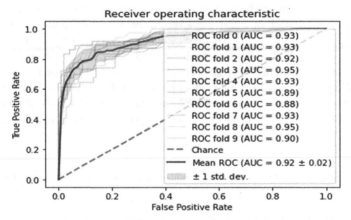

Fig. 2. Receiver Operating Characteristic (ROC) curve for the weighted RF classifier. Each curve denotes the ROC of one-fold of the 10-fold cross validation: AUC is displayed for each fold and mean AUC for the 10-fold.

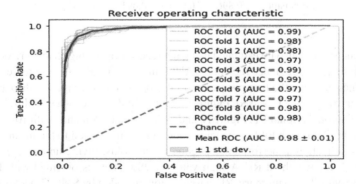

Fig. 3. Receiver Operating Characteristic (ROC) curve for RF classifier preceded with SMOTE. Each curve denotes the ROC of one-fold of the 10-fold cross validation: AUC is displayed for each fold and mean AUC for the 10-fold.

As can be seen from results in Tables 3 and 4, the proposed hybrid method (combination of Hjorth descriptor, SMOTE and RF) outperforms the weighted RF with consistent improvement of 5% in classification accuracy. The method achieved an accuracy of 92.3% for the focal and generalized seizures classification. The precision and recall were also good. These results demonstrate the advantage in balancing the input feature space using SMOTE before classification, instead of giving each class a mis-classification cost. With regard to the window size, the results show a slight difference in accuracy, recall and precision as the window size varies between 5 and 20 s. The best results were obtained for a 10 s window size in both experiments.

4 Conclusion

In this study, we investigated focal vs. generalized seizure classification using a subset of the TUSZ corpus. We investigated two ways to address imbalanced data, Random Forest supervised classification, and Hjorth data description extracted from 19 EEG channels. Weighted Random Forest classification was compared to a conventional Random Forest classifier preceded by SMOTE oversampling. Results indicate a good separation between focal and generalized seizure using SMOTE applied on EEG segments of 10 s window size. A system for classifying seizure types could be a clinically relevant tool for experts to have better diagnosis. In future work, we intend to expand our study to include classification of specific types of generalized and focal seizures such as tonic, clonic, tonic-clonic, complex partial, and simple partial seizures. In addition, we will include a cross-database evaluation to generalize our proposed method.

Acknowledgment. Special thanks to Youssef Ouakrim for his technical contribution in coding stage. This research was supported by funding from Fonds de recherche du Quebec- Nature et technologies (L.A.A) and the Canada Research Chair on Biomedical Data Mining (950–231214).

References

1. Stafstrom, C.E., Carmant, L.: Seizures and epilepsy: an overview for neuroscientists. Cold Spring Harb. Perspect. Biol. **7**, 1–19 (2015). https://doi.org/10.1101/cshperspect.a022426
2. Shoeb, A.H.: Application of machine learning to epileptic seizure onset detection and treatment MASS NSl of technology. Massachusetts Institute of Technology (2009)
3. Song, Y., Crowcroft, J., Zhang, J.: Automatic epileptic seizure detection in EEGs based on optimized sample entropy and extreme learning machine. J. Neurosci. Methods **210**, 132–146 (2012). https://doi.org/10.1016/j.jneumeth.2012.07.003
4. Sharma, M., Dhere, A., Pachori, R.B., Acharya, U.R.: An automatic detection of focal EEG signals using new class of time–frequency localized orthogonal wavelet filter banks. Knowl.-Based Syst. **118**, 217–227 (2017). https://doi.org/10.1016/j.knosys.2016.11.024
5. Bhattacharyya, A., Sharma, M., Pachori, R.B., Sircar, P., Acharya, U.R.: A novel approach for automated detection of focal EEG signals using empirical wavelet transform. Neural Comput. Appl. **29**(8), 47–57 (2016). https://doi.org/10.1007/s00521-016-2646-4
6. Zeng, W., Li, M., Yuan, C., Wang, Q., Liu, F., Wang, Y.: Classification of focal and non focal EEG signals using empirical mode decomposition (EMD), phase space reconstruction (PSR) and neural networks. Artif. Intell. Rev. **52**(1), 625–647 (2019). https://doi.org/10.1007/s10 462-019-09698-4

7. Saputro, I.R.D., Maryati, N.D., Solihati, S.R., Wijayanto, I., Hadiyoso, S., Patmasari, R.: Seizure type classification on EEG signal using support vector machine. In: Journal of Physics: Conference Series, p. 12065. IOP Publishing (2019). https://doi.org/10.1088/1742-6596/1201/1/012065

8. Roy, S., Asif, U., Tang, J., Harrer, S.: Seizure type classification using EEG signals and machine learning: setting a benchmark. In: 2020 IEEE Signal Processing in Medicine and Biology Symposium, SPMB (2020). https://doi.org/10.1109/SPMB50085.2020.9353642

9. Das, A.B., Bhuiyan, M.I.H.: Discrimination and classification of focal and non-focal EEG signals using entropy-based features in the EMD-DWT domain. Biomed. Signal Process. Control **29**, 11–21 (2016). https://doi.org/10.1016/j.bspc.2016.05.004

10. Obeid, I., Picone, J.: The Temple University Hospital EEG data corpus. Front. Neurosci. **10**, 196 (2016). https://doi.org/10.3389/fnins.2016.00196

11. Hjorth, B.: EEG analysis based on time domain properties. Electroencephalogr. Clin. Neurophysiol. **29**, 306–310 (1970). https://doi.org/10.1016/0013-4694(70)90143-4

12. Oh, S.-H., Lee, Y.-R., Kim, H.-N.: A novel EEG feature extraction method using Hjorth parameter. Int. J. Electron. Electr. Eng. **2**(2), 106–110 (2014). https://doi.org/10.12720/ijeee.2.2.106-110

13. Jemal, I., Mitiche, A., Mezghani, N.: A study of EEG feature complexity in epileptic seizure prediction. Appl. Sci. **11**, 1579 (2021). https://doi.org/10.3390/app11041579

14. Fraiwan, L., Lweesy, K., Khasawneh, N., Wenz, H., Dickhaus, H.: Automated sleep stage identification system based on time-frequency analysis of a single EEG channel and random forest classifier. Comput. Methods Programs Biomed. **108**, 10–19 (2012). https://doi.org/10.1016/j.cmpb.2011.11.005

15. Lehmann, C., et al.: Application and comparison of classification algorithms for recognition of Alzheimer's disease in electrical brain activity (EEG). J. Neurosci. Methods **161**, 342–350 (2007). https://doi.org/10.1016/j.jneumeth.2006.10.023

16. Breiman, L.: Random forests. Mach. Learn. **45**, 5–32 (2001). https://doi.org/10.1023/A:1010933404324

17. Chawla, N.V., Bowyer, K.W., Hall, L.O., Kegelmeyer, W.P.: SMOTE: Synthetic minority over-sampling technique. J. Artif. Intell. Res. **16**, 321–357 (2002). https://doi.org/10.1613/jair.953

18. Chen, C., Liaw, A., Breiman, L.: Using random forest to learn imbalanced data. Department of Statistics (2004)

19. Shah, V., et al.: The Temple University Hospital seizure detection corpus. Front. Neuroinform. **12**, 83 (2018). https://doi.org/10.3389/fninf.2018.00083

20. Donos, C., Dümpelmann, M., Schulze-Bonhage, A.: Early Seizure Detection Algorithm Based on Intracranial EEG and Random Forest Classification. Int. J. Neural Syst. **25**, 1550023 (2015). https://doi.org/10.1142/S0129065715500239

Event Related Potential Analysis Using Machine Learning to Predict Diagnostic Outcome of Autism Spectrum Disorder

Lina Abou-Abbas[1][(✉)], Stefon van Noordt[2], and Mayada Elsabbagh[1]

[1] Montreal Neurological Institute-Hospital, McGill University, Montreal, QC H3A 2B4, Canada
Lina.abou-abbas.1@etsmtl.net
[2] Department of Psychology, Mount Saint Vincent University, Halifax, NS B3M 2J6, Canada

Abstract. Identifying diagnostic biomarkers for autism spectrum disorder (ASD) is one of the challenges in autism research today. Recent studies using visual Event Related Potentials (ERPs) have identified abnormal patterns of brain activity in high-risk infants who go onto ASD diagnosis. In this study, we used well-established ERP components related to face processing. Features of these ERPs were used to explore the performance of machine learning algorithms in classifying ASD diagnostic outcomes. Data were used from the EEG Integrated Platform (EEG-IP). ERPs were recorded from six-months infants in response to static faces that dynamically changed between direct and averted eye gaze. Amplitude and latency measures of prominent ERP peaks including P100, N290 and P400 were derived across five scalp regions. Difference Scores between stimulus conditions (direct versus indirect eye gaze, toward versus away and face versus noise) were considered. Features were selected by weight correlation and used as inputs to three classifiers: k-Nearest Neighbor, Support Vector machines and Decision tree. Performance of these classifiers was compared. The results showed that the Decision tree classifier had the greatest average accuracy rate of 78.09% in classifying ASD diagnosis in high-risk infants.

Keywords: Autism spectrum disorder · Event Related Potential · P100 · N290 · P400 · Support Vector Machine · k-Nearest Neighbor · Decision tree

1 Introduction

Autism Spectrum Disorder (ASD) is a complex neurodevelopmental condition that affects communication, social interaction, and behavior. Intervention during infancy and early childhood can improve outcomes by changing developmental pathways across the lifespan. Even though ASD has its roots in very early perturbation of brain development, it is rarely diagnosed in children younger than 3 years of age [1]. Thus, identifying early risk and diagnostic biomarkers for ASD is of critical importance. According to a population-based study of medical records, infants have an elevated risk of future diagnosis if they have an older sibling who has been diagnosed with ASD [2]. These "infant siblings" cohorts are needed in order to investigate signs of neurological disorders from early infancy. Through these infants siblings studies, ASD has been linked to abnormal

© Springer Nature Switzerland AG 2021
I. Rojas et al. (Eds.): BIOMESIP 2021, LNCS 12940, pp. 71–79, 2021.
https://doi.org/10.1007/978-3-030-88163-4_7

electrocortical patterns of brain function [3, 4]. Most relevant to the current study, several groups have investigated high-risk infants' response to faces and eye gaze using event-related potentials (ERPs), which reflect dynamic brain responses that are time-locked to a specific event [5]. ERPs have become increasingly important for studying neurodevelopmental disorders such as ASD [6–8]. The overall goal of this line of work is to examine whether there are ERP differences that distinguish between high-risk infants who went on to develop ASD versus those who did not. In particular, the association between ERPs and ASD has focused largely on visually evoked ERPs, including early responses such as the P100 (approximately 100-290ms after stimulus onset), as well as later responses including the N290 (approximately 200-320ms after stimulus onset) and P400 (approximately 320-540ms after stimulus onset). Previous results show that characteristics of face-related ERP components at early and later temporal processing stages could distinguish high-risk from typically developing infants and that ERPs to dynamic eye gaze shifts (away versus towards) were associated with autism diagnosed at 36 months [7]. Other studies have found that cortical processing of faces versus objects are atypical in 10-month-old high-risk infants [8], and 6-month-old high-risk infants who went on to develop ASD had significantly faster cortical responses to faces [9]. The majority of previous ERP studies on siblings' cohorts have relied on more traditional parametric tests to evaluate group differences and found that neural measures could be considered valuable biomarkers for the early prediction of risk or clinical outcome. Recently, efforts have focused on expanding analysis pipelines to include automatic classification in order to discriminate subgroups of participants by risk status and/or diagnostic outcomes. For example, non-linear complexity computed from resting state EEG signals was used as a feature input to multiclass support vector machine algorithm to distinguish between typically developing and high-risk infants with accuracies approaching 80% as early as 9 months [10, 11]. Using behavioral and developmental measures, some studies have applied machine learning methods (ML) to show its robustness in improving ASD screening and diagnostic instruments [10, 12, 13]. In [12], authors used multi-level SVM model to differentiate verbal ASD individuals and found 89.2% accuracy with only five behavioral codes. In [13], authors used Mullen Scales of Early learning and Vineland Adaptive Behavior scales from multiple time points as input for 10-fold cross-validation least-square SVM, and reported that prediction of ASD clinical outcome is possible with moderate accuracy at 14 months. To date, two studies have investigated the use of ERP data with ML techniques [14, 15]. By analyzing ERPs elicited during eye gaze processing (direct versus averted), SVM achieved 64% of global accuracy in discriminating high-risk infants from typically developing at 6 months [14]. In [15], authors used also SVM and found a maximum accuracy of 75.7% for distinguishing high-risk infants who went on to develop ASD from those who did not. Given that atypical face and gaze processing could be considered an early marker of ASD, the present study explored the use of various computational and engineering ML methods with previously established ERPs in infants [7]. We extracted as features several ERP peaks and latencies including P100, N290 and P400 across five scalp regions. We applied three widely used machine learning methods, k-Nearest Neighbor (KNN), Support Vector machines (SVM), and Decision tree (DT) to test whether ERP parameters were capable of classifying infants by risk status and diagnostic outcomes.

2 Methods and Materials

2.1 Participants

EEG data were drawn from the EEG Integrated Platform database (EEG-IP- not currently publicly available due to privacy or ethical restrictions) [16]. Participants included a subset of infants who participated in a longitudinal study (BASIS: British Autism Study of Infant Siblings) to investigate developmental differences between infants who have siblings with ASD (high-risk group: HR) and those who did not. Fifty-six-month-old infants provided sufficient data for ERP analysis. Seventeen infants were diagnosed with ASD at approximately 3 years of age, based on clinical assessment including the Autism Diagnostic Observation Schedule (ADOS) and the Autism Diagnostic Interview (ADI). Therefore, two groups were considered in this study: high-risk infants who went on to develop ASD (HR-ASD; n = 17; 6 girls), high-risk infants who did not go on to develop ASD (HR-noASD; n = 33; 24 girls). See Table 1.

Table 1. The number of participants available for analysis

	HR-noASD	R-ASD	All
Male	9	11	20
Female	24	6	30
Total	33	17	50

2.2 ERP Procedure

EEG was recorded at 500 Hz sampling rate using 128-channel Geodesic sensor nets. Infants were presented with visual stimuli to yield three main contrasts: face (static face versus noise control face stimulus), static gaze (direct versus averted) and dynamic gaze shifts (toward versus away). Stimuli were presented for 800 ms and trials began with the presentation of a static face followed by a sequence of 3 to 6 gaze shifts. Trials were presented continuously in a pseudorandom order for as long as the infant attended. Detailed information about the groups including data collection, clinical assessment, measures and different contrasts is presented in [7]-(Supplemental Data).

2.3 ERP Pre-processing

For the current study, EEG data were pre-processed using the EEG-IP Lossless (EEG-IP-L) pipeline [17], which provides comprehensive annotation of the raw EEG data to identify channels, time periods, and independent components that contain unreliable or non-stationary signals. Data identified as artifacts were purged, and a 1 Hz high pass and 30 Hz low pass filter was applied. The scalp data were then interpolated to 19 channels corresponding to the 10–20 montage and re-referenced to the average of all electrodes.

From the remaining continuous EEG, we extracted 800ms fixed-length epochs, time locked to the onset of each visual stimulus. ERP segments were corrected with the 200 ms pre-stimulus baseline. Five brain regions were selected based on previous studies indicating the sensitivity of ERP components during face and eye gaze processing [6, 18]. These were a frontal, temporal, occipital, central and posterior regions. Based on previous research [6, 7, 14] three prominent ERP peaks sensitive to face and eye-gaze processing were considered in this work: P100-maximum positive peak between 100 and 219 ms, N290-maximum negative peak between 220 and 319 ms and P400- maximum positive peak between 320 and 540 ms. In addition, two other peaks were considered: maximum negative peak (MNP between 0 and 219ms) and late positive response (LPR between 541 and 789 ms). Figure 1 shows ERP peaks of interest on an averaged ERP waveform at occipital region of one HR-noASD subject.

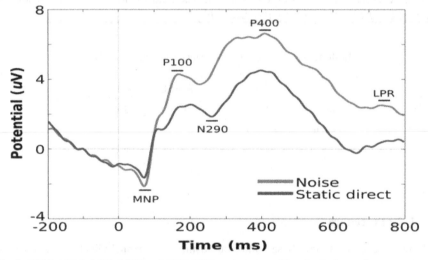

Fig. 1. P100, N290, P400, MNP and LPR- ERP components. The graph shows the average over trials of ERP response to face (in solid line) and to noise (dashed line) for an HR-noASD subject at occipital region.

2.4 ERP Features Extraction and Selection

A total of 300 features were extracted automatically for each subject, including amplitude and latency of five peaks (P100, N290, P400, MNP, LPR), five brain regions (frontal, temporal, central, occipital and parietal) and six stimulus conditions (static gaze direct/averted, gaze shift toward/away, face and noise). To reduce the number of features, we derived the difference score between each of the three contrasts (static gaze direct versus averted, face versus noise and gaze shift toward versus away). Therefore, the number of features was reduced to 150. All steps of ERP peaks extraction were performed using MATLAB and EEGLab [19]. To further avoid over-fitting due to the high number of features and low sample size we added a feature selection step based on the correlation of the features in the training group. A selection approach is used to measure the relevance of features before the use of the classifier according to the value of correlation between each feature and its respective class. A feature is considered to be more significant if the weight of that feature is larger. The feature subset is obtained by choosing the top ranked features of the binary classification problem (HR-ASD versus HR-noASD). The highest-ranking 10, 20 and 30 features were sub-grouped and considered separately for each experiment. Table 2 lists top-10 features for the classification of HR-ASD vs HR-noASD.

Table 2. Top 10 best features in classification of HR-ASD and HR-noASD groups- ranked by variable importance- Amp for Amplitude and Lat for Latency

Classification of HR-ASD and HR-noASD

Rank	Feature	Region	Contrast
1	Amp of P400	Temporal	Face Vs Noise
2	Lat of MNP	Central	Face Vs Noise
3	Lat of N290	Frontal	Static Gaze Direct Vs Indirect
4	Lat of MNP	Occipital	Face Vs Noise
5	Lat of P100	Posterior	Gaze Shift Toward Vs Away
6	Lat of P100	Occipital	Gaze Shift Toward Vs Away
7	Amp of LPR	Occipital	Gaze Shift Toward Vs Away
8	Lat of LPR	Central	Gaze Shift Toward Vs Away
9	Lat of P400	Central	Face Vs Noise
10	Amp of N290	Posterior	Static Gaze Direct Vs Indirect

2.5   Classification Procedure

The generalized ML strategy of our work is presented in Fig. 2. The automatic classification method includes two stages: training and testing. In both stages, for each subject, the whole ERP extraction procedure is applied to produce a feature vector, which is followed by a feature selection step to pick only the highest ranked features based on weight correlation. The classification is then carried out using three classifiers for comparison purpose: SVM, k-NN and DT. In a final step, the validation accuracy was calculated for each set of features. The accuracy corresponds to the ratio of the number of correctly classified samples to the total number of samples. Sensitivity represents the ratio of samples correctly classified in the positive group (HR-ASD in our case). Specificity represents the ratio of samples correctly classified in the negative group (HR-noASD).

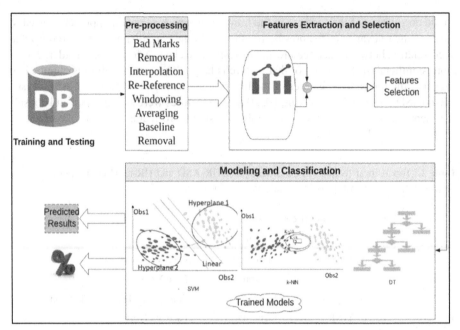

Fig. 2. A schematic block diagram of the classification method. EEG was first pre-processed to extract ERPs in response to visual stimuli. Peak extraction procedure is followed by feature selection step to pick highly discriminative features as input for three classifiers separately

3　Results

Based on results obtained in previous work [7, 14], we extended our research to compare the performance of three classifiers SVM, k-NN and DT and study the effect of using different features subsets on classifiers' performance. Due to the relatively small sample size in our main group of interest (n = 17 h-ASD) and to avoid class imbalance issue in the dataset (1:2 ratios between HR-ASD and HR-noASD), we used repeated under-sampling and 5-fold cross-validation. Under-sampling consists of selecting randomly, without replacement, an equal number of samples in each class by removing inputs that belong to the majority class (in our cases: HR-noASD) and 5-fold cross validation, which consists of splitting data randomly into 5 folds then using 4 folds for training and one for testing to ensure the accuracy of results. The steps of under-sampling and cross validation were repeated 100 times. Top groups of features (10, 20 and 30) having high weight correlation to classes were considered as optimal features at each iteration. Classification performance was calculated as the means of cross validation. The metrics of classifiers' performance in terms of overall mean accuracies, sensitivity and specificity are presented in Table 3. The results are grouped with respect to the top 10, 20 and 30 features by classifier. SVM, k-NN and DT are employed for each subset to identify which one contributed toward the best classification. Table 3 shows the results of the classification of HR-ASD and HR-noASD groups. DT achieves a greater overall mean accuracy rate of 78.09% compared to 75.7% with k-NN and SVM in classification of

HR-ASD and HR-noASD. Among the three subsets of features, the second subgroup of 20 features achieves the best classification rate while the subset of 10 and 30 lead to a lower classification rate when using DT. Compared to other classifiers, k-NN provided a better sensitivity of 85.4% to HR-ASD group and DT provided a better specificity of 76.8% to HR-noASD group. The accuracy of k-NN decreases from 75.7% to 70.6% with an increased number of features.

Table 3. Classification performance of HR-ASD and HR-noASD groups with different features subsets and three classifiers. The results correspond to the average of many iterations.

| | HR-ASD vs HR-noASD | | | | | | | | |
| | SVM | | | K-NN | | | DT | | |
Nb feat	cc %	Sens %	Spec %	Acc %	Sen s%	Spec %	Acc %	Sens %	Spec %
10	75.5	76.8	74.2	**75.7**	85.4	65.9	77.4	78.6	76.8
20	**75.7**	77.5	73.8	71.9	81.3	62.5	**78.1**	80.7	75.5
30	72.1	70.7	73.5	70.6	81.5	59.7	77.1	78.1	76.0

4   Discussion and Limitation

In this study, we used established ERP features to investigate the classification performance of three widely used machine learning techniques in distinguishing high-risk infants who went on to develop ASD from those who did not. To prevent overfitting due to the lower sample size of HR-ASD population and given the large number of candidate features, we choose to keep the number of features smaller than the total number of samples. A feature selection step based on weight correlation was used to reduce the number of features (subgroups don't exceed 30) and to improve system accuracy. Three feature subgroups with respect to the top 10, 20, and 30 ranked features were considered as input to classifiers. Five well defined ERP peaks namely: P100, N290, P400, MNP and LPR have been chosen in this study to classify HR-ASD vs HR-noASD. A previous study highlighted the advantage of applying ML to ERP data by employing an expanded feature extraction, selection algorithms, consider wider application [14]. As such, this study used ERP peaks originally investigated by [7, 14], but applied different pre-processing step, grouping options, and a more expanded feature extraction step followed by ML to predict outcome at an individual level. Visual ERPs in high-risk infants have been studied using P100, N290 and P400 [7, 20, 21]. Results from previous studies were based on group level comparisons and differed between studies due to the difference in datasets, scalp regions selected, and the condition contrasts that were used. At a group level, results showed a slower latency of P400 in HR-ASD infants for gaze shift (towards versus away) and slower N290 latency to faces compared to noise, in addition to greater P400 amplitude to gaze shift towards versus away. Our findings are in line with previous results and show that the aforementioned peaks are predictive features as they were among the top 30 ranked features (as shown in Table 2). The difference in findings between this current work and the previous studies is the use of peaks across all scalp regions as well as all experimental contrasts that could contribute to the performance of classifying outcomes at an individual level. Our results indicate a good separation between the studied classes. Therefore, ML can be applied to aid in classifying diagnostic outcome of ASD using event related potentials elicited by face stimuli with accuracy of 78.1%. We found that the number of chosen features, when less than 30, can slightly influence classification performance specifically with DT. K-NN is more sensitive to the number of features as accuracy rate was inversely related to the number of features. There are some limitations due to the small sample size used in this study. A larger cohort can validate the effectiveness of the proposed method for diagnostic outcome prediction. In future studies, we aim to expand our sample size and method to include resting state analysis of spectral power as these features were reported in previous studies to be efficient at discriminating at-risk group who went on to develop ASD.

Acknowledgment. Special thanks to all the families and their infants who participated in research related to identifying risk for ASD. Special thanks to the BASIS team for the data used in this study. We would also like to extend our thanks to Samantha Wunderlich for proofreading the article. The study was supported by funding from Fonds de recherche du Quebec- Nature et technologies (L.A.A), Brain Canada (M.E.), and NARSAD Young Investigator grant (S.v.N.). The British Autism Study of Infant Siblings (BASIS) was funded by the Medical Research Council and Autistica.

References

1. Courchesne, E., et al.: Mapping early brain development in autism . Neuron **56**(2), 399–413 (2007). https://doi.org/10.1016/j.neuron.2007.10.016
2. Charman, T., Jones, E.J.H.: Later sibling recurrence of autism spectrum disorder and attention-deficit/hyperactivity disorder: clinical and mechanistic insights. JAMA Pediatr. **173**, 128–130 (2019). https://doi.org/10.1001/jamapediatrics.2018.4345
3. Orekhova, E.V., et al.: EEG hyper-connectivity in high-risk infants is associated with later autism. J. Neurodev. Disord. **6**, 1–11 (2014). https://doi.org/10.1186/1866-1955-6-40
4. Jones, E.J.H., et al.: Reduced engagement with social stimuli in 6-month-old infants with later autism spectrum disorder: a longitudinal prospective study of infants at high familial risk. J. Neurodev. Disord. **8**, 1–20 (2016). https://doi.org/10.1186/s11689-016-9139-8
5. Luck, S.J.: An Introduction to Event-Related Potentials and Their Neural Origins. An introduction to the event-related potential technique. 11 (2005). https://doi.org/10.1007/s10409-008-0217-3.
6. Elsabbagh, M., et al.: Neural correlates of eye gaze processing in the infant broader autism phenotype. Biol. Psychiatry. **65**(1), 31–38 (2009). https://doi.org/10.1016/j.biopsych.2008.09.034
7. Elsabbagh, M., et al.: Infant neural sensitivity to dynamic eye gaze is associated with later emerging autism. Curr. Biol. **22**(4), 338–342 (2012). https://doi.org/10.1016/j.cub.2011.12.056
8. McCleery, J.P., Akshoomoff, N., Dobkins, K.R., Carver, L.J.: Atypical face versus object processing and hemispheric asymmetries in 10-month-old infants at risk for autism. Biol. Psychiat. **66**(10), 950–957 (2009). https://doi.org/10.1016/j.biopsych.2009.07.031

9. Jones, E.J.H., Venema, K., Earl, R.K., Lowy, R., Webb, S.J.: Infant social attention: an endophenotype of ASD-related traits? J. Child Psychol. Psychiatry. **58**(3), 270–281 (2017). https://doi.org/10.1111/jcpp.12650

10. Bosl, W.J., Tager-Flusberg, H., Nelson, C.A.: EEG analytics for early detection of autism spectrum disorder: a data-driven approach. Sci. Rep. **8**(1), 1–20 (2018). https://doi.org/10.1038/s41598-018-24318-x

11. Abou-Abbas, L., van Noordt, S., Desjardins, J.A., Cichonski, M., Elsabbagh, M.: Use of empirical mode decomposition in ERP analysis to classify familial risk and diagnostic outcomes for autism spectrum disorder. Brain Sci. **11**, 409 (2021). https://doi.org/10.3390/brainsci11040409

12. Bone, D., Bishop, S.L., Black, M.P., Goodwin, M.S., Lord, C., Narayanan, S.S.: Use of machine learning to improve autism screening and diagnostic instruments: effectiveness, efficiency, and multi-instrument fusion. J. Child. Psychol. Psychiatry. Allied. Discipl. **57**(8), 927–937 (2016). https://doi.org/10.1111/jcpp.12559

13. Bussu, G., Jones, E.J.H., Charman, T., Johnson, M.H., Buitelaar, J.K.: Prediction of autism at 3 years from behavioural and developmental measures in high-risk infants: a longitudinal cross-domain classifier analysis. J. Autism Dev. Disord. **48**(7), 2418–2433 (2018). https://doi.org/10.1007/s10803-018-3509-x

14. Stahl, D., Pickles, A., Elsabbagh, M., Johnson, M.H.: Novel machine learning methods for ERP analysis: a validation from research on infants at risk for autism. Dev. Neuropsychol. **37**(3), 274–298 (2012). https://doi.org/10.1080/87565641.2011.650808

15. Tye, C., et al.: Understanding the nature of face processing in early autism: a prospective study . J. Abnorm. Psychol. (2020). https://doi.org/10.1101/2020.05.06.20092619

16. van Noordt, S., et al.: EEG-IP: an international infant EEG data integration platform for the study of risk and resilience in autism and related conditions. Mol. Med. **26**, 40 (2020). https://doi.org/10.1186/s10020-020-00149-3

17. Desjardins, J.A., van Noordt, S., Huberty, S., Segalowitz, S.J., Elsabbagh, M.: EEG integrated platform lossless (EEG-IP-L) pre-processing pipeline for objective signal quality assessment incorporating data annotation and blind source separation. J. Neurosci. Methods **347**, 108961 (2021). https://doi.org/10.1016/j.jneumeth.2020.108961

18. Johnson, M.H., et al.: The emergence of the social brain network: evidence from typical and atypical development. Dev. Psychopathol. **17**(3), 599–619 (2005). https://doi.org/10.1136/bmj.38519.678148.8F

19. Delorme, A., Makeig, S.: EEGLAB: an open source toolbox for analysis of single-trial EEG dynamics including independent component analysis. J. Neurosci. Methods. **134**(1), 9–21 (2004). https://doi.org/10.1016/j.jneumeth.2003.10.009

20. Bentin, S., Allison, T., Puce, A., Perez, E., McCarthy, G.: Electrophysiological studies of face perception in humans. J. Cogn. Neurosci. **8**(6), 551–565 (1996). https://doi.org/10.1162/jocn.1996.8.6.551

21. De Haan, M., Johnson, M.H., Halit, H.: Development of face-sensitive event-related potentials during infancy: a review. Int. J. Psychophysiol. **51**(1), 45–58 (2003). https://doi.org/10.1016/S0167-8760(03)00152-1

Natural Cellulosic Fiber Reinforced Bio-Epoxy Based Composites and Their Mechanical Properties

Rajesh Mishra[1] and Michal Petru[2(✉)]

[1] Faculty of Engineering, Czech University of Life Sciences, Prague, Czech Republic
[2] Faculty of Mechanical Engineering, Technical University of Liberec, Liberec, Czech Republic
`michal.petru@tul.cz`

Abstract. The current research deals with bio-composites which are fabricated by using natural cellulosic fibers as reinforcements. A multifunctional bio-resin derived from epoxy is used as matrix. Four different types of fibers e.g., jute, sisal, coconut/coir and sugarcane (bagasse) were used for reinforcement. Fibers were used with three different loading levels by volume i.e., 20%, 25% and 30% respectively. Mechanical properties e.g., impact strength, flexural strength, tensile strength, and modulus etc. were evaluated and analyzed for the developed samples. The results reveal that there is improvement of mechanical properties by increasing fiber loading which is important requirement for several structural engineering applications. Among all the different types of cellulosic fibrous reinforcement, jute fiber-based composites exhibit superior tensile, impact and flexural properties as compared to all other fiber types. This is attributed to the jute fiber mechanical properties, morphology and surface roughness which contribute significantly towards the interfacial bonding with resin.

Keywords: Natural fiber · Bio-epoxy · Bio-composite · Tensile · Bending · Impact

1 Introduction

Composite materials are classified into different classes, out of which polymer composites find many applications in civil, automobiles, aircraft, sporting goods etc. due to their exceptionally low weight to strength ratio. There is a great demand for low cost, high strength composite materials in current time. Synthetic fiber reinforced composites are widely used for structural applications. The main problem with them remains non eco friendliness in terms of biodegradability and renewability. Different types of high-performance synthetic fibers e.g., Kevlar, Carbon and Nomex etc. have been developed which are practically used in all load bearing applications. However, widespread use of such materials becomes a serious issue for disposal in the form of solid waste. The landfill of such non-biodegradable waste becomes unbearable stress for environment [1, 2].

© Springer Nature Switzerland AG 2021
I. Rojas et al. (Eds.): BIOMESIP 2021, LNCS 12940, pp. 80–96, 2021.
https://doi.org/10.1007/978-3-030-88163-4_8

With the increasing demand of environmentally friendly materials and higher cost of conventional reinforcing fiber materials like (aramid, carbon, and glass), new low cost and environmentally friendly natural fiber reinforced composites has emerged as an alternative [3, 4].

Researchers are focusing on natural fiber reinforced, bio-based composites which impose minimal environmental impact as compared to conventional fiber-based composites. During the last few years, researchers and industrialists show great interest to use natural fibers as reinforcement in the composites. Natural fiber composites offer great environmental advantage like lower CO_2 emission, relatively easier/quicker biodegradability and are obtained from renewable sources. Furthermore, natural fibers have lower density, relatively high strength, and high stiffness. The epoxy composites reinforced by natural fibers can potentially replace existing fossil plastics and shall serve for electrical applications [5–7]. The environmentally friendly nature is a very important driver to increase the future use of natural fibers in the composites used in components with enhanced electrical insulation [4]. Bio-fiber reinforced composites are used in multiple applications which result in improvement of fuel efficiency. They can be used in commercial vehicles with decreased weight ranges, boats, interior of automotive which are bio-degradable and serve as an alternative of glass fiber-based composites. Jute fiber based composite has application in the areas like underground drainpipes, water pipes, different shaped beams, windows, doors, furniture, floor tiles and roofing etc. [8, 9]. The natural fiber reinforced composites are excellent among applications which are commercially used in interior and exterior of automobiles, example of which is usage of jute reinforced matrix in door panels of E-class Mercedes-Benz [10]. Natural fiber reinforced composites like flax fiber/polypropylene, hemp fiber/epoxy are particularly used for automotive applications due to their low density and low cost. The application of composite materials in hi-tech engineering as components in electrical/electronic appliances is becoming increasingly important. Epoxy reinforced composites are suitable for different industrial applications such as circuit board, electronic encapsulation etc. but their low strength is problematic [11–14]. Glass fibers for Printed Circuit Boards are already studied and used extensively [15]. Therefore, investigation of mechanical properties of composites that are produced by natural fiber-based reinforcement is widely important [16–18].

Researchers have studied the mechanical properties of polypropylene composites which are made by Jute fiber reinforcement. The results revealed that by increasing fiber content tensile strength and tensile modulus also increases [19]. Others investigated the effect of fiber orientation on the strength of jute fiber reinforced epoxy composites. They used four different orientations 45°/-45°, 30°/-60°, 15°/-75° and 0/90°. Results revealed that the composite with fiber orientation of 0/90° has the highest strength and stiffness. Compressive strength of jute-based composite was found to be higher than bamboo fiber composite [20–22]. Some researchers studied about mechanical properties of reinforced polyester resin composites with glass, sisal, and jute fibers. Results revealed that jute and sisal fiber reinforced composites have relatively good tensile, impact and flexural strength and are able to replace glass fiber as reinforcement [23].

From investigation of sisal fiber reinforced composites, it was concluded that the specific strength is almost comparable to that of glass fiber reinforced composites [24–26]. Bagasse fibers are gathered from sugarcane milling process, when juice is extracted from sugarcane. Composites reinforced with sugarcane bagasse exhibit relatively good modulus and higher stiffness than glass fiber reinforced composite with similar weight fraction [27]. Sugarcane bagasse composite incurs much lower cost due to its abundance, environmentally friendly nature because obtained from renewable and otherwise waste agro-product [28]. In another study, the researcher revealed that 40–60% coir fiber content results in satisfactory flexural properties. However, further increase of fiber content shows significant decrease in flexural strength. The optimal fiber content for automotive interior was found to be 60% coir fiber, 37% polypropylene and 3% maleic anhydride-grafted polypropylene (MAPP) [29]. Coir-jute hybrid composites found applications in the areas like backrest in buses, railway sleeper birth backing, doors and buildings interiors etc. [30]. As most of the natural fiber-based composites show negligible conductivity, they can be used as an insulator in various electrical circuits. Researchers have investigated the electrical resistivity of coir fiber reinforced polypropylene composites [31–33].

Polymer composites are widely used due to good mechanical properties, chemical resistance, and corrosion resistance behavior, but their fire resistance behavior is a threat. In order to achieve such properties, thermoset resins e.g. epoxies are used which show good fire resistance properties, high strength and modulus. Epoxy resins have a reasonably good ignition temperature (around 430 °C) as compared to thermoplastic resins e.g. unsaturated polyester (ignition temperature 300-3500C) [34, 35].

In the present study, effect of four different types of natural fiber reinforcements namely jute, sugarcane bagasse, sisal and coir in composites is studied in detail. Influence of fiber volume fraction (Vf) on mechanical properties e.g. tensile, flexural and impact properties is investigated. Bio-epoxy was chosen as the resin. They have very good electrical insulation properties, moisture resistance and high mechanical, chemical resistance, and heat resistance [36]. Thermal stability of BPF epoxy composite is as high as 375–450 °C [37]. A lot of work has been reported about mechanical properties of natural fiber-based composites with different types of matrices, but no literature was found about multifunctional polymer composites with BPF epoxy resins.

2 Materials and Methods

2.1 Materials

All the fibers were cut into short lengths ranging between 3–9 mm. The inherent properties of these fibers are given in Table 1. The matrix material was based on Bioepoxy. The epoxy resin was supplied by Sigma-Aldrich, China which has an epoxide equivalent weight (EEW) of 180 g/eq. Aradur HY-159 based on aliphatic amine curing agent was also purchased from Sigma-Aldrich, China.

Four different types of cellulosic fibers were selected for manufacturing of composite samples. Jute is from the bast fiber category. It shows good thermal insulation, high strength to weight ratio and high aspect ratio. Sisal was chosen from category of leaf fibers, coconut/coir fibers from category of fruit fiber and sugarcane bagasse which is the by-product of the sugar cane industry was selected from cane fiber category. Jute and coconut/coir was obtained from tropical country, sisal fiber was imported from China and sugarcane fibers were extracted from bagasse by manual process as mentioned in literature [38–40].

Table 1. Properties of fibers.

Properties	Jute	Sisal	Bagasse	Coir
Fiber fineness/diameter (μ)	18 + 1.1	20 + 1.2	22 + 1.2	21 + 1.1
Fiber linear density (Tex, g/km)	17 + 1.1	21 + 1.2	32 + 1.2	30 + 1.3
Fiber length (mm)	3–6	4–8	3–7	3–9
Fiber aspect ratio	167–344	200–400	136–318	143–429
Density (g/cm^3)	1.3	1.5	0.82	1.2
Cellulose content (%)	61–72	66–78	45–55	32–43
Lignin content (%)	12–13	8–11	19–24	41–45
Crystallinity (%)	60–70	60–70	51.1	27–33
Angle of orientation (^{0})	8–10	10–25	14–15	30–49
Tensile strength (MPa)	480 + 16.2	681 + 23.6	18 + 09.1	175 + 8.2
Elongation at break (%)	2.3 + 0.1	2.45 + 0.1	1.5 + 0.1	4.5 + 0.2
Young's modulus (GPa)	37.5 + 1.4	15.5 + 0.8	15.9 + 0.8	6 + 0.2
Tenacity (cN/Tex)	20.02 + 1.5	17.7 + 0.9	11.5 + 0.6	11.2 + 0.6

2.2 Methods

2.2.1 Samples Preparation

In order to develop the composite samples, a mold of 20×20 cm^2 (length $\times$ width) was fabricated. The fibers were uniformly distributed within the boundaries of the mold by layering and averaging technique so as to ensure uniform distribution. The mixture of epoxy and hardener was prepared as per manufacturer suggested ratio of 100:22 and was stirred well for uniform mixing. The matrix was dispensed over the fibers in the mold very carefully to ensure uniform distribution/impregnation of epoxy throughout the composite sample. Teflon sheet was placed on both sides of the sample and was pressed in a hydraulic compression device under 1 bar pressure for 30 min at 110 °C. Subsequently, the samples were cured at room temperature. In total twelve different samples were developed by repeating the same procedure with different fiber volume fraction (Vf) of 20%, 25% and 30% for all four types of fibers. Pure epoxy sample was also prepared for reference and comparison purpose.

2.2.2 Scanning Electron Microscopy

Scanning electron microscopy (SEM) was carried out for the fiber samples as well as the composites after mechanical (tensile) testing. The samples for scanning electron microscope were prepared with Quorum Q150R ES, which is a sputter and uses gold-plating with argon gas atmosphere. The thickness of gold plating was kept at 2 nm using a current of 20 mA. The scanning electron microscope MIRA 3 TESCAN was used for this purpose. The samples were visualized in nitrogen atmosphere with SE (secondary electron) detector, using acceleration voltage of 5–10 kV. The working distance was maintained at 16–32 mm with scan mode. The 500x magnification was used for all the samples.

2.2.3 Characterization of Mechanical Properties

The developed composite samples were cut into appropriate sizes for different testing and characterization as per required standards. All the samples were conditioned at 55% RH and 23 + 2 °C for 24 h before testing. All mechanical tests were conducted under the same controlled condition of humidity and temperature.

To measure the tensile properties, samples were cut in the size of 200 mm × 2.50 mm x 2.6 mm and the test was carried out on universal testing machine Zwick/Roell Z100 as per ASTM-D 3039 standard. The testing device works on principle of constant rate of elongation (CRE) which was set to 2 mm/min. Vernier caliper was used before testing to measure the thickness of each specimen. The effective gauge length of test samples was set as 100 mm. The maximum load applied was 1000 kN. Maximum load of the specimens was noted before fracture or failure. By monitoring the strain and load of the specimens, the stress strain response was plotted. From this plot, the tensile modulus and ultimate tensile stress were calculated. For each sample 10 measurements were carried out. The mean and standard deviation were calculated.

The flexural properties of composite samples were evaluated using 3-point bending test according to standard test method ASTM-D7264. The samples were cut into size of 120 mm × 13 mm × 2.6 mm and test was performed by universal testing machine Zwick/Roell Z100. The distance between supporting spans of 80mm and test speed of 1 mm/min was maintained. For each sample 10 measurements were carried out. The mean and standard deviation were calculated.

In order to investigate the impact properties of the samples, Zwick/Roell HIT 50P Charpy impact tester was used according to ISO-179–1 standard. Samples were cut in size 80 mm × 10 mm x 2.6 mm for testing. The thickness and width of samples were measured by Vernier caliper before testing. Specimens were notched on one side for initiation of a predetermined crack. They were placed on specific slot and a pendulum with 50J energy was allowed to hit and break the specimens.

3 Results and Discussion

3.1 Morphological Analysis by Scanning Electron Microscopy (SEM)

The samples were developed with randomly oriented short fibers of natural origin. They have inherent natural unevenness and thus cannot be assumed to show consistent morphological features. When such fibrous systems are impregnated with resin, there are chances that voids will appear, and the fiber surfaces will not be uniformly covered by the resin. It is therefore extremely important to analyze the fractured surfaces of the composites by scanning electron microscopy in order to ascertain that the failure is not because of any such void which is a possible site for tensile or impact fracture. The microscopic analysis of composite samples after tensile testing was carried out with the help of SEM images. Figure 1 shows images of jute-bio-epoxy composite samples with different wt% taken at a 500x magnification.

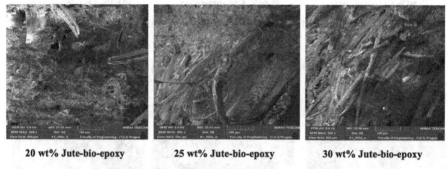

| 20 wt% Jute-bio-epoxy | 25 wt% Jute-bio-epoxy | 30 wt% Jute-bio-epoxy |

Fig. 1. SEM images of jute-bio-epoxy composites.

It can be observed that with 20 wt% of jute fibers, there are some voids near thr fiber surface. These voids might create sites of failure during mechanical loading. With increase in fiber wt%, there is more uniformity. Figure 2 shows images of sisal-*bio-epoxy* composite samples.

| 20 wt% Sisal-bio-epoxy | 25 wt% Sisal-bio-epoxy | 30 wt% Sisal-bio-epoxy |

Fig. 2. SEM images of sisal-bio-epoxy composites.

As can be seen from Fig. 2, there is more randomness in the fibers in the composite sample reinforced with 20% sisal fibers. With increase in weight% to 35% and 30%, there is more uniform distribution of fibers. This is good for mechanical performance of composites. Figure 3 shows images of coir-*bio-epoxy* composite samples.

20 wt% Coir-bio-epoxy   **25 wt% Coir-bio-epoxy**   **30 wt% Coir-bio-epoxy**

Fig. 3. SEM images of coir-bio-epoxy composites.

Coir fiber based composites show more voids as compared to jute and sisal based composites. This might result in lower strength and other mechanical properties. Figure 4 shows images of bagasse-*bio-epoxy* composite samples.

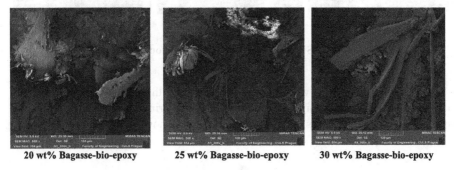

20 wt% Bagasse-bio-epoxy   **25 wt% Bagasse-bio-epoxy**   **30 wt% Bagasse-bio-epoxy**

Fig. 4. SEM images of bagasse-bio-epoxy composites.

Similar to coir-based bio-epoxy composites, the bagasse-bio-epoxy samples also show higher levels of fiber non-uniformity.

In general, it is visible from the SEM images that in each fiber category, with 20 wt% of reinforcement there are some voids between the fibers and the matrix. As the wt% increases to 25% and 30%, there is improvement of uniformity. Further, in case of jute and sisal fibers, there is more even distribution of fibers pertaining to finer fiber cross-section (smaller diameter) as compared to coir and bagasse fibers. The uneven distribution of coir and bagasse might lead to uneven stress distribution in the composites during mechanical loading.

3.2 Mechanical Properties

The key mechanical properties e.g., tensile strength, tensile modulus, flexural strength and modulus, impact strength etc. were investigated and summarized. As all the reinforcing fibers have different densities, their composites with bio-epoxy also show variable densities. Therefore, specific strength and modulus were calculated for each category of mechanical property in order to understand the performance with respect to unit density of the material. This gives idea about material strength to weight ratio which is very important in composite applications.

3.2.1 Tensile Properties

Tensile strength and modulus values are compared in Fig. 5.

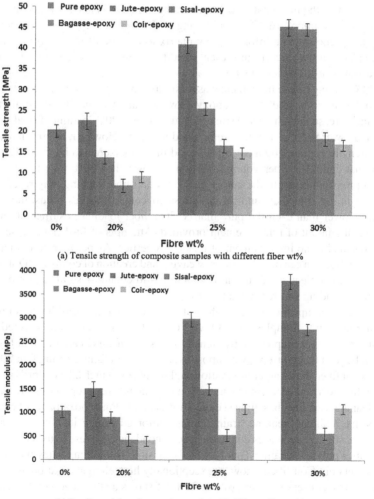

(a) Tensile strength of composite samples with different fiber wt%

(b) Tensile modulus of composite samples with different fiber wt%

Fig. 5. Tensile strength and modulus of composite samples.

The amount of maximum load that a material can survive before failure or breaking is called tensile strength. Tensile strength and modulus of jute fiber reinforced composites was found to be higher than other composite samples investigated. In a fiber reinforced composite material, the main load bearing component is reinforcement i.e., fiber [41–43]. Due to higher cellulose content and lower orientation angle in jute fiber, it exhibits higher strength as compared to other fibers used in the present study. Further, among the different fiber types, the jute fiber shows highest tenacity due to minimum fiber fineness/fiber diameter. It can also be observed that as fiber loading % increases, tensile properties are improved. The results revealed that pure epoxy has higher tensile strength and modulus than sugarcane bagasse-epoxy and coir-epoxy composites. Similar results were also reported by other researchers [44, 45]. In a fiber reinforced composite system, the matrix is brittle, and reinforcement is ductile. In the initial phase of loading, the stress is absorbed by the matrix. Once the matrix starts to fracture, the fibers act as crack stoppers to delay catastrophic failure of the composite materials until their breaking point. In this context, if the fiber-matrix adhesion at the interface is good, overall mechanical properties will be improved. The results suggest that sugarcane bagasse and coir fibers are not strong enough to reinforce epoxy matrix as they don't make strong interfacial bonding/adhesion with matrix in present condition. The resultant composites of these fibers become brittle and less ductile.

At 20% loading of jute fiber, there was no significant improvement in tensile strength and modulus. as compared to pure epoxy. However, at 25% and 30% loading, there is significant increase in both tensile strength and modulus. 20% loading of sisal fiber also results in a lower value of tensile strength and modulus. However, at 30% loading, the tensile strength increases by almost 117% and modulus increases by 50%. The results indicate that cellulosic fiber volume fraction of lower than 30% fails to provide any significant reinforcement to the epoxy resin. A small fiber loading may result in very weak links in the composite and creates stress concentration sites. Thus, the resultant strength is lower than even the pure matrix. 30% fiber loading is sufficient and there is significant amount of reinforcement provided. Attempts of further increase in fiber loading resulted in no improvement of tensile properties. As per literature, increase of fiber volume fraction can be achieved by weaving and creation of compact 3D structures. However, as the objective of current research was to create loose fiber reinforcement, the optimum loading was restricted to 30%.

Fracture of composites occurs when stress exceeds fracture/ultimate strength of the reinforcing fiber. Samples with 30 wt% of reinforcing fibers were selected to plot stress-strain behavior. Representative tensile stress-strain curves are given in Fig. 6.

It can be seen that coir-epoxy composites show highest failure strain % at 20% fiber fraction. Coir fibers have larger orientation angle of fibrils, which allows fibrils to untwist and straighten to a higher extent when stretched. From the fiber properties shown in Table 1, it is clear that coir fiber has highest elongation at break. Pure epoxy panel of equivalent thickness has a higher breaking strain than its reinforced composites. With the addition of fibers, the strain% decreases due to interfacial bondages and restrictions in movement of molecules/polymer chains. This fact is also visible from composites with all other fibers except coir. Coir fibers show an exceptionally high elongation at break%. That is the reason why coir-epoxy composite at 20% Vf shows a strain even higher than pure

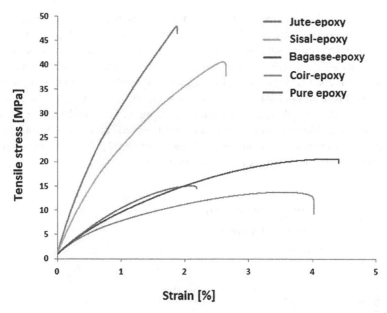

Fig. 6. Stress-strain behavior of the composite samples.

epoxy panel. However, this fiber volume fraction is relatively small to develop enough interfacial linkage, which is reflected in very low tensile strength. With increase of Vf to 25% and 30%, there is decrease in strain% of all composites. In general, it can be seen that the cellulosic fibers with lower orientation angle and higher cellulose content exhibit relatively higher strength and modulus and a lower strain at failure.

Further, representative tensile stress-strain curves are shown in Fig. 6, where it may be seen that jute-epoxy composite shows maximum slope followed by sisal-epoxy. Fracture of composites occurs when stress exceeds fracture/ultimate strength of the reinforcing fiber. Samples with 30% fiber loading were selected to plot stress-strain behavior. From the stress-strain curves, it is clear that jute fiber-based samples show highest stress value. This is attributed to better stress transfer from matrix to fiber and thus resulting in better mechanical properties.

The specific tensile strength and specific tensile modulus are shown in Fig. 6. Among the various fiber types, jute-based composite shows highest specific strength as well as modulus followed by sisal. This is pure reflection of the fiber mechanical properties as compared to pure epoxy resin. Increase of fiber volume fraction in such composites increases the specific tensile properties making them suitable for load bearing and durable. Sugarcane bagasse and coir-based epoxy composites fail to produce any favorable results.

3.2.2 Flexural Properties

Flexural modulus is product of tensile modulus and moment of inertia. The values are higher than tensile properties as load is applied at a single point, where least number of flaws can be available. However, for the tensile test the load is applied over a longer length where many flaws are possible. Flexural strength of the developed samples was tested on composite universal testing machine and the graphical representation of the obtained results is shown in Fig. 6. After being subjected to bending force, the pure epoxy sample as well as epoxy composites reinforced with bagasse and coir fiber were fractured while the reinforced composites with jute and sisal didn't show any sign of fracture. The broken samples show brittle surface fracture indicating uniform load/stress distribution and good interface. Flexural properties of a fiber reinforced composite depend upon the properties of reinforcement and interface with the matrix used. The flexural strength and modulus for all composite samples are compared in Fig. 7.

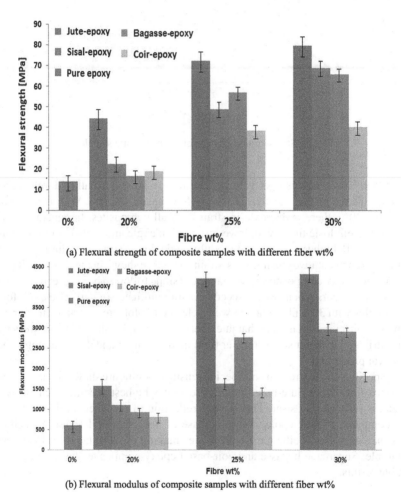

(a) Flexural strength of composite samples with different fiber wt%

(b) Flexural modulus of composite samples with different fiber wt%

Fig. 7. Bending strength and modulus for composite samples.

The flexural strength of the cellulosic fiber composite samples is presented in Fig. 7 which shows the effect of fiber loading. Results revealed that by increasing fiber loading, flexural strength and modulus increases. All the samples with fiber reinforcement have higher bending strength and modulus than pure epoxy due to higher stiffness of the cellulosic fibers as compared to epoxy resin. The rigidity is a function of the orientation angle of fibrils in the fiber cross-section. Epoxy composite samples having 30% fiber fraction show the highest flexural properties for all four types of fibers. Flexural properties increase linearly with increasing fiber loading. It is interesting to observe the performance of bagasse and coir reinforced composites under the bending stress, which is quite different from normal stress applied during tensile testing. Even at 20% fiber loading, composites have better resistance to bending than pure epoxy. Almost in all types of bio-composites samples developed, the ultimate strain was slightly lower than pure epoxy except at 20% bagasse and coir reinforced composites. This indicates that cellulosic fiber reinforcement enhances the properties of epoxy matrix in flexural mode.

Figure 7 indicate that maximum flexural strength and modulus was observed for jute fiber reinforced composites followed by sisal, bagasse, and coir respectively. This has direct proportionality with the tensile properties of these reinforcing fibers. The angle of orientation in the fiber structure decides the stiffness properties. Further the content of cellulose is responsible for fiber bending stiffness. Cellulose has a more linear structure in comparison to lignin or hemicellulose. Thus, the inter-molecular bonds are shorter and stronger which results in enhancement of stiffness. As the content of cellulose in jute and sisal fibers is much higher as compared to bagasse and coir, the flexural properties of the reinforced epoxy composites are also superior. The fiber diameter has a direct implication on flexural properties. Higher the diameter, higher is the rigidity and modulus. Thus, the sugarcane bagasse fiber reinforced epoxy composites offer some promising results. As far as the specific bending strength and modulus are concerned, they are dependent on the density. Due to lowest density of bagasse fiber, the corresponding composites offer highest specific strength and modulus. 20% fiber volume fraction is not enough to contribute substantially towards enhancement of bending properties. However, with 25% and 30% fiber fraction, there is significant improvement of specific bending strength and modulus as shown in Fig. 7.

3.2.3 Impact Properties

During Charpy impact testing, energy is transferred from the impactor/pendulum to the sample and if the sample material is not able to absorb the energy, it leads to fracture. Impact strength is the ability of a material to withstand against sudden applied impact load. The impact strength and specific impact strength (SIS) of all the samples are given in Fig. 8.

The impact strength in increased with increase in fiber loading% as shown in Fig. 8. The impact strength increases when the resistance of the material to the impact deformation increases. It means energy absorption capacity increases. Metals generally undergo elasto-plastic deformation prior to failure so they absorb energy in both regions. In composite materials major energy absorption occurs in the elastic region. Composites are generally brittle in nature. By the addition of fibers, it shows better resistance to the plastic deformation in the transverse direction of the fiber. The impact strength for jute,

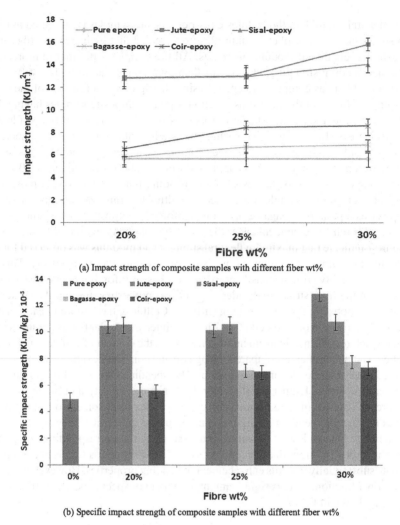

(a) Impact strength of composite samples with different fiber wt%

(b) Specific impact strength of composite samples with different fiber wt%

Fig. 8. Impact properties of bio-epoxy resin and bio-composites developed.

sisal, bagasse, and coir fiber reinforced epoxy composites increases by 176%, 145%, 20% and 50% respectively when fiber loading is increased from 0% to 30%. Due to superior load bearing capacity of fibers as compared to the epoxy resin, they serve to inhibit crack propagation and induce significant deflection in the path of the crack. Maximum impact strength is observed for jute-epoxy composites followed by sisal-epoxy, among all the cellulosic fiber reinforcements. This is due to superior mechanical properties of jute and sisal fiber as compared to bagasse and coir fibers. Further, the relatively finer diameter of jute and sisal fibers offer higher surface area for the interfacial bonding with epoxy resin. A stronger interface is responsible for efficient load/stress transfer in the microscale from resin to the reinforcement. Impact loading is a phenomenon which leads to sudden transfer of energy at the molecular level. Stronger fiber-matrix interface is responsible for absorbing the energy at molecular level. The specific impact strength shown in Fig. 8 is dependent on the absolute impact strength and the density of the composites. It follows almost similar trend as the impact strength itself. Thus, the jute and sisal fiber reinforced epoxy composite samples prove to be superior to sugarcane bagasse and coir based samples in terms of overall impact energy absorption capacity.

4 Conclusions

Results revealed that tensile properties of jute and sisal fiber reinforced epoxy composite panels are superior as compared to their bagasse and coir counter parts. Among the various fiber types, jute-based composite shows highest specific strength as well as modulus followed by sisal. This is pure reflection of the fiber mechanical properties as compared to pure epoxy resin. Increase of fiber volume fraction in such composites increases the specific tensile properties making them suitable for load bearing and durable. Sugarcane bagasse and coir-based epoxy composites fail to produce any favorable results. By increasing fiber content/ loading, the flexural strength of all types of composite samples is improved. It is due to the increase of load bearing components in the composite. All the samples with fiber reinforcement have higher bending strength and modulus than pure epoxy due to higher stiffness of the cellulosic fibers as compared to epoxy resin. The rigidity is a function of the orientation angle of fibrils in the fiber cross-section. The fiber diameter has a direct implication on flexural properties. Higher the diameter, higher is the rigidity and modulus. Thus, the sugarcane bagasse fiber reinforced epoxy composites offer better results. Impact properties of all the cellulosic fiber reinforced composites increases with the fiber loading. The impact strength of jute-epoxy and sisal-epoxy composites is much superior in comparison to other two fiber types. This is due to superior mechanical properties of jute and sisal fiber as compared to bagasse and coir fibers. The relatively finer diameter of jute and sisal fibers offers higher surface area for the interfacial bonding with epoxy resin.

Acknowledgements. The result was obtained through the financial support of the Ministry of Education, Youth and Sports of the Czech Republic, the European Union (European Structural and Investment Funds - Operational Program Research, Development and Education) in the frames of the project "Modular platform for autonomous chassis of specialized electric vehicles for freight and equipment transportation", Reg. No. CZ.02.1.01/0.0/0.0/16_025/0007293 and Internal grant agency of Faculty of Engineering, Czech University of Life Sciences Prague (no. 2021:31140/1312 /3108).

References

1. Hu, R., Lim, J.K.: Fabrication and mechanical properties of completely biodegradable hemp fiber reinforced polylactic acid composites. J. Compos. Mater. **41**(13), 1655–1669 (2007). https://doi.org/10.3390/ma12060854
2. Thomason, J., Yang, L., Gentles, F.: Characterization of the anisotropic thermoelastic properties of natural fibers for composite reinforcement. Fibers. **5**(4), 36 (2017). https://doi.org/10.3390/fib5040036

3. Cavalcanti, D., Banea, M., Neto, J., et al.: Mechanical characterization of intralaminar natural fiber-reinforced hybrid composites. Compos. Part B-Eng. **175**, 107–149 (2019)
4. Arumugam, V., Mishra, R., Militky, J., Salacova, J.: Investigation on thermo-physiological and compression characteristics of weft-knitted 3D spacer fabrics. J. Text. Inst. **108**(7), 1095–1105 (2017)
5. Behera, B.K., Mishra, R.K.: Artificial neural network-based prediction of aesthetic and functional properties of worsted suiting fabrics. Int. J. Clothing Sci. Technol. **19**, 259–276 (2007)
6. Zhang, Z., Cai, S., Li, Y., et al.: High performances of plant fiber reinforced composites—a new insight from hierarchical microstructures. Compos. Sci. Technol. **194**, 108151 (2020). https://doi.org/10.1016/j.compscitech.2020.108151
7. Venkataraman, M., Mishra, R., Wiener, J., Kotresh, T.M., Vaclavik, M.: Novel techniques to analyze thermal performance of aerogel-treated blankets under extreme temperatures. J. Text. Inst. **106**(7), 736–747 (2015)
8. Balachandar, M., Ramnath, B., Barath, R., Sankar, S.: Mechanical characterization of natural fiber polymer composites. Mater. Today Proc. **16**(2), 1006–1012 (2019)
9. Koronis, G., Silva, A., Fontul, M.: Green composites: a review of adequate materials for automotive applications. Compos. Part B-Eng. **44**(1), 120–127 (2013)
10. Saba, N., Jawaid, M., Alothman, O.Y., Tahir, P.M., Hassan, A.: Recent advances in bio-epoxy resin, natural fiber-reinforced bio-epoxy composites and their applications. J. Reinf. Plast. Comp. **35**(6), 447–470 (2016)
11. Longobardo, A.V.: Glass fibers for printed circuit boards. In: Wallenberger, F., Bingham, P. (eds.) Fiberglass and Glass Technology. Springer, USA (2010)
12. Kabir, M., Huque, M.M., Islam, M.R., Islam, R.: Mechanical properties of jute fiber reinforced polypropylene composite: effect of chemical treatment by benzenediazonium salt in alkaline medium. J. Reinf. Plast. Comp. **29**(20), 3111–3114 (2010)
13. Patel, B.C., Acharya, S.K., Mishra, D.: Environmental effect of water absorption and flexural strength of red mud filled jute fiber/polymer composite. Int. J. Eng. Sci. Technol. **4**(4), 49–59 (2012)
14. Venkataraman, M., Mishra, R., Jasikova, D., Kotresh, T.M.: Thermodynamics of aerogel-treated nonwoven fabrics at subzero temperatures. J. Ind. Text. **45**(3), 387–404 (2015)
15. Ramesh, M., Palanikumar, K., Reddy, K.H.: Mechanical property evaluation of sisal–jute–glass fiber reinforced polyester composites. Compos. Part B-Eng. **48**(1), 1–9 (2013)
16. Nagaraj, C., Mishra, D., Reddy, J.D.P.: Estimation of tensile properties of fabricated multi layered natural jute fiber reinforced E-glass composite material. Mater. Today. Proc. **27**(2), 1443–1448 (2020)
17. Chandekar, H., Chaudhari, V., Waigaonkar, S.: A review of jute fiber reinforced polymer composites. Mater. Today Proc. **26**(2), 2079–2082 (2020)
18. Behera, B.K., Pattanayak, A.K., Mishra, R.: Prediction of fabric drape behaviour using finite element method. J. Text. Eng. **54**, 103–110 (2008)
19. Crina, B., Blaga, M., Luminita, V., Mishra, R.: Comfort properties of functional weft knitted spacer fabrics. Tekstil v Konfeksiyon. **23**(3), 220–227 (2013)
20. Valarmathi, T., Arputhabalan, J., Ravichandran, S., et al.: Studies on mechanical properties of jute fiber composite panels. Mater. Today Proc. **16**(2), 1239–1243 (2019)
21. Plackett, D., Andersen, T., Pedersen, W., Nielsen, L.: Biodegradable composites based on l-polylactide and jute fibers. Compos. Sci. Technol. **63**(9), 1287–1296 (2003)
22. Mishra, R., Behera, B.K.: Recycling of textile waste into green composites: performance characterization. Polym. Compos. **35**, 1960–1967 (2014). https://doi.org/10.1002/pc.22855
23. Magarajan, U., Dharanikumar, S., Arvind, D., et al.: A comparative study on the static mechanical properties of glass fiber vs glass-jute fiber polymer composite. Mater. Today Proc. **5**(2), 6711–6716 (2018)

24. Bisaria, H., Gupta, M., Shandilya, P., et al.: Effect of fiber length on mechanical properties of randomly oriented short jute fiber reinforced bio-epoxy composite. Mater. Today Proc. **2**(4–5), 1193–1199 (2015)

25. Mishra, V., Biswas, S.: Physical and mechanical properties of bi-directional jute fiber bio-epoxy composites. Procedia Eng. **51**, 561–566 (2013)

26. Ramnath, B., Kokan, S., Raja, R.: Evaluation of mechanical properties of abaca–jute–glass fiber reinforced bio-epoxy composite. Mater. Design. **51**, 357–366 (2013)

27. Jamshaid, H., Mishra, R., Militky, J., Pechociakova, M., Noman, M.T.: Mechanical, thermal and interfacial properties of green composites from basalt and hybrid woven fabrics. Fibers. Polym. **17**(10), 1675–1686 (2016). https://doi.org/10.1007/s12221-016-6563-z

28. Mishra, R., Behera, B.K., Pal, B.P.: Novelty of bamboo fabric. J. Text. Inst. **103**(3), 320–329 (2012)

29. Doan, T., Brodowsky, H., Mäder, E.: Jute fiber/polypropylene composites II. Thermal, hydrothermal and dynamic mechanical behavior. Compos. Sci. Technol. **67**(13), 2707–2714 (2007)

30. Islam, M., Ahmed, S.: Influence of jute fiber on concrete properties. Constr. Build. Mater. **189**, 768–776 (2018)

31. Sharif, S., Shikkeri, S., Rajanikanth, K.: Mechanical characterization of Jute/Banana/Bio-epoxy reinforced laminate composite. Mater. Today Proc. **27**(2), 835–839 (2020)

32. Reddy, M., Kumar, M., Raju, C.: Tensile and flexural properties of jute, pineapple leaf and glass fiber reinforced polymer matrix hybrid composites. Mater. Today Proc. **5**(1), 458–462 (2018)

33. Mishra, R., Wiener, J., Militky, J., Petru, M., Tomkova, B., Novotna, J.: Bio-composites reinforced with natural fibers: comparative analysis of thermal, static and dynamic-mechanical properties. Fibers Polym. **21**(3), 619–627 (2020)

34. Sivakandhan, C., Murali, G., Tamiloli, N., Ravikumar, L.: Studies on mechanical properties of sisal and jute fiber hybrid sandwich composite. Mater. Today Proc. **21**(1), 404–407 (2020)

35. Ansari, A., Dhakad, S., Agarwal, P.: Investigation of mechanical properties of sisal fiber and human hair reinforced with bio-epoxy resin hybrid polymer composite. Mater. Today Proc. **26**(2), 2400–2404 (2020)

36. Vishnuvardhan, R., Kothari, R., Sivakumar, S.: Experimental investigation on mechanical properties of sisal fiber reinforced bio-epoxy composite. Mater. Today Proc. **18**(7), 4176–4181 (2019)

37. Senthilkumar, K., Saba, N., Rajini, N.: Mechanical properties evaluation of sisal fiber reinforced polymer composites: a review. Constr. Build. Mater. **174**, 713–729 (2018)

38. Mishra, R., Militky, J., Gupta, N., Pachauri, R., Behera, B.K.: Modelling and simulation of earthquake resistant 3D woven textile structural concrete composites. Compos B: Eng. **81**, 91–97 (2015)

39. Venkataraman, M., Mishra, R., Militky, J., Hes, L.: Aerogel based nanoporous fibrous materials for thermal insulation. Fibers. Polym. **15**(7), 1444–1449 (2014). https://doi.org/10.1007/s12221-014-1444-9

40. Rana, R., kumre, A., Rana, S., Purohit, R.: Characterization of properties of bio-epoxy sisal / glass fiber reinforced hybrid composite. Mater. Today Proc. **4**(4), 5445–5451 (2017)

41. Mishra, R., Huang, J., Kale, B., Zhu, G., Wang, Y.: The production, characterization and applications of nanoparticles in the textile industry. Text. Prog. **46**, 133–226 (2014). https://doi.org/10.1080/00405167.2014.964474

42. Towo, A., Ansell, M.: Fatigue evaluation and dynamic mechanical thermal analysis of sisal fiber–thermosetting resin composites. Compos. Sci. Technol. **68**(3–4), 925–932 (2008)

43. Ramires, E., Megiatto, J., Gardrat, C., et al.: Biobased composites from glyoxal–phenolic resins and sisal fibers. Bioresour. Technol. **101**(6), 1998–2006 (2010)

44. Reis, M.L.: Sisal fiber polymer mortar composites: Introductory fracture mechanics approach. Constr. Build. Mater. **37**, 177–180 (2012)
45. Saravanan, N.: Mechanical and fracture study of hybrid natural fiber reinforced composite – Coir and sugarcane leaf sheath. Mater. Today. Proc. (2020). https://doi.org/10.1016/j.matpr.2020.02.677

Modelling Brain Connectivity Networks by Graph Embedding for Dyslexia Diagnosis

Marco A. Formoso[1]([✉]), Andrés Ortiz[1,3], Francisco J. Martínez-Murcia[2,3],
Nicolás Gallego-Molina[1], Juan L. Luque[4], Juan J. Escobar[5],
and Francisco G. Montoya[6]

[1] Department of Communications Engineering, University of Málaga, Malaga, Spain
marco.a.formoso@ic.uma.es
[2] Department of Signal Theory, Telematic and Communications,
University of Granada, Granada, Spain
[3] Andalusian Data Science and Computational Intelligence Institute (DasCI),
Granada, Spain
[4] Department of Developmental Psychology, University of Málaga, Malaga, Spain
[5] Department of Computer Architecture And Technology, CITIC,
University Of Granada, Granada, Spain
[6] Department of Engineering, University of Almeria, Almeria, Spain

Abstract. Several methods have been developed to extract information from electroencephalograms (EEG). One of them is Phase-Amplitude Coupling (PAC) which is a type of Cross-Frequency Coupling (CFC) method, consisting in measure the synchronization of phase and amplitude for the different EEG bands and electrodes. This provides information regarding brain areas that are synchronously activated, and eventually, a marker of functional connectivity between these areas. In this work, intra and inter electrode PAC is computed obtaining the relationship among different electrodes used in EEG. The connectivity information is then treated as a graph in which the different nodes are the electrodes and the edges PAC values between them. These structures are embedded to create a feature vector that can be further used to classify multichannel EEG samples. The proposed method has been applied to classified EEG samples acquired using specific auditory stimuli in a task designed for dyslexia disorder diagnosis in seven years old children EEG's. The proposed method provides AUC values up to 0.73 and allows selecting the most discriminant electrodes and EEG bands.

Keywords: Dyslexia · Phase-amplitude coupling · Classification · Graph embedding

1 Introduction

EEGs record the electric field fluctuations generated by the neurons as result of their activity [8]. These recordings provide a non-invasive way to record the brain

© Springer Nature Switzerland AG 2021
I. Rojas et al. (Eds.): BIOMESIP 2021, LNCS 12940, pp. 97–106, 2021.
https://doi.org/10.1007/978-3-030-88163-4_9

activity as it reacts to stimuli and can be split in several subsignals of different frequencies called brainwaves. There are several brainwaves defined according to their frequency: Delta (0.5–4) Hz, Theta (4–8) Hz, Alpha (8–13) Hz, Beta (13–30) Hz, Gamma (30–100) Hz and Epsilon (100–200) Hz. How and where this bands interact between them in the brain can be measured and used to gain insights on how the brain behaves. We quantified this interaction in terms of phase-amplitude coupling, i.e. how the phase of one signal is synchronized with the amplitude of another [3].

In this paper we extract the PAC values from the EEGs and are then used to built a graph where every node of this graph correspond to an electrode from the EEG montage. Graphs are powerful mathematical tools that combined with deep learning result in new methods capable of gathering knowledge. Among them is node2vec [6], a technique derived from natural language processing (NPL) where the node information and its neighbours is embedded into a N-dimensional vector. We use these embeddings to classify subjects who suffer from developmental dyslexia while performing a selection of the best bands and electrodes.

Developmental Dyslexia (DD) is a learning disorder affecting between 5% and 13% of the population [11]. Early diagnosis of DD in children results essential for their correct intellectual and emotional development. However, it is a challenging task since usually the diagnosis is made after behavioral tests. These tests depend on the child's motivation affecting the result and could only be applied to reading and writing children since they include several tasks based on these skills. The need for diagnosis in pre-reading children has led to the use of biomedical signals without such requirements and disadvantages as EEGs. Thus, the main aim of this work is to provide an effective tool for objective diagnosis using EEG signals.

The rest of the document is organized as follows. In Sect. 2 we present the data and how it was obtained along with the methods used. Then, in Sect. 3 the results are discussed and finally, in Sect. 4, we present the conclusions and the future work.

2   Materials and Methods

2.1   Database and Stimulus

EEG data used in this work was provided by the Leeduca Reserch Group at the University of Málaga [10]. EEG signals were recorded using the Brainvision acticHamp Plus with 32 active electrodes (actiCAP, Brain Products GmbH, Germany) at a sampling rate 500 Hz during 15-minute sessions, while presenting an auditory stimulus to the subject. A session consisted of a sequence of white noise stimuli modulated in amplitudes at rates 4.8, 16, 40 Hz presented sequentially for 5 min each.

The database is composed of Forty-eight participants, including 32 skilled readers (17 males) and 16 dyslexic readers (7 males) matched in age ($t(1) = -1.4$, $p > 0.05$, age range: 88–100 months). The mean age of the control group was 94, 1 $\pm$ 3.3 months, and 95, 6 $\pm$ 2.9 months for the dyslexic group. All participants are right-handed Spanish native speakers with no hearing impairments and normal or corrected–to–normal vision. Dyslexic children all received a formal diagnosis of dyslexia in the school. None of the skilled readers reported reading or spelling difficulties or have received a previous formal diagnosis of dyslexia. The locations of 32 electrodes used in the experiments is in the 10–20 standardized system, whose names are shown in Fig. 1.

The present experiment was carried out with the understanding and written consent of each child's legal guardian and in the presence thereof, and was approved by the Medical Ethical Committee of the Malaga University (ref. 16–2020-H) and according to the dispositions of the World Medical Association Declaration of Helsinki.

2.2 Signal Prepocessing

Recorded EEG signals were processed to remove artifacts related to eye blinking using the EOG channel and impedance variation due to movements. This was addressed using blind source separation by means of Independent Component Analysis (ICA). Then, EEG signal of each channel was referenced to the Cz electrode and normalized independently to zero mean and unit variance. Baseline correction was also applied.

2.3 Phase-Amplitude Coupling (PAC)

Phase-Amplitude Coupling is a type of Cross-Frequency Coupling. In Canolty et al. [3] they propose that CFC arises as a sort of cross-domain connectivity. The high-frequency oscillations reflect local domain cortical processing, and the low-frequency rhythms are *dynamically entrained across distributed brain regions*. Several measures have been proposed over time to quantify this connectivity and compared in Hülsemann et al. [7] (Phase-Locking Value, Mean Vector Length (MVL), Modulation Index (MI), and Generalized-Linear-Modeling-Cross-Frequency-Coupling). Their recommendation is to use MVL-based descriptors for signals recorded at high sample rate and high signal-noise ratio. In addition, they advise to use MI as it complements the weaknesses of MVL. The main hissue wit MVL is its dependency on the amplitude of the signal providing amplitude. Amplitude outliers can strongly affect the final result of the measure. However, these issues can be partially addressed by means of permutation testing.

PAC is a way to quantify the interaction between the phase of low-frequency components and the amplitude of high-frequency components in a EEG. To this end, the first step consist in decomposing the signal into its frequency components. The classical approach using Fourier methods require the signal to meet the requirements of periodicity and stationarity, both of which are not present in EEG signals. Instead, Hilbert transform is used posterior to a band-pass filter for every brainwave frequency range, obtaining the corresponding analytic signal to derive the amplitude, phase and frequency of the signal over time. As explained in the following, phase-synchronization measurements can be computed from the instantaneous, unwrapped phase.

As previously stated, there are several methods to quantify the synchronization of two signals. The selected one in this work is MVL introduced in [2] and defined as follows:

$$MVL = \left| \frac{\sum_{t=1}^{n} a_t e^{i(\theta_t)}}{n} \right| \qquad (1)$$

where n is the total number of data points, a_t is the amplitude at point t of the signal providing amplitude and θ_t is the phase angle at point t of the signal providing phase. Additionally, spurious coupling values are discarded by a permutation test using surrogates computed by swapping amplitude values in the former signal [1].

2.4 Connectivity Estimation by Phase-Amplitude Coupling

Once MVL values are computed, a connectivity matrix can be defined as shown in Fig. 1. This matrix shows inter and intra node connectivity, allowing the composition of a directed graph by using the computed PAC matrix as an adjacency matrix. The values represent the degree of synchronization between bands and also the weight of the edges when the graph is built.

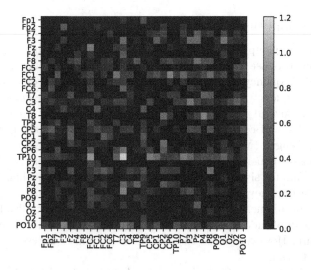

Fig. 1. PAC Matrix for Delta-Theta. The nodes on the Y axis are the nodes for Delta band providing phase and the nodes on X axis are the nodes for Theta band providing amplitude. Higher values represent a higher synchronization between bands.

2.5   Graph Embedding

Several algorithms have been recently developed in order to extract information from graphs. They can be classified into different categories depending on the technique to process the connectivity matrix that represents the graph: factorization, random walk and deep learning [5]. The algorithm used in this work is *node2vec*. It is classified in the group of random walks, although it uses a NPL embedding method we commonly encounter in deep learning architectures called word2vec [9]. In node2vec as in word2vec, we try to find a representation of the word/node while preserving as much information as possible. As a result, similar objects have similar embeddings. In this context, and to show the equivalence to NPL, the graph can be seen as a document of which we can extract sentences. These sentences are composed by a finite set of nodes.

The selection of nodes in order to build a sentence in node2vec is performed by means of a random walk through the graph: starting in a node, we select one of its neighbour with bias (2) and it is added to the set. The same operation is repeated but starting from the last added node. The number of repetitions of this operation is called walk length, and it is one of the hyperparameters of node2vec algorithm. In addition, there are two more hyperparameters, q and p that control how the graph is traversed. If the walk is in a node v coming from a node x and $t \in neighbours(v)$, being d_{tx} the distance from x to t, the likelihood $\alpha_{pq}(t, x)$ of adding t to the set is as follows:

$$\alpha_{pq}(t, x) \begin{cases} \frac{1}{p} & \text{if } d_{tx} = 0 \\ 1 & \text{if } d_{tx} = 1 \\ \frac{1}{q} & \text{if } d_{tx} = 2 \end{cases} \tag{2}$$

This procedure is applied for all the neighbours t of v. The number of walks is another adjustable parameter and sets the number of walks which will be available to train the aforementioned skip-gram model thus obtaining the embedding for each node.

2.6   Classification

The classification task consist of two major steps, node sorting and ensemble classification. In Fig. 2 we can see a visual representation as well as the pseudocode in Algorithm 1.

- **Node sorting**: As a first step, node selection is performed by a one-class support vector machine (OCSVM). This algorithm is typically used to detect outliers in a dataset. In this work, for the embeddings of every single node, a OCSVM is trained with control samples, and it is then used to predict dyslexia samples. In this way, we can determine the most discriminant nodes (i.e. those which detect a larger number of outliers). Then, a list is created with the nodes. This list is sorted based on the numbers of detected outliers.

– **Ensemble classification**: This step consist of a number X of iterations, being X the number of nodes. Begin with the embeddings of the first node in the previous list, we perform a classification task using an ensemble of a random forest and gradient boosting. Cross-validation is used to evaluate the performance of the classifier. In the next iteration, the embeddings of the next node in the list is added and a new classification step is performed.

Algorithm 1. Classification

1: $Nodes$ = Set of nodes
2: $Embeddings$ = Data with shape (#Subjects, #Nodes, EmbeddingDimension)
3: $Outliers = []$
4: **for** $node$ **in** $Nodes$ **do**
5:     $Outliers.append(GetNumberOutliers(node))$
6: **end for**
7: $Indices = Outliers.argumentsort()$
8: **for** $index$ **from** 0 **to** $Length(Indices)$ **do**
9:     $DataSet = Embeddings[:, Indices[: index]]$
10:     $VotingClassifier(Dataset)$
11: **end for**

---

3 Results

In this section, experimental results through the entire classification pipeline are shown, using PAC to compose the connectivity matrix and embedding the corresponding graph. PAC is obtained with the tensorpac library [4]. As explained in the introduction, PAC is used to measure the synchronization between the phase of one band and the amplitude of another. Typically, PAC is computed between a low frequency band providing phase and a higher frequency band providing amplitude meaning it is not necessary to calculate all the permutations for the bands. We computed the PAC between the following bands:

– Bands providing phase: Delta, Theta, Alpha, Beta
– Bands providing amplitude: Beta, Gamma, Epsilon

As a result, we obtain twelve 31 × 31 PAC matrices for each subject like the one in Fig. 1. These matrices are used as adjacency matrices to construct a directed graph that is then processed with the *node2vec* algorithm. Moreover, experiments varying the node embedding dimension from 1 to 9 have been carried out, as it is related to the representation capability of the embedding. In the classification step, the depth was 3 and the number of estimators was 20 for the gradient boosting classifier and the estimators for the random forest was 100.

Maximum AUC values for different embedding dimension and band combinations are shown in Table 1. The best values are found for 1 and 9 embedding dimensions, with a maximum AUC of 0.73 for the 9 dimension embedding in the Delta-Gamma band. In Fig. 3 a comparative between these two bands is shown for every number of nodes. The best values are obtained using 4 nodes in

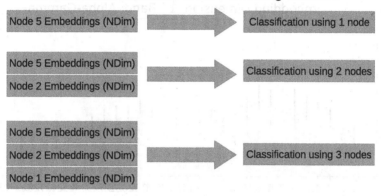

Fig. 2. Classification. This process is done for every embedding dimension N ranging from 1 to 9.

Table 1. Maximum AUC obtained for embeddings from 1 to 9 dimensions

	1	2	3	4	5	6	7	8	9
Delta-Beta	0.69	0.47	0.57	0.66	0.54	0.55	0.53	0.65	0.62
Delta-Gamma	0.68	0.55	0.59	0.58	0.54	0.55	0.55	0.59	**0.73**
Delta-Epsilon	0.47	0.57	0.59	0.66	0.62	0.55	0.69	0.66	0.58
Theta-Beta	0.56	0.62	0.45	0.60	0.56	0.52	0.44	0.50	0.48
Theta-Gamma	0.60	0.66	0.57	0.48	0.51	0.59	0.58	0.65	0.55
Theta-Epsilon	0.53	0.63	0.53	0.67	0.55	0.59	0.61	0.56	0.52
Alpha-Beta	0.68	0.54	0.50	0.48	0.48	0.58	0.55	0.62	0.72
Alpha-Gamma	**0.72**	0.62	0.65	0.53	0.57	0.44	0.61	0.55	0.62
Alpha-Epsilon	0.61	0.59	0.52	0.59	0.64	0.65	0.51	0.57	0.51
Beta-Beta	0.58	0.55	0.66	0.60	0.46	0.55	0.58	0.56	0.53
Beta-Gamma	0.59	0.64	0.59	0.68	0.67	0.59	0.64	0.67	0.60
Beta-Epsilon	0.58	0.67	0.51	0.61	0.52	0.63	0.58	0.59	0.56

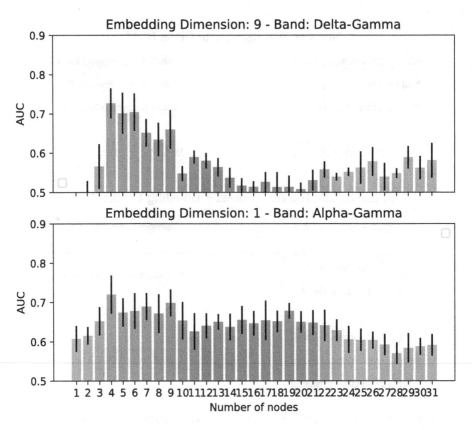

Fig. 3. AUC values for Delta-Gamma and Alpha-Gamma. (Color figure online)

both situations. Moreover, it can be seen that not all nodes carry discriminant information, so adding more may be counterproductive.

In Fig. 4 we can see the distribution of the embeddings for Delta-Gamma and Alpha-Gamma PACs. For Delta-Gamma we use TSNE to reduce the 9D embeddings to 2D. We can see clusters for both groups that explain the results in Fig. 4.

Finally, although Delta-Gamma provides the best AUC value, it is worth noting that we are dealing with 9 dimension embeddings while getting similar results using only 1D. This is the trade-off that we will have to take into account for future experiments.

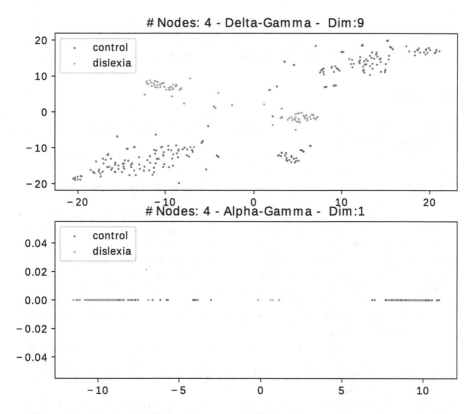

Fig. 4. Distribution for Delta-Gamma and Alpha-Gamma. (Color figure online)

4 Conclusions and Future Work

In this work we present a classification method that relies on PAC-based connectivity to construct directed graph explaining the connectivity patterns found in EEG signals. Moreover, a graph embedding technique was used to compress all the information on the graph in a feature set representing it. Then, a feature space consisting of descriptors for the graphs of each subject is composed and then used for subject classification. The methodology used demonstrated that graphs computed from PAC matrices provide discriminative enough information to separate dyslexia and control groups, especially in certain EEG bands as Alpha-Gamma and Delta-Gamma with AUC values in the 0.7–0.73 range.

As future work we plan to use another metrics to describe the graph structure and to extract features as well as to use specific deep learning methods for graphs such as graph neural networks.

Acknowledgments. This work was supported by projects PGC2018-098813-B-C32 (Spanish "Ministerio de Ciencia, Innovación y Universidades"), and by European Regional Development Funds (ERDF) and BioSiP (TIC-251) research group. We gratefully acknowledge the support of NVIDIA Corporation with the donation of one of the

GPUs used for this research. Work by F.J.M.M. was supported by the MICINN "Juan de la Cierva - Incorporación" Fellowship. We also thank the *Leeduca* research group and Junta de Andalucía for the data supplied and the support.

References

1. Aru, J., et al.: Untangling cross-frequency coupling in neuroscience. Curr. Opin. Neurobiol. **31**, 51–61 (2015)
2. Canolty, R.T., et al.: High gamma power is phase-locked to theta oscillations in human neocortex. Science **313**(5793), 1626–1628 (2006)
3. Canolty, R.T., Knight, R.T.: The functional role of cross-frequency coupling. Trends Cogn. Sci. **14**(11), 506–515 (2010)
4. Combrisson, E., et al.: Tensorpac: an open-source Python toolbox for tensor-based phase-amplitude coupling measurement in electrophysiological brain signals. PLoS Comput. Biol. **16**(10), (2020). https://doi.org/10.1371/journal.pcbi.1008302
5. Goyal, P., Ferrara, E.: Graph embedding techniques, applications, and performance: a survey. Knowl. Based Syst. (2018). https://doi.org/10.1016/j.knosys.2018.03.022. http://www.sciencedirect.com/science/article/pii/S0950705118301540
6. Grover, A., Leskovec, J.: node2vec: scalable feature learning for networks. In: Proceedings of the 22nd ACM SIGKDD International Conference on Knowledge Discovery and Data Mining, pp. 855–864 (2016)
7. Hülsemann, M.J., Naumann, E., Rasch, B.: Quantification of phase-amplitude coupling in neuronal oscillations: comparison of phase-locking value, mean vector length, modulation index, and generalized-linear-modeling-cross-frequency-coupling. Front. Neurosci. **13**, 573 (2019)
8. Kirschstein, T., Köhling, R.: What is the source of the eeg? Clin. EEG Neurosci. **40**(3), 146–149 (2009)
9. Mikolov, T., Chen, K., Corrado, G., Dean, J.: Efficient estimation of word representations in vector space. arXiv preprint arXiv:1301.3781 (2013)
10. Ortiz, A., Martinez-Murcia, F.J., Luque, J.L., Giménez, A., Morales-Ortega, R., Ortega, J.: Dyslexia diagnosis by eeg temporal and spectral descriptors: An anomaly detection approach. Int. J. Neural Syst. **30**, 2050029–2050029 (2020)
11. Peterson, R.L., Pennington, B.F.: Developmental dyslexia. Lancet **379**(9830), 1997–2007 (2012)

Causal Coupling of Low Frequency Oscillations During Movement Imagination – A Multimodal Study

Katarzyna J. Blinowska[1,2](✉) , Piotr Lachert[1], Maciej Kamiński[2] ,
Jarosław Żygierewicz[2] , and Adam Liebert[1]

[1] Nalecz Institute of Biocybernetics and Biomedical Engineering Polish Academy of Sciences,
Ks. Trojdena 4 St., 02-109 Warsaw, Poland
kjbli@fuw.edu.pl

[2] Faculty of Physics, University of Warsaw, Pasteura 5, 02-093 Warsaw, Poland

Abstract. The study aimed to determine the causal coupling between electrical brain activity, heart rate, hemodynamic signals, and blood supply in ~0,1 Hz frequency range during movement imagination. The relationships between the signals were found using Directed Transfer Function based on the Granger causality principle. The study yielded a comprehensive scheme of reciprocal interactions, which was compared with the scheme obtained for the real movement. The persistent feedback loop between heart rate and blood pressure was identified.

Keywords: Causal coupling · Mayer waves · Electroencephalogram · fNIRS · Heart rate · Directed Transfer Function

1 Introduction

In several body signals, oscillations ~0.1 Hz were observed. They were first detected in blood pressure (BP) by Sigmund Mayer (hence their name Mayer Waves). Later Mayer Waves (MW) were identified in: heart rate variability (HRV), modulation of the EEG rhythms, the concentration of oxy- and deoxyhemoglobin, and fMRI signals. MW were observed in several species. In humans, their frequency does not alter depending on body posture, age, or gender. The fact that oscillations in the MW frequency range were detected in several body signals and their occurrence in different physiological time series seems to be phase-locked indicates that they may play a role in controlling vital body functions.

Despite the extensive repertoire of studies, the MW generation mechanisms and their role are still elusive [1, 2]. Two hypotheses of MW generation were proposed: the central pacemaker and the baroreflex theory [1]. The pacemaker theory assumes the existence of a central MW pacemaker presumably located in the spinal cord or brain stem. The baroreflex theory is based on the action of the feedback loop involving baroreceptors, efferent and afferent nerves, and the heart. The interrelations between different body signals comprising MW were investigated to reveal the mechanisms behind the generation of MW. The studies involving cross-spectral methods showed coherences between

© Springer Nature Switzerland AG 2021
I. Rojas et al. (Eds.): BIOMESIP 2021, LNCS 12940, pp. 107–111, 2021.
https://doi.org/10.1007/978-3-030-88163-4_10

pairs of signals, e.g., HRV and blood pressure (BP), and brain signals; however, they supplied only an incomplete picture of interactions since bivariate measures are not able to identify reciprocal connections and unequivocally determine the precedence of signals. The Directed Transfer Function (DTF) is a method, which allows determining causal relations between multiple signals as a function of frequency, including reciprocal connections. As an extension of the Granger causality principle to the multichannel case, DTF makes it possible to determine the comprehensive coupling scheme between multiple signals [3]. It was applied to establish interrelations between blood pressure, electrophysiological and hemodynamic signals for spontaneous activity and movement [4]. Herein we shall report the coupling scheme between the above signals in the case of the movement imagination.

2 Material and Methods

Our multimodal study involved simultaneous measurement of blood pressure (BP), electrocardiogram (ECG), electroencephalogram (EEG), and fNIRS (functional near-infrared spectroscopy) signal during movement imagination for a group of 10 healthy adults. After the acoustic signal, the subject had to imagine during 20 s grasping of a glass of water. The task was repeated ten times with a 30 s break after each repetition.

The time-resolved fNIRS system used in the study [5] consisted of 2 laser light sources operating at 687 nm and 832 nm and 8 detectors fitted between EEG electrodes overlying the motor cortex. The distance between sources and detectors was 3.5 cm. From the distributions of times of flight of diffusely reflected photons, the mean path length and the relative changes in the total number of the detected photons obtained at both wavelengths were determined. Using the modified Beer-Lambert law, the oxyhemoglobin (HbO) and deoxyhemoglobin (HbR) concentration changes were found.

From the EEG signals (10–10 system), the envelopes of the filtered alpha (EEGalpha) and beta (EEGbeta) rhythms were obtained using the Hilbert transform as the instantaneous amplitudes of absolute values of the analytical signal. Heart rate (HRV) was obtained as a reciprocal of the time difference between two consecutive R waves in the ECG signal. Blood pressure was measured continuously from the left index finger using Finometer. Along with the positions of R waves, diastolic (dBP) and systolic pressure (sBP) values were obtained. A more detailed description of the experimental setup may be found in [4].

Multivariate Autoregressive Model (MVAR) was fitted to EEGalpha, EEGbeta, HbO, HbR, HRV, sBP, and dBP signals resampled at 2 Hz. Next, DTF based on the transfer matrix of the MVAR model was determined [6]. MVAR may be considered as a black-box model with white noise as an input, time series as an output; the relations between signals are contained in the transfer matrix of the model $H_{ji}(f)$. Herein DTF modification – ffDTF involving the integration of normalizing factor over frequencies was used:

$$\text{ffDTF}_{ji}(f) = \frac{\left|H_{ji}(f)\right|^2}{\sum_f \sum_{m=1}^{k} |H_{im}(f)|^2} \tag{1}$$

DTF describes the causal influence of channel j on channel i at frequency f and takes values in the range [0,1]. The ffDTF functions were integrated within the frequency range of MW: 0.05–0.15 Hz, and in this way, the coupling strengths C_{ji} between signals were found. The significance of C_{ji} values was found through surrogate data tests and corrected for false discovery rate (FDR) as in [4].

3 Results

The values of coupling strengths in the MW frequency range are shown in Table 1.

Table 1. The averaged strengths of couplings in the range of 0.05–0.15 Hz. The significant interactions are printed in bold on a gray background. FDR is controlled at the 5% level. The direction of interaction from the variable marked below the column to the variable marked on the left.

EEG Alpha		0,25	0,36	0,39	0,82	**1,20**	**1,31**
EEG Beta	0,17		0,29	0,41	0,68	**1,10**	**1,22**
HbO	0,24	0,34		0,50	**1,04**	0,95	**1,41**
HbR	0,20	0,21	0,61		**1,19**	1,08	**1,52**
HRV	0,15	0,19	0,42	0,36		0,75	**1,50**
sBP	0,21	0,19	0,55	0,54	**1,58**		**1,15**
dBP	0,26	0,23	**0,63**	0,62	**1,67**	1,01	
	EEG Alpha	EEG Beta	HbO	HbR	HRV	sBP	dBP

The obtained scheme of couplings (Fig. 1) showed the predominant influence of dBP on all the signals. The sBP influenced in a significant way EEG alpha and EEGbeta signals only. An important role played HRV, driving HbO and HbR and strongly influencing dBP and sBP.

In comparison to the real movement, the direct connection between HbO and HbR was weakened. These signals became coupled through HRV instead. The connection from sBP to HRV was only two times smaller than from dBP to HRV; however, it did not reach a significance level.

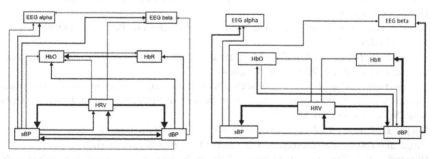

Fig. 1. The schemes of causal coupling between signals; on the left for real movement (from ref. [4]) on the right for the imagination. Only connections of $p < 0.05$ (including correction for FDR) are plotted. The thickness of arrows corresponds to the strengths of coupling.

4 Discussion

Comparing the scheme of couplings during real and imaginary movements, we can observe that some connections disappeared or were weakened in the case of imagination. In [4], the comparison of couplings between spontaneous and movement activity also revealed a reduction of some connections during movement, e.g., the disappearance of EEGalpha and EEGbeta influence on the other variables and weakening of the influence of sBP on HBR. In the case of movement imagination, the influence of EEGalpha and EEGbeta on the other variables is absent too, which can be explained by the desynchronization of alpha and beta rhythms. In the case of imagination, the prevailing action of dBP, which is driving other signals, may be observed. It can be explained by the high need for blood supply during mental action requiring more effort than rest state or self-paced finger movements.

The remarkable feature of the coupling scheme is the persistence of the loop involving HRV and dB observed for all tasks. This observation supports the baroreflex theory. However, our experimental design did not allow the recording of signals from subcortical structures, which might influence the relationships between the investigated variables. The fMRI technique makes it possible to probe the autonomic brain structures. The possible localization of central pacemaker in subcortical brain atructures was reported [7, 8], in particular the brain stem was proposed as responsible for MW oscillations on the ground of phase-coupling analysis between BOLD (blood oxygenation level-dependent) fluctuations in pons/brain stem and low-frequency oscillations in HRV [8]. However, the effect was present only in 50% of investigated cases. Nevertheless, even if the central pacemaker was responsible for MW generation, its direct feedforward effect on arterial blood pressure would be modulated without doubt by the baroreceptor effect. The problem of MW generation is still open and under investigation. However, it can be assumed that the MW generation involves complex mechanisms that synchronize the cardiovascular, hemodynamic, and electrophysiological variables, helping to exert flexible control over the body functions.

References

1. Julien, C.: The Enigma of Mayer Waves: Facts and Models. Cardiovascular Research. Oxford University Press, pp. 12– 21 (2006)
2. Julien, C.: An update on the enigma of Mayer waves. Cardiovasc. Res. (2019). https://doi.org/10.1093/cvr/cvz327
3. Blinowska, K.J., Kuś, R., Kamiński, M.: Granger causality and information flow in multivariate processes. Phys. Rev. E **70**(51), 50902 (2004)
4. Lachert, P., et al.: Causal coupling between electrophysiological signals, cerebral hemodynamics and systemic blood supply oscillations in mayer wave frequency range. Intern. J. Neural Syst. **29**(5), 1850033 (2018)
5. Kacprzak, M., et al.: Application of a time-resolved optical brain imager for monitoring cerebral oxygenation during carotid surgery. J. Biomed. Opt. **17**(1), 016002 (2012)
6. Blinowska, K.J., Żygierewicz, J.: Practical Biomedical Signal Analysis using Matlab. CRC Press, Boca Raton, London, New York (2012)

7. Pfurtscheller, G., et al.: Brain-heart communication: evidence for "central pacemaker" oscillations with a dominant frequency at 0.1Hz in the cingulum. Clin. Neurophysiol. **128**(1), 183–193 (2017). https://doi.org/10.1016/j.clinph.2016.10.097
8. Pfurtscheller, G., Schwerdtfeger, A.R., Rassler, B., Andrade, A., Schwarz, G., Klimesch, W.: Verification of a central pacemaker in brain stem by phase-coupling analysis between HR interval- and BOLD-oscillations in the 0.10–0.15 Hz frequency band. Front. Neurosci. **14**, 922 (2020)

Methodological Approaches to the Comparison of Left Ventricular Stroke Volume Values Measured by Ultrasonic Technique or Estimated via Transfer Functions

Andrey P. Pugovkin⬭, Valeriy O. Erkudov(✉) ⬭, and Sergey A. Lytaev⬭

St. Petersburg State Pediatric Medical University, St. Petersburg 194100, Russia

Abstract. The development of high tech approaches for clinical monitoring, diagnostics and treatment requires implication of contemporary biometric methods comparing the data obtained by measurement of hemodynamic parameters. In previous publications we suggested the experimental approach for assessment of cardiac output and systemic arterial pressure using experimental data obtained via measurements of the pulse waveform in peripheral arteries under steady-state and transitive conditions. A methodological basis for two approaches in estimation of left ventricular stroke volume in humans are presented: «classic» according to Teichholz ultrasonic echocardiography and «experimental» according to reconstruction via transfer functions created by means of computer Fourier waveform analysis of the peripheral pulse curves obtained using Penaz volume-clump method. Checking and analysis of differences in data obtained with both approaches was provided biometrically according to the following protocol: checking of availability of significant differences in the results of both techniques; calculation and analysis of 95% confidence intervals for differences between mean values; estimation of Spearman's rank correlation; linear regression analysis; Bland-Altman analysis; estimation of the mean measurement error. The values obtained via both methods revealed no significant differences according to two different statistical algorithms. The results of the research confirm the possibility for implication of volume-clump method in non-invasive monitoring of the cardiac output.

Keywords: Left ventricular stroke volume · Ultrasonic technique · Transfer functions · Comparison of two methods

1 Introduction

The development of high tech approaches for clinical monitoring, diagnostics and treatment requires implication of contemporary biometric methods comparing the data obtained by measurement of hemodynamic parameters [1, 2, 10]. This can be obtained via non-invasive waveform analysis in peripheral arteries with further reconstruction of the pressure and flow pulse waveforms in major arterial vessels. In previous publications we suggested the experimental approach for assessment of cardiac output (CO)

© Springer Nature Switzerland AG 2021
I. Rojas et al. (Eds.): BIOMESIP 2021, LNCS 12940, pp. 112–120, 2021.
https://doi.org/10.1007/978-3-030-88163-4_11

and systemic arterial pressure using experimental data obtained via measurements of the pulse waveform in peripheral arteries under steady-state [13] and transitive conditions: aftermath of infusions of vasoactive pharmacological agents [12], dextran solution or acute experimental hemorrhage [3, 13]. Correlation between corresponded periodical processes in the vascular system that follow pulsatile heart performance can be expressed in terms of transfer functions (TF) – differential operators that describe such correlations. The following paper suggests a methodological basis for comparison of two methods in estimation of the left ventricular stroke volume (LVSV) in humans: «classic» according to Teichholz ultrasonic echocardiography and «experimental» according to reconstruction via transfer functions created by means of computer Fourier waveform analysis of the peripheral pulse curves.

2   Methods

2.1   LVSV and Arterial Pressure Data Obtaining

In 34 adult volunteers M-modal echocardiography (SA 9900, Samsung-Medison, 2–5 MHz) followed by estimation of the LVSV according to Teichholz ultrasonic technique was accompanied by simultaneous computing LVSV according to reconstruction via TF created by computer Fourier waveform analysis of the peripheral pulse curves using Penaz volume-clump method (spirocardiorhythmograph SACR-2) [6, 8, 13]. This device works according to the principle of «unloaded vessel» which provides a continuous indirect photoplethysmographic measurement of systolic, diastolic and mean AP simultaneously with registration of the pulse wave-form curve in the forefinger vascular bed by means of clamping the volume of arteries by fast changes of pressure by a special finger cuff connected to a pump and equipped with built-in photoelectric plethysmograph to measure the vascular volume. The latter was measured when the external pressure was automatically kept continuously equal to the AP so that transmural pressure was equal to zero. The pressure in the cuff was measured by means of tachooscillography [8]. Monitoring of the established counterpressure level was provided by the built-in electronic control system adjustable to changes of blood filling of vascular bed aftermath every cardiac cycle or in response to external stimuli [13].

2.2   Calculation of TF

Another approach used for the AP measurement was applanation tonometry (Sphygmocor, AtCor Medical, Australia) for detection of instant pressure values in the forefinger artery [11]. This allowed the creation of two TFs expressing the correspondence between pulse curves in forefinger, radial and carotid arteries. TFs were determined by Fourier transforms of pulse waveforms as the ratios between the frequency spectra of pressure waveforms. The first was used for reconstruction of pulse curve in radial artery on the basis of the data obtained according to Penaz method.

The pressure in the carotid artery was estimated with two methods. The first was based on the built-in algorithm of the Sphygmocor device [11]. The another approach included calculation of the parameters mentioned above, in the carotid artery via second

TF corresponding pressure curve in the radial artery to that in the carotid artery obtained via applanation tonometry or reconstructed using data, obtained by built-in algorithm of the Sphygmocor device on the basis of forefinger artery pressure values revealed using Penaz method.

Estimation of TFs was followed by calculation of generalized vascular impedance as a ratio between the frequency spectra of averaged pulse waveforms which, in turn, made possible further estimation of LVSR. These estimations were based on the multibranched model of vascular bed. Multibranched mathematical model of hemodynamics is used in studies of pressure and flow waveforms in pathology, of relations between central and peripheral waves and their repulse [9, 14].

The main concept for application of this model was based on the consecutive di-vision of the vascular bed that connects radial or forefinger arterial pressure with ascending aorta into nodal points with certain shape and mechanical properties and further con-struction of TFs between them [15]. Mathematical multibranched model is a system of differential equations describing pressure and flow changes by means of Fourier trans-forms of pressure and flow waveforms as a ratio between spectra of measured pressure waveforms [9, 15]. Pressure and flow in each time domain were ensemble-averaged with periodicity normalized to the mean frequency of a cycle onset systole/start of the next systole. General vascular impedance was estimated as ratio between the frequency spectra of averaged pressure and flow waveforms [9, 14, 15]. Estimation and application of TFs and vascular impedance were provided using function libraries of the computer software MATLAB R2012b (8.00).

2.3 Statistical Analysis

Checking and analysis of differences in data obtained with both approaches was provided biometrically according to the following protocol:

1. Checking of availability of significant differences in the results of both techniques, interpreted as independent excerpts using Mann-Whitney test (software: Past version 2.17, Norway, Oslo, 2012).
2. Calculation and analysis of 95% confidence intervals (CI) for differences between mean values of LVSR obtained via «classic» and «experimental» methods (Microsoft Office 2010 Exploratory Software for Confidence Intervals (ESCI-JSMS), Melbourne, Australia, 2001).
3. Estimation of Spearman's rank correlation coefficient [7] for LVSV values obtained via «classic» and «experimental» methods (Past version 2.17, Norway, Oslo, 2012).
4. Analysis of proportionality between the results obtained via «classic» and «experimen-tal» methods admitting non-variability of data for «classic» approach (semi-calibration conditions [7]). Linear regression analysis was provided using software: Past version 2.17, Norway, Oslo, 2012.
5. Bland-Altman analysis [4, 5] was applied for estimation the mean difference between values obtained via both methods for the analysis of systemic discrepancy between mean values and standard deviation for the mean difference and comparison of the standard deviation and values of LVSV obtained via «experimental» approach (software: Statistica 10, StatSoft Inc, USA, 2010).

6. Estimation of the mean measurement error (1), fractions of error lower than 10%, 10%–19%, 20–39% and 50%–99% and higher than 100% towards the total number of coupled data obtained via different methods [3]. In addition, share of coupled data with positive (underestimation) or with negative (overestimation) measurement errors in relation to the total number (software: StatXact-8, shell Cytel Studio version 8.0.0). A value of p < 0.05 was taken as significant.

$$SE\% = \frac{\text{LVSRmes} - \text{LVSRtf}}{\text{LVSRdir}} \times 100 \tag{1}$$

SE–relative error; LVSVmes–values of LVSV obtained via ultrasonic measurement; LVSVtf – values of LVSV estimated via TF.

3   Results

LVSV values obtained via ultrasonic technique (μ; 95%CI) 72.46 (65.36; 79.57) ml/min, or estimated via TF 74.07 (62.16; 85.98) ml/min possessed no significant differences (p = 0.8297). This means that, if the null hypothesis (absence of differences) is valid, the probability for obtaining observed values was higher than 80%.

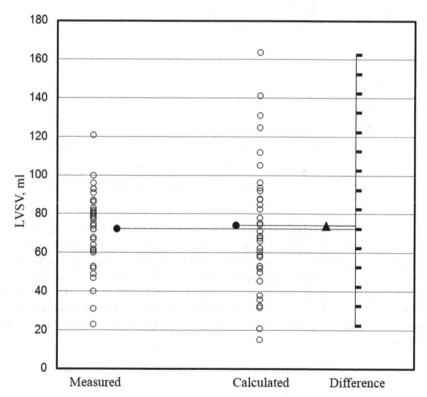

Fig. 1. Difference and 95% CI for mean difference in mean values of LVSV revealed with different approaches

Figure 1 represents the mean difference (18.08 ml) and 95% CI for the difference between the mean values. The obtained 95% CI for the difference in the mean LVSV values measured in different ways includes the value of zero, which means that the values of the difference in the mean do not differ statistically from zero.

Spearman's rank correlation coefficient between two groups of values $r_s = 0.74$, (p $= 5.0633 \times 10^{-7}$), reflecting moderate positive link (Fig. 2).

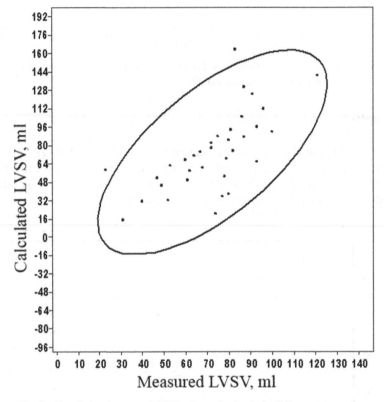

Fig. 2. Correlation between LVSV values obtained via different approaches

Linear regression analysis (2) revealed proportionality for both groups of data. Figure 3 represents the results of regression analysis of interdependence between the data obtained via different approaches. The resulting regression equation has the form: $y = b + ax$ (2) where b – intercept, marking the cross between the line and axis Y when $x = 0$; a – slope, tilt angle tangent (2). The values obtained by means of «experimental» approach for LVSV measurement are proportional to those obtained via «classical» approach (2) which is concluded from overlap of 95% CI for $a = 1$ and for $b = 0$, and $p < 0.01$ [7].

$$y = -7,38\,(95\%CI: -34,32;\ 20,81) + 1,12(95\%CI: 0,72;\ 1,50)x,\ R2 = 0,67,\ p = 0,000014155) \quad (2)$$

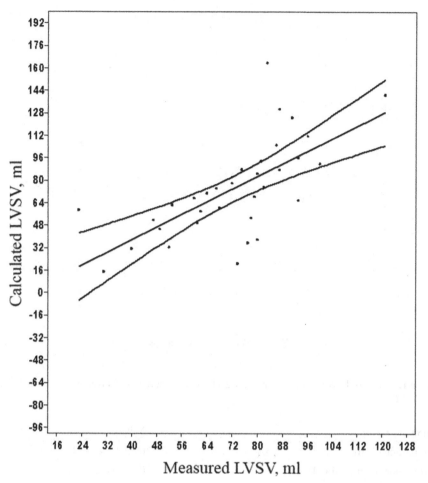

Fig. 3. Results of regression analysis of interdependence between the LVSV values obtained by different approaches

According to the Bland–Altman plot (Fig. 4) mean difference between pairs of LVSV values was 1.6 ml which indicated that «experimental» approach produced values overestimated by this quantity in absence of the systemic deviations from the results of «classical» approach. Standard deviation in mean difference constituted 25.43 ml/min which is relatively low in relation to ultrasonically measured LVSV.

Distribution of paired data with different levels of error was relatively uniform: «low» (<10%–32% cases, «medium» (<40%–42%, «high» (>50%)–26%. Positive error (underestimation) occurred in 40% cases, negative (overestimation) – in 60% (Table 1).

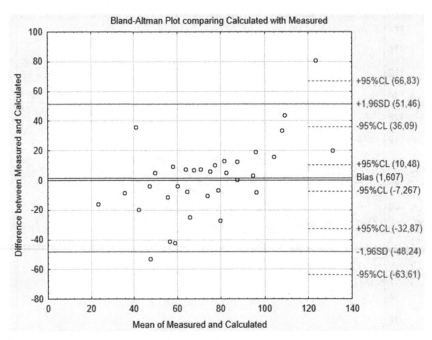

Fig. 4. The Bland–Altman plot

Table 1. Errors of LVSV values estimated via TFs and measured by ultrasonic echocardiography (μ; 95%CI)

Systemic error	Values
Proportion of error <10%	0.32 (0.14; 0.54)
Proportion of error 10%–19%	0.21 (0.07; 0.41)
Proportion of error 20–39%	0.21 (0.07; 0.41)
Proportion of error 40%–99%	0.14 (0.04; 0.36)
Proportion of error >100%	0.12 (0.03; 0.31)
Proportion of data pairs with a positive error	0.41 (0.22; 0.62)
Proportion of data pairs with a negative error	0.59 (0.38; 0.78)

4   Conclusions

Matching of measured and estimated LVSV data for coordination of approaches revealed necessity for application of not a single but a combination of statistical criteria. Still, it was not possible to fulfill solution of the problem of their interchangeability within the framework of this study. On one side, these approaches are corresponded, which follows from the absence of significant differences if they are compared at least by two statistical methods (Mann-Whitney test and analysis of 95% CI for difference in mean values of LVSV). Additionally, «experimental» LVSV values are proportional to the «classical» in the «calibration» regime in the absence of systematical differences. On the other side, only moderate statistical link between two groups of data has been detected alongside with relatively high measurement error (up to 35%, mean 15%) and equal probability for obtaining «high» or «low» error if the experiment is repeated. The presented results indicate that none of the approaches for comparison of the experimental methods can be regarded as universal criterion of their interchangeability. At the same time, taken together or separately, they compose nothing more than collection of biometrical «markers» that reflect expediency of further physiological and clinical justification, approbation and introduction of the method into routine practice. Only after such trial and on the basis of practical data about factors that affect instrumental errors, like, for example, transitory processes of hemodynamics, pathology or operator dependence an approach can be recommended for common use.

References

1. Adji, A., Kachenoura, N., Bollache, E., Avolio, A.P., O'Rourke, M.F., Mousseaux, E.: Magnetic resonance and applanation tonometry for noninvasive determination of left ventricular load and ventricular vascular coupling in the time and frequency domain. J. Hypertens. **34**(6), 1099–1108 (2016)
2. Bogert, L., et al.: Pulse contour cardiac output derived from non-invasive arterial pressure in cardiovascular disease. Anaesthesia **65**(11), 1119–1125 (2010)
3. Erkudov, V., Pugovkin, A., Verlov, N., Sergeev, I., Ievkov, S.: Systemic errors in the estimation of systemic arterial pressure via transfer functions after experimental changes of the circulating blood volume. Pathological Physiol. Exp. Ther. **60**(2), 45–49 (2016)
4. Gerke, O.: Reporting standards for a bland-altman agreement analysis: a review of methodological reviews. Diagnostics (Basel) **10**(5), 334 (2020)
5. Giavarina, D.: Understanding bland altman analysis. Biochem. Med. (Zagreb) **25**(2), 141–151 (2015)
6. Guelen, I., et al.: Validation of brachial artery pressure reconstruction from finger arterial pressure. J. Hypertens. **26**(7), 1321–1327 (2008)
7. Ludbrook, J.: Confidence in Altman-Bland plots: a critical review of the method of differences. Clin. Exp. Pharmacol. Physiol. **37**(2), 143–149 (2010)
8. Novák, L., Penáz, J., Kotovskaya, A., Vil-Vilyams, I., Lukjanuk, V., Nikolashin, G.: Perspectives for the application of the Penáz's method for a non-invasive continuous blood pressure measurement in space medicine. Physiologist. **34**(1 Suppl), S230–231 (1991)
9. O'Rourke, M., Avolio, A.: Pulsatile flow and pressure in human systemic arteries. Studies in man and in a multibranched model of the human systemic arterial tree. Circ. Res. **46**(3), 363–372 (1980)
10. O'Rourke, M., Winter, D.: Transfer function-derived central pressure and cardiovascular disease events: the Framingham Heart Study. J. Hypertens. **34**(12), 2487–2489 (2016)
11. O'Rourke, M.: Calibration of sphygmoCor. J. Hypertens. **35**(3), 645 (2017)
12. Pugovkin, A., Erkudov, V., Sergeev, I., Khananashvili, Y.: The physiological basis for assessment of haemodynamic parameters by means of arterial pressure pulse waveform analysis in peripheral arteries. Georgian Med. News **7–8**(304–305), 127–134 (2020)
13. Pugovkin, A., Erkudov, V., Verlov, N.: Non-invasive methods in the circulatory physiology. SpetsLit. St-Peterburg (2018)

14. Schumacher, J., Kaden, J., Trinkmann, F.: Multiple coupled resonances in the human vascular tree: refining the Westerhof model of the arterial system. J. Appl. Physiol. (1985) **124**(1), 131–139 (2018)
15. Westerhof, N., Stergiopulos, N., Noble, M., Westerhof, B.: Snapshots of Hemodynamics. 3nd edn. Springer International Publishing AG, New York (2019)

Investigation of Gastroparesis Using Multichannel Electro Gastro Gram – A Study

R. Chandrasekaran[1]([⊠]) [iD], S. Vijayaraj[2] [iD], and G. R. Jothi Lakshmi[2] [iD]

[1] Department of EEE, Vels Institute of Science, Technology and Advanced Studies, Chennai, India
[2] Department of ECE, Vels Institute of Science, Technology and Advanced Studies, Chennai, India

Abstract. In this study the various investigation for the Gastroparesis condition is discussed. The Gastroparesis is a disease/pathological condition in which the food inside the stomach cannot able to digest or empty in a normal way. The Symptoms of the Gastroparesis includes heart burn, nausea, vomiting sensation, fullness feeling quickly after the intake of meal, abdominal bloating. This kind of medical condition is common in people having diabetes for the long term. This phenomenon is common in people for some other conditions also like damage in the vagnus nerve. The vagnus nerve is responsible for the stomach contraction and relaxation. Any damage in the vagnus nerve creates this medical condition called Gastroparesis. In most cases the Gastroparesis condition is caused by prolonged diabetes and viral infections. The Gastroparesis condition is diagnosed using EGG – ElectroGastroGram. In this study, the various methodologies used to diagnose the Gastroparesis condition is reviewed.

Keywords: Gastroparesis · Electrogastrogram · Vagnus nerve

1 Introduction

Electrogastrography refers to acquisition of Gastric Signals [1,2]. The Diagnosis of Gastroparesis is not easy. The Exact location of injury or accurate location of the palsy is very tough to identify. The Diagnosis of Gastroparesis aims at identification of the location of injury and methodology to be followed for curing & Treatment [3,4]. The various events of stomach digestion process and its records are discussed and sensitive galvanometer is used as alternative for EGG [1].

2 Histroy

Electrogastrography technique was Initially proposed by Dr. Alvarez in the year 1922, later on the technique was altered and further developed by davis et al. Electrogastrography is used by most of the physicians as bio marker for detection of Gastroparesis [5–8]. It is clearly established that Electrogastrography technique is used to

I. Rojas et al. (Eds.): BIOMESIP 2021, LNCS 12940, pp. 121–129, 2021.
https://doi.org/10.1007/978-3-030-88163-4_12

diagnose the various gastric disorders clinically before the 1960s, thus the Electrogas-trography technique is an accurate diagnostic procedure for gastric motility disorders [9–13] (Table 1).

Table 1. Pathological conditions that influence the Gastroparesis

S/no	Pathological conditions that influences the Gastroparesis
1	Abnormal Ddgestion
2	Diabetes
3	Stroke
4	Nervous system injury or damage
5	After surgery like translplantation, Bypass surgery etc
6	Thyroidism
7	Ischemia
8	Edema

The Measuring parameters of Electrogastrograms includes measuring of digestion rate, stomach motility rate, gastric cycles rate. The Measuring procedure involves patient preparation initially. The surface electrodes are mostly involved to acquire the signals from the surface of the stomach. The various merits and demerits of EGG were discussed in [2] and the advantages are really appreciable. Myoelectric activity is present in the stomach, just as it is in the heart. The stomach's myoelectrical behavior is made up of sluggish waves and spike potentials. Spike potentials are also known as action potentials or electrical reaction activity, while slow waves are known as pacesetter potentials or electrical control activity (Table 2).

Table 2. Drugs that influence the Gastroparesis

S/no	Drugs that influences the Gastroparesis
1	Tobaco
2	Alcohol
3	Calcium channel blockers
4	Opioids
5	Proton pump Inhibitors
6	Cyclosporine
7	H2 receptors antogonists
8	Sucralfate

3 Procedures for Diagnosis of Gastroparesis

There are various procedure followed for the diagnosis of the Gastroparesis in Humans.

3.1 Esophagogastroduodenoscopy

This is one of the earliest scanning and diagnosing technique for Gastroparesis. The Subject is asked to undergo fasting for two hours. The Esophagogastroduodenoscopy is used to check whether the food particles are located in the same intestine region or whether the food particles are digested completely, any residue are present etc. The same procedure is repeated for the second time but this time after the fasting scanning the subject is advised to take heavy food. The scanning procedure takes place in post prandial state. The digestion process, gastric emptying, gastric delaying, fullness of stomach, irritation, stomach ulcer reaction, etc. can be monitored using this procedure.

3.2 GI Radiography

One of the Oldest Methodology for diagnosis of Gastroparesis. This Methodology is not exactly proposed for the diagnosis of the Gastroparesis. This Methodology of radiography is initially used to diagnose the Pathology of Hernia and its abnormalities. The contrast agent will be injected or mixed with the food of the testing subject. The subject is asked to swallow the food or get injected. The contrast agent popularly used are Barium. In general, this methodology is also called as Barium X ray Procedure. This Barium X ray radiography is also used for chest x ray scanning. This Methodology is not very accurate. The main highlight of the procedure is to add contrast imaging in radiography. The Barium is an inert chemical compound. It does not harm the subject & it will be digested along with the food.

The Electrogastrogram is one of the cost-effective methodologies for the diagnosis of the gastroparesis condition in humans. The EGG has single to multi-channel number of electrodes acquisition system. Based on the acquisition modality, the region of analysis of stomach and acquisition clarity is defined. Through Electrogastrogram the digestion rate can be predicted. The digestion process of the each and every type of food can be calculated. This analysis of food digestion will be very much useful for patients who are suffering from gastroparesis.

3.3 Gastric Myo – Electrical Activity

The leahy et al., conducted various experiments in evaluating EGG signal as biomarker for GERD syndrome for diabetic peoples.

The Electrogastrogram is used to identify the most pathological conditions of the Gastroparesis named as Tachygastria and Bradygastria. These abnormalities are observed in patients having Gastroparesis condition and these conditions are often seen in Diabetic patients.

The various useful features are extracted from the signal of ElectroGastroGram. The signal gives the exact information regarding the electrical activity of stomach. The Digestion cycle in rates or cycles per minute can be calculated from this signal. Various other useful information are extracted from the signals. The PPG signals have influences in EGG signals. It is been proved that at various kinds of food that is been taken, the EGG cycle differs in diabetic patients. [11–15].

A number of studies have discovered a connection between the EGG and gastric emptying. The EGG and gastric emptying scintigraphy were found to be complementary for the assessment of dyspepsia in patients. The rate of stomach emptying was found to be significantly associated with the postprandial shift in EGG dominant power in pediatric patients with gastroesophageal reflux.

4 Methodology

This Paper is a complete review about Electrogastrogram & Electrogastrography. The Electrogastrography signals should be considered as one of the vital parameters of the body. More number of useful information can be extracted from one single gastric waveform.

5 Study of Electrogastrography

5.1 Electrogastrography - Recording

As we all know that bio signals are very weak to record. The Electrogastrography signals are very weak in potential. In order to record the gastric signals suitable amplifiers should be implemented to amplify the signals. If the system is multichannel electrogastrogram then the proper electrode montage is used to select the number of electrode channel used for recording the bio potential [16–20].

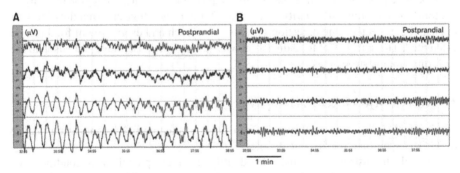

Fig. 1. Sample Electrogastrography waveform of postprandial state

5.2 Patient Preparation

The Hairs that are present on the abdomen skin should be removed before recording the EGG signal. Before the placement of the electrode, suitable electrolyte should be used to affix the electrode. The usage of appropriate electrolyte is most important for better recording of the signal. If the electrolyte solution is applied more then the electrodes cannot fix firm on the skin. If multiple electrodes are used then the impedance has to be verified before recording the signal. The subject is prepared to not to make shake or feel disturbed during the recording the bio potential (Fig. 1).

5.3 Placement of Electrodes

If the recording of signal is single channel, then one active electrode and one reference electrode and one ground electrode is used. The active electrode is placed at the midline of stomach near xiphoid or near umbilicus [21–23]. The reference electrode is placed far from the stomach. If the system for recording is multichannel, then two or more electrodes are used. The electrodes are placed completely around the stomach. The array of electrodes are sticked all around the stomach for recording high resolution gastric signals.

5.4 Patient State of Recording Signal

The most important points that should be remembered during the subject preparation is,
* avoid usage of any other electronic gadgets like cell phone during recording the signal. The subject should be in resting state, calm and peaceful for better recording of signal [24, 25]. Any radiational disturbances should be avoided during recording of signal. The subject should co operate while recording the signal for smooth recording of signal.

5.5 Recording Duration

The most common mistakes that everybody does while recording the signal is short duration of signal is recorded. For example, two to three minutes recording duration is insufficient for analyzing the signals. The normal cycle of EGG signal is 3–4 cycles per minute, hence it requires minimum thirty minutes to record the signal at both fasting and postprandial states. Below an average of thirty minutes of recording would give lesser information for diagnosing if any abnormalities are present in the subject. Therefore, the duration of recording is most important for recording, diagnosing, analyzing the gastric signals [26–28].

5.6 Gastric Signals

The patient preparation is most important before the recording of EGG signal. The patient is asked to undergo fasting before the recording of the signal. The subject is not allowed to drink water or any liquid or solid foods for two hours before recording. Compulsory fasting has to be carried out before recording the signal. After successful recording of the signal, the subject can take food but the number of calories is measured before eating. The number of calories that is commonly prescribed is between 400–250 kcal. The food is a mixture of proteins, carbohydrates, fats, liquid foods. The exact kcal of food is noted. After eating the subject is asked to record the signal. This kind of recoding signal is called as postprandial state of recording the signal. After fasting and postprandial state recording signal is recorded then the signal can be further processed for analysis. The most important condition during recording of the signal is the subject should not sleep during the recording process. If the subject fall asleep during recording process, then the pattern of gastric waveforms get differs from normal state. Subject should not sleep during any state of recording of signal [25, 29–31].

5.7 Flaws in EGG Recording

The EGG recording may get completely flawed if the following happens.

- Noises in the signal
- Mismatching of skin impedance
- Disturbance during recording
- Electrical or radiation interference
- Over usage of electrolyte gel
- Wrong placement of electrodes
- Poor recording or short-term recording of signal
- Non-cooperation of subject

5.8 EGG Signal Analysis

The Electrogastrogram is one of the most important clinical diagnostic tools for many abnormalities of stomach. The Various useful diagnostic information can be extracted from the gastric signals. The EGG signal analysis can be done in various methodologies and domains. The new algorithm are developed to analyse all the forms, domains and exploring new parameters of the gastric waves. The usual methodology of analyzing the spectrum of the signal gives frequency distribution of the signal. Using this spectral analysis tool we can able to find the dominant frequency of the signals. Using the dominant signals we can able to diagnose the gastroparesis condition in patients. The patients digestive rate can also be calculated using this spectral analysis [31, 32].

The various other techniques like mathematical modelling, in vivo modelling, can be used to analyse to the various other parameters of the signals. Usually the extraction of the slow wave is most important and difficult task in analysing the signal. Using suitable filters the noise and other errors of the signals are removed. The basic preprocessing of signal is most important. Based on the sample length factor, sample time period, the suitable filters are applied. The most used filters are band pass filter which is used to remove the unwanted components of the signals. After filtering, the signal is used for further processing and extraction of useful parameters from the signal. Many parameters are un explored in terms of the gastric signals.

6 Other Disorders

The most frequent gastric disorders that often hits the clinical side is irregular digestion rate, gastroparesis, dyspepsia, tachygastria, bradygastria, bloating of stomach, early fullness of stomach etc. The normal gastric cycles for human is three cycles per minute. Due to irregularity in sleeping patterns, stress and other conditions the pathophysiology of the gastroparesis differs. Gastric dsyrthmia is also a common gastric disorders that happens in early days of pregnancy, which results in irregular bowel movements [33–35].

7 Summary

In this paper we have reviewed about Electrogastrogram and its application over diagnosis of various abnormalities of stomach. The most important disorder of stomach is gastroparesis. The pathophysiology of the gastroparesis can be analyzed using the EGG signal and it can be prevented. The EGG is a very important clinical diagnostic tool for analyzing and diagnosing the electrogastrogram and other disease conditions.

The various other abnormalities of the stomach is also discussed in this paper. This paper revolves around a complete theoretical survey of EGG and the gastric signals. Using this review of EGG signals the various procedures difficulties and abnormalities are discussed here.

8 Conclusion

The Electrogastrogram provides in depth information about the gastric slow waves and myoelectric activity of the stomach. The methods for acquisition of signal from stomach differs based on the channels of electrodes used. The digestion rate and various other stomach disorders can be diagnosed using the Multichannel EGG. The Gastroparesis condition is most commonly found in diabetic peoples which creates quick stomach paralysis and makes the food to get digested in prolonged state. However this MEGG is one of the best tool used to diagnose the pathological condition and make judgement on the condition of the subject.

References

1. Alvarez, W.C., et al.: The Electrogastrogram and what it shows. JAMA. **78**, 1116–1119 (1922)
2. Chen, J.D., et al.: Electrogastrographic parameters and their clinical significance. In: Chen, J.D., McCallum, R.W. (eds.) Electrogastrography: Principles and Applications, pp. 45–73. Raven, New York (1994)
3. Davis, R.C., Carafolo, L., Gault, F.P.: An exploration of abdominal potentials. J. Comp. Physiol. Psychol. **50**, 519–523 (1957)
4. Bharucha, A.E.: Epidemiology and natural history of gastroparesis. Gastroenterol. Clin. North Am. **44**(1), 9–19 (2015)
5. Usai-Satta, P., Bellini, M., Morelli, O., Geri, F., Lai, M., Bassotti, G.: Gastroparesis: new insights into an old disease. World J. Gastroenterol. **26**(19), 2333–2348 (2020). https://doi.org/10.3748/wjg.v26.i19.2333

6. Thomas, A., de Souza Ribeiro, B., Malespin, M., de Melo, S.W.: Botulinum toxin as a treatment for refractory gastroparesis: a literature review. Curr. Treatment Opt. Gastroenterol. **16**(4), 479–488 (2018). https://doi.org/10.1007/s11938-018-0187-x

7. Rhee, P.L., Lee, J.Y., Son, H.J., et al.: Analysis of pacemaker activity in the human stomach. J. Physiol. **589**(Pt 24), 6105–6118 (2011)

8. Manolakis, A.C., Inoue, H., Ueno, A., Shimamura, Y.: 2007–2019: a "Third"-space odyssey in the endoscopic management of gastrointestinal tract diseases. Curr. Treatment Opt. Gastroenterol. **17**(2), 202–220 (2019). https://doi.org/10.1007/s11938-019-00233-6

9. Camilleri, M., Parkman, H.P., Shafi, M.A., Abell, T.L., Gerson, L.: American college of Gastroenterology. Clinical guideline: management of gastroparesis. Am. J. Gastroenterol. **108**, 18–37 (2013)

10. Cohen, M.S.: Clinical practice. Eur. J. Pediatr. **171**(8), 1145–1150 (2012). https://doi.org/10.1007/s00431-012-1736-2

11. Tougas, G., Eaker, E.Y., Abell, T.L., et al.: Assessment of gastric emptying using a low fat meal: establishment of international control values. Am. J. Gastroenterol. **95**, 1456–1462 (2000)

12. Patterson, D., Abell, T., Rothstein, R., et al.: A double-blind multicenter comparison of domperidone and metoclopramide in the treatment of diabetic patients with symptoms of gastroparesis. Am. J. Gastroenterol. **94**, 1230–1240 (1999)

13. Abell, T.L., Bernstein, R.K., Cutts, T., et al.: Treatment of gastroparesis: a multidisciplinary clinical review. Neurogastroenterol. Motil. **18**, 263–283 (2006)

14. Komorowski, D., Pietraszek, S., Tkacz, E., Provaznik, I.: The extraction of the new components from electrogastrogram (EGG), using both adaptive filtering and electrocardiographic (ECG) derived respiration signal. Biomed. Eng. Online. **23**(14), 60 (2015). https://doi.org/10.1186/s12938-015-0054-0

15. Komorowski, D., Pietraszek, S.: The use of continuous wavelet transform based on the fast fourier transform in the analysis of multi-channel electrogastrography recordings. J. Med. Syst. **40**(1), 1–15 (2015). https://doi.org/10.1007/s10916-015-0358-4

16. Lin, X., Chen, J.Z.: Abnormal gastric slow waves in patients with functional dyspepsia assessed by multichannel elctrogastraphy. Am. J. Physiol. Gastrointest. Liver Physiol. **280**, G1370–G1375 (2001)

17. Yin, J., Levanon, D., Chen, J.D.: Inhibitory effects of stress on postprandial gastric myoelectrical activity and vagal tone in healthy subjects. Neurogastroenterol. Motil. **16**, 737–774 (2004)

18. Qian, L.W., Pasricha, P.J., Chen, J.D.: Origin and patterns of spontaneous and drug-induced canine gastric myoelectrical dysrhythmias. Dig. Dis. Sci. **48**, 508–515 (2003)

19. Ouyang, H., Xing, J., Chen, J.D.: Tachygastria induced by gastric electrical stimulation is mediated via alpha- and beta-adrenergic pathway and inhibits antral motility in dogs. Neurogastroenterol. Motil. **17**, 846–853 (2005)

20. O'Grady, G., Angeli, T.R., Du, P., et al.: Abnormal initiation and conduction of slow-wave activity in gastroparesis, defined by high-resolution electrical mapping. Gastroenterology **143**(3), 589–598 (2012)

21. McNearney, T., Lin, X., Shrestha, J., Lisse, J., Chen, J.D.: Characterization of gastric myoelectrical rhythms in patients with systemic sclerosis using multichannel surface electrogastrography. Dig. Dis. Sci. **47**, 690–698 (2002)

22. Koch, K.L., Hong, S.P., Xu, L.: Reproducibility of gastric myoelectric activity and the water load test in patients with dysmotility-like dyspepsia symptoms and in control subjects. J. Clin. Gastroenterol. **31**, 125–129 (2000)

23. Wang, Z.S., Elsenbruch, S., Orr, W.C., Chen, J.D.: Detection of gastric slow wave uncoupling from multi-channel electrogastrogram: validations and applications. Neurogastroenterol. Motil. **15**, 457–465 (2003)

24. Qian, L., Orr, W.C., Chen, J.D.: Inhibitory reflexive effect of rectal distention on postprandial gastric myoelectrical activity. Dig. Dis. Sci. **47**, 2473–2479 (2002)
25. Chen, J., Song, G.Q., Yin, J., Koothan, T., Chen, J.D.: Electroacupuncture improves impaired gastric motility and slow waves induced by rectal distension in dogs. Am. J. Physiol. Gastrointest. Liver Physiol. **295**, G614–G620 (2008)
26. Liu, J., Huang, H., Xu, X., Chen, J.D.: Effects and possible mechanisms of acupuncture at ST36 on upper and lower abdominal symptoms induced by rectal distension in healthy volunteers. Am. J. Physiol. Regul. Integr. Comp. Physiol. **303**, R209–R217 (2012)
27. Yin, J., Chen, J.D.: Gastrointestinal motility disorders and acupuncture. Auton. Neurosci. **157**, 31–37 (2010)
28. Chen, J.D., Ke, M.Y., Lin, X.M., Wang, Z., Zhang, M.: Cisapride provides symptomatic relief in functional dyspepsia associated with gastric myoelectrical abnormality. Aliment Pharmacol. Ther. **14**, 1041–1047 (2000)
29. Orr, W.C., Zhang, M., McClanahan, J., Sloan, S., Chen, J.D.: Gastric myoelectric activity in older adults treated with cisapride for gastro-oesophageal reflux disease. Aliment Pharmacol. Ther. **14**, 337–343 (2000)
30. DiBaise, J.K., Park, F.L., Lyden, E., Brand, R.E., Brand, R.M.: Effects of low doses of erythromycin on the 13C Spirulina platensis gastric emptying breath test and electrogastrogram: a controlled study in healthy volunteers. Am. J. Gastroenterol. **96**, 2041–2050 (2001)
31. Faure, C., Wolff, V.P., Navarro, J.: Effect of meal and intravenous erythromycin on manometric and electrogastrographic measurements of gastric motor and electrical activity. Dig. Dis. Sci. **45**, 525–528 (2000)
32. Franzese, A., Borrelli, O., Corrado, G., et al.: Domperidone is more effective than cisapride in children with diabetic gastroparesis. Aliment Pharmacol. Ther. **16**, 951–957 (2002)
33. Talley, N.J., Camilleri, M., Burton, D., et al.: Double-blind, randomized, placebo-controlled study to evaluate the effects of tegaserod on gastric motor, sensory and myoelectric function in healthy volunteers. Aliment Pharmacol. Ther. **24**, 859–867 (2006)
34. Jackson, A.L., Rashed, H., Cardoso, S., et al.: Assessment of gastric electrical activity and autonomic function among diabetic and nondiabetic patients with symptoms of gastroesophageal reflux. Dig. Dis. Sci. **45**, 1727–1730 (2000)
35. Jung, K.T., Park, H., Kim, J.H., et al.: The relationship between gastric myoelectric activity and SCN5A mutation suggesting sodium channelopathy in patients with Brugada syndrome and functional dyspepsia - a pilot study. J. Neurogastroenterol. Motil. **18**, 58–63 (2012)

Computerized Medical Imaging
and Graphics

3D Tomosynthesis Evaluation of Pixel Intensity Values of Breast Masses

Sneha Ravichandran[1] (iD) and Rohini Avantsa[2](✉) (iD)

[1] Department of Medical Imaging Technology, K S Hegde Medical Academy, Mangalore, Karnataka, India
[2] Department of Radiodiagnosis and Imaging, Justice K S Hegde Charitable Hospital, Mangalore, Karnataka, India

Abstract. Breast cancer remains the most commonly diagnosed cancer among women in India and globally. For women 30 years old and older, current evidence supports evaluation with diagnostic mammography combined with targeted breast ultrasound for palpable or non-palpable lumps because of the surrounding attenuating breast tissue. Higher breast density is associated with both decreased sensitivity of mammography and an elevated risk of breast cancer. Hence there is a need for identifying additional characteristics of breast lumps on mammography or a new tool which could higher up the possibility of detecting the cancerous lumps and thereby increasing the sensitivity of mammography in identifying the breast cancer. With this idea we aimed for finding the pixel intensity values for benign and malignant breast masses.
Results. Our study showed that breast masses with pixel value below 2100 (N-10) were all benign masses and pixel values above 2390 were all belonged to malignant masses (n = 11). Majority of the breast masses (N = 89) in our study were falling under the range of 2100 to 2390 which contained both benign and malignant masses with most (N = 75) of them were benign and 14 were malignant.
Conclusion. Our study concluded that benign and malignant masses can be diagnosed using pixel values alone when they are falling in the category of <2100 and >2390. However the masses falling into the indeterminate category with values of 2100–2390, require additional mammography features for differentiating and diagnosing cancerous lumps from benign.

Keywords: Breast tomosynthesis · Breast lump · Breast density · Benign breast masses · Malignant breast masses · Pixel intensity

1 Introduction

Worldwide breast cancer is the commonest cancer in women with variable incidence between developed and developing countries with 50% of diagnosed in developed countries and lowest in far Eastern and South-East Asian countries [1, 2, 4]. The incidence of breast cancer is less in developing countries of Asia, but there is steady increase in the disease and thereby increased burden on the health care. India being a subcontinent with diverse ethnic, cultural, religious and economic structure and also variation in health care

© Springer Nature Switzerland AG 2021
I. Rojas et al. (Eds.): BIOMESIP 2021, LNCS 12940, pp. 133–140, 2021.
https://doi.org/10.1007/978-3-030-88163-4_13

infrastructure, the pattern of health care facilities varies between different regions and also between urban and rural area. The illiteracy, lack of awareness and myths regarding the disease are still prevailing in the rural and also in some parts of urban women which results in an unrealistic fear about the disease. And added to this the financial constraints are preventing women from attend breast clinical at an early stage. Hence it is crucial to diagnose the disease in time and to minimize the number of investigations in order to reduce the financial burden.

Imaging plays a crucial role in breast cancer diagnosis and invasive procedures like BIOPSY and FNAC are the gold standards, provides the tissue diagnosis of tumors [5]. Breast Imaging Reporting And Database System (BIRADS) is an internationally accredited scoring system for the diagnosis and classification of breast masses ranging from inconclusive to malignant tumors [6]. The BIRADS scoring helps in reducing the HPE burden to all the patients with a lump and therefore low monetary burden on diagnosis [5].BIRADS II masses are benign with 0% probability of malignancy which require no further investigation and BIRADS IV masses have 2–94% probability of malignance which require tissue diagnosis. Whereas BIRADS III masses are categorized as indeterminate with < 2% probability of malignance which require short interval follow-up to either upgrade or downgrade the lesion.

To the best of our knowledge, no study has been conducted and published on the pixel intensity values of breast masses. Therefore the main aim of our study is to evaluating the pixel intensity values of the breast masses using the 3D tomosynthesis and to categorize the lesion according to pixel intensity values. The quantification technique by using pixel intensity values might help to lower the invasive procedures, also faster diagnosis and treatment and thereby reducing the monetary burden. Having this in mind, as the first research initiation, this study was conducted to quantify the breast masses on basis of attenuation values of the tumor and to compare with BIRADS.

2 Methodology

The study was conducted between November 2019 to April 2021 in our hospital. 232 patients were referred for mammography which was performed using Siemens Mammo-mat Inspiration mammography machine. The routine mammogram consisted of Cranio-caudal (CC) and Medio-lateral Oblique (MLO) views. Out of 232 patients, the study included 69 patients who had clinically and/or radiologically diagnosed breast masses. The patients with breast masses in the pectoralis major muscle, enlarged lymph nodes and those without histopathological results were excluded from the study. A total of 110 breast masses were assessed using ultrasound and mammography for characterization according to BIRADS followed by FNAC/Biopsy/Excision biopsy of the breast lesion for tissue diagnosis as malignant or benign for the final assessment. Single radiologist assessed both the images from the X-ray mammogram and the ultrasound for the final reporting and the BIRADS scoring and was blinded for the histopathological results. The breast mass viewed in CC and MLO views for the lesion localization, margins, and the pixel intensity value measurements. The circle ROI tool in the system was used for assessing the pixel values at a window width of 1804 and centered at 2108 as a standard set protocol. The ROI of maximum of 0.5 cm^2 of area coverage was used to measure pixel intensity in 3 different locations within the lesion in both the views to find an average pixel intensity value of the masses. However due to the compression pressure difference between CC and MLO view, the pixel intensity values were significantly differed leaving CC view as an ideal view for the measurements (Fig. 1).

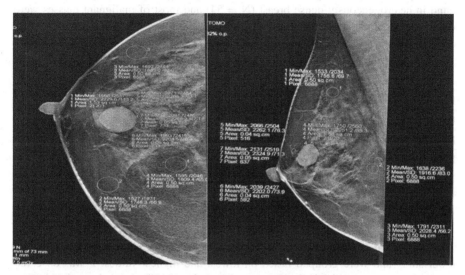

Fig. 1. Representation of the pixel intensity value measurements within the breast mass

3   Results

The study included 69 patients and 110 breast masses. Among the 69 patients included in this study 6 patients were below the age of 40 years and 2 patients were above 70 years age. Majority of the patients (39%) were within the age group of 40–50 (N = 27) followed by 32% of patients in the age group of 50–60 years (N = 22). 17% of patients were in the age group of 60–70 years (N = 12) [Table 1].

Table 1. Age group distribution

Age group	Frequency (N)	Percent (%)
Below 40	6	9
40–50	27	39
50–60	22	32
60–70	12	17
Above 70	2	3
Total	69	100.0

Among 110 breast masses, 12 masses were found in fatty parenchyma, 38 masses in fibroglandular parenchyma, 58 masses in heterogeneously dense parenchyma and 2 masses were found in extremely dense parenchyma. This signifies that occurrence of breast masses in heterogeneously dense breast were most common (53%) followed by the fibroglandular parenchyma (34%) in our study. Majority of benign masses were found in heterogeneously dense breast (N = 54) and most of malignant masses were found in fibroglandular parenchyma (N = 12) [Table 2].

Table 2. Distribution of patients according to breast parenchyma pattern

Breast tissue architecture	Number (N)	Percentage (%)	Benign (N)	Malignant (N)
Fatty	12	11	6	6
Fibroglandular	38	34	26	12
Heterogeneously dense	58	53	54	4
Hyperdense	2	2	2	0
Total	110	100	88	22

A wide [total of 970] range of pixel intensity values of breast masses were observed in our study and were grouped based on lowest and highest values. It was observed that the breast mass with pixel intensity values below 2100 were belonged to benign and the values above 2390 were fallen into the category of malignant masses. The pixel intensity values between 2100 and the 2390 were seen in 80.9% of cases which contained 75 benign and 14 malignant masses. The study showed weak positive correlation between pixel intensity values and type of mass (benign/malignant) [Table 3].

Table 3. Distribution of Pixel Intensity values of breast masses according to HPE (benign/malignant)

Pixel intensity	Mass type		Total
	Benign	Malignant	
Below 2100	10	0	10
2100–2390	75	14	89
Above 2390	0	11	11
Total	85	25	110

Table 4. Distribution of patients according to lesions in the breast

Occurrence	Frequency (N)	Percent (%)
Unilateral	48	69.5
Bilateral	21	30.5
Total	69	100

Table 5. Distribution of patients according to lesion multiplicity

Occurrence	Frequency (N)	Percent (%)
Single	43	62.5
Multiple	26	37.5
Total	69	100.0

Table 6. BIRADS score comparison with the pixel intensity values

Pixel intensity values	BIRADS score								
	0	2	3	4	4a	4b	4c	5	6
CC	2094.51	2282.95	2301.93	2226.58	2227.58	2278.86	2251.40	2667.50	2547.18
Total	10	53	25	7	2	3	1	5	4
P value- 0.529									

4 Discussion

This was a cross sectional study conducted at Justice K S Hegde Charitable Hospital from March 2020–May 2021, with an objective to find out the pixel intensity values of breast masses on mammogram which probably help in diagnosing the breast masses there by increasing the acucracy of mammogram in diagnosing breast masses especially in breasts with heterogenously dense and extermely dense parenchyma. Further it might reduce the unnecessary invasive diagnostic procedures and to fasten up the cancer treatment. Our study mainly focused on female patients who had either symptomatic or asymptomatic breast masses. We excluded the breast masses that were found in the pectoralis major muscle and the enlarged lymph nodes. This exclusion was made for three reasons. First one was the observed difference in pixel intensity values of the muscle as compared to that of the normal breast parenchyma. The second reason was enlarged overlapping axillary lymph nodes and the third reason was the partial visualization of the breast mass which has to be evaluated in both CC and MLO views. Because of this margins of the masses were often partially delineated which made incomplete assessment of the pixel intensity values. The study evaluated 4 factors, the frequency of normal breast parenchymal pattern in the study group, pixel intensity values of breast masses, lesion type [benign or malignant] and the relation with BIRADS score (Fig. 2).

71% of 69 patients included in our study were in 40–60 age groups. This shows occurrence of breast masses, both benign and malignant at a younger age compared

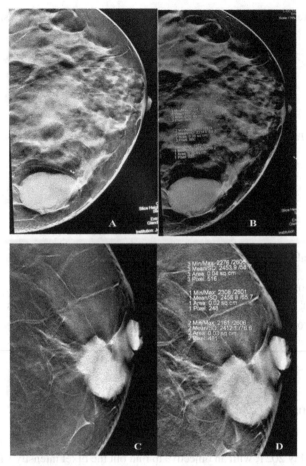

Fig. 2. Benign and malignant lesion pixel intensity values evaluation **A and B**-Left breast palpable lesion Mammography + USG = Fibroadenoma BIRADS = 3 Pixel value = 2320 HPE = Fibroadenoma, **C and D** - Left breast palpable lesion Mammography + USG = malignant BIRADS = 5 Pixel value = 2412 HPE = Lobar carcinoma

to the study conducted by Etta Pisano D et al. [7] in United States of America which observed in 42,760 patients. In their study majority (47%) of the breast masses were in the age group of 50–65 followed by the age group of below 50 years (33%). In our study left breast masses (59%) were more frequent compared to right breast masses (41%) and unilateral presentation was more [69.5%] frequent than that of bilateral [30.5%] [Table 4]. 37.5% of our patients were presented with multiple masses and 64.5% had single masses. All the patients with multiple masses had benign masses [Table 5]. Our study results were similar to previous study conducted among African population by Uchechukwu I Nwadike et al. [8].

The breast parenchymal pattern was classified as fatty, fibroglandular, heterogeneously dense and hyperdense depending upon the predominant appearance on mammogram following ACR criteria. Heterogeneously dense parenchyma was the most frequent [53%] pattern of parenchyma observed in our study, followed by fibroglandular pattern [34%], Extremely dense parenchyma [2%] and fatty parenchyma [11%]. This could be explained by breast disease in younger population and also supported by the 39% percentage of study population below 50 years age group.

In our study we classified all 110 breast masses on the basis of the internationally accredited BIRADS where the masses were separated based on different scores. Our study observed 80% benign masses and 20% malignant masses. This distribution of breast masses was also observed in previous study conducted in Bihar, India, by Dr. N.K. Srivastava et al. [9], which showed 79.5% benign and 20.5% malignant masses. Another interesting observation in our study was there is difference in pixel intensity values between the CC and MLO views of the same mass. The reason for this difference could be due to the amount of compression i.e. the CC view had more compression than the MLO view [because of the position and also added muscle], because of which the MLO view showed variable pixel intensities values due to the non uniformity of the breast. In general if both the views were given the same amount of compression, then the values would be equal. In our study BIRADS 2 and 3 masses showed a steady increase in pixel intensity values from 2100 to 2390. All the BIRADS 2 masses were under 2300 and BIRADS 3 were above 2300. BIRADS 4 was on contrary has shown a decline in the pixel intensity values as compared to BIRADS 3 [Table 6]. The pixel intensity values were under 2300 in all cases. BIRADS 5 and 6 had an elevated pixel intensity values and were above 2390. Our study showed that breast masses with pixel intensity value below 2100 (N = 10) were all benign masses and pixel intensity value above 2390 were all belonged to malignant masses (N = 11). Majority of the breast masses (N = 89) in our study were falling under the range of 2100 to 2390 which contained both benign and malignant masses with most (N = 75) of them were benign and 14 were malignant.

5   Conclusion and Recommendations

The breast masses with pixel intensity values below 2100 were all benign and the masses above the pixel intensity values of 2500 were all malignant in our study. Many breast masses in our study with pixel intensity values between 2100–2390 were indeterminate with predominantly benign category. However the values towards the higher side were predominantly malignant. The breast masses in this group can be further characterized based on other mammography features as benign or malignant. This study has opened a wide room for further study to assess the masses in the pectoralis muscle and difference in two basic views.

6   Limitations of Study

The study did not include the masses that were not observed in CC view since CC view was taken as our primary view for the pixel intensity evaluation. Those masses which were being overlapped on the pectoralis major muscle were also excluded due to the difference in the pixel intensity values of muscle to the breast parenchyma. The masses with indistinct margins and architectural distortion were also not considered. The major setback was seen due Covid pandemic which decreased the patient inflow for our study causing lower number breast masses for evaluation.

Acknowedgement. We would like to thank the staff of Dept of Radiodiagnosis and Imaging and also the hospital ethical committee for their support to the study.

References

1. National Cancer Registry Program: Ten year consolidated report of the Hospital Based Cancer Registries, 1984–1993, an assessment of the burden and care of cancer patients. Indian Council of Medical Research, New Delhi (2001)
2. Agarwal, G., Pradeep, P.V., Aggarwal, V., Yip, C.H., Cheung, P.S.: Spectrum of breast cancer in Asian women. World J. Surg. **31**, 1031–1040 (2007)
3. Aggarwal, V., et al.: Feasibility study of safe breast conservation in large and locally advanced cancers with use of radiopaque markers to mark pre-neoadjuvant chemotherapy tumor margins. World J. Surg. **32**(12), 2562–2569 (2007)
4. Parkin, D.M.: Global cancer statistics in the year 2000. Lancet Oncol. **2**, 533 (2001)
5. Attia, R., Kotb, F., Rabie, O.M.: Role of fine-needle aspiration cytology in the diagnosis of thyroid diseases. Egypt J. Surg. **38**, 439–450 (2019)
6. Burnside, E.S., Sickles, E.A., Bassett, L.W., et al.: The ACR BI-RADS experience: learning from history. J. Am. CollRadiol. **6**(12), 851–860 (2009)
7. Pisano, E.D., et al.: DMIST investigators group. Diagnostic accuracy of digital versus film mammography: exploratory analysis of selected population subgroups in DMIST. Radiology. **246**(2), 376–83 (2008)
8. Nwadike, U.I., Eze, C.U., Agwuna, K., Mouka, C.: Mammographic classification of breast lesions amongst women in Enugu. South East Nigeria. Afr. Health Sci. **17**(4), 1044–1050 (2017)
9. Srivastava, D.N.K.: Clinico-pathological study 200 cases of Breast lesions in a tertiary care centre of Rohtas, Bihar. India. Trop. J. Pathol. Microbiol. **5**(6), 338–342 (2019)

Trident U-Net: An Encoder Fusion for Improved Biomedical Image Segmentation

Rajdeep Chatterjee[1]($\boxtimes$) ⓘ, Soham Roy[1] ⓘ, and SK Hafizul Islam[2] ⓘ

[1] School of Computer Engineering, KIIT Deemed to be University,
Bhuvaneswar 751024, Odisha, India
`rajdeepfcs@kiit.ac.in`
[2] Department of Computer Science and Engineering, Indian Institute of Information Technology Kalyani, Kalyani 741235, West Bengal, India

Abstract. Image segmentation is a fundamental requirement in biomedical image analysis. Recent advances in deep learning have resulted in optimistic results on many biomedical image segmentation benchmark datasets. However, there is a need to propagate and improve biomedical image analysis due to significant variations in biomedical images in recent days. As with the rapid growth of technology in medical equipment, more variations of biomedical data of various tests/scans are being generated rapidly. There is a growing vacuum of quick technical analysis on these biomedical data. Biomedical image segmentation is at the forefront of them. Manual analysis results in outrageous efforts and costs because only biomedical experts can annotate effectively and are often subjected to human error. Various deep learning-based solutions are being created to leverage machine learning capabilities and effectively address this problem. In this paper, We propose a deep learning framework built on the U-Net architecture and use a combination (triplet) of encoder models to address the semantic segmentation of a biomedical image effectively. An extensive experiment of our proposed Trident U-Net architecture has been done using the CVC-612 and ETIS datasets. The overall performance of the proposed Trident U-Net on both datasets outperforms the existing reportedly best performing models. The results obtained from the ETIS dataset are 0.66, 0.68, and 0.59 for the evaluation metrics Recall, Dice Coefficient, and IoU Score, respectively. Similarly, the results achieved on the CVC-612 dataset are 0.91, 0.89, and 0.83 for the same evaluation metrics, respectively.

Keywords: Efficientnet · MobileNetV2 · ResNet50 · Semantic segmentation · U-Net

1 Introduction

Since late 2019, the World has witnessed a new virus called COVID-19. It started in Wuhan city of China and then began spreading to the rest of the World. It is a deadly virus, and one generally catches it if one comes within proximity of an infected person. According to WHO, the only way to contain this virus is *"Physical distancing helps limit the spread of COVID-19 – this means we keep a distance of at least 1 m."* Due to this pandemic and growing cases of covid patients, there is an ever-increasing need for

I. Rojas et al. (Eds.): BIOMESIP 2021, LNCS 12940, pp. 141–154, 2021.
https://doi.org/10.1007/978-3-030-88163-4_14

communications to go contactless as much as possible. Generally, in Biomedical image analysis, a certified professional analyzes a biomedical image in the presence of an individual/patient where the primary task is to classify the ROI, e.g., diseased region or healthy region. There is ample opportunity and need for biomedical image segmentation to go contactless and remote. Many deep learning-based models are coming up trying to address this problem. However, with the Covid situation, the onus is on researchers to improve these machine learning-based image segmentation models to deliver the transition from semi-automatic to fully automatic segmentation methods.

1.1 Motivation

Here, We have focussed only on polyp segmentation. The purpose of this is to detect colorectal polyps, which are highly related to colorectal cancer. Detecting polyp is a difficult task mainly because of two reasons. First, there is no well-defined edge and separation between the affected region and the surroundings. Secondly, polyp comes in various shapes, sizes, colors, and textures, making it particularly difficult to recognize that very limited datasets are available for training the model for polyp segmentation.

1.2 Contribution

A deep learning architecture has been proposed, which is created on the underlying U-Net architecture. Our proposed Trident model is using the same decoder architecture as the U-Net. Nevertheless, we have used a Trident encoder model where three encoders are combined to downsample the image and to use the standard U-Net upsampling arm for the decoding part. Because of these, ensemble Trident encoder fusion introduces diversity and improves the encoding of a biomedical image. We believe that more powerful encoders are needed to capture the intricate features from the image before it heads up to the decoding arm. Our belief has been ascertained by the results of the proposed Trident U-Net model.

1.3 Organization

The paper has been organized into a total of six sections. Section 2 discusses the related research works. The background concepts have been explained in Sect. 3. The proposed model has been described in Sect. 4. It is followed by Sect. 5 which contains details of the datasets, experimental set-up, and results. Finally, the paper has been concluded in Sect. 6.

2   Related Work

In the paper by Zhou et al. [1], a organ segmentation model is built, Jaccard Similarity index of 79% and 67% are achieved.

In [2], the authors have proposed a ResNet model-based approach for brain tissue segmentation. The model performed 86.15%, 89.46%, and 84.25%, respectively,

Xu et al. in [3], a CNN model has been used on 3D UltraSonography image segmentation, which achieved accuracy, F1, Recall metrics above 80%. When it comes to polyp detection, very early works of Mamonov et al. [4] are based on manual extraction of features like texture, shape, color, etc., and then training a machine learning classifier to distinguish the polyp from the surroundings. However, this is inefficient as manual intervention is needed and has a high chance of misclassification rate.

Among deep learning-based approaches, Yu et al. [5]. They have presented a way to detect polyps using bounding boxes. However, the drawback of this approach is that it fails to find a hard boundary for the affected region. To address this issue, Brando et al. [6] used an FCN with a pretrained model to identify and segment polyps. Precision and recall of 73.61% and 86.31% are achieved, respectively, and Akbari et al. [7] used convolution networks fully to increase the accuracy of the segmentation using a novel image patch selection method in the training phase of the network. Later revolutionary image segmentation architectures U-Net [8], U-Net++ [9] came into the picture. Eventually, U-Net-based models became the center stage for all image segmentation works as they gave the most promising results.

So over the years, many models and solutions came up for different polyp detection datasets. However, as the diversity of biomedical images increases, it is challenging for the research community to develop tailor-made solutions for every category of biomedical images. It is also a very time and effort-consuming task to determine which type of network architecture works best with which specific type of problem, and eventually, there will be so many that it will be arduous to keep track of all. To mitigate this problem in hand, we propose Trident U-Net, where we use a fusion of encoders to capture the varying features in varying datasets where the architecture can cater to different sorts of biomedical image datasets.

3   Background Concepts

The proposed Trident model is based on the U-Net skeleton architecture. Before we dive into the U-Net architecture, a few background concepts are important for a convolution neural network perspective that needs to be mentioned first. The first is the convolution operation. A convolution operation has two inputs. One is the input image of size $n \times n \times c$. where n is the height and width and c is the depth of the channel. The second input to a convolution operation is a set of k filters (kernels), each one of size ($f \times f \times channels$). Another thing to note is the receptive field of a convolution operation, which is the input image that the filter covers at any given point in time.

The U-Net has been developed by Olaf Ronneberger et al. for Biomedical Image Segmentation. The architecture contains two paths. The first path is called the contraction path; interchangeably, this is also known as the encoder. The encoder arm of the U-Net is primarily used to capture the image's features and context. As an image propagates through the encoder arm, the size(dimension) of the image gradually reduces while the depth gradually increases. It is just a traditional stack of convolutional and max-pooling layers. The second path is the symmetric expanding path, also known as the decoder. The aim of the decoder is used to enable precise localization using transposed convolutions for upsampling. In the decoder arm, the size of the image gradually increases, and the depth gradually decreases. To get better precise locations, we skip connections by concatenating the output of the transposed convolution layers with the feature maps from the encoder at the same level at every step of the decoder. After every concatenation, we again apply two successive regular convolutions so that the model can learn to assemble a more precise output. It is what gives the architecture a symmetric U-shape, hence called the U-Net.

We have used two ways to test and evaluate the trident model. The first one we are calling a non-binarised category evaluation. When an input image of an original sized mask is reshaped into a different image dimension with a number of channels being constant to match the input shape of the network (256×256 in our case), the binary values of the original image mask is converted into a stream of continuous values (between 0 and 1). The model is trained on these continuous values. One set of evaluations is also performed on these raw masks without any conversion. It is being referred to as a non-binarised evaluation. In the second category, we convert this continuous value into binary values by keeping 0.5 as the threshold and thus doing a second round of evaluation. It is being called binarised evaluation. All previous works in this domain have been done and evaluated on binarised values. However, we are showing for both binarised and non-binarised categories. The purpose is that both these sets of evaluation categories give a better representation of the readability of the model. Again, its ability has been improved to learn and adapt to different types of training data.

For our Trident fusion encoder arm, we will be using three pre-trained encoder models. A pre-trained model has been trained on a large benchmark dataset to solve a problem similar to what needs to be solved. Accordingly, due to the computational cost of training such models, it is common practice to import and use models from published literature. We have used ResNet50, EfficientnetB0, and MobileNetV2 pre-trained models trained on the Imagenet dataset. The pre-trained models give the model a head start, and then the model can fine-tune the weights and parameters through learning and backpropagation. Resnet50 [10] is a heavyweight model and has a depth of 152 layers. The other two pre-trained models used are EfficientNet [11] and MobileNetV2 [12].

AlexNet is an improvement on the traditional convolutional neural networks. It was proposed in 2012. Since then, many deep nets have been developed to solve various types of problems. Each of the deep nets has its own merits and demerits. In this line, VGG is the successor of the AlexNet, and different variants of VGG are available in practice. However, ResNet50, MobileNetV2, and the latest EfficientNetB0 are a few top-rated image classification deep neural networks with fewer hyper-parameters.

3.1 ResNet50

Deeper neural networks are recommended as a potential solution to image-related tasks, but they are challenging to train. Most deep nets suffer from the vanishing gradients problem. In this case, typically, while backpropagation through longer paths, the gradient tends to turn to 0. It poses a significant challenge in training deep networks. However, the Residual Networks, commonly called ResNet [10, 13], is a suitable alternative to the problem mentioned above. The ResNet50 has 50 layers and is used to win the ImageNet competition in 2015.

3.2 MobileNetV2

MobileNets are depthwise separable convolution architecture used to downsize the model's size and reduce the overall complexity of the network [12]. It is used for embedded device-based and mobile applications. In this type of network, two global hyper-parameters have been introduced by the author. It makes an efficient balance between latency and accuracy of the model. The hyper-parameters also provide the functionality to select an appropriately sized model depending on the problem constraints.

3.3 EffcicientNetB0

In 2019, Google came forward with a series of optimized deep neural network architectures known to maximize the accuracy with the minimization of computational complexity [11]. This family of architectures is known as the EfficientNet family.

EfficientNet architectures' family is developed through optimal balancing between the network depth, width, and resolution. Eventually, it leads the network to perform better, using fewer hyper-parameters and low computational constraints. A new uniform scaling technique has been proposed that applies to all the variations in network depth, width, and resolution dimensions aimed at achieving higher-performing versions of similar network architectures. Thus the base network EfficientNet "B0" has been scaled up to create EfficientNet "B1", a system with roughly twice the processing power. The same scaling is applied successively to create EfficientNet B2, B3, B4, B5, B6, and B7. We have used EfficientNetB0 in our model as it is the baseline model in the EfficientNet family.

3.4 Evaluation Matrices

For evaluation purposes of the model, we have used the following metrics:

The *Intersection over Union* (IoU) metric, also called the Jaccard index, is a method to quantify the overlap percentage between the target mask and the prediction output. The IoU metric measures the number of standard pixels between the actual and prediction masks divided by the total number of pixels present across both masks

$$IoU = \frac{Actual \cap Predicted}{Actual \cup Predicted} \qquad (1)$$

Another metric is *Dice coefficient*. It is essentially a measure of the overlapping region between two samples. This measure ranges from 0 to 1, where a Dice coefficient of 1 denotes perfect and complete overlap. The Dice coefficient can be calculated as

$$Dice = \frac{2(|Actual \cap Predicted|)}{|Actual| + |Predicted|} \qquad (2)$$

Recall (True Positive Rate) has also been used to evaluate and compare different models. Here, recall is computed as the ratio between the predicted mask and the actual mask (see Eq. 3).

$$Recall/TPR = \frac{Predicted}{Actual} \qquad (3)$$

To formulate a loss function to train the model, "1 - Dice" has been calculated. It is also called the *Dice Loss*.

4 Proposed Model

A straightforward approach towards building a network architecture for image segmentation is to stack several convolution layers, preserve the input's dimension, and output a segmentation map. It is already a proven way to learn feature mapping by transforming the feature maps; however, a drawback to using this approach is that it is quite computationally expensive to preserve the full resolution throughout the network. This computational burden can be reduced by periodically downsampling our feature maps through max-pooling and compression of spatial resolution without concern. We would like our model to produce a full-resolution semantic prediction that is generally the mask for image segmentation.

These particular constraints lay down the setting for an encoder/decoder structure where the spatial resolution of the image is downsampled, developing lower-resolution feature mappings which are learned to be highly efficient at discriminating between positive and negative classes in case of polyp segmentation, and the upsample the feature representations into a full-resolution segmentation map. Transpose convolutions are the most popular approach as they allow for us to develop a learned upsampling. As the encoder module downsamples the resolution, the decoder module struggles to produce fine-grained segmentation, adding skip connections into the picture. The encoded representation is upsampled using transposed convolution, adding "skip connections" from earlier layers and concatenating these two feature maps. Ronneberger et al., in their paper on the U-Net architecture, improved upon the "fully convolutional" architecture primarily through expanding the capacity of the decoder module of the network. They propose the U-Net architecture, which "consists of a contracting path to capture context and a symmetric expanding path that enables precise localization." This simpler architecture has grown to be very popular and has been adapted for various segmentation problems.

Our proposed Trident model is based on this architecture. We have redesigned the encoding arm of the traditional U-Net shown in Fig. 1. We are using a fusion of three pre-trained encoders for the downsampling of the spatial resolution. The input shape of the image is 256×256. We have downsampled it to $256 \Rightarrow 128 \Rightarrow 64 \Rightarrow 32 \Rightarrow 16$ image resolution before heading up to the decoder arm. The three pre-trained encoders used are ResNet50, MobileNetV2, and EfficientNetB0. All three of them are trained on the Imagenet dataset. ResNet50 has around 9.5M trainable params , MobileNetV2 and EfficientNetB0 has both around 1.5M params each. So our Trident encoder has a total of 12M trainable params. The input image is fed parallelly to all three encoder arms; the output of the three encoder arms is of the shape $16 \times 16 \times 2272$ where 16×16 is the downsampled spatial image resolution, and 2272 is the channel width of the encoder—the output channel width results from the concatenation of the output of the three individual encoders. These are 672 for MobileNetV2, 576 for EfficientNetB0, and 1024 for ResNet50. A similar exercise is done for all the other four skip connections used in this model. In the decoder arm, the upsampled feature representation of the previous layer is concatenated with the three skip connections of the three encoder arms and then followed by two layers of convolution operation, which is then topped by batch normalization followed by a relu activation function. The output of the decoder is the output of the model. It is of the shape $256 \times 256 \times 1$, where 256×256 is the spatial resolution of the image and 1 is the channel width depicting the segmentation mask.

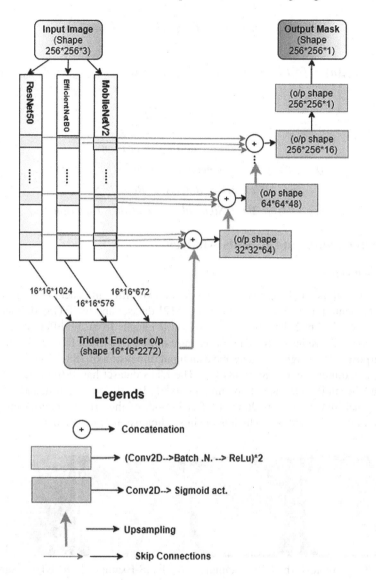

Fig. 1. A block diagram visualization of the proposed Trident U-Net architechure with encoder fusion between ResNet50, EfficientNetB0 and MobileNetV2 primary models

The outputs of different primary encoders has been concatenated into a single output and passed it to the decoder arm using Eqs. 4, 5 and 6. A common mathematical expression for a concatenation operation of two vectors X and Y is as follows: assume two vectors $X \in \Re^m$ and $Y \in \Re^n$. Let, $x \in X \subset \Re^m$ and $y \in Y \subset \Re^n$. Therefore, $Z := \{X \frown \langle y \rangle : \forall y \ and \ y \in Y\}$ (here, the length of two vectors X and Y are equal, m=n).

$$F_{encoder} = F_{resnet50} \frown F_{efficientnetb0} \frown F_{mobilenetv2} \tag{4}$$

$$F_{decoder}^{k}(n) = fc(F_{decoder}(n-1) \frown \phi_{resnet50}^{k} \frown \phi_{efficientnetb0}^{k} \frown \phi_{mobilenetv2}^{k}) \tag{5}$$

$$F_{trident} = fe(F_{decoder}^{n}) \tag{6}$$

$$\frown: \quad concatenation \quad operation$$
$$\phi: \quad k^{th} \quad skip \quad connection \quad from \quad n^{th} \quad encoder$$
$$fc: \quad (Conv2D \Rightarrow BatchN \Rightarrow Relu) \quad \times \quad 2$$
$$fe: \quad Conv2D \Rightarrow Sigmoid \quad Activation \quad Function$$

5 Experiments and Results Analysis

5.1 Used Dataset

We have tested the applicability of the model on two different benchmark datasets. For polyp segmentation we have used the CVC-612[1] dataset and the ETIS[2] dataset (see in Fig. 2). The CVC-612 dataset contains 612 still images from 29 different sequences. Among the 612, we have divided it into a ratio of 80 : 10 : 10 for train, test, and validation purposes. The original images have an input dimension of $288 \times 384 \times 3$ while the mask has a dimension of $288 \times 384 \times 1$. The ETIS dataset has 196 images and again followed the similar practice of dividing it into 80 : 10 : 10 for train, test, and validation. The original image shape is $966 \times 1225 \times 3$. Both of the original dataset images are reshaped into $256 \times 256 \times 3$ which is the input dimension of our model.

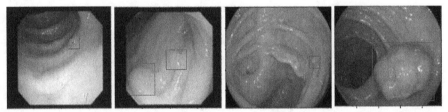

(a) CVC-Example-1 (b) CVC-Example-2 (c) ETIS-Example-1 (d) ETIS-Example-2

Fig. 2. Few examples from CVC-612 and ETIS datasets; a bounded box indicates the actual polyp segmentation area

We have divided the experiment into two parts. The first part is done with the ETIS dataset and the second one with the CVC-612 dataset. We have used data augmentation, mainly flipping the image bottom-up and right-left, and used random brightness adjustments for the images.

---

[1] https://polyp.grand-challenge.org/CVCClinicDB/.
[2] https://polyp.grand-challenge.org/EtisLarib/.

5.2 System

The paper is implemented using Python 3.6 and on the Keras Tensorflow framework 2.4.1. We have used the cloud virtual machine provided by Google Colab to train the model. It has 12 GB RAM, and the GPU provided is NVidiaK80.

We have used Adam optimizer for training with a learning rate of ($lr = 1e - 4$) and $eps = 1e - 16$ and $betas = (0.9, 0.999)$). For the calculation of the dice coefficient, a smoothing coefficient of $1e - 15$ is used.

5.3 Results Analysis and Discussion

Our main objective is to show the general applicability of the Trident model along with the individual models and study their outcomes and then conclude as to which model gives the best overall on varied datasets (two different datasets in our case). Here individual models are the models where only one individual pre-trained encoder is used instead of the ensemble Trident encoder. We have studied four models overall. First is the Trident model with ResNet50, MobileNetV2, and EfficientNetB0 as the encoder. The second model is only the ResNet50 as the encoder. Similarly, the third and fourth model consists of MobilenetV2 and the EfficientNetB0 as the encoder respectively.

Similarly, we will evaluate the non-binarised metrics of the models. Here it is referred to as the scores, which are not binarized to 0/1 masks after evaluation. When the images and masks are reshaped and rescaled for the models, the binary data got converted into continuous data. The model is trained on this continuous data itself, and two rounds of evaluation have been performed, that is, on the non-binarized data and then the binarized data, that is, after the conversion.

Table 1 and 2 show the results of non binarized version. Here it can be seen that the Trident model has outperformed the other three individual encoder models, albeit with a small margin, which is an indication that the Trident model has adapted better to the data than the other three. Table 3 and 4 show the binarized evaluation of the models. It is here that we have compared our approach to other works of similar nature. Here, for the CVC-612 dataset, EfffcientNetB0 has a slightly better True Positive score than Trident by a margin of 0.01, and for the ETIS dataset, ResNet50 encoder has a better True Positive score than Trident by a margin of 0.07. so this is evident from the results that some encoders work better with some datasets than others.

However, if we see the overall results, the Trident model has a better generalization capability for diverse datasets than the others. The main reason for this is the ensemble approach that is taken for the Trident fusion encoders. This architecture reduced its reliance on any specific encoder for any specific dataset and can consider the ensemble outcome instead of a specific one.

Table 1. Results obtained from the non-binarized ETIS dataset (higher is good ⇑)

Model	Dice coefficient	IoU score	Recall	Precision
ResNet50 U-Net	0.32	0.19	0.94	0.90
EffcientNetB0 U-Net	0.19	0.10	0.95	0.77
MobileNetV2 U-Net	0.24	0.13	0.94	0.78
Trident U-Net (ours)	0.35	0.21	0.95	0.92

Table 2. Results obtained from the non-binarized CVC-612 dataset (higher is good ⇑)

Model	Dice coefficient	IoU score	Recall	Precision
ResNet50 U-Net	0.83	0.72	0.82	0.93
EffcientNetB0 U-Net	0.75	0.61	0.83	0.93
MobileNetV2 U-Net	0.86	0.76	0.83	0.93
Trident U-Net (ours)	0.90	0.82	0.86	0.94

In Table 5 and 6, it can be seen that, as our Trident model has more parameters (12M) compared to the other three, it took more time to train, but the convergence rate is quicker than the other three as expected. We have used early stopping with the patience of 30 epochs in the training process, so it exits the training process when there is no improvement in the validation loss for a length of 30 epochs. Thus we have a varying number of convergence epochs for all the types of models evaluated. On the downside, it has been noticed that the proposed Trident U-Net model takes a fewer number of epochs to train. However, due to its hybrid encoder architecture, the time taken to complete the training is higher than the other used models. In biomedical image segmentation, segmentation accuracy is vital for efficient diagnosis.

Table 3. Results obtained from the binarized ETIS dataset (higher is good ⇑)

Model	Recall/TP	Dice coefficient	IoU score
U-Net (MICCAI'15) [8]	NA	0.43	0.28
U-Net++ (TMI'19) [9]	NA	0.49	0.33
SFA (MICCAI'19) [14]	NA	0.29	0.11
ResNet50 U-Net	0.63	0.65	0.56
EffcientNetB0 U-Net	0.63	0.56	0.46
MobileNetV2 U-Net	0.62	0.67	0.56
Trident U-Net (ours)	0.66	0.68	0.59

Table 4. Results obtained from the binarized CVC-612 dataset (higher is good ⇑)

Model	Recall/TP	Dice coefficient	IoU score
U-Net (MICCAI'15) [8]	NA	0.82	0.69
U-Net++ (TMI'19) [9]	NA	0.79	0.65
SFA (MICCAI'19) [14]	NA	0.67	0.51
ResUNet++ [15]	NA	0.79	0.79
ResNet50 U-Net	0.89	0.87	0.82
EffcientNetB0 U-Net	0.92	0.89	0.82
MobileNetV2 U-Net	0.89	0.88	0.81
Trident U-Net (ours)	0.91	0.89	0.83

Table 5. Time taken to achieve results from the non-binarized CVC-612 dataset

Model	Time (Min.)	Epoch
ResNet50 U-Net	30	120
MobileNetV2 U-Net	28	117
EffcientNetB0 U-Net	27	115
Trident U-Net (ours)	40	090

Table 6. Time taken to acheive results from the non-binarized ETIS dataset

Model	Time (Min.)	Epoch
ResNet50 U-Net	40	140
MobileNetV2 U-Net	35	125
EffcientNetB0 U-Net	36	130
Trident U-Net (ours)	55	110

Some random samples from each of the datasets (CVC-612 and ETIS) are shown in the Figs. 3, 4, 5 and 6, respectively. Each example contains the original image, the actual mask (ground truth), the masks obtained from ResNet50, MobileNetV2, EfficientNetB0 (EffNetB0) and the proposed Trident U-Nets architectures, respectively. It is found that our Trident U-Net model captures the original segments very effectively than the primary models due to its encoder fusion. The results are very competitive in its fist adaptation against the existing SOTA techniques. The significant improvements can be found in Figs. 3, 4, and 5.

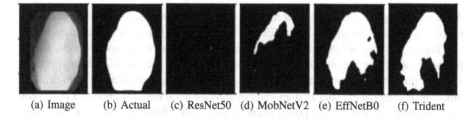

(a) Image   (b) Actual   (c) ResNet50   (d) MobNetV2   (e) EffNetB0   (f) Trident

Fig. 3. Example-1 from CVC-612 dataset: a comparison between segmentations obtained from different used U-Net models

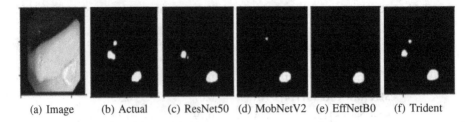

(a) Image   (b) Actual   (c) ResNet50   (d) MobNetV2   (e) EffNetB0   (f) Trident

Fig. 4. Example-2 from CVC-612 dataset: a comparison between segmentations obtained from different used U-Net models

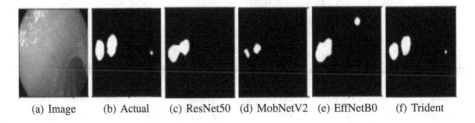

(a) Image   (b) Actual   (c) ResNet50   (d) MobNetV2   (e) EffNetB0   (f) Trident

Fig. 5. Example-1 from ETIS dataset: a comparison between segmentations obtained from different used U-Net models

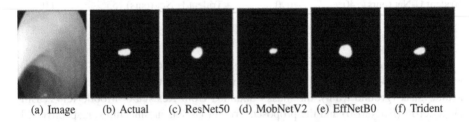

(a) Image   (b) Actual   (c) ResNet50   (d) MobNetV2   (e) EffNetB0   (f) Trident

Fig. 6. Example-2 from ETIS dataset: a comparison between segmentations obtained from different used U-Net models

6   Conclusion

A deep learning mechanism for biomedical image segmentation is a typical computer vision application. As the automatic diagnosis deals with life-critical decisions, therefore higher accuracy is always preferred. Thus, it motivates the research community for further improvements in accuracy. It is already established that the U-Net architectures are very promising in these tasks. Usually, one single pre-trained/new (from scratch) model is used as the encoder in the U-Net models. Many other new encoders have been used individually, but the proposed encoder fusion, a Trident U-Net, is a new solution. An encoder fusion, in simple words, ensemble encoders, brings diversity due to the combination of the advantages of its primary models. The proposed Trident fusion encoder captures the details of the image segmentation better than the other existing alternatives. The first adaption of the Trident U-Net architecture provides competitive and consistent results in the field of biomedical image segmentation.

In the future, this model can be examined with other types of encoders and observe the performance with other variations in the architecture, such as with dense connections and attention mechanism, etc. One more region to focus on is reducing the training time of the model. As the Trident model is having more parameters than others so evidently, it takes longer to converge. Future efforts will also focus on making this model more lightweight by tuning hyperparameters and depth tuning of pre-trained models used in encoders.

References

1. Zhou, X., et al.: Performance evaluation of 2d and 3d deep learning approaches for automatic segmentation of multiple organs on CT images. In: Medical Imaging 2018: Computer-Aided Diagnosis, vol. 10575, p. 105752C. International Society for Optics and Photonics (2018)
2. Chen, H., Dou, Q., Yu, L., Qin, J., Heng, P.A.: Voxresnet: deep voxelwise residual networks for brain segmentation from 3d MR images. NeuroImage **170**, 446–455 (2018)
3. Xu, Y., Wang, Y., Yuan, J., Cheng, Q., Wang, X., Carson, P.L.: Medical breast ultrasound image segmentation by machine learning. Ultrasonics **91**, 1–9 (2019)
4. Mamonov, A.V., Figueiredo, I.N., Figueiredo, P.N., Tsai, Y.H.R.: Automated polyp detection in colon capsule endoscopy. IEEE Trans. Med. Imaging **33**(7), 1488–1502 (2014)
5. Yu, L., Chen, H., Dou, Q., Qin, J., Heng, P.A.: Integrating online and offline three-dimensional deep learning for automated polyp detection in colonoscopy videos. IEEE J. Biomed. Health Inf. **21**(1), 65–75 (2016)
6. Brandao, P., et al.: Fully convolutional neural networks for polyp segmentation in colonoscopy. In: Medical Imaging 2017: Computer-Aided Diagnosis, vol. 10134, p. 101340F. International Society for Optics and Photonics (2017)
7. Akbari, M., et al.: Polyp segmentation in colonoscopy images using fully convolutional network. In: 2018 40th Annual International Conference of the IEEE Engineering in Medicine and Biology Society (EMBC), pp. 69–72. IEEE (2018)
8. Ronneberger, O., Fischer, P., Brox, T.: U-Net: convolutional networks for biomedical image segmentation. In: Navab, N., Hornegger, J., Wells, W.M., Frangi, A.F. (eds.) MICCAI 2015. LNCS, vol. 9351, pp. 234–241. Springer, Cham (2015). https://doi.org/10.1007/978-3-319-24574-4_28
9. Zhou, Z., Rahman Siddiquee, M.M., Tajbakhsh, N., Liang, J.: UNet++: a nested u-net architecture for medical image segmentation. In: Stoyanov, D., et al. (eds.) DLMIA/ML-CDS -2018. LNCS, vol. 11045, pp. 3–11. Springer, Cham (2018). https://doi.org/10.1007/978-3-030-00889-5_1
10. Targ, S., Almeida, D., Lyman, K.: Resnet in resnet: generalizing residual architectures. arXiv preprint arXiv:1603.08029 (2016)
11. Tan, M., Le, Q.: Efficientnet: rethinking model scaling for convolutional neural networks. In: International Conference on Machine Learning, pp. 6105–6114. PMLR (2019)
12. Howard, A.G., et al.: Mobilenets: efficient convolutional neural networks for mobile vision applications. arXiv preprint arXiv:1704.04861 (2017)
13. Wu, Z., Shen, C., Van Den Hengel, A.: Wider or deeper: revisiting the resnet model for visual recognition. Pattern Recogn. **90**, 119–133 (2019)

14. Fang, Y., Chen, C., Yuan, Y., Tong, K.: Selective feature aggregation network with area-boundary constraints for polyp segmentation. In: Shen, D., et al. (eds.) MICCAI 2019. LNCS, vol. 11764, pp. 302–310. Springer, Cham (2019). https://doi.org/10.1007/978-3-030-32239-7_34
15. Jha, D., et al.: Resunet++: an advanced architecture for medical image segmentation. In: 2019 IEEE International Symposium on Multimedia (ISM), pp. 225–2255. IEEE (2019)

COVID-19 Detection Method from Chest CT Scans via the Fusion of Slice Information and Lung Segmentation

Jesús Toledano Pavón[✉], Juan Carlos Morales Vega, Francisco Carrillo-Perez,
Luis Javier Herrera, and Ignacio Rojas

Department of Computer Architecture and Technology, University of Granada.
C.I.T.I.C., Periodista Rafael Gómez Montero, 2, 18014 Granada, Spain
jesutolepa@ugr.es

Abstract. Due to the high spread of the COVID-19 virus, several diagnosis support systems are being developed in order to detect the disease in a faster and accurate way. In this paper, a stacking method for Computed Tomography (CT) scans has been implemented for the preprocessing step. The method combines both slice normalization and lung segmentation in a single output image using RGB color channels, providing more information from the input slices to the CNN models. The binary classification step starts with a slice-level prediction, which applies fine-tuning to the whole model and dense layers are changed by a custom scheme to improve the performance. Then, a patient-level prediction is performed by fixing a threshold percentage of COVID positive slices that allows to make the final prediction, classifying patients as COVID or NORMAL. The accuracy and metrics obtained show the robustness of the presented method in comparison to using the normalised slices or the masks independently. Given the results obtained, the proposed method can accurately detect the COVID-19 disease and the fusion of information improves the results obtained.

Keywords: COVID-19 · CT scans · Image preprocessing · Lung segmentation · CNN · Slice-level prediction · Patient-level prediction

1 Introduction

COVID-19 is a highly contagious viral lung disease whose symptoms range from coughing, wheezing, breath shortness to pneumonia or pulmonary fibrosis, which may lead to severe sequelae or even death. COVID-19 first appeared by the end of 2019 and rapidly spread leaving 178 million people infected and 3.84 million deaths around the world so far. As a result of the high incidence of the COVID-19 pandemic, researchers have put efforts on developing diagnosis support systems for the detection of the disease. Thus, by using these systems an early diagnosis can be provided, which can improve the prognosis of the patient in the first stages of the disease. The most widely used diagnostic methods are Antigen Detection and Reverse Transcription Polymerase Chain Reaction (RT-PCR) tests, offering

© Springer Nature Switzerland AG 2021
I. Rojas et al. (Eds.): BIOMESIP 2021, LNCS 12940, pp. 155–165, 2021.
https://doi.org/10.1007/978-3-030-88163-4_15

results in a short time. However, other screenings such as X-ray images and Computed Tomography (CT) scans are also used to assess the presence and evolution of the disease in the lungs. In this paper, a binary classification problem is faced between COVID and NORMAL patients using 3D CT images, which are divided into multiple 2D slices in the axial plane. The images are provided by the COVID-CT-MD database which allows a deeper feature extraction compared to X-ray images [1]. This study propose a method for the pre-processing step of these images that combines both slice normalisation and lung segmentation methods in an single output image through its RGB color channels.

2   Related Work

Several works have been presented in literature for COVID classification using the database released by Parnian et al. [1]. Heidarian et al. developed a novel framework called COVID-FACT that is based on Capsule Networks [4]. The model has two main stages. After performing the lung segmentation, in the first stage potential infected slices in COVID patients (or CAP if used) are identified. Then, in the second stage the potential infected slices are used to perform a slice-level classification and a final prediction of the patient is carried out by using a majority voting or a threshold method. For a binary classification of 54 COVID and 43 Non-COVID patients at the slice level, using 0.5 probability threshold and 5-fold cross-validation, authors reached an accuracy of $87.61\% \pm 2.00\%$, a sensitivity of $88.30\% \pm 3.22\%$ and a specificity of $86.75\% \pm 1.91\%$. Anbarasi et al. proposed to use the VGG16 architecture and transfer learning in a small subset of 449 COVID and 463 NORMAL input slices from the COVID-CT-MD database, using the weights of a network trained on a much larger dataset in order to increase the performance when less data is available for training. Only a basic normalisation was performed to the slices, reaching an accuracy of 98.33% in a single train-test split [2]. Finally, Chaudhary et al. presented a similar approach to the one presented by Heidarian et al. [4], but using a plain CNN [3]. By using a subset of 80 pre-processed central slices per patient the authors followed a two stages approach. In the first phase authors labelled infected COVID or CAP slices by training the Huang et al. DenseNet architecture [5]. Then, different architectures were tested for a slice-level classification between COVID, CAP and Normal. The best architecture was Tan et al. Efficientnet [12], reaching a slice-level validation accuracy of 89.9% in a single split and reaching a final patient-level classification accuracy performance of 84%. All in all, COVID-CT-MD database provides good results and allows a more reliable slice-level training by offering a subset where infected and healthy slices are labelled by medical experts one by one.

3   Materials and Methods

3.1   Dataset

COVID-CT-MD database [1] includes CT lung slices from 169 COVID, 60 Community Acquired Pneumonia (CAP) and 76 NORMAL patients. COVID cases were collected from February to April 2020 whereas CAP and NORMAL cases were acquired from April 2018 to December 2019 and January 2019 to May 2020, respectively, in Tehran, Iran. Patient division analysis was performed by 3 radiologist who analysed a subset of 54 COVID and 25 CAP cases to identify slices with infection evidence. Thus, 3779 of 8048 total slices were labelled showing infection in COVID cases and 1178 of 3896 total infected slices in CAP cases. CT slices on the database are initially presented on DICOM format (Digital Imaging and Communication On Medicine). This standard stores a variety of data related to the patient and the acquisition settings together with medical images, providing further information when these images are evaluated. In order to respect the privacy of the patients, personal data were removed from CT studies. However, information such as age, gender and weight of patients, clinical history and positive RT-PCR of some covid patients was maintained for statistical purposes. For example, gender and age distribution in COVID-CT-MD database are displayed in Table 1.

Table 1. Gender and age distribution

Diagnosis	Cases	Gender	Age (year)
COVID-19	169	108 M/61 F	51.96 ± 14.39
CAP	60	35 M/25 F	57.7 ± 21.7
NORMAL	76	40 M/ 36 F	43.4 ± 14.1

3.2 Pre-processing Step

Our method starts with a pre-processing step, where we first perform a slice extraction over the DICOM image to obtain a 2D array of pixels, which is then transformed to Hounsfield Units (HU) by a histogram normalisation. HU scale describes the intensity level according to the different tissues which are found in CT images (see Fig. 1). With centre in 0 HU corresponding to water, it ranges between -1000 HU and $+1000$ HU referring to air and the bones, respectively. A intensity normalisation is performed over the slices to enhance the regions inside the lungs. We used a 1500 HU window with a -600 HU center.

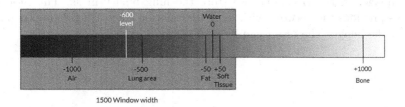

Fig. 1. Intensity normalisation for CT lung images.

Subsequently, binary segmentation is performed to obtain lung masks according to the method presented by Zaffino et al. [13]. The automatic segmentation extracts lungs islands first by setting a -110 HU threshold followed by a second filtering that fixes a minimum amount of voxels along slices in each patient, in order to eliminate any possible noise outside the lungs. The resulting images are shown in Fig. 2.

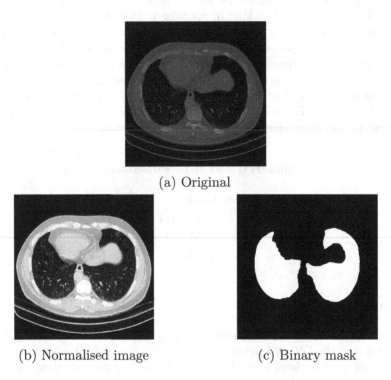

(a) Original

(b) Normalised image   (c) Binary mask

Fig. 2. Preproccessing methods applied. (a) shows the original image. (b) presents the image after applaying the normalisation step. (c) shows the binary mask obtained from the original image.

The resulting grayscale image is then stored in the R and G channels of a RGB image. In the B channel we store the lung binary mask. This stacking process provides the network with more information since it highlights the main area of the image. The result can be seen in Fig. 3.

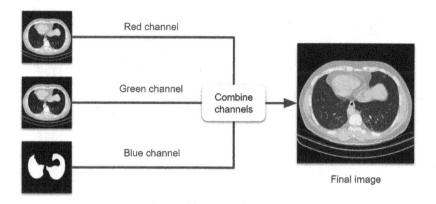

Fig. 3. Stacking method scheme. The information is fused on the RGB channels in order to obtain a new representation of the image.

3.3 Classification Slices and Final Patient Prediction

Once the pre-processing step has been carried out, the data is ready for classification. We first resize the slices from 512×512 to 256×256 to fit the network. Then, we apply a data augmentation stage consisting of random shifts, random rotations and random zooms to improve the generalisation capabilities of the model (see Fig. 4). For the backbone of our model, we have tried the VGG16 architecture [11], displayed in Fig. 5. It is composed by 13 Convolutional layers together with 5 Max Pooling layers and finally 3 Dense layers on the top. Other models were tried, such as Resnet50 or a custom models, but better results were obtained when using VGG16.

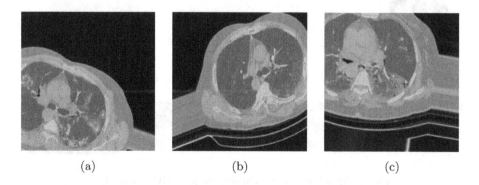

Fig. 4. Augmented images for input CNN models

For the training phase, whose scheme is shown in Fig. 6, the VGG16 model uses the ImageNet weights as the starting point and fine tuning is applied through the whole network in order to improve the performance over the slices

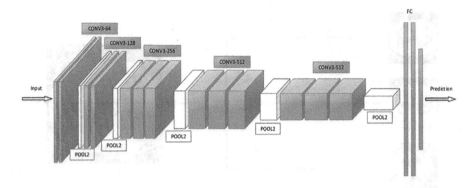

Fig. 5. Diagram of the VGG16 architecture [6].

generated by our method. In addition, the final dense layers are changed by a custom scheme involving overfitting reduction methods. This scheme starts with a batch normalization layer together with a Dropout layer with a rate of 0.5 to prevent overfitting and improve the generalisation of the model. Then, a convolutional 2D layer with 128 filters and ReLU activation function is used, followed by other batch normalization layer. In addition, 2D Max Pooling layer is applied which down-samples the input along its spatial dimensions, followed by two dense layers. The first dense layer is formed by 128 and the ReLU activation function, including a L2 regularisation parameter. The second dense layer is formed by 2 neurons and uses the Softmax activation function. Thus, the model generates one-hot-encoder output predictions for COVID or NORMAL slices.

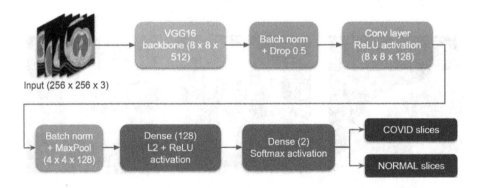

Fig. 6. Slice-level prediction scheme for VGG16 model.

After that, we moved to the patient-level prediction. It is performed by choosing a minimum percentage of COVID-positive slices (less than 0.5) from which patients are classified as COVID. The scheme for patient-level prediction is shown in Fig. 7. If the percentage of infected slices exceeds the fixed cutoff, the patient is predicted as COVID. Otherwise, it would be predicted as healthy.

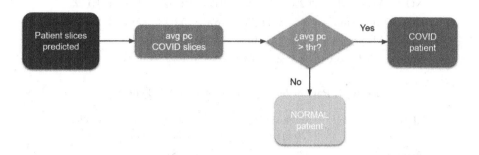

Fig. 7. Patient-level prediction scheme for final decision.

4   Results and Discussion

In order to evaluate the performance of CNN models, a subset of the COVID-CT-MD database of 54 COVID patients together with 76 NORMAL patients is used. For training and validation (60%–20%) splits we consider those slices that have been labelled as infected in COVID cases (3401 COVID slices), and we include all slices in NORMAL cases (7384 NORMAL slices). Using a 5-fold cross-validation, metrics were computed on the test set. Recall is a critical factor in this problem since it represents the percentage of true positives that are identified by the model. Thus, our aim is to classify as many correctly infected slices as possible by achieving a high COVID recall rate.

An enhancement of the model with a COVID recall of 76% ± 4.79% by using the stacking of normalised slices and masks in 20 epochs is achieved (see Table 2), in comparison with using the normalised slices or the masked slices independently. The extra information provided by our method involves a higher number of COVID slices which are classified correctly compared to the full normalised slices and the product of the masks and slices in 30 epochs. However, NORMAL recall for stacked slices is smaller than the other cases, although the percentage is quite high. This behaviour is due to the fact that NORMAL is the class with the most slices, so the model barely fails to predict COVID slices as NORMAL. Precision shows the quality of the model when classifying each class by calculating the true positives/negatives rate according to the false positives/negatives. COVID precision results in a lower percentage than NORMAL precision since the different number of total slices between classes. This is not relevant to evaluate the model performance because class weights are used for every class [7]. This method establishes a higher weight for the minority class (COVID slices) while

Table 2. Slice-level results metrics for 20% test.

Metrics	Stacked slices (20 epochs)	Norm slices (30 epochs)	Masks × slices (30 epochs)
Accuracy	88% ± 4.01%	88% ± 1.34%	90% ± 0.55%
COVID recall	76% ± 4.79%	68% ± 3.61%	70% ± 5.67%
NORMAL recall	92% ± 6.07%	94% ± 2.56%	97% ± 1.12%
COVID precision	76% ± 11.75%	78% ± 5.89%	86% ± 2.89%
NORMAL precision	93% ± 1.10%	91% ± 0.77%	92% ± 1.39%
Weighted F1-score	88% ± 3.54%	88% ± 1.12%	90% ± 0.76%

Table 3. Patient-level results metrics for 0.2 cut-off.

Metrics	Stacked slices (20 epochs)	Norm slices (30 epochs)	Masks × slices (30 epochs)
Accuracy	83% ± 4.44%	83% ± 1.81%	84% ± 1.81%
COVID recall	75% ± 3.64%	69% ± 4.45%	69% ± 4.45%
NORMAL recall	89% ± 10%	93% ± 2.50%	94% ± 0.00%
COVID precision	84% ± 9.84%	87% ± 3.34%	88% ± 0.68%
NORMAL precision	84% ± 0.51%	81% ± 2.02%	82% ± 2.15%
Weighted F1-score	83% ± 4.24%	83% ± 1.92%	83% ± 1.99%

a lower weight is applied for the majority class (NORMAL slices). Thus, both classes are considered in a balanced way by the model for slice-level prediction.

For the patient-level prediction, a threshold was set in order to determine the minimum percentage of slices predicted as COVID in order to label a patient as infected. Otherwise, the prediction would be healthy. In Table 3, the results obtained for a 5-fold cross-validation for a patient-level prediction can be observed. A significant increase in COVID recall (75% ± 3.64%) is obtained by using stacked slices in comparison to normalised slices and the product of slices and masks cases. This effect is mainly due to the better performance achieved in the aforementioned slice-level prediction, which allows a more accurate final decision of the patients predicted as infected or healthy. NORMAL recall obtained by stacked slices has a slightly lower rate similar to slice-level prediction compared to the other cases. Therefore, COVID patients predicted as healthy are low. Precision rate for COVID and NORMAL classes are similar for patient-level prediction in all cases. This is due to the fact that the number of patients is balanced between classes for final prediction.

Finally, the GradCAM method [10] is applied in order to check the activations of the network. GradCAM method is a generalisation of CAM (Class Activation Mapping) method [14], which allows to visualise the activations for one of the convolutional layers of the network. The main interest of this algorithm resides in the fact that larger activations corresponds to the regions of the image where the model is paying more attention to, so we can "see what the model is seeing". Figure 8 shows the output slices generated by the GradCAM method. We can note that the highlighted areas inside the lungs correspond to nodules and opacity areas approximately. Thus, those slices are properly classified as COVID showing that the model has been successfully trained.

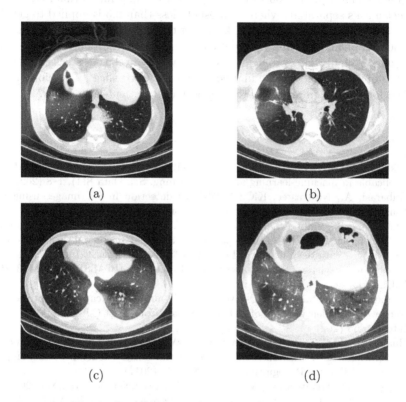

(a)   (b)

(c)   (d)

Fig. 8. GradCAM visualisation in obtained slices.

Additionally, other methods to reduce the imbalance between classes can be tried in an attempt to enhance the aforementioned results instead of weighting the classes. The focal loss function is quite effective when classes are highly unbalanced [8]. This function enhances the Cross -Entropy loss [9] by allowing the model to assume more risk in the prediction of minority class. This is achieved by employing a γ factor which sets a rate that controls the attention level of the model to classify those classes that are harder. Finally, it is possible to apply data augmentation in order to oversampling the minority class. As a result, the model is trained with more images whose classes are balanced, allowing to reach a more accurate classification.

5   Conclusion and Future Work

In this paper, we have presented a pre-processing method that combines normalised CT slices and their respective binary masks in an single output image along color RGB channels. This approach offers an improved performance in COVID slice-level prediction terms compared to taking full normalised slices or product masks separately, where a threshold less than 0.5 is applied to get final decision. As future work we would like to test this method in the multi-class classification problem, including CAP patients, in order to test its performance when facing a more challenging problem. The imbalance between classes is greater than binary problem because of the limited number of CAP slices. Therefore, results reached for prediction are lower than expected at patient-level so far.

References

1. Afshar, P., et al.: COVID-CT-MD, COVID-19 computed tomography scan dataset applicable in machine learning and deep learning. Sci. Data **8**(1), 1–8 (2021)
2. Anbarasi, A., Nithyasree, K.C.: COVID-19 detection in CT images using deep transfer learning. Int. Trans. Electr. Eng. Comput. Sci. **1**(1), 1–7 (2020)
3. Chaudhary, S., Sadbhawna, S., Jakhetiya, V., Subudhi, B.N., Baid, U., Guntuku, S.C.: Detecting COVID-19 and community acquired pneumonia using chest CT scan images with deep learning. In: ICASSP 2021–2021 IEEE International Conference on Acoustics, Speech and Signal Processing (ICASSP), pp. 8583–8587. IEEE (2021)
4. Heidarian, S., et al.: COVID-FACT: a fully-automated capsule network-based framework for identification of COVID-19 cases from chest CT scans. Front. Artif. Intell. **4**, 65 (2021)
5. Huang, G., Liu, Z., Van Der Maaten, L., Weinberger, K.Q.: Densely connected convolutional networks. In: Proceedings of the IEEE Conference on Computer Vision and Pattern Recognition, pp. 4700–4708 (2017)
6. Kaggle. CNN Architectures: VGG, Resnet, InceptionNet, XceptionNet (2018)
7. King, G., Zeng, L.: Logistic regression in rare events data. Polit. Anal. **9**(2), 137–163 (2001)
8. Lin, T.Y., Goyal, P., Girshick, R., He, K., Dollár, P.: Focal loss for dense object detection. In: Proceedings of the IEEE International Conference on Computer Vision, pp. 2980–2988 (2017)
9. Rubinstein, R.: The cross-entropy method for combinatorial and continuous optimization. Methodol. Comput. Appl. Probab. **1**(2), 127–190 (1999)
10. Selvaraju, R.R., Cogswell, M., Das, A., Vedantam, R., Parikh, D., Batra, D.: Gradcam: visual explanations from deep networks via gradient-based localization. Int. J. Comput. Vision **128**(2), 336–359 (2019)
11. Simonyan, K., Zisserman, A.: Very deep convolutional networks for large-scale image recognition. arXiv preprint arXiv:1409.1556 (2014)
12. Tan, M., Le, Q.: Efficientnet: rethinking model scaling for convolutional neural networks. In: International Conference on Machine Learning, pp. 6105–6114. PMLR (2019)

13. Zaffino, P., et al.: An open-source COVID-19 CT dataset with automatic lung tissue classification for radiomics. Bioengineering **8**(2), 26 (2021)
14. Zhou, B., Khosla, A., Lapedriza, A., Oliva, A., Torralba, A.: Learning deep features for discriminative localization. In: 2016 IEEE Conference on Computer Vision and Pattern Recognition (CVPR), pp. 2921–2929 (2016)

DenseNet for Breast Tumor Classification in Mammographic Images

Yuliana Jiménez Gaona[1,2,3](✉) 🄳, María José Rodriguez-Alvarez[2] 🄳,
Hector Espino-Morato[2,5] 🄳, Darwin Castillo Malla[1,2,3] 🄳,
and Vasudevan Lakshminarayanan[3,4](✉) 🄳

[1] Departamento de Química y Ciencias Exactas, Universidad Técnica Particular de Loja,
San Cayetano Alto s/n CP1101608, Loja, Ecuador
{ydjimenez,dpcastillo}@utpl.edu.ec
[2] Imagen Molecular i3M, Universitat Politècnica de València (UPV), 46022 Valencia, Spain
{mjrodri,hespinos}@i3m.upv.es
[3] Theoretical and Experimental Epistemology Lab, School of Optometry and Vision Science,
Waterloo, Canada
vengulak@uwaterloo.ca
[4] Department of Systems Design Engineering, Physics, and Electrical and Computer
Engineering, University of Waterloo, Waterloo, ON N2L3G1, Canada
[5] Consejo Superior de Investigaciones Científicas (CSIC), 46022 Valencia, Spain

Abstract. Breast cancer screening is an efficient method to detect breast lesions early. The common screening techniques are tomosynthesis and mammography images. However, the traditional manual diagnosis requires an intense workload for pathologists, and hence is prone to diagnostic errors. Thus, the aim of this study was to build a deep convolutional neural network method for automatic detection, segmentation, and classification of breast lesions in mammography images. Based on deep learning the Mask-CNN (RoIAlign) method was developed to automate RoI segmentation. Then feature extraction, selection and classification were carried out by the DenseNet architecture. Finally, the precision and accuracy of the model was evaluated by the AUC, accuracy and precision metrics. To summarize, the findings of this study show that the methodology may improve the diagnosis and efficiency in automatic tumor localization through medical image classification.

Keywords: Breast tumor classification · Convolutional neural network · Mammography · RoI align · DenseNet · Deep learning

1 Introduction

By screening for indeterminate breast lesions, it is possible to detect breast cancer [1–6]. Clinically, the most common and best techniques are images captured from ultrasound [7] and mammography [8, 9] procedures, if there are suspicious lesions. Then further analyses using biopsies [10], histopathological images [11–13] and magnetic resonance imaging (MRI) are performed [14].

© Springer Nature Switzerland AG 2021
I. Rojas et al. (Eds.): BIOMESIP 2021, LNCS 12940, pp. 166–176, 2021.
https://doi.org/10.1007/978-3-030-88163-4_16

The ultrasound allows obtaining high quality images, without the need for ionizing radiation, and enables detection of very small lesions, even masses and microcalcifications. However, mammography (x-rays) is currently the most used imaging method to detect breast cancer early in both, symptomatic and asymptomatic patients [2], reducing unnecessary biopsies. Also, World Health Organization recommends it as the standard imaging procedure for early diagnosis.

Specialists can interpret the breast images using the latest breast imaging reporting and data system (BI-RADS) version [15–17]. Nevertheless, the traditional manual diagnosis is time consuming and prone to diagnostic errors [18, 19]. Digital images from physiological structures can be processed to visualize hidden diagnostic features [20].

Automated techniques based on Deep Learning (DL) and Machine Learning (ML) [20–25], can be utilized for classification, diagnostic accuracy and improvement of localization and tumor process monitoring. Convolutional neural networks (CNN), have been extensively used to analyze medical images [27–33]. A recent paper [27] by Jimenez et al., reviews DL applications in breast cancer using ultrasound and mammography images.

There are many semi-automated breast tumor classification methodologies [34, 35]. For instance, Ragab et al. [2] used a deep CNN technique and replacing the last fully connected layer with a SVM as breast tumor classifier. However, these semi-automated methods cannot totally relieve the diagnosis burden of the pathologist. Thus, recently automatic DL techniques are gaining attention due to their superior performance in automatic feature extraction, selection and better features discrimination for breast lesions classification [16, 36–38]. There are a number of CNN architectures e.g. AlexNet [39], VGGNet [40], ResNet [41], Inception (GoogleNet) [42], DenseNet [43], ImageNet [43] that are of great value in screening and reduces the need for manual processing by experts, thus saving time and resources. In this work we selected DenseNet to solve the vanishing-gradient problem, strengthen feature propagation, feature reuse and reduce the number of parameters as indicated by Huang et al. [18].

Therefore, the principal contribution of this paper is to present a novel Deep CNN method for automatic segmentation and a DenseNet for feature selection and classification of breast lesions in both Cranio-Caudal (CC) and Medio Lateral Oblique (MLO) mammography views, and discuss the results obtained from this network.

2 Materials and Methodology

The workflow for this methodology is illustrated in Fig. 1 and consists of the following steps: (1) Breast Dataset acquisition and preprocessing. (2) RoI (Region of Interest) image segmentation using a Mask R-CNN with RoIAlign technique. (3) Feature selection, extraction and classification using DenseNet architecture. (4) Evaluation of performance metrics. The Mask R-CNN and RoIAlign are discussed below.

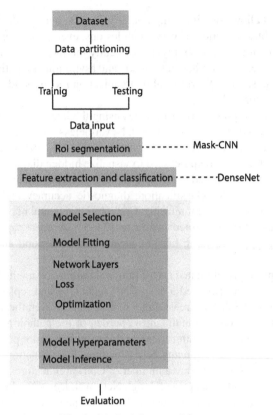

Fig. 1. Methodology workflow.

2.1 Dataset

Images from a public Breast Cancer Digital Repository (BCDR) were used for training and evaluation of the CNN. The BCDR-DM [44] mammography dataset contains 724 (723 female and 1 male). In addition to individual patient clinical data, the patient mammograms had both CC and MLO image views as well as the coordinates of the lesion contours. The images are grey-level mammograms with a resolution of 3328 (width) by 4084 (height) or 2560 (width) by 3328 (height) pixels, depending on the compression plate used in the acquisition (according to the breast size of the patient).

2.2 Segmentation

Preprocessing consists of breast border extraction, pectoral muscle removal and tumor delineation from the background [24]. This is followed by Region of Interest (RoI) segmentation. The operation is necessary to target and crop the bounding box of the lesions automatically. For that, a statistical cross-validation technique (hold-out splits) was used to divide the dataset into training 80% (579 images) and testing 20% (145 images) where 579 segmentations were manually made by specialized radiologists based on BI-RADS criteria (Fig. 2).

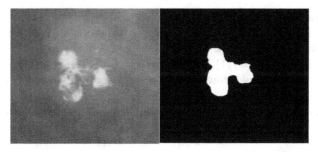

Fig. 2. Illustration of RoI binary mask contour, selected by radiologists.

Once the RoI is detected and cropped, we extract the features maps of the tumor contour by a Mask R-CNN [45] network trained using RoI alignment (RoI Align) technique. This technique is based on bilinear interpolation to smoothly crop a patch from a full-image feature maps based on a region proposal network (RPN), and then resize the cropped patch to a desired spatial size using a loss function. This has shown to outperform the use of RoI pooling [28].

The four sampling points in each bin dashed grid represents the RoIAlign method (Fig. 3).

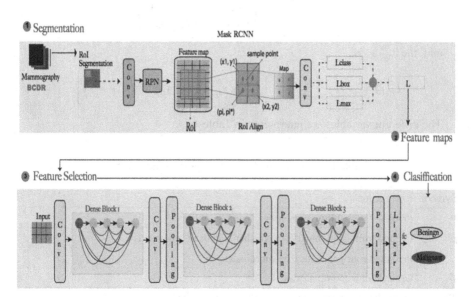

Fig. 3. Breast-Dense workflow for breast tumor classification (1) image is input into Mask RCNN for feature extraction (2) The Region Proposal Network (RPN) is used to generate N proposal windows for each image; (3) The Align RoI layer, generates for each RoI a fixed-size characteristic map and are assigned to the CNN Convolution, and finally (4) The RoI map feature selection and classification steps are carried out by Densenet architecture.

Here the value of each sampling point is computed by bilinear interpolation from the nearby grid points on the feature map. The maxpooling procedure is used by RoI Pooling to convert features in the projected region of the image of any size, (x1) × (y1), into a small fixed window, [x1] × [y1]. The input region is divided into [x1] and [y1] grids, giving approximately every sub-window of size ([x1]/x1) ([y1]/y1). Then maxpooling is applied to every grid.

During the Mask R-CNN training, the loss function L (Eq. 1) is minimized,

$$L = L_{class} + L_{box} + L_{mask} \tag{1}$$

where L_{class} is the classification loss, L_{box} is the bounding-box loss regression and. L_{mask} is the average binary cross-entropy loss mask prediction. The parameters L_{class} + L_{box}, and L_{class} are defined by Eqs. (2) and (3).

$$L_{class} + L_{box} = \frac{1}{N_{class}} \sum_i L_{class}\left(p_i, p_i^*\right) + \frac{1}{N_{box}} \sum_i p_i^* L_1^{smooth}\left(t_{i,} - t_i^*\right) \tag{2}$$

$$L_{class}\left(\{p_i, p_i^*\}\right) = -p_i^* \log p_i^* - (1 - p_i^*) \log(1 - p_i^*) \tag{3}$$

where, *smooth* in Eq. (2) is given by:

$$smooth_{L1}(x) = \begin{cases} 0.5x^2 & if\, |x| < 1 \\ |x| - 0.5 & otherwise, \end{cases} \tag{4}$$

and, the L_{mask}, is:

$$L_{mask} = -\frac{1}{m^2} \sum_{1 \le i, j \le m} \left[y_{ij} \log \widehat{y}_{ij}^k + (1 - y_{ij}) \log\left(1 - \widehat{y}_{ij}^k\right) \right] \tag{5}$$

The different variables are interpreted in Table 1.

Table 1. Definition of different variables of Eqs. (1–5).

Symbol	Explanation
P_i	Predicted probability of anchors i, being an object
p_i^*	Ground truth label (binary) of whether anchor i is an object
t_i	Predicted four parameterized coordinates
t_i^*	Ground truth coordinates
N_{Class}	Normalization term, set to be mini batch size ~ 256
N_{box}	Normalization term, set the number of anchor locations ~ 2400
y_{ij}	Is the label of a cell (i, j) in the mask for the region of size m × m
$\widehat{y}_{ij}^k$	Is the predicted value of the same cell in the mask learned for the ground truth class k

2.3 Feature Extraction and Classification: DenseNet Architecture

After Mask R-CNN segmented each RoI, DensetNet carried out the features extraction and classification process. DenseNet presents several advantages over other pretrained CNN methods. These include more accuracy, less prone to overfitting and is efficient to train a cross-layer connections structure because it contain shorter connections between layers [18].

In addition, the CNN consists of a number of feedforward layers implementing convolutional filters and pooling layers. After the last pooling layer, the CNN has a number of several fully connected layers that convert the 2D feature maps of the previous layers into a 1D vector for classification [22]. This is represented as:

$$G(X) = g_N(g_N - 1(\ldots(g_1(x))))\tag{6}$$

Here, N is the number of hidden layers, X, the input signal and g_N is the corresponding function to the layer N. A typical CNN model convolutional layer consists of a function g, with multiple convolutional kernels $(h_1,\ldots h_{k-1}, h_k)$. Every h_k denotes a linear function in k_{th} kernel, given by:

$$h_k(x, y) = \sum_{s=-m}^{m} \sum_{t=-n}^{n} \sum_{v=-d}^{w} V_k(s, t, v)X(x - s, y - t, z - v)\tag{7}$$

where (x, y, z) represents pixel position of input X, m represents height, n denotes width, w is depth of the filter, and V_k represents weight of k_{th} kernel. The CNN schematic is shown in Fig. 3.

2.4 Evaluation Metrics

Various metrics are used to quantitatively evaluate the classifier performance of a DL system [33]. These include *Accuracy* (Acc), *Sensitivity* (Sen), *Specificity* (Spe), *Area Under the Curve* (AUC), *Precision, and F1 score*.

The trained Mask R-CNN model performance was quantitatively assessed by the mean average precision (MAP), namely the accuracy of lesion detection/segmentation on the validation set:

$$MAP = \frac{A \cap B}{A \cup B} = \frac{1}{N_T} \sum_{i}^{N_i} \left(\frac{N_i^{DR}}{N_i^{D}}\right)\tag{8}$$

where A is the model segmentation result, and B is the contour tumor delineated by the radiologist (the ground truth). In the above equation, N_T is the number of images; N_i^{DR} represents the area overlap between the model detected lesion and the true clinical lesion regions and N_i^{D} is the size of the true clinical lesion.

3 Results

To test the model, we used the training dataset. The left side of Fig. 3 the original cropped image, and the right side the mask produced by a radiologist. The performance of the trained Mask R-CNN model achieved a MAP value of 0.75 for the automatic lesion delineation in the testing dataset.

3.1 Breast DenseNet

Table 2 summarizes the results of the Breast DenseNet model and their comparison performance evaluation with different pre-trained models in terms of the Acc, Sen, Spe and AUC .

Table 2. Summary of pre-trained DL model results in mammograms.

Reference	Method	Database	Sen (%)	Spe (%)	AUC	Acc (%)
Al-Masni et al. [46]	YOLO5- Fold cross validation	DDSM	100	94	96.5	97
Ragab et al. [2]	CNN + Linear SVM	DDSM	77	84	88	80.5
Duggento et al. [21]	CNN	CBIS-DDSM	84.4	62.4	77	71
Choudgrad et al. [23]	CNN	DDSM	-	-	98	97.4
Debelee et al. [47]		MIAS	96.26	100	-	97.46
		DDSM	99.48	98.16	-	99
Ahmed et al. [48]		Inbreast	80	-	78	80.10
This work	DenseNet	BCDR	99	94	97	97.7

4 Discussion

In this work we used a BCDR dataset is one of the most utilized mammography databases for processing images; the others being MIAS, DDSM, and Inbreast [33]. The BCDR database contains 1734 total cases of patients with mammography and ultrasound images, clinical history and lesion segmentation, and has been used to train convolutional networks.

Thus, with respect to the segmentation process, several traditional methodologies have been used for extract the RoI area: i) threshold-based segmentation, (ii) region-based (iii) pixel-based, (iv) model-based (v) edge-based (vi) fuzzy theory, (vii) artificial neural network (ANN) and (viii) active contour-based [27]. But those studies used manually segmentation and the errors in the accuracy of the tumor deliniation can affect the results of the classificfation. This is one of the several reasons why researchers are using DL arquitectures. For example, Chiao et al. [25] built an automatic segmentation and classification model based on Mask RCNN in ultrasound images. It reached a mean average precision (MAP) of 0.75 for the detection and segmentation, which is similar to our results, and a benign or malignant classification accuracy of 85%.

For detection and classification process some traditional studies used support vector machine (SVM) [2, 49] methodology. Those methods extracted features manually from the RoI in breast ultrasound images and then these features were input to the SVM classifier.These were classified as benign or malignant lesions using texture morphological and fractal features. However, in the present work it was not necessary.

DL methods, have been used for their excellent performance in medical image classification. AlMasni [46], trained the YOLO method in clinical mammography images, which successfully (Acc = 97%) identified breast masses. Alkhaleefah et al., [50] used transfer learning technique to classify benign and malignant breast cancer by various CNN architectures: AlexNet, VGGNet, GoogleNet, and ResNet. However, these networks had been trained on large datasets such as ImageNet, which do not contain labeled breast cancer images and therefore lead to poor performance. Huang et al. [18] used a dense CNN to object recognition task and obtained significant improvements over other state-of-the-art [50, 51] with less computation to achieve high performance. He et al. [50] and Huang et al. [51] showed that not all layers may be needed and highlighted the fact there exist a great amount of redundancy in deep residual (ResNet) networks.

Based on these observations, our work used the DenseNet architecture.The Breast-DenseNet DL system presented here can detect the locations of masses on mammograms and classify them as benign or malignant, from the automatically segmented region which successfully accuracy of 97.7%. Also, the proposed methodology successfully identified breast masses in the dense tissues. We did not require filtering and noise elimination before segmentation and feature extraction to improve the accuracy [46]. The RoI regions were automatically delineated and the feature extraction tumor was done via YOLO using Mask RCNN.

5   Conclusions

We conclude that DL promises an improvement over other approaches. The Breast-Dense strategy is state-of-the-art and improves the state-of-the-art classification accuracy when using the BCDR dataset. The YOLO + DenseNet model trained on the dataset, achieved the best accuracy rate overall, and was used to develop a tumor lesion classification tool.

Breast-DenseNet provided highly accurate diagnoses when classifying benign from malignant tumors. Therefore, its predictor could be used as a preliminary tool to assist the diagnosis by the radiologist. Our future research includes deeper architectures as well as ultrasound, histopathology and PET images to deal with problems encountered in mammography images of highly dense breasts. It will be helpful to include other imaging techniques, in combination with mammography during the learning process, to help to model work as a robust breast mass predictor. In conclusion, Table 2 demonstrated that Breast DenseNet achieved better results compared to other state-of-the-art methods, which used the same public dataset.

Acknowledgement. VL would like to thank the natural sciences and engineering research council of Canada (NSERC) for a discovery grant. Y.J.G. and D.C.M. acknowledge the research support of Universidad Técnica Particular de Loja through the project PROY_INV_QUI_2020_2784 and the CSIC grant PTA2019–017113-1/AEI/https://doi.org/10.13039/501100011033.

References

1. Ferlay, J., et al.: Cancer incidence and mortality worldwide: sources, methods and major patterns in GLOBOCAN 2012. Int. J. Cancer. **136**(5), E359–E386 (2015)
2. Ragab, D.A., Sharkas, M., Marshall, S., Ren, J.: Breast cancer detection using deep convolutional neural networks and support vector machines. Peer J. **7**, e6201 (2019)
3. Shieh, S.H., Hsieh, V.C.R., Liu, S.H., Chien, C.R., Lin, C.C., Wu, T.N.: Delayed time from first medical visit to diagnosis for breast cancer patients in Taiwan. J. Formos. Med. Assoc. **113**(10), 696–703 (2014)
4. Nahid, A.A., Kong, Y.: Involvement of machine learning for breast cancer image classification: a survey. Comput. Math. Methods Med. **2017**, 29 (2017). https://doi.org/10.1155/2017/378 1951
5. Bardou, D., Zhang, K., Ahmad, S.M.: Classification of breast cancer based on histology images using convolutional neural networks. IEEE Access **6**, 24680–24693 (2018)
6. Skandalakis, J.E.: Embryology and anatomy of the breast. In: Shiffman, M. (eds) Breast Augmentation, pp. 3–24. Springer, Berlin, Heidelberg (2009). https://doi.org/10.1007/978-3-540-78948-2_1
7. Huang, Y.L., Chen, D.R., Lin, Y.C.: 3D Contouring for Breast Tumor in Sonography. arXiv preprint arXiv:1901.09407 (2019)
8. Al Rahhal, M.M.: Breast cancer classification in histopathological images using convolutional neural network. Int. J. Adv. Comput. Sci. Appl. **9**(3), 64–68 (2018)
9. Lim, C.N., Suliong, C., Rao, C.V., et al.: Recent advances in breast cancer diagnosis entering an era of precision medicine. Borneo J. Med. Sci. (BJMS) **13**(1), 3–9 (2019)
10. Karthiga, R., Narasimhan, K.: Automated diagnosis of breast cancer using wavelet based entropy features. In: Second International Conference on Electronics, Communication and Aerospace Technology (ICECA), pp. 274–279. IEEE, Coimbatore, India (2018). https://doi.org/10.1109/ICECA.2018.8474739.
11. Han, Z., Wei, B., Zheng, Y., Yin, Y., Li, K., Li, S.: Breast cancer multi-classification from histopathological images with structured deep learning model. Sci. Rep. **7**(1), 1–10 (2017)
12. Xie, J., Liu, R., Luttrell IV, J., Zhang, C.: Deep learning based analysis of histopathological images of breast cancer. Front. Gene. 10(80), 19 (2019). https://doi.org/10.3389/fgene.2019.00080
13. Toğaçar, M., Özkurt, K.B., Ergen, B., Cömert, Z.: BreastNet: a novel convolutional neural network model through histopathological images for the diagnosis of breast cancer. Physica A: Stat. Mech. App. **545**,123592 (2020)
14. Pan, Y., et al.: Brain tumor grading based on neural networks and convolutional neural networks. In: 37th Annual International Conference of the IEEE Engineering in Medicine and Biology Society (EMBC), pp. 699–702. IEEE, Milan, Italy (2015)
15. Camacho-Piedra, C., Espíndola-Zarazúa, V.: Actualización de la nomenclatura BI-RADS® por mastografía y ultrasonido. Anales de Radiología, (México). **17**(2), 100–108 (2018)
16. Huang, Y., Han, L., Dou, H., et al.: Two-stage CNNs for computerized BI-RADS categorization in breast ultrasound images. BioMed. Eng. OnLine **18**, 8 (2019). https://doi.org/10.1186/s12938-019-0626-5
17. Liberman, L., Menell, J.H.: Breast imaging reporting and data system (BI-RADS). Radiol. Clin. **40**(3), 409–430 (2002)
18. Huang, G., Liu, Z., Van Der Maaten, L., Weinberger, K.Q.: Densely connected convolutional networks. In: Proceedings of the IEEE conference on computer vision and pattern recognition, pp. 4700–4708. IEEE, Honolulu, Hawaii (2017)
19. Kerlikowske, K., et al.: Performance of screening mammography among women with and without a first-degree relative with breast cancer. Ann. Internal Med. **133**(11), 855–863 (2000)

20. Cao, Z., Duan, L., Yang, G., Yue, T., Chen, Q.: An experimental study on breast lesion detection and classification from ultrasound images using deep learning architec-tures. BMC Med. Imaging, **19**(51), 9 (2019). https://doi.org/10.1186/s12880-019-0349-x

21. Duggento, A., et al.: An Ad Hoc random initialization deep neural network architecture for discriminating malignant breast cancer lesions in mammographic images. Contrast Media Mol. Imaging, **2019**, 5982834 (2019). https://doi.org/10.1155/2019/5982834

22. Munir, K., Elahi, H., Ayub, A., Frezza, F., Rizzi, A.: Cancer diagnosis using deep learning: a bibliographic review. Cancers, **11**(9), 1235, (2019). https://doi.org/10.3390/cancers11091235

23. Chougrad, H., Zouaki, H., Alheyane, O.: Deep convolutional neural networks for breast cancer screening. Comput. Methods Programs Biomed. **157**, 19–30 (2018)

24. Das, K., Conjeti, S., Roy, A.G., Chatterjee, J., Sheet, D.: Multiple instances learning of deep convolutional neural networks for breast histopathology whole slide classification. In: 2018 IEEE 15th International Symposium on Biomedical Imaging (ISBI 2018), pp. 578–581. IEEE, Washington, USA (2018)

25. Chiao, J.Y., et al.: Detection and classification the breast tumors using mask R-CNN on sonograms. Medicine. **98**(19), e15200 (2019)

26. Jiang, Y., Chen, L., Zhang, H., Xiao, X.: Breast cancer histopathological image classifica-tion using convolutional neural networks with small SE-ResNet module. PloS ONE. **14**(3), e0214587 (2019)

27. Jiménez-Gaona, Y., Rodríguez-Álvarez, M.J., Lakshminarayanan, V.: Deep-learning-based computer-aided systems for breast cancer imaging: a critical review. Appl. Sci. **10**(22), 8298 (2020). https://doi.org/10.3390/app10228298

28. Duraisamy, S., Emperumal, S.: Computer-aided mammogram diagnosis system using deep learning convolutional fully complex-valued relaxation neural network classifier. IET Comput. Vision **11**(8), 656–662 (2017)

29. Litjens, G., et al.: A survey on deep learning in medical image analysis. Med. Image Anal. **42**, 60–88 (2017)

30. Castillo, D., Lakshminarayanan, V., Rodríguez-Álvarez, M.J.: MRI images, brain lesions and deep learning appl. Science **11**, 1675 (2021). https://doi.org/10.3390/app11041675

31. Ravì, D., et al.: Deep learning for health informatics. IEEE J. Biomed. Health Inform. **21**(1), 4–21 (2016)

32. Mohsen, H., El-Dahshan, E.S.A., El-Horbaty, E.S.M., Salem, A.B.M.: Classification using deep learning neural networks for brain tumors. Future Comput. Inf. J. **3**(1), 68–71 (2018)

33. Matta, S.: Various image segmentation techniques. Int. J. Comput. Sci. Inf. Technol. (IJCSIT) **5**(6), 7536–7539 (2014)

34. Zhou, Z., Wu, W., Wu, S., Tsui, P.-H., Lin, C.-C., Zhang, L., et al.: Semi-automatic breast ultrasound image segmentation based on mean shift and graph cuts. Ultrasound Imaging **36**(4), 256–276 (2014)

35. Levman, J., Warner, E., Causer, P., Martel, A.: Semi-automatic region-of-interest segmentation based computer-aided diagnosis of mass lesions from dynamic contrast-enhanced magnetic resonance imaging based breast cancer screening. J. Digit. Imaging **27**(5), 670–678 (2014)

36. Yap, M.H., et al.: Automated breast ultrasound lesions detection using convolutional neural networks. IEEE J. Biomed. Health Inform. **22**(4), 1218–1226 (2017)

37. Cheng, B., Ran, L., Chou, Y.H., Cheng, J.Z.: Boundary regularized convolutional neural net-work for layer parsing of breast anatomy in automated whole breast ultrasound. In: Inter-national Conference on Medical Image Computing and Computer-Assisted Intervention. Springer International Publishing, Cham, pp. 259–266 (2017). ISBN 978–3–319–66179–7

38. Huynh, B., Drukker, K., Giger, M.: MO-DE-207B-06: computer-aided diagnosis of breast ultrasound images using transfer learning from deep convolutional neural networks. Med. Phys. **243**(6), 3705 (2016)

39. Nahid, A.A., Mehrabi, M.A., Kong, Y.: Histopathological breast cancer image classification by deep neural network techniques guided by local clustering. Biomed. Res. Int. **2018**, 2362108 (2018). https://doi.org/10.1155/2018/2362108

40. Ragab, D.A., Sharkas, M., Marshall, S., Ren, J.: Breast cancer detection using deep convolutional neural networks and support vector machines. Peer J. **7**, e6201 (2019). https://doi.org/10.7717/peerj.6201

41. Simonyan, K., Zisserman, A.: Very deep convolutional networks for large-scale image recognition. In: ICLR, (2015). arXiv preprint arXiv:1409.1556 (2014)

42. He, K., Zhang, X., Ren, S., Sun, J.: Deep residual learning for image recognition. In: Proceedings of the IEEE Conference on Computer Vision and Pattern Recognition, 2016 IEEE Conference on Computer Vision and Pattern Recognition (CVPR), pp. 770–778 (2016). https://doi.org/10.1109/CVPR.2016.90.

43. Huang, G., Liu, Z., Van Der Maaten, L., Weinberger, K.Q.: Densely connected convolutional networks. In: Proceedings of the 2017 IEEE Conference on Computer Vision and Pattern Recognition 2017 IEEE Conference on Computer Vision and Pattern Recognition (CVPR), 2017, pp. 2261–2269 (2017). https://doi.org/10.1109/CVPR.2017.243

44. Russakovsky, O., et al.: ImageNet large scale visual recognition challenge. Int. J. Comput. Vision **115**(3), 211–252 (2015). https://doi.org/10.1007/s11263-015-0816-y

45. Lopez, M.G., et al.: BCDR: a breast cancer digital repository. In: 15th International Conference on Experimental Mechanics, Porto, Portugal, vol. 1215, pp.1–5 (2012). https://bcdr.eu/

46. Marcomini, K.D., Carneiro, A.A., Schiabel, H.: Application of artificial neural network models in segmentation and classification of nodules in breast ultrasound digital images. Int. J. Biomed. Imaging. **2016**, 13 (2016). https://doi.org/10.1155/2016/7987212

47. Al-Masni, M.A., et al.: Simultaneous detection and classification of breast masses in digital mammograms via a deep learning YOLO-based CAD system. Comput. Methods Programs Biomed. **157**, 85–94 (2018)

48. Debelee, T.G., Schwenker, F., Ibenthal, A., Yohannes, D.: Survey of deep learning in breast cancer image analysis. Evol. Syst. **11**(1), 143–163 (2019). https://doi.org/10.1007/s12530-019-09297-2

49. Ahmed, A.H., Salem, M.A.M.: Mammogram-Based cancer detection using deep convolutional neural networks. In: 2018 13th International Conference on Computer Engineering and Systems (ICCES), pp. 694–699. IEEE, Egypt (2018). https://doi.org/10.1109/ICCES.2018.8639224

50. Prabhakar, T., Poonguzhali, S.: Automatic detection and classification of benign and malignant lesions in breast ultrasound images using texture morphological and fractal features. In: 2017 10th Biomedical Engineering International Conference (BMEiCON), pp. 1–5. IEEE, Japan (2017)

51. Alkhaleefah, M., Ma, S.C., Chang, Y.L., Huang, B., Chittem, P.K., Achhannagari, V.P.:https://doi.org/10.3390/app10113999 Double-shot transfer learning for breast cancer classification from X-ray images. Appl. Sci. **10**(11), 3999 (2020).

52. He, K., Zhang, X., Ren, S., Sun, J.: Deep residual learning for image recognition. In: Proceedings of the IEEE Conference on Computer Vision and Pattern Recognition, pp. 770–778 (2016)

53. Huang, G., Sun, Y., Liu, Z., Sedra, D., Weinberger, K.Q.: Deep Networks with Stochastic Depth. In: Leibe, B., Matas, J., Sebe, N., Welling, M. (eds) Computer Vision – ECCV 2016. ECCV 2016. Lecture Notes in Computer Science, vol 9908. Springer, Cham. (2016). https://doi.org/10.1007/978-3-319-46493-0_39https://doi.org/10.1007/978-3-319-46493-0_39

Disease Control and Diagnosis

Analysing Large Repositories of Medical Images

Ivan Štajduhar[1,2]($\boxtimes$)(iD), Teo Manojlović[1,2](iD), Franko Hržić[1,2](iD),
Mateja Napravnik[1], Goran Glavaš[3](iD), Matija Milanič[4,5](iD),
Sebastian Tschauner[6](iD), Mihaela Mamula Saračević[7], and Damir Miletić[7](iD)

[1] Faculty of Engineering, University of Rijeka, Rijeka, Croatia
{istajduh,tmanojlovic,fhrzic,mnapravnik}@riteh.hr
[2] Center for Artificial Intelligence and Cybersecurity,
University of Rijeka, Rijeka, Croatia
[3] School of Business Informatics and Mathematics, University of Mannheim,
Mannheim, Germany
goran@informatik.uni-mannheim.de
[4] Faculty of Mathematics and Physics, University of Ljubljana, Ljubljana, Slovenia
matija.milanic@fmf.uni-lj.si
[5] Jozef Stefan Institute, Ljubljana, Slovenia
[6] Division of Pediatric Radiology, Department of Radiology,
Medical University of Graz, Graz, Austria
sebastian.tschauner@medunigraz.at
[7] Clinical Hospital Centre Rijeka, Rijeka, Croatia
damir.miletic@medri.uniri.hr

Abstract. In clinical analysis, medical radiology is a widely used technique to make a noninvasive medical diagnosis that establishes the presence of an injury or disease without requiring invasive surgery. The purpose of computer-aided diagnosis (CAD) is to assist the clinician in interpreting the acquired data. In recent years, the application of machine learning techniques in this field has greatly increased, leading to increased accuracy or even complete replacement of manually created models. The main reason for the increased use of these techniques in medical image analysis is due to the fact that medical data has become increasingly available, the computational power of computers has increased, and significant advances have been made in machine learning, especially in machine vision applications. This development is a driving force behind major changes in the field of medicine, both in the laboratory and in the clinic. Unlike filtering techniques, machine learning can open up new methods for diagnosing diseases that were previously unthinkable. Moreover, the implementation of personalised medicine in the clinic, i.e. modelling specific conditions closely related to patient characteristics, requires the use of machine learning. In this paper, we give an overview of the field and present a set of guidelines that can be helpful in analysing large collections of medical images using data-driven techniques.

© Springer Nature Switzerland AG 2021
I. Rojas et al. (Eds.): BIOMESIP 2021, LNCS 12940, pp. 179–193, 2021.
https://doi.org/10.1007/978-3-030-88163-4_17

Keywords: Information fusion · Clinical medicine · Big data · Machine learning · Deep learning · Transfer learning · Image analysis · DICOM · Natural language processing

1   Introduction

The physician's work in diagnosing injuries and pathologies from medical scans is demanding, expensive, and prone to error. The purpose of computer-aided diagnosis (CAD) is to reduce the impact of these problems by assisting physicians in interpreting the acquired data [5,17,65]. Some of the more interesting problems we face today in implementing successful CAD systems are: (1) detecting the presence of a specific event, e.g. a lesion or pathology, and (2) segmenting an area of interest, e.g. determining the exact space occupied by an organ in a three-dimensional scan. CAD systems are usually created by exploiting expertise. For medical image analysis, this typically requires careful design of solutions (e.g. rules or filters) suitable for solving specific problems [25]. With the development of high-quality metrics to evaluate detection, classification, and segmentation performance, the application of machine learning (ML) in this field is becoming more common, as it has the inherent ability to automatically search for new and better models by optimising the chosen metric [29,66].

In the clinic, medical radiology is often used to establish a medical diagnosis noninvasively. Radiologists can diagnose injury or disease without invasive intervention by considering the morphological characteristics of the observed area. Computed tomography (CT), magnetic resonance imaging (MRI), as well as other radiological imaging modalities have become inexhaustible sources of immense amounts of complex, high-quality data. These data must be approached from multiple perspectives and used entirely to determine the correct diagnosis of patient conditions in a timely and accurate manner, placing great pressure on both radiologists and clinicians in general. In response to the information overload in healthcare [3], numerous decision support systems [17] (DSSs) have been developed in recent years [5], confirming that CAD has become important in the modern clinical decision-making process [65].

Recently, the use of ML techniques has greatly increased in this field, enhancing or substituting manually created models [41,62,66]. This has been fuelled by greater availability of data [31,48], increased computer processing power, and more significant advances through the use of deep learning (DL) [23,39] techniques in machine vision (MV) applications. The emergence of data driven modelling has the potential to introduce radical improvements in biology and medicine – both in the laboratory and in the clinic [11,30]. One of the greatest advantages of ML techniques, compared to filtering techniques, in medicine is the ability to uncover new, previously unthinkable procedures for diagnosing disease [51].

One of the challenges we face today is the use of genetic and other molecular mechanisms to introduce personalised health care (personalised medicine) [21]. Personalised medicine implies identifying patients who will benefit from a particular targeted therapy tailored specifically to them. Moreover, due to the complexity of modelling specific conditions closely related to patient characteristics, ML techniques are becoming the driving force behind the implementation of personalised medicine in the clinic, e.g. in the application of radiation oncology [6], or in predictive modelling from electronic health records (EHR) [54].

To get the most out of data-driven modelling techniques, all available data sources must be used. Looking at the Picture Archiving and Communication System (PACS) repositories of medical radiology images, there are three main sources of information that are commonly available: (1) pixel data (i.e. images), (2) DICOM headers, and (3) narrative diagnoses. To be used efficiently, each of these sources requires special attention. When dealing with large datasets, the data cannot be manually filtered to remove noise or outliers. Furthermore, with medical data, ground truth or labelling for a specific target is rarely available. Therefore, the data is often used as is.

In this paper, we review current methods useful for analysing large datasets of (unlabelled) medical images using these three data sources. We give an overview of available medical data modelling techniques and guidelines for selecting appropriate data transformation methods.

Our motivation is to point out the challenges a researcher must consider when acquiring and preprocessing medical and biomedical data stored in different forms. The work presented here can be used by researchers unfamiliar with the field as a starting point when considering how to approach solving a particular problem with big data sources using data-driven techniques.

The remainder of the work is as follows. In Sect. 2 we give an overview of the common modelling techniques used to extract knowledge from data, including the traditional ML approaches as well as DL and transfer learning (TL). We also give some general practical tips on how to approach the modelling problem. In Sect. 3, we extend these concepts by describing how to use available data sources to extract knowledge from PACS repositories. Finally, in Sect. 4 we provide some final considerations and conclude the paper.

2   Making Sense Out of the Data

Clinical DSSs are typically constructed by manually collecting, formalising, and implementing specialist knowledge [25]. This approach is limited both by existing human knowledge about modelling clinical conditions, diagnosis, and therapy, and by the variations and complexities inherent to clinical data [63]. ML techniques can overcome the above limitations, provided that sufficient amounts of data are available. Given the widespread availability of high-quality data today [26], accurate predictive models for automatic detection, localisation, and classification of disease or injury can be built from medical scans by applying recent knowledge from ML and MV fields.

ML is data-driven, as opposed to model-based techniques. However, highly complex distributions – which are of greatest interest for building DSSs for medical imaging – require large amounts of data for modelling. Moreover, models are often very prone to getting stranded in local optima, producing suboptimal solutions. One remedy is to use high-quality feature extractors (encoders) that are invariant to specific undesirable variations in the data (e.g., noise, within-class variations, repetitions, etc.) and allow the creation of highly accurate and robust predictive models, e.g. bag-of-visual-words (BoVW) [47,60]. Various feature selection techniques can be used to determine the most informative features, but this method is not very robust. Alternatively, multimodal learning, also known as information fusion, can be used to exploit multiple data representations simultaneously. This expands the input data space, but in return allows the modelling of simpler, preferably linear hypotheses using maximum margin separation, e.g. support vector machine (SVM) [12]. While model variance can be contained by ensemble models obtained by sampling with replacement (e.g. bagging), e.g. random forests (RF) [10], model bias required to represent complex distributions can be lowered by boosting weak learners, e.g. gradient boosting (GB) [14]. The usefulness of parameterised feature extractors often depends on the correct choice of parameters. These parameters can be estimated together with the parameters of the ML model in an embedded optimisation pipeline to obtain even more accurate predictive models. Specific underlying distributions require the use of different approaches, such as multiple-instance learning (MIL) [2]. When data is scarce, TL [49] can be used to bridge the gap between the required model complexity and the underlying distribution. When data is abundant compared to the complexity of the underlying distribution, DL techniques [39] can be used instead.

2.1 Deep Learning

In recent years, the scientific community has been informed of the excellent results obtained in numerous fields using the DL methodology. Published results of various empirical studies indicate that DL outperforms existing approaches in numerous highly complex domains, including natural language processing (NLP), speech modelling, and image classification [4]. A variant of an artificial neural network (NN) is a convolutional neural network (CNN), which is popular for performing image analysis tasks. A CNN contains in its shallow layers the filters that transform and decompose the input images into relevant features (e.g., edge, texture, and shape detectors) that are more suitable for modelling the problem at hand. A similar concept of model architecture has been observed in the brains of living creatures [27]. The role of the deeper layers of a CNN is to extract the meanings of these indirect features and reveal their correlation with the features of interest. Deep networks are capable of modelling highly complex concepts, such as recognising or categorising a scene or object in a real-world photograph. However, this requires the correct setting of a large number of hyperparameters that control these models. Some of the recent state-of-the-art techniques used for DL are CNNs [36], autoencoders (AEs) [64], recurrent neural networks (RNNs) [20] – long short-term memory (LSTMs) [18,24] and gated recurrent units (GRUs) [15] – attention neural networks [68], and generative adversarial networks (GANs) [19,53]. RNN, LSTM, and GRU architectures are particularly well suited for modelling temporal sequences, which makes them very useful for NLP.

Although the above methods are capable of solving various tasks, they all lack interpretability (so-called black box models) [40]. To deal with this, which is of utmost importance for use of clinical DSSs, researchers come up with various solutions, most of which focus on interpreting the results of the models [32, 61]. Nevertheless, there are many works that provide useful applications of DL methods in medicine where the result of DL methods is self-explanatory, e.g., segmentation of skin lesions [33] or various segmentation and classification tasks of chest X-ray images [1,59].

2.2 Transfer Learning

TL is a ML concept that focuses on applying knowledge acquired by solving one problem to solving another (similar) problem [9,49]. Besides the fact that less data is needed, this form of learning is also more time efficient. In TL, complex models are trained from large amounts of readily available data and then applied to problem domains with much smaller amounts of data through the concept of fine-tuning the pretrained model. TL has recently gained enormous popularity, especially in the application of deep CNNs to model complex problems with limited datasets [56,69]. One of the most famous pretrained model types commonly used for TL was created from a dataset of hierarchically organised photographs of the real world – ImageNet [58].

2.3 Nooks and Crannies of Model Learning

When working with ML models, one of the most challenging tasks is the choice of appropriate hyperparameter values. For example, the potential of an NN model for learning the underlying distribution encoded in the data is largely defined by the choice of its architecture (type and structure) and the appropriate optimisation parameters such as the choice of optimiser (e.g., first or second order, SGD, AdaGrad, Adam [34], RMSProp, etc.) and the regularisation penalty. Several factors must be considered when determining the hyperparameter values that are appropriate for modelling a target distribution. For example, when considering image classification, the following factors should be considered: the number of classes, the hierarchical structure (if any), the number of available instances per class (numerousness of individual classes), and the distribution of image dimensions and colour depth (e.g. radiology images are predominantly 12-bit but vary in spatial dimensions).

A good starting point for determining these values are examples of good practise identified through review of the literature (e.g. cross-validated greedy search over a reasonable hyperparameter subspace). Noise present in both inputs and outputs should be removed using regularisation techniques, such as L2 regularisation and dropout [22] (NNs), and/or batch normalisation [28] (useful for optimisers who can use mini-batches of data instances). Model architectures and appropriate optimisation algorithms can be easily implemented using existing publicly available tools and libraries (Python, Scikit-Learn, Dask, Tensorflow).

3   Using Available Data Sources for Mining PACS Repositories

As mentioned earlier, there are three interrelated sources of information that can be used in mining PACS repositories: (1) DICOM headers, (2) narrative diagnoses, and (3) pixel data. In the following, we describe how each of these sources should be approached to extract the most information from them.

3.1   Analysing Individual Data Sources

DICOM (Digital Imaging and Communications in Medicine)[1] standard defines how medical images, often supplemented by additional information, should be stored. This information is contained in numerous meta tags recorded during exams, measured in thousands (approximately 4,000 different tags in total). These tags are structured according to their function, which is not necessarily true for their content. An example of a partial DICOM header is shown in Fig. 1. Tags are entered either manually by a medical professional or automatically by a device [7]. Although the data stored in the tags may seem uninformative, they can be used to derive meaningful associations between semantically similar images [44].

Tags can be analysed both functionally (manually) and content-wise (manually and automatically) to determine the most effective ways to extract informative features that can be used for data-driven modelling. Record-parsing rules can be implemented by combining regular expressions (e.g. for text fields), information (entropy) measures (e.g. to determine appropriate thresholds and/or cutoff points), and one-hot encoding or similar to encode nominal variables. Due to the heterogeneity of DICOM tag domains, record parsing rules should be manually tailored for each specific tag that is considered potentially useful. To make this effort computationally feasible, for large datasets, representative validation subsets of appropriate size (smaller for decision making and medium for confirming the validity of the decisions made) can be used for this purpose instead. When using supervised evaluation metrics to measure the informativeness of individual DICOM tags, one can use a separate test subset of images labelled with respect to the modelling goal. It should be noted here that labelling is usually done by visual inspection of each data instance, preferably by multiple radiologists – to counteract subjective interpretations.

The use of unprocessed (raw) data can be problematic for ML modelling if proper handling of missing values, noise reduction, outlier removal, feature space transformation, and variable selection is not performed. Tags having a large proportion of missing values, where the absence of a value is considered

---

[1] https://www.dicomstandard.org/ (last accessed July 26, 2021).

(Group,Ele...	TAG Description	Value
(0002,0000)	FileMetaInformationGroupLength	218
(0002,0001)	FileMetaInformationVersion	
(0002,0002)	MediaStorageSOPClassUID	1.2.840.10008.5.1.4.1.1.2
(0002,0003)	MediaStorageSOPInstanceUID	
(0002,0010)	TransferSyntaxUID	1.2.840.10008.1.2.4.70
(0002,0012)	ImplementationClassUID	1.2.276.0.7230010.3.0.3.6.0
(0002,0013)	ImplementationVersionName	OFFIS_DCMTK_360
(0002,0016)	SourceApplicationEntityTitle	SH_DICOMD
(0008,0005)	SpecificCharacterSet	
(0008,0008)	ImageType	ORIGINAL\PRIMARY\AXIAL
(0008,0016)	SOPClassUID	1.2.840.10008.5.1.4.1.1.2
(0008,0018)	SOPInstanceUID	
(0008,0020)	StudyDate	
(0008,0021)	SeriesDate	
(0008,0022)	AcquisitionDate	
(0008,0023)	ContentDate	
(0008,0030)	StudyTime	
(0008,0031)	SeriesTime	
(0008,0032)	AcquisitionTime	
(0008,0033)	ContentTime	
(0008,0050)	AccessionNumber	
(0008,0060)	Modality	CT
(0008,0070)	Manufacturer	SHIMADZU CORPORATION
(0008,0080)	InstitutionName	
(0008,0090)	ReferringPhysicianName	
(0008,1010)	StationName	SCT-7800TX

Fig. 1. An illustration of a partial DICOM header.

uninformative, should be removed from the dataset. Noise reduction in free-form (manual input) tags values can be performed either by manual inspection or preferably using empirical metrics, e.g. string edit distance, to pinpoint and correct the noisy records. Outlier removal can be used to mitigate unwanted variation in the data, e.g. using (multivariate) Gaussian anomaly detection or isolation forests [42]. To evaluate the influence of particular feature groups, PCA and its nonlinear counterpart, t-SNE [43], can be used to view the data in feature space (Fig. 2).

Intentionally added noise can pose a significant security risk in ML modelling [13]. Augmenting the input with tailored noise can lead to a completely different prediction result – which is a known problem for adversarial attacks in ML. Therefore, it is important to be aware of its presence when developing a model to be used in medical practice [38].

For narrative diagnoses feature extraction, the use of representations of text diagnoses obtained by using pretrained semantic representations of words [8,46, 50] and/or sentences [16,35] can be extremely helpful. One can do this by using a specialised corpus of medical-diagnosis words and/or unspecialised sources like the web corpus [37]. RNNs (e.g., LSTM or GRU cells) are suitable for modelling semantics of sequences, because each new input in a sequence is combined with the knowledge aggregated from all previous inputs. Such distinctive mechanism

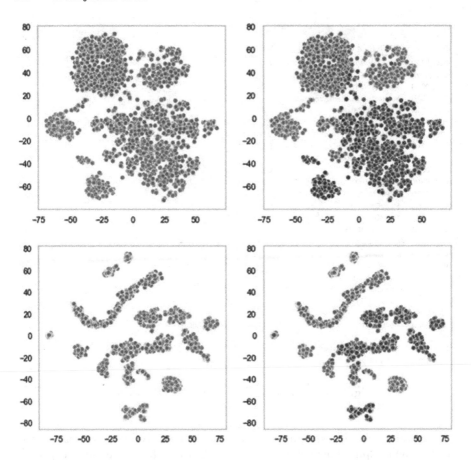

Fig. 2. An illustration of the 2D t-SNE visualisation for the comparison of the clustering results obtained with two different clustering techniques (vertical) while using a different number of clusters (horizontal).

of sequential memory enables enviable performance in modelling the behaviour of sequential data, such as unstructured texts (sentences are sequences of words, paragraphs are sequences of sentences, and so on).

Merging pixel data information with other information sources has to be conducted carefully, bearing in mind the source variation, as well as the data dimensionality. Namely, some of the challenges involving image analysis involves the variation induced by perspective, deformations, partial occlusion, background noise, within-class variability, and so on. These challenges are highly dependent on the image acquisition parameters, which, in turn, depend on the type of utilised diagnostic procedure. Convolution-based models are commonly used to mitigate the influence of unwanted variation and escalating dimensionality in images. When no trustworthy labels in the data exist, convolutional AEs [67] can be used for learning feature extractors from unlabelled data. AEs learn latent

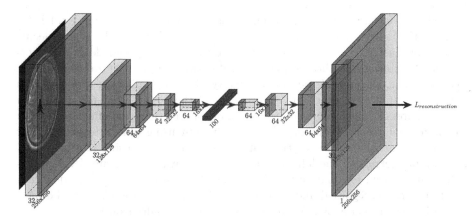

Fig. 3. An illustration of a convolutional autoencoder architecture that can be used, e.g. for empirical evaluation of clustering in the pixel space [44].

data representations (typically in a vector space of reduced dimensionality), from which the original data can be reproduced. Learning more concise semantic representations using AEs can also be used for initialising parameter values of more complex supervised models, in order to ensure both faster and better parameter convergence. However, convolutional AEs can also be used to learn embeddings, which can be useful for measuring morphological (dis)similarities of images [45] (Fig. 3). Because embeddings are commonly highly non-linear (distant points in the Euclidean-space are not necessarily far apart), using t-SNE can be helpful for determining their usefulness.

3.2 Fusing Multimodal Data Sources

In the previous section, we described several approaches that can be used for suppressing noise, mitigating the unwanted variation and cutting back the dimensionality of the data. This process of feature extraction gives us homogeneous encodings of data instances, in terms of data types (e.g. producing a vector of real values from several data sources). To get the most out of the available data, following feature extraction, an appropriate approach for fusing the data with respect to a target modelling goal needs to be chosen. One approach would be to form groups, or clusters, of data instances that are morphologically, or semantically, similar. We will discuss this approach further.

High quality encoders mitigate the variation among instances belonging to the same cluster, while enhancing the variation between the instances belonging to clusters we would like to differentiate. Subsets of the most informative features can be selected to capture the maximum desired variation in the data. Clustering quality can be evaluated qualitatively through PCA/t-SNE visualisations in the feature space, as well as by using supervised evaluation metrics (e.g. classification accuracy, F1 score, confusion matrix, and so on) on a labelled data subset, if available.

Selected feature subsets can then be used to build a clustering model, for binding the images that are morphologically similar to one another, into specific groups or clusters. Unsupervised learning techniques, e.g. k-medoids and hierarchical clustering, can be suitable for dealing with large-scale problems in the feature space. Because of the dimensionality of the optimisation problem, it is generally sound to conduct the experiments in the hyperparameter space on a smaller subset of the available dataset. Quantitative evaluation of clustering can be performed automatically on a larger sample, by using silhouette score [57] or a similar evaluation metric on the feature space, as well as using the supervised evaluation metrics on the labelled data subset, if available. Again, PCA and t-SNE can be used for qualitative assessment of clusterings. If the encoded data contains both categorical and numerical features, Gower distance can be used as a distance measure, as it is able to handle both simultaneously.

An alternative way to fuse multimodal data sources is to jointly train the encoders using contrastive pretraining and zero-shot prediction to learn transferable visual models from natural language supervision [52]. This novel system has yet to realise its full potential in various medical applications where the anamnesis given as text is combined with the pixel data provided by the medical examination [55].

Another test used for measuring the model clustering quality, with respect to the target goal, involves manual labour by radiologists (preferably two or more). The radiologists assign their concordance scores to randomly sampled images falling into each cluster (e.g., 10 images) in a blind fashion, to confirm the inter- and intra-cluster (dis)agreements. A control mechanism should randomly introduce mixtures of groups. The concordance score obtained this way reflects both the morphological homogeneity of specific clusters, as well as morphological heterogeneity between clusters.

4   Conclusion

This paper presents current methods that are useful in analysing potentially large datasets of medical images. To get the most out of available data, researchers must first recognise the nature of their sources. For data sources from PACS, the data types are typically pixel data, DICOM headers, and narrative diagnoses. Creating a good representation of the data can reduce dimensionality and mitigate unwanted variation and noise in the data. This can be done with various approaches that include data extraction and preprocessing, visualisation, and clustering techniques. High quality data and their representation are crucial for training DL models, which are commonly used for classification and segmentation tasks on medical images. Although DL models can be very accurate, their lack of explainability is a non-negligible problem. Moreover, these models are often vulnerable to induced data perturbation, i.e. adversarial attacks. Both of these problems can be addressed by various methods available to researchers. We believe that the work presented here may be useful as a starting point for medical researchers who wish to participate in a data science project involving the use of large datasets from PACS repositories.

Acknowledgement. This work has been supported in part by Croatian Science Foundation [grant number IP-2020-02-3770]; and by the University of Rijeka, Croatia [grant number uniri-tehnic-18-15].

References

1. Abdel-Basset, M., Chang, V., Mohamed, R.: HSMA_WOA: a hybrid novel slime mould algorithm with whale optimization algorithm for tackling the image segmentation problem of chest X-ray images. Appl. Soft Comput. **95**, 106642 (2020)
2. Babenko, B., Yang, M.-H., Belongie, S.: Robust object tracking with online multiple instance learning. IEEE Trans. Pattern Anal. Mach. Intell. **33**(8), 1619–1632 (2011). https://doi.org/10.1109/TPAMI.2010.226
3. Beasley, J.W., et al.: Information chaos in primary care: implications for physician performance and patient safety. J. Am. Board Fam. Med. **24**(6), 745–751 (2011). http://www.jabfm.org/content/24/6/745.short
4. Bengio, Y., Courville, A., Vincent, P.: Representation learning: a review and new perspectives. IEEE Trans. Pattern Anal. Mach. Intell. **35**(8), 1798–1828 (2013). https://doi.org/10.1109/TPAMI.2013.50
5. Berner, E.S. (ed.): Clinical Decision Support Systems: Theory and Practice, 3rd edn. Springer, Cham (2016). https://doi.org/10.1007/978-3-319-31913-1
6. Bibault, J.E., Giraud, P., Burgun, A.: Big data and machine learning in radiation oncology: state of the art and future prospects. Cancer Lett. **382**(1), 110–117 (2016). https://doi.org/10.1016/j.canlet.2016.05.033
7. Bidgood, W.D., Horii, S.C., Prior, F.W., Van Syckle, D.E.: Understanding and using DICOM, the data interchange standard for biomedical imaging. J. Am. Med. Inform. Assoc. **4**(3), 199–212 (1997). https://doi.org/10.1136/jamia.1997.0040199
8. Bojanowski, P., Grave, E., Joulin, A., Mikolov, T.: Enriching word vectors with subword information. Trans. Assoc. Comput. Linguist. **5**, 135–146 (2017). https://doi.org/10.1162/tacl_a_00051
9. Bozinovski, S.: Reminder of the first paper on transfer learning in neural networks, 1976. Informatica **44**(3) (2020). https://doi.org/10.31449/INF.V44I3.2828
10. Breiman, L.: Random forests. Mach. Learn. **45**(1), 5–32 (2001)
11. de Bruijne, M.: Machine learning approaches in medical image analysis: from detection to diagnosis. Med. Image Anal. **33**, 94–97 (2016). https://doi.org/10.1016/j.media.2016.06.032
12. Burges, C.J.C., Schölkopf, B.: Improving the accuracy and speed of support vector machines. In: Advances in Neural Information Processing Systems 9, pp. 375–381 (1997). https://papers.nips.cc/paper/1253-improving-the-accuracy-and-speed-of-support-vector-machines
13. Chen, S.-T., Cornelius, C., Martin, J., Chau, D.H.P.: ShapeShifter: robust physical adversarial attack on faster R-CNN object detector. In: Berlingerio, M., Bonchi, F., Gärtner, T., Hurley, N., Ifrim, G. (eds.) ECML PKDD 2018. LNCS (LNAI), vol. 11051, pp. 52–68. Springer, Cham (2019). https://doi.org/10.1007/978-3-030-10925-7_4
14. Chen, T., Carlos, G.: Xgboost: a scalable tree boosting system. In: Proceedings of the 22nd ACM SIGKDD International Conference on Knowledge Discovery and Data Mining (2016)
15. Chung, J., Gulcehre, C., Cho, K., Bengio, Y.: Gated feedback recurrent neural networks. In: 32nd International Conference on Machine Learning, ICML 2015, vol. 3 (2015)

16. Devlin, J., Chang, M.W., Lee, K., Toutanova, K.: BERT: pre-training of deep bidirectional transformers for language understanding. In: NAACL HLT 2019-2019 Conference of the North American Chapter of the Association for Computational Linguistics: Human Language Technologies - Proceedings of the Conference, vol. 1 (2019)

17. Doi, K.: Computer-aided diagnosis in medical imaging: historical review, current status and future potential. Comput. Med. Imaging Graph. **31**(4–5), 198–211 (2007). https://doi.org/10.1016/j.compmedimag.2007.02.002

18. Gers, F.: Learning to forget: continual prediction with LSTM. In: 9th International Conference on Artificial Neural Networks: ICANN 1999, vol. 1999, pp. 850–855. IEEE (1999). https://doi.org/10.1049/cp:19991218

19. Goodfellow, I., et al.: Generative adversarial nets. In: Advances in Neural Information Processing Systems 27, pp. 2672–2680 (2014)

20. Graves, A., Mohamed, A.R., Hinton, G.: Speech recognition with deep recurrent neural networks. In: 2013 IEEE International Conference on Acoustics, Speech and Signal Processing, pp. 6645–6649. IEEE (2013). https://doi.org/10.1109/ICASSP.2013.6638947

21. Hamburg, M.A., Collins, F.S.: The path to personalized medicine. N. Engl. J. Med. **363**(1), 1–3 (2010). https://doi.org/10.1056/NEJMp1002530

22. Hinton, G.: Dropout: a simple way to prevent neural networks from overfitting. J. Mach. Learn. Res. (JMLR) **15**, 1929–1958 (2014)

23. Hinton, G.: Deep learning-a technology with the potential to transform health care. JAMA **320**(11), 1101 (2018). https://doi.org/10.1001/jama.2018.11100

24. Hochreiter, S., Schmidhuber, J.: Long short-term memory. Neural Comput. **9**(8), 1735–1780 (1997). https://doi.org/10.1162/neco.1997.9.8.1735

25. Hržić, F., Štajduhar, I., Tschauner, S., Sorantin, E., Lerga, J.: Local-entropy based approach for X-ray image segmentation and fracture detection. Entropy **21**(4), 338 (2019). https://doi.org/10.3390/E21040338

26. Hržić, F., Tschauner, S., Sorantin, E., Štajduhar, I.: XAOM: a method for automatic alignment and orientation of radiographs for computer-aided medical diagnosis. Comput. Biol. Med. **132**, 104300 (2021). https://doi.org/10.1016/j.compbiomed.2021.104300

27. Hubel, D.H., Wiesel, T.N.: Receptive fields, binocular interaction and functional architecture in the cays visual cortex. J. Physiol. **160**(1), 106–154 (1962)

28. Ioffe, S., Szegedy, C.: Batch normalization: accelerating deep network training by reducing internal covariate shift. In: Proceedings of the 32nd International Conference on Machine Learning, vol. 37 (2015)

29. Jain, V., Seung, H.S., Turaga, S.C.: Machines that learn to segment images: a crucial technology for connectomics. Curr. Opin. Neurobiol. **20**(5), 653–666 (2010). https://doi.org/10.1016/j.conb.2010.07.004

30. Kalinin, A.A., et al.: Opportunities and obstacles for deep learning in biology and medicine. J. R. Soc. Interface **15**(141), 20170387 (2018). https://doi.org/10.1098/rsif.2017.0387

31. Kansagra, A.P., et al.: Big data and the future of radiology informatics. Acad. Radiol. **23**(1), 30–42 (2016)

32. Kaur, H., Nori, H., Jenkins, S., Caruana, R., Wallach, H., Wortman Vaughan, J.: Interpreting interpretability: understanding data scientists' use of interpretability tools for machine learning. In: Proceedings of the 2020 CHI Conference on Human Factors in Computing Systems, pp. 1–14 (2020)

33. Khan, M.A., Sharif, M., Akram, T., Damaševičius, R., Maskeliūnas, R.: Skin lesion segmentation and multiclass classification using deep learning features and improved moth flame optimization. Diagnostics **11**(5), 811 (2021)
34. Kingma, D.P., Ba, J.L.: Adam: a method for stochastic optimization. In: 3rd International Conference on Learning Representations, ICLR 2015 - Conference Track Proceedings (2015)
35. Kiros, R., et al.: Skip-thought vectors. In: Advances in Neural Information Processing Systems 28 (NIPS 2015), pp. 3294–3302 (2015)
36. Krizhevsky, A., Sutskever, I., Hinton, G.E.: ImageNet classification with deep convolutional neural networks. Adv. Neural. Inf. Process. Syst. **25**, 1097–1105 (2012)
37. Krsnik, I., Glavaš, G., Krsnik, M., Miletic, D., Štajduhar, I.: Automatic annotation of narrative radiology reports. Diagnostics **10**(4), 196 (2020). https://doi.org/10.3390/diagnostics10040196
38. Lal, S., et al.: Adversarial attack and defence through adversarial training and feature fusion for diabetic retinopathy recognition. Sensors **21**(11), 3922 (2021)
39. LeCun, Y., Bengio, Y., Hinton, G.: Deep learning. Nature **521**(7553), 436–444 (2015). https://doi.org/10.1038/nature14539
40. Lipton, Z.C.: The mythos of model interpretability: in machine learning, the concept of interpretability is both important and slippery. Queue **16**(3), 31–57 (2018)
41. Litjens, G., et al.: A survey on deep learning in medical image analysis. Med. Image Anal. **42**, 60–88 (2017). https://doi.org/10.1016/J.MEDIA.2017.07.005
42. Liu, F.T., Ting, K.M., Zhou, Z.H.: Isolation forest. In: 2008 Eighth IEEE International Conference on Data Mining, pp. 413–422. IEEE (2008). https://doi.org/10.1109/ICDM.2008.17. http://ieeexplore.ieee.org/document/4781136/
43. van der Maaten, L., Hinton, G.: Visualizing data using t-SNE. J. Mach. Learn. Res. **9**(Nov), 2579–2605 (2008). https://doi.org/10.1007/s10479-011-0841-3
44. Manojlović, T., Ilić, D., Miletić, D., Štajduhar, I.: Using DICOM tags for clustering medical radiology images into visually similar groups. In: ICPRAM 2020 - Proceedings of the 9th International Conference on Pattern Recognition Applications and Methods (2020). https://doi.org/10.5220/0008973405100517
45. Manojlović, T., Milanič, M., Štajduhar, I.: Deep embedded clustering algorithm for clustering PACS repositories. In: 2021 IEEE 34th International Symposium on Computer-Based Medical Systems (CBMS). IEEE (2021). https://doi.org/10.1109/CBMS52027.2021.00091
46. Mikolov, T., Sutskever, I., Chen, K., Corrado, G.S., Dean, J.: Distributed representations of words and phrases and their compositionality. In: Advances in Neural Information Processing Systems 26 (NIPS 2013), pp. 3111–3119 (2013)
47. Niebles, J.C., Wang, H., Fei-Fei, L.: Unsupervised learning of human action categories using spatial-temporal words. Int. J. Comput. Vis. **79**(3), 299–318 (2008). https://doi.org/10.1007/s11263-007-0122-4
48. Obermeyer, Z., Emanuel, E.J.: Predicting the future - big data, machine learning, and clinical medicine. New Engl. J. Med. **375**(13), 1216–1219 (2016). https://doi.org/10.1056/NEJMp1606181
49. Pan, S.J., Yang, Q.: A survey on transfer learning. IEEE Trans. Knowl. Data Eng. **22**(10), 1345–1359 (2010)
50. Pennington, J., Socher, R., Manning, C.: Glove: global vectors for word representation. In: Proceedings of the 2014 Conference on Empirical Methods in Natural Language Processing (EMNLP), pp. 1532–1543. Association for Computational Linguistics, Stroudsburg (2014). https://doi.org/10.3115/v1/D14-1162

51. Poplin, R., et al.: Prediction of cardiovascular risk factors from retinal fundus photographs via deep learning. Nat. Biomed. Eng. **2**(3), 158–164 (2018). https://doi.org/10.1038/s41551-018-0195-0
52. Radford, A., et al.: Learning transferable visual models from natural language supervision. arXiv preprint arXiv:2103.00020 (2021)
53. Radford, A., Metz, L., Chintala, S.: Unsupervised representation learning with deep convolutional generative adversarial networks. In: 4th International Conference on Learning Representations, ICLR 2016 - Conference Track Proceedings (2016)
54. Rajkomar, A., et al.: Scalable and accurate deep learning for electronic health records. NPJ Digital Med. **1**(Jan), 1–10 (2018). https://doi.org/10.1038/s41746-018-0029-1
55. Ramasamy, L.K., Padinjappurathu, S.G., Kadry, S., Damaševičius, R.: Detection of diabetic retinopathy using a fusion of textural and ridgelet features of retinal images and sequential minimal optimization classifier. PeerJ Comput. Sci. **7** (2021)
56. Razavian, A.S., Azizpour, H., Sullivan, J., Carlsson, S.: CNN features off-the-shelf: an astounding baseline for recognition. In: IEEE Computer Society Conference on Computer Vision and Pattern Recognition Workshops, pp. 512–519. IEEE Computer Society (2014)
57. Rousseeuw, P.J.: Silhouettes: a graphical aid to the interpretation and validation of cluster analysis. J. Comput. Appl. Math. **20**, 53–65 (1987). https://doi.org/10.1016/0377-0427(87)90125-7
58. Russakovsky, O., et al.: ImageNet large scale visual recognition challenge. Int. J. Comput. Vis. **115**(3), 211–252 (2015). https://doi.org/10.1007/s11263-015-0816-y
59. Sahlol, A.T., Abd Elaziz, M., Tariq Jamal, A., Damaševičius, R., Farouk Hassan, O.: A novel method for detection of tuberculosis in chest radiographs using artificial ecosystem-based optimisation of deep neural network features. Symmetry **12**(7), 1146 (2020)
60. Sánchez, J., Perronnin, F., Mensink, T., Verbeek, J.: Image classification with the fisher vector: theory and practice. Int. J. Comput. Vis. **105**(3), 222–245 (2013). https://doi.org/10.1007/s11263-013-0636-x
61. Selvaraju, R.R., Cogswell, M., Das, A., Vedantam, R., Parikh, D., Batra, D.: Grad-cam: visual explanations from deep networks via gradient-based localization. In: Proceedings of the IEEE International Conference on Computer Vision, pp. 618–626 (2017)
62. Štajduhar, I., Mamula, M., Miletić, D., Ünal, G.: Semi-automated detection of anterior cruciate ligament injury from MRI. Comput. Methods Programs Biomed. **140**, 151–164 (2017). https://doi.org/10.1016/j.cmpb.2016.12.006
63. Štajduhar, I., Tomić, M., Lerga, J.: Mirroring quasi-symmetric organ observations for reducing problem complexity. Expert Syst. Appl. **85**, 318–334 (2017). https://doi.org/10.1016/j.eswa.2017.05.041
64. Vincent, G., Wolstenholme, C., Scott, I., Bowes, M.: Fully automatic segmentation of the knee joint using active appearance models. In: Medical Image Analysis for the Clinic: A Grand Challenge, pp. 224–230. CreateSpace (2010)
65. Wagholikar, K.B., Sundararajan, V., Deshpande, A.W.: Modeling paradigms for medical diagnostic decision support: a survey and future directions. J. Med. Syst. **36**(5), 3029–3049 (2012)
66. Wang, S., Summers, R.M.: Machine learning and radiology. Med. Image Anal. **16**(5), 933–951 (2012). https://doi.org/10.1016/j.media.2012.02.005
67. Xie, J., Girshick, R., Farhadi, A.: Unsupervised deep embedding for clustering analysis. In: 33rd International Conference on Machine Learning, ICML 2016, vol. 1 (2016)

68. Xu, K., et al.: Show, attend and tell: neural image caption generation with visual attention. In: Proceedings of the 32nd International Conference on Machine Learning, vol. 37, pp. 2048–2057 (2015). https://doi.org/10.1016/j.scitotenv.2016.07.196
69. Yosinski, J., Clune, J., Bengio, Y., Lipson, H.: How transferable are features in deep neural networks? In: Advances in Neural Information Processing Systems, pp. 3320–3328 (2014)

Fat Mass is Negatively Associated with Composite Indices of Femoral Neck Strength in Elderly Lebanese Subjects

Amal Antoun[1,2], Antonio Pinti[3(✉)], Hayman Saddik[1,4], Emneh Hammoud[1], Eric Watelain[2], and Rawad El Hage[1]

[1] Department of Physical Education, Division of Education, Faculty of Arts and Sciences, University of Balamand, El-Koura, Lebanon
[2] Laboratoire Impact de l'Activité Physique sur la Santé (IAPS), Université de Toulon, 83041 Toulon Cedex 9, Toulon, France
[3] DeVisu – Design, Visuel, Urbain, EA 2445, UPHF, Valenciennes, France
antonio.pinti@uphf.fr
[4] I3MTO, EA4708, Université d'Orléans, Orléans, France

Abstract. The aim of the current study was to explore the relationships between fat mass and composite indices of femoral neck strength ((compressive strength index (CSI), bending strength index (BSI) and impact strength index (ISI)) in a group of elderly Lebanese subjects. 59 elderly women and 39 elderly men whose ages range between 60 and 85 years participated in this study. Height and weight were measured, and body mass index (BMI) was calculated. Body composition and femoral neck bone mineral density were measured by DXA. Handgrip strength was measured by a hand dynamometer. In women, fat mass was negatively correlated to CSI and ISI. In men, fat mass was negatively correlated to CSI, BSI and ISI. The negative correlations between fat mass and composite indices of femoral neck strength remained significant after controlling for age. In conclusion, the current study suggests that fat mass is a negative determinant of composite indices of femoral neck strength in elderly Lebanese subjects. Implementing strategies to reduce fat mass excess seems important to prevent osteoporotic fractures in elderly subjects.

Keywords: Ageing · Adiposity · Hip fractures · Femoral neck strength

1 Introduction

Osteoporosis is a prevalent disease in the elderly Lebanese population [1–3]. Previous studies conducted on elderly Lebanese subjects and young adults demonstrated that body weight and body mass index (BMI) are positively correlated to bone mineral density (BMD) values [3–9]. The relative importance of lean mass and fat mass on BMD values has been previously described by several studies, and potential mechanisms

© Springer Nature Switzerland AG 2021
I. Rojas et al. (Eds.): BIOMESIP 2021, LNCS 12940, pp. 194–206, 2021.
https://doi.org/10.1007/978-3-030-88163-4_18

have been proposed [4, 10, 11]. Low BMD is an important risk factor for hip fractures [1–3]. Independent of BMD, bone size and body size also play important roles in hip fracture risk and contribute differentially to fracture risk in different populations [12–16]. Karlamangla et al. [14] have shown that composite indices of femoral neck strength, constructed from DXA measurements, have the potential to improve hip fracture risk assessment. An interesting study has suggested that higher compressive strength index (CSI) values in Chinese subjects may partially help explain the lower incidence of hip fractures in this population compared to Caucasian subjects [15]. Previous studies conducted on young Lebanese adults demonstrated that body weight, BMI and fat mass are negatively correlated to composite indices of femoral neck strength while serum vitamin D and physical activity level are positive determinants of these bone indices [17–21]. However, the relationships between fat mass and composite indices of femoral neck strength in the elderly Lebanese population remain unclear. The main aim of this study was to explore the relationships between fat mass and composite indices of femoral neck strength (compressive strength index (CSI), bending strength index (BSI) and impact strength index (ISI)) in a group of elderly Lebanese subjects. The secondary aim of the current study was to investigate whether these relationships are similar in both genders in this population.

2 Material and Methods

2.1 Subjects and Study Design

59 elderly women and 39 elderly men whose ages range between 60 and 85 years participated in this study. The subjects were randomly chosen from Tripoli, Lebanon. The subjects that were excluded from the study were those suffering from any medical condition which could potentially affect bone metabolism such as history of chronic disease with vital organ involvement or intake of medications that may affect bone metabolism (i.e., steroid intake for more than 6 months and/or treatment with bone antiresorptive drugs). In addition, other subjects that were excluded were those with a radiotherapy or chemotherapy history or those who had been in bed rest for more than 1 month 6 months prior to the study. Other excluded subjects were those with conditions that technically interfere with dual-energy X-ray absorptiometry (DXA) assessment (i.e., previous spine or hip surgery). The present study was carried out in accordance with the declaration of Helsinki (regarding human experimentation developed for the medical community by the World Medical Association). An informed written consent was obtained from the participants.

2.2 Anthropometrics and Bone Measurements

Height (m) and weight (kg) were measured, and body mass index (BMI; kg/m^2) was calculated. Body composition and BMD were assessed by DXA (DXA; GE Healthcare, Madison, WI). Appendicular lean mass (ALM, in kg) was calculated by summing the muscle masses of the 4 limbs, assuming that all non-fat and none-bone mass is lean muscle [22]. Skeletal muscle mass index (SMI = ALM/height^2) and ALM/BMI were then calculated [22]. BMD was measured by DXA at whole body, total hip (TH) and femoral neck (FN). The coefficients of variation were <1% for BMC and BMD in our center [1–11]. Composite indices of femoral neck strength were calculated as previously described by Karlamangla et al. [14]. CSI ([FN BMD * FN width/weight]) and BSI ([FN BMD * FN width^2]/[hip axis length * weight]) express the forces that the FN has to withstand in axial compressive and bending forces, whereas ISI ([FN BMD * FN width * hip axis length]/[height * weight]) expresses the energy that the FN has to absorb in an impact from standing height [14]. The three indices (CSI, BSI and ISI) are expressed in g/kg-m.

2.3 Handgrip Measurements

Handgrip strength was measured by a hand dynamometer (CAMRY Model: EH101-37, China) using a validated protocol [22]. The highest value from 3 trials separated by 2 min of rest on the right hand was used for analysis.

2.4 Statistical Analysis

The means and standard deviations were calculated for all clinical data and for the bone measurements. Comparisons between the 2 groups (women and men) were made after checking for Gaussian distribution. If Gaussian distribution was found, parametric unpaired t-tests were used. In other cases, Mann-Whitney U-tests were used. Correlations between clinical characteristics and bone data were given as Pearson correlation coefficients. Multiple linear regression analysis models were used to test the relationship of obesity indices/handgrip and age with bone variables, and r^2 values were reported. Data were analyzed with Number Cruncher Statistical System (NCSS, 2001; NCSS, Kaysville, UT). A level of significance of $p < 0.05$ was used.

3 Results

3.1 Clinical Characteristics and Bone Variables of the Study Population

Age, weight, height, lean mass, ALM, SMI, ALM/BMI, WB BMC, WB BMD, L1-L4 BMD, TH BMD, FN BMD, CSA, CSMI, Z and handgrip were significantly higher in men compared to women (Table 1). The differences between the two groups regarding TH BMD values are shown in Fig. 1.

Table 1. Clinical characteristics and bone variables of the study population.

	Women (n = 59) Mean ± SD	Men (n = 39) Mean ± SD	p-value
Age (years)	69.1 ± 7.1	75.9 ± 6.7	<0.001
Weight (Kg)	68.219 ± 13.362	81.00 ± 13.461	<0.001
Height (m)	1.57 ± 0.075	1.68 ± 0.06	<0.001
BMI (Kg/m^2)	27.56 ± 4.38	28.55 ± 4.04	0.258
Fat mass (%)	43.79 ± 5.72	34.41 ± 5.76	<0.001
Fat mass (Kg)	29.974 ± 8.777	27.735 ± 8.247	0.209
Lean mass (Kg)	34.306 ± 5.459	45.700 ± 6.670	<0.001
SMI (Kg/m^2)	5.73 ± 0.88	7.15 ± 0.83	<0.001
ALM (Kg)	13.97 ± 2.16	20.27 ± 2.99	<0.001
ALM/BMI (m^2)	0.509 ± 0.0757	0.716 ± 0.0996	<0.001
WB BMC (kg)	1.80 ± 0.56	2.348 ± 0.439	<0.001
WB BMD (g/cm^2)	0.940 ± 0.114	1.087 ± 0.129	<0.001
L1-L4 BMD (g/cm^2)	0.923 ± 0.128	1.050 ± 0.206	<0.001
TH BMD (g/cm^2)	0.805 ± 0.108	0.887 ± 0.129	0.001
FN BMD (g/cm^2)	0.747 ± 0.113	0.827 ± 0.143	0.003
CSA (mm^2)	114.6 ± 12.6	131.4 ± 24.4	<0.001
CSMI (mm^4)	7.8 ± 1.6	11.4 ± 3.4	<0.001
Z (mm^3)	466.5 ± 68.3	661.9 ± 144.3	<0.001
SI	1.29 ± 0.27	1.32 ± 0.35	0.632
BR	3.79 ± 1.38	4.336 ± 1.79	0.093
CSI (g/kg-m)	3.54 ± 0.71	3.63 ± 0.71	0.546
BSI (g/kg-m)	1.11 ± 0.28	1.13 ± 0.27	0.744
ISI (g/kg-m)	0.231 ± 0.048	0.244 ± 0.050	0.177
Handgrip (Kg)	17.6 ± 3.5	27.4 ± 6.8	<0.001

ALM, Appendicular lean mass; BMC, bone mineral content; BMD, bone mineral density; BMI, body mass index; BR, buckling ratio; BSI, bending strength index; CSA, cross sectional area; CSI, compressive strength index; CSMI, cross-sectional moment of inertia; FN, femoral neck; ISI, impact strength index; L1-L4, Lumbar spine; SD, standard deviation; SI, strength index; SMI, skeletal muscle mass index; TH, total hip; WB, whole body; Z, section modulus.

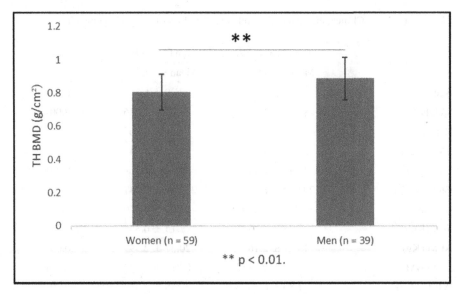

Fig. 1. Total hip bone mineral density values in both groups.

3.2 Correlations and Multiple Linear Regressions in Women

In women, weight and BMI were negatively correlated to CSI (r = −0.41; p < 0.01 and r = −0.43; p < 0.001 respectively), BSI (r = −0.28; p < 0.05 and r = −0.34; p < 0.01 respectively) and ISI (r = −0.43; p < 0.001 and r = −0.44; p < 0.001 respectively); these negative correlations remained significant after controlling for age (Tables 2 and 3). In addition, fat mass was negatively correlated to CSI (r = −0.31; p < 0.05) and ISI (r = −0.33; p < 0.01); these negative correlations remained significant after controlling for age (Tables 2 and 3). Age, fat mass percentage and handgrip were not significantly correlated to composite indices of femoral neck strength (Table 2).

Table 2. Correlation coefficients between clinical characteristics and composite indices of femoral neck strength in women.

	CSI (g/kg-m)	BSI (g/kg-m)	ISI (g/kg-m)
Age (years)	0.153	0.214	0.210
Weight (kg)	−0.410**	−0.286*	−0.436***
Lean mass (kg)	−0.386**	−0.302*	−0.401**
BMI (kg/m^2)	−0.436***	−0.347**	−0.449***
Fat mass (%)	−0.0527	−0.212	−0.067
Fat mass (kg)	−0.309*	−0.217	−0.326*
Handgrip (kg)	−0.166	−0.156	−0.185

BMI, body mass index; BSI, bending strength index; CSI, compressive strength index; ISI, impact strength index; * p < 0.05; ** p < 0.01; *** p < 0.001.

Table 3. Multiple linear regression analysis for the effect of independent variables on composite indices of femoral neck strength in women.

	Coefficient ± SE	t value	p-value
Dependent variable: CSI ($R^2 = 0.213$)			
Constant	4.503 ± 0.960	4.690	<0.001
Age (years)	0.016 ± 0.011	1.390	0.170
BMI (Kg/m^2)	−0.0759 ± 0.0190	−4.001	<0.001
Dependent variable: CSI ($R^2 = 0.128$)			
Constant	4.526 ± 1.098	4.124	<0.001
Age (years)	0.0098 ± 0.0125	0.789	0.433
Lean mass (Kg)	−0.0486 ± 0.0162	−2.997	0.004
Dependent variable: CSI ($R^2 = 0.000$)			
Constant	2.752 ± 1.189	2.315	0.024
Age (years)	0.0152 ± 0.0133	1.145	0.257
Fat mass (%)	−0.0060 ± 0.016	−0.367	0.715
Dependent variable: CSI ($R^2 = 0.0735$)			
Constant	3.554 ± 1.004	3.538	<0.001
Age (years)	0.0101 ± 0.0130	0.779	0.439
Fat mass (Kg)	−0.0237 ± 0.0105	−2.269	0.027
Dependent variable: BSI ($R^2 = 0.140$)			
Constant	1.130 ± 0.403	2.806	0.007
Age (years)	0.0089 ± 0.0049	1.814	0.075
BMI (Kg/m^2)	−0.0230 ± 0.007	−2.886	0.006
Dependent variable: BSI ($R^2 = 0.0892$)			
Constant	1.129 ± 0.450	2.509	0.015
Age (years)	0.0070 ± 0.0051	1.367	0.177
Lean mass (Kg)	−0.014 ± 0.0066	−2.183	0.033
Dependent variable: BSI ($R^2 = 0.285$)			
Constant	0.552 ± 0.472	1.169	0.247
Age (years)	0.0086 ± 0.00528	1.635	0.108
Fat mass (%)	−0.0007 ± 0.0065	−0.116	0.908
Dependent variable: BSI ($R^2 = 0.0457$)			
Constant	0.790 ± 0.409	1.932	0.058
Age (years)	0.0073 ± 0.0052	1.386	0.171
Fat mass (Kg)	−0.00602 ± 0.0042	−1.413	0.163

(*continued*)

Table 3. (*continued*)

	Coefficient ± SE	t value	p-value
Dependent variable: ISI ($R^2 = 0.223$)			
Constant	0.265 ± 0.0649	4.079	<0.001
Age (years)	0.0015 ± 0.0007	1.893	0.064
BMI (Kg/m^2)	−0.0050 ± 0.0012	−3.920	<0.001
Dependent variable: ISI ($R^2 = 0.155$)			
Constant	0.272 ± 0.0735	3.708	<0.001
Age (years)	0.0010 ± 0.0008	1.264	0.211
Lean mass (Kg)	−0.0033 ± 0.001	−3.101	0.003
Dependent variable: ISI ($R^2 = 0.000$)			
Constant	2.752 ± 1.189	2.315	0.024
Age (years)	0.0152 ± 0.0133	1.145	0.257
Fat mass (%)	−0.0060 ± 0.0165	−0.367	0.715
Dependent variable: ISI ($R^2 = 0.0991$)			
Constant	0.205 ± 0.0673	3.051	0.003
Age (years)	0.0010 ± 0.0008	1.234	0.223
Fat mass (kg)	−0.00165 ± 0.000	−2.354	0.022

BMI, body mass index; BSI, bending strength index; CSI, compressive strength index; ISI, impact strength index.

3.3   Correlations and Multiple Linear Regressions in Men

In men, age was negatively correlated to CSI (r = −0.39; p < 0.05), BSI (r = −0.37; p < 0.05) and ISI (r = −0.36; p < 0.05) (Table 4). Weight and BMI were negatively correlated to CSI (r = −0.52; p < 0.001 and r = −0.56; p < 0.001 respectively), BSI (r = −0.47; p < 0.001 and r = −0.55; p < 0.001 respectively) and ISI (r = −0.50; p < 0.001 and r = −0.51; p < 0.001 respectively); these negative correlations remained significant after controlling for age (Tables 4 and 5). In addition, fat mass and fat mass percentage were negatively correlated to CSI (r = −0.50; p < 0.01 and r = −0.50; p < 0.001 respectively), BSI (r = −0.45; p < 0.01 and r = −0.46; p < 0.001 respectively) and ISI (r = −0.50; p < 0.01 and r = −0.51; p < 0.001 respectively); these negative correlations remained significant after controlling for age (Tables 4 and 5). Handgrip was positively correlated to CSI (r = 0.37; p < 0.05), BSI (r = 0.35; p < 0.05) and ISI (r = 0.41; p < 0.01); the positive correlation between handgrip and ISI remained significant after controlling for age (Tables 4 and 5).

Table 4. Correlation coefficients between clinical characteristics and composite indices of femoral neck strength in men.

	CSI (g/kg-m)	BSI (g/kg-m)	ISI (g/kg-m)
Age (years)	−0.394*	−0.371*	−0.365*
Weight (kg)	−0.524***	−0.479***	−0.502***
Lean mass (kg)	0.0732	0.0365	0.159
BMI (kg/m^2)	−0.564***	−0.550***	−0.511***
Fat mass (%)	−0.508***	−0.464**	−0.516***
Fat mass (kg)	−0.501**	−0.459**	−0.503**
Handgrip (kg)	0.375*	0.358*	0.415**

BMI, body mass index; BSI, bending strength index; CSI, compressive strength index; ISI, impact strength index; * p < 0.05; ** p < 0.01; *** p < 0.001.

Table 5. Multiple linear regression analysis for the effect of independent variables on composite indices of femoral neck strength in men.

	Coefficient ± SE	t value	p-value
Dependent variable: CSI ($R^2 = 0.460$)			
Constant	9.883 ± 1.157	8.540	<0.001
Age (years)	−0.044 ± 0.012	−3.463	0.001
BMI (kg/m^2)	−0.102 ± 0.0211	−4.840	<0.001
Dependent variable: CSI ($R^2 = 0.109$)			
Constant	6.682 ± 1.545	4.324	<0.001
Age (years)	−0.041 ± 0.016	−2.532	0.016
Lean mass (kg)	0.0024 ± 0.016	0.147	0.884
Dependent variable: CSI ($R^2 = 0.284$)			
Constant	7.597 ± 1.146	6.631	<0.001
Age (years)	−0.028 ± 0.0153	−1.841	0.074
Fat mass (%)	−0.053 ± 0.0178	−2.970	0.005
Dependent variable: CSI ($R^2 = 0.369$)			
Constant	7.9671 ± 0.88	7.319	<0.001
Age (years)	−0.0414 ± 0.0137	−3.014	0.005
Fat mass (kg)	−0.043 ± 0.0112	−3.856	<0.001

(continued)

Table 5. (*continued*)

	Coefficient ± SE	*t* value	*p*-value
Dependent variable: CSI ($R^2 = 0.186$)			
Constant	5.329 ± 1.433	3.720	<0.001
Age (years)	−0.0331 ± 0.0163	−2.032	0.050
Handgrip	0.0298 ± 0.0160	1.861	0.071
Dependent variable: BSI ($R^2 = 0.425$)			
Constant	3.415 ± 0.454	7.521	<0.001
Age (years)	−0.015 ± 0.004	−3.170	0.003
BMI (kg/m^2)	−0.037 ± 0.008	−4.577	<0.001
Dependent variable: BSI ($R^2 = 0.0902$)			
Constant	2.303 ± 0.594	3.880	<0.001
Age (years)	−0.0151 ± 0.0063	−2.390	0.022
Lean mass (kg)	−0.00047 ± 0.0063	−0.0745	0.941
Dependent variable: BSI ($R^2 = 0.234$)			
Constant	2.546 ± 0.450	5.651	<0.001
Age (years)	−0.010 ± 0.006	−1.710	0.096
Fat mass (%)	−0.018 ± 0.007	−2.602	0.013
Dependent variable: BSI ($R^2 = 0.309$)			
Constant	2.677 ± 0.433	6.181	<0.001
Age (years)	−0.0148 ± 0.0054	−2.716	0.010
Fat mass (kg)	−0.0150 ± 0.0044	−3.373	0.002
Dependent variable: BSI ($R^2 = 0.162$)			
Constant	1.735 ± 0.553	3.139	0.003
Age (years)	−0.0118 ± 0.006	−1.880	0.068
Handgrip (kg)	0.0108 ± 0.00618	1.755	0.088
Dependent variable: ISI ($R^2 = 0.374$)			
Constant	0.649 ± 0.0882	7.366	<0.001
Age (years)	−0.0028 ± 0.00096	−2.975	0.005
BMI (kg/m^2)	−0.0065 ± 0.0016	−4.077	<0.001
Dependent variable: ISI ($R^2 = 0.0984$)			
Constant	0.405 ± 0.110	3.679	<0.001
Age (years)	−0.00264 ± 0.0011	−2.253	0.030
Lean mass (kg)	0.00086 ± 0.0011	0.736	0.467

(*continued*)

Table 5. (*continued*)

	Coefficient ± SE	*t* value	*p*-value
Dependent variable: ISI ($R^2 = 0.276$)			
Constant	0.510 ± 0.0815	6.260	<0.001
Age (years)	−0.0017 ± 0.0010	−1.590	0.121
Fat mass (%)	−0.0039 ± 0.00127	−3.083	0.004
Dependent variable: ISI ($R^2 = 0.347$)			
Constant	0.534 ± 0.0783	6.820	<0.001
Age (years)	−0.0027 ± 0.0009	−2.740	0.009
Fat mass (kg)	−0.0030 ± 0.0008	−3.804	<0.001
Dependent variable: ISI ($R^2 = 0.195$)			
Constant	0.328 ± 0.101	3.250	0.003
Age (years)	−0.0020 ± 0.0011	−1.749	0.089
Handgrip	0.0025 ± 0.0011	2.217	0.033

BMI, body mass index; BSI, bending strength index; CSI, compressive strength index; ISI, impact strength index.

4 Discussion

The current study conducted on a group of elderly Lebanese subjects mainly shows that indices of obesity such as body weight, BMI and fat mass are negatively associated with composite indices of femoral neck strength; most of these associations remained significant after controlling for age.

In our study, weight, lean mass, ALM, SMI, handgrip, BMC, BMD, CSA, CSMI and Z were higher in men compared to women. Our results confirm several previous reports conducted on elderly subjects [1–7]. However, CSI, BSI and ISI were not significantly different between the two genders. Further studies are necessary to better understand why composite indices of femoral neck strength are not different between elderly men and elderly women.

Although body weight and BMI are positive predictors of BMD, previous reports conducted on healthy adults showed that fat mass and BMI are negatively correlated to CSI, BSI and ISI [17–21]. These indices take into account FN BMD and body dimensions; when FN BMD is not enough to compensate for body weight excess, CSI, BSI and ISI values are low [14, 17–21].

In the current study, many negative correlations have been found between obesity indices (weight, BMI and fat mass) and composite indices of femoral neck strength. Our results are in line with those of our previous studies conducted on young healthy adults [17–21]. Moreover, the results of the current study confirm those of several studies that showed that indices of metabolic syndrome are negatively associated with composite indices of femoral neck strength in middle-aged and elderly subjects [23–27]. Kim et al. [23] showed that indicators of total and abdominal obesity are negatively associated with femoral neck strength in Korean adults. Ahn et al. [24] showed that insulin resistance is associated with low femoral neck strength, particularly against the compressive load. Ishii et al. [25] demonstrated that diabetic women have lower indices of femoral neck strength relative to load, consistent with their documented higher fracture risk. Srikanthan et al. [26] suggested that insulin resistance and in particular, hyperinsulinemia, may negatively affect bone strength relative to load in middle-aged Americans. Ishii et al. [27] demonstrated that composite strength indices are inversely related to C-reactive protein levels and partially explain the increased fracture risk associated with inflammation in premenopausal or early perimenopausal women.

Interestingly, fat mass percentage was negatively correlated to composite indices of femoral neck strength in men but not in women. In addition, lean mass was negatively correlated to these indices in women but not in men. Accordingly, there are some gender differences regarding the relationships between anthropometrics and composite indices of femoral neck strength in the elderly Lebanese population. More importantly, the negative associations between fat mass/fat mass percentage and these indices seem to be stronger in men compared to women. Endocrine reasons could explain these results. After menopause, fat mass excess is associated with increased estrogen and insulin circulating levels which positively influence bone health in women [3–7]. In elderly men, fat mass excess including abdominal obesity is associated with lower GH and testosterone circulating levels which negatively affect bone health [4, 23, 24]. Accordingly, the relative importance of lean mass and fat mass on CSI, BSI and ISI seems to be gender specific in elderly subjects.

Handgrip was positively correlated to these indices in men while no significant correlations have been observed in women. Previous studies conducted on young adults have shown positive correlations between physical activity level/physical performance level and composite indices of femoral neck strength [16, 20, 28–30].

The current study has several limitations. First, the cross-sectional design of this study cannot completely confirm causal relationships between obesity indices and femoral neck strength in the studied population. Second, the size of the studied population is relatively small; however, power values were sufficient to run the different statistical analyses. Third, we did not evaluate several factors (hormones, nutritional factors, physical activity level and sun exposure) associated with bone mass in adults and elderly subjects [31, 32].

5 Conclusion

In conclusion, the present study suggests that fat mass is a negative determinant of composite indices of femoral neck strength in elderly women and men. To our knowledge, this is the first study to demonstrate such correlations in the elderly Lebanese population and to detect gender differences regarding the associations between anthropometrics and composite indices of femoral neck strength. The results of the current study could be easily extrapolated to other populations since the relationships between fat mass and composite indices of femoral neck strength do not seem to be influenced by ethnicity/origin. Implementing strategies to reduce fat mass seems to be important in elderly women and men to prevent osteoporotic fractures. In addition, implementing strategies to reduce fat mass percentage and to increase muscular strength seems to be important in elderly men to prevent osteoporotic fractures. Future longitudinal studies which include different types of physical training programs are necessary to better understand the effectiveness of these programs on fat mass, composite indices of femoral neck strength and fracture incidence in the elderly.

Disclosure of Interest. The authors declare that they have no competing interest.

References

1. Maalouf, G., et al.: Epidemiology of hip fractures in Lebanon: a nationwide survey. Orthop. Traumatol. Surg. Res. **99**(6), 675–680 (2013)
2. Ayoub, M.L., et al.: DXA-based variables and osteoporotic fractures in Lebanese postmenopausal women. Orthop. Traumatol. Surg. Res. **100**(8), 855–858 (2014)
3. El Hage, R., Baddoura, R.: Anthropometric predictors of geometric indices of hip bone strength in a group of Lebanese postmenopausal women. J. Clin. Densitom. **15**(2), 191–197 (2012)
4. El Hage, R., Mina, F., Ayoub, M.L., Theunynck, D., Baddoura, R.: Relative importance of lean mass and fat mass on bone mineral density in a group of Lebanese elderly men. J. Med. Liban. **60**(3), 136–141 (2012)
5. El Hage, R., Bachour, F., Sebaaly, A., Issa, M., Zakhem, E., Maalouf, G.: The influence of weight status on radial bone mineral density in Lebanese women. Calcif. Tissue Int. **94**(4), 465–467 (2014)
6. El Hage, R., et al.: The influence of obesity and overweight on hip bone mineral density in Lebanese women. J. Clin. Densitom. **17**(1), 216–217 (2014)
7. El Hage, R., et al.: Lumbar spine bone mineral density in obese, overweight, and normal-weight Lebanese postmenopausal women. J. Clin. Densitom. **17**(1), 215–216 (2014)
8. El Hage, R.: Geometric indices of hip bone strength in obese, overweight, and normal-weight adolescent boys. Osteoporos. Int. **23**(5), 1593–1600 (2012)
9. Al Rassy, N., et al.: The relationships between bone variables and physical fitness across the BMI spectrum in young adult women. J. Bone Miner. Metab. **37**(3), 520–528 (2018). https://doi.org/10.1007/s00774-018-0949-5
10. El Hage, R., Courteix, D., Benhamou, C.L., Jacob, C., Jaffré, C.: Relative importance of lean and fat mass on bone mineral density in a group of adolescent girls and boys. Eur. J. Appl. Physiol. **105**(5), 759–764 (2009)
11. El Hage, R., Jacob, C., Moussa, E., Baddoura, R.: Relative importance of lean mass and fat mass on bone mineral density in a group of Lebanese postmenopausal women. J. Clin. Densitom. **14**(3), 326–331 (2011)
12. Allolio, B.: Risk factors for hip fracture not related to bone mass and their therapeutic implications. Osteoporos. Int. **9**(Suppl 2), S9–S16 (1999)
13. Faulkner, K.G., Cummings, S.R., Black, D., Palermo, L., Glüer, C.C., Genant, H.K.: Simple measurement of femoral geometry predicts hip fracture: the study of osteoporotic fractures. J. Bone Miner. Res. **8**(10), 1211–1217 (1993)
14. Karlamangla, A.S., Barrett-Connor, E., Young, J., Greendale, G.A.: Hip fracture risk assessment using composite indices of femoral neck strength: the Rancho Bernardo study. Osteoporos. Int. **15**(1), 62–70 (2004)
15. Yu, N., et al.: Evaluation of compressive strength index of the femoral neck in Caucasians and Chinese. Calcif. Tissue Int. **87**(4), 324–332 (2010)

16. Kim, B.-J., Ahn, S.H., Kim, H.M., Lee, S.H., Koh, J.-M.: Low skeletal muscle mass associates with low femoral neck strength, especially in older Korean women: the fourth Korea National Health and Nutrition Examination Survey (KNHANES IV). Osteoporos. Int. **26**(2), 737–747 (2015). https://doi.org/10.1007/s00198-014-2959-z

17. El Khoury, C., et al.: Decreased composite indices of femoral neck strength in young obese men. J. Clin. Densitom. **20**(2), 268–270 (2017)

18. Berro, A.J., Alwan, A., Zouhal, H., Maalouf, G., Rizkallah, M., El Hage, R.: Vitamin D level and composite indices of femoral neck strength in a group of young Lebanese women. J. Clin. Densitom. **21**(2), 308–309 (2018)

19. Alwan, A., et al.: Vitamin D level and composite indices of femoral neck strength in a group of young Lebanese men. J. Clin. Densitom. **19**(4), 492–493 (2016)

20. El Hage, R.: Composite indices of femoral neck strength in adult female soccer players. J. Clin. Densitom. **17**(1), 212–213 (2014)

21. Zakhem, E., et al.: Influence of physical activity level on composite indices of femoral neck strength in a group of young overweight men. J. Clin. Densitom. **23**(4), 596–603 (2020)

22. Sutter, T., Toumi, H., Valery, A., El Hage, R., Pinti, A., Lespessailles, E.: Relationships between muscle mass, strength and regional bone mineral density in young men. PLoS One **14**(3), e0213681 (2019)

23. Kim, H., Lee, S.H., Kim, B.J., Koh, J.M.: Association between obesity and femoral neck strength according to age, sex, and fat distribution. Osteoporos. Int. **28**(7), 2137–2146 (2017). https://doi.org/10.1007/s00198-017-4015-2

24. Ahn, S.H., Kim, H., Kim, B.J., Lee, S.H., Koh, J.M.: Insulin resistance and composite indices of femoral neck strength in Asians: the fourth Korea National Health and Nutrition Examination Survey (KNHANES IV). Clin. Endocrinol. (Oxf.) **84**(2), 185–193 (2016)

25. Ishii, S., et al.: Diabetes and femoral neck strength: findings from the hip strength across the menopausal transition study. J. Clin. Endocrinol. Metab. **97**(1), 190–197 (2012)

26. Srikanthan, P., et al.: Insulin resistance and bone strength: findings from the study of midlife in the United States. J. Bone Miner. Res. **29**(4), 796–803 (2014)

27. Ishii, S., et al.: C-reactive protein, bone strength, and nine-year fracture risk: data from the Study of Women's Health Across the Nation (SWAN). J. Bone Miner. Res. **28**(7), 1688–1698 (2013)

28. El Khoury, G., et al.: Maximal oxygen consumption and composite indices of femoral neck strength in a group of young overweight and obese men. J. Clin. Densitom. **21**(2), 310–311 (2018)

29. El Hage, R., Zakhem, E., Zunquin, G., Theunynck, D., Moussa, E., Maalouf, G.: Does soccer practice influence compressive strength, bending strength, and impact strength indices of the femoral neck in young men? J. Clin. Densitom. **17**(1), 213–214 (2014)

30. Berro, A.-J., et al.: Maximal oxygen consumption and composite indices of femoral neck strength in a group of young women. In: Rojas, I., Ortuño, F. (eds.) IWBBIO 2017. LNCS, vol. 10208, pp. 369–375. Springer, Cham (2017). https://doi.org/10.1007/978-3-319-56148-6_32

31. Chawla, J., Sharma, N., Arora, D., Arora, M., Shukla, L.: Bone densitometry status and its associated factors in peri and post menopausal females: a cross sectional study from a tertiary care centre in India. Taiwan. J. Obstet. Gynecol. **57**(1), 100–105 (2018)

32. Vitale, S.G., Caruso, S., Rapisarda, A.M.C., Cianci, S., Cianci, A.: Isoflavones, calcium, vitamin D and inulin improve quality of life, sexual function, body composition and metabolic parameters in menopausal women: result from a prospective, randomized, placebo-controlled, parallel-group study. Prz. Menopauzalny **17**(1), 32–38 (2018)

Neuroimaging

Image Fusion to Guide Decision-Making Towards Minimally Invasive Epilepsy Treatment

Pauly Ossenblok[1,2]([✉]) [ID], Stephan Meesters[1,2], Raf van Hoof[3], Albert Colon[1,3], and Louis Wagner[3]

[1] Foundation: Clinical Neuro-Science Projects, Amsterdam, Netherlands
P.P.W.Ossenblok@tue.nl
[2] Mathematics and Computer Science, Eindhoven University of Technology, Eindhoven, Netherlands
[3] Academic Center for Epileptology, Kempenhaeghe and Maastricht UMC+, Maastricht, Netherlands

Abstract. For the work-up of epilepsy surgery candidates, various medical imaging data are acquired for diagnosis. Software applications were designed for multimodality mapping of non-invasive and invasive imaging data to support the decision-making process towards minimally invasive treatment of these candidates.

The multi-modal imaging software imports from disparate sources of data the anatomical, functional and structural medical imaging datasets, brings the datasets in the same co-ordinate system and allows the user to browse through the medical imaging datasets obtained with the distinct imaging modalities. Convergence with 3D-mapping of depth electrode or stereo-EEG (SEEG) recordings completes the image fusion that may guide the decision for minimally invasive treatment.

Shown are the results of several pre-programmed sequences for creating multi-modal visualizations used to identify epileptic tissue versus functional areas, combining e.g., magnetic resonance images (MRI), Positron Emission Tomography (PET), Single Photon Emission Computed Tomography (SPECT), inverse solutions of high-density EEG and functional MRI. Regions of interest can be set to mark abnormalities visible at the images, while integration with depth electrodes translate the neurophysiology recordings into a 3D-space.

The applications are designed to provide the clinician with an easy-to-use tool to visualize in a multi-modal fashion the images acquired during the work-up of epilepsy surgery candidates. Integration with visualization of SEEG recordings in a 3D-space completes the decision-making process towards invasive treatment, aimed at rendering a patient seizure free while avoiding damage to eloquent cortex.

Keywords: Multi-modal imaging · Medical imaging data · Epilepsy · Stereo-EEG · Minimally invasive treatment

1 Introduction

The treatment of epilepsy surgery candidates is changing from open, surgical resections towards minimally invasive, image guided treatment procedures. There is no single diagnostic test for identifying the epileptogenic zone. Patients who are eligible for epilepsy

© Springer Nature Switzerland AG 2021
I. Rojas et al. (Eds.): BIOMESIP 2021, LNCS 12940, pp. 209–217, 2021.
https://doi.org/10.1007/978-3-030-88163-4_19

surgery commonly go through a lengthy research trajectory, from the initial diagnosis based on video-EEG and various magnetic resonance images (MRI), followed by a battery of imaging studies, such as positron emission tomography (PET), interictal-ictal single photon emission computed tomography (SPECT) and for a selection of patients by invasive EEG assessment. Apart from the technological advanced medical imaging systems others were developing hybrid solutions that integrate different layers of information, including neurological hardware and multi-model imaging software. Thus, currently, the acquisition and image registration procedures during an epilepsy surgery trajectory are clearly defined. However, the process of medical decision-making towards treatment is still highly intuitive and dependent on personal expertise and reports (still mainly on paper) of the professionals involved. A recent study showed that simultaneous visualization of different modalities, including PET, source mapping of high-resolution EEG and functional MRI (fMRI), compared to the visual assessment of the individual modalities, contributes to better postoperative outcomes and to a decrease in invasive examinations [1]. Therefore, in order to objectify the decision-making process towards invasive treatment, clinically easy-to-use multi-modal imaging software was developed for merging of anatomical, functional and structural brain imaging data of the individual patient. This contribution describes the procedures to bring together the different imaging modalities in the same coordinate system, to explore the images and visualize them together with stereo-EEG (SEEG) data into a 3D-space against the cortical anatomy.

2 Methods

The multi-modal imaging software was designed for multimodality mapping of the analysis results of non-invasive and invasive brain imaging studies and for visualization of these results against the cortical anatomy. The software will not include steps that involve operations on the data itself, like source mapping of surface EEG and MEG recordings and fMRI analysis. Figure 1 gives an overview of the data import, processing and visualization steps of the software. The software is capable of:

- Easy to use I/O options for medical imaging data.
- Pre-processing of medical imaging data.
- Presentation of fused brain imaging datasets in 2D- and 3D-MRI viewports.
- 4D-visualization of EEG source mapping data against the cortical anatomy.
- Depth electrode detection and visualisation against the cortical anatomy.
- Setting of custom regions/markers for identifying abnormalities.

2.1 Application Database

The multi-modal imaging software imports from disparate sources of data the anatomical, functional and structural medical imaging datasets and imports when eligible the data in the application database (Fig. 1, Layer I). The imported DICOM files are converted by the application into the NIfTI format internally used for all operations, which are saved in the application database. A project file is created containing in each entry the patient information as well as the project information. Furthermore, the project file contains a list of references to all the imported and processed data, together with their visual settings and registration information. The importance of this is that the creation of a project can be done by e.g., technical staff, while the clinician subsequently can explore the imaging data and select the most relevant of these datasets for diagnosis. As output 3D-images can be exported in a DICOM format to be used for guidance in the operating theatre.

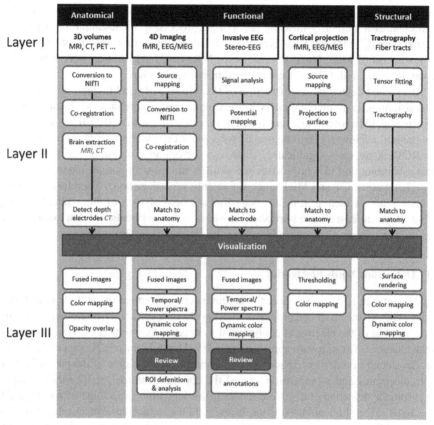

Fig. 1. An overview of the data import (layer I) processing (layer II) and visualization (layer III) steps of the multi-modality software applications (red framed boxes indicate external processing steps). (Color figure online)

2.2 Pre-processing

The medical imaging datasets are usually not recorded at the same time and/or location and may come from different scanners. The multi-modal imaging software brings the datasets in the same co-ordinate system using the Aladin algorithm, which maximizes a measure of similarity in intensity between corresponding pixels, using the correlation coefficient as a similarity measure [2]. For preprocessing we resample the Computer Tomography (CT) images to an isotropic spatial resolution of 1 mm^3 in order to match the resolution of MRI. Optimal settings for MRI-to-CT registration were investigated by van Rooijen et al. [3] and were adopted in our application.

Automated detection and extraction of skull from MR head images, also known as skull stripping, is a key component in most neuroimage pipelines [4]. In the study of Iglesias et al. [5] a robust, learning-based brain extraction system (ROBEX) is proposed. The method achieved a high degree of robustness on a variety of datasets, indicating that ROBEX provides significantly improved performance measures for almost every dataset combination [5]. In practice the skull is the most important landmark for the co-registration of CT and MRI, since CT mainly visualizes bone. Therefore, to ensure accurate brain extraction, it is necessary that the field of view of the medical imaging data contains at least a large portion of the skull. In our application 'brain extraction' is also used to remove electrode cables from the CT-data (Fig. 2a).

2.3 Detection Depth Electrodes

Depth electrode EEG or SEEG is the percutaneous placement of multiple depth electrodes to record the onset and propagation networks of seizure activity. Knowledge of the exact location of the electrodes is important as to properly interpret the EEG in relation to the anatomy. The software application DENS (Depth Electrode Navigator Software) was developed in order to provide fast and accurate identification of the position of the depth electrodes and visualization against the cortical anatomy [6]. The initial step of the automatic detection of depth electrodes is the detection of guiding screws in the CT-data, fixed to the skull and used to guide and hold the intracerebral electrodes (Fig. 2b). From a guiding screw, the software can extract the initial location and orientation of the depth electrode, which is used as a starting point to detect the entire electrode. Next, a region in the raw CT-data is sampled using a scoring algorithm to find the most probable tip of the electrode (Fig. 2c). Results indicate that in the vast majority of cases the depth electrodes can be automatically found. The localization of the electrodes versus the anatomy showed an acceptable small error when compared to manual positioning, with a deviation between the detected tip locations and the manually verified locations of 1.2 ± 0.5 mm [6]. Furthermore, interactive visualization software is developed to show the detected electrodes together with pre-operative MR-images, which enables the physician to confirm that the electrode is placed at the expected anatomical location (Fig. 2d).

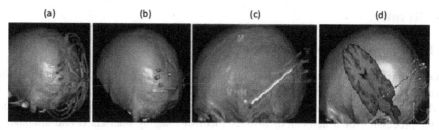

Fig. 2. The subsequent steps to detect the positions of the depth electrodes (a, c and d were taken from Meesters et al. [6]).

2.4 Exploration and Visualization of the Images

The (CE certified) software applications developed are used for image integration and advanced visualization to support the strategic decision-making during an epilepsy surgery trajectory (https://cnsprojects.nl/products/). One of the applications (MIND or Multi-modal Imaging for Neurological Diagnostics) was developed for bringing together brain images in the same co-ordinate system, for exploration (browsing) of these data and for visualization in support of minimally invasive treatment of neurological disorders. The user interface consists of three 2D-viewports, providing sagittal, coronal and axial views that are commonly used in medical visualization, a 3D-viewport used to visualize renderings of patient-specific models and supporting controls for data import and export. The user is allowed to browse through the medical imaging data types obtained with the distinct imaging modalities ((f)MRI, PET, SPECT, diffusion-weighted images (DWI), EEG/MEG source activity etc.) and set regions of interest (ROIs) to mark abnormalities visible at the images. The user is also able to assess the changes of resting state fMRI or EEG/MEG source maps as a function of time by browsing through the 4D-datasets: the 3D-images and the signal changing as a function of time, for example, in a given voxel or averaged for a ROI.

For a selection of patients with a complex type of epilepsy SEEG recordings may be considered. The challenge of SEEG is to translate the data from the neurophysiology recordings into a 3D-space and by showing together with the multimodality images created in MIND intuitive and insightful 2D-/3D-visualizations that may guide minimally invasive treatment. Following recording of seizure activity, the result of advanced analysis tools (equipotential or time-frequency maps) creates the possibility of dynamic source mapping of the activated epileptic networks in 3D-images. Furthermore, the clinician also is allowed when browsing through the 3D-images of the depth electrodes to highlight electrode contacts of interest by setting markers to annotate abnormal or evoked discharges identified in the SEEG-data.

Both applications (MIND and DENS) save its state in a project file, which can be imported by the viewer software (VIEWER), which has the same functionality for visualization of the medical imaging datasets as MIND and DENS. VIEWER allows multiple users to visualize the content of a prepared project to adapt, add or remove ROIs or markers at the depth electrodes for fine tuning together with colleagues or to discuss the strategy for treatment at the patient management meeting.

3 Results

3.1 Output of the Applications

As output MIND generates multi-modal visualizations of either voxel-based images (e.g., MRI, CT, PET, SPECT, DWI) or projections of EEG/MEG source mapping data or fMRI activation maps. In Fig. 3A the 3D-images are shown for a single patient obtained after processing of a number of distinct medical imaging datasets (Fluid-attenuated inversion recovery (FLAIR) MRI, PET and SPECT), all indicating an abnormality at the left frontal cortex. Concentric circles are set to zoom in on the abnormality visible at each of the images: red for the abnormality visible at Flair MRI, purple indicating the area reflecting the hypometabolism of the PET-image and green for the clear hypermetabolism of the SPECT-image. The ROIs visualized in the rendering of the cortex and patient's head illustrate how different diagnostic techniques depict different areas that might reveal different aspects of the epileptogenic tissue, but which ideally converge together with the electro-clinical information of the patient to a clinical hypothesis about the area to be resected to render a patient seizure free.

Creating a projection of functional activation maps on a cortical rendering requires an anatomical MRI volume in the patient-specific co-ordinate system. The pre-processed activation maps of fMRI and the EEG/MEG source maps are projected color coded on the cortical rendering. Figure 3B shows the fMRI activation maps associated with the language areas (left), which are dominant in the right hemisphere for the patient with the results shown in Fig. 3A. The EEG source (ESI) maps, which are the output of the BESA Research software (BESA GmbH, München), shown here superimposed with the equivalent dipole sources, localize the left and right auditory areas and the primary visual cortex of a healthy control (right).

Intracranial depth electrodes are commonly used to confirm the clinical hypothesis with regard to the regions of the brain that are responsible for epileptic seizures. In Fig. 3C (left) the depth electrodes implanted for a second patient are visualized as projections in the axial and sagittal slice and as a 3D-image of the Flair MRI. Visual review of the SEEG recordings indicated seizure onset at electrode LD (placed mid parietal), at the contacts 1–4 highlighted here in red. The primary spreading was maximal at electrode LL (placed parietal vertical) at the contacts 1–2 indicated here in blue. In VIEWER all the selected imaging datasets, including the depth electrodes are brought together and can be visualized as fused images (Fig. 3C, right), giving the clinician an immediate overview of the most relevant combinations of conceptual zones that might indicate epileptogenic tissue. For this patient the fused images of Flair MRI, the EEG correlated fMRI (EEG-fMRI) activation map and PET are shown, together with the highlights at the electrodes LD and LL. The ROI (in green) indicates the maximal values of the EEG-fMRI activation map, whereas PET reflects a widespread hypometabolism in the left central-parietal-occipital region.

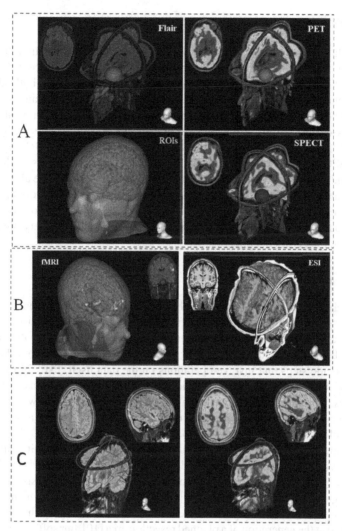

Fig. 3. A. Clockwise, the 3D-perpendicular slices and as insert an axial slice of Flair MRI, PET and SPECT and the ROIs, respectively colored red, blue and green, visualized in a 3D-rendering of cortex and skull. B. Projection of fMRI at the cortical rendering (left), with positive (red) and negative (blue) correlations and the EEG source (ESI) mapping results superimposed with the equivalent dipoles projected in the 3D-perpendicular slices (right). As insert is shown for both images the intersection with a coronal slice. C. The depth electrodes visualized as projection in an axial and coronal slice (upper left) and in the 3D-perpendical slices (bottom left) of the patients Flair MRI. The highlighted contacts 1–4 of electrode LD (red) indicate the seizure onset zone, while the blue highlighted contacts of electrode LL indicate primary spreading. Right, results for the same patient, but now shown as fused images with the result of the EEG-fMRI analysis (indicated by the green circle in the 2D-images and as a sphere in 3D) and with PET. (Color figure online)

4   Discussion

We report the combined use of distinct multi-modality imaging applications that provide the clinician with easy-to-use tools in the strategic decision-making process towards minimally invasive epilepsy treatment. Various techniques, encompassing both advances in existing techniques and new combinations of technologies, are enhancing the ability to define the optimal resection strategy for epilepsy treatment. The multi-modality applications discussed here are able to handle most of the techniques, distinguished by Zijlmans et al. [7] as 'established' diagnostics that are used by most centers (MRI, PET, SPECT, ESI and SEEG) and 'upcoming' diagnostics that are used in some centers and have shown clinical validity (task and resting state fMRI, MEG and EEG-fMRI. We already are able to incorporate tract representations of the optic radiation and plan to work on important white matter pathways, such as the uncinate fasciculus, inferior fronto-occipital fasciculus and arcuate fasciculus, to further aid planning and improve the safety of surgery for the more complex types of epilepsy.

4.1   Limitations

The applications developed import all the medical imaging data, enable to browse through these data and visualize the 3D-fused images for a range of different modalities and enable to pinpoint the area that most likely is responsible for the epilepsy of the patient by setting ROIs or markers at the depth electrodes. However, the software does not include steps that involve operations on the data itself, like, for example, the 'Multi-Modal Visualization Tool' [8], which is one of the available opensource software applications for multi-modality imaging. Data analyzed in external software can be visualized, reflecting e.g., the spatiotemporal dynamics of seizure activity as 4D-images in MIND or color coded at the depth electrode contacts in DENS [9].

Our challenge was to develop easy-to-use clinical tools to create intuitive and insightful 2D-/3D-visualizations of the multimodality imaging data together with SEEG, translated into a 3D-space, to come to the most accurate clinical hypothesis, which might define the so-called conceptual zones [7]. Contrary to EpiNavTM, which is software developed at the National Hospital for Neurology and Neurosurgery (https://www.kcl.ac.uk/) aimed at the generation of a planned resection area [10], our software applications are aimed to support the clinician (e.g., the neurologist, neurophysiologist, neuroradiologists etc.) at an earlier stage of the decision-making process and not for planning the resection area or guiding during surgery. Our applications might be the missing link between higher-level data analysis software and the neuronavigational systems for resection planning.

4.2   Conclusions

The significance of the applications discussed here is that they provide the clinician with an easy-to-use tool to visualize in a multi-modal fashion the images acquired during the pre-surgical trajectory to come, together with the electro-clinical information of the patient, to the most accurate clinical hypothesis. Integration with the visualization of invasive SEEG recordings in a 3D-space completes the decision-making process towards invasive epilepsy treatment, aimed at rendering a patient seizure free while avoiding damage to eloquent cortex.

Acknowledgements. The software applications were originally developed and evaluated at the Academic Center for Epileptology, Kempenhaeghe for patients who are candidate for epilepsy surgery. The Depth Electrode Navigator Software' (DENS) was developed as part of the Central Nervous System and Imaging (CSI) project and the Devices for NeuroControl and NeuroRehabilitation (DeNeCor) project funded by ENIAC Joint Undertaking (grant numbers 120209, 324257). A prototype of the software product Multi-modal Imaging for Neurological Diagnostics (MIND) was developed as part of the "Advancing Smart Optical Imaging and Sensing for Health" (ASTONISH) project that has received funding from ECSEL Joint Undertaking (grant no 692470).

References

1. Perry, M.S., Bailey, L., Freedman, D., Donahue, D., Malik, S., Head, H.: Coregistration of multimodal imaging is associated with favourable two-year seizure outcome after paediatric epilepsy surgery. Epileptic. Disord. **19**, 40–48 (2017). https://doi.org/10.1684/epd.2017.0902
2. Ourselin, S., Roche, A., Subsol, G., Pennec, X., Ayache, N.: Reconstructing a 3D structure from serial histological sections. Image Vis. Comput. **9**(1–2), 25–31 (2001). https://doi.org/10.1016/S0262-8856(00)00052-4
3. van Rooijen, B.D., Backes, W., Schijns, O.E.M.G., Colon, A., Hofman, P.A.M.: Brain imaging in chronic epilepsy patients after depth electrode (stereoelectroencephalography) implantation: magnetic resonance imaging or computed tomography? Neurosurgery **73**(3), 543–549 (2013). https://doi.org/10.1227/01.neu.0000431478.79536.68
4. Goceri, E., Songül, C.: Automated detection and extraction of skull from MR head images: preliminary results. In: International Conference on Computer Science and Engineering (UBMK), pp. 171–176 (2017). https://doi.org/10.1109/UBMK.2017.8093370
5. Iglesias, J.E., Liu, C., Thompson, P.M., Tu, Z.: Robust brain extraction across datasets and comparison with publicly available methods. IEEE Trans. Med. Imaging **30**(9), 617–1634 (2011). https://doi.org/10.1109/TMI.2011.2138152
6. Meesters, S., Ossenblok, P., Colon, A., Schijns, O., Florack, L., Boon, P.: Automated identification of intracranial depth electrodes in computed tomography data. In: IEEE 12th International Symposium on Biomedical Imaging (ISBI), pp. 976–979. IEEE Press, New York (2015). https://doi.org/10.1109/ISBI.2015.7164034
7. Zijlmans, M., Zweiphenning, W., van Klink, N.: Changing concepts in presurgical assessment for epilepsy surgery. Nat. Rev. Neurol. **15**, 594–606 (2019). https://doi.org/10.1038/s41582-019-0224-y
8. Felsenstein, O., Peled, N., Hahn, E., Rockhill, A.P., Folsom, L., Gholipour, T.: Multi-modal neuroimaging analysis and visualization tool (MMVT). arXiv:1912.10079 (2019)
9. Meesters, S., Ossenblok, P., Colon, A., Wagner, L., Schijns, O., Boon, P.: C modeling of intracerebral interictal epileptic discharges: evidence for network interactions. Clin. Neurophysiol. **129**(6), 1276–1290 (2018). https://doi.org/10.1016/j.clinph.2018.03.021
10. Nowell, M., Sparks, R., Zombori, G., Miserocchi, A., Rodionov, R., Diehl, R.: Resection planning in extratemporal epilepsy surgery using 3D multimodality imaging and intraoperative MRI. Br. J. Neurosurg. **31**(4), 468–470 (2017). https://doi.org/10.1080/02688697.2016.1265086

Data-Driven EEG Informed Functional MRI Combined with Network Analysis Successfully Identifies the Seizure Onset Zone

Pauly Ossenblok[1,2]([envelope]) [ORCID], Albert Colon[1], Liesbeth Geerts[3], Paul Boon[1],
Petra van Houdt[1], and Jan de Munck[4]

[1] Department of Research and Development, Academic Center for Epileptology,
Kempenhaeghe/MUMC+, Heeze, The Netherlands
P.P.W.Ossenblok@tue.nl
[2] Department of Mathematics and Computer Sciences, Eindhoven University of Technology,
Eindhoven, The Netherlands
[3] MR Clinical Science, Philips Healthcare, Best, The Netherlands
[4] Department of Radiology, University Medical Center, Amsterdam, The Netherlands

Abstract. A data-driven network analysis strategy was developed to apply EEG-informed functional MRI to identify the seizure onset zone in the presurgical work-up of epilepsy patients (n = 10). Instead of voxel-wise general linear model analysis the time series of independent components were correlated with the inter-ictal epileptic discharges density function, yielding the so-called epileptic network. We used eigenvector centrality mapping and a symmetry index to detect the epileptic independent component (ICE) out of the epileptic network. The location of the ICE was for 9 of the 10 patients studied concordant with the clinical hypothesis. Moreover, the clinical evaluation including the outcome of surgery indicated successful localization of the ICE for 6 out of 8 patients who had a resection. The robustness of the methods used to identify the ICE was demonstrated by evaluating the results of the patient study against the results of similar network analysis procedures applied to the functional MRI sequences of 10 healthy controls. In conclusion, the data-driven network analysis strategy successfully identifies the ICE. The concordance of the ICE with the clinical information, including outcome of the resection of the patients, is in support of the usefulness of EEG-fMRI as initial diagnostic tool in the presurgical work-up of epilepsy patients.

Keywords: Epilepsy · EEG-informed fMRI · Network analysis · Outcome of surgery · Resting-state fMRI

1 Introduction

Epilepsy patients who are candidate for epilepsy surgery usually go through an extensive work-up, from the initial diagnosis (history, video-EEG and MRI) followed by a battery of imaging studies, usually consisting of Positron Emission Tomography (PET), Single Photon Emission Computed Tomography (SPECT), inverse solutions of high-density

© Springer Nature Switzerland AG 2021
I. Rojas et al. (Eds.): BIOMESIP 2021, LNCS 12940, pp. 218–230, 2021.
https://doi.org/10.1007/978-3-030-88163-4_20

EEG and/or MEG and functional MRI. Additionally, quite a number of studies have shown that EEG-informed functional MRI (EEG-fMRI) may be helpful in the assessment of epilepsy surgery candidates [1–5], especially, in case of the involvement of more deep lying anatomical structures [6]. In most of the EEG-fMRI studies a voxel-wise general linear model (GLM) analysis was applied to fMRI sequences, with an Interictal Epileptic Discharges (IEDs) density function used as regressor, yielding the so-called EEG-fMRI activation pattern. However, this pattern can be complex, because it may reflect the region of onset of the IEDs, but also the sometimes widely distributed propagation areas [2]. In addition to those areas also spurious areas may be found related to noise, what makes fMRI activation patterns difficult to interpret, hampering the use in daily clinical practice. An alternative data-driven strategy for the analysis of fMRI sequences is the application of Independent Component Analysis (ICA). ICA is a technique that yields spatially independent components (ICs), with their associated time series [7], which can be related to resting-state-networks (RSNs) [8], but also to the epileptic network of a patient [9, 10]. Van Houdt et al. [10] used a priori spatial information derived from the resected area which rendered the patient seizure free plus the EEG-fMRI activation pattern to identify the IC which was related to the seizure onset zone, the so-called epileptic IC (ICE). Hermans et al. [11] showed that the ICE was similar for the condition before and after complete withdrawal of anti-epileptic drugs, independent whether IEDs occurred in the simultaneously recorded EEG or not. However, if there is no prior information available it is an open problem to determine which of the ICs resulting from ICA can be identified as the ICE.

To identify the ICE from the large number of ICs obtained from ICA without the use of a priori knowledge we here consider the use of network analysis. A multitude of studies have been published with a network analysis perspective using fMRI data of epilepsy patients [12, 13]. To study networks derived from brain imaging basic concepts of graph theory were introduced [14], suggesting that the seizure onset zone might be a hub, i.e., a node densely connected with neighboring nodes, in the epileptic network [15]. Eigenvector centrality can be used to indicate how densely the neighboring nodes are connected to other nodes [16], which could help to identify hubs in a network. Eigenvector centrality analysis was successfully applied to determine functional network differences between patients with Alzheimer's disease and multiple sclerosis compared to healthy controls [17, 18]. In this study we investigate whether eigenvector centrality analysis could be used to study functional networks on the individual level of epilepsy patients.

The goal of the present study is to develop and test a data analysis strategy to identify the ICE without the need of prior information. Spatial ICA was performed yielding the ICs and their corresponding time series, which were related to the IEDs using GLM analysis. From the ICs which were significantly related to the IEDs density function the IC was selected with the highest eigenvector centrality. However, it is well known that there may be an interaction between connectivity changes associated with epileptic transients and those associated with RSNs [12], with as most well-known example the lifting of the default mode network during the generalized spike-and-wave discharges [19]. By introducing a symmetry index as additional criterion we aimed at distinguishing the ICE from the RSNs, which are in most cases symmetrical. The concordance of the

ICE was evaluated against clinical information and for a number of patients studied (n = 8) the outcome after a resection.

At last, the robustness of the procedures for the selection of the ICE was evaluated against the results of eigenvector centrality analysis applied to the fMRI sequences of healthy controls. Based on the evaluation results the question will be addressed whether the identification of the ICE has added value as a tool to determine at an early diagnostic stage the suitability of the patient as an epilepsy surgery candidate.

2 Materials and Methods

2.1 Subjects

EEG-fMRI data were selected retrospectively for 10 patients with focal epilepsy who were candidates for epilepsy surgery. All patients underwent MRI assessment according to the epilepsy protocol used at the Academic Center for Epileptology, Kempenhaeghe/MUMC+ and a presurgical video-EEG examination (Heeze, the Netherlands). The inclusion criteria for this study were: (1) localization-related epilepsy established by standard electro-clinical examinations, and (2) a sufficient number of IEDs to yield an EEG-fMRI result [20].

Patients 1 till 5, and 8 and 9 were selected from an EEG-fMRI study which was approved by the Medical Ethics Committee of the University Medical Centre Utrecht and the local committee of the Academic Center for Epileptology, Kempenhaeghe/MUMC+. The recording of patients 6, 7 and 10 were clinical recordings. All patients gave informed consent for the study. Patients were notified that the EEG-fMRI study was not part of the standard pre-surgical evaluation and that it did not influence any of the clinical decisions.

The clinical characteristics of the patients included (5 male and 5 female, age range 22–60 years) are summarized in Table 1, including MRI abnormalities and the electro-clinical hypothesis based on previous EEG-recordings outside the MR scanner (including long term video-EEG monitoring), the resected brain area, and the outcome of the resection. The 10 healthy controls ((36.7 ± 18.2; 4 male) included for comparison participated also in the EEG-fMRI study of van Houdt et al. [10] and Hermans et al. [11]. The healthy controls study was approved by the Medical Ethics Committee of Maastricht University Medical Center. All volunteers gave informed consent for the study.

2.2 Data Acquisition

Data acquisition of the patients and subjects was identical to those described by Hermans et al. [11]. During the EEG-fMRI registration the resting-state fMRI data were acquired for 45 min using a T2*-weighted EPI sequence (TR = 2.5 s; TE = 35 ms; voxel size $3.2 \times 3.2 \times 3$ mm^3; 29–33 adjacent slices; bottom-to-top). Patients were instructed to lay still inside the scanner (Philips Achieva 3T, Philips, Best, The Netherlands) with their eyes closed. EEG data were acquired simultaneously with an MR-compatible EEG amplifier (MicroMed, Treviso, Italy) and an EEG cap containing 64 Ag/AgCl electrodes positioned according to an extended 10/20 system. Additionally, three current loops were attached to the cap to measure subtle movements inside the scanner [21]. Respiratory signals were obtained using a belt measuring abdominal expansion and vector cardio graphic (VCG) signals were recorded using MR compatible sensors connected to the MR-scanner. The VCG signal and the respiratory signal were both sampled with a sample frequency of 500 Hz. In addition, a T1-weighted MRI was acquired using a spin-echo sequence (reconstructed voxel size $1 \times 1 \times 1$ mm^3, 170 slices, TR 8.4 ms, TE 3.9 ms, flip angle 90°). For the healthy controls resting state fMRI datasets were acquired with a minimal length of 15 min using the same T2*-weighted EPI sequence as was used in the patient study.

Table 1. Summary of patient clinical data of patient 1..10 (P1,..P10): age/sex, MRI abnormalities and electroclinical hypothesis (column 1–4). Listed on the lobe level is the EEG-fMRI activation pattern, the ICE and the resected area (column 5–7). The last column lists the outcome of the resection according to the Engel classification. [Abbreviations: HS-R = hippocampal sclerosis-right; MTS- R/L = multiple temporal sclerosis-right/left; (F)CD = (focal) cortical dysplasia; O-L = Occipital-left; TP-R = Temporal Parietal-right; T-R/L = temporal-right/left; F-R/L = frontal-right/left; Ins-R/L = Insular-right/left; P-L/R = Parietal left/right; mT-R/L = mesioTemporal-right/left; Ci = Cinguli; AMT = Anterior MesioTemporal; MTR/MTL = Maximal Temporal Right/Left].

Patient	Age/Sex	MRI	Electroclinical hypothesis	EEG-fMRI (#ICs)	ICE	Resected	Outcome
P1	60/male	-	T-R	T-R, P (4)	T-R	T-R (AMT)	Engel II
P2	49/male	-	T-L	T-L, P-L, F (4)	T-L	NA	
P3	43/female	HS-R, 2 drains R	T-R, F-R	F-R (1)	F-R	T-R (MTR)	Engel Ia
P4	22/female	MTS-L	Ins-L, T-L	T-L, Ins-L, Ci (6)	Ins-L	T-L (MTR)	Engel IV
P5	51/male	CD T-L m	T-L	T-L, T-R (6)	T-L	T-L (AMT)	Engel 1b
P6	35/female	MTS-L	Ins-L, T-L	T-L, P-L (4)	P-L	Ins-L, T-L	Engel 1b
P7	33/female	-	F-L, T-L / generalized	F-L, F-R, P (8)	F-L	T-L (AMT)	Engel 1a/ Engel III
P8	24/male	MTS L; infarct O-L	T-L	T-L, P-L (5)	T-L	T-L (MTR)	Engel 1a
P9	42/female	Porencephalic cyst TP-R; MTS-R	mT-R and/or Ins-R	T-R, P-R (6)	Ins-R, T-R	Ins-R, T-R (MTR)	Engel II
P10	28/male	-	F-L	F-R, F-L, P (9)	F-L	NA	

2.3 Data Analysis

Preprocessing of the Data

An overview of the analysis pipeline used in this study is schematically depicted in Fig. 1A. fMRI data were spatially realigned, registered and spatially smoothed (Gaussian kernel with standard deviation 5 mm), while data points with abrupt head movement (> 0.5 mm) were ignored in the later GLM analysis. Confounders as described by Glover et al. [22] and de Munck et al. [23] and seven motion regressors resulting from realignment were extracted. Spatial ICA was performed using the MELODIC toolbox [7] and the FEAT toolbox [24] of FSL for removal of the confounding effects from the fMRI time series. Resulting in the IC maps which are the nodes of a functional network, as illustrated in Fig. 1B (bottom left), while correlation of the time series of the ICs establishes the edges. Preprocessing of the EEG removes the gradient and ballistocardiographic artifacts using average template subtraction and hierarchical clustering as described in de Munck et al. [25]. Current loop signals were used during visual review to avoid identification of motion artifacts as epileptic events [26]. Finally, IEDs (spikes, sharp waves, or spike-and-wave discharges) were visually identified in the EEG by an experienced EEG specialist, which resulted in an IED density function (no. of IEDs per volume scan).

Selection of IEDs-Related Components

To detect the IEDs related ICs a GLM analysis was applied according to the same procedure as for the standard voxel-wise GLM analysis as described by de Munck et al. [27]. The GLM analysis was performed in Matlab ((R2016a, The Mathworks, Inc.), while the time series of the IC as output of MELODIC were taken as input for the GLM analysis. P-values were corrected for multiple comparisons by the False Discovery Rate [28]. ICs that were significantly correlated to the IEDs density function were defined as IC_{IEDs}, the so-called epileptic network, as illustrated in Fig. 1B (upper right) for one of the patients studied. The p-threshold used for determining the IC_{IEDs} was usually lower than 0.01, depending on the number of significantly correlating ICs, but if in that case no ICs were selected the p-threshold was increased to at most 0.05.

Determining the ICE

Next, eigenvector centrality is computed for each node of the network. The IC with the highest eigenvector centrality was selected from the set of ICs of the IC_{IEDs}. To assure that all eigenvector centralities are positive values, the correlation $r_{nn'}$ between components n and n' are scaled as follows:

$$c_{nn'} = \frac{1 + r_{nn'}}{2} \tag{1}$$

In this way all matrix elements of the matrix C were positive and therefore also the components of the eigenvector with largest eigenvalue were positive [16].

A symmetry index (S) was calculated to distinguish the ICE from the default mode network components, which are, apart from the left and right executive control network, mostly symmetric.

$$S = \frac{IC_L \cdot IC_{R,Mirrored}}{|IC_L||IC_{R,Mirrored}|} \tag{2}$$

The IC_L were the spatial maps of the left side of the brain (in MNI space), and $IC_{R,Mirrored}$ were the spatial maps of the right side of the brain that were mirrored.

The IC of the set of ICs of the IC_{IEDs} with the highest eigenvector centrality (EC = 0.96) and a symmetry index less than 0.5 (S = 0.14) was chosen as the ICE, which is located for the example shown in Fig. 1B (bottom right) in the left insular area.

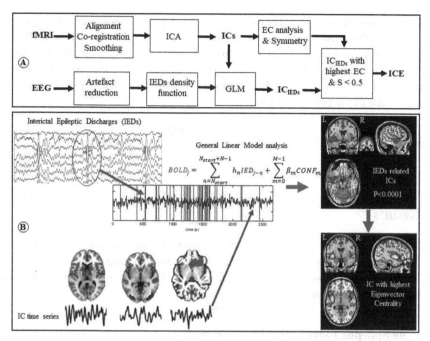

Fig. 1. A. Schematic overview of the pre-processing and analysis pipeline used in this study. [GLM = general linear model, ICA = independent component analysis, ICs = independent components, ICE = epileptic independent component, IED = interictal epileptic discharges, EC = eigenvector centrality, S = symmetry index; IC_{IEDs} are components which are significantly correlated to the IED density function] B. GLM analysis using the time series of the ICs and the interictal epileptic density function to create the regressor of interest to select IEDs related ICs, shown color coded in a coronal, sagittal and axial MR scan (upper right). The insert is the coronal view of the component maximal in the anterior cinguli. The location of the ICE is displayed in the coronal, sagittal and axial view of the MRI (bottom right).

2.4 Comparison with Healthy Control Networks

Eigenvector centrality analysis was applied to the ICs obtained for the fMRI sequences of 10 healthy controls, following the same procedures as for the patients. To determine whether the ICs of the healthy controls with the highest eigenvector centrality are part of an intrinsic RSN the fraction of overlap between these ICs and the RSN templates was calculated,

$$R_{RSN}^{IC} = \frac{N(IC \cup RSN)}{N(RSN)}, \tag{3}$$

where N(S) is the number of voxels of set S. The templates from FIND lab [29] were used for the detection of the RSNs. In order to be able to use these generic templates the spatial maps of the ICs were first normalized to MNI space using SPM5.

To determine the interaction between connectivity changes associated with epileptic transients and those associated with RSNs the overlap of the IC_{IEDs} and the RSNs was computed. Furthermore, to assess the robustness of the procedures for the selection of the ICE we calculated the overlap between the ICE and the RSNs and, on the other hand, the overlap of the ICs with the highest eigenvector centrality of healthy controls and the IC_{IEDs} of each of the patients studied.

$$R_{RSN}^{ICIEDs} = \frac{N(ICIEDs \cup RSN)}{N(RSN)}; \quad R_{RSN}^{ICE} = \frac{N(ICE \cup RSN)}{N(RSN)} \quad R_{ICIEDs}^{IC} = \frac{N(IC \cup ICIEDs)}{N(ICIEDs)}$$

$$(4)$$

3 Results

The ICE identified for each of the 10 patients studied is shown (Fig. 2) and discussed in relation to the clinical information of the patients. Furthermore, results are presented for the computation of overlap of IC_{IEDs} and RSNs and the overlap of the ICs with these networks of either patients or healthy controls.

3.1 The Epileptic Independent Component

Figure 2 summarizes the analysis results of the 10 patients studied, with in the first column the epileptic network (IC_{IEDs}) and in the second column the ICE. If we compare the results presented in Fig. 2 with the clinical information of the patients, including the outcome of the resection of 8 out of 10 patients studied as listed in Table 1, we may come to the following conclusions. The IC of the set of ICs of the IC_{IEDs} with the highest eigenvector centrality and $S < 0.5$ selected per patient as the ICE, is for 9 of the 10 patients studied concordant with the clinical hypothesis. 8 of the 10 patients had a resection. For 6 of these patients the Engel score was II or less, with for 4 of these 6 patients a resection which was concordant with the location of the ICE. For patient 6 (P6) the ICE with an eigenvector centrality of 0.91 and symmetry index $S = 0.09$ was, according to the clinical information, wrongly identified in the parietal lobe. Intracerebral video-EEG recordings guided for this patient the left-sided resection of the temporal lobe and the basal part of the anterior insula rendering the patient seizure free (Engel 1b). Patient 3 (P3) had a right hippocampus sclerosis and had implanted right frontal drains. The presurgical examinations mainly indicated a temporal seizure onset zone (SOZ), therefore a right temporal lobe resection was performed, which rendered the patient seizure free (Engel 1a). The resection of the patients who had an Engel score > II was not concordant with the ICE. Patient 4 (P4) developed insular and parieto-temporo-occipital seizures half a year after initial seizure freedom as result of a left temporal lobe resection. Patient 7 did not agree to pre-operative intracranial recordings and opted for a temporal lobe resection, with as result that frontal lobe seizures persisted. In conclusion, the clinical evaluation including the outcome of surgery indicated concordance with the clinical hypothesis for 9 out of 10 patients studied and successful localization of the ICE for 6 out of 8 patients who had a resection.

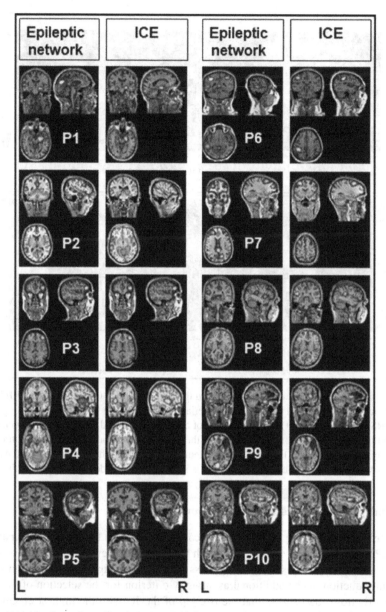

Fig. 2. Displayed are the epileptic network (IC_{IEDs}) and the epileptic independent component (ICE) (from top to bottom and left to right) of the 10 patients (P1...P10) studied in a coronal, sagittal and axial MR-scan.

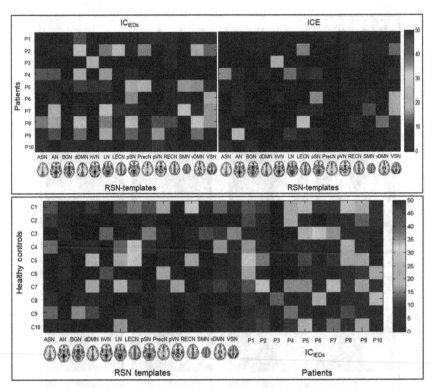

Fig. 3. Upper row: Fraction of overlap between the IC_{IEDs} of the 10 patients (P1,....P10) with the RSN-templates (left) and the fraction of overlap of the ICE of the 10 patients (P1,.......P10) and the RSN-templates (right). The percentage of overlap is indicated color coded between 0 and 50%. Bottom row: Fraction of overlap between the ICs with the highest eigenvector centrality of 10 healthy controls (C1,---C10) with the RSN-templates (left) and the IC_{IEDs} of the 10 patients studied (P1, ---P10). The percentage of overlap is indicated color coded between 0 and 50%.

3.2 Epileptic Versus Resting State Networks

From the upper part of Fig. 3 (upper left) it can be derived that the IC_{IEDs} of the patients (P1, ...P10) may overlap considerably with the RSNs. However, the overlap between the ICE and the RSNs was considerably less (Fig. 3, upper right), most likely because of the introduction of the additional asymmetry criterion for the selection of the ICE. Figure 3 (bottom row) shows that the overlap of the IC with the highest eigenvector centrality of the 10 healthy controls (C1,....C10) with the templates of the RSNs is high (the percentage of overlap is 65% $\pm$ 19%). However, when the overlap between the IC with the highest eigenvector centrality of healthy controls was determined with the IC_{IEDs} of the 10 patients (P1,.....P10) the percentage of overlap is much lower (26% $\pm$ 6%). Thus, apparently, the ICs of healthy controls with the highest eigenvector centrality overlap significantly with RSNs and less with the epilepsy related ICs (IC_{IEDs}) of the patients (Wilcoxon rank sum: p = 0.0002).

4 Discussion

The data-driven EEG-informed fMRI analysis strategy used in our study together with the chosen well founded network parameters enabled us to identify the ICE with high specificity. The concordance of the ICE with the clinical information, including outcome of the resection of the patients, is in support of the usefulness of EEG-fMRI as initial diagnostic tool in the presurgical work-up of epilepsy patients.

4.1 Analysis Strategy

The data-driven approach followed in our study reduces the problem of complex and diffuse fMRI activation patterns, because the number of statistical tests decreases and the signal-to-noise ratio of each statistical comparison increases, while this approach is in line with the assumption that all voxels of one component behave similarly [30]. However, the main challenge of our approach was to identify out of the set of ICs of the IC_{IEDs} the ICE, without the need of a priori knowledge. We introduced eigenvector centrality as a measure to study the connectivity in functional brain networks on the individual level of epilepsy patients by attributing network properties to ICs extracted from fMRI sequences. Eigenvector centrality mapping is a fully data-driven functional connectivity analysis at the single-subject level by computing nodes that may identify regional changes of a global brain network, which was shown for example for patients with Alzheimer disease [18]. In our study we demonstrated that eigenvector centrality mapping together with a symmetry index can be readily used to detect the ICE in an epileptic network. It was shown that despite the huge overlap of the IC_{IEDs} and the RSNs (see Fig. 3), which is in line with earlier reports of e.g. Centeno and Carmichael [12] and Gotman et al. [19], the overlap of the ICE and the RSNs is low. In conclusion, the overlap of the IC with the highest eigenvector centrality appeared to be specific for both, for patients and for healthy controls (see Fig. 3). For our study we choose a single network parameter (eigenvector centrality) to identify the ICE, because it seemed the most promising parameter for identifying the SOZ as node of the epileptic network.

4.2 Clinical Evaluation

The goal of this study was to develop tools to identify the fMRI activation pattern, the ICE, related to the SOZ, in order to predict at an early stage whether the patient might be a successful epilepsy surgery candidate. A simultaneous EEG and fMRI examination can be readily done within three hours, including preparations. Furthermore, the result of the present study demonstrated the usefulness of EEG-fMRI in the presurgical work-up of epilepsy patients. Preliminary results of a recently published systematic review and meta-analysis of Chakaborty et al. [31] show that there are no significant differences in surgical outcome between traditional standards of SOZ localization and resting state fMRI with ICA. Moreover, when adding to the initial diagnostics EEG-fMRI analysis the clinician may end up with a more precise localization of the presumed SOZ, which is especially important at this stage in case the patient is MRI negative, with the hope of moving towards less invasive screening methods.

4.3 Limitations and Future Directions

Demonstrating the usefulness of ICA as a fully independent technique for the detection of the epileptic network is still work in progress. We were able to unravel the quite often complex and diffuse fMRI activation patterns by using the time series of the ICs in the GLM and extract out of the IC_{IEDs}, without the use of prior information, the ICE. However, for our analysis approach we still depend on the occurrence of IEDs in the EEG, recorded during the limited time of fMRI scanning, to be used as regressor in the GLM. It has been reported, amongst others by Iannotti et al. [32], that epileptic networks are strongly connected with and without the effects of IEDs. However, most of the studies who reported on fMRI activation patterns obtained without the use of IEDs as regressor in the GLM were based on a priori knowledge [9–11]. Future studies should investigate whether other characteristics of the ICs can distinguish epilepsy related ICs from the ICs of healthy volunteers, without the use of an IEDs density function.

4.4 Conclusions

Data-driven EEG informed functional MRI combined with network analysis successfully identifies the ICE. Moreover, the ICE is identified with high specificity compared to the results of network analysis applied to fMRI sequences obtained for healthy controls. This result together with the concordance of the ICE with the clinical information, including outcome of the resection of the patients, argues for the use of EEG-fMRI as initial diagnostic tool in the presurgical work-up of epilepsy patients.

Acknowledgements. This study was part of the Central Nervous System and Imaging (CSI) project and the Devices for NeuroControl and NeuroRehabilitation (DeNeCor) project funded by ENIAC Joint Undertaking (grant numbers 120209, 324257). The authors thank, especially, the Academic Center for Epileptology, Kempenhaeghe for the contribution to the data collection, Kees Hermans for his contribution to the fMRI data analysis and Jan Verwoerd (clinical scientist at Philips Health Care, Best) for his contribution to the EEG-related fMRI sequences development.

References

1. Zijlmans, M., Huiskamp, G., Hersevoort, M., Seppenwoolde, J.H., van Huffelen, A.C., Leijten, F.S.S.: EEG-fMRI in the preoperative work-up for epilepsy surgery. Brain **130**, 2343–2353 (2007). https://doi.org/10.1093/brain/awm141
2. van Houdt, P.J., de Munck, J.C., Leijten, F.S.S., Huiskamp, G.J.M., Colon, A.J., Boon, P.A.J.M.: EEG-fMRI correlation patterns in the presurgical evaluation of focal epilepsy: a comparison with electrocorticographic data and surgical outcome measures. Neuroimage **75**, 238–248 (2013). https://doi.org/10.1016/j.neuroimage.2013.02.033
3. Tousseyn, S., Dupont, P., Goffin, K., Sunaert, S., Van Paesschen, W.: Correspondence between large-scale ictal and interictal epileptic networks revealed by single photon emission computed tomography (SPECT) and electroencephalography (EEG)-functional magnetic resonance imaging (fMRI). Epilepsia **56**(3), 382–392 (2015). https://doi.org/10.1111/epi.12910
4. Coan, A.C., Chaudhary, U.J., Grouiller, F., Campos, B.M., Perani, S., De Ciantis, A.: EEG-fMRI in the presurgical evaluation of temporal lobe epilepsy. J. Neurol. Neurosurg. Psychiatry **87**(6), 642–649 (2016). https://doi.org/10.1136/jnnp-2015-310401

5. Ito, Y., Maesawa, S., Bagarinao, E., Okai, Y., Nakatsubo, D., Yamamoto, H.: Subsecond EEG-fMRI analysis for presurgical evaluation in focal epilepsy. J. Neurosurg. **13**, 1–10 (2020). https://doi.org/10.3171/2020.1.JNS192567

6. van Houdt, P.J., Ossenblok, P.P.W., Colon, A.J., Boon, P.A.J.M., de Munck, J.C.: A framework to integrate EEG-correlated fMRI and intracerebral recordings. Neuroimage **60**, 2042–2053 (2012). https://doi.org/10.1016/j.neuroimage.2012.02.023

7. Beckmann, C.F., Smith, S.M.: Probabilistic independent component analysis for functional magnetic resonance imaging. IEEE Trans. Med. Imaging **23**, 137–152 (2004). https://doi.org/10.1109/TMI.2003.822821

8. Damoiseaux, J.S., Rombouts, S.A.R.B., Barkhof, F., Scheltens, P., Stam, C.J., Smith, S.M.: Consistent resting-state networks. Proc. Natl. Acad. Sci. USA **103**, 6 (2006). https://doi.org/10.1073/pnas.0601417103

9. Hunyadi, B., Tousseyn, S., Mijovic, B., Dupont, P., Van Huffel, S., Van Paesschen, W.: ICA extracts epileptic sources from fMRI in EEG-negative patients: a retrospective validation study. PLoS ONE **8**(11), e78796 (2013). https://doi.org/10.1371/journal.pone.0078796

10. van Houdt, P.J., Ossenblok, P.P.W., Colon, A.J., Hermans, K.H.M., Verdaasdonk, R.M., Boon, P.A.J.M.: Are epilepsy-related fMRI components dependent on the presence of interictal epileptic discharges in scalp EEG? Brain Topogr. **28**(4), 606–618 (2014). https://doi.org/10.1007/s10548-014-0407-1

11. Hermans, K., Ossenblok, P., Van Houdt, P., Geerts, L., Verdaasdonk, R., Boon, P.: Network analysis of EEG related functional MRI changes due to medication withdrawal in focal epilepsy. Neuroimage Clin. **9**(8), 560–571 (2015). https://doi.org/10.1016/j.nicl.2015.06.002

12. Centeno, M., Carmichael, D.W.: Network connectivity in epilepsy: resting state fMRI and EEG-fMRI contributions. Front. Neurol. **5**, 93 (2014). https://doi.org/10.3389/fneur.2014.00093

13. Dansereau, C.L., Bellec, P., Lee, K., Pittau, F., Gotman, J., Grova, C.: Detection of abnormal resting-state networks in individual patients suffering from focal epilepsy: an initial step toward individual connectivity assessment. Frontiers Neurosci. **8**, 419 (2014). https://doi.org/10.3389/fnins.2014.00419

14. Bernhardt, B.C., Bonilha, L., Gross, D.W.: Network analysis for a network disorder: the emerging role of graph theory in the study of epilepsy. Epilepsy Behav. **50**, 162–170 (2015). https://doi.org/10.1016/j.yebeh.2015.06.005

15. Crossley, N.A., Mechelli, A., Scott, J., Carletti, F., Fox, P.T., McGuire, P.: The hubs of the human connectome are generally implicated in the anatomy of brain disorders. Brain **137**, 2382–2395 (2014). https://doi.org/10.1093/brain/awu132

16. Wink, A.M., De Munck, J.C., van der Werf, Y.D., van den Heuvel, O.A., Barkhof, F.: Fast eigenvector centrality mapping of voxel-wise connectivity in functional magnetic resonance imaging: implementation, validation, and interpretation. Brain Connect. **2**(5), 265–274 (2012). https://doi.org/10.1089/brain.2012.0087

17. Schoonheim, M., Geurts, J., Wiebenga, O., De Munck, J., Polman, C., Stam, C.: Changes in functional network centrality underlie cognitive dysfunction and physical disability in multiple sclerosis. Mult. Scler. **20**, 1058–1065 (2013). https://doi.org/10.1177/1352458513516892

18. Binnewijzend, M.A.A., Adriaanse, S.M., Van der Flier, W.M., Teunissen, C.E., de Munck, J.C., Stam, C.J.: Brain network alterations in Alzheimer's disease measured by eigenvector centrality in fMRI are related to cognition and CSF biomarkers. Hum. Brain Mapp. **35**, 2383–2393 (2014). https://doi.org/10.1002/hbm.22335

19. Gotman, J., Grova, C., Bagshaw, A., Kobayashi, E., Aghakhani, Y., Dubeau, F.: Generalized epileptic discharges show thalamocortical activation and suspension of the default state of the brain. PNAS **102**(42), 15236–15240 (2005). https://doi.org/10.1073/pnas.0504935102

20. van Houdt, P.J., de Munck, J.C., Zijlmans, M., Huiskamp, G., Leijten, F.S., Boon, P.A.: Comparison of analytical strategies for EEG-correlated fMRI data in patients with epilepsy. Magn. Reson. Imag. **28**(8), 1078–1086 (2010). https://doi.org/10.1016/j.mri.2010.03.022

21. Masterton, R.A.J., Abbott, D.F., Fleming, S.W., Jackson, G.D.: Measurement and reduction of motion and ballistocardiogram artefacts from simultaneous EEG and fMRI recordings. Neuroimage **37**, 202–211 (2007). https://doi.org/10.1016/j.neuroimage.2007.02.060

22. Glover, G.H., Li, T.Q., Ress, D.: Image-based method for retrospective correction of physiological motion effects in fMRI: RETROICOR. Magn. Reson. Med. **44**, 162–167 (2000). https://doi.org/10.1002/1522-2594(200007)44:1%3c162::aid-mrm23%3e3.0.co;2-e

23. de Munck, J.C., van Houdt, P.J., Gonçalves, S.I., van Wegen, E., Ossenblok, P.P.W.: Novel artefact removal algorithms for co-registered EEG/fMRI based on selective averaging and subtraction. Neuroimage **64**, 407–415 (2013). https://doi.org/10.1016/j.neuroimage.2012.09.022

24. Beall, E.B., Lowe, M.J.: The non-separability of physiologic noise in functional connectivity MRI with spatial ICA at 3T. J. Neurosci. Methods **191**, 263–276 (2010). https://doi.org/10.1016/j.jneumeth.2010.06.02

25. de Munck, J.C., Gonçalves, S.I., Faes, T.J.C., Kuijer, J.P., Pouwels, P.J.W., Heethaar, R.M.: A study of the brain's resting state based on alpha band power, heart rate and fMRI. Neuroimage **42**, 111–121 (2008). https://doi.org/10.1016/j.neuroimage.2008.04.244

26. Hermans, K., de Munck, J.C., Verdaasdonk, R., Boon, P., Krausz, G., Prueckl, R.: Effectiveness of reference signal-based methods for removal of EEG artifacts due to subtle movements during fMRI scanning. IEEE Trans. Biomed. Eng. **63**(12), 2638–2646 (2016). https://doi.org/10.1109/TBME.2016.2602038

27. de Munck, J.C., Gonçalves, S.I., Huijboom, L., Kuijer, J.P.A., Pouwels, P.J.W., Heethaar, R.M.: The hemodynamic response of the alpha rhythm: an EEG/fMRI study. Neuroimage **35**, 1142–1151 (2007). https://doi.org/10.1016/j.neuroimage.2007.01.022

28. Benjamini, Y., Hochberg, Y.: Controlling the false discovery rate: a practical and powerful approach to multiple testing. J. R. Stat. Soc. Series B **57**, 289–300 (1995). https://doi.org/10.1016/s0166-4328(01)00297-2

29. Shirer, W.R., Ryali, S., Rykhlevskaia, E., Menon, V., Greicius, M.D.: Decoding subject-driven cognitive states with whole-brain connectivity patterns. Cereb. Cortex **22**, 158–165 (2012). https://doi.org/10.1093/cercor/bhr099

30. Heller, R., Stanley, D., Yekutieli, D., Rubin, N., Benjamini, Y.: Cluster-based analysis of FMRI data. Neuroimage **33**, 599–608 (2006). https://doi.org/10.1016/j.neuroimage.2006.04.233

31. Chakraborty, A.R., Almeida, N.C., Prather, K.Y., O'Neal, C.M., Wells, A.A., Chen, S.: Resting-state functional magnetic resonance imaging with independent component analysis for presurgical seizure onset zone localization: a systematic review and meta-analysis. Epilepsia **00**, 1–11 (2020). https://doi.org/10.1111/epi.16637

32. Iannotti, G.R., Grouiller, F., Centeno, M., Carmichael, D., Abela, E., Wiest, R.: Epileptic networks are strongly connected with and without the effects of interictal discharges. Epilepsia **57**(7), 1086–1096 (2016). https://doi.org/10.1111/epi.13400

Modern Neurophysiological Research of the Human Brain in Clinic and Psychophysiology

Sergey Lytaev[(✉)] [ID]

St. Petersburg Federal Research Center of the Russian Academy of Sciences, St. Petersburg
199178, Russia
mail@physiolog.spb.ru

Abstract. The article presents a comparative classification of most of the known methods for studying the human brain in clinic and psychophysiology. The informativeness of methods for assessing the state of the brain by electric and magnetic dipoles, as well as by various parameters of blood flow, is discussed. In conclusion, a comparative table of the main methods of neuroimaging is given. The table is based on research levels and time – from milliseconds to several years. The most sensitive methods are EEG, ERPs, MEG, ECoG, the less sensitive ones are fMRI, USDG, NIRS, EDA. PET is even less sensitive. A number of methods exist for the study of nuclei, neurons, synapses and separate sections in biophysics and molecular biology.. Along with general methodological approaches, some historical aspects of the development of methods of clinical neurophysiology are highlighted.

Keywords: EEG · Evoked potentials · Brain computer interface · Electro-dermal activity · Near-infrared spectroscopy

1 Introduction

Neurosciences in the XXI century characterized by the simultaneous development of new technologies of surgical neurosurgical interventions and visualization systems (neuronavigation, neuromonitoring, mapping, etc.) of the brain state. Preoperative morphological diagnostics is carried out according to the data of magnetic resonance imaging (MRI), computed tomography, angiography and MRI angiography. Physiological support is provided by functional MRI, positron emission tomography (PET), magnetoencephalography, traditional electroencephalography (EEG), evoked potentials (EP). Doppler ultrasound (USDG), functional MRI, PET, functional stereotaxis (using the methods of dipole localization, neuronavigation and 3-dimensional Lissajous trajectory), neurovideoendoscopy allow recording the brain state in real time [8, 9, 12, 18].

2 Electroencephalography. Neurophysiological Basis

Electroencephalography is a method for brain research based on recording its electrical potentials. According to its intended purpose, the EEG can be divided into clinical and

© Springer Nature Switzerland AG 2021
I. Rojas et al. (Eds.): BIOMESIP 2021, LNCS 12940, pp. 231–241, 2021.
https://doi.org/10.1007/978-3-030-88163-4_21

physiological. Clinical EEG is used to diagnose brain diseases. These are verification of electrical activity disorders, localization of injuries, prediction of outcomes of brain damage, etc. Physiological EEG allows one to reveal correlates of mental functions in the state of electrical activity of the brain. This makes it possible to reveal the regularities of the functioning of a healthy brain, and the results obtained can be used for professional selection, dynamic observation of the functional state of people during their professional activities [19].

The concept of statistical display of the activity of multiple neural potentials based on the total EEG data seems to be the most adequate at present. The concept suggests that EEG is the result of a complex summation of the electrical potentials of many neurons working independently. The bioelectrical activity of the brain reflects the gradual fluctuations of somatodendritic potentials corresponding to postsynaptic excitatory and inhibitory potentials.

The EEG in summary reflects the functional activity of huge populations of neurons. As a result, EEG is a process caused by the activity of a huge number of neural generators. The generated electric field appears to be heterogeneous throughout the brain and changing over time. In this regard, between two points above the brain or between points above the brain and distant from it, there are variable potential differences (dipoles), the registration of which is the subject of electroencephalography.

The priority in recording the electrical activity of the brain is shared by the England surgeon and physiologist Richard Caton (1842–1926) and the Russian physiologist Vasily Danilevsky (1852–1939). At 1875, independently of each other, Caton and Danilevsky have recorded the total bioelectric activity on the open brain of a dog in an acute experiment. Thus, 1875 can reasonably be considered one of the key points in the history of neurophysiology – the total electrical activity of the cortex was recorded in an animal with an open brain [3].

The creation of the electroencephalography method is closely related to the name of the Russian physiologist Vladimir Pravdich-Neminsky (1879–1952). In 1912–1913 he has completed and published articles in which he proved the possibility of recording the electrical activity of the brain from the surface of the head through the meninges, the bones of the skull and intact skin. In studies carried out in acute experiments on immobilized anesthetized dogs, Pravdich-Neminsky registers the electrical activity of the cerebral cortex from the intact scalp.

Thus, the date of birth of the experimental EEG can be safely recognized as 1912–1913, when the electrical activity of the brain in an animal was first recorded through the bones of the skull and intact skin.

Modern clinical EEG begins in 1929, when the German psychiatrist Hans Berger publishes an article "Uber das Elektroenzephalogramm des Menschen" [1]. Since the 1920s, Berger has been developing a method for recording the electrical activity of the human brain. For work, he independently designed an original device ("Berger's EEG machine"). Berger identified two types of electrical activity – with a frequency of about 10 Hz, which he designated as the alpha rhythm, and with a higher frequency (beta rhythm). For the first time, the characterization of the alpha rhythm was given, which occurs when the eyes are closed, and when the eyes are opened or upon sensory stimulation, the alpha rhythm is replaced by beta activity. It was also reported that the nature of the "brain waves" changes depending on the functional state of the brain, during sleep, under general anesthesia and hypoxia. It was shown that the nature of activity in a healthy person and in a patient with epilepsy is significantly different. Berger proposed not only the term "electroencephalogram" itself, but also the term "EEG".

The method of clinical EEG gained recognition only after the work of Berger was supported by the master of electrophysiology Lord Edgar Douglas Adrian – Nobel winner in Physiology or Medicine (1932), which he received together with Charles Sherrington for researching the functional activity of neurons. At a meeting of the Physiological Society in Cambridge in May 1934, Adrian and Matthews demonstrated with their demonstration the connection between the "Berger's rhythm", as they called the alpha rhythm, with the bioelectrical activity of the brain. The period from the second half of the 1930s to the early 1950s was marked by the rapid development of the EEG. The method was widely introduced into clinical practice. "Pioneers of electroencephalography": Gray Walter, Herbert Jasper and Wilder Penfield, spouses Frederick and Erna Gibbs, Nathaniel Kleitman – laid the foundations of classical neurophysiology [3, 10].

3   Brain Evoked Potentials

One of the techniques that are most successfully used in the study of perception processes is the method of recording the evoked potentials (EP) of the brain. Described for the first time by Richard Caton, above mentioned, in 1875, almost 50 years before the discovery of the EEG, the EP method now represents a "spatio-temporal window" of brain activity [19]. EP is the electrical response of the brain structure to a stimulus or to a certain event, a change in the internal or external situation. Therefore, in psychophysiological research, there is another name – event-related potentials (ERPs). As a rule, an oscillation in response to a certain event is recorded within a time interval of 300–400 ms.

EP registration is carried out in two ways: in response to single stimuli (single EP) and in response to a series of stimuli with simultaneous summation of evoked responses (averaged EP). In the latter case, the use of special computing devices is required, which extract a useful signal from the noise generated by spontaneous brain activity.

Before a wave self-oscillatory process, called EP, is formed, the registered dipoles must undergo a series of transformations in the biological amplifier. In addition to increasing the apparent amplitude of the signal, the amplifier performs the function of filtering (not removing artifacts and network noise) of the signal in a certain frequency range. So, for example, if the EEG is recorded in the bandwidth of frequencies from 0.5 to 30 Hz, then EPs require an expansion of the upper frequency up to 100 Hz for visual EPs and even up to 1000–2000 Hz for auditory (see Fig. 1) and somatosensory EPs during intraoperative monitoring in neurosurgery [9, 12].

The registered EP consists of a number of components reflecting the alternation of successive phases of polarization and depolarization of neuronal populations and the inclusion of an increasing number of brain structures in the analysis of the incoming signal. The time interval from the moment the signal is applied to the completion of the formation of the analyzed components is called the analysis epoch. Typically, studies requiring an assessment of the state of cognitive functions use an analysis epoch of 400 ms, although this can be extended to 1000 and 2000 ms [14]. Depending on the stimulus used and, accordingly, on the objectives of the study, cerebral EPs are subdivided by modality into visual (VEP), auditory (AEP), and somatosensory (SEP). These three basic modalities have been adapted in both clinical and psychophysiological research.

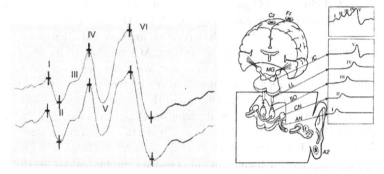

Fig. 1. The original short-latency auditory evoked potential registered during neurosurgery (left) and brain generators (right). AN – acoustical nerve, CN – cochlear nucleus, SO – top olive, LL – lateral lemniscuses, MG – medial geniculus. Epoch of analyze – 10 ms.

3.1 Evoked Potentials and Perception

The registered EP consists of a number of components reflecting the alternation of successive phases of polarization and depolarization of neuronal populations and the inclusion of an increasing number of brain structures in the analysis of the incoming signal. The time interval from the moment the signal is applied to the completion of the formation of the analyzed components is called the analysis epoch. Typically, studies requiring an assessment of the state of cognitive functions use an analysis epoch of 400 ms, although this can be extended to 1000 and 2000 ms [14]. Depending on the stimulus used and, accordingly, on the objectives of the study, cerebral EPs are subdivided by modality into visual (VEP), auditory (AEP), and somatosensory (SEP). These three basic modalities have been adapted in both clinical and psychophysiological research.

In terms of their physiological genesis, EP components are heterogeneous. Early waves (up to 70–100 ms) represent the primary response of nerve structures (nuclei of the brain stem, projection cortex) to the arrival of impulses along sensory pathways. Later components are associated with complex processes of intracerebral interaction, including the arrival of impulses from other parts of the cortex and subcortical structures, including nonspecific centers of the brain stem, centers of emotions and motivations. Between the early and late EP waves, there is a group of waves of mixed genesis due to sensory and non-sensory influences. In many psychophysiological studies carried out over the past 2–3 decades in various laboratories around the world, and during neurosurgical operations, the nature of the relationship between physiological and psychological indicators of perception had much in common. Early sensory EP waves (with PL up to 100 ms) show a high correlation with the indicator of sensory sensitivity, and the late ones, including the P300 wave, with the indicator of the decision criterion. Intermediate EP components with a PL of 100–200 ms revealed a double correlation – both with the sensitivity index and the decision criterion [3].

Informative data on the essence of mental processes that make up the content of the third stage of perception were obtained in studies devoted to the analysis of the functional meaning and informational significance of the wave P300, which shows the highest correlation with the decision-making criterion. It should be said that over the past 40 years a phenomenon, and even a paradigm "P300" (see Fig. 2), has formed in the literature, combining not one positive oscillation with a peak latency of 300 ms, but a whole complex of waves following this period of time. The generalizing result of these works was the proposition that P300 reflects an important stage of cognitive processes associated with the recognition of a stimulus based on the comparison of available information with memory and the expectation formed on its basis [15].

3.2 Registration of Magnetic Fields

In addition to recording the electric component of the field generated around the head, systems for assessing the magnetic fields of the brain are being actively developed. It is believed that their possible sources are electrical currents arising in synapses and synchronously activating pyramidal neurons. The apical dendrites of these cells are located parallel to each other and perpendicular to the surface of the cortex, where primary intracranial currents are generated, forming an electric circle in the surrounding tissues. Consequently, the magnetoencephalogram (MEG) of a living brain is mainly a sensor of the activity of the fissural cortex.

The most interesting results were obtained in the study of magnetic EPs in response to auditory stimulation. It was found that the localization of the source of cortical auditory magnetic EPs moves with a change in the frequency of stimuli. This phenomenon is called the tonotopic organization of the auditory cortex. In order to localize the dipole of the pathological focus, according to the MRI data, the dimensions of the Hershel's gyrus (the primary projection zone of the auditory analyzer located in the temporal lobe) in different people were determined [6].

One of the essential features of MEG registration is the use of superconducting quantum interferometric device (SQUID). Such devices have the highest sensitivity among all existing magnetic flux detectors. Their principle of operation is based on the use of the magnetic flux quantization effect and the Josephson tunneling effect. Thus, the SQUID is a "magnetic flux-voltage" converter, which generates a voltage at the output that periodically changes depending on the applied magnetics flux with a period equal to one flux quantum. By analogy with bioelectric EPs, the registration of magnetic EPs in order to suppress the noise of SQUIDs and spontaneous MEG requires a large number of accumulations (tens and hundreds). To build brain maps, you need to use from 30 to 70 (up to 200) registration points.

The cost of devices for recording brain magnetic fields is tens of times higher than the cost of traditional EEG-EP.

3.3 Systems "Brain-Computer Interface" Based on P300

Last two decades practical studies of the P300 ERP component have been associated with brain-computer interface (BCI) systems, which, in addition to solving physiological and psychological problems, have medical and social significance. Modern BCI systems can use a number of electrophysiological signals – visual EPs, slow cortical potentials, alpha and beta EEG rhythm, and the P300 component of evoked potentials [16]. In Fig. 2 shows the original visual event-related potential during perception of oddball visual image. The red circle marks the late components that make up the P300 paradigm.

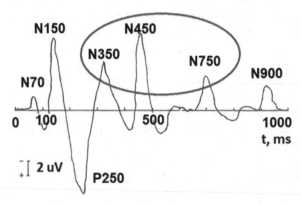

Fig. 2. Visual evoked potential (numbers – time, ms) according to the 10–20 system during the perception of visual image (oddball). Analysis time – 1000 ms.

In the BCI system, the digitized bioelectric signal recorded from the scalp is sent to the processing level, where the necessary features are extracted by applying spatial filtering and spectral analysis [23]. To extract useful information BCI can use temporal parameters of the signal (peak latency of the EP, P300 components), frequency characteristics of the EEG rhythms, spatial parameters, as well as a combination of all of the above characteristics [4].

The P300 wave attracted a lot of attention in BCI studies [7, 20]. Since the P300 only elicits oddball (strange) stimuli that require special attention from the user, it can be used as control signals in the BCI to select the desired choice. Users (subjects) can influence the amplitude of the P300, paying more attention to a specific event. Therefore, the P300 is used in many BCI systems to reveal intentions or information hidden in the EEG [16].

Persons with disabilities can use the P300-based BCI for communication [21]. The P300 spelling system (speller) is proposed, which allows subjects to transmit a sequence of letters to a computer. To create a "weird" oddball paradigm, a 6x6 matrix containing letters of the alphabet and numbers is displayed on the computer screen. A person can choose a specific sign by focusing attention on it. The BCI can also be used to drive a wheelchair. With the P300 BCI system, the user can select a destination in the menu by counting the number of flashes of the destination. Further, the wheelchair moves to the selected and desired destination along a predetermined path [16].

In addition to the wheelchair, an important application for people with severe motor impairments is the control of neuroprosthetic devices. BCIs can be used to control limb movements, for example, a robotic arm. It has been shown that BCIs based on the activity of cortical neurons are able to control three-dimensional movements of a robot arm [13].

BCI systems can communicate in paralyzed patients suffering from neurological or neuromuscular diseases (eg, amyotrophic lateral sclerosis (ALS). As the disease progresses, various conditions can be distinguished. In a completely blocked state, voluntary muscle control is lost. Many ALS patients achieve this conditions, have visual impairments and may not be able to use BCIs through the visual sensory system. Usually in these patients the auditory system is not damaged, therefore, studying the possibility of using BCIs based on auditory signals may be of great importance [23].

In the future, P300-based BCI systems are being considered for controlling combat information posts and computer virtual games.

4 Electrodermal Reactions. Super-Slow Physiological Processes

Electrodermal activity (EDA) is a set of bioelectric phenomena recorded from the skin surface. The potential level, conductivity and resistance of the skin reflect the state of the autonomic nervous system and are widely used in psychophysiology to assess the emotional sphere, neuropsychic tension, selective attention, etc.

E. Dubois-Reymond was the first to describe the potentials of the skin in 1848. He showed that the biocurrents of the isolated frog skin are superior in magnitude to the nervous and muscular ones [5].

Carl Jung (1907) showed the connection between galvanic skin response (GSR) and the degree of emotional experience. In GSR, Jung saw an objective physiological "window" into unconscious processes postulated by his teacher Sigmund Freud. Thus, from the beginning of the twentieth century GSR has become one of the most common indicators. This was due to the ease of its registration and the seeming simplicity of the interpretation of measurements. It has been widely and relatively successfully used to control the state of a person when performing various types of activities, in the research of the emotional-volitional sphere and intellectual activity. Galvanic skin response is one of the main indicators in "lie detectors".

Sweat glands are the source of EDA generation. Simultaneous recording of EDA from the skin and the secretion of sweat by a single sweat gland revealed that sweat secretion coincides with the deviation of the skin potential in the negative direction, and the latter, in turn, coincides with a decrease in skin resistance in response to a stimulus [2].

Although acetylcholine is the neurotransmitter for sweat glands, they are under the control of the sympathetic nervous system (for example, destruction of the sympathetic nervous system on one side of the body leads to the destruction of EDA only on that side). The sweat glands receive influences from the cortex and deep structures of the brain – the hypothalamus and the reticular formation. EDA is a suprasegmentally somato-vegetative reflex, the effector organ of which is the sweat glands, and the "generator" of the response is the posterior hypothalamus.

Super-slow physiological processes (SSPP) are in the same frequency range (less than 1 Hz) with the EDA. The study of the SSPP dynamics showed that they reflect the level of stable functioning and are a physiological indicator that determines the state of brain structures and the course of a number of other bioelectric processes. To date, numerous studies have shown that SSPPs are an adequate physiological method for studying the cerebral system for providing emotions and mental activity.

So the EDA evaluates skin resistance, which is determined by the state of the sweat glands. Sweating, in turn, depends on the state of the autonomic nervous system. The study of the dynamics of skin resistance is used in devices called "lie detector". A person, answering the questions posed in monosyllables, is already in a state of heightened emotional stress. Control over the autonomic nervous system by the higher parts of the central nervous system is practically absent, which is reflected in the dynamics of the EDA with correct and incorrect answers. It should be said that a real boom in research using the "lie detector" was observed in the 50s and 70s of the 20th century in the practice of professional selection. EDA registration has also found its application in the practice of psychophysiological correction – in biofeedback devices. EDA registration data (possibly other indicators – ECG, EEG, electromyogram, etc.) are displayed on a display that is visible to the subject [22]. Conditions that modulate positive emotions are created for the patient for a certain period of time. At the end of the action of positive stimulants, neutral conditions are created, where a person, according to the values of GSR, controls his state, trying to maintain at the level of positive emotions.

5   Other Methods in Clinical Neurophysiology and Applied Psychophysiology (USDG, PET-Scan, NIRs)

The above research methods have found wide application in clinical and diagnostic practice, and are also widely used in assessing human conditions in various conditions, especially when testing new technology and new conditions of activity.

Fundamentally new data on the role of subcortical formations in the provision of neurophysiological mechanisms of mental activity made it possible to obtain the method of implanted electrodes, which was used for therapeutic and diagnostic purposes in clinical practice in the 70s–80s. It has been established that in the activity of the subcortical formations of the brain, the interaction of analyzers and systems that provide programming of purposeful behavior is clearly observed. However, despite the use of both gold and platinum electrodes implanted into the brain structures, this method turned out to be unnecessarily invasive for humans and is currently practically not used.

Austrian physicist Christian Doppler (1803–1853) in 1842 formulated a principle that makes it possible to assess the direction and speed of movement of any object by changes in the echo signal reflected from it. If this object is stationary, then the echo signal reflected from it returns to the radiation source after a time T, which is directly proportional to the doubled path from the radiation source to the object (2L) and inversely proportional to the propagation speed of this type of radiation C ($T = 2L/C$). If the object moves at a certain speed, then the time after which the echo signal returns to the radiation source changes, which makes it possible to estimate the speed and direction of the object movement. In medicine, the use of ultrasound radiation is widespread to assess the speed and direction of movement of red blood cells in blood vessels. Almost a century and a half later, in 1982, the method of transcranial ultrasound Doppler (USDG) was proposed, which evaluates blood flow in the great intracranial vessels of the brain.

When examining blood circulation by the USDG method, the Doppler signal frequency spectrum represents the range of the linear velocity of red blood cells in the measured volume and is displayed as a spectrogram in real time on a unidirectional or bidirectional frequency analyzer. The signal is evaluated using a fast Fourier transform, the maximum frequency is plotted along the vertical axis in cm/s or kHz, and the time is either continuously or in freeze frame mode horizontally. The method allows one to simultaneously measure the maximum linear (systolic) velocity, the minimum linear (diastolic) velocity, the average blood flow velocity and the pulsation index (the ratio of the difference between the systolic and diastolic linear blood flow velocity to the average velocity).

Changes in the parameters of cerebral blood flow allows in psychophysiological studies to quantitatively assess the degree of participation of certain parts of the brain in providing cognitive activity of varying degrees of intensity.

Positron emission tomography is one of the most modern, promising and powerful neuroimaging methods. According to a line of authors, it is called "functional neuroanatomy of the human brain." The first publications on PET date back to 1975–1979, but the main stream of work appeared in the 80s. The main purpose of PET-scan is to study the distribution in the living brain of various (more than 200) chemicals it utilizes in order to assess one or another of its functions. Among them are blood flow, pH, metabolism, molecular diffusion, protein synthesis, activity of membrane receptors, and a number of others. Amino acids, carboxylic acids, amines, sugars, steroids, metabolites, drugs, and their derivatives are used as injected substances. The principle of the method is registration of radioactive decay (positron emission) of short-lived (2–110 min) isotopes (C, N, O or F), combined with a substance-tracer. Based on the principles of computed tomography, a three-dimensional display of brain radioactivity is constructed, consisting of huge number (up to 230 thousand) discrete points. The sensitivity of PET is very high – it allows the detection of test substances in the brain in concentrations of up to several picomoles per gram [11].

Modern technologies for registration of near infrared light (Near Infra-Red Spectroscopy – NIRS) allow detecting changes in blood flow and metabolic activity of the brain (similar to functional MRI), since these physiological processes are associated with the scattering of light infrared light. NIRS technology evaluates the neural and vascular activity of brain structures. The technique is based on changes in light scattering arising in the dynamics of blood oxygen saturation and local activity of neurons. In this way, safe infrared light is transformed through the bones of the skull and adjacent tissues from the superficial layers of the brain. Then it is removed from the scalp using a fiber-optic cable, turning into an electrical signal and transforming into a brain map [17].

The positive aspects of NIRS technology are the ability to assess local hemodynamics associated with neural activity in real time, the absence of artifacts and the portability of devices. NIRS studies of parental recognition ability in 2–3 month old infants have been described. One of the limitations of this innovative technology is the low penetrating ability to deep brain structures. However, the developers consider this shortcoming temporary. The future in NIRS technologies lies in increasing the temporal resolution and depth of signal detection. Recent research indicates that light infrared light is also dependent on ion currents and water in neurons and glia, which brings closer real-time measurement of brain activity. Thus, the study of mental processes using objective methods opens up broad prospects for understanding the mechanisms of the brain. In turn, when assessing the prospects for studying each of the methods, it is important to emphasize that the complex application of an adequate set of economically feasible techniques greatly increases the effectiveness of research.

Research in time	Research level				
	Brain	**Mapping**	**Layers/ Nuclei**	**Cells**	**Synapses**
Milliseconds/ seconds	EEG, ERPs, MEG, ECoG		Neural activity		Biophysics
Seconds/ hours	fMRI, USDG, NIRS, EDA		Vascular video microscopy		
Days	PET-scan		Angiography		Molecular biology
Years	CT, MRI				

Fig. 3. Diagnostic methods for brain mapping.

As a result, let us consider what place the approaches of clinical neurophysiology occupy among the methods of brain mapping (see Fig. 3). Research levels are divided from the whole brain to cells and synapses. Research in time may vary from milliseconds to several years. The main feature of clinical neurophysiology diagnostics is time. As a rule, these are fractions of a second (ERPs), seconds (EEG, MEG, ECoG), minutes (fMRI). Only positron emission tomography reflects the state of the brain over several days, which is associated with the life cycle of radioactive isotopes. The level of research corresponds to the whole brain, maps, microelectrode (neural activity) allow you to explore individual neurons and nerve centers – nuclei.

References

1. Berger, H.: Uber das Elektroenzephalogramm des Menschen. Arch. f. Psychiat. u. Nervenkrankh. **87**, 527–570 (1929)
2. Boucsein, W.: Electrodermal Activity. Springer, Boston, MA (2012)
3. Daube, J.R. (ed.): Clinical Neurophysiology, 2nd ed. Oxford University Press, Oxford, New York (2002)
4. Donchin, E., Spencer, K.M., Wijesinghe, R.: The mental prosthesis: assessing the speed of a P300-based brain–computer interface. IEEE Trans. Rehabil. Eng. **8**, 174–179 (2000)
5. Gabriel, F.: Emil du Bois-Reymond: Neuroscience, Self, and Society in Nineteenth-Century Germany. The MIT Press, Cambridge, Massachusetts, London (2013)
6. Hari, R., Baillet, S., Barnes, G., Burgess, R., Forss, N., Gross, J.: IFCN-endorsed practical guidelines for clinical magnetoencephalography (MEG). Clin. Neurophysiol. **129**, 1720–1747 (2018)
7. Hoffmann, U., Vesin, J., Ebrahimi, T., Diserens, K.: An efficient P300-based brain–computer interface for disabled subjects. J. Neurosci. Methods **167**, 115–125 (2008)

8. Höller, Y.: Quantitative EEG in cognitive neuroscience. Brain Sci. **11**, 517 (2021)
9. Intraoperative monitoring of neural function. In: Nuwer, M.R. (ed.), Handbook of Clinical Neurophysiology. Elsevier B.V., Amsterdam, Boston, London, New York (2008)
10. Jasper, H.H.: The ten-twenty electrode system of the International Federation. Electroencephalogr. Clin. Neurophysiol. **10**, 371–375 (1958)
11. Khil'ko, V., et al.: The topographic mapping of evoked bioelectrical activity and other methods for the functional neural visualization of the brain. Vestnik Rossiiskoi akademii meditsinskikh nauk. **3**, 36–41 (1993)
12. Khil'ko, V.A., Lytaev, S.A., Ostreiko, L.M.: Clinical physiological significance of intraoperative evoked potential monitoring. Hum. Physiol. **28**, 619–626 (2002)
13. Levi-Aharoni, H., Shriki, O., Tishby, N.: Surprise response as a probe for compressed memory states. PLoS Comput. Biol. **16**, e1007065 (2020)
14. Lytaev, S.: Modeling and estimation of physiological, psychological and sensory indicators for working capacity. Adv. Intell. Syst. Comput. **1201**, 207–213 (2021)
15. Lytaev, S., Aleksandrov, M., Lytaev, M.: Estimation of emotional processes in regulation of the structural afferentation of varying contrast by means of visual evoked potentials. Adv. Intell. Syst. Comput. **953**, 288–298 (2020)
16. Lytaev, S., Vatamaniuk, I.: Physiological and medico-social research trends of the wave P300 and more late components of visual event-related potentials. Brain Sci. **11**, 125 (2021)
17. McGrath, M.C.: Near-infrared spectroscopy (NIRS). In: Goldstein, S., Naglieri, J.A. (eds.) Encyclopedia of Child Behavior and Development. Springer, Boston, MA (2011)
18. Hallett, M. (ed.), Movement disorders. Handbook of Clinical Neurophysiology. Elsevier B.V., Amsterdam, Boston, London, New York (2003)
19. Niedermeyer, E., Lopes da Silwa, F.: Electroencephalography. Basis, Principles, Clinical Applications Related Fields. Lippincott Williams & Wilkins, Philadelphia, Baltimore, New York (2005)
20. Rebsamen, B., et al.: Controlling a wheelchair indoors using thought. IEEE Intell. Syst. **22**(2), 18–24 (2007). https://doi.org/10.1109/MIS.2007.26
21. Sellers, E., Donchin, E.: P300-based brain–computer interface: initial tests by ALS patients. Clin. Neurophysiol. **117**, 538–548 (2006)
22. Society for Psychophysiological Research Ad Hoc Committee on Electrodermal Measures: Publication recommendations for electrodermal measurements. Psychophysiology **49**, 1017–1034 (2012)
23. Wolpaw, J.R., et al.: Brain–computer interfaces for communication and control. Clin. Neurophysiol. **113**, 767–791 (2002)

Application of Resting Brain Frontal Lobe Complexity in Depression Screening

Zhilin Gao[1], Wang Wan[1], Zhongze Gu[1,3], and Xingran Cui[1,2(✉)]

[1] State Key Laboratory of Bioelectronics, School of Biological Science & Medical Engineering, Southeast University, Nanjing 210096, China
cuixr@seu.edu.cn
[2] Key Laboratory of Child Development and Learning Science, Ministry of Education, School of Biological Science & Medical Engineering, Southeast University, Nanjing 210096, China
[3] Institute of Biomedical Devices (Suzhou), Southeast University, Suzhou 215000, China

Abstract. The increase in the number of depressed people worldwide has put forward higher requirements for higher accuracy and efficiency of depression screening. In this study, the wearable EEG devices were applied to improve screening efficiency, and the complexity attenuation rate (CAR) based on the large-scale and small-scale indexes of multivariate multiscale entropy (MMSE) were proposed, in order to improve the accuracy of screening. The EEG resting state recordings including 22 depressed patients and 20 healthy people was collected using a four-channel frontal lobe portable device. The results showed that, compared with healthy people, depressed patients had higher small-scale complexity and lower large-scale complexity, which means that depressed patients have a greater CAR. The study also verified depressed patients had lower alpha and higher beta power. Compared to other features, CAR had the highest correlation with depression scale scores. The leave-one-subject-out classification results showed that the accuracy of combined features (CAR, MMSE, multiscale entropy, and power spectral density (PSD)) reaches 88.63%, which was much higher than the traditional PSD accuracy of 79.60%. To further verify the reliability and robustness of the above results, the proposed method was verified in the public depression dataset, and the accuracy rate was increased to 87.05%. The conclusions proved that the depression screening method based on portable EEG devices proposed in this study is universal and has great practical application value.

Keywords: EEG · Depression · Frontal region · Multivariate multiscale entropy · Multiscale entropy · Wearable device

1 Introduction

Nowadays, more and more people of all ages suffered from depression disorder which is one of the main causes of the global burden. As a serious neurological disease, depression is characterized by sadness, loss of interest, and suicidal tendencies in severe cases. There are two major unstable factors in traditional methods of inquiry and scale diagnosis: (1)

© Springer Nature Switzerland AG 2021
I. Rojas et al. (Eds.): BIOMESIP 2021, LNCS 12940, pp. 242–254, 2021.
https://doi.org/10.1007/978-3-030-88163-4_22

subjectivity; and (2) heterogeneity of depression [1]. Therefore, quantitative assessment based on physiological signals is essential.

Non-invasive scalp EEG is one of the most important tools for brain science research. With its advantages of high time resolution, high safety, and low cost, it has become a promising auxiliary evaluation solution for depression. In the past few decades of research on depression, theta, alpha and beta were commonly used bands. Grin-Yatsenko et al. [2] discovered 111 depressive patients in the early stages had higher power in theta, alpha, and beta bands at occipital and parietal regions than 526 non-depressed subjects. Mumtaz et al. [3] compared 33 major depressive disorder (MDD) patients and 30 healthy people and found lower theta and alpha power, lower delta in the frontal and occipital regions as well as higher delta and beta in central, temporal, and parietal regions. Lee et al. [4] found that compared with healthy people, young people aged 18 to 25 with depressive tendencies have increased alpha band energy in the left hemisphere, and decreased beta band energy in the central brain area and left hemisphere. Lin et al. [5] found that, compared MDD with the healthy group, major depressive disorder (MDD) group had lower delta and theta power, and higher beta power in the resting state. Previous results have shown that, in different studies, the results of the differences in power between the depression group and the healthy group at different frequency bands are often contradictory. The conflicting results may come from different data collection equipment, environments, and data preprocessing methods. Therefore, in the study to demonstrate the difference between the depression group and the healthy group, multi-database verification is necessary.

In addition to the linear Fourier transform-based power calculation, nonlinear analysis algorithms are also widely used as quantitative physiological indicators in EEG based depression research. Hosseinifard et al. [6] extracted the fractal dimension, lyapunov index, correlation dimension and detrend fluctuation analysis features of theta and alpha bands, and used them to distinguish depressed patients and healthy people with an accuracy rate of 90%. Chen et al. [7] found MDD had the higher quantitative electroencephalography approximate entropy during a test of variables of attention than healthy group. Čukić et al. [8] also demonstrated depressed patients had higher higuchi's fractal dimension and sample entropy in frontal and parietal regions compared to healthy subjects. The brain is a nonlinear and unstable chaotic system. Entropy evaluates the uncertainty of chaotic systems. The traditional entropy analysis method only analyzes the uncertainty on a fixed time scale. The multiscale entropy (MSE) analysis method proposed by Peng et al. [9] evaluated the complexity of time series on multiple time scales. Ahmed et al. [10] proposed multivariate multiscale entropy (MMSE) on the basis of MSE to access structural complexity of multivariate physical or physiological systems, together with more degrees of freedom and enhanced rigor in the analysis.

With the development of wearable devices, the development of depression assessment systems based on portable devices has begun to appear in the past few years. The phenomenon of frontal alpha lateralization in patients with depression, which is different from ordinary people, is also a commonly used indicator [11]. Studies have found that the frontal alpha of depressive disorder patients is lateralized to the right, and healthy people are lateralized to the left. Cai et al. [12] collected EEG signals at Fp1, Fp2, and Fpz electrodes from 178 subjects including 92 healthy people and 86 depressed patients.

The classification accuracy reached 78.24%, combining the deep belief network and the absolute power of beta wave. Shen et al. [13] collected the Fp1, Fp2, and Fpz EEG signals of 170 subjects including 89 healthy people and 81 depressed patients. The average accuracy reaches 83.07% in support vector machine (SVM). Wan et al. [14] obtained the highest accuracy of 86.67% based on leave-one-participant-out cross in the classification and regression tree combining genetic algorithm on Fp1.

The above research proves that depression screening based on portable devices has potential. In this study, multiple frontal lobe channels are regarded as a whole, and the complexity of each frontal lobe channel and the entire frontal lobe area is evaluated to improve the accuracy of depression classification. The Fp1, Fp2, F7, and F8 four-channel EEG data of depression group and healthy control group on portable devices were collected. The proposed method for diagnosing depression in this study was validated both in the portable device dataset and a public depression dataset.

2 Materials and Methods

2.1 Datasets

2.1.1 Wearable Device Dataset——Mindeep Dataset

In this study, 22 depression disorder patients were recruited in Zhongda Hospital as depression group and 20 healthy students were recruited in Southeast University as the healthy group (Table 1). All participants were informed about the experimental protocol and matters needing attention, then signed the informed consent before the experiment. This study was approved by IEC for Clinical Research of Zhongda Hospital, affiliated to Southeast University. The depressed patients were diagnosed by the psychiatrist of Zhongda Hospital and meet the clinical diagnostic criteria for depression. All participants completed the self-rating depression scale (SDS) [15] and 17-item hamilton depression rating scale (HAMD-17) [16] before the experiment for depression assessment under the guidance of professional doctors. In the healthy group, the subjects whose SDS score $\geq$ 50 or HAMD-17 score $\geq$ 7 have been eliminated.

The experiment was carried out in a quiet and dimly lit room and includes 3 min rest with eyes closed and 3 min with eyes open. 4 channels (Fp1, Fp2, F7, F8) EEG was recorded by wearable EEG monitor device Mindeep (co-developed by School of Biological Science and medical Engineering, Southeast University and Mindoop Company). The sample rate of EEG signals was 1000 Hz and the reference was the average of FT7 and FT8.

2.1.2 Public MDD Dataset——Malaysia Dataset

The public MDD dataset was collected by Aamir Saeed Malik of Petronas University of Technology in Malaysia (https://figshare.com/articles/EEG_Data_New/4244171) [17]. The database contains resting EEG data of 34 MDD patients and 30 healthy people, including 5 min with eyes closed and 5 min with eyes open (Table 1). The 19 channels of EEG data (Fp1, F3, C3, P3, O1, F7, T3, T5, Fz, Fp2, F4, C4, P4, O2, F8, T4, T6, Cz, Pz) were recorded by Brain Master Discovery EEG equipment with the left ear (A1) reference, 256 Hz sample rate, 50 Hz notch, and 0.5–70 Hz band-pass filter.

Table 1. Subjects' basic information of Mindeep dataset and Malaysia dataset

Info	Mindeep		Malaysia	
	Depression	Healthy	Major depression	Healthy
Gender (female/male)	11/11	8/12	17/17	9/21
Age (years), mean ± SD	27.7 ± 9.1	22.8 ± 2.5	40.3 ± 12.9	38.3 ± 15.6
SDS	56.1 ± 14.4	37.4 ± 6.5	--	--
HAMD	11.3 ± 7.0	1.75 ± 1.6	--	--
Data length	3 min eyes-closed, 3min eyes-open		5 min eyes-closed, 5min eyes-open	
Channels	4 (Fp1, Fp2, F7, F8)		19	
Sample rate	1000		256	
Reference	FT7, FT8		A1	
Preprocessed	Raw		50 Hz notch, 0.1–70 Hz bandpass	

2.2 EEG Preprocessing

In this study, wearable device dataset and public dataset were preprocessed and then the data was divided into 10-s epochs.

2.2.1 Wearable Device Dataset

Baseline and high frequency noise were removed by 0.3 Hz high pass filter and 45 Hz low pass filter. The spower frequency was removed by 50 Hz notch filter. Since the limitation of wearable device's number of channels, eye movement artifacts were removed by wavelet transform [18].

2.2.2 Public MDD Dataset

The public MDD dataset was re-referenced to zero reference. The eye movement artifacts were removed by independent component analysis (ICA) [19] after the detecting and rebuilding of bad channels.

2.3 Feature Extraction

2.3.1 Multiscale Entropy (Sample Entropy)

The process of MSE is as follows for time series $x_i = (x_1, x_2, x_3, \ldots, x_N) i = 1, 2, 3, \ldots, N$.

Step 1. The coarse-graining series was obtained in scale τ from 1 to s:

$$x(\tau) = (mean(x_1, x_2, x_3, \ldots, x_\tau), mean(x_{\tau+1}, x_{\tau+2}, x_{\tau+3}, \ldots, x_{2*\tau}), \ldots) \tau = 1, 2, 3, \ldots, s, \quad (1)$$

Step 2. Sample entropy (SE) was then calculated for each coarse-graining time series in different scale factors.

$$MSE(\tau) = SpEn(x(\tau), m, r), \tag{2}$$

where SpEn denotes SE, m denotes the vector of length, and r denotes the tolerance of similarity.

When all SE for time scale τ from 1 to s are calculated, the $MSE(\tau)$ series was the multiscale entropy of the original time series.

If time scale $\tau = 1$, MSE is the SE of the original signal.

In our previous EEG-based emotion recognition research, we compared different values of m and r, and found that m = 2 and r = 0.2 were the most appropriate values for EEG signals [20].

In this paper, the sample rate of Mindeep wearable device dataset is 1000 Hz, there are 10,000 points of each 10-s epoch. The number of data points in the coarse-grained sequence at the largest scale is still enough to use sample entropy. Therefore, the maximum scale was set as 50, which means there are still 200 points of the coarse-graining series in scale 50. The sample rate of public dataset is 256 Hz, there are 2560 points of each 10-s epoch. The maximum scale was set as 20, there are 128 points of the coarse-graining series in scale 20.

2.3.2 Multivariate Multiscale Entropy (Sample Entropy)

Since MMSE is the improved algorithm of MSE, the procedure of MMSE is similar with MSE.

Step 1. The coarse-grained multivariate $y_{k,j}^{\in}$ in scale $\in$:

$$y_{k,j}^{\in} = \frac{1}{\in} \sum_{i=(j-1)\in+1}^{j\in} x_{k,i}, \tag{3}$$

where $1 \leq j \leq \frac{N}{\in}$ and the channel index $k = 1, \ldots, p$.

Step 2. The reconstructed multivariate embedded series is computed:

$$
\begin{aligned}
X_m(i) = \big[& x_{1,i}, x_{1,i+\tau_1}, \ldots, x_{1,i+(m_1-1)\tau_1}, \\
& x_{2,i}, x_{2,i+\tau_2}, \ldots, x_{2,i+(m_2-1)\tau_2}, \\
& \cdots, \\
& x_{p,i}, x_{p,i+\tau_p}, \ldots, x_{p,i+(m_p-1)\tau_p} \big],
\end{aligned} \tag{4}
$$

where $M = [m_1, m_2, \ldots, m_p]$ is the embedding vector and $\tau = [\tau_1, \tau_2, \ldots, \tau_p]$ is the time lag vector.

Step 3. Finally, the *SpEn* of all scales are calculated.

The settings of the parameters m, r, and the maximum scale in MMSE were consistent with the values in MSE.

2.3.3 Complexity Attenuation Rate

According to the MMSE curve as shown in Fig. 1, the area under the curve in the ascending phase which called *area*1 and the area under the curve in the descending phase which called *area*2 are used as features. What's more, the complexity attenuation rate (CAR) of complexity curve, which means the area ratio of *area*1 and *area*2 are also being extracted as a feature:

$$CAR = (area1 - area2)/(area1 + area2), \tag{5}$$

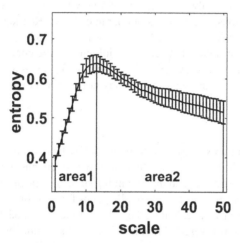

Fig. 1. MMSE curve with standard error and the area under the curve *area*1 and *area*2.

2.3.4 Power Spectral Density

The Power Spectral Density (PSD) [21] is a linear analysis method based on Fourier transform, which is the most commonly used method in conventional EEG analysis. For the EEG oscillations $x_i = (x_1, x_2, x_3, \ldots, x_N)$ $i = 1, 2, 3, \ldots, N$, the PSD is:

$$p(k) = \left| F \sum_{i=1}^{n} f(i) e^{-j2\pi ik/N}(k) \right|^2 / N, \tag{6}$$

The relative power RP of [f1, f2] frequency band is the ratio of the sum PSD in [f1, f2] frequency range to the sum PSD in [0.3 Hz, 30 Hz] frequency range:

$$RP = \sum_{f1}^{f2} p / \sum_{0.3}^{30} p, \tag{7}$$

The frequency band power ratio FP of [f1, f2] frequency band to [f3, f4] frequency band is:

$$FP = \left(\sum_{f1}^{f2} p - \sum_{f3}^{f4} p \right) / \left(\sum_{f1}^{f2} p + \sum_{f3}^{f4} p \right), \tag{8}$$

The interhemispheric power asymmetry PA in frequency band $[f1, f2]$ is:

$$PA = (RP(leftchannel) - RP(rightchannel))/(RP(leftchannel) + RP(rightchannel)) \tag{9}$$

2.4 Statistical Analysis

In this paper, the significance test was analyzed on Matlab R2019 (a). First, we tested whether the data satisfied the assumption of normality and homogeneity of variance. The parametric test one-way analysis of variance (ANOVA) [22] was chosen when the data satisfied the assumptions, otherwise, a nonparametric test Kruskal-Wallis was chosen. The significant difference was defined as the p-value < 0.05.

To explore the correlation between physiological indicators and behavioral scale results, the nonparametric Spearman's rank correlation [23] was used in this study, since the physiological features and scale scores may not conform to the normal distribution.

2.5 Classification

Leave-one-subject-out cross was used to better solve depression screening across subjects. The EEG data in EC state was divided into 10-s epochs. One subject's all 10-s epochs were used as testing set and the remaining subjects' epochs were used as training set. The predicted label and target label of all epochs for all subjects were recorded after leave-one-subject-out cross to calculate the total accuracy and model evaluation indexes.

The extracted features were fed into SVM which has promising properties in many fields. In our study, a library for support vector machines (LIBSVM) [24] is implemented for the SVM classifier with radial basis kernel function.

3 Results

3.1 Multivariate Multiscale Entropy and Complexity Attenuation Rate

MMSE curves with r $= 0.2$ of the healthy and depression group were calculated and shown in Fig. 2 from scale 1 to scale 50. As we can see, the entropy of depression EEG was higher than the healthy group before scale 9, the difference between the depression group and healthy group reduced along with the scale. While the entropy of depression EEG was lower than the healthy group after scale 10, the difference increased and then stabilized since scale 20. According to the statistic results, the area under the MMSE curve from scale 1 to 2 and the area under the MMSE curve from scale 20 to 50 were calculated as MMSE indexes MMSE1–2 and MMSE20–50.

On the basis of MMSE1–2 and MMSE20–50, CAR was acquired as a feature for the attenuation rate. Compared with healthy group, depression group had higher MMSE1–2 complexity and lower MMSE20–50 complexity. These phenomena demonstrated depressed patients had higher CAR than healthy people.

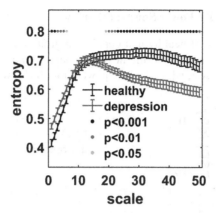

Fig. 2. MMSE curves of healthy group and depression group. The black line with standard error is the curve of the healthy group. The red line with standard error is the curve of depression group. Three different colored circles represent different degrees of significant differences. No circles indicate no significant difference, light gray circles indicate $p < 0.05$, dark gray circles indicate $p < 0.01$, and black circles indicate $p < 0.001$.

3.2 Multiscale Entropy (Sample Entropy)

MSE curve with $r = 0.2$ of healthy and depression group were also calculated from scale 1 to scale 50. The results of four channel average MSE curve was shown in Fig. 3, compared with healthy group, the complexity of depression group's neural activity in prefrontal region was lower after scale 20. According to the statistic results, the area under the MSE curve from scale 28 to scale 47 was computed as MSE indexes on Fp1, Fp2, F7, F8, and the whole prefrontal region.

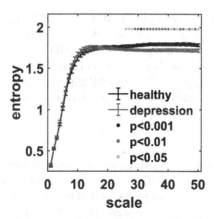

Fig. 3. MSE curves of healthy group and depression group. The black line with standard error is the curve of healthy group. The red line with standard error is the curve of depression group. Three different colored circles represent different degrees of significant differences. No circles indicate no significant difference, light gray circles indicate $p < 0.05$, dark gray circles indicate $p < 0.01$, and black circles indicate $p < 0.001$.

3.3 Traditional Relative Power Spectral Density

The relative PSD curves of healthy and depression group were shown in Fig. 4. The results indicated that, compared to the healthy group, the alpha power (9–13 Hz) of depression group was lower, while the beta power (14–30 Hz) was higher.

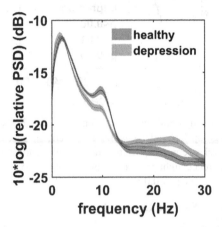

Fig. 4. PSD curves of healthy group and depression group. The black line with standard error is the curve of healthy group. The red line with standard error is the curve of depression group. (Color figure online)

3.4 Correlation Between Features and Depression Scales

The Spearman correlation results of CAR, MMSE1–2, MMSE20–50, MSE, PSDα, and PSDβ was shown in Fig. 5, as we can see, CAR had the highest correlation with SDS and HAMD-17 (SDS: r = 0.567, p < 0.001; HAMD: r = 0.530, p < 0.001), while MMSE1–2 had the positive correlation with SDS and HAMD-17 (SDS: r = 0.553, p < 0.001; HAMD: r = 0.445, p = 0.002), and MMSE20–50 had the negative correlation with SDS and HAMD-17 (SDS: r = 0.405, p = 0.004; HAMD: r = 0.429, p = 0.003).

3.5 Classification

The accuracy of traditional PSD features and combined features (CAR, MMSE, MSE, and PSD) on leave-one-subject-out SVM were computed and shown in Table 2 and Fig. 6. There were 17 PSD features including PSDα, PSDβ, and PSDα/β of four channels and PSD asymmetry of five bands. There were 24 combined features, including 17 PSD features, 1 CAR feature, 2 MMSE features, and 4 MSE features with different channels. The results demonstrated that, compared with PSD, the accuracy on combined features were increased to 88.63% in Mindeep dataset. The verification result on the public database Malaysia also proves that, the combined features had the highest performance 87.05%.

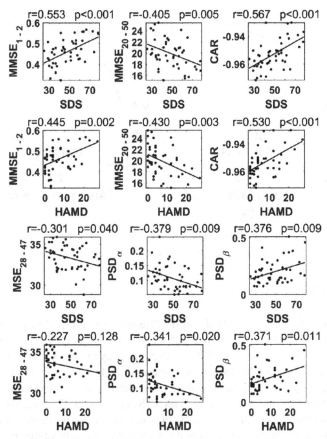

Fig. 5. Correlations of features (CAR, $MMSE_{1-2}$, $MMSE_{20-50}$, MSE, PSD_{α}, and PSD_{β}) and scale scores (SDS and HAMD-17).

Table 2. Accuracy of PSD features and combined features on Mindeep dataset and Malaysia dataset.

		Mindeep	Malaysia
Prefrontal region (Fp1, Fp2, F7, F8)	PSD	79.60%	75.15%
	CAR + MMSE + MSE + PSD	88.63%	87.05%

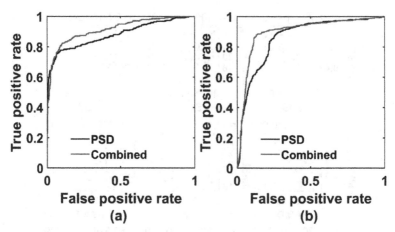

Fig. 6. Receiver operating characteristic curve of PSD features and combined features. (a) Mindeep dataset and (b) Malaysia dataset.

4   Conclusion

According to the CAR, MMSE, MSE, and PSD results of Mindeep dataset, the following conclusions were obtained. Compared with the healthy group, the depression group has lower complexity of large scale MMSE, lower complexity of large scale MSE, and higher complexity of small-scale MMSE, which indicated the higher CAR. Depression group had lower relative power of alpha band and higher relative power of beta band than healthy group. CAR had the highest correlation with SDS and HAMD-17 score, MMSE1–2 had a high positive correlation, and MMSE20–50 had a high negative correlation.

The depression classification accuracy with leave-one-subject-out indicated that, compared with the accuracy of the traditional power-related features, by combining MMSE-related features, MSE-related features, and PSD-related features, the accuracy of Mindeep dataset increased to 88.63%, and the accuracy of Malaysia dataset increased to 87.05%.

5   Discussion

In previous studies, the power, non-linear characteristics, and brain function connection differences between depressed patients and healthy people have been demonstrated in the whole brain electricity. Considering the practical application of depression screening, a depression screening system based on portable EEG will be an inevitable trend. Therefore, this study proved the application prospects of prefrontal lobe EEG data in depression screening on two databases. In order to further improve the accuracy of screening, the CAR index was proposed in this study on the basis of MMSE. The highest accuracy of Mindeep and Malaysia dataset were 88.63% and 87.05%.

In previous studies of the Malaysian public depression database, based on EEG signal power and EEG alpha interhemispheric asymmetry features, all 19 channels were used, and the accuracy of the 10-fold cross-validated SVM model reached 98.4% [25].

However, in this study, in order to be consistent with the Mindeep database, only four prefrontal channels (Fp1, Fp2, F7, and F8) were selected. In order to avoid the information leakage problem of model training and testing, and to verify the generalization of features and models on different subjects, leave-one-subject-out cross was used instead of 10-fold cross. As a result, the accuracy was 87.05%. The results of this study proved that frontal lobe portable EEG devices can actually be used for depression screening in daily life.

The Mindeep dataset includes patients with different degrees of depression, but due to the sample size of the dataset, only two categories (depression and healthy) have been predicted, and the prediction of different degrees of depression was not achieved. In the future study, the number of depressed patients with different levels will be increased, and the classification of mild, moderate, and severe depression and health will be improved, as well as the corresponding regression models.

In this study, the number of subjects in wearable device dataset and public dataset are small. Nowadays, most EEG databases have small sample size, especially those related to mental illness or brain diseases. The currently widely used deep learning model is not suitable for small sample databases. The widespread promotion of portable EEG devices will help the establishment of large sample size EEG databases which can accelerate the development of scientific research in various fields.

Acknowledgement. This work was supported in part by the National Natural Science Foundation of China under Grant 61807007, in part by National Key Research and Development Program of China under Grant 2018YFC2001100, 2018YFB1305200.

References

1. Fried, E.I.: The 52 symptoms of major depression – lack of content overlap among seven common depression scales. J. Affect. Disord. **208**, 191–197 (2017)
2. Grin-Yatsenko, V.A., Baas, I., Ponomarev, V.A., Kropotov, J.D.: Independent component approach to the analysis of EEG recordings at early stages of depressive disorders. Clin. Neurophysiol. **121**, 281–289 (2010)
3. Mumtaz, W., Xia, L., Ali, S.S.A., Yasin, M.A.M., Hussain, M., Malik, A.S.: Electroencephalogram (EEG)-based computer-aided technique to diagnose major depressive disorder (MDD). Biomed. Signal Process. Control **31**, 108–115 (2017)
4. Lee, P.F., Kan, D.P.X., Croarkin, P., Phang, C.K., Doruk, D.: Neurophysiological correlates of depressive symptoms in young adults: a quantitative EEG study. J. Clin. Neurosci. **47**, 315–322 (2018)
5. Lin, I.M., Chen, T.C., Lin, H.Y., Wang, S.Y., Sung, J.L., Yen, C.W.: Electroencephalogram patterns in patients comorbid with major depressive disorder and anxiety symptoms: pProposing a hypothesis based on hypercortical arousal and not frontal or parietal alpha asymmetry. J. Affect. Disord. **282**, 945–952 (2021)
6. Hosseinifard, B., Hassan, M., Rostami, R.: Classifying depression patients and normal subjects using machine learning techniques and nonlinear features from EEG signal. Comput. Methods Programs Biomed. **109**, 339–345 (2012)
7. Chen, S.-T., Li-Chi, K., Chen, S.-J., Shen, T.-W.: The changes of qEEG approximate entropy during test of variables of attention as a predictor of major depressive disorder. Brain Sci. **10**(11), 828 (2020). https://doi.org/10.3390/brainsci10110828

8. Čukić, M., Stokić, M., Radenković, S., Ljubisavljević, M., Simić, S., Savić, D.: Nonlinear analysis of EEG complexity in episode and remission phase of recurrent depression. Int. J. Methods Psychiatr. Res. **29**, 1–11 (2020)

9. Costa, M., Goldberger, A.L., Peng, C.K.: Multiscale entropy analysis of biological signals. Phys. Rev. E. Stat. Nonlinear Soft Matter Phys. **71**, 1–18 (2005)

10. Humeau-Heurtier, A.: Multivariate generalized multiscale entropy analysis. Entropy **18**, 411 (2016)

11. Koo, P.C., et al.: Combined cognitive, psychomotor and electrophysiological biomarkers in major depressive disorder. Eur. Arch. Psychiatry Clin. Neurosci. **269**(7), 823–832 (2018). https://doi.org/10.1007/s00406-018-0952-9

12. Cai, H., Sha, X., Han, X., Wei, S., Hu, B.: Pervasive EEG diagnosis of depression using deep belief network with three-electrodes EEG collector. In: Proc. – 2016 IEEE Int. Conf. Bioinforma. Biomed. BIBM 2016, pp. 1239–1246 (2017)

13. Shen, J., Zhao, S., Yao, Y., Wang, Y., Feng, L.: A novel depression detection method based on pervasive EEG and EEG splitting criterion. In: Proc. – 2017 IEEE Int. Conf. Bioinforma. Biomed. BIBM 2017, pp. 1879–1886 (2017 Jan).

14. Wan, Z., Zhang, H., Huang, J., Zhou, H., Yang, J., Zhong, N.: Single-channel EEG-based machine learning method for prescreening major depressive disorder. Int. J. Inf. Technol. Decis. Making **18**, 1579–1603 (2019)

15. Zung, W.W.K.: A self-rating depression scale. Arch. Gen. Psychiatry **12**(1), 63 (1965). https://doi.org/10.1001/archpsyc.1965.01720310065008

16. Fleck, M.P.A., Poirier-Littre, M.F., Guelfi, J.-D., Bourdel, M.C., Loo, H.: Factorial structure of the 17-item Hamilton Depression Rating Scale. Acta Psychiatr. Scand. **92**, 168–172 (1995)

17. Mumtaz, W., Xia, L., Yasin, M.A.M., Ali, S.S.A., Malik, A.S.: A wavelet-based technique to predict treatment outcome for major depressive disorder. PLoS ONE **12**, 1–30 (2017)

18. Krishnaveni, V., Jayaraman, S., Aravind, S., Hariharasudhan, V., Ramadoss, K.: Automatic identification and removal of ocular artifacts from EEG using wavelet transform. Meas. Sci. Rev. **6**, 45–57 (2006)

19. Delorme, A., Sejnowski, T., Makeig, S.: Enhanced detection of artifacts in EEG data using higher-order statistics and independent component analysis. Neuroimage **34**, 1443–1449 (2007)

20. Gao, Z., Cui, X., Wan, W., Gu, Z.: Recognition of emotional states using multiscale information analysis of high frequency EEG oscillations. Entropy **21**(6), 609 (2019). https://doi.org/10.3390/e21060609

21. Martin, R.: Noise power spectral density estimation based on optimal smoothing and minimum statistics. IEEE Trans. Speech Audio Process. **9**, 504–512 (2001)

22. Sthle, L., Wold, S.: Analysis of variance (ANOVA). Chemom. Intell. Lab. Syst. **6**, 259–272 (1989)

23. Zar, J.H.: Significance testing of the spearman rank correlation coefficient. J. Am. Stat. Assoc. **67**, 578–580 (1972)

24. Chang, C.-C., Lin, C.-J.: LIBSVM: a library for support vector machines. ACM Trasn. Intell. Syst. Technol. **2**(3), 1–27 (2011). https://doi.org/10.1145/1961189.1961199

25. Mumtaz, W., et al.: Biomedical signal processing and control electroencephalogram (EEG)-based computer-aided technique to diagnose major depressive disorder (MDD). Biomed. Signal Process. Control **31**, 108–115 (2020)

Local Contrast Normalization to Improve Preprocessing in MRI of the Brain

Giuseppe Placidi$^{(\boxtimes)}$ ⓘ and Matteo Polsinelli ⓘ

A2VI-Lab, c/o Department of Life, Health and Environmental Science,
University of L'Aquila, L'Aquila, Italy
giuseppe.placidi@univaq.it, matteo.polsinelli@graduate.univaq.it
http://www.giuseppeplacidi.org

Abstract. Magnetic resonance imaging (MRI) is a fundamental medical tool for its versatility and richness of parameters. This allows the implementation of several imaging sequences capable to create high contrast images. However, contrast is also modified by magnetic field strength, system manufacturer and internal properties of the imaged body. This implies that MR images have not standardized amplitudes, though contrast normalization could help in processing and interpretation, especially when these are performed by automated strategies. We present a local contrast normalization strategy for a specific MRI imaging sequence, the FLuid Attenuated Inverse Recovery (FLAIR), one of the imaging sequence used to study inflammatory processes of the brain. The application of the proposed strategy on the images from different MRI scanners are reported and compared. Results are reported and discussed. The proposed strategy could greatly improve automatic interpretation because it reduces data variability.

Keywords: MRI · Local contrast normalization · Medical imaging · Image segmentation · Image interpretation

1 Introduction

MRI is recognized to be one of the most important medical advances of the 20th century [1]. It was developed with the joint efforts of physicists, chemists, engineers and further improved with the contribution of physicians. In fact, physicians use MRI in several diagnosis and clinical practice, given the richness of parameters combined in several imaging sequences, that open MRI to a large number of possible applications. These include high-resolution real-time imaging (regarding, for example, functional MRI, cardiac imaging, angiography), diagnosis and follow up of inflammatory diseases affecting brain (such as multiple sclerosis, Alzheimer, Parkinson diseases, etc.), cancer and other diseases also affecting other tissues and organs. In order to fulfill these requests,

Research supported by the Department of Life, Health and Environmental Science, University of L'Aquila, ITALY.

© Springer Nature Switzerland AG 2021
I. Rojas et al. (Eds.): BIOMESIP 2021, LNCS 12940, pp. 255–266, 2021.
https://doi.org/10.1007/978-3-030-88163-4_23

though, further technological improvements have regarded the implementation of real-time imaging sequences, the improvement of spatial resolution, the reduction of artifacts due to magnetic field in-homogeneity, and the design of whole body scanners. Hundreds of images are normally collected for each single examination, often referred to different imaging sequences, used to collect complete information, to increase spatial-temporal information, resolution and contrast. In order to obtain an exhaustive evaluation, radiologists are forced to manually evaluate this huge amount of information which make the task long, boring and prone to subjective interpretations, errors, oversights, etc. For this reason, automated classification/segmentation strategies [2,3] are increasingly used to support radiologists, to reduce errors and subjectivity, while increasing repeatability. However, though the richness of parameters makes MRI so special, it results in a huge variability in image contrast, also collected with the same instrument and with the same imaging sequence, due to the fact that variability is also implicit on the imaged sample, on how it interacts with the MRI system and its chemical intrinsic properties. Contrast variability is greatly enhanced in images from scanners of different manufacturers, magnetic field strength, electromagnetic field homogeneity, etc. [4]. This make MRI very different from other imaging techniques, such as Computed Tomography (CT) where images, depending just on one parameter (X-ray attenuation), can be easily normalized for different tissues and organs, both in healthy and pathological conditions, in Hounsfield units. Contrast instability in MRI makes identification/segmentation task very difficult also for expert radiologists but, in particular, for automated strategies. Indeed, automated strategies which are trained to cope very well with data from one scanner, could completely fail with data from another. To make automated segmentation strategies robust to contrast variability, a lot of images from different scanners have to be used for training thus making this process very long, and the segmentation results are suboptimal. For this reason, images are preprocessed before they are passed to automatic segmentation. Though several strategies have been proposed to standardize MRI similarly to CT [5–7], results are not enough accurate because a general MRI normalization, feasible both for each imaging sequence and for each anatomical district, was attempted while preprocessing, due to huge MRI variability, has to be specific for each imaging sequence and for each imaged anatomical region. In what follows we present a local contrast normalization strategy for MRI of the brain, related to a specific MRI imaging sequence, the FLuid Attenuated Inverse Recovery (FLAIR), one of the imaging sequences used for inflammatory diseases. The generalization of the technique to other imaging sequences and to other anatomical regions is out the scope of the manuscript. The remaining of the manuscript describes the usual preprocessing pipeline in MRI (Sect. 2), the proposed local contrast stabilization strategy and its collocation in the preprocessing pipeline (Sect. 3), experimental results and discussion (Sect. 4) and, finally, conclusion and future developments (Sects. 5).

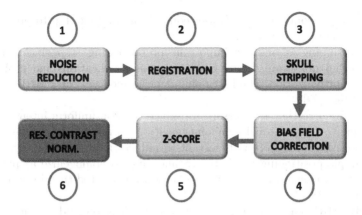

Fig. 1. MRI preprocessing pipeline: the first 5 steps are usually applied to MRI; the last step (n.6) is the contrast normalization that we improve with a local contrast matching to reduce residual contrast mismatch.

2   MRI Preprocessing

Preprocessing refers to a series of mathematical adjustments to MR images before segmentation [8] for reducing the effects of noise and imaging artifacts, equalizing space, eliminating outliers and stabilizing contrast. Though it is well known [9] how important is to match image contrast before segmentation, due to variable sequences, overlapping intensities, noise, field inhomogeneity, partial volume, gradients, motion, echoes, blurred edges, anatomical variations and susceptibility artifacts [4,10]. Some of this variability can be reduced with specific hardware [11–15] but most has to be correctly with appropriate software [4,10,16–20]. For this reason, MRI has to undergo preprocessing to stabilize and make effective segmentation.

Preprocessing for MRI (Fig. 1) consists of: registration and alignment of images, noise reduction, skull stripping, bias field correction, and contrast normalization. Step 6 in Fig. 1 represents the proposed technique for local contrast normalization.

Rigid registration and alignment are necessary because images obtained by different imaging modalities are not registered and might have different spacing and thickness. Robust methods are used for this scope [21,22] to obtain images in axial orientation, the orientation used therein, with the same resolution along the three spatial axes and we used MRITOTAL [23] whose source code is available at https://github.com/bic-mni.

Experimental noise affects MRI [4,24], whose power is inversely proportional to the magnetic field strength: noise reduction would serve to make images more robust to MRI equipment at different magnetic field strength and to reduce segmentation outliers. Anisotropic diffusion noise reduction filtering to preserve edges is routinely applied in MRI and we merged the strategies in [19,25,26] to keep advantage from each one. Noise reduction is the first step to prepare data at best for the following steps.

Skull stripping is another important preprocessing step since fat, skull, skin and other non-brain tissues may cause misclassifications and problems to amplitude normalization. Skull stripping is performed via the FMRIB Software Library (FSL) [27].

Bias field correction is necessary to reduce the non-uniform intensity effects in MRI due to magnetic fields inhomogeneity or applied radio-frequency fields within the scanner: it is very important to reduce them to make segmentation robust sample positioning inside the scanner and to homogenize amplitude for the same grain tissue. In-homogeneity effects are corrected therein by using the N4 algorithm [28].

Finally, MR images undergo contrast normalization and all the intensity levels of the various scans are rearranged and normalized in the same interval through the z-score [7], that is by subtracting the mean value of the image to the image itself and by dividing the result for its standard deviation.

Due to the extreme variability in parameters settings, MR images collected with the same sequence could have variable contrast in equipment from different manufacturers or when the same system is used for different patients (reciprocal amplitudes are not standardized in MRI) and residual contrast difference often remains after z-score. Residual amplitude variations between different brain tissues could negatively influence the following image analysis. To this aim, Fig. 2 shows a comparison between FLAIR images collected by different systems on different patients before (A) and after their preprocessing with z-score (B). The other preprocessing steps have yet been applied to all the proposed images. In particular, the first column shows the images and the second column shows the corresponding histograms. As can be noticed, contrast differences are high in original images. Moreover, though attenuated, these differences remain after z-score calculation, as confirmed by histograms. In fact, z-score eliminates scaling between images but internal reciprocal contrast differences between soft brain tissues are almost unaltered. This is explainable because z-score normalization acts on the whole image by displacing and stretching (or enlarging) its histogram, but it leaves unchanged reciprocal amplitude displacement between different soft brain tissues, as can be noticed from the reciprocal peaks positions on the histograms both before and after z-score. However, a whole image histogram equalization would not be feasible since it would tend to eliminate the contrast gained by the imaging sequence.

3   The Proposed Strategy

We introduce a specific reinforcement for the standard preprocessing (the first 5 steps in Fig. 1), summarized by Step 6 of Fig. 1: a local histogram matching strategy for FLAIR images which differentiates between white matter (WM), grey matter (GM) and cerebrospinal fluid (CSF). Images (sub-images) corresponding to WM, GM and CSF segmentation, respectively, are treated separately (due

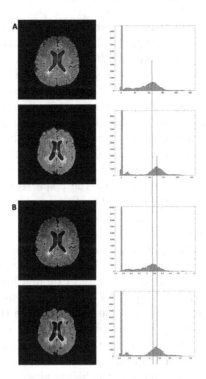

Fig. 2. (A) Brain FLAIR images from different MRI scanners (Philips 3T and Siemens 3T, respectively) and related histograms. (B) z-score results of the images in (A) and related histograms. Relevant intensity mismatch remains after z-score. In the histograms, vertical axis was cut at 10.000 to better highlight lower details.

to MRI variability, in one the amplitude shift could be in one direction and in another could follow the opposite direction) and then recombined to obtain the whole contrast normalized image.

The technique we propose aims at comparing the grey levels of WM, GM and CSF of an axial FLAIR image of the current patient examination, central in the brain where all the three classes are well recognizable, with the corresponding classes of a reference central image r, whose values, once calculated, are fixed, stored in memory and used as a ground truth, being the reference image selected between those of an examination collected with a MRI system used for reference (it is important to note that the choice of the reference scanner is irrelevant). To calculate the reference values, first the z-score is applied to r, then the soft brain tissues are segmented and separated in three complementary classes, corresponding to three images (WM, GM, and CSF), and the peak positions in the histograms are calculated of the three resulting sub-images and stored in memory. The Flow-chart of the method is reported in Fig. 3, where the operations performed on r are not shown because it undergoes steps 1 and 2 of the same Flow-chart. The method collects the central image k of the FLAIR data set to be treated and does the same as in the reference image r (steps 1 and 2). Then, for each class $H \in \{WM, GM, CSF\}$, the shift of the maximum in k with respect to r, DH, and the gray-scale band, BH, are calculated (steps 3 and 4). The band BH is necessary to collect the gray scale range allowing to each class H without repeating classification. DH and BH are calculated just once, for k and then applied to all the image of the current examination. In fact, for each image i, the sub-image allowing to each histogram range BH is realigned in amplitude for compensating the shift (step 5). Finally (step 6), the realigned sub-images are summed together to recreate the final image. Note that the segmentation is necessary just for image k and not for the other images it because the selection of the three classes is made by choosing the respective ranges of amplitudes, BH, which are complementary each other. Some points are important: 1) We need to use segmentation to separate different brain tissues from the histogram of the whole image both to find the position of local maximum amplitude and to calculate the range of amplitudes allowing to each class. The segmentation strategy we used therein is that proposed in [29] which has been proven to be one of the best. 2) For each image of the current examination, we divide the three sub images by using BH and apply DH to each of them (the correction could be different for each range) and then we recombine the three corrected images into the whole image (images in which one of the three classes is absent would not be corrected, having it no pixels for the corresponding amplitude range). In this way, all the images of the current examination undergo the same process. 3) The calculation of the maximum in the histograms is performed on a filtered version of the histogram plot (3 points CAR filter [30] is used) to force stability and reducing unjustified over or under corrections. 4) The ground truth image and its respective histogram ranges and amplitude peaks for the three classes are selected from a central image of an examination collected with the reference scanner and saved. 5) Data from all patients, including those collected with the reference scanner, are processed by the proposed histogram correction algorithm to stabilize data also coming from the reference equipment: this could help to reduce patient and scanner dependencies. The fact that contrast normalization is applied for last is to avoid that noise, bias field, skull presence, differences in dynamic range and other disturbing effects could negatively influence normalization.

4   Experimental Evaluation

To test the effectiveness of the proposed strategy in the context of preprocessing pipeline, we applied both the traditional MRI preprocessing pipeline (steps 1–5 in Fig. 1) and that integrated with the local contrast normalization (steps 1–6 in Fig. 1) on 1500 FLAIR brain images from a public dataset of data coming from patients affected by multiple sclerosis. In what follows, the used dataset is described and the results presented and discussed.

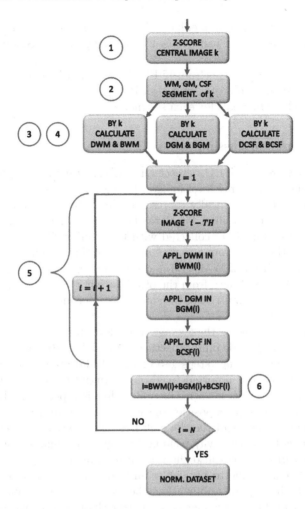

Fig. 3. Amplitude realignment procedure. DH, for $H \in \{WM, GM, CSF\}$, are the amplitude displacements calculated on the sub-images WM, GM and CSF of the image k, respectively. BH, for $H \in \{WM, GM, CSF\}$, are the histogram band sub-images WM, GM and CSF of the image k, respectively. BWM(i), BGM(i) and BCSF(i) are the histogram ranges of sub-images WM, GM and CSF of the image i, respectively.

4.1   The Used Dataset

To test the proposed method, we have used the publicly available large-scale benchmark MRI database and corresponding ground truth proposed in MICCAI MS Lesion Segmentation Challenges: MSSEG [31].

In MSSEG data were acquired by several MRI scanners using different magnetic field strengths: a Siemens Aera 1.5T, a Siemens Verio 3T and a Philips Ingenia 3T. The images were made anonymous and furnished both in original form and pre-processed for the convenience of the users. The database contained

T_1-w weighted, T_1-w gadolinium enhanced (T_1-w Gd), T_2-w, T_2-FLAIR and PD-w images. For our purposes, just the T_2-FLAIR images, denoted simply FLAIR, were used.

In our tests, we used images from 15 FLAIR examinations, 1 for each patient, being the patients in groups of 5 for each MRI scanner. The total set of analyzed images was 1500, 500 images for each scanner.

4.2   Results and Discussion

The 1500 images from MSSEG dataset all undergo standard preprocessing. Of the original images, 256 grey-level images, histograms were calculated in single amplitude values, but graphically represented in 64 bins (4 intensity levels for each bin) to improve readability. The data of a patient, selected randomly among the patients whose data were collected with the Philips 3T scanner, were used for reference. To this aim, from a central image r of the chosen examination, the histogram peak position of WM, GM and CSF are calculated and stored to be used for the correction of data from the other patients and scanners. At the end of the process all images must have the same internal contrast between the three segmented tissues.

The final results, showing the average peak shift and the corresponding standard deviation, in amplitude units, affecting original data (before preprocessing), after standard preprocessing (steps 1–5 of Fig. 1) and after final preprocessing (steps 1–6 of Fig. 1), are reported in Table 1. Amplitude displacements could be, for each class, positive, negative or null. What is reported in Table 1 is the average of the histogram peak position of the final image, after it has been recombined from the sub-images of the three classes, once they have been separately realigned. This is the reason why residual histogram mismatch also occur after correction. As can be noted, also the reference scanner Philips 3T expressed a non zero displacement due to patient/scanner dependencies. Note that we are interested to the histogram stabilization, the local contrast equalization, not to the amount of the shift (a scanner is not better than another when the shift is lower: shift just depends on the scanner used for reference and it is not a quality parameter).

Results in Table 1 demonstrates that the amplitude shift has been almost completely corrected (residual final displacement remains inside a single bin, consisting of 4 intensity values, for all the considered scanners): obviously, the amplitude shift starting differences were so huge, also after the application of the z-score, that images appeared too different (see Fig. 2) and needed to be corrected.

As an example, Fig. 4 shows the images of Fig. 2, with the application of the method to the image of second row in order to make it normalized to that in the first row. The histograms of the resulting images are also reported for comparison (right column). As can be noticed, images have very similar contrast and the original differences, clearly visible in Fig. 2 also after the application of z-score, is greatly reduced as confirmed by the histogram. Note that the proposed

Table 1. Average displacement and standard deviation, in intensity units, without preprocessing (second column), after standard preprocessing (third column) and after final preprocessing (fourth column), separately for each scanner (rows).

Scanner type	No Prep.	Prep.	Prep. + C. norm.
Siemens 1.5T	15 ± 3	12 ± 2	2 ± 1
Siemens 3T	18 ± 4	14 ± 3	2 ± 1
Philips 3T	4 ± 2	3 ± 1	1 ± 1

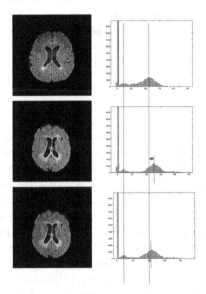

Fig. 4. Local contrast normalization. The image in the third row represents the local amplitude realignment of the image in the second row to the image in the first row. Lines connecting histograms (right column) serve to evaluate the respective positions of the peak, before and after correction, with respect to the reference image. Vertical axis of the histogram was cut to zoom low values.

strategy has been applied to translate a higher contrast image to a lower contrast one: the opposite could have been done without any limitation.

The effect of preprocessing on segmentation is important because it stabilizes data and, pushing toward generalization, simplifies the role of the following segmentation/interpretation process. The proposed local contrast normalization method, as an integration to the general preprocessing strategy, greatly contribute to homogenize FLAIR images from different scanners. In this way, a relevant gain is furnished to radiologists, who are not forced to retrain themselves when using data from different scanners, but, more important, to automatic segmentation/interpretation strategies which could be trained by using lower data sets (being data yet equalized to different scanners, the automatic strategies would not need to be trained with data from several scanners) and, hence, the training process could be faster. Finally, as a really good consequence, the automatic strategies could result more general (data coming from a scanner which is completely new to the automatic systems would be effectively treated) and final accuracy would improve.

It is important to note that, with the exception of FLAIR in which the three above classes show well separated intensities, as shown in Fig. 2, the proposed strategy has not been tested on other imaging modalities and it does not necessarily performs well in all of them, for example when the contrast among classes in the original image is very low, though a similar strategy could be also attempted to translate images from one imaging modality to the others. This could be very helpful in reducing acquisition time while maintaining the advantage of using information by different modalities (some modality could be calculated from others and not directly acquired).

5   Conclusion

A new local contrast normalization strategy has been proposed for MRI FLAIR images of the brain. It is based on the preliminary segmentation of a reference image in WM, GM and CSF and on the calculation of the peak positions of the histograms of these segmented images. These values are used as reference amplitude positions. When using a new examination, its central image undergoes the same procedure as the reference image and the displacements from the reference images are calculated for the classes WM, GM and CSF. Finally, for each image, corrections are applied to the histogram of each class separately and then recombined in a single image. The proposed histogram normalization strategy has been experimentally tested on 1500 images from 3 different MRI scanners: its good performance has been numerically demonstrated and graphically illustrated.

The proposed strategy could be very effective to generalize and improve the training process and the final accuracy of automated segmentation/identification strategies due to its good property of reducing scanner and patient specific mismatches.

However, the proposed method is sequence (FLAIR) and organ (brain) specific: its application to other imaging sequences has not been attempted and, as it is, we think it could be easily extended to those imaging sequences whose original contrast between WM,GM and CSF is well defined; its application to different body districts is out the scope of the research, being it included in a project for the study of the inflammatory processes of the brain [32].

In the future, we aim to adapt the strategy to other imaging sequences and to apply a similar strategy to transform images from one imaging sequence to another, thus reducing acquisition time while maintaining the richness of details. Finally, we aim at using it in the pipeline of an automated segmentation/identification strategy in order to verify the gain it can allow in terms of generality, robustness, training speeding up and accuracy improvement.

References

1. Rinck, P.A.: European Magnetic Resonance Forum: Magnetic resonance in medicine: a critical introduction: the basic text book of the European Magnetic Resonance Forum (2019). ISBN 9783746095189
2. Kaur, A., Kaur, L., Singh, A.: State-of-the-art segmentation techniques and future directions for multiple sclerosis brain lesions. Arch. Comput. Methods Eng. **28**(3), 951–977 (2020). https://doi.org/10.1007/s11831-020-09403-7
3. Placidi, G., Cinque, L., Polsinelli, M.: Guidelines for effective automatic multiple sclerosis lesion segmentation by magnetic resonance imaging. In: ICPRAM, pp. 570–577 (2020)
4. Placidi, G.: MRI: Essentials for Innovative Technologies, 1st edn. CRC Press, Boca Raton (2012)
5. Shinohara, R.T., Sweeney, E.M., et al.: Statistical normalization techniques for magnetic resonance imaging. NeuroImage: Clin. **6**, 9–19 (2014)
6. Ford, J., Dogan, N., Young, L., Yang, F.: Quantitative radiomics: impact of pulse sequence parameter selection on MRI-based textural features of the brain. Contrast Media Mol. Imaging **2018**, 1–9 (2018)
7. Carré, A., et al.: Standardization of brain MR images across machines and protocols: bridging the gap for MRI-based radiomics. Sci. Rep. **10**(1), 1–15 (2020)
8. Ravnik, D., Jerman, T., Pernuš, F., Likar, B., Špiclin, Ž.: Dataset variability leverages white-matter lesion segmentation performance with convolutional neural network. In: Medical Imaging 2018: Image Processing (2018)
9. Commowick, O., et al.: Objective evaluation of multiple sclerosis lesion segmentation using a data management and processing infrastructure. Sci. Rep. **8**(1), 1–17 (2018)
10. Bosc, M., Heitz, F., Armspach, J.P., Namer, I., Gounot, D., Rumbach, L.: Automatic change detection in multimodal serial MRI: application to multiple sclerosis lesion evolution. Neuroimage **20**(2), 643–656 (2003)
11. Alecci, M., Brivati, J.A., Placidi, G., Testa, L., Lurie, D.J., Sotgiu, A.: A submicrosecond resonator and receiver system for pulsed magnetic resonance with large samples. J. Magn. Reson. **132**(1), 162–166 (1998)
12. Di Giuseppe, S., Placidi, G., Brivati, J.A., Alecci, M., Sotgiu, A.: Pulsed EPR imaging: image reconstruction using selective acquisition sequences. Phys. Med. Biol. **44**(6), N137–N144 (1999)
13. Di Giuseppe, S., Placidi, G., Sotgiu, A.: New experimental apparatus for multimodal resonance imaging: initial EPRI and NMRI experimental results. Phys. Med. Biol. **46**(4), 1003–1016 (2001)
14. Placidi, G., Alecci, M., Sotgiu, A.: First imaging results obtained with a multimodal apparatus combining low-field (35.7 mT) MRI and pulsed EPRI. Phys. Med. Biol. **47**(10), N127–N132 (2000)
15. Alfonsetti, M., et al.: Versatile coil design and positioning of transverse-field RF surface coils for clinical 1.5-T MRI applications. Magn. Reson. Mater. Phys. Biol. Med. **18**(2), 69–75 (2004)
16. Placidi, G., Alecci, M., Sotgiu, A.: Angular space-domain interpolation for filtered back projection applied to regular and adaptively measured projections. J. Magn. Reson. Ser. B **110**(1), 75–79 (1996)
17. Placidi, G., Alecci, M., Colacicchi, S., Sotgiu, A.: Fourier reconstruction as a valid alternative to filtered back projection in iterative applications: implementation of fourier spectral spatial EPR imaging. J. Magn. Reson. **134**(2), 280–286 (1998)

18. Placidi, G., Alecci, M., Sotgiu, A.: Omega-space adaptive acquisition technique for magnetic resonance imaging from projections. J. Magn. Reson. **143**(1), 197–207 (2000)
19. Placidi, G., Alecci, M., Sotgiu, A.: Post-processing noise removal algorithm for magnetic resonance imaging based on edge detection and wavelet analysis. Phys. Med. Biol. **48**(13), 1987–1995 (2003)
20. Placidi, G., Sotgiu, A.: A novel algorithm for the reduction of undersampling arte-facts in magnetic resonance images. Magn. Reson. Imaging **22**(9), 1279–1287 (2000)
21. Dadar, M., Fonov, V.S., Collins, D.L.: A comparison of publicly available linear MRI stereotaxic registration techniques. Neuroimage **174**, 191–200 (2018)
22. Zhang, X., et al.: Linear registration of brain MRI using knowledge-based multiple intermediator libraries. Front. Neurosci. **13**, 909 (2019)
23. Collins, D.L., Neelin, P., Peters, T.M., Evans, A.C.: Automatic 3D intersubject registration of MR volumetric data in standardized Talairach space. J. Comput. Assist. Tomogr. **18**(2), 192–205 (1994)
24. Dietrich, O., Raya, J.G., Reiser, M.F.: Magnetic resonance noise measurements and signal-quantization effects at very low noise levels. Magn. Reson. Med. **60**(6), 1477–1487 (2008)
25. Bao, P., Zhang, L.: Noise reduction for magnetic resonance images via adaptive multiscale products thresholding. IEEE Trans. Med. Imaging **22**(9), 1089–1099 (2003)
26. Coupé, P., Yger, P., Prima, S., Hellier, P., Kervrann, C., Barillot, C.: An optimized blockwise nonlocal means denoising filter for 3-D magnetic resonance images. IEEE Trans. Med. Imaging **27**(4), 425–441 (2008)
27. Jenkinson, M., Beckmann, C.F., Behrens, T.E., Woolrich, M.W., Smith, S.M.: FSL. Neuroimage **62**(2), 782–790 (2012)
28. Tustison, N.J., et al.: N4ITK: improved N3 bias correction. IEEE Trans. Med. Imaging **29**(6), 1310–1320 (2010)
29. Li, C., Gore, J.C., Davatzikos, C.: Multiplicative intrinsic component optimization (MICO) for MRI bias field estimation and tissue segmentation. Magn. Reson. Imaging **32**(7), 913–923 (2014)
30. Villar, S.A., Torcida, S., Acosta, G.G.: Median filtering: a new insight. J. Math. Imaging Vis. **58**(1), 130–146 (2017)
31. Commowick, O., Cervenansky, F., Ameli, R.: MSSEG challenge proceedings: multiple sclerosis lesions segmentation challenge using a data management and processing infrastructure. In: International Conference on Medical Image Computing and Computer-Assisted Intervention (2016)
32. Placidi, G., Cinque, L., Polsinelli, M., Splendiani, A., Tommasino, E.: Automatic framework for multiple sclerosis follow-up by magnetic resonance imaging for reducing contrast agents. In: Ricci, E., Rota Bulò, S., Snoek, C., Lanz, O., Messelodi, S., Sebe, N. (eds.) ICIAP 2019. LNCS, vol. 11752, pp. 367–378. Springer, Cham (2019). https://doi.org/10.1007/978-3-030-30645-8_34

Morphological Characteristics Analysis of Working Memory Tracts Using BOLD-fMRI and HARDI Based Tractography in Healthy Human Brains

Abir Troudi[✉], Ines Ben Alaya, and Salam Labidi

University of Tunis El Manar, Higher Institute of Medical Technologies of Tunis, Research
Laboratory of Biophysics and Medical Technologies , 1006 Tunis, Tunisia
abir.troudi@etudiant-istmt.utm.tn, ines.benalaya@istmt.utm.tn

Abstract. The neuroimaging field has newly become a drift with multimodal neuroimaging findings to study brain connectivity through the combination of High Angular Resolution Diffusion Imaging (HARDI) based tractography, and functional activation maps using functional Magnetic Resonance Imaging (fMRI) task-related. The reconstruction of Working Memory (WM) fibers bundle is an important goal for many clinical applications such as brain tumors, gliomas, traumatic brain injury, schizophrenia, and Alzheimer Disease.

In the present paper, we propose to study the anatomical variability of the WM bundle by focusing on the quantification of the track and testing for correlations with sex and local reconstruction methods.

The dataset used for the experiment is based on in vivo data from the Human Connectome Project (HCP). We used fifty normal volunteers (25 males, 25 females; mean age $= 25 \pm 2.81$ years). We computed the shape similarity, the volume, the mean length, and the number of streamlines, to evaluate the variability of macro structural measures between subjects.

Firstly, this study demonstrates that there is a significant difference between the reconstruction of WM fiber bundle using the Diffusion Tensor Imaging (DTI) model and the High Angular Resolution Diffusion Imaging (HARDI) model, with a mean correlation coefficient r of 0.43 and a p-value of 0.09 for all measured parameters. Also, the WM bundle has a complex architecture with crossing fibers. Therefore, we can conclude that the HARDI model is the most relevant model for the reconstruction of the WM fiber bundle. Secondly, there were a slight sex differences in WM fiber bundles morphology between healthy subjects, with a 0.95 shape similarity average. Finally, we find a slight difference between the measured macrostructural parameters inter-subjects (Normalized Volume, Mean Length of streamlines (MLS), and Number of streamlines). We conclude that the statistical measures show that the MLS is the well-correlated parameter.

Keywords: Working memory bundle · HARDI · fMRI · Tractography

I. Rojas et al. (Eds.): BIOMESIP 2021, LNCS 12940, pp. 267–280, 2021.
https://doi.org/10.1007/978-3-030-88163-4_24

1 Introduction

The Working Memory (WM) fasciculus was first described by Baddeley and Hitch in 1974. It is a white matter fiber bundle in the human brain that connect the prefrontal cortex, the parietal lobe, and the occipital lobe. WM is a temporary Short-Term Memory (STM) that provides the temporary storage and manipulation of the information necessary for the execution of a wide range of complex cognitive tasks [1].

It is divided into three subcomponents: the central executive (expected to be an attentional-controlling system (important in skills), on the prefrontal lobes), the visuospatial sketch pad (manipulate visual images on the occipital lobe), and the phonological loop (stores and rehearses speech-based information, on the parietal lobe) [2]. The Episodic buffer was an attentionally-based control system, this had the advantage of focusing attention on the fractionation of executive processes [3]. WM has proved to be an important part of the cognitive system, providing the ability to maintain and manipulate information in the process of guiding and executing complex cognitive tasks [4].

The depiction of the working memory network, its organization, and disruption represent one of the central themes of cognitive neuroscience, and in many clinical applications among the most frequent we find brain tumors [5], gliomas [6], traumatic brain injury [7], schizophrenia [8], and Alzheimer disease [9].

Several approaches have been followed to extract a fiber bundle, such as manual extraction, or extraction based on a choice of a manual Region Of Interest (ROI) [10, 11], the extraction according to a Template [12], or atlas [13]. However, it has been proved that these methods cannot be very specific, and relevant, because they can lead to a loss of the information which is carried by the original data (during the manual selection of the ROIs for example) [14, 15].

Therefore, to overcome these problems, our extraction of the WM fiber bundle and tractography features will be based on the combination of fMRI BOLD and Diffusion MRI. This combination allows a more comprehensive analysis of the WM bundle characteristics and represent the relationship between the neural dynamics and the anatomical network. It remains indistinct with single imaging modality analyses [16, 17].

Diffusion Magnetic Resonance Imaging (MRI) based tractography has been recognized as a valuable tool to study the architecture of the white matter fiber bundle in vivo implicated in WM, and the extraction of quantitative measures of the tractography [18].

Probabilistic fiber reconstruction based High Angular Resolution Diffusion Imaging (HARDI), was demonstrated as the appropriate method for the reconstruction of fiber bundles with complex configurations [19].

HARDI technique is based on the acquisition of a series of diffusion-weighted signals with the application of N diffusion gradients (60 or more) of different forces and directions, the N directions of which are regularly distributed over the q-space [20].

Functional Magnetic Resonance Imaging (fMRI) is an imaging technique based on the changes in the signal depending on the level of oxygenation of the blood (BOLD: Blood Oxygenation Level Dependent). It is the most popular non-invasive functional neuroimaging technique in clinical practice and cognitive neuroscience.

BOLD fMRI technique is designed to measure the neuronal activity when performing a cognitive or experimental task according to a well-defined experimental paradigm. It allows the localization of functional brain areas [21, 22].

The extraction of different scalar metrics of WM fiber tract such as Axial Diffusivity (AD), Fractional Anisotropy (FA), Mean Diffusivity (MD) and Radial Diffusivity (RD), represent the microstructural properties of the fiber bundle [12].

From the HARDI data, it is possible to estimate the number of fiber orientations (NuFO) from local maxima of fiber orientation distribution (FOD) [12], Number of tracts, Mean tract length, approximate tract volume, and standard deviation [23]. Also, the Apparent Fiber Density measure [24], and Shape similarity [25] were extracted.

However, the ability of this combination to study the entire WM fiber bundle is still a matter of debate. Most of the research work has focused on a single type of fiber bundle from the entire WM fiber bundles seen as its complex architecture and depending on the medical application in study [26].

In our work, we propose a method that allows us to extract the whole WM fiber bundle. Then, we visualize and quantify this WM bundle in healthy subjects. Next, we'll be able to assess the cognitive impairment caused by a tumor for which we don't know which part of the WM bundle it will damage (such as low-grade gliomas, and glioblastomas) as our future application.

The present study aims to describe the anatomical variability of WM fiber tract more accurately by focusing on the shape of the tract, the number of the streamlines, the normalized volume, and mean length of streamlines, and testing for correlations with sex, and the diffusion model.

Thus, this paper will be structured as follows: we present in the second section our proposed pipeline to extract WM bundle features. Moreover, we present our datasets designed for our methodology. In the third section, we present the experimental results. Finally, we discuss the results.

2 Materials and Methods

In this section, we present the used database. Then, we describe our proposed processing pipeline to extract the WM bundle and its macro-structural features.

2.1 HCP Database

The Human Connectome Project (HCP) database is a public database for storing and propagating human brain connectivity data. The HCP brings multiple MRI modalities together to acquire and analyses connectivity, behavioral and genetic data.

A subset of 50 healthy subjects from the HCP were enrolled in this study (25 Female and 25 Male with mean age $= 25 \pm 2.81$ years). They were scanned on a Skyra 3T MRI scanner; 1.25 mm isotropic resolution scans. The acquisition parameters of HARDI data and BOLD data are described in (www.connectomedb.com). Also, all the data collected from HCP database were preprocessed using the HCP pipelines, that correct the raw images for most common sources of noise and artifacts [27].

2.2 Processing Pipeline Description

Our pipeline is organized in such a way as to collect the data of the two MRI acquisitions. From the whole brain tractography, we have extracted the WM bundle based on the extracted brain-activated areas.

Finally, we were able to extract shape similarity, normalized volume, Mean length of streamlines, and number of streamlines for the WM bundle (Fig. 1).

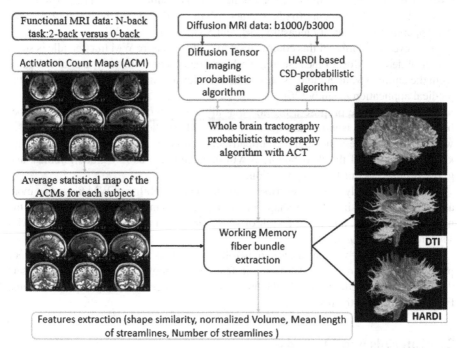

Fig. 1. A flowchart of the WM bundle extraction and the estimation of the morphological characteristics.

2.2.1 Diffusion MRI Processing

The diffusion MRI data were gathered with two diffusion gradients (b-value = 1000 s/mm^2 and b-value = 3000 s/mm^2). The application of Constrained Spherical Deconvolution (CSD) allows estimating the fiber Orientation Distribution Functions (fODFs) [28]. Using the MRtrix3' software, the whole brain tractography was processed based on a probabilistic tractography algorithm with Anatomically Constrained Tractography (ACT) [29]. The ACT was proposed by Smith et al. [30]. It uses the T1w to limit potential false-negative and improves white matter coverage taking the advantage of the tissue Partial Volume Effect. The stopping criterion was suggested by using white matter, grey matter, and CSF maps to determine when a streamline should stop and if it is included or excluded from the reconstruction [12].

2.2.2 Functional MRI Processing

We used the N-back task (2BK-0BK block paradigm), to visualize all the cortical areas that are involved in WM [31].

From the collected fMRI data, we have extracted the Activation Count Maps (ACM). The ACMs were created to demonstrate, for each contrast of interest, the proportion of participants that showed activation (or deactivation) at a z-threshold of 1.96. Specifically, for each contrast of interest, a binary mask for each participant was created from voxels with z-values greater than $z = 1.96$.

For each subject, we have extracted the functional active brain areas when performing the WM task, to obtain the average statistical map of the activation count maps. Then, these statistical maps will be used as a seeded mask to extract the WM fiber bundles [31].

2.2.3 WM Fiber Bundle Extraction

The WM fiber bundle was extracted using the combination of the statistical maps and the whole tractography generated of the whole brain, using the MRtrix3 software.

2.2.4 Working Memory Fiber Bundle Parameters Extraction

We were able to extract the WM fiber bundle macro-structural measures. Through the DIPY library (www.dipy.org) [32], we have calculated the shape similarity. The mean length of streamlines, the volume of the bundle, and the number of fibers were extracted using the MRtrix3 software (www.mrtrix.org).

3 Results

In this section, we present the experimentation procedure. In the first part, we compare the reconstruction of the WM fiber bundles obtained from HARDI data to those with DTI data. In the second part, we calculate, for the extracted fiber bundle based HARDI data, the shape similarity for Males and Females, the normalized volume, Mean length of streamlines (MLS), and the normalized number of streamlines.

3.1 Comparison Between Local Models

We present in Table 1, a visualization of the extracted WM fiber bundle in four healthy Males subjects for the two tractography methods (HARDI and DTI models).

As well illustrated in Table 1, the shape of the reconstructed bundle based on the DTI model is less than the shape of the reconstructed bundle based on HARDI data.

Thus, using the Pearson test, we have compared the two models for the tractography reconstruction. (The Pearson's correlation coefficient measures the statistical relationship between two continuous groups of variables, whose for a p-value < 0.05 and an r ≈ 1 means the best correlation).

Table 1. Qualitative comparison between WM fiber tracts reconstructed using HARDI data, and DTI data, in four representative healthy subjects.

Subjects	Subject1	Subject2	Subject3	Subject4
HARDI reconstruction				
DTI reconstruction				

We present in Table 2, the correlation coefficients r, and the p-values of the compared macrostructural measures between HARDI and DTI reconstructions.

Table 2. Statistical measures comparing HARDI and DTI reconstruction

Macro-measures	Tract volume	Mean length of streamlines	Number of streamlines	Mean values
p-value	0.1	0.07	0.1	0.09
r-value	0.2	0.5	0.6	0.43

In Table 2, we have calculated the correlation values scores between the two reconstruction models (DTI and HARDI).

The results in Table 2 reveal statistically significant differences (p-values > 0.05 and mean correlation coefficient = 0.43) between the two models. Although, the WM fiber bundle is arranged in a complex architecture with crossing fibers.

Moreover, the volumes of the reconstructed tracts based on HARDI calculated for the 50 healthy subjects show a slight variation. While the volumes of the reconstructed tracts-based DTI calculated for the same 50 healthy subjects are not stable and show a significant variation. Also, the mean length of streamlines (MLS) and the number of streamlines for the reconstructed tracts based on HARDI were superior and have better stability inter-subjects, than the mean length of streamlines and the number of streamlines for the reconstructed tracts-based DTI. We can conclude that the most relevant tractography model to reconstruct the WM fiber bundle is the ACT-CSD-probabilistic tractography-based HARDI data.

3.2 Comparison Between Subjects

We compare, in this section, the macrostructural measures of the WM fiber bundle reconstructed by the HARDI model between fifty healthy subjects.

a) Shape similarity

Shape similarity is a confined measure that takes values between 0 to 1 so that for subjects with values close to 0 means no shape similarity and 1 means maximum similarity. As it is shown in Fig. 2, a fully connected graph with similarity scores between five healthy subjects presents a slight variation. That is to say that the shapes of the bundles are very similar.

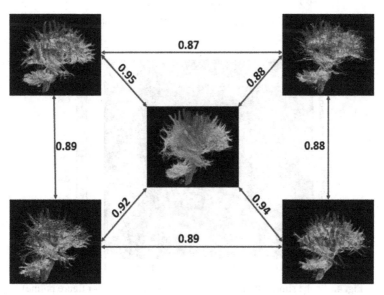

Fig. 2. Shape similarity between working memory fiber bundles of five healthy subjects.

The shape similarity matrix information is computed for fifty healthy subjects (Fig. 3, Fig. 4, Fig. 5). Dark blue colors mean higher shape similarity and light blue colors mean less shape similarity.

A three-shape similarity matrix was illustrated. In Fig. 3, the shape matrix presents the variation of the shape between 25 Males. In the diagonal the shape is equal to 1 since we have measured the shape between the bundle and itself, the rest of the matrix presents very close shape values with a mean value of 0.91. In Fig. 4, the shape matrix presents

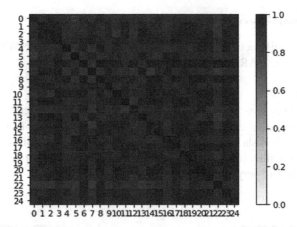

Fig. 3. Shape similarity matrix between 25 males. (Color figure online)

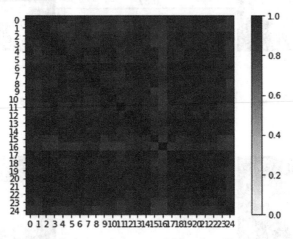

Fig. 4. Shape similarity matrix between 25 females. (Color figure online)

the variation of the shape between 25 Females. In the diagonal the shape is equal to 1 since we have measured the shape between the bundle and itself, the rest of the matrix presents very close shape values with an average of 0.93. The last shape matrix in Fig. 5, presents the variation of the shape between 25 Males and 25 Females. It's a homogenous matrix that presents very close shape values with an average of 0.92. Consequently, the shapes of the extracted WM fiber bundles in fifty healthy subjects are very adjacent.

b) Macrostructural measures

We present the box plots of the normalized volume (Fig. 6) of the WM bundle for tractography-based HARDI, the number of the streamlines (Fig. 7), and the Mean length of streamlines (Fig. 8), for Males and Females.

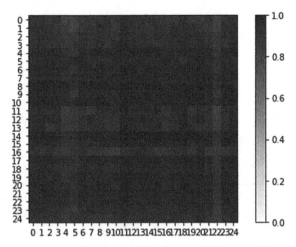

Fig. 5. Shape similarity matrix between 25 males and 25 females. (Color figure online)

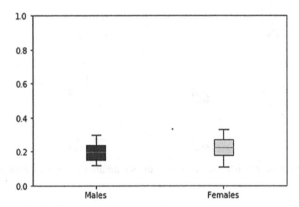

Fig. 6. Box plot of normalized volume variation for males and females.

Three box plots are shown, and the horizontal orange lines illustrate the median values for each measurement. The first box plot (Fig. 6), shows the normalized volume for Males and Females where the variation of the volume is close with an average value of 0.22 ± 0.05 mm^3 for Males and 0.23 ± 0.06 for Females. The second box plot (Fig. 7), displays the MLS between Males and Females, where the MLS average value is 38.43 ± 3.38 mm for Males, and for Females is 41.72 ± 5.14 mm. The last box plot (Fig. 8) represents the normalized number of streamlines between Males and Females, where the average number for Males is 9203.79 ± 2967.15, and for Females is 11269.52 ± 3337.07.

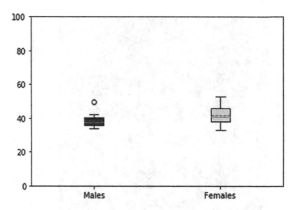

Fig. 7. Box plots of Mean length of streamlines variation for males and females.

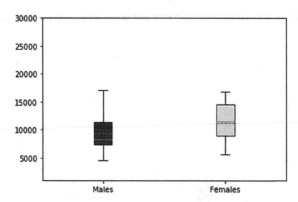

Fig. 8. Box plots of the normalized number of the streamlines variation for males and females.

Table 3. Comparison of the statistical parameters calculated for males and females.

		Normalized volume	Mean length of streamlines (MLS)	Number of streamlines
Males	Mean value and standard deviation	0.22 ± 0.05 mm^3	38.43 ± 3.38 mm	9203.79 ± 2967.15
	Coefficient of variation	0.23	0.08	0.3
Females	Mean value and standard deviation	0.23 ± 0.06 mm^3	41.72 ± 5.14 mm	11269.52 ± 3337.07

(*continued*)

Table 3. (*continued*)

	Normalized volume	Mean length of streamlines (MLS)	Number of streamlines
Coefficient of variation	0.26	0.12	0.3

Table 3 resumes all the statistical parameters calculated for both Males and Females. This table presents the mean values, the standard deviations, and the coefficient of variation for each quantitative parameter. As it is shown, the MLS and the normalized volume offer good correlation inter-subjects for both Males and Females. From all these representations, we can conclude that the WM fiber bundle could be characterized by its normalized volume and MLS.

4   Discussion

The combination of fMRI and diffusion MRI tractography is currently the only method that offers the best reconstruction of white matter fiber bundles in vivo. Its ability to map the human connectome has made it quite popular in the field of neuroscience. For this reason, we used the combination to reconstruct the WM fiber bundle.

Macro-structural measures of WM bundle provide complementary information to characterize white matter integrity in many neurological diseases, which includes the total streamline counts, the normalized volume of the fiber tracts and the mean length of streamlines (MLS).

The current study aimed to explore how macro-structural parameters of WM fiber bundle correlates between local models and between healthy subjects.

The data of the two MRI acquisitions were obtained on a group of healthy subjects collected from the HCP database.

Firstly, the results demonstrate that the reconstructed fiber bundles based on HARDI data present a significant difference with the reconstructed fiber bundles based on DTI data. This difference is expressed by the mean correlation coefficient $r = 0.43 < 1$, and p-values $= 0.09 > 0.05$, calculated from the statistical Pearson's test. The WM fiber bundle presents an architecture of complex fibers (crossing fibers). However, the tensor model can assume only one orientation of the fiber in each voxel. Therefore, it is inappropriate to describe diffusion data in voxels containing complex fiber configurations or multiple fiber populations [33], which is the case for the WM fiber bundle.

In our study, we used HARDI-based on the ACT and probabilistic tracking algorithms, which have the aptitude to yield completer, longer bundles that reach the cortex [34]. It reduces variability and overcomes the limits of the tensor model.

Secondly, tract-specific measures, as the shape similarity showed good overlap between Males and Females. As well as the macrostructural measures such as the mean length of streamlines that showed best correlation between healthy subjects with a coefficient of variation equal to 0.08 for Males and 0.12 for Females. The bundle volume, another macrostructural feature, showed good reproducibility for most fiber bundles with a coefficient of variation equal to 0.23 for Males and 0.26 for Females. However, the number of streamlines, presents feeble reliability for all reconstructed fiber bundles. It was the order of 0.3 for both Males and Females. Thus, our results confirm the reproducibility of the normalized volume, and MLS extracted from WM tracts. Additionally, our findings were consistent with previous studies that reported the organization of WM fiber bundles using probabilistic CSD tractography-based HARDI data [7, 10].

Using this combinatorial approach, we were able to visualize the WM tracts and calculate the macrostructural measures which are the most used in diffusion MRI studies of different fiber bundles, such as language fiber bundles [12], and different WM bundles [35]. This shows a valuable step towards the validation of this approach in the analysis and the quantification of WM fiber bundles. These results represent a first validation protocol for the study of the whole WM fiber bundle. Our study shows a good correlation of the extracted macrostructural bundle measures for Males and Females.

To the best of our knowledge, there are not many studies that have investigated the whole WM bundles. Our findings seem to encourage more in-depth studies on the parameters that offer good inter-subject correlation for the WM fiber bundle to better understand the neuropathological basis of WM deficits.

5   Conclusion and Perspectives

In conclusion, we have evaluated a combining approach using fMRI and diffusion MRI-based CSD probabilistic tractography to reconstruct the WM fiber bundle. Then, we have extracted macrostructural measures such as, shape similarity, mean length of streamlines, normalized bundle volume, and streamlines count. We have shown that the HARDI fiber reconstruction model is more efficient and more reliable than the DTI fiber reconstruction model. The present study supports the use of probabilistic CSD-tractography combined with fMRI to study WM fiber bundles in healthy and clinical populations. Even though the present results are very encouraging for the extraction of macrostructural measures, future studies should focus on the confirmation of our results. First, these results should be reproduced in a larger number of healthy subjects. Secondly, we should increase the number of parameters that can quantify the WM fiber bundle and find the best parameters that offer the best correlation inter-subjects. Thirdly, we should study the symmetry of the WM tract between the two hemispheres. Finally, we would design our study to quantify the WM deficits.

References

1. Baddeley, A.: Working Memory Components of Working Memory Individual Differences in Working Memory The Slave Systems of Working Memory, vol. 255
2. Chai, W.J., Abd Hamid, A.I., Abdullah, J.M.: Working memory from the psychological and neurosciences perspectives: a review. Front. Psychol. **9**, 1–16 (2018)
3. Baddeley, A.: Working memory. Curr. Biol. **20**(4), 136–140 (2010)
4. Charlton, R.A., Barrick, T.R., Lawes, I.N.C., Markus, H.S., Morris, R.G.: White matter pathways associated with working memory in normal aging. Cortex **46**(4), 474–489 (2010)
5. Lapointe, S., Perry, A., Butowski, N.A.: Primary brain tumours in adults. Lancet **392**(10145), 432–446 (2018)

6. Acharya, S., et al.: Neuro-oncology survivors of childhood or adolescent low-grade glioma: a 10-year neurocognitive longitudinal study **21**, 1175–1183 (2019)

7. Guberman, G.I., Houde, J., Ptito, A., Gagnon, I.: Structural abnormalities in thalamo-prefrontal tracks revealed by high angular resolution diffusion imaging predict working memory scores in concussed children (2019)

8. Sugranyes, G., et al.: Multimodal analyses identify linked functional and white matter abnormalities within the working memory network in schizophrenia. Schizophr. Res. **138**(2–3), 136–142 (2012)

9. Huntley, J.D., Howard, R.J.: Working memory in early Alzheimer's disease: a neuropsychological review. Int. J. Geriatr. Psychiatry **25**(2), 121–132 (2010)

10. Cahn, A.J., Little, G., Beaulieu, C., Tétreault, P.: Diffusion properties of the fornix assessed by deterministic tractography shows age , sex, volume , cognitive , hemispheric , and twin relationships in young adults from the Human Connectome Project. Brain Struct. Funct. (2021)

11. Yeatman, J.D., Dougherty, R.F., Myall, N.J., Wandell, B.A., Feldman, H.M.: Tract profiles of white matter properties: automating fiber-tract quantification. PLoS One **7**(11) (2012)

12. Boukadi, M., et al.: Test-retest reliability of diffusion measures extracted along white matter language fiber bundles using Hardi-based tractography. Front. Neurosci. **13** (2019)

13. Sinke, M.R.T., et al.: Diffusion MRI-based cortical connectome reconstruction: dependency on tractography procedures and neuroanatomical characteristics. Brain Struct. Funct. **223**(5), 2269–2285 (2018). https://doi.org/10.1007/s00429-018-1628-y

14. Fan, J., Milosevic, R., Li, J., Bai, J., Zhang, Y.: The impact of neuroimaging advancement on neurocognitive evaluation in pediatric brain tumor survivors: a review. Brain Sci. Adv. **5**(2), 117–127 (2019)

15. Azad, T.D., Duffau, H.: Limitations of functional neuroimaging for patient selection and surgical planning in glioma surgery. Neurosurg. Focus **48**(2), E12 (2020)

16. Vassal, F., Schneider, F., Boutet, C., Jean, B., Sontheimer, A., Lemaire, J.J.: Combined DTI tractography and functional MRI study of the language connectome in healthy volunteers: extensive mapping of white matter fascicles and cortical activations. PLoS One **11**(3), 1–19 (2016)

17. Yang, Z., He, P., Zhou, J., Ding, Z., Wu, X.: Functional informed fiber tracking using combination of diffusion and functional MRI. IEEE Trans. Biomed. Eng. **66**(3), 794–801 (2019)

18. Takemura, H., Caiafa, C.F., Wandell, B.A., Pestilli, F.: Ensemble tractography. PLoS Comput. Biol. **12**(2), 1–22 (2016)

19. Descoteaux, M.: High Angular Resolution Diffusion MRI: From Local Estimation to Segmentation and Tractography (2008)

20. Webster, J.G., Descoteaux, M.: high angular resolution diffusion imaging (HARDI). Wiley Encycl. Electr. Electron. Eng., pp. 1–25 (2015)

21. Brown, G.G., Perthen, J.E., Liu, T.T., Buxton, R.B.: A primer on functional magnetic resonance imaging. Neuropsychol. Rev. **17**(2), 107–125 (2007)

22. Li, M., Newton, A.T., Anderson, A.W., Ding, Z., Gore, J.C.: Characterization of the hemodynamic response function in white matter tracts for event-related fMRI. Nat. Commun. **10**(1), 1–11 (2019)

23. El Kininy, W., Tcd, S., Roddy, D., Hanlon, E.O., Barry, D.: Magnetic resonance diffusion weighted imaging using constrained spherical deconvolution-based tractography of the extracranial course of the facial nerve. Oral Surg. Oral Med. Oral Pathol. Oral Radiol. **130**(2), e44–e56 (2020)

24. Raffelt, D., et al.: Apparent fibre density: a novel measure for the analysis of diffusion-weighted magnetic resonance images. Neuroimage **59**(4), 3976–3994 (2012)

25. Chandio, B.Q., et al.: Bundle analytics, a computational framework for investigating the shapes and profiles of brain pathways across populations. Sci. Rep. **10**(1), 1–18 (2020)
26. Chung, S., et al.: Working memory and brain tissue microstructure : white matter tract integrity based on multi-shell diffusion MRI. Sci. Rep. 1–7 (2018)
27. Glasser, M.F., et al.: The minimal preprocessing pipelines for the Human Connectome Project. Neuroimage **80**, 105–124 (2013)
28. Tournier, J.D., Calamante, F., Gadian, D.G., Connelly, A.: Direct estimation of the fiber orientation density function from diffusion-weighted MRI data using spherical deconvolution. Neuroimage **23**(3), 1176–1185 (2004)
29. Tournier, J.D., Calamante, F., Connelly, A.: MRtrix: diffusion tractography in crossing fiber regions. Int. J. Imaging Syst. Technol. **22**(1), 53–66 (2012)
30. Smith, R.E., Tournier, J., Calamante, F., Connelly, A.: NeuroImage anatomically-constrained tractography: improved diffusion MRI streamlines tractography through effective use of anatomical information. Neuroimage **62**(3), 1924–1938 (2012)
31. Barch, D.M., et al.: Function in the human connectome: task-fMRI and individual differences in behavior. Neuroimage **80**, 169–189 (2013)
32. Garyfallidis, E., Brett, M., Amirbekian, B., Rokem, A., Van Der Walt, S.: Dipy, a library for the analysis of diffusion MRI data. **8**, 1–17 (2014)
33. Hardi, D.I.: Moving beyond DTI. Introd. to Diffus. Tensor Imaging, pp. 65–78 (2014)
34. Descoteaux, M., Deriche, R., Knösche, T.R., Anwander, A.: Deterministic and probabilistic tractography based on complex fibre orientation distributions. IEEE Trans. Med. Imaging **28**(2), 269–286 (2009)
35. Guberman, G.I., Houde, J.-C., Ptito, A., Gagnon, I., Descoteaux, M.: Structural abnormalities in thalamo-prefrontal tracks revealed by high angular resolution diffusion imaging predict working memory scores in concussed children. Brain Struct. Funct. **225**(1), 441–459 (2020)

Pattern Recognition and Machine Learning for Biosignal Data

Analysis of Accuracy and Timing
in Decision-Making Tasks

Olga Georgieva[1]($\boxtimes$) (iD), Nadejda Bocheva[2] (iD), Miroslava Stefanova[2],
and Bilyana Genova[2]

[1] Sofia University "St. Kliment Ohridski", 1164 Sofia, Bulgaria
o.georgieva@fmi.uni-sofia.bg
[2] Institute of Neurobiology, Bulgarian Academy of Sciences, 1113 Sofia, Bulgaria
nadya@percept.bas.bg

Abstract. The present study investigates the separation abilities by age and gender based on raw data of two-alternative force choice decision-making task in visuo-motor experiment. The applied methodology is based on machine learning procedure for finding, assessing, and interpreting existing dependencies in interested data spaces. The procedure applies fuzzy cluster analysis to discrimate the biosignal data of the visual task where the location of the pattern center is determined by form cues, motion cues, or by their combination. The obtained grouping results are assessed according to the participants' age and gender. Further, these results are compared against the results obtained of statistical parameters data of a hierarchical drift-diffusion model (HDDM) processed by the same machine learning methodology. Differences in the subjects' capabilities to perform the visuo-motor task are summarized. It was found that age groups could be recognized with similar success by both raw and HDDM data clustering analyses. Between factors analysis strongly underlines the informativity of the reaction time. Dynamic conditions are better performed for age distinction in both cases. However, the gender is better recognizable in HDDM data space. The group of young people is characterized by low reaction time and middle value of accuracy in their responce, whereas the reverse is valid for the middle-aged participants.

Keywords: Decision making · Visuo-motor task · Cluster analysis · Fuzzy clustering

1 Introduction

Nowadays, biosignal data sensing, acquisition, analyzing is a subject of significant research that aims to reveal dependencies and hidden knowledge and by that to improve the peoples' health, physical activity, nutrition, psychological and mental state or environment [16]. The exploratory data analysis is applied through machine learning technologies both to gain insights of individuals for personalized care and to provide the technical and functional background for effective health activities as tracking, analysis, acting and visualization of the results [7, 8, 13].

© Springer Nature Switzerland AG 2021
I. Rojas et al. (Eds.): BIOMESIP 2021, LNCS 12940, pp. 283–296, 2021.
https://doi.org/10.1007/978-3-030-88163-4_25

Sophisticated data mining techniques need to be used, in order to uncover hidden meaningful patterns both in an unsupervised and supervised manner. These methods find structures within complex data sets as biosignal data are. By that they could increase the knowledge about the biological mechanizms and their application can surely improve patient outcomes [13, 15]. Thus, the obtained results indicate that machine learning algorithms can be used to effectively differentiate between healthy subjects and affected patients [14]. Important implementation of these methods is for diagnosis and disease classification, risk prediction, and solution of patient management tasks.

In particular, the potential of the unsupervised learning algorithms as cluster analysis has been proven in the years as a reliable technique for biosignal discrimination. These methods find the structure of the data space by identifying specific groups and thus enable to conclude about existing relations within and between groups. They are powerful in dealing with complex and uncertain information as they enable to handle little available information. Different brain states have been benefited by this approach being a basis for theoretical and experimental evidence for a scientific forecast of the human condition [7, 8, 15].

In this study we implement a methodology based on cluster analysis to evaluate whether, based on the raw data of visuo-motor experiment, it is possible to estimate the contribution of between-subject factors and to get information about the different characteristics of the stimulus conditions to form age and gender groups. The other research aim is to compare the raw data results and the results of statistical parameters' data for grouping and to conclude the possible practical implementation of the applied discrimination methodology.

2   Related Works of Human Decision Data Analysis

Human decision-making involves a multitude of processes – from coding stimulus information to organizing a response based on the decision choice [2]. A successful approach to separate the contribution of these processes is the drift diffusion model [4–6]. The model is applicable for two-alternative choice decision tasks and assumes that the decision is reached by a sequential accumulation of evidence in support of the two decision choices. Its main parameters include the non-decision time t-c needed to code the stimulus information and prepare the response, the drift rate v-c characterizing the speed of evidence accumulation, and the decision boundary a-c between the two choices. A Python toolbox named Hierarchical Drift Diffusion Model (HDDM) [9] applies the drift-diffusion model by using Bayesian parameter estimation. It allows estimation of both individual and group parameters, tolerates missing values, and requires fewer data to estimate model parameters.

In seeking to extend the usability of HDDM the grouping abilities were investigated [10]. The findings show that application of machine learning technique as clustering analysis to the HDDM parameters is helpful for understanding and explaining the decision-making process. The cluster separation implies that in a visual task where the location of the pattern center could be determined by form cues (orientation), motion cues (direction of motion), or by their combination, the dynamic conditions provide better separation of the age groups. Also, the non-decision time (t-c parameter) provides better separation of the age groups than any other parameter of the drift-diffusion model. Between-factors not studied by HDDM can be evaluated based on the individual values for cluster membership, allowing a simplification of the coding and estimation derived by the model.

Despite the detailed information that HDDM could retrieve, its drawbacks are connected to the variability of the model parameters due to instability to keep a constant criterion in the decision process, the random variations in evidence accumulation from trial to trial, and the variability in the non-decision processes. Coding mixed-effects models with the toolbox is a challenge, as well as evaluating the interaction in between-subject factors. More complex models are also time-consuming. In addition, it is unclear whether and to what extent using the parameters of the drift-diffusion model has advantages for subject grouping compared to raw data estimates of response time and accuracy and in what conditions. For this research we aplly the same methodology of cluster analysis [10] to raw data for finding and assess the age and gender groups in different conditions of the visio-motor experiment. Further these results are compared with the results of HDDM parameters grouping obtained by the same methodology in order to conclude the possible practical implementation of the investigated discrimination methodology.

In the sequel, after specifying briefly the experiments and the raw data collected, the study presents the applied methodology for assessing the informativeness of different experimental conditions and distinguishing by age and gender. The next study part explains the extracted information about age and gender effects from the performance of the visuo-motor task. Further, comparison analysis with the results obtained by grouping based on the HDDM parameters is commented. The last part summarizes the results and draws conclusions about the practical applicability of the analyzes.

3   Experiments and Data Description

Data from four types of visual experiments have been examined. A detailed description of the experiments is given in [11]. Here we will present the experimental conditions and the task briefly. The stimuli were the so-called Glass patterns [1] in which randomly scattered dot pairs' orientations are consistent with a globally coherent structure. In our study, the dot pairs formed radial patterns with a center shifted to the left or the right from the mid-point of the image in a horizontal direction. Out of 25 pairs of points, 18 pointed to the pattern center, and seven pairs were randomly oriented. This description corresponds to the static condition.

Three other conditions were used: combined, flicker and motion. In all of them, the lifetime of the dots was three frames (100 ms). In the flicker condition, one-third of the pairs were re-generated elsewhere on every frame keeping their initial orientation. This gives the impression of movement, but it is not related to the orientation of the pairs. In the combined condition, the pairs moved in the direction of their orientation; those pointing to the pattern center moved away from it, whereas the others (7) moved randomly. Again, each frame updated the position of one-third of the pairs. In motion condition, there were no pairs, and 18×2 (36) points in the pattern moved away from a common center, while the remaining 7×2 (14) moved randomly. In all conditions, the simulated shifts of the pattern centers were from 0.67 to 4.69 cm with a step of 0.67.

Data of 35 participants in the four experiments were collected. The subjects were classified into three age groups: 12 young (19 to 34 years, median = 23 years); 11 middle-aged (36 to 52 years, median = 44 years); 12 old (57 to 84 years, median = 72), having a parity representation of both sexes in each group. Each pattern was presented to each participant 20 times in random order. Each condition was performed on a separate day. The task of the participants was to determine whether the center of the patterns was to the left or right of the screen mid-point. They had to make a saccade to the perceived pattern center and to press a mouse button according to their decision.

1. The reaction time of the mouse button press measured in milliseconds, the response accuracy and the eye-movement data were recorded for each condition and participant for the twenty repetitions of each center shift. Some preliminary data processing is necessary in order to get a reliable and useful data set. Following activities in consequent order are important stages of data preparation:
2. Downloading and collecting data by the experimental equipment in a relational database [12].
3. Data filtering was needed to reduce the effect of the individual's ability to answer correctly at the expense of the group's ability. For this, we use data only from the largest center displacement of 4.69 cm.
4. The median of reaction time denoted as RT is calculated as a summary statistic of the measurements obtained for a distinct set of the condition parameters of a participant. This characteristic is preferred against the mean value due to the existing data asymmetry.
5. Accuracy Ac is calculated as a relative value of the number of correct answers to the number of experiments done for a condition set of a participant.
6. Data organization appropriated for clustering analysis: respective tables of 35×4 dimensions were organized for the data of RT and Ac, where rows correspond to the participants and the columns to the four visual conditions.

4   Methodology

For the purpose of the research aim, four-dimensional data spaces of the key variables data – RT, Ac or both, measured at respective combined, motion, flicker, and static experiments were used to evaluate their ability to detect the grouping and contribution of the age and gender to the investigated decision process. Due to the lack of a reference model, studies of these spaces can be carried out using cluster analysis. This machine learning technique does not need preliminary information about the data structure. An effective solution could be found by objective function clustering. The defined groups are clusters, each of which is represented by a cluster center – a point that is most representative of it in the probabilistic sense. Among the large number of this type of clustering algorithms, here we apply fuzzy clustering as a good opportunity to deal with the existing uncertainty of the spaces and lack of a clear boundary between groups. Another advantage is that it provides information for the degree of belonging of the data to each cluster.

For each formed data space, the research procedure follows several steps:

a) *Data clustering by Fuzzy-C-Means* (FCM) algorithm

FCM is an objective function-based algorithm with clustering criteria J that iteratively minimizes the following sum [3]:

$$J = \sum_{i=1}^{c} \sum_{k=1}^{N} u_{ik}^{m} |x_k - v_i|^2 \tag{1}$$

where u_{ik} denotes the membership degree of the data point x_k, $k = 1,\ldots, N$, to the i-th cluster with a center v_i, $i = 1,\ldots, c$. Every point of the data space belongs to the clusters with membership degree u_{ik}, which is a value between 0 and 1. If the data is close to the cluster center, the membership degree is closer to one. Here N is the number of data, and c is the number of clusters. In our case, $N = 35$ is the number of participants, and the number of clusters c is defined based on further data analysis. The coefficient $m \in [1,\infty)$ determines how much clusters may overlap and its default value is $m = 2$. As we don't have preliminary knowledge about the shape and orientation of the searched clusters, Euclidean distance is incorporated as a data distance measure in Eq. (1).

b) *Evaluation of clustering quality* by indexes to find the right number of clusters

1) Average within-cluster distance (AWCD) value is estimated by the weighted distances of the data to the cluster centers. The minimum value is preferred but the "knee" principle is applied to determine the best clustering:

$$AWCD = \frac{1}{c} \sum_{i=1}^{c} \frac{\sum_{k=1}^{N} u_{ik}^{m} |x_k - v_i|^m}{\sum_{k=1}^{N} u_{ik}^{m}} \tag{2}$$

2) Average partition density (APD) assesses the density of the clusters. An index assesses the fuzziness of the partition. Good partitions are indicated by large values of APD.

$$APD = \frac{1}{c} \sum_{i=1}^{c} \frac{S_i}{\sum_{k=1}^{N} u_{ik}} \tag{3}$$

where $S_i = \sum_{k=1}^{N} u_{ik}$ or every point k that $(x_k - v_i)(x_k - v_i)^T < 1$.

3) The cluster volume V_i, $i = 1,\ldots, c$, calculated by a sum of the membership values of a cluster, is another measure to estimate the cluster density. The maximum value indicates better clustering

c) *Comparative analysis of the obtained grouping*

The AWCD, APD, and V_i indexes are parameters that evaluate the quality of the obtained data grouping itself but not the classification capabilities of the obtained grouping. The extent to which the obtained clusters cover actual age and gender groups needs to investigate. It is necessary to explicate the membership degree of each person's data to each cluster obtained. Due to the affiliation of the data to multiple clusters, the highest membership degree is used to determine belonging to a unique cluster.

d) *Visualization and interpretation of the results* is a step that describes and explains the dependences identified by the groups found

This methodology was already applied for the investigation of HDDM statistical parameters defined for the same experimental data set [10]. The reason for this application is twofold. First, the methodology successfully reveals knowledge about data grouping, and second, this is a premise for reliable comparison analysis about the applicability of statistical and raw data.

5 Data Analysis

5.1 Age Grouping Assessment According to *RT* Data

Values of AWCD and APD indexes allow setting appropriate data separation (Table 1). The results of AWCD enable to set the proper number of clusters. By applying the knee method to AWCD values for division in 2, 3, 4, and 5 we found that most representative is clustering in 3 and 4 clusters. Due to the number of data points, division in more than five clusters does not give reliable information.

Clustering in 3 and 4 clusters as the most representative, obtained for the HDDM parameter data [10] is valuable as well for the raw data of *RT* values (Table 1). However, the values APD index of *RT* data structuring are commensurate with the respective values of the least informative space defined by a-c parameter. This means that the raw data clusters are less compact than those obtained by the most representative HDDM parameters.

Table 1. Clustering indexes results of the HDDM parameters [10] and *RT* data

Index\c	2	3	4	5
t-c data				
AWCD	0.279133	0.179799	0.129162	0.053895
APD	0.887900	0.886915	0.910591	0.913007
a-c data				
AWCD	0.710794	0.489768	0.377499	0.261670
APD	0.638586	0.766424	0.769378	0.779237
v-c data				
AWCD	0.555400	0.351397	0.270981	0.217894
APD	0.752245	0.855247	0.827687	0.851103
***RT*data**				
Index\c	2	3	4	5
AWCD	0.987363	0.505178	0.396061	0.334074
APD	0.648173	0.731065	0.772663	0.831175

The coordinates of the cluster centers give some more inside information about the obtained grouping. Main conclusions done for t-c clustering ability for recognizing the age groups (Table 2A) are valid for RT clustering. Young participants form the most compact group. In the three clusters' division, eleven of them belong to the first cluster of people having the quickest response (small RT) (Table 2B). Out of them, 8 strongly belong to this group with membership degree over 0.87. In the case of division in 4 clusters, the group of people having the quickest answer comprises 8 young people, seven of which with strong membership with degree over 0.7. One middle-aged person also belongs to this first cluster. Old persons are recognized in a group with the largest response time (Table 2B) – cluster 3 for division in three clusters and cluster 4 for division in four clusters. Again, only part of the elderly persons is recognized by these groups as the rest of the old individuals are spread over the other groups. The middle-aged people in practice are not identified by division in three clusters as they are separated in the first (7 subjects) and third group (4 subjects). In a division in four clusters, the second cluster that presents the second in magnitude RT value predominantly is formed by middle-aged subjects (six persons). The third cluster collects individuals from all three age groups, whereas the cluster of longest RT comprises only elderly people (Fig. 1).

Assuming that the difference Δ between the maximal and minimal value of the respective cluster center coordinates to some extent is a measure of the separation ability of the corresponding experimental condition, then the following could be summarized. The largest difference is presented by the dynamic conditions, these are more sensitive in separating the individuals than the static one (Table 2B). Nevertheless, the dynamic conditions are not that much delimited according to Δ values, it should be marked that

Table 2A. Cluster centers of t-c parameter data clustering into 3 and 4 clusters [10]

c	Combined	Flicker	Motion	Static	c	Combined	Flicker	Motion	Static
1	0.3219	0.3314	0.3340	0.3264	1	0.2786	0.2589	0.2479	0.2534
2	0.9736	1.0641	1.3208	0.6849	2	0.3993	0.4169	0.4737	0.4298
3	0.5477	0.5353	0.5965	0.5439	3	0.5865	0.5795	0.6284	0.5729
–	–	–	–	–	4	0.9609	1.0519	1.3070	0.7344
Δ	0.6517	0.7327	0.9868	0.3585		0.6823	0.7930	1.0590	0.4810

Table 2B. Cluster centers of RT data clustering into 3 and 4 clusters

c	Combined	Flicker	Motion	Static	c	Combined	Flicker	Motion	Static
1	0.7777	0.8125	0.9887	0.7705	1	0.6625	0.6884	0.7729	0.6735
2	2.9675	3.0050	3.2023	2.1785	2	0.9127	0.9819	1.2418	0.9206
3	1.3087	1.3834	1.7425	1.3371	3	1.3676	1.4283	1.8047	1.3943
–	–	–	–	–	4	3.0051	3.0451	3.2292	2.1926
Δ	2.1899	2.1925	2.2136	1.4081	Δ	2.3426	2.3567	2.4563	1.5191

the motion condition is represented highly. This in fact confirms the general conclusions done based on the HDDM parameter analysis (Table 2A) [10].

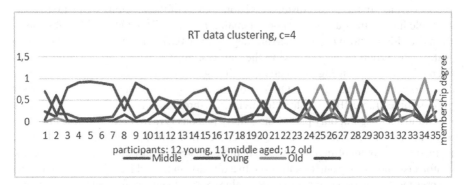

Fig. 1. Membership degrees values of the participants to each of the four clusters. Three of the clusters could be identified as corresponding to an age group. whereas the fourth (violet color) covers data of all age groups. (Color figure online)

5.2 Age Grouping Assessment According to *Ac* Data

The other point of interest is assessing the ability to group the participants accounting for the accuracy *Ac* of their responses. The clustering ability of this parameter shows low abilities as no well-formed clusters are recognized, and thus no good covering of the real age groups is found. For clustering in three clusters, $c = 3$ the young people are in parity separated in the first and third clusters. The larger part of the middle-aged (8 persons) are also assigned to the third cluster and the rest three – to the first cluster. Elderly people do not present any assignment as they are spread over all clusters. Clustering in 4 clusters also does not reveal much information about the grouping. For instance, the second cluster attracts 5 of the young, 8 of the middle-aged, and 5 of the old subjects. The rest of each group is scattered over the other clusters and does not present any valuable grouping (Table 2C).

A reason for the low grouping ability is the lack of diversity of *Ac* values. In fact, the larger part of the participants has a similar behavior as they didn't make any mistakes or showed only a few. Only a few people have presented a larger and different number of wrong answers. According to the Δ values (Table 2C and Table 2D), the combined condition is represented highly.

5.3 Age Grouping Assessment According to Joint *RT* and *Ac* Data

More informative is the space organized by both interesting factors of the visuo-motor task – *RT* and *Ac*. The eight-dimensional data space is formed by the *RT* and *Ac* values of the four conditions. It gives the opportunity to find groups that are dependent on both factors.

Table 2C. Cluster centers of *AC* data clustering into 3 and 4 clusters

c	Combined	Flicker	Motion	Static	c	Combined	Flicker	Motion	Static
1	0.8951	0.8903	0.6196	0.7343	1	0.7560	0.8361	0.6904	0.5625
2	0.4261	0.6636	0.6026	0.3164	2	0.9919	0.9773	0.8549	0.8808
3	0.9887	0.9722	0.8389	0.8684	3	0.9644	0.9237	0.6329	0.7894
					4	0.3493	0.6275	0.5691	0.2620
Δ	0.5626	0.3086	0.2363	0.5519	Δ	0.6426	0.3497	0.2859	0.6187

Table 2D. Cluster centers of *RT-Ac* data clustering into 3 clusters

c	*RT*-combined	*RT*-flicker	*RT*-motion	*RT*-static	*Ac*-combined	*Ac*-flicker	*Ac*-motion	*Ac*-static
1	2.8260	2.7308	2.9215	1.9826	0.5892	0.7412	0.6996	0.4360
2	1.1275	1.2255	1.5197	1.1151	0.9771	0.9617	0.8376	0.8533
3	0.8076	0.8423	1.0528	0.8292	0.9415	0.9365	0.6827	0.7957
Δ	2.0184	1.8885	1.8686	1.1533	0.3878	0.2205	0.1549	0.4174

Clustering in three clusters, c = 3 distinguishes well the three age groups. Nine of the young participants and three of the middle-aged ones strongly belong to one cluster (third cluster, Table 2D). This cluster presents the fastest answers. However, people included in this cluster are in mid according to the accuracy of their responses. The second cluster is formed predominantly by middle-aged (8 persons). This group of participants are in mid according to *RT* but most accurate in their responses. The elderly are difficult to recognize as they are scattered among the three clusters. The tendency for young and middle-aged to form separate clusters is kept in case of division in four clusters (Fig. 2). However, unlike the *RT* clustering (Sect. 5.1) the elderly people are more scattered and could not form a representative cluster group.

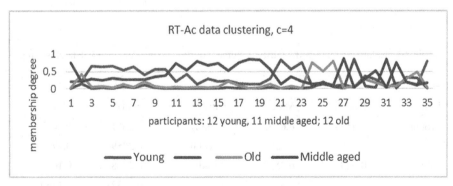

Fig. 2. Membership degrees values of the participants to each of the four clusters. Three of the clusters are identified as corresponding to an age group, whereas the fourth (red color) covers data of all age groups. (Color figure online)

5.4 Gender Grouping Assessment

The assessment of the gender differentiation can be done by comparison of the volume of clusters, V_i, $i = 1,..., c$ formed by the two genders. The respective relative volume values are calculated in order to account for the different number of female and male participants in each group. Here, the analysis is given for the two valuable spaces – the division of RT and RT-Ac data spaces.

The relative value of the cluster volumes of HDDM t-c data separation shows that males are more represented in the clusters of young people and part of the middle-aged, whereas women predominantly form the cluster of elderly (Table 3A). In contrast to these results, the contribution of both sexes in the formation of cluster volume obtained by the RT data separation shows some differences. The relative cluster volumes could not distinguish well females and males as both they are highly presented in the same clusters (Table 3B), although the tendency for men to participate more in the formation of the youth cluster persists. The most represented volume values given in the tables are in bold.

By the same method, the two genders are distinguished for each group separately (Table 4A, Table 4B, Table 4C). For drift-diffusion model spaces, the genders are quite well separated. The females are less likely to form the group of young people, while males are strongly represented in it: 0.559 vs. 0.8799 for division into 3 clusters and 0.3645 vs. 0.6945 for division into 4 clusters. Conversely, women more strongly form the elderly group, whereas males are less represented.

Table 3A. Relative values of the cluster volumes for the two genders of t-c data clustering [10]

c = 3			c = 4		
Cluster	Female	Male	Cluster	Female	Male
1	0.3019	**0.5844**	1	0.1598	0.3268
2	0.1544	0.0834	2	0.3178	**0.4033**
3	**0.5438**	0.3322	3	**0.3855**	0.2110
			4	0.1369	0.0589

Table 3B. Relative values of the cluster volumes for the two genders of RT data clustering

c = 3			c = 4		
Cluster	Female	Male	Cluster	Female	Male
1 (young)	**0.4824**	**0.6202**	1 (mid)	0.2661	0.3477
2 (mid)	0.1683	0.1260	2 (young)	**0.3059**	**0.3711**
3 (old)	0.3493	0.2538	3 (old)	0.2748	0.1673
			4	0.1532	0.1139

Table 3C. Relative values of the cluster volumes for the two genders of *RT-Ac* data clustering

c = 3			c = 4		
Cluster	Female	Male	Cluster	Female	Male
1 (old)	0.1743	0.1258	1 (young)	0.2919	0.3790
2 (mid)	**0.4391**	0.4130	2	0.1015	0.0913
3 (young)	0.3867	**0.4612**	3 (old)	0.2160	0.0979
			4 (mid)	**0.3914**	**0.4318**

The participation of the two genders in forming the *RT* clusters accounting for the age of the participants confirms the general dependency already discovered by HDDM parameter analysis. Again, young males are more involved in forming the cluster of young subjects but the difference with females is not such exceeding (Table 3B). The gender of middle-aged people is almost equally represented in all obtained clusters. Unlike the statistical parameter clustering, the *RT* clustering presents the female participation in the elderly group more expressively (Table 4B).

The low level of distinguishing between the two genders is seen for *RT-Ac* clustering as well (Table 3C). The gender effect within different clusters presents a result that differs from *RT* space distinguishing. Young and middle-aged females are better presented than males in forming the clusters of young and middle-aged (Table 4C). This result could be explained by better accuracy of women responses than males, which difference is especially strongly expressed for the middle-aged group.

Table 4A. Relative volumes of clusters calculated for the two genders in t-c space; a) division in three clusters; b) division in four clusters [10]

a)	Young		Middle-aged		Elderly	
Cluster	Female	Male	Female	Male	Female	Male
1	**0.5590**	**0.8799**	0.3104	**0.5859**	0.079	0.2384
2	0.0213	0.0191	0.0291	0.0211	0.3906	0.2105
3	0.4197	0.1011	**0.6605**	0.3931	**0.5304**	**0.5511**
b)	Young		Middle-aged		Elderly	
Cluster	Female	Male	Female	Male	Female	Male
1	**0.3645**	**0.6957**	0.1048	0.0969	0.0443	0.0881
2	0.3223	0.2507	**0.4896**	**0.6369**	0.109	**0.3866**
3	0.2614	0.0444	0.3853	0.2572	**0.4891**	0.3669
4	0.0118	0.0092	0.0204	0.0091	0.3576	0.1585

Table 4B. Relative volumes of clusters calculated for the two genders in *RT* data space; a) division in three clusters; b) division in four clusters

a)	Young		Middle-aged		Elderly	
Cluster	Female	Male	Female	Male	Female	Male
1	**0.7394**	**0.8581**	**0.6755**	**0.5837**	0.0750	**0.3732**
2	0.0316	0.0134	0.0150	0.0148	0.4356	0.3500
3	0.2290	0.1286	0.3096	0.4015	**0.4894**	0.2767
b)	Young		Middle-aged		Elderly	
Cluster	Female	Male	Female	Male	Female	Male
1	**0.4172**	**0.6134**	0.1662	0.2703	0.0525	0.1021
2	0.3852	0.3199	**0.4859**	**0.4492**	0.1120	**0.3659**
3	0.1617	0.0602	0.2056	0.2707	**0.4306**	0.2061
4	0.0226	0.0065	0.0174	0.0098	0.4049	0.3259

Table 4C. Relative volumes of clusters calculated for the two genders in *RT-Ac* data space; a) division in three clusters; b) division in four clusters

a)	Young		Middle-aged		Elderly	
Cluster	Female	Male	Female	Male	Female	Male
1	0.1118	0.0377	0.0270	0.0163	0.3736	0.3199
2 mid	0.2830	0.4011	**0.6079**	**0.4939**	**0.4002**	**0.3595**
3 young	**0.6052**	**0.5612**	0.3651	0.4899	0.2261	0.3206
b)	Young		Middle-aged		Elderly	
Cluster	Female	Male	Female	Male	Female	Male
1 young	**0.3878**	0.4496	0.2266	0.4308	0.1333	0.2536
2	0.0648	0.0239	0.0213	0.0112	0.2204	0.2367
3	0.2112	0.0566	0.1889	0.0564	**0.4090**	0.1806
4 mid	0.2025	**0.4698**	**0.5295**	**0.5015**	0.2372	**0.3292**

6 Discussion and Conclusion

Comparison of division abilities of HDDM parameter and raw data spaces to identify subject age and gender could be summarized as follows.

- Age groups could be recognized with similar success by both HDDM and raw data clustering analyses. Between factors analysis strongly underlines the informativity of *RT* factor as well as *RT-Ac* space. However, we have to note that additional experiments are needed in order to conclude about the ability of the accuracy to be a distinguishing factor.

- Dynamic conditions are better performed for the distinction of the age of both data space types.
- The gender is better recognizable in HDDM data space.
- The *RT-Ac* space enriches the grouping accounting for both factors. In this space, the group of young is characterized by low *RT* and middle value of *Ac*, whereas the reverse is valid for the middle-aged participants.
- The elderly people are not so well separated in comparison to the young participants as their cluster is more sparse.
- It could not recognize any (strong) dependency of the particular subject's age and the respective level of belonging to the identified clusters. This means that the process of ageing is not defined only by age but other factors should be considering in visio-motor decision-making task.

Acknowledgment. This research work has been supported by GATE project, funded by the Horizon 2020 WIDESPREAD-2018-2020 TEAMING Phase 2 programme under grant agreement No. 857155 and and Operational Programme Science and Education for Smart Growth under Grant Agreement No. BG05M2OP001-1.003-0002-C01 as well as by the Science Fund of Sofia University "St. Kliment Ohridski", Bulgaria under grant FNI-SU-80-10-152/05.04.2021.

References

1. Bocheva, N., Genova, B., Stefanova, M.: Drift diffusion modeling of response time in heading estimation based on motion and form cues. Int. J. Biol. Biomed. Eng. **12**, 75–83 (2018)
2. Goodale, M.A., Milner, A.D.: Separate visual pathways for perception and action. Trends Neurosci. **15**, 20–25 (1992)
3. Bezdek, J.C.: Pattern Recognition with Fuzzy Objective Function Algorithms. Plenum Press, NY (1981)
4. Ratcliff, R., Smith, P., Brown, S., MacKoon, G.: Diffusion decision model: current issues and history. Trends Cogn. Sci. **20**(4), 260–281 (2016)
5. Ratcliff, R., Smith, P.: Perceptual discrimination in static and dynamic noise: the temporal relation between perceptual encoding and decision-making. J. Exp. Psychol. Gen. **139**(1), 70–94 (2010)
6. Ratcliff, R., MacKoon, G.: The diffusion decision model: theory and data for two-choice decision tasks. Neural Comput. **20**(4), 873–922 (2008)
7. Viswanathan, M., Whangbo, T.K., Yang, Y.K.: Data mining in ubiquitous healthcare. In: Funatsu, K. (ed.) New Fundamental Technologies in Data Mining. InTech (2011). ISBN: 978-953-307-547-1
8. Di, W., Zhu, D.: Study on brainfag based on EEG signal analysis. In: Proc. of ETP International Conference on Future Computer and Communication, pp. 134–137. June (2009)
9. Wiecki, T.V., Sofer, I., Frank, M.J.: HDDM: hierarchical bayesian estimation of the drift-diffusion model in python. Front. Neuroinform. **7**, 1–10 (2013)
10. Georgieva, O., Bocheva, N., Genova, B., Stefanova, M.: Eye movement data analysis. In: Iliadis, L., Angelov, P.P., Jayne, C., Pimenidis, E. (eds.) EANN 2020. PINNS, vol. 2, pp. 460–470. Springer, Cham (2020). https://doi.org/10.1007/978-3-030-48791-1_36

11. Glass, L.: Moire effect from random dots. Nature **223**, 578–580 (1969)
12. Kraleva, R., Kralev, V., Sinyagina, N., Koprinkova-Hristova, P., Bocheva, N.: Design and analysis of a relational database for behavioral experiments data processing. Int. J. Online Eng. **14**(2), 117–132 (2018)
13. Chousiadas, D., Menychtas, A., Tsanakas, P., Maglogiannis, I.: Advancing quantified-self applications utilizing visual data analytics and the internet of things. In: Iliadis, L., Maglogiannis, I., Plagianakos, V. (eds.) AIAI 2018. IAICT, vol. 520, pp. 263–274. Springer, Cham (2018). https://doi.org/10.1007/978-3-319-92016-0_24
14. Poddar, M.G., Birajdar, A.C., Virmani, J., Kriti: Automated classification of hypertension and coronary artery disease patients by PNN, KNN, and SVM classifiers using HRV analysis. In: Dey, N., Borra, S., Ashour, A.S., Shi, F. (eds.) Machine Learning in Bio-Signal Analysis and Diagnostic Imaging, pp. 99–125. Academic Press (2019)
15. Sevakula, R.K., Au-Yeung, W.T.M., Singh, J.P., Heist, E.K., Isselbacher, E.M., Armoundas, A.A.: State-of-the-art machine learning techniques aiming to improve patient outcomes pertaining to the cardiovascular system. J. Am. Heart Assoc. **9**(4) (2020)
16. Swan, M.: The quantified self: fundamental disruption in big data science and biological discovery. Big Data **1**(2), 85–99 (2013)

Recurrent Neural Networks and Efficiency in High-Dimensional EEG Classification

Javier León[1]([✉])(iD), Juan José Escobar[1](iD), Jesús González[1](iD), Julio Ortega[1](iD), Francisco Manuel Arrabal-Campos[2](iD), Andrés Ortiz[3](iD), and Miguel Damas[1](iD)

[1] Department of Computer Architecture and Technology, CITIC,
University of Granada, Granada, Spain
{jleon,jjescobar,jesusgonzalez,jortega,mdamas}@ugr.es
[2] Department of Engineering, University of Almería, Almería, Spain
fmarrabal@ual.es
[3] Department of Communications Engineering, University of Málaga, Málaga, Spain
aortiz@ic.uma.es

Abstract. The performance of neural networks has granted deep learning a place at the forefront of machine learning in the last decade. Although these models are computationally intensive, their advantage is recognized in a wide array of applications. Nonetheless, the large amount of learnable parameters in neural networks can be a disadvantage for small and high-dimensional datasets. In this context, the relationship between solution quality and model complexity gains significance due to overfitting concerns. This is precisely the case of Electroencephalography (EEG), where the data consists in relatively few patterns obtained from multiple electrode readings. In this paper, we take a look at two widely-known types of Recurrent Neural Networks (RNNs), namely Gated Recurrent Unit (GRU) and Long Short-Term Memory (LSTM), which are evaluated on three EEG Motor Imagery (MI) datasets by measuring not only classification accuracy, but also time and energy consumption. Although the results are not entirely competitive with the state-of-the-art in the datasets considered, the interaction that occurs between the size of the networks and their accuracy provides us with valuable insight about network structure design in the context of the curse of dimensionality.

Keywords: Recurrent Neural Networks · Gated Recurrent Unit · Long Short-Term Memory · Electroencephalography · Energy-time analysis

1 Introduction

High-dimensional datasets with few training examples available are a common occurrence in Electroencephalography (EEG), along with many other applications in bioinformatics. For the case of EEG, this is due to the nature of the data acquisition process: Brain-Computer Interface (BCI) subjects are required

© Springer Nature Switzerland AG 2021
I. Rojas et al. (Eds.): BIOMESIP 2021, LNCS 12940, pp. 297–310, 2021.
https://doi.org/10.1007/978-3-030-88163-4_26

to perform certain tasks during which their brain activity is recorded, which becomes cumbersome for a high number of repetitions.

In the last years, the problem of EEG classification has often been tackled through deep learning approaches. Neural networks of various kinds have been employed in the state-of-the-art: for instance, Convolutional Neural Networks (CNNs) can be found in [1–3], Recurrent Neural Networks (RNNs) in [4] or a recurrent-convolutional hybrid network in [5].

Whereas, understandably, high classification accuracy is the most sought-after metric of performance, the use of neural networks in EEG applications often sees time and energy consumption relegated to the background. This can detract from the practical value of an otherwise powerful solution, but it is seldom addressed. For instance, in [5] the authors consider two models of similar accuracy by running a real-time experiment where the smaller model has a delay of 1.4 seconds, against 2.5 of the bigger one. Although there should still be room for improvement, it serves to highlight the importance of computational efficiency. With this concern in mind, this paper takes a look at two common types of recurrent units (Gated Recurrent Unit and Long Short-Term Memory) and analyzes both their classification accuracy and energy-time cost; a Feature Selection (FS) step is first carried out, and then a hyperparameter tuning procedure is used to find the size of the recurrent layer. The assessment of the accuracy-cost trade-off is particularly relevant in small but high-dimensional datasets (such as EEG), where the curse of dimensionality [6] is likely to occur. In this context, increasing the complexity of the models could detract from their performance as overfitting starts to prevail over generalization capabilities.

The remaining sections are organized as follows: Sect. 2 describes the datasets; Sect. 3 explains the recurrent models, the optimization procedure, the performance measurements, and the statistical analysis; Sect. 4 presents and discusses the experimental results; finally, the conclusions and future work can be found in Sect. 5.

2   The Datasets Used in This Work

In this paper, three EEG datasets are used to evaluate the accuracy and energy-time cost of two widely-known RNN alternatives. The datasets, which correspond to three human subjects (104, 107, and 110), were recorded at the BCI Laboratory of the University of Essex, UK [7]. 12 healthy subjects between 24 and 50 years old (58% female, half of them naive to BCI) were recruited for the experiment. The subjects gave their written informed consent beforehand and were paid for their participation.

The EEG data corresponds to the MI paradigm, which focuses on the brief amplifications and attenuations (Event-Related Desynchronization and Synchronization, respectively) that limb movement imagination produces. EEG trials were recorded through 15 electrodes (placement shown in Fig. 1) at a sampling rate of

256 Hz. These trials were used to build patterns through a type of Multiresolution Analysis (MRA) [8] called Discrete Wavelet Transform, as seen in [7].

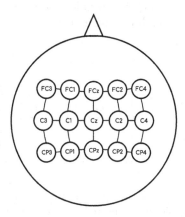

Fig. 1. Electrode placement in the extension of the International 10–20 system.

To build each pattern, the signal obtained from each electrode (a time series) was divided into 20 consecutive and partially overlapping segments. At every segment, MRA was performed with 6 wavelet levels to produce 6 sets of coefficients. These sets are of two types (approximation and details) and their sizes are powers of two (128, 64, 32, 16, 8, and 4 coefficients for levels 6 to 1). In total, an EEG pattern has $2 \times S \times E \times L$ sets of coefficients, where S indicates the number of segments, E the number of electrodes, and L the number of wavelet levels. Thus, with $S = 20$, $E = 15$, and $L = 6$, there are $3,600$ sets of coefficients and a total of $151,200$ coefficients. This number can be reduced to $3,600$ coefficients by computing the within-set variance [7]. The resulting patterns are also normalized between 0 and 1, with no missing values present.

There are 178 patterns available for training and a further 178 for testing, each containing $3,600$ features, for every one of the three datasets. The datasets have three balanced classes that correspond to imagined left and right hand movements and imagined feet movement.

3   Methodology

3.1   Recurrent Neural Networks and Model Optimization

Recurrent Neural Networks (RNNs) can be seen as an extension of the basic feedforward model that is able to work with inputs of variable length. A working memory in the form of a recurrent internal state makes it possible to use not only the information contained in each isolated value but also its surrounding context.

The basic recurrent unit involves a loop that adds a variable amount of feedback from previous values to the processing of subsequent ones. The loop can be unrolled as shown in Fig. 2, where x_t is a value of the input vector, o_t is the output of the unit (which has a hidden state h_t), and c_f is the context preserved in some form through the different units.

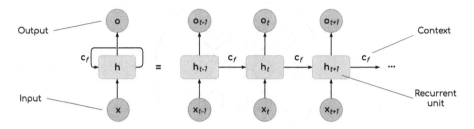

Fig. 2. An unrolled RNN loop with inputs at the bottom and outputs at the top. Recurrent units are in the middle, connected by a one-way context loop.

A simple recurrence scheme where the context (c_f) is just the hidden state from the previous unit (h_{t-1}) is described by Eqs. 1 and 2, with θ representing the set of hyperparameters of the model. Note that there exist other schemes of recurrence, such as bi-directional [9].

$$h_t = f(h_{t-1}, x_t, \theta), \tag{1}$$

$$o_t = f(h_t, \theta), \tag{2}$$

The equations show that the output of the unit is obtained solely from its hidden state. The current hidden state is computed by taking into account the input and the hidden state from the previous unit. This allows the network to keep utilizing previous inputs.

However, this architecture comes with some issues: as the context needed for an application grows, basic RNNs become progressively worse at handling dependencies among inputs [10]. Two of the most successful variants that were designed to solve this problem are the Long Short-Term Memory (LSTM), introduced in [11], and the more recent Gated Recurrent Unit (GRU), proposed in [12]. It has been shown that, although GRU is computationally cheaper, LSTM is strictly more powerful [13]. In order to tackle long-term dependencies, LSTM units have five elements:

- Input gate (Eq. 3), which controls the extent to which new information is stored in the cell.

$$i_t = \sigma_{\log}(W^i x_t + U^i h_{t-1} + b^i). \tag{3}$$

- Forget gate (Eq. 4), which decides the fragments of existing context that will be forgotten based on the current input. This element was added to the architecture in [14].

$$f_t = \sigma_{\log}(W^f x_t + U^f h_{t-1} + b^f). \tag{4}$$

- Output gate (Eq. 5), which controls how relevant the information from the current unit is to the output.

$$o_t = \sigma_{\log}(W^o x_t + U^o h_{t-1} + b^o). \tag{5}$$

- Cell state (Eq. 6), where important contextual information is stored. The contents do not change substantially once stored, and thus the network is able to keep track of details for a relatively long time.

$$c_t = f_t \circ c_{t-1} + i_t \circ \tanh(W^c x_t + U^c h_{t-1} + b^c). \tag{6}$$

- Hidden state (Eq. 7), where the output of the unit is computed.

$$h_t = o_t \circ \tanh(c_t). \tag{7}$$

In Eqs. 4, 5, 6, and 7, lowercase variables are vectors (with x_t being the input vector of the unit) and uppercase variables are weight matrices learned during training (W matrices contain weights associated with the input and U matrices contain weights for the connections coming from network units). $\sigma_{\log}$ represents logistic sigmoid functions. The operator $\circ$ is the Hadamard product, or element-wise product.

The GRU is a simplified variant of the LSTM. The cell element disappears, and only two gates are required: the reset and update gates, shown in Eqs. 8 and 9. The reset gate is in charge of merging existing information with new inputs, whereas the update gate decides what should be discarded from the current context. The output of the unit is given by Eqs. 10 and 11.

$$r_t = \sigma_{\log}(W^r x_t + U^r h_{t-1} + b^r). \tag{8}$$

$$z_t = \sigma_{\log}(W^z x_t + U^z h_{t-1} + b^z). \tag{9}$$

$$\tilde{h}_t = \tanh(W^h x_t + U^h(r_t \circ h_{t-1} + b^h). \tag{10}$$

$$h_t = z_t \circ h_{t-1} + (1 - z_t) \circ \tilde{h}_t. \tag{11}$$

Figure 3 depicts the operations taking place inside LSTM and GRU units according to the equations described above.

Due to the high computational complexity of recurrent networks and the high ratio of features to training examples, an FS procedure is carried out before optimizing any network hyperparameters. As suggested by the experimental results in [15], FS may not significantly impact classification accuracy for these datasets,

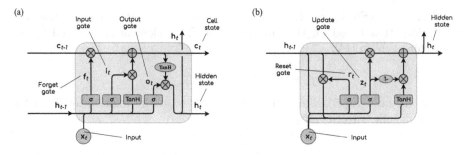

Fig. 3. (a) LSTM unit. (b) GRU unit.

as the potential context loss of having fewer features could be offset by a reduction in overfitting. In addition, and in line with efficiency concerns, FS makes RNN models several times more efficient in terms of energy-time consumption.

A Genetic Algorithm (GA) is employed in two separate steps: first, to perform the FS procedure; second, to optimize the structure of both GRU and LSTM networks. The GA carries out an iterative search procedure using a population of candidate solutions that compete through a set number of generations guided by a fitness measure. For FS, a much faster model (Logistic Regression) evaluates populations of feature subsets. The structure of the RNNs is optimized by finding and evaluating the amount of recurrent units in a recurrent layer. In both steps, the fitness function uses cross-validation as defined in Sect. 3.2. Binary tournament is used for parent selection, and population replacement is elitist. For more information on GAs and evolutionary computation in general, see [16].

3.2   Performance Measurement and Estimation

EEG pattern classification into the three data classes is used at both the training and the evaluation stages: 5-fold cross-validation accuracy is used inside the GA to guide the optimization, and the Kappa coefficient is used to compare final models to each other:

- Cross-validation accuracy: the training set is split into n partitions, iteratively using $n-1$ of them for model training and the remaining one for testing. The final value is the average of the n test accuracies, with a range of possible values of $[0, 1]$.
- Cohen's Kappa coefficient [17]: it is similar to the accuracy metric, but it also takes into account the possibility of correctly classifying by chance. It is computed as:

$$\kappa = \frac{p_0 - p_c}{1 - p_c}, \tag{12}$$

where p_0 is the measured accuracy, and p_c is the sum of the probabilities of random agreement for all possible classes. The range of values is $[-1, 1]$.

The computational efficiency of the solutions is addressed with measures of time and accumulated energy consumption.

3.3 Analysis of Results

As previously stated, the resulting networks are compared in terms of several measures. In particular, classification accuracy is evaluated through statistical testing in addition to regular discussion. In order to compare GRU with LSTM, the Bayesian Signed-Rank test [18] is used. This test computes the probability of either algorithm winning and the probability of a practical equivalence. The output can be represented as a point cloud in barycentric coordinates contained within a triangle, where each vertex is associated with a possibility (i.e., one of them wins, the other one wins, or they are equivalent). The closer the point cloud is to a vertex, the higher the probability given to that possibility.

More formally, the test calculates the distribution (assumed to be a Dirichlet distribution) of a parameter z. Let A and B be the sets of measurements of two alternatives. By counting the occurrences in the sample of $b - a > 0$, $b - a < 0$, and $b - a \approx 0$, where a and b are elements of A and B, the test is able to build a Dirichlet distribution. $b - a \approx 0$ represents the Region of Practical Equivalence (rope), which contains non-significant differences within the interval $[\text{rope}_{\min}, \text{rope}_{\max}]$. The distribution is then sampled to obtain triplets of the form shown in Eq. 13:

$$[P(z < \text{rope}_{\min}), P(z \in \text{rope}), P(z > \text{rope}_{\max})]. \tag{13}$$

The elements of these triplets are treated as barycentric coordinates, so that every triplet can be seen as a point in the aforementioned triangle.

4 Experimental Results

4.1 Experimental Setup

The code was written in *Python v3.6.8*. Some of the state-of-the-art machine learning libraries available for the language are also used: *Scikit-Learn v0.22.1* [19], *NumPy v1.18.5* [20], and *TensorFlow v2.3.0* [21] as a backend for *Keras v2.4.0* [22]. The Bayesian Signed-Rank test is implemented in the R library rNPBST [23]. The experiments have been carried out on a cluster node with the following hardware specifications:

- 2x Intel® Xeon® Silver 4214 @ 2.20 GHz: 24 cores/48 threads and a Thermal Design Power (TDP) of 85W.
- 64 GB of DDR4 RAM memory.
- NVIDIA Quadro RTX 6000: $4,608$ CUDA cores, 24 GB of GDDR6 RAM memory, and a TDP of 295W.

Since FS is performed as a previous step, both GRU networks and LSTM networks deal with a small subset of the 3,600 original features: 25 for dataset 104 and 30 for datasets 107 and 110. The GA uses 1,000 individuals and 100 generations, and Logistic Regression inside a 5-fold cross-validation fitness function. An individual of the population consists of 3,600 boolean values which, on their own, represent whether a certain feature is part of that particular subset.

Regarding hyperparameter optimization, 30 individuals are evolved through 10 generations and evaluated with 5-fold cross validation. Each individual encodes the size of the recurrent layer in a recurrent network, i.e., the number of units it contains (whether it be GRU or LSTM).

For both GAs, selection is done by binary tournament, replacement is elitist, and initialization is done by sampling from a normal distribution centered at the middle of the allowed value ranges.

The hyperparameter optimization experiments have been repeated 5 times for each type of network and dataset to enable statistical analysis and more reliable conclusions.

4.2   Results

In order to analyze the effect of recurrence in model accuracy and cost, two different types of recurrent units (GRU and LSTM) are tested. Every RNN consists in a first recurrent layer followed by a fully-connected softmax layer for three-class classification. Table 1 holds average and peak values obtained in the three datasets, and Fig. 4 represents this information.

Table 1. Test-set Kappa comparison for GRU and LSTM. SD: Standard Deviation.

Dataset	Measure	GRU	LSTM
104	Avg. ± SD	0.6494 ± 0.0227	0.5948 ± 0.0215
104	Best	0.6737	0.6272
107	Avg. ± SD	0.5567 ± 0.0125	0.5451 ± 0.0166
107	Best	0.5705	0.5648
110	Avg. ± SD	0.5850 ± 0.0081	0.5906 ± 0.0181
110	Best	0.5947	0.6140

As can be observed, GRU clearly outperforms LSTM in dataset 104, but the difference is not as clear for the other two datasets (one win for each). On balance, it would be reasonable to conclude that GRU prevails, which could be attributed to several causes. For instance, a first hypothesis would be that the features chosen by the FS procedure are somehow be more beneficial for GRU. In addition, perhaps the mathematical transformations applied to the

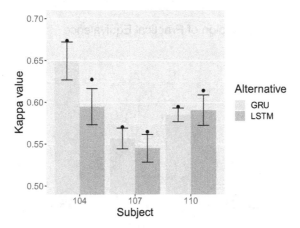

Fig. 4. Comparison of test-set Kappa values for GRU and LSTM. Bars represent averages, points mean peak performance, and lines delimit the range of the standard deviation.

original raw data to obtain the current datasets do not have significant synergy with context-based networks. In this respect, the greater complexity that LSTM needs to better track contextual information could be detrimental in the form of overfitting. Theoretically, excessive complexity can be mitigated by regularization mechanisms such as dropout [24], although it would increase training time.

The Bayesian Signed-Rank test supports what can be seen in the results: GRU tends to achieve higher overall classification accuracy in the datasets considered. This can be seen in the posterior probabilities: the test assigns a mere 8.9% probability to the dominance of LSTM in the general case. In contrast, GRU has a 59.9% probability of being better, and the practical equivalence of the two is at 31.2% probability. The corresponding heatmap is illustrated in Fig. 5: the point cloud is noticeably closer to the GRU vertex, which indicates its higher probability of prevalence.

However, regardless of their relative quality, it should be noted that they do not fare that well when compared to other deep learning-based proposals. For instance, in [15] a Convolutional Neural Network (CNN) with only one convolutional layer achieves higher classification accuracy in the same datasets, although it uses not a feature subset but the 3, 600 original features. A comparison of the three can be seen in Fig. 6. It is worth noting that, in the same paper, the experimental results suggest that the recurrent networks would not benefit in the same way from using the full feature set.

The discussion on the use of feature subsets against the entire feature set links with the topic of energy-time efficiency. When computationally intensive algorithms and machine learning models are employed, the quality of the solutions should not be the only way of estimating practicality. Time constraints

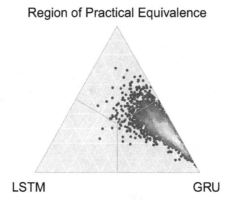

Fig. 5. Bayesian Signed-Rank test heatmap of GRU vs. LSTM. 2,000 points sampled from the Dirichlet distribution. Red represents lower density, and increasingly brighter colors mean higher densities. (Color figure online)

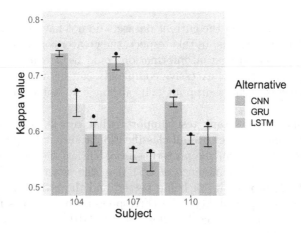

Fig. 6. Comparison of test-set Kappa values for the CNN in [15], GRU and LSTM.

and hardware limitations are usual, and should also be factored in: for example, responsiveness is valuable in BCI applications since they are often meant to provide quality-of-life improvements for disabled patients; just as it would not be reasonable to have a system that regularly misclassifies inputs, it would not be reasonable to have a system that takes too long before performing the desired action. Moreover, economic and environmental issues are also relevant on a more general note.

Dimensionality reduction, as FS does, would be a potential first step to decrease computational costs. In particular, the hyperparameter optimization procedure for the recurrent networks in this paper needed almost an hour to finish (see Fig. 7). However, our early experimentation showed that it would take ten times that amount without FS, given that model training and evaluation inside the fitness function is the bottleneck of the algorithm.

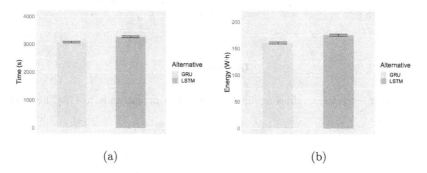

(a)   (b)

Fig. 7. Average time (a) and energy (b) behavior for the hyperparameter optimization procedure of GRU and LSTM. Measured for all datasets.

Another detail that stands out in Fig. 7 is how time and energy do not scale the same: the two GRU bars purposely have the same height to make this more noticeable. What causes the difference is that LSTM networks not only require more computation time but also more GPU usage for equivalent periods of time. In summary, the results suggest that GRU outperforms LSTM for these datasets both in classification accuracy and in energy-time cost.

Nonetheless, there is another phenomenon worthy of study: the relationship between network complexity (i.e., the amount of recurrent units) and classification accuracy. Many deep learning applications tackle large datasets through highly complex networks, which hints at a positive correlation between model complexity and accuracy. However, in small but high-dimensional datasets such as those found in bioinformatics, these dynamics may stop working much earlier as a consequence of overfitting.

Figures 8 and 9 show the evaluated networks in terms of the trade-off between the amount of recurrent units and the Kappa values each of them achieves.

There are no discernible positive slopes in either of them, for any dataset, that reveal a clear correlation between the width of the network and the quality of the solutions it produces. Although this is only an isolated piece of empirical evidence, it could serve as a guideline to have in mind when applying deep learning to datasets of similar characteristics: wider networks do not always lead to higher accuracy, and sometimes smaller networks (simpler models) are not only more computationally efficient but also more accurate.

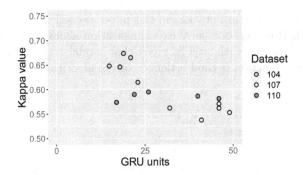

Fig. 8. Test-set Kappa values against amount of recurrent units in GRU networks.

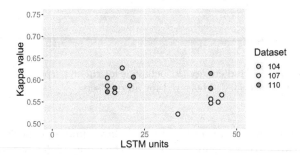

Fig. 9. Test-set Kappa values against amount of recurrent units in LSTM networks.

5   Conclusions and Future Work

In this paper, we have studied the performance of two common types of recurrent units (GRU and LSTM) in the context of small and high-dimensional EEG datasets. On balance, the results appear to point in the direction of GRU being more adequate than LSTM in this particular case. Nonetheless, the results in general are not as competitive as they could be in light of the comparison with a CNN. This could be attributed to: (i) overfitting (since RNNs introduce additional computations in the network); (ii) to a poor match between the nature of the data and the strengths of recurrence; or (iii) to insufficient hyperparameter tuning, which would probably benefit at least from a larger scale.

In addition to accuracy-oriented conclusions, we can also gain some insight on the interaction between accuracy and its computational cost. Deep learning has, without a doubt, a wide scope of application, but its resource requirements are easy to overlook in favor of solution quality. When resources are limited or concerns about responsiveness are not just secondary, taking a look at the efficiency of the proposals could be highly beneficial. Moreover, in certain problems such as those with the curse of dimensionality, focusing on efficiency could also lead to superior overall solutions. The energy-time results of this paper point in this direction.

To conclude, there are some shortcomings to this work that are worth high-lighting for future work. The conclusions would have a more solid statistical basis with experiments of a larger scale; this larger scale could mean more repetitions, more datasets (including the BCI competition IV), and larger amounts of individuals and generations in the genetic algorithm used for hyperparameter tuning. Furthermore, the energy-cost issues could be explored in terms of parallelism: a heterogeneous cluster offers opportunities to distribute model training and evolutionary computation among multiple CPU-GPU devices and also among multiple independent nodes.

Acknowledgments. This research has been funded by the Spanish Ministry of Science, Innovation, and Universities under grants PGC2018-098813-B-C31 and PGC2018-098813-B-C32, and ERDF fund. We would like to thank the BCI laboratory of the University of Essex, especially Dr. John Q. Gan, for allowing us to use their datasets. We also thank the NVIDIA Corporation for the donation of the two TITAN Xp GPUs used for this research.

References

1. Amin, S.U., Alsulaiman, M., Muhammad, G., Mekhtiche, M.A., Hossain, M.S.: Deep Learning for EEG motor imagery classification based on multi-layer CNNs feature fusion. Future Gener. Comput. Syst. **101**, 542–554 (2019)
2. Sakhavi, S., Guan, C., Yan, S.: Learning temporal information for brain-computer interface using convolutional neural networks. IEEE Trans. Neural Netw. Learn. Syst. **29**(11), 5619–5629 (2018)
3. Acharya, U.R., Oh, S.L., Hagiwara, Y., Tan, J.H., Adeli, H.: Deep convolutional neural network for the automated detection and diagnosis of seizure using EEG signals. Comput. Biol. Med. **100**, 270–278 (2018)
4. Wang, P., Jiang, A., Liu, X., Shang, J., Zhang, L.: LSTM-based EEG classification in motor imagery tasks. IEEE Trans. Neural Syst. Rehabilitation Eng. **26**(11), 2086–2095 (2018)
5. Tayeb, Z., et al.: Validating deep neural networks for online decoding of motor imagery movements from EEG signals. Sensors **19**(1), 210 (2019)
6. Raudys, S., Jain, A.: Small sample size effects in statistical pattern recognition: recommendations for practitioners. IEEE Trans. Pattern Anal. Mach. Intell. **13**(3), 252–264 (1991)
7. Asensio-Cubero, J., Gan, J.Q., Palaniappan, R.: Multiresolution analysis over simple graphs for brain computer interfaces. J. Neural Eng. **10**(4), 046014 (2013)
8. Daubechies, I.: Ten lectures on wavelets, vol. 61. Siam (1992)
9. Graves, A., Schmidhuber, J.: Framewise phoneme classification with bidirectional LSTM and other neural network architectures. Neural Netw. **18**(5–6), 602–610 (2005)
10. Bengio, Y., Simard, P., Frasconi, P., et al.: Learning long-term dependencies with gradient descent is difficult. IEEE Trans. Neural Netw. **5**(2), 157–166 (1994)
11. Hochreiter, S., Schmidhuber, J.: Long short-term memory. Neural Comput. **9**(8), 1735–1780 (1997)
12. Cho, K., et al.: Learning phrase representations using RNN encoder-decoder for statistical machine translation. In: Conference on Empirical Methods in Natural Language Processing, pp. 1724–1734 (2014)

13. Weiss, G., Goldberg, Y., Yahav, E.: On the practical computational power of finite precision RNNs for language recognition. In: 56th Annual Meeting of the Association for Computational Linguistics, vol. 2, pp. 740–745 (2018)
14. Gers, F., Schmidhuber, J., Cummins, F.: Learning to forget: continual prediction with LSTM. Neural Comput. **12**(10), 2451–2571 (2000)
15. León, J., et al.: Deep learning for EEG-based motor imagery classification: accuracy-cost trade-off. PLoS ONE **15**(6), e0234178 (2020)
16. Eiben, A.E., Smith, J.E., et al.: Introduction to Evolutionary Computing, vol. 53, 2nd edn. Springer, Heidelberg (2015). https://doi.org/10.1007/978-3-662-44874-8
17. Cohen, J.: A coefficient of agreement for nominal scales. Educ. Psychol. Meas. **20**(1), 37–46 (1960)
18. Benavoli, A., Corani, G., Demšar, J., Zaffalon, M.: Time for a change: a tutorial for comparing multiple classifiers through Bayesian analysis. J. Mach. Learn. Res. **18**(1), 2653–2688 (2017)
19. Pedregosa, F., et al.: Scikit-learn: machine learning in Python. J. Mach. Learn. Res. **12**, 2825–2830 (2011)
20. Oliphant, T.E.: A guide to NumPy, vol. 1. Trelgol Publishing USA (2006)
21. Abadi, M., et al.: TensorFlow: large-scale machine learning on heterogeneous systems (2015)
22. Chollet, F., et al.: Keras (2015)
23. Carrasco, J., García, S., del Mar Rueda, M., Herrera, F.: rNPBST: an R package covering non-parametric and Bayesian statistical tests. In: Martínez de Pisón, F.J., Urraca, R., Quintián, H., Corchado, E. (eds.) HAIS 2017. LNCS (LNAI), vol. 10334, pp. 281–292. Springer, Cham (2017). https://doi.org/10.1007/978-3-319-59650-1_24
24. Srivastava, N., et al.: Dropout: a simple way to prevent neural networks from overfitting. J. Mach. Learn. Res. **15**(1), 1929–1958 (2014)

Energy-Time Profiling for Machine Learning Methods to EEG Classification

Juan Carlos Gómez-López[1]([✉]) ⓘ, Juan José Escobar[1] ⓘ, Jesús González[1] ⓘ,
Francisco Gil-Montoya[2] ⓘ, Julio Ortega[1] ⓘ, Mike Burmester[3] ⓘ,
and Miguel Damas[1] ⓘ

[1] Department of Computer Architecture and Technology,
CITIC University of Granada, Granada, Spain
{goloj,jjescobar,jesusgonzalez,jortega,mdamas}@ugr.es
[2] Department of Engineering, University of Almería, Almería, Spain
pagilm@ual.es
[3] Department of Computer Science, Florida State University, Tallahassee, USA
burmester@cs.fsu.edu

Abstract. The Electroencephalography discipline studies a type of signals called Electroencephalograms (EEGs), which represent the electrical activity of different parts of the brain. EEGs are composed of a massive number of features that could be used to create an intelligent recognition system. Nevertheless, the high number of available features difficult the correct classification of the signals as most of them do not contain relevant information. The use of Feature Selection (FS) techniques allows the reduction of the number of features by extracting a reduced but powerful feature subset. Afterwards, the problem can be addressed by using both the reduced features along with classification methods. In this sense, this work proposes a comparison of five supervised classifiers to solve an Electroencephalography problem in the context of Motor Imagery-based BCI tasks. The predictive models are evaluated in terms of classification rate and performance (execution time and energy consumption), with the idea of determining which alternative offers the best trade-off among all the objectives.

Keywords: BCI tasks · EEG classification · Motor imagery · Machine learning methods · Energy-aware computing

1 Introduction

Bioinformatics is an interdisciplinary field of study where biological data is analyzed using computer science and statistics. In recent years, this field has experienced an exponential growth due to the increment in computing power [24]. However, this progress has also caused biological datasets to increase greatly in size, like EEG signals, so that disciplines such as Machine Learning (ML) [22] have emerged to address this issue. In this way, recognizing the underlying patterns of these signals is the main objective of EEG classification.

© Springer Nature Switzerland AG 2021
I. Rojas et al. (Eds.): BIOMESIP 2021, LNCS 12940, pp. 311–322, 2021.
https://doi.org/10.1007/978-3-030-88163-4_27

Conversely, the problem with this type of signals is the so-called *curse of dimensionality problem* [4] in which the few EEGs available are composed of a large number of features, so that any type of metaheuristic is needed to find the best subset of features. In this context, ML became increasingly relevant to tackle this problem in a compelling way because it is designed to detect patterns from a massive set of data to predict future behaviors. According to the methodology and dataset to be used, ML methods can be classified into three groups: reinforcement, supervised, and unsupervised. Classification methods used in this study are framed within the second group, where the class to which each sample belongs during the training stage is known. From this knowledge a model will be generated to classify new signals and identify their class.

After this introduction, Sect. 2 describes the ML methods used to solve the Electroencephalography problem, whereas Sect. 3 describes the methodology followed. Then, Sect. 4 carries out the experimental work and provide the classification rate and performance of each method. Finally, the conclusions and future work are given in Sect. 5.

2   Methods Used to EEG Classification

A total of five supervised classification methods have been used to evaluate the EEG dataset: KNN, SVM, Naive Bayes, Random Forest, and a Convolutional Neural Network (CNN). This section describes the characteristics of each method and points out their advantages and disadvantages.

2.1 K-Nearest Neighbors (KNN)

KNN [12] assigns to the new instance the predominant class among the K neighbors. The steps of this classification method are described herein:

1. Calculate the distance between the new instance to be classified and the rest of the samples.
2. Sort the distances in increasing order.
3. Select the K nearest distances (neighbors).
4. Determine the predominant class among the K nearest distances and assign it to the new instance.

The interpretability is the main advantage of this method. However, the computation time is linearly dependent on the size of the dataset since each new instance has to be compared with all the existing samples.

2.2   Support Vector Machine (SVM)

Although SVM [23] was originally created for binary classification, its use has been extended to multi-class classification and regression problems. The design of SVM resides in the *Maximal Margin Classifier* [15], which is based on the hyperplane concept and tries to separate the n-dimensional space into two halves.

Depending on the number of dimensions, the representation of the hyperplane changes. As the ideal recognition is not feasible in most cases, the solution is to assume some classification errors, handling two complementary *Support Vectors* or *Soft Margin*. The hyperparameter that tunes these errors is known as C. The higher the value of C, the more errors are allowed. Due to the complexity of some problems, the data space has been transformed into a different dimensional space by using a radial kernel that is adjusted with a *gamma* hyperparameter. The EEG problem addressed in this paper, which contains three classes, has followed the *One-versus-one* strategy (OVO) [19]. Here, $\frac{K \cdot (K-1)}{2}$ SVMs are generated, comparing all possible pairs of classes. At the time of classifying a new instance, the number of times that this instance appears in each class is recorded, and the one that appears more frequently will be the chosen class.

The main advantage of SVM is the great versatility [14], but the final model is difficult to understand for the programmer. Moreover, the memory required to store the hyperplanes and the time to generate the model is greater than in KNN.

2.3 Random Forest

Random Forest [11] is an evolution of the decision tree classification method [8], which is based on `if-this-then-that` decisions. Its highlights are listed below:

1. For each tree a subset of features is selected, which provides N_T new trees.
2. Then, each sample is classified through all trees.
3. Finally, the class is determined by the predominant class along the "forest".

In this method, the concept of randomness comes from two different sources: (i) the F features that are selected to create the different trees are chosen randomly and (ii) the number of samples used to train the tree also changes. This randomness, along with the creation of tens or hundreds of trees is the main advantage of this method since it works well for both regression or classification problems, avoiding overfitting in most cases. However, creating too many trees is also its weak point because it can require a lot of computation time. In addition, Random Forest does not work well with small datasets since its model is complex and difficult to understand.

2.4 Naive Bayes

Naive Bayes [2] is based on the world-renowned Bayes Theorem [13]. The common use is to calculate the probability of an event occurring once the probabilities of previous events are known. This method is called "naive" because it assumes that the predictor variables are independent of each other. The steps of this method are as follows:

1. Transform the dataset into a frequency table.
2. Create a table with the probabilities of all possible events occurring.

3. Calculate for each class the posterior probability using the Bayes equation [5].
4. The class with the highest posterior probability is the outcome of the prediction.

The main advantage of this method is that it predicts classes quickly and easily for both binary and multi-class classification problems [18]. On the contrary, the main disadvantage of Naive Bayes lies in the way it works: assuming that all features are independent of each other, the model created does not reflect in most cases what the data looks like in the real world.

2.5   Convolutional Neural Network (CNN)

Artificial Neural Networks (ANNs) [10] have become one of the main classifiers nowadays due to their versatility and ability to obtain good classification rates in several problems. Although there are different types of neural networks, in this work a CNN has been chosen because of its suitability for EEG classification [17]. Unlike other neural networks where their density often leads to overfitting, CNNs are sparse and more flexible. Here, the network progressively transforms the information from detailed to abstract through a series of chained convolutional operations, which are carried out over different number of iterations or epochs (e) [16]. The topology of the network implemented in this paper is as follows:

1. The first layer is a 2D-Convolutional operation whose input shape is a 240×15 matrix since an EEG signal is composed of 240 samples from 15 electrodes. The convolution applies N_F filters with a kernel size of $K_S \times K_S$.
2. A max-pooling operation with a size of 2×1 is applied to reduce the size of the sample dimension.
3. A flattening operation is used to reshape the output of the convolutional layer to vectors. This is mandatory before using any Fully-Connected layer (FC).
4. Finally, one FC layer is connected to the output layer, which has three units since the EEG problem studied in this research is composed of three classes.

The main advantage of neural networks lies in the fact that they are able to create robust learning models with high fault tolerance [1]. Conversely, their main disadvantage is the high computational time needed to generate the model.

3   Methodology

3.1   Data Description

The EEG dataset used to evaluate the proposed predictive models was recorded in the BCI Laboratory at the University of Essex, UK [3]. Specifically, it corresponds to a human subject coded as 104. The samples are split into two different datasets: one for training and one for testing, which are composed of 178 EEG signals with 3,600 features each. These signals belong to three types of imagined limb movements: left and right hand, and feet. The class distribution in both datasets is detailed in Table 1.

Table 1. Class distribution in test and training datasets.

Dataset	Left hand	Right hand	Feet
Training	60	66	52
Test	58	65	55

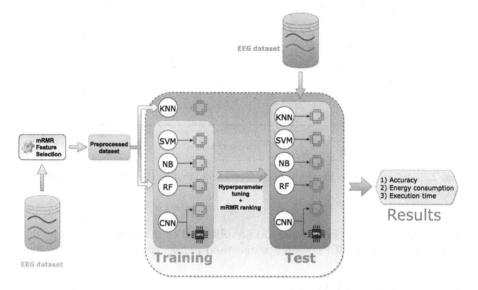

Fig. 1. Workflow implemented for the different supervised classification methods.

3.2 Implemented Workflow

Figure 1 represents the designed pipeline, which is in-depth explained as follows: the first step is to implement a FS technique on the dataset to be used since the most of the features are considered as noise, being necessary to obtain a subset with the most relevant ones. For this research, the minimum Redundancy Maximum Relevance mRMR technique [20] has been selected because is one of the most powerful and widespread FS techniques among the ML community. mRMR returns a ranked features that maximizes the relevance while minimizing the redundancy. Then, a subset of the most informative features is taken with the aim of optimizing the posterior classification phase. The different methods will use the training dataset with the subset of features obtained to create the model, optimizing the hyperparameters through a grid search strategy, which returns the means of the cross-validated score (5-fold). The only method that does not need to optimize its hyperparameters is Naive Bayes as there are no hyperparameters to tune. After applying FS and tuning the hyperparameters, the models can now be evaluated using the test dataset.

After applying FS and tuning the hyperparameters, the models can now be evaluated using the test dataset. Now, the execution time, energy consumption,

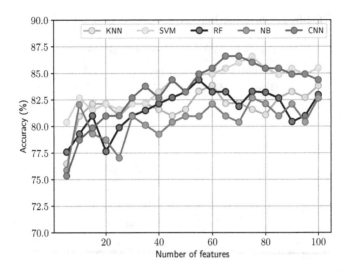

Fig. 2. Incremental classification when increasing the number of selected features at intervals of 5.

and accuracy results of each method are obtained to determine which one provides the best trade-off between accuracy and performance.

4 Experimental Work

This section analyzes the classification rate and energy-time performance of the five methods used to cope with the EEG classification problem. Section 4.1 shows the setup used to carry out the experiments, which are provided in Sect. 4.2.

4.1 Setup Used

The platform used is a PC with two CPUs Intel(R) Xeon(R) Silver 4214 and a GPU Quadro RTX 6000. The operating system used is CentOS (v7.9.2009). All methods have been developed using the Python language (v3.6.8). On the one hand, the *Scikit-learn* library (v0.24.1) [6] was chosen to implement KNN, SVM, Naive Bayes, and Random Forest. On the other hand, neural networks have been implemented with *Keras* (v2.4.3) [7] and *TensorFlow* (v2.4.1) [9]. It is important to highlight that although all methods have been run on CPU, the CNN has also been executed on GPU. All experiments have been repeated 30 times to obtain more reliable measurements on the behavior of the procedure.

The energy measurements have been obtained by a wattmeter based on Arduino Mega and developed specifically for the experiments. The wattmeter provides a measure of energy accumulated, $E\,(\mathrm{W \cdot h})$, every second.

Table 2. Hyperparameters of each classification method after optimizing them with a grid search.

Method	Hyperparameter	Value
KNN	K	25
SVM	$decision\_function\_shape$	ovo
	C	0.75
	$gamma$	0.25
Naive Bayes	–	–
Random Forest	N_T	128
CNN	N_F	32
	K_S	16
	e	75

4.2 Results

Figure 2 illustrates the training accuracy obtained by each classifier when using different number of selected features. The CNN begins as the worst method but ends up outperforming the rest of them with a relatively low number of features. Nevertheless, it is important to note that SVM always surpass CNN with few features and at some points when the features increase as well. In addition, from 35 features ahead, following the Akaike criterion [21], the gain in accuracy does not justify the increment of features to classify. For this reason, to evaluate the different methods with the test dataset, the first 35 features of the mRMR ranking have been used. On the contrary, as an optimization of hyperparameters has been performed through a grid search strategy in this incremental classification, there is no need to optimize them again. The specific hyperparameters for each method can be found in Table 2.

Figure 3 illustrates the accuracy, execution time, and energy consumption of each method when 35 features are used. In first place, observing the different accuracy measurements, SVM provides the best accuracy results. The rest of the methods reach similar values, all of them above 80%. This figure also reveals that, at least for the dataset used in this work, all methods achieve a high classification rate when a powerful FS technique such as mRMR is implemented.

Focusing on performance, it is noticeable that the CNN is, despite obtaining the second best accuracy, the heaviest method, not only in execution time but also in energy consumption due to its high complexity. Nevertheless, Naive Bayes is the most efficient method because once the probability table is created, the model construction is very fast. In the case of CNN, to create the classification model the network needs to perform thousands and thousands of mathematical operations throughout different epochs to complete the learning process, which increases execution time. It is worth noting that running CNN on GPU entails higher execution times and energy consumption than running on CPU. This can be explained taking into account the feature selection step and

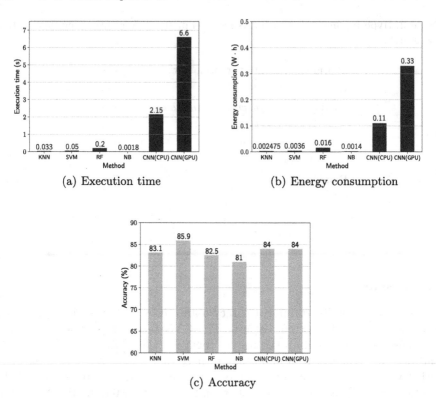

(a) Execution time   (b) Energy consumption

(c) Accuracy

Fig. 3. Average performance and accuracy values obtained by the different supervised classification methods when using 35 features.

network topology. Firstly, thanks to FS only 35 of the initial 3, 600 features were selected. Second, the complexity of the neural network used is low, so the program would not be taking advantage of the GPU architecture. In fact, using the `nvidia-smi` command, it was observed during the execution that GPU usage rarely exceeded 19%. Finally, to clarify which method is better, we are going to establish the energy-time, time-accuracy, energy-accuracy, and energy-time-accuracy products as quality measures to compare the methods:

$$P_{et} = energy \cdot time \qquad (1)$$

$$P_{ta} = time \cdot (1 - accuracy) \qquad (2)$$

$$P_{ea} = energy \cdot (1 - accuracy) \qquad (3)$$

$$P_{eta} = energy \cdot time \cdot (1 - accuracy) \qquad (4)$$

Table 3. Energy-time, time-accuracy, energy-accuracy, and energy-time-accuracy product obtained by each method. The execution time, energy consumption, and accuracy are also given.

Method	P_{et}	P_{ta}	P_{ea}	P_{eta}	Time (s)	Energy ($W \cdot h$)	Accuracy (%)
KNN	$8.1 \cdot 10^{-5}$	0.56	0.042	$1.3 \cdot 10^{-3}$	0.033	$2.4 \cdot 10^{-3}$	83.1
SVM	$1.8 \cdot 10^{-4}$	0.71	0.051	$2.5 \cdot 10^{-3}$	0.05	$3.6 \cdot 10^{-3}$	**85.9**
RF	$3.2 \cdot 10^{-3}$	3.5	0.28	0.056	0.2	0.016	82.5
NB	$\mathbf{2.52 \cdot 10^{-6}}$	**0.034**	**0.023**	$\mathbf{4.8 \cdot 10^{-5}}$	$\mathbf{1.8 \cdot 10^{-3}}$	$\mathbf{1.4 \cdot 10^{-3}}$	81
CNN (CPU)	0.24	34.4	1.76	3.79	2.15	0.11	84
CNN (GPU)	2.18	105.6	5.25	34.85	6.6	0.33	84

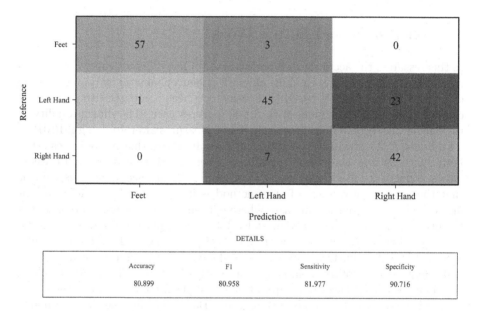

Fig. 4. Confusion matrix of Naive Bayes when using 35 features. The green color corresponds to successes, while the red color corresponds to failures. The higher the intensity of the red color, the more failures there will have been in that prediction. (Color figure online)

The goal is to minimize time and energy, while maximizing accuracy. Since this is a multi-objective problem, all objectives must be maximized or minimized. In this case, the easiest thing is to transform the accuracy into a minimization problem by replacing *accuracy* with $(1 - accuracy)$. Table 3 shows the values of these products obtained by each method. For this particular problem, one method is considered better than another if it has a lower P_{eta} value since it contains the three metrics. With this in mind, the lowest P_{eta} value is achieved by Naive Bayes despite being the method with the worst accuracy. This is because it is the most efficient method, both in execution time and energy consumption. On the contrary, the worst are obtained by CNN, first in its GPU version followed by the CPU version. In any case, choosing the best method will be the responsibility of the user or programmer. For example, in cases where precision needs to be prioritized, SVM would be the best version.

As Naive Bayes is the best method to the problem addressed, Fig. 4 provides its confusion matrix when using 35 features. Furthermore, not only the accuracy is given, but also the F1-Score (mean classification rate per classes), the Sensitivity (true positive), and the Specificity (true negative). One point to highlight is that the classification errors are not homogeneously distributed among classes: the figure illustrates that there is a higher number of failures between the left hand and right hand class pair.

5   Conclusions and Future Work

In this research, the accuracy and performance of five different supervised classification methods to address a multi-class Electroencephalography problem in the context of Motor Imagery-based BCI tasks have been compared using a dataset composed of 178 EEG signals with 3,600 features each. The dimensionality of the dataset has been reduced to a subset of 35 features after applying mRMR as a FS method. With this feature subset, the results reveal that Naive Bayes is the best choice for this classification problem when the three objectives are taken into account: execution time, energy consumption, and accuracy. It is evident that the greatest advantage of this method is its speed and simplicity, reaching to be an ideal solution in cases where efficiency is the primary premise. On the other hand, SVM has proven, at least for the application addressed, to be the method that best classifies with optimum performance. Finally, the results obtained by CNN illustrates its major weakness: a much higher execution time and energy consumption compared to the other methods. Thus, we conclude that in cases where powerful computational systems are not available, the use of classical classification methods such as Naive Bayes is a suitable choice. Finally, the results lead to the conclusion that a classical classification method can outperform other more complex ones such as CNN when a rigorous FS method is applied before. However, this may also depend on the dataset used, so it is proposed as future work to compare the results obtained in this paper with those obtained using more standardized datasets such as the BCI Competition IV.

Acknowledgments. This research has been funded by the Spanish Ministry of Science, Innovation, and Universities under grant PGC2018-098813-B-C31 and ERDF fund. We would like to thank the BCI laboratory of the University of Essex, especially Dr. John Q. Gan, for allowing us to use their datasets.

References

1. Dertat, A.: Applied deep learning - part 4: convolutional neural networks. https://medium.com/@ardendertat

2. Amra, I., Maghari, A.: Students performance prediction using KNN and naïve bayesian. In: 2017 8th International Conference on Information Technology. ICIT 2017, Amman, Jordan, pp. 909–913. IEEE, October 2017. https://doi.org/10.1109/ICITECH.2017.8079967

3. Asensio-Cubero, J., Gan, J.Q., Palaniappan, R.: Multiresolution analysis over simple graphs for brain computer interfaces. J. Neural Eng. 10(4), 21–26 (2013). https://doi.org/10.1088/1741-2560/10/4/046014

4. Bellman, R.E.: Adaptive Control Processes: A Guided Tour. Princeton University Press (1961)

5. Crellin, G.L.: The philosophy and mathematics of bayes' equation. IEEE Trans. Reliab. $\mathbf{R} - \mathbf{21}$, 131–135 (1972). https://doi.org/10.1109/TR.1972.5215975

6. Cournapeau, D.: Machine learning in Python. https://scikit-learn.org/stable/. Accessed 15 Sept 2020

7. Chollet, F.: The Python deep learning API. https://keras.io/. Accessed 25 Feb 2021

8. Friedl, M.A., Brodley, C.E.: Decision tree classification of land cover from remotely sensed data. Remote Sens. Environ. 61, 399–409 (1997). https://doi.org/10.1016/S0034-4257(97)00049-7

9. Google Brain Team: An end-to-end open source machine learning platform. https://www.tensorflow.org/. Accessed 25 Feb 2021

10. Gurney, K.: An Introduction to Neural Networks. CRC Press (1997)

11. Hengl, T., Nussbaum, M., Wright, M.N., Heuvelink, G., Gräler, B.: Random forest as a generic framework for predictive modeling of spatial and spatio-temporal variables. PeerJ 6, e5518 (2018). https://doi.org/10.7717/peerj.5518

12. Imandoust, S.B., Bolandraftar, M.: Application of k-nearest neighbor (KNN) approach for predicting economic events theoretical background. Int. J. Eng. Res. Appl. 3, 605–610 (2013)

13. Joyce, J.: Bayes' theorem. https://stanford.library.sydney.edu.au/archives/sum2016/entries/bayes-theorem/#4

14. Karamizadeh, S., Abdullah, S.M., Halimi, M., Shayan, J., Rajabi, M.J.: Advantage and drawback of support vector machine functionality. In: 2014 International Conference on Computer, Communications, and Control Technology, Langkawi, Malaysia. I4CT 2014, pp. 63–65. IEEE, September 2014. https://doi.org/10.1109/I4CT.2014.6914146

15. Krupal, S.P., Trupti, P.S.: Support vector machine - a large margin classifier to diagnose skin illnesses. Procedia Technol. 23, 369–375 (2016). https://doi.org/10.1016/j.protcy.2016.03.039

16. LeCun, Y., Bengio, Y., Hinton, G.: Deep learning. Nature, 436–444 (2015). https://doi.org/10.1038/nature14539

17. León, J., et al.: Deep learning for EEG-based motor imagery classification: accuracy-cost trade-off. PLoS ONE 15, 1–30 (2020). https://doi.org/10.1371/journal.pone.0234178

18. Li, L.L.C.: Research and improvement of a spam filter based on naive bayes. In: 2015 7th International Conference on Intelligent Human-Machine Systems and Cybernetics, Hangzhou, China. IHMSC 2015, vol. 2, pp. 361–364. IEEE, November 2015. https://doi.org/10.1109/IHMSC.2015.208

19. Milgram, J., Cheriet, M., Sabourin, R.: "one against one" or "one against all": which one is better for handwriting recognition with SVMS? In: Tenth International Workshop on Frontiers in Handwriting Recognition, La Baule, France. IWFHR 2006. IEEE, October 2006

20. Peng, H., Long, F., Ding, C.: Feature selection based on mutual information criteria of max-dependency, max-relevance, and min-redundancy. IEEE Trans. Pattern Anal. Mach. Intell. **27**, 1226–1238 (2005). https://doi.org/10.1109/TPAMI.2005.159

21. Sakamoto, Y., Ishiguro, M., Kitagawa, G.: Akaike information criterion statistics. D. Reidel **81**, 26853 (1986). https://doi.org/10.1080/01621459.1988.10478680

22. Shastry, K.A., Sanjay, H.A.: Machine Learning for Bioinformatics, pp. 25–39. Springer Singapore (2020). https://doi.org/10.1007/978-981-15-2445-5_3

23. Sha'abani, M.N.A.H., Fuad, N., Jamal, N., Ismail, M.F.: kNN and SVM classification for EEG: a review. In: Kasruddin Nasir, A.N., et al. (eds.) InECCE2019. LNEE, vol. 632, pp. 555–565. Springer, Singapore (2020). https://doi.org/10.1007/978-981-15-2317-5_47

24. Yin, Z., Lan, H., Tan, G., Lu, M., Vasilakos, A.V., Liu, W.: Computing platforms for big biological data analytics: perspectives and challenges. Comput. Struct. Biotechnol. J. **15**, 403–411 (2017). https://doi.org/10.1016/j.csbj.2017.07.004

Performance Study of Ant Colony Optimization for Feature Selection in EEG Classification

Alberto Ortega[1]([✉]) [ID], Juan José Escobar[1] [ID], Julio Ortega[1] [ID],
Jesús González[1] [ID], Alfredo Alcayde[2] [ID], Jorge Munilla[3] [ID],
and Miguel Damas[1] [ID]

[1] Department of Computer Architecture and Technology, CITIC,
University of Granada (Spain), Granada, Spain
{aoruiz,jjescobar,jortega,jesusgonzalez,mdamas}@ugr.es
[2] Department of Engineering, University of Almería (Spain), Almeria, Spain
aalcayde@ual.es
[3] Communications Engineering Department, University of Málaga (Spain),
Malaga, Spain
munilla@ic.uma.es

Abstract. Feature Selection (FS) is a contemporary challenge for the
scientific community since new methods are being discovered and new
forms of algorithmic design are required. In this sense, classic bio-inspired
swarm intelligence algorithms can be explored to get a new suitable feature selection application where simple agents interact locally with each
other while searching a global solution. Therefore, this work proposes
an innovative utilization of the ant colony optimization algorithm for FS
(ACO-FS) with the objective of reducing the high number of features
present in Electroencephalogram (EEG) signals. Specifically, a base ant
colony optimization algorithm and two variants have been implemented
and evaluated in terms of execution time, energy consumption, and classification rates to point out the strength and weakness of each variant.
The preliminary results demonstrate that the proposed method provides
a classification rate close to 86% when the whole dataset is reduced from
3,600 features to only 22.

Keywords: Ant colony optimization · Feature selection · Energy-time
analysis · Electroencephalography · Swarm intelligence · Bio-inspired
algorithm

1 Introduction

In the last decade, the appearance of large input datasets has brought an extensive variety of classification problems in bioinformatics applications. Electroencephalography is one of the disciplines that normally faces classification problems with high-dimensional datasets, since Brain-Computer Interfaces (BCI) are
devices designed to collect multiple EEG signals from a subject. As each signal

© Springer Nature Switzerland AG 2021
I. Rojas et al. (Eds.): BIOMESIP 2021, LNCS 12940, pp. 323–336, 2021.
https://doi.org/10.1007/978-3-030-88163-4_28

is composed of a significant number of features and few samples are available, EEG classification faces what is known as the *curse of dimensionality* [5]: when the dimensionality increases, the volume of the space increases so quickly that the data become sparse. To deal with this problem, it is necessary to reduce the number of features before the classification phase. This can be achieved by FS techniques, which should generate a new subset of features with the same consistency and better possibilities than the original set could have.

So far, most contemporary FS methods have been inspired by mathematics techniques and evolutionary algorithms using different approaches called *wrappers* and *filters* [4]. *Wrapper* approaches assume a predetermined learning model, where features are selected for improving the learning performance of that model. On the contrary, *filter* approaches apply statistical analysis to the feature set even before choosing any model. Today, it is common to explore new methodologies that mix wrappers and filters approaches to find new solutions or simply complement existing ones. With this in mind, this work presents a new bio-inspired FS algorithm based on Ant Colony Optimization (ACO) to cope with an EEG classification problem [8,10].

After this introduction, Sect. 2 describes the ACO algorithm [12], while Sect. 3 explains how to extrapolate the original ACO algorithm to the FS proposed in this paper. Later, Sect. 4 proposes some variants to the ACO algorithm, which are experimentally evaluated in Sect. 5. Finally, the conclusions and future work are given in Sect. 6.

2   Ant Colony Optimization

As a source of bio-inspired approaches, biological collective behaviors are able to construct complex systems instinctively. These systems are called Swarm Intelligence (SI) [19], like those found in insect colonies [3]. Colonies manage to cooperatively complete simple but necessary tasks, such as getting out of their nest of finding food for the colony. Focusing on how a wild ant colony could search the shortest path between the food source and the anthill, the ACO algorithm was originally proposed as a technique to solve the widely-known Travelling Salesman Problem (TSP) [9,11].

The ACO algorithm uses the terms *ant* and *colony*, which refer to individual agents [21], and families of ants of the same anthill, respectively. When a colony starts its execution, every ant is assigned to an unique city by an adjustable rule. Then, each ant searches the next city to visit, depositing the so-called *pheromones* [16] on its path and leaving a trail. After all ants have completed their tour, the colony finishes and the next one will start in the same way, but from now the ants will contemplate not only their own estimates but also the pheromone trails. On account of this, former ant colonies have influence over their successors.

2.1   Probabilistic Function

The decision of which path to choose is based upon a probabilistic function defined by the original algorithm proposal. The probability $p_{i,j}$ of choosing the path from city i towards city j can be written as:

$$p_{i,j} = \begin{cases} \frac{(\tau_{i,j})^\alpha \cdot (\eta_{i,j})^\beta}{\sum (\tau_{i,j})^\alpha \cdot (\eta_{i,j})^\beta}, & \text{if } j \in C \\ 0, & \text{otherwise} \end{cases} \qquad (1)$$

where $\tau_{i,j}$ is the amount of pheromones, $\eta_{i,j}$ is the heuristic function, and parameters α and β represents the user-adjustable weights of $\tau_{i,j}$ and function $\eta_{i,j}$, respectively [23]. If city j is in the set of non-visited cities C, $p_{i,j}$ is calculated as indicated. Otherwise, $p_{i,j}$ is 0.

It is convenient to explain in more detail the parameter $\tau_{i,j}$ and the $\eta_{i,j}$ function. On the one hand, $\tau_{i,j}$ is the amount of pheromone deposited on the path (i,j) and represents how ideal that path was in past colonies. On the other hand, $\eta_{i,j}$ points out a heuristic function $\eta(i,j)$ designed specifically to optimize the algorithm. In the TSP problem, this heuristic returns $1/d_{i,j}$, with d distance between the i-th and j-th cities.

2.2   Pheromones Update Function

The biological behavior that defines this algorithm is the existence of pheromones and how they are put down on the ant paths: when all ants of the colony complete its tour, the colony finishes and the trails are re-calculated as Eqs. (2), (3) and (4) indicate:

$$\tau_{i,j}^{t+1} = \rho \cdot \tau_{i,j}^t + \Delta\tau_{i,j} \qquad (2)$$

where the updated pheromones $\tau_{i,j}^{t+1}$ will depend on the old pheromones $\tau_{i,j}^t$, a *decay* value ρ, and pheromone increment $\Delta\tau_{i,j}$, which is defined as:

$$\Delta\tau_{i,j} = \sum_{k=1}^{N_A} \Delta\tau_{i,j}^k \qquad (3)$$

where N_A is the number of ants in the colony and $\Delta\tau_{i,j}^k$ the pheromone increment of the k-th ant, which is defined as:

$$\Delta\tau_{i,j}^k = \begin{cases} \frac{Q}{\mu}, & \text{if the } k\text{-th ant uses path } (i,j) \\ 0, & \text{otherwise} \end{cases} \qquad (4)$$

$\Delta\tau_{i,j}^k$ is calculated as $\frac{Q}{\mu}$ for the ants that used the path, or 0 otherwise. Q is an user-defined constant and μ is the quality measure of the ant path [23] [20], which is usually defined as the current tour distance [9].

3   ACO for Feature Selection

In recent years [13], multiple ACO-based algorithms have emerged for a large number of different problems [1,2,7,17,18,24,25]. Insect colonies allow the design of new algorithms that can be applied to other fields such as EEG classification.

As FS is necessary to address this problem, this paper proposes the use of the ACO algorithm for FS. Throughout this section, the changes required in the ACO algorithm to adapt it to FS will be detailed. Basically, the changes are mainly related to the probabilistic function and the pheromones update function, which now operate on features instead of cities.

3.1   Probabilistic Function Applied to FS

In this case, the probabilistic function should return a probability for each non-visited feature, showing which one will be the best for the ant. To achieve that, the previous Eq. (1) is replaced by the following:

$$
p_f = \begin{cases} \frac{(\tau_f)^\alpha \cdot (\eta_f)^\beta}{\sum (\tau_f)^\alpha \cdot (\eta_f)^\beta}, & \text{if } f \in F \\ 0, & \text{otherwise} \end{cases} \tag{5}
$$

where τ_f is the amount of pheromones deposited on feature f, and $F = [0, N_F) \cap \mathbb{N}$, where N_F is the number of features of the input dataset. However, the heuristic function η needs to be redefined for FS. As commented in Sect. 1, in FS there are *wrapper* approaches which depend on a specific classifier to estimate their goodness. Here, a *wrapper* approach based on a logistic regression classifier [14] that uses the *logit* function [6] has been used. The use of *LogReg* model guarantees the isolation of the algorithm from the final classification method, since *LogReg* is used as a maximum entropy statistical classifier.

In FS, the main purpose is reducing the number of features while keeping or even increasing the classification accuracy. That is why a solution in FS is a subset of features. Since each ant of the colony will construct a whole solution from an empty set, it is possible to convert η into an appropriate heuristic for FS. The heuristic function will test all non-visited features for each ant and it will return a value based on how much a non-visited feature f maximizes the classification accuracy of the subset of features selected by the ant. In this way, the better classification accuracy achieved with the addition of f, the higher value for η_f. For this reason, η_f has been redefined as:

$$
\eta_f = \begin{cases} LogReg(X \cup \{f\}) - LogReg(X), & \text{if } LogReg(X \cup \{f\}) > LogReg(X) \\ 0, & \text{otherwise} \end{cases}
$$
$$\tag{6}$$

where X is the subset of features currently selected by the ant and *LogReg* is the logistic classifier.

3.2   Pheromones Update Function Applied to FS

As pheromones trails are now designed to be put down on features, Eqs. (2), (3) and (4) are replaced by the following:

$$\tau_f^{t+1} = \rho \cdot \tau_f^t + \Delta\tau_f \tag{7}$$

$$\Delta\tau_f = \sum_{k=1}^{N_A} \Delta\tau_f^k \tag{8}$$

$$\Delta\tau_f^k = \begin{cases} \frac{Q}{\mu}, & \text{if the } k\text{-th ant has feature } f \text{ in its subset} \\ 0, & \text{otherwise} \end{cases} \tag{9}$$

As seen above, pheromones trail has been redefined for FS as τ_f because pheromones will be put down in feature f and not in path (i, j). Moreover, the adjustable parameter μ in Eq. (9) has also to be redefined since in FS it is necessary to measure the quality of the subset of features of the ant instead of the path traveled. In this way, μ has been redefined as:

$$\mu = LogReg(X) \tag{10}$$

3.3   The Proposed ACO-FS Algorithm

This section presents the proposed ACO algorithm for Feature Selection (ACO-FS), whose pseudocode can be found in Algorithm 1. Although Fig. 1 shows the flowchart of the proposed algorithm, its operation is as follows: firstly, once the algorithm starts its execution, the colonies start sequentially and parameters such as the ants and their initial subset of features are reset with random values. Then, each ant of a colony computes its subset of features as Fig. 1 presents. It calculates the probability for all non-visited features as Eqs. 5 and (6) indicate. The feature with the highest probability is chosen to be added to the current subset of features of the ant, and is also deleted from the non-visited feature set. This is repeated until none of the remaining features improves the subset of features of the ant. When the last ant finishes, pheromones trails must be updated as Eqs. (7), (8), (9) and (10) indicate. Finally, when the last colony finishes, the algorithm returns the subset of features of the ant with the best *LogReg* rate as the final solution.

4   ACO-FS Variants

In Sect. 4 the ACO algorithm has been modified and expanded to two more variants.

Algorithm 1: Pseudocode of the proposed ACO-FS algorithm.

---

1 **Function** ACO-FS(N_C, N_A, DS, α, β, Q, ρ):

    Input : Number of colonies, N_C

    Input : Number of ants, N_A

    Input : EEG dataset, DS

    Input : Weight of τ_f, α

    Input : Weight of function η_f, β

    Input : Constant for the pheromone update function, Q

    Input : Rate of pheromones decay, ρ

    Output: Ant with the best *LogReg* rate, S_a

2   **for** $c \leftarrow 0$ **to** N_C **do**

3   resetInitialValues()

4   **for** $a \leftarrow 0$ **to** N_A **do**

5        $F \leftarrow$ getFeatureIndex(DS)

6        $N_F \leftarrow$ getNumberFeatures(F)

      // Ant Internal Compute

7        $run \leftarrow$ true

8   **while** run **do**

9   resetValues()

10   **for** $f \leftarrow 0$ **to** N_F **do**

11           $\eta_f \leftarrow$ heuristicCost(X, f, F, DS)

12           $\tau_f \leftarrow$ getPheromones(f, F)

13           $pnum_f \leftarrow \tau_f^{\alpha} \cdot \eta_f^{\beta}$

14           $pden \leftarrow pden + pnum_f$

15   **end**

16   **if** $pden = 0$ **then** $run \leftarrow$ false

17   **else**

18   **for** $f \leftarrow 0$ **to** N_F **do** $p_f \leftarrow pnum_f / pden$

19           $f_b \leftarrow$ selectBestFeature()

20           $X \leftarrow X \cup \{f_b\}$

21   removeVisitedFeature(f_b, F)

22   **end**

23   **end**

24   **end**

25   updatePheromones(Q, ρ)

26   **end**

27   $S_a \leftarrow$ selectBestFinalAnt()

28   **return** S_a

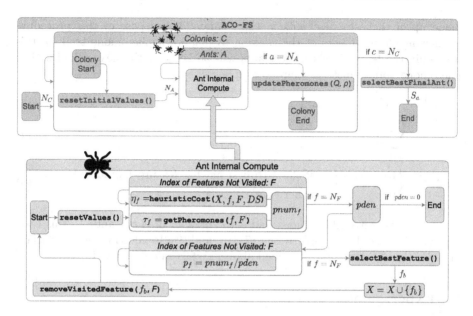

Fig. 1. Flowchart of ACO-FS algorithm. *pnum* and *pden* represent the numerator and denominator of function *p*, respectively.

4.1 Elitist

Elitist ACO for Feature Selection (EACO-FS) is a new variant based on the addition of *elitism* concept [15]. From this section, the *best ant* concept will be introduced: the ant with the subset of features that gets the best *LogReg* rate of the actual colony. On the other hand, *elitist* ants are extra ants which put more pheromones on the features of the *best ant*, enhancing that subset of features. The purpose of this modification is enhancing the best ants of each colony through elitist ants. Again, the pheromone update method has to be modified to add elitist ants pheromones ($\Delta\tau_f^e$):

$$\tau_f^{t+1} = \rho \cdot \tau_f^t + \Delta\tau_f + \Delta\tau_f^e \tag{11}$$

$$\Delta\tau_f^e = \begin{cases} \sigma \cdot \dfrac{Q}{\mu_{best}}, & \text{if } f \text{ is part of the best ant} \\ 0, & \text{otherwise} \end{cases} \tag{12}$$

where μ_{best} is the *LogReg* of the best ant and σ the number of elitist ants. If feature f is in the best path, $\Delta\tau_f^e$ is calculated as $\sigma \cdot \frac{Q}{\mu_{best}}$. In this variant, Eq. (11) replaces Eq. (7).

4.2 Rank-Based

Rank-based ACO for Feature Selection (RACO-FS) is another variant based on the combination of the elitist variant with an *ant ranking*. This *ant ranking* is made up of the λ-th best ants in the colony. The purpose of this procedure is allowing the best ants of the ranking to put down pheromone trail. In this way, only the features of the best ants will be kept for the next colonies. The pheromone update method changes as follows:

$$\tau_f^{t+1} = \rho \cdot \tau_f^t + \Delta\tau_f + \Delta\tau_f^e \tag{13}$$

$$\Delta\tau_f = \sum_{\lambda=1}^{\sigma-1} \Delta\tau_f^\lambda \tag{14}$$

$$\Delta\tau_f^\lambda = \begin{cases} (\sigma - \lambda) \cdot \frac{Q}{\mu_\lambda}, & \text{if the } \lambda\text{-th best ant has feature } f \text{ in its subset} \\ 0, & \text{otherwise} \end{cases} \tag{15}$$

where λ is the ant ranking index and σ the number of elitist ants. In this case, Eqs. (13), (14) and (15) replace Eqs. (7), (8) and (9). In addition, as this variant includes the elitist variant described above, $\Delta\tau_f^e$ is calculated as Eq. (12).

5   Experimental Work

5.1   Setup and Methodology

Hardware and Software. For the experimental phase of the work, programs have been run on a computer that executes CentOS Linux (v7.9). This platform is composed of two Intel Xeon E5-2620 v4 with 16 cores and 32 threads running at 2,100 MHz. The variants of ACO-FS have been coded in Python (v3.6.8) using different Machine Learning libraries such as *TensorFlow* (v2.3) and *Scikit-learn* (v0.22.3). The energy consumed by the procedures has been obtained with a wattmeter based on Arduino Mega, which is able to provide an energy value every second.

EEG Dataset. Obtained from the BCI laboratory at the University of Essex, it consists of a training dataset and a testing dataset. Both correspond to a human subject: the training dataset contains 178 EEG signals with 3,600 features each and the testing dataset contains 179 EEG signals with 3,600 features each. The objective is to classify these EEGs into three different classes that correspond to imagined limb movements: left and right hands, and feet.

Program Parameters. The parameter values of all algorithms are $N_C = 5$ and $N_A = 10$. However, EACO-FS and RACO-FS variants have another specific parameter: the number of elitist ants (σ), whose value is $\sigma = 4$. Although higher values of the parameters could improve the results, due to the computational demand of the procedures the values could not be increased.

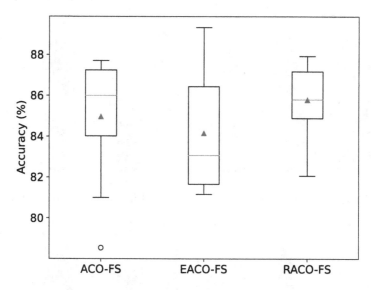

Fig. 2. Classification rate obtained by the ACO-FS algorithm and its variants for the testing dataset

Table 1. Mean classification rate and standard deviation obtained by each algorithm for the testing dataset

Algorithm	Mean classification rate	Standard deviation
ACO-FS	84.97%	3.08
EACO-FS	84.16%	3.00
RACO-FS	85.79%	1.84

Classification Method. To get a comparable measurement between algorithms it is necessary to define a classification method. In this way, a classifier based on a mono-layer Neural Network (NN) with 64 *sigmoid* function neurons has been used. The network has been executed 10 times per program execution to get a stable accuracy value. In turn, all programs have been executed 10 times to get the average execution time, energy consumption, and accuracy.

5.2   Results

Figure 2 and Table 1 show the classification rate obtained by all algorithms for the testing dataset. ACO-FS and RACO-FS are the best options. Nevertheless, RACO-FS presents the best statistical behavior, with a lower standard deviation and a higher mean classification rate, while the median keeps stable, near to the arithmetic average and leaving a symmetric distribution. On the other hand, Fig. 3 shows the mean execution time for each algorithm. ACO-FS is the fastest program while RACO-FS is the one which requires more time to complete its

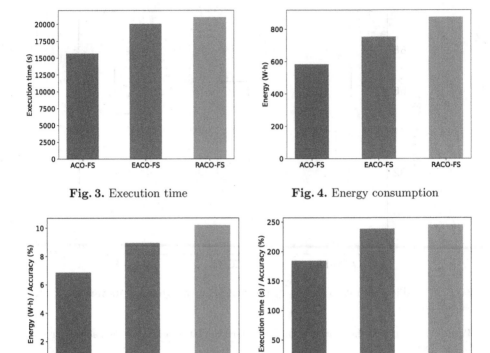

Fig. 3. Execution time   **Fig. 4.** Energy consumption

Fig. 5. Energy-accuracy relation   **Fig. 6.** Time-accuracy relation

execution. The energy consumption associated with the execution times of Fig. 3 is exposed in Fig. 4. Here, we can see how RACO-FS requires much more energy than the other algorithms. It is worth mentioning that it is not strange to see that the energy is roughly proportional to the execution time. This makes sense since the longer the execution time, the greater the accumulated energy.

In view of the results, new questions could be raised as the methods have been evaluated taking into account three different metrics: time, energy, and accuracy. So which method is really the best? Before answering this question we are going to look at Figs. 5 and 6, which shows the energy-accuracy and time-accuracy relation, respectively. From Fig. 5, it is stated that in RACO-FS, for every 1% accuracy, 10 W·h of energy are needed. However, in ACO-FS, only 7 W·h. A similar behavior can be found in Fig. 6.

The previous figures have shown that each method is better or worse depending on the observed measure. However, we are going to establish a new metric that allows accuracy and performance to be taken into account simultaneously. In this way, the energy-time-accuracy product is established as:

$$S = Energy \cdot Time \cdot (1 - Accuracy) \tag{16}$$

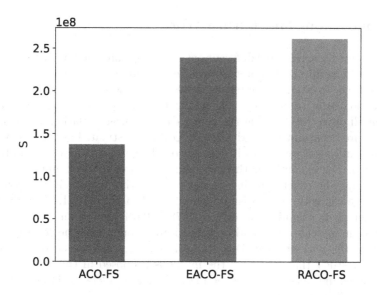

Fig. 7. Energy-time-accuracy product

Table 2. Average number of selected features for each algorithm

Algorithm	Mean number of features
ACO-FS	17.9
EACO-FS	22.2
RACO-FS	21.9

Table 3. Average K-fold cross validation accuracy in each algorithm for the training dataset

Algorithm	K-Fold CV
ACO-FS	73.28%
EACO-FS	71.43%
RACO-FS	74.06%

The goal is to minimize time and energy, while maximizing accuracy. Since this is a multi-objective problem, all objectives must be maximized or minimized. In this case, the easiest thing is to transform the accuracy into a minimization problem by replacing *Accuracy* with $(1 - Accuracy)$. Figure 7 shows the results obtained by each algorithm taking into account the new metric, S. Looking at the figure, it can be clearly seen that ACO-FS is the best option.

Finally, Table 2 shows the average number of selected features in each algorithm. In order to keep the consistency of the subsets solutions, program parameters have been selected according to a K-fold cross-validation value near to the original feature set. Also, Table 3 presents the average K-fold cross-validation accuracy obtained by each algorithm with $K = 10$ [22] for the training dataset.

6   Conclusions and Future Work

Throughout this work, three different ant colony optimization algorithms applied to an EEG classification problem have been proposed and analyzed. All algorithms have been evaluated in terms of execution time, energy consumption, and classification rates (accuracy) to identify which one provides the best trade-off between all objectives. Taking the energy-time-accuracy relation as a comparative measure between the algorithms, ACO-FS is postulated as the best version. However, this is subjective, as it depends on the circumstances surrounding the application. For example, if the procedures are executed on multi-node clusters, perhaps the execution time is not an objective to take into account due to the large capacity of these supercomputers. In this sense, RACO-FS will be the winner as its classification rate is 85.79%, 0.6% more than that reached by ACO-FS. In any case, it should be taken into account that the results will also depend on the dataset used. Due to its importance, we are currently working on another study that evaluates the methods proposed in this paper with the datasets used in the BCI Competition IV, which are widely used in the literature to test classification methods.

Regarding the algorithms themselves, the original ACO algorithm was proposed twenty years ago, so that today it has a multitude of variants. For example, the elitist variant proposed in this work essentially proposes a form of rewarding the best ant of the colony. Consequently, this develops other impairments: a highly influenced result by the path of the first colonies or a worse exploration of new features. The way to alter the behavior of ACOs to search for new methodologies goes beyond its own algorithmic nature, since with the appearance of parallel programming new computing paradigms have been opened. In Swarm Intelligence systems, individual agents work separately but have a collective conscience and capacity for cooperation. This is doubly beneficial for a possible parallelization because: (i) the computation associated with an agent could be carried out in parallel as it does not depend on that of other agents. This is not exclusive to SI systems, since evolutionary algorithms also have this feature; (ii) the way agents cooperate can change. By using different threads or processes, the search space is really being explored in parallel, so there could be real-time communication between agents to quickly report an event such as the non-viability of a subset of features or to request some kind of help. In addition to this, parallelizing the application would lead to reductions in execution time and consequently also in energy consumption, which would allow exploring more subset of features and increasing the size of the program parameters, something that has not been possible in this work due to the high computational cost that this would entail.

Acknowledgments. This research has been funded by the Spanish Ministry of Science, Innovation, and Universities under grant PGC2018-098813-B-C31 and ERDF fund. We would like to thank the BCI laboratory of the University of Essex, especially Dr. John Q. Gan, for allowing us to use their datasets.

References

1. Bauer, A., Bullnheimer, B., Hartl, R., Strauss, C.: Minimizing total tardiness on a single machine using ant colony optimization. Cent. Eur. J. Oper. Res. **8**(2), 125–141 (2000)
2. Blum, C.: Beam-aco-hybridizing ant colony optimization with beam search: an application to open shop scheduling. Comput. Oper. Res. **32**(6), 1565–1591 (2005). https://doi.org/10.1016/j.cor.2003.11.018
3. Bonabeau, E., Dorigo, M., Theraulaz, G.: Swarm intelligence: from natural to artificial systems. Oxford University Press (1999). https://doi.org/10.1093/oso/9780195131581.001.0001
4. Chandrashekar, G., Sahin, F.: A survey on feature selection methods. Comput. Electr. Eng. **40**(1), 16–28 (2014). https://doi.org/10.1016/j.compeleceng.2013.11.024
5. Chen, L.: Curse of dimensionality, pp. 545–546. Springer, US, Boston, MA (2009). https://doi.org/10.1007/978-0-387-39940-9_133
6. Cramer, J.S.: The origins and development of the logit model, pp. 149–157. Cambridge University Press, Cambridge (2003). https://doi.org/10.1017/CBO9780511615412.010
7. Deng, W., Xu, J., Zhao, H.: An improved ant colony optimization algorithm based on hybrid strategies for scheduling problem. IEEE Access **7**, 20281–20292 (2019). https://doi.org/10.1109/ACCESS.2019.2897580
8. Dorigo, M.: Optimization, learning and natural algorithms. Ph.D. thesis, Politecnico di Milano (1992)
9. Dorigo, M., Birattari, M., Stutzle, T.: Ant colony optimization. IEEE Comput. Intell. Mag. **1**(4), 28–39 (2006). https://doi.org/10.1109/MCI.2006.329691
10. Dorigo, M., Caro, G.A.D.: Ant colony optimization: a new meta-heuristic. In: Proceedings of the 1999 Congress on Evolutionary Computation-CEC99 (Cat. No. 99TH8406). vol. 2, pp. 1470–1477. IEEE, Washington, DC, USA (1999). https://doi.org/10.1109/CEC.1999.782657
11. Dorigo, M., Gambardella, L.M.: Ant colony system: a cooperative learning approach to the traveling salesman problem. IEEE Trans. Evol. Comput. **1**(1), 53–66 (1997). https://doi.org/10.1109/4235.585892
12. Dorigo, M., Maniezzo, V., Colorni, A.: Ant system: optimization by a colony of cooperating agents. IEEE Trans. Syst. Man Cybern. Part B Cybern. **26**(1), 29–41 (1996). https://doi.org/10.1109/3477.484436
13. Dorigo, M., Stützle, T.: Ant colony optimization: overview and recent advances, pp. 311–351. Springer International Publishing, Cham (2019). https://doi.org/10.1007/978-3-319-91086-4_10
14. Dreiseitl, S., Ohno-Machado, L.: Logistic regression and artificial neural network classification models: a methodology review. J. Biomed. Inf. **35**(5), 352–359 (2002). https://doi.org/10.1016/S1532-0464(03)00034-0
15. Du, H., Wang, Z., Zhan, W., Guo, J.: Elitism and distance strategy for selection of evolutionary algorithms. IEEE Access **6**, 44531–44541 (2018). https://doi.org/10.1109/ACCESS.2018.2861760
16. Fujisawa, R., Dobata, S., Sugawara, K., Matsuno, F.: Designing pheromone communication in swarm robotics: Group foraging behavior mediated by chemical substance. Swarm Intell. **8**(3), 227–246 (2014). https://doi.org/10.1007/s11721-014-0097-z

17. Gambardella, L.M., Taillard, E., Agazzi, G.: Macs-vrptw: a multiple ant colony system for vehicle routing problems with time windows. Tech. Rep. 1, Istituto Dalle Molle Di Studi Sull Intelligenza Artificiale, Lugano, Switzerland (1999)
18. Uthayakumar, J., Metawa, N., Shankar, K., Lakshmanaprabu, S.: Financial crisis prediction model using ant colony optimization. Int. J. Inf. Manage. **50**, 538–556 (2020). https://doi.org/10.1016/j.ijinfomgt.2018.12.001
19. Kennedy, J.: Swarm Intelligence, pp. 187–219. Springer, US, Boston, MA (2006). https://doi.org/10.1007/0-387-27705-6
20. Ling, W., Luo, H.: An adaptive parameter control strategy for ant colony optimization. In: International Conference on Computational Intelligence and Security (CIS). vol. 1, pp. 142–146. IEEE, Harbin, China (2007). https://doi.org/10.1109/CIS.2007.156
21. Monmarché, N.: Swarm Intelligence, pp. 179–202. Springer International Publishing, Cham (2016). https://doi.org/10.1007/978-3-319-45403-0_7
22. Refaeilzadeh, P., Tang, L., Liu, H.: Cross-Validation, pp. 532–538. Springer, US, Boston, MA (2009). https://doi.org/10.1007/978-0-387-39940-9
23. Stützle, T., et al.: Parameter adaptation in ant colony optimization, pp. 191–215. Springer, Berlin Heidelberg, Berlin, Heidelberg (2012). https://doi.org/10.1007/978-3-642-21434-9_83
24. Sun, Y., Dong, W., Chen, Y.: An improved routing algorithm based on ant colony optimization in wireless sensor networks. IEEE Commun. Lett. **21**(6), 1317–1320 (2017). https://doi.org/10.1109/LCOMM.2017.2672959
25. Zhao, D., et al.: Chaotic random spare ant colony optimization for multi-threshold image segmentation of 2d kapur entropy. Knowledge-Based Systems **216**,(2021). https://doi.org/10.1016/j.knosys.2020.106510

Personalized Medicine

Comparison of Fusion Methodologies Using CNV and RNA-Seq for Cancer Classification: A Case Study on Non-Small-Cell Lung Cancer

Francisco Carrillo-Perez[✉], Juan Carlos Morales, Daniel Castillo-Secilla, Alberto Guillen, Ignacio Rojas, and Luis Javier Herrera

Department of Computer Architecture and Technology, University of Granada. C.I.T.I.C., Periodista Rafael Gómez Montero, 2, 18014 Granada, Spain
franciscocp@ugr.es

Abstract. Lung cancer is one of the most frequent cancer types, and one among those causing more deceases worldwide. Nowadays, in order to improve the diagnosis of cancer more screenings are performed to the same patient and various biological sources are being gathered. Fusing the information provided by these sources can lead to a more robust diagnosis, which can improve the prognosis of the patient. In this work, a comparison of fusion methodologies (early and intermediate) using RNA-Seq and Copy Number Variation data for Non-Small-Cell Lung Cancer classification is performed. We found that great results can be attained using both fusion methodologies, with an AUC of 0.984 for the early fusion and 0.989 for the intermediate fusion, improving those obtained by each source of information independently (0.978 RNA-Seq and 0.910 Copy Number Variation). This work shows that fusion methodologies can enhance the classification of non-small-cell lung cancer, and that these methodologies can be promising for the diagnosis of other cancer types.

Keywords: Information fusion · NSCLC · Machine learning

1 Introduction

Cancer is one of the most deadly diseases worldwide, just behind cardiovascular diseases. Lung cancer is one of the most frequent types, with a total of 2.2 million new cancer cases and 1.8 million deaths worldwide in 2020 [27], representing the 18.0% of total cancer related deceases. Non-Small-Cell Lung Cancer (NSCLC) is the most prevalent of the lung cancer cases, representing around 80–85% of the total [29]. Within NSCLC two different sub-types can be observed: adenocarcinoma (LUAD), which usually comes from peripheral lung tissue [26], and squamous-cell-carcinoma (LUSC), which is usually centrally located [13,28]. The treatment used for a diagnosed patient differs between these two cancer sub-types, therefore, an accurate diagnosis is crucial in order to improve the prognosis of the patient [11].

© Springer Nature Switzerland AG 2021
I. Rojas et al. (Eds.): BIOMESIP 2021, LNCS 12940, pp. 339–349, 2021.
https://doi.org/10.1007/978-3-030-88163-4_29

In recent years the availability and gathering of biological information has increased dramatically. Experts use different screenings for the identification of lung cancer, such as Whole-Slide Imaging (WSIs), the identification of biomarkers in next-generation sequencing (NGS) data (e.g. gene expression analysis using RNA-Seq or Copy Number Variation -CNV- analysis) or the use of clinical information from the patient. However, manually analyzing these sources can be a time-consuming task, so in recent years different automatic approaches have been proposed in literature for the design of decision-support systems which fall in the area of precision medicine [9,21]. Two sources of information that have been used in literature are RNA-Seq and CNV. RNA-Seq measures gene expression, and CNV measures the number of copies of specific genes along segments of the genome. It has been shown in literature that both are highly correlated with cancer development [23,24], therefore, an integration of the information provided from these two sources for cancer classification is of great significance.

Information Fusion has been a topic of interest in machine learning (ML) in recent years, given the increasing gathering of multimodal data. Depending on in which stage the fusion takes place, three different approaches can be differentiated: late, early and intermediate fusion. In this work we are going to focus on two of them, early and intermediate fusion. In the early fusion, different features are obtained from each data type, and then are joined and fed to a classification model that learns from them [25]. The intermediate fusion is more related to Artificial Neural Networks (ANNs) models. For this type of fusion, typically independent ANNs are used for each data type, and the features provided by them are fused in the middle layers of an ANN that performs the classification. The optimization of all the ANNs is performed searching for classification performance [12]. A graphical representation of these fusion methodologies can be observed in Fig. 1.

The aim of this work is to present a comparison of the two aforementioned fusion methodologies for the task of LUAD, LUSC and healthy classification when using RNA-Seq and CNV data. In this section and introduction to the problem has been outlined. In Sect. 2, an overview of the the related works will be reported. In Sect. 3, the methodology and data used in this work will be presented. In Sect. 4, the results obtained will be presented and discussed. Finally, in Sect. 5 conclusions will be drawn and future work will be presented.

2   Related Work

In recent years several works have been presented using RNA-Seq and CNV in lung cancer related problems.

For lung cancer subtypes classification using RNA-Seq, Gonzalez et al. studied differentially expressed genes (DEGs) between SCLC, LUAD, LUSC and Large Cell Lung Carcinoma. Then, different feature selectors and predictive models were used in order to compare their classification performance [9]. Authors reached an accuracy of 88.23% using k-NN and the Random Forest feature selector. For a similar task but using CNV, Qiu et al. presented a CNV signature for

LUAD, LUSC and healthy classification formed by thirty-three genes reaching an accuracy of 84% in the validation set [21].

Different works have been presented using the fusion of heterogeneous sources of biological information for lung cancer, including RNA-Seq and CNV. Lee et al. used an autoencoder for the obtention of a feature representation using mRNA, miRNA, CNV and DNA Methylation for prognosis prediction [16]. Dong et al. proposed to use a late fusion methodology along with a gcForest model for predicting the stage of lung adenocarcinoma by fusing RNA-Seq, DNA Methylation and CNV [6]. Authors reached an F1-Score of 88.9% on the task.

3   Materials and Method

3.1   Data Acquisition and Models Evaluation

In this work we have used two different types of biological data: RNA-Seq and CNV. The data were gathered from the The Cancer Genome Atlas (TCGA) program [30], located in the GDC portal [10].

The TCGA contains information from 33 different cancer types and GDC have performed an harmonization of all the available samples in the program. Moreover, various data types are available for each sample (e.g. gene expression, copy number variation, histology imaging, etc.). In GDC, each patient has a Patient ID that identifies them, and each screening performed on the same biological sample from a patient has a defined Case ID. Then, we have the Sample ID, which represents the information from a given sample. Therefore, for each Sample ID we can have different biological information (CNV, RNA-Seq or both). Those Case IDs used in this work are available in this Github repository: https://github.com/pacocp/RNA-CNV-fusion-comparison. Table 1 shows the Sample IDs availability per class and considered data type.

Table 1. Number of samples per class and data type.

Data type	LUAD	Healthy	LUSC	Total
RNA-Seq	457	44	479	980
CNV	465	919	472	1856
In common	433	23	448	904

For the case of gene expression, RNA-Seq from Illumina HTSeq data is used in TCGA. In the specific case of GDC data, it harmonizes RNA-Seq data by aligning raw RNA reads to the GRCh38 reference genome building and calculating gene expression levels with standardized protocols [20]. The KnowSeq R-Bioc package was used in order to obtain the DEGs [3].

For CNV data, Affymetrix SNP 6.0 array data is used to identify genomic regions that are repeated and infer the copy number of these repeats. Then, sequences are mapped to the GRCh38 reference genome. The R-Bioc package Genomic Ranges [15] was used for obtaining the gene matrix where each gene has its associated mean segment value.

Models were implemented in Python using the Pytorch [17], Scikit-Learn [18] and XGBoost [4] packages. ANNs model training was performed using a Intel(R) Xeon(R) CPU E5-2620.

In order to avoid a result bias due to a reduced test set and the data imbalance, the whole dataset was divided using a 10-Fold Cross-Validation (10-Fold CV) for different training-test assessments, in order to obtain a more thorough assessment. In each iteration, the training set was used for feature selection, to train the models, and also for hyperparameter tuning, while a final assessment of models performance was done in the test set. No information from the test set was included in the feature selection phase nor for hyperparameter tuning. The hyperparameter tuning strategy followed was a classic training-validation split, including a Grid Search in the case of the early fusion. All the splits were performed both in a patient-wise way and in a stratified way. With a patient-wise splitting we are ensuring that, even if a patient has more than one case, they could only belong to one of the splits, being this training or validation. Imposing this restriction prevents any kind of information leakage during training. On the other hand, through stratified splitting the proportion of classes in each fold is maintained.

3.2 RNA-Seq Pre-processing

In order to analyze the HTSeq-Counts data provided, we used the KnowSeq R-Bioc package [3]. This package provides a pipeline to obtain DEGs based on the HTSeq-Counts files and finally perform a machine learning assessment of the selected DEGs. KnowSeq relies on limma [22], which is the state-of-the-art for finding genes with differential expressions. However, limma is usually employed to biclass problems, where two classes need to be compared. Thus, additional tasks need to be perform to achieve DEGs when there are more than two classes. In order to deal with this problem, Castillo et al. presented the coverage (COV) parameter, which uses limma to a perform binary comparisons of the N presented classes and finally select a set of genes that are differentially expressed in COV binary comparisons [1].

Therefore, we used the *DEGsExtraction* function from the KnowSeq package over the training set to obtain the DEGs matrix. As parameters, a *Log_2 Fold Chain* (*LFC*) value of 2 (early fusion) and 1.5 (intermediate fusion), a p-value of 0.05, and a COV value of 2, were set. Once we obtained the DEGs matrix, we used the minimun Redundancy Maximum Relevance (mRMR) algorithm to obtain a ranking of the genes [19]. The mRMR algorithm uses information theory to obtain a ranking of features which are highly correlated with the classes but with a minimum redundancy between them. It has been previously used in literature as feature selector for gene expression [1,2,5,7]. The smaller value of *LFC* is used in the intermediate fusion to not have a huge imbalance with the number of CNV input features.

3.3   Copy Number Variation Pre-processing

The level 3 CNV data of LUAD and LUSC patients measured by the Affymetrix Genome-Wide Human SNP Array 6.0 were used in our study. The CNV value of a gene was defined as the average value of all of the segments' CNV values corresponding to the gene. This correspondence between the segments files and the gene files was performed using the R-Bioc package Genomic Ranges [15].

Once the gene matrix was obtained, where for each sample and gene we obtained the average value of all the segments', we proceeded to obtain those genes with significant differences between the groups of samples. Firstly, genes with missing CNV values were removed, leaving 46, 585 genes. In order to investigate the global differences of CNV patterns among the three different groups (LUAD, LUSC and Healthy), a two-tailed t-test was employed, also using Bonferroni correction as a way to control for the family-wise error rate (p-value ≤ 0.001). Those genes that were significantly different for the three two-tailed t-test (LUAD vs LUSC, LUAD vs Healthy, LUSC vs Healthy) and where the difference of the mean was greater or equal to 0.1 were selected in each split. Finally, the mRMR algorithm was used to obtain a ranking of the genes for the classification task.

3.4   Early Fusion

In an early fusion methodology, the features are obtained and then fed to a classification model for its training. Therefore, after following the pre-processing steps explained in Subsect. 3.2 and 3.3, those obtained features were concatenated and used as input for the classification model. A diagram representing this type of fusion can be observed in Fig. 1 (a).

For the early fusion methodology, the hyperparameters of the models were chosen using a Grid Search over each training set. As the classification model, XGBoost was chosen based on its good performance on mid-size and tabular datasets. A 10% of the training set was used as validation set for early stopping for the XGBoost model (in order to prevent an overfitting of the model), and the values used for the Grid Search were:

- **max_depth**: $2, 4, 6, 8$
- **n_estimators**: $20, 30, 50, 100, 200$
- **alpha**: $0, 0.1, 0.2, 0.3$

In order to test the capabilities of the model when both sources of information were available, only those samples that fulfill this requirement were used for training and testing (see Table 1).

3.5   Intermediate Fusion

For the intermediate fusion methodology, the feature selection and fusion is performed while training the model. Therefore, the DEGs selected by limma (in the case of RNA-Seq) and those selected in the two-tailed t-test (for CNV) are used as inputs for two different ANNs (sub-networks). Then, the features obtained by each sub-network were concatenated and fed to a classification ANN. The whole optimization is performed based on the classification performance of the ANN. The architecture is depicted in Fig. 2, indicating the layers used as well as the inputs' size of the first split. A diagram of this type of fusion can be observed in Fig. 1 (b).

Different sets of hyperparameters were tested for the architecture optimization, using a 10% of the training set as validation set. Finally, Adam [14] was used as the optimizer with a learning rate of 0.001 and the Cross Entropy Loss was used as loss function. Also, the network weights were initialized using the Xavier weight initialization [8], since it has been shown to provide with a good starting point for the optimization. The model was trained for 15 epochs using an early stopping strategy, saving the best weights for later use in the prediction phase.

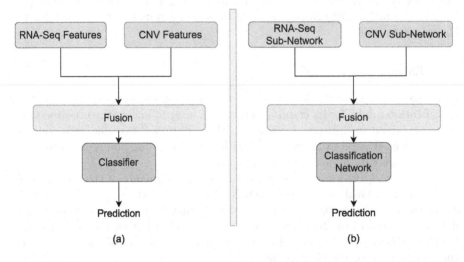

Fig. 1. Diagrams representing each fusion methodology. In Fig. 1 a, an early fusion methodology is depicted, where the features are fused and fed to a classification model that uses them for training and predicting. In Fig. 1 b, the intermediate fusion methodology is shown, where the feature selection and classification is performed by ANNs, and the whole optimization is performed based on the classification performance.

4   Results and Discussion

In this section the different results obtained with each methodology are going to be shown and discussed. It must be noted that, in order to make a fair comparison, all the results presented have been obtained using those samples where both sources of information were available. For the RNA-Seq and CNV independent models' results, the methodology used for their training and testing

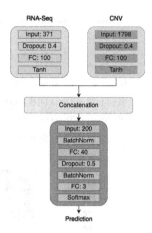

Fig. 2. Architecture used for the intermediate fusion methodology. Each subnetwork learn a feature representation for each data type. These representations are concatenated and fed to the classification network. The optimization of the weights is based on the classification performance, therefore, the feature selection is driven by improving the classification. FC is the abbreviation of Fully Connected Layer. The number of RNA-Seq and CNV inputs are those from the first split.

is the one depicted in Subsect 3.4. After several experiments in the training sets, the first six genes of the RNA-Seq mRMR ranking and the first twelve for the CNV mRMR ranking were selected for training the model in the early fusion in each split. For each model and fusion methodology, the accuracy, F1-score and AUC metrics were computed (see Table 2) as well as the ROC Curves per class (see Fig. 4) and the confusion matrices (see Fig. 3).

The results obtained by the fusion methodologies are very similar in terms of AUC (see Table 2), being the intermediate fusion methodology the one that obtains the best performance (0.984 for the early fusion and 0.989 for the intermediate fusion). On this metric, the two fusion strategies outperform the results obtained by each independent model, reducing the standard deviation across the ten splits (a 0.978 (0.010) obtained by the RNA-Seq model and a 0.910 (0.013) obtained by the CNV model).

In terms of F1-Score (see Table 2), the intermediate fusion reaches the best performance and similar results are obtained with the early fusion (95.13% and 95.01% respectively). In addition, the minimum standard deviation on both F1-Score and accuracy is obtained with the early fusion, making it the most robust methodology of the two (with an standard deviation of 1.32% for both F1-score and accuracy).

Using an early or intermediate fusion methodology improves the results over using each data type independently for all metrics (see Table 2). The ANNs are able to select those genes that are useful for the classification, and the proposed pre-processing steps in the case of the early fusion provides relevant features for training a classification model. Given these results, the use of one of these

Table 2. Results obtained by each fusion methodology and each data type independently.

	F1-Score	AUC	Acc.
RNA-Seq	94.41 (1.67)	0.978 (0.010)	94.46 (1.68)
CNV	80.71 (3.83)	0.910 (0.013)	80.74 (3.81)
Early fusion	95.01 (1.32)	0.984 (0.008)	95.02 (1.32)
Intermediate fusion	95.13 (1.73)	0.989 (0.007)	95.01 (1.76)

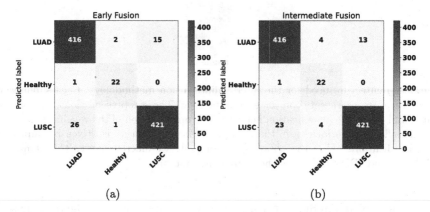

(a)   (b)

Fig. 3. Confusion matrices over the whole dataset for the early (a) and intermediate (b) fusion methodologies.

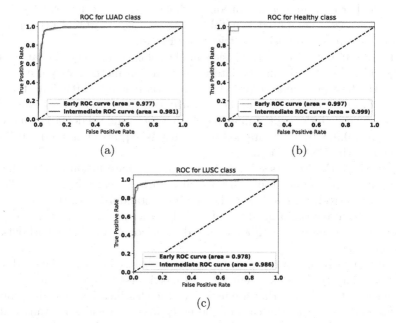

(a)   (b)

(c)

Fig. 4. ROC Curves over the whole dataset for the LUAD (a), Healthy (b) and LUSC (c) for the two fusion methodologies.

two methodologies can be useful for the diagnosis. An early fusion should be used if we care about the interpretability, since the genes selected by mRMR are provided, and the intermediate fusion should be selected if we only care about the performance in the classification.

5   Conclusions

In this work we have performed a comparison of fusion methodologies for RNA-Seq and CNV data in a case study of NSCLC. Promising results are obtained with each source of information, showing their potential to find cancer biomarkers. Nevertheless, it has been shown that using a fusion methodology can improve the results obtained by independent models. The early and intermediate fusion methods obtained the best results in the classification task, showing their potential for cancer classification. As future work, we would like to increase the number of cancer types where the different methodologies are applied, in order to test their capabilities on different scenarios. In addition, we want to integrate more heterogeneous sources of information in order to investigate the potential of these fusion strategies when more data types are present.

Acknowledgements. The results published here are in whole or part based upon data generated by the TCGA Research Network: https://www.cancer.gov/tcga.

This work was funded by the Spanish Ministry of Sciences, Innovation and Universities under Grant RTI2018-101674-B-I00 as part of project "Computer Architectures and Machine Learning-based solutions for complex challenges in Bioinformatics, Biotechnology and Biomedicine" and by the Government of Andalusia under the grant CV20-64934 as part of the project "Development of an intelligence platform for the integration of heterogenous sources of information (images, genetic information and proteomics) for the characterization and prediction of COVID-19 patients' virulence and pathogenicity". The funders had no role in study design, data collection and analysis, decision to publish, or preparation of this manuscript.

References

1. Castillo, D., et al.: Leukemia multiclass assessment and classification from microarray and rna-seq technologies integration at gene expression level. PloS One **14**(2), e0212127 (2019)
2. Castillo, D., Gálvez, J.M., Herrera, L.J., San Román, B., Rojas, F., Rojas, I.: Integration of rna-seq data with heterogeneous microarray data for breast cancer profiling. BMC Bioinf. **18**(1), 506 (2017)
3. Castillo-Secilla, D., et al.: Knowseq r-bioc package: the automatic smart gene expression tool for retrieving relevant biological knowledge. Comput. Biol. Med. **133**, 104387 (2021)
4. Chen, T., Guestrin, C.: Xgboost: a scalable tree boosting system. In: Proceedings of the 22nd ACM Sigkdd International Conference on Knowledge Discovery and Data Mining, pp. 785–794 (2016)
5. Ding, C., Peng, H.: Minimum redundancy feature selection from microarray gene expression data. J. Bioinf. Comput. Biol. **3**(02), 185–205 (2005)

6. Dong, Y., et al.: Mlw-gcforest: a multi-weighted gcforest model towards the staging of lung adenocarcinoma based on multi-modal genetic data. BMC Bioinf. **20**(1), 1–14 (2019)

7. Gálvez, J.M., et al.: Towards improving skin cancer diagnosis by integrating microarray and rna-seq datasets. IEEE J. Biomed. Health Inf. **24**(7), 2119–2130 (2019)

8. Glorot, X., Bengio, Y.: Understanding the difficulty of training deep feedforward neural networks. In: Proceedings of the Thirteenth International Conference on Artificial Intelligence and Statistics, pp. 249–256. JMLR Workshop and Conference Proceedings (2010)

9. González, S., Castillo, D., Galvez, J.M., Rojas, I., Herrera, L.J.: Feature selection and assessment of lung cancer sub-types by applying predictive models. In: International Work-Conference on Artificial Neural Networks, pp. 883–894. Springer (2019)

10. Grossman, R.L., et al.: Toward a shared vision for cancer genomic data. New England J. Med. **375**(12), 1109–1112 (2016)

11. Hanna, N., et al.: Systemic therapy for stage iv non-small-cell lung cancer: american society of clinical oncology clinical practice guideline update. J. Clin. Oncol. (2017)

12. Huang, S.C., Pareek, A., Seyyedi, S., Banerjee, I., Lungren, M.P.: Fusion of medical imaging and electronic health records using deep learning: a systematic review and implementation guidelines. NPJ Digital Med. **3**(1), 1–9 (2020)

13. Kenfield, S.A., Wei, E.K., Stampfer, M.J., Rosner, B.A., Colditz, G.A.: Comparison of aspects of smoking among the four histological types of lung cancer. Tobacco Control **17**(3), 198–204 (2008)

14. Kingma, D.P., Ba, J.: Adam: a method for stochastic optimization. arXiv preprint arXiv:1412.6980 (2014)

15. Lawrence, M., et al.: Software for computing and annotating genomic ranges. PLoS Comput. Biol. **9**(8), e1003118 (2013)

16. Lee, T.Y., Huang, K.Y., Chuang, C.H., Lee, C.Y., Chang, T.H.: Incorporating deep learning and multi-omics autoencoding for analysis of lung adenocarcinoma prognostication. Comput. Biol. Chem. **87**, 107277 (2020)

17. Paszke, A., et al.: An imperative style, high-performance deep learning library. In: Wallach, H., Larochelle, H., Beygelzimer, A., d' Alché-Buc, F., Fox, E., Garnett, R. (eds.) Advances in Neural Information Processing Systems 32, pp. 8024–8035. Curran Associates, Inc. (2019), http://papers.neurips.cc/paper/9015-pytorch-an-imperative-style-high-performance-deep-learning-library.pdf

18. Pedregosa, F., et al.: Scikit-learn: machine learning in Python. J. Mach. Learn. Res. **12**, 2825–2830 (2011)

19. Peng, H., Long, F., Ding, C.: Feature selection based on mutual information criteria of max-dependency, max-relevance, and min-redundancy. IEEE Trans. Patt Anal. Mach. Intell. **27**(8), 1226–1238 (2005)

20. Portal, G.: Gdc rna-seq analysis pipeline. https://docs.gdc.cancer.gov/Data/Bioinformatics_Pipelines/Expression_mRNA_Pipeline/. Accessed 4 Jul 2020

21. Qiu, Z.W., Bi, J.H., Gazdar, A.F., Song, K.: Genome-wide copy number variation pattern analysis and a classification signature for non-small cell lung cancer. Genes Chromosom. Cancer **56**(7), 559–569 (2017)

22. Ritchie, M.E., et al.: Limma powers differential expression analyses for rna-sequencing and microarray studies. Nucleic Acids Res. **43**(7), e47–e47 (2015)

23. Ross, D.T., et al.: Systematic variation in gene expression patterns in human cancer cell lines. Nat. Genet. **24**(3), 227–235 (2000)

24. Shlien, A., Malkin, D.: Copy number variations and cancer. Genome Med. **1**(6), 1–9 (2009)
25. Snoek, C.G., Worring, M., Smeulders, A.W.: Early versus late fusion in semantic video analysis. In: Proceedings of the 13th Annual ACM International Conference on Multimedia, pp. 399–402 (2005)
26. Subramanian, J., Govindan, R.: Lung cancer in never smokers: a review. J. Clin. Oncol. **25**(5), 561–570 (2007)
27. Sung, H., et al.: Global cancer statistics 2020: globocan estimates of incidence and mortality worldwide for 36 cancers in 185 countries. CA: a cancer J. Clin. **71**(3), pp. 209-249 (2021)
28. Heigener, D.F., Reck, M.: Der Internist **58**(12), 1258–1263 (2017). https://doi.org/10.1007/s00108-017-0339-4
29. UK, C.R.: Types of lung cancer. https://www.cancerresearchuk.org/about-cancer/lung-cancer/stages-types-grades/types
30. Weinstein, J.N., et al.: The cancer genome atlas pan-cancer analysis project. Nat. Genet. **45**(10), 1113 (2013)

Artificial Corneal Transplantation and the Safe Recovery of Vision in the COVID-19 Pandemic

Carlos Eduardo Ximenes da Cunha[1](✉) ⓘ, Laís Rytholz Castro[1] ⓘ,
Marina Maria Gonzaga Moreira[1,2,3] ⓘ, Paloma da Silva de Santana[1] ⓘ,
Marina Viegas Moura Rezende Ribeiro[1] ⓘ, Luciano Timbó Barbosa[1] ⓘ,
Eugênia Mirza Queiroz Ferreira Barboza da Silveira[2] ⓘ,
and Ana Ramalho Gameleira Soares[3] ⓘ

[1] Tiradentes University Center (UNIT), Maceió-Al, Brazil
[2] University of Fortaleza (UNIFOR), Fortaleza-Ce, Brazil
[3] Maceió's Eyes Institute (IOM), Maceió-Al, Brazil

Abstract. In March 2020 the WHO announced the pandemic due to the new coronavirus nCoV-19, which uses the ACE-2 enzyme, present in several body tissues, to infect the host. The presence of ACE-2 in the corneal limbus makes the eyeball an important route of infection for the virus, which is why corneal transplantation is precluded in cases of suspected COVID-19 donors. Also in 2020, The Global Alliance of Eye Bank Association (GAEBA) developed restrictive measures aimed at preventing the spread of the new coronavirus between eye tissue donors and recipient patients, consequently, there was a reduction in effective donors and a global increase in the waiting lines for corneal transplantation worldwide. On the other hand, artificial corneal implantation presents itself as a positive alternative for the current moment, since it makes it impossible for the donor and the recipient of the eye tissue to become infected. In this sense, the present study aims to describe the use of artificial corneas in keratoplasties, considering this a safe and effective method for restoring vision during the COVID-19 pandemic.

Keywords: Corneal transplantation · Corneal diseases · Artificial cornea · Novel coronavirus pandemic

1 Introduction

In December 2019, the advent of a zoonotic agent in Wuhan, China, was related to the emergence of Severe Acute Respiratory Syndrome in some individuals infected with the pathogen [1–3]. From then on, it was found that the flu-like symptoms presented by these patients with dry cough, fever, and dyspnea were symptoms of COVID-19. This is considered a respiratory disease with systemic repercussions caused by the new coronavirus, nCoV-19 [1, 4].

Following the emergence of cases of COVID-19 on several continents, the World Health Organization (WHO) announced in March 2020 a pandemic caused by nCoV-19. This virus is a single-stranded RNA that circulates among mammals via bats [5, 6].

© Springer Nature Switzerland AG 2021
I. Rojas et al. (Eds.): BIOMESIP 2021, LNCS 12940, pp. 350–358, 2021.
https://doi.org/10.1007/978-3-030-88163-4_30

Furthermore, it was realized that the new coronavirus infects host cells via angiotensin-converting enzyme 2 (ACE-2) receptors and that these are localized to a greater extent in the lower respiratory tract [7].

In this perspective, the existence of ACE-2 receptors in organs other than the lungs suggested the possibility of infection through different histological sites [8]. Given that the ocular surface serves as a gateway for various pathogens, the presence of ACE-2 in the corneal limbus facilitates coronavirus entry through the visual system, making the eyeball an important source of nCoV-19 contagion [9].

In this scenario, The Global Alliance of Eye Bank Association (GAEBA) guided measures that aim to prevent infection between eye tissue donors and recipient patients [9]. Therefore, corneal transplantation is not possible in cases of suspect donors for COVID-19 or in those where an immunological test has not been performed [10]. As a consequence of this event, there has been an overall reduction in the number of keratoplasties performed due to restrictive measures adopted to contain the pandemic's progress [10, 11].

In January 2021, the first successful artificial cornea transplant in the world was performed in Israel. For this, an inert, synthetic and non-degradable substitute was used, compatible with the extracellular matrix of the receptor patient. Considering that synthetic cornea transplantation prevents contamination between donor patients and recipients of ocular tissues, this article aims to describe the use of artificial corneas in keratoplasties, considering this a safe and effective method to reestablish vision during the COVID-19 pandemic.

2   Methodology

This is a bibliographic study, of the narrative review type, guided by the following steps: recognition of the topic and formation of the research question; definition of sample inclusion and exclusion criteria; categorization of studies; evaluation of studies included in the review; discussion of results and synthesis of knowledge.

The guiding research question was the use of artificial corneas in keratoplasties during the COVID-19 pandemic. The object of analysis consisted of papers from journals indexed in the Latin American and Caribbean Literature on Health Sciences (LILACS), Scientific Electronic Library Online (SciELO) and United States National Library of Medicine (PubMed) databases.

The search for papers took place between March and April 2021, using the keywords: corneal transplantation; COVID-19; keratoplasty and artificial cornea using AND, we established the following relation: "corneal transplantation, COVID-19, keratoplasty AND artificial cornea". We used language (Portuguese and English texts) and time filters for the review, considering papers published in the last 15 years.

The following inclusion criteria were used: articles available on the Internet; articles published in English; articles published in Portuguese. Non-scientific resources were excluded from this review, as well as articles whose full texts were not available and texts that, after reading the abstracts, did not present significant content on the proposed theme.

3 Discussion and Results

3.1 Corneal Transplantation

The cornea is the ophthalmic tissue that forms the transparent outer layer covering the iris, and is the tissue most closely related to the refractive power of the human eye. [12, 13]. As it is an avascular structure, the cornea is relatively sensitive to infections and ocular trauma, situations that can permanently damage this tissue and indicate the need for corneal transplantation to re-establish vision [12].

Corneal transplantation (CT) or keratoplasty is the most performed allogeneic transplant worldwide and presents a high success rate, being the main means of vision restoration when the corneal transparency has already been compromised [14]. The main pathologies that lead to keratoplasties are: keratoconus, aphasic and pseudophasic bullous keratopathy, dystrophies, infections and trauma, with keratoconus and keratitis being the pathologies that most lead to CTs in the world [15, 16].

Currently, there are four surgical techniques of keratoplasty: penetrating technique (PKP), anterior lamellar technique (DALK), Descemet's membrane automated denudation (DSAEK) and Descmet's membrane endothelial keratoplasty (DMEK) [17]. What differentiates one technique from another is the selectivity of the tissue that will be removed, for example: in penetrating keratoplasty, the recipient has about two thirds of his cornea removed and receives all the five layers of the donor cornea. In the other techniques, only the receiver's dysfunctional layers are removed and replaced by graft (Fig. 1) [17].

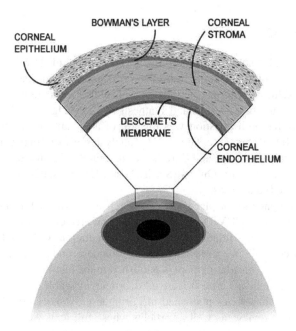

Fig. 1. Corneal tissue layers. Author: CUNHA, C.E.X (2020)

3.2 Impact of the Covid-19 Pandemic on Corneal Transplants

Since the beginning of the new coronavirus pandemic, medical societies around the world have released guidelines aiming to make organ transplantation safer, thus avoiding contamination among tissue donors, healthcare professionals and organ recipients [18]. However, taking into consideration that the COVID-19 is a recent disease, the studies are still insufficient about the virus contagion in solid organ transplantation and, thus, the procedures considered non-emergency have presented a marked reduction since the beginning of the pandemic [19].

Even though recent studies indicate a lower probability of SARS-CoV-2 infection through the conjunctival surface, The Global Alliance of Eye Bank Association (GAEBA) has issued some safety measures related to ocular tissue transplantation, such as: proscription of organ donation by donors positive for COVID-19, suspicious individuals who died less than 14 days after symptom resolution or those who did not undergo immunological testing, and donors who had contact with suspected or confirmed cases of COVID-19 [20, 21]. Such restrictive measures adopted by GAEBA were based on the current scarcity of standardized studies linking ocular coronavirus infection and corneal transplantation [20, 21].

In addition to discouraging elective keratoplasty, the operation of eye banks was affected worldwide due to the onerous screening process for tissue donor patients, the extensive list of contraindications for transplants and the redirection of efforts to fight the pandemic [22]. Thus, there was a significant reduction of effective donors of ocular tissue and, consequently, a global increase in waiting lines for cornea transplantation [11, 23].

3.3 Artificial Corneal Transplantation

The cornea is the most transplanted tissue worldwide and the only widely accepted treatment to promote corneal transparency and restore vision [22, 23]. However, this procedure suffers from the scarcity of good quality donated tissue, as well as the lack of public policies that encourage the practice of organ donation and the lack of preparation of health professionals to approach families with requests for donation at death [24]. Considering the above, a series of artificial replacements for corneas have been developed around the world. Proof of this is the first artificial corneal implant – called Kpro – performed in Israel for a 78-year-old man, in which the lens of the device was designed to integrate with ocular tissue using a patented synthetic nanofabric skirt that is placed under the conjunctiva [24].

Additionally, choosing the artificial method has the advantage of eliminating the possibility of transplant rejection and, consequently, the need for the patient to use immunosuppressive oral medications [12]. Currently, thanks to clinical and pre-clinical trials, artificial corneal transplantation can be divided into three main categories: keratoprosthesis, artificial biosynthetic cornea and 3D bioprint [12, 24].

Keratoprosthesis
Keratoprostheses are made of transparent plastic and have excellent human tissue tolerance. They vary in design, size and even implantation technique [25]. Although many

keratoprostheses have been developed, only four models are currently in commercial use: the Boston keratoprosthesis, the Osteo-Odonto-Ceratoprosthesis (OOKP), the AlphaCor and the KeraKlear Artificial Cornea [25, 26]. Importantly, this type of artificial cornea can be made with a range of organic, inorganic, and metal materials [26].

The Boston keratoprosthesis (BKPro, Massachusetts Eye and Ear Infirmary, Boston, MA, USA), developed in 1974, is the most widely used type of artificial cornea worldwide [27]. This prosthesis is made of organic glass made of polymethyl methacrylate (PMMA) and has a central optical zone of 3.35 mm in diameter [11, 27]. The Dohlman-Doane keratoprosthesis (Fig. 2), the main prototype of the artificial cornea produced in Boston, presents 90% of success in non-immune diseases and 50% in immune pathologies, being considered the most evolved in the last years [28]. The structure of this keratoprosthesis is assembled on two platforms of viscoelastic material, anterior and posterior, made of Polymethylmethacrylate (PMMA), having a central area normally made of titanium, and up to 16 fenestrations on its surface, with the purpose of providing adequate nutrition of the cornea by the aqueous humor [29]. It has a 0.9 mm thick and 7.0 mm diameter posterior platform, with 8 to 16 fenestrations to allow better nutrition of the cornea [30]. Such procedure is considered simple, with an outpatient character and realized and only one surgical time only [29].

The osteo-odonto-ceratoprosthesis is the procedure in which it is necessary to implant the acrylic keratoprosthesis in a tooth of the patient for subsequent implantation in the receiving cornea [28]. It is considered a laborious surgery, being performed in two stages, with approximately 3 months of interval between them [28].

CeratpróteseAlphaCor, produced in Australia, presents limitations for some pathologies, such as: cases of dry eye, post hepatic leukoma and immune diseases of mucous membranes, however, it is similar to a hydrophilic contact lens [11].

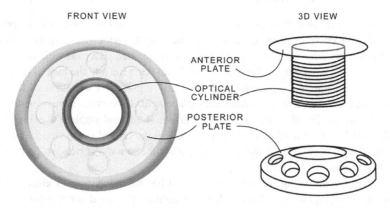

Fig. 2. The Dohlman-Doane keratoprosthesis. Author: CUNHA, C.E.X (2020)

Biosynthetic Cornea

Biosynthetic implants are defined as a procedure in which synthetic and natural components are mixed with materials that mimic structures found in nature [31]. Examples of artificial materials used in the biosynthetic cornea are: poly-L-lactic acid (PLA or PLLA), poly-lactic-co-glycolic acid (PLGA) and poly-2-hydroxyethyl methacrylate (PHEMA) [31]. On the other hand, examples of natural polymers are alginates, chitosan, collagen, fibrin, keratin and silk [31].

In relation to other types of artificial corneas, the biosynthetic one has the advantage of having biomaterials with well-defined chemical and structural composition, besides the ability to customize its properties according to the patient's needs [32]. An example of this is that depending on the intended use, materials that are rapidly or slowly degraded – such as Polyglycerol Sebacate – or non-degradable materials – such as polyethylene terephthalate – are produced. It is worth mentioning that a disadvantage of this type of artificial cornea is that non-degradable materials may suffer an inflammatory reaction by the patient's defense mechanism when relating the material as a foreign body [32].

In addition, numerous synthetic and natural biomaterials have been made with an eye surface reconstruction applicability in mind. However, when tested in vitro and in vivo clinically, the biosynthetic cornea showed to have problems related to the epithelization of the surface, which generates a lack of integration between the receptor tissue and the external material [33]. This fact generated inflammatory reactions, turbidity and consequent neovascularization in the area of the implants [33, 34].

An example of a biosynthetic cornea is the one being developed at the University of Granada, Spain, which consists of a fibrin and agarose structure containing human corneal fibroblasts and covered by an epithelial layer [33]. Such nanostructuring ensures stiffness and strength necessary for human use. Furthermore, studies in the tissue engineering field have been developing autologous cells since 1999 to use them as artificial corneal transplantation [33]. However, due to the limitations of the technology, the use of the biosynthetic cornea is still in the clinical stage, and, therefore, its use in humans is forbidden [33].

3D Bioprint

For science to find a substitute for the cornea, such element needs to be equivalent to the natural one in terms of structure, function and shape [34]. Considering the above, studies in the field of medical engineering have been developing artificial corneas through three-dimensional printing technologies. Compared to other types of artificial corneas, 3D bioprinting has the advantage of high quality and low cost [34].

Thus, it is worth remembering that the 3D printed cornea has high transparency and micropores that support the diffusion of oxygen, carbon, and other nutrients [35]. Moreover, because this type of artificial cornea has its shape consistent with the natural cornea, it can be closely linked to autologous tissue.

The flexibility and sagacity of 3D printing can realize the integral structure of the artificial cornea with several layers, cells and some specific arrangement of element with curved surface [36]. In in vitro corneal model building and ultrastructural studies, 3D printing has the potential advantages of building complex structures such as epithelium, stroma, endothelium and limbic stem cells [36].

4 Final Considerations

Since the pandemic scenario caused by the SARS-CoV-2 virus, organ donation has become even more difficult due to the possible risk of disease transmission to the recipient, if the donor is a carrier of the pathogen. Thus, the debate about artificial cornea transplantation has become more and more important as the safest way to recover vision nowadays.

A review of the literature on artificial corneal transplantation shows that this category has been developing over the years and offers possibilities to minimize transplant rejection. To this end, there are three main types of artificial corneas: keratoprosthesis, artificial biosynthetic cornea and 3D bioprint. The first is the most used and has four models in commercial use; the second has the ability to adapt according to the patient's individual needs, however, the disadvantage is the risk of increased inflammatory reaction due to the possibility of the individual's immune system recognizing the synthetic material as a foreign body. Finally, 3D bioprinting has the advantage of high quality, low cost, and its good adaptation to autologous tissue.

Despite recent studies showing a low risk of SARS-CoV-2 infection through ocular tissue, major associations such as The Global Alliance of Eye Bank As-sociation (GAEBA) report the need for some safety measures for eye transplantation. Thus, besides the difficulties already experienced before, with the addition of the pandemic, this process has become even more delicate.

5 Conclusion

The artificial cornea transplant appears as a therapeutic option for patients who need it, and it is growing due to the growth of research in the area, as well as the search for the development of a cornea as similar as possible to human tissue in an attempt to reduce the risks of rejection and reactions against the foreign body.

Considering the high worldwide demand for corneal transplants and its limiting factors, such as: lack of effective corneal donors and organic tissue rejection in transplanted patients, the artificial cornea represents a safe solution for vision recovery during the pandemic, and is also a tool to reduce the waiting list for corneal transplants and the numbers of blindness rates in the post-pandemic period.

References

1. Sohrabi, C., et al.: World Health Organization declares global emergency: a review of the 2019 novel coronavirus (COVID-19). Int. J. Surg. **76**, 71–76 (2020)
2. Morales, A.J.R., et al.: Clinical, laboratory and imaging features of COVID-19: a systematic review and meta-analysis. Travel Med. Infect. Dis. **34**, 1–13 (2020)
3. Lake, M.A.: What we know so far: COVID-19 current clinical knowledge and research. Clin. Med. **17**(6), 124–128 (2020)
4. Yoshimoto, F.K.: The proteins of severe acute respiratory syndrome Coronavirus-2 (SARS CoV-2 or n-COV19), the cause of COVID-19. Protein J. **39**(3), 198–216 (2020). https://doi.org/10.1007/s10930-020-09901-4

5. Lana, R.M., et al.: The novel coronavirus (SARS-CoV-2) emergency and the role of timely and effective national health surveillance. Cad Saude Publica **36**(3), e00019620 (2020)
6. Tortorici, M.A., Veesler, D.: Structural insights into coronavirus entry. Adv. Virus Res. **105**, 93–116 (2019). https://doi.org/10.1016/bs.aivir.2019.08.002
7. Scialo, F., et al.: ACE2: the major cell entry receptor for SARS-CoV-2. Lung **198**(6), 867–877 (2020). https://doi.org/10.1007/s00408-020-00408-4
8. Bourgonje, A.R., et al.: Angiotensin-converting enzyme 2 (ACE2), SARS-CoV-2 and the pathophysiology of coronavirus disease 2019 (COVID-19). J. Pathol. **251**(3), 228–248 (2020). https://doi.org/10.1002/path.5471
9. Torres, B.R.S., Cunha, C.E.X., Castro, L.R., Brito, P.L.M., Ferreira, C.V.O., Ribeiro, M.V.M.R.: Ocular manifestations of COVID-19: a literature review. Revista da Associação Médica Brasileira **66**(9), 1296–1300 (2020). https://doi.org/10.1590/1806-9282.66.9.1296
10. Global Alliance of Eye Bank Associations. ALERT UP-DATE: Coronavirus (COVID-2019) and Ocular Tissue Donation. http://www.gaebaorg/2020/alert-coronavirus-2019-ncov-and-ocular-tissue-donation. Accessed 18 Apr 2020
11. Ang, M., Moriyama, A., Colby, K., et al.: Corneal transplantation in the aftermath of the COVID-19 pandemic: an international perspective. Br. J. Ophthalmol. **104**(11), 1477–1481 (2020). https://doi.org/10.1136/bjophthalmol-2020-317013
12. Polisetti, N., Islam, M.M., Griffith, M.: The artificial cornea. Methods Mol. Biol. **1014**, 45–52 (2013). https://doi.org/10.1007/978-1-62703-432-6_2
13. Almeida, H.G.: Transplante de córnea no Brasil: progresso e dificuldades em 16 anos. Orientador: Newton Kara José Junior. 83 f. Tese (Doutorado) – Faculdade de Medicina da Universidade de São Paulo, São Paulo (2018)
14. Ple-Pakon, P.A., Shtein, R.M.: Trends in corneal transplantation: indications and techniques. Curr. Opin. Ophthalmol. **25**, 300–305 (2014)
15. Mathews, P.M., Lindsley, K., Aldave, A.J., Akpek, E.K.: Etiology of global corneal blindness and current practices of corneal transplantation: a focused review. Cornea **37**(9), 1198–1203 (2018). https://doi.org/10.1097/ICO.0000000000001666
16. Boynton, G.E., Woodward, M.A.: Evolving techniques in corneal transplantation. Curr. Surg. Rep. **3**(2), 1–8 (2014). https://doi.org/10.1007/s40137-014-0079-5
17. Wang, J., Li, X., Cao, G., Wu, X., Wang, Z., Yan, T.: COVID-19 in a kidney transplant patient. Eur. Urol. **77**(6), 769–770 (2020)
18. Nacif, L.S., et al.: COVID-19 in solid organ transplantation patients: a systematic review. Clinics (Sao Paulo) **75**, e1983 (2020). https://doi.org/10.6061/clinics/2020/e1983
19. Ali, M.J.: The SARS-CoV-2, tears, and ocular surface debate: what we know and what we need to know. Indian J. Ophthalmol. **68**(7), 1245–1246 (2020). https://doi.org/10.4103/ijo.IJO_1881_20
20. Cho, P., Boost, M.: COVID 19 – an eye on the virus. Cont. Lens Anterior Eye **43**(4), 313–314 (2020). https://doi.org/10.1016/j.clae.2020.05.011
21. Chaurasia, S., Sharma, N., Das, S.: COVID-19 and eye banking. Indian J. Ophthalmol. **68**(6), 1215–1216 (2020). https://doi.org/10.4103/ijo.IJO_1033_20
22. CorNeat [Internet]. CorNeat EverPatch. https://www.corneat.com/corneat-everpatch-for-physicians (2021). Cited 24 May 2021
23. Alzahrani, K., et al.: Corneal clarity measurements in healthy volunteers across different age groups. Medicine **96**(46), 1–6 (2017)
24. Bachmann, B.O., Keratin, S.S.: Kollagen oder doch Spendergewebe – wo liegt die Zukunft in der Entwicklung neuer Biomaterialien zur Hornhautrekonstruktion? [Biomaterials or donor tissue – what is the future of tissue engineering for cornea reconstruction?]. Klin. Monbl. Augenheilkd. **234**(6), 758–762 (2017). https://doi.org/10.1055/s-0043-109024. German
25. Bradley, J.C., Hernandez, E.G., Schawb, I.R., Mannis, M.J.: Boston type I keratoprosthesis: the University of California Davis experience. Cornea **28**(3), 321–327 (2009)

26. Kim, M.J., Yu, F., Aldave, A.J.: Microbial keratitis after Boston type I keratoprosthesis implantation: incidence, organisms, risk factors, and outcomes. Ophthalmology **120**(11), 2209–2216 (2013)

27. Saeed, H.N., Shanbhag, S., Chodosh, J.: The Boston keratoprosthesis. Curr. Opin. Ophthalmol. **28**(4), 390–396 (2017). https://doi.org/10.1097/ICU.0000000000000373

28. Zarei-Ghanavati, M., Avadhanam, V., Vasquez Perez, A., Liu, C.: The osteo-odonto-keratoprosthesis. Curr. Opin. Ophthalmol. **28**(4), 397–402 (2017). https://doi.org/10.1097/ICU.0000000000000388

29. Kwitko, Sérgio e Stolz, Andressa Prestes Ceratoprótese de Boston. Revista Brasileira de Oftalmologia **71**(6), 403–406 (2012). Acessado 12 Junho 2021. Epub 04 Jan 2013. ISSN 1982-8551. https://doi.org/10.1590/S0034-72802012000600014

30. Harissi-Dagher, M., Slim, E.: La kératoprothèse de Boston type 1 [Boston keratoprosthesis type 1]. J. Fr. Ophtalmol. **42**(3), 295–302 (2019). https://doi.org/10.1016/j.jfo.2018.08.010. French

31. Xie, R.Z., Stretton, S., Sweeney, D.F.: Artificial cornea: towards a synthetic only for correction of refractive error. Biosci. Rep. **21**(4), 513–536 (2001). https://doi.org/10.1023/a:1017900111663

32. Griffith, M., et al.: Biosynthetic alternatives for corneal transplant surgery. Expert Rev. Ophthalmol. **15**(3), 129–143 (2020). https://doi.org/10.1080/17469899.2020.1754798

33. Griffith, M., et al.: Biosynthetic alternatives for corneal transplant surgery. Expert Rev. Ophthalmol. (2020). https://doi.org/10.1080/17469899.2020.1754798

34. Zhang, B., et al.: 3D bioprinting for artificial cornea: challenges and perspectives. Med. Eng. Phys. **71**, 68–78 (2019). https://doi.org/10.1016/j.medengphy.2019.05.002

35. Hos, D., Matthaei, M., Bock, F., et al.: Immune reactions after modern lamellar (DALK, DSAEK, DMEK) versus conventional penetrating corneal transplantation. Prog. Retin. Eye Res. **73**, 100768 (2019). https://doi.org/10.1016/j.preteyeres.2019.07.001

36. Cruz, G.K.P., Ferreira-Júnior, M.A., Azevedo, I.C., Santos, V.E.P., Flores, V.G.T., Gonçalves, E.A.P.: Clinical and surgical factors and intraoperative complications in patients who underwent penetrating keratoplasty. Rev. Latino-Am. Enfermagem. **27**, e3141 (2019). https://doi.org/10.1590/1518-8345.2733-314

COVID-19. Disease

PEAK: A Clever Python Tool for Exploratory, Regression, and Classification Data. A Case Study for COVID-19

Giuseppe Sgroi[1], Giuseppe Alessandro Parasiliti Palumbo[1], Valentina Di Salvatore[2], Giulia Russo[2], and Francesco Pappalardo[2(✉)]

[1] Department of Mathematics and Computer Science, University of Catania, Catania, Italy
giuseppe.sgroi@unict.it, giuseppe.parasilitipalumbo@phd.unict.it
[2] Department of Drug and Health Sciences, University of Catania, Catania, Italy
{valentina.disalvatore,giulia.russo,
francesco.pappalardo}@unict.it

Abstract. Researchers often face the need to collect, explore, correlate, analyze, and classify different data sources to discover unknown relationships while performing basic steps of pattern recognition and regression analysis with classification. PEAK is a Python tool designed to make easier all of these the basic steps of pattern recognition, allowing less experienced users to reduce the time required for analysing data and promoting the discovery of unknown relationships between different data. As a working example, we applied PEAK to a specific case study dealing with a well-defined dataset representing a cohort of COVID-19 10000 digital twins with different immunological characteristics.

PEAK is a freely available open-source software. It runs on all platforms that support Python3. The user manual and source code are accessible following this link: https://github.com/Pex2892/PEAK.

Keywords: SARS-CoV-2 · UISS-SARS-CoV-2 · Python3 · Data analysis

1 Introduction

The severe acute respiratory syndrome coronavirus 2 (SARS-CoV-2) is the virus that causes coronavirus disease 2019 (COVID-19), a contagious disease plaguing the world for over a year and a half. Despite the great multitude of critical situations and difficulties, this pandemic also made the possibility to highlight the importance of specific tools based on artificial intelligence to predict the spread of COVID-19 [1, 2]. The main open issue of these tools deals with the requirement of advanced knowledge of regression and classification algorithm theory. Hence researchers are often looking for tools and software solutions able to satisfy this important aspect of data analysis. Here, we present Pattern rEcognition frAmeworK (PEAK), a newly developed tool for data analysis through the use of specially designed open-source tools and Python libraries [3], such as Pandas, Joblib, Matplotlib, and Scikit.

© Springer Nature Switzerland AG 2021
I. Rojas et al. (Eds.): BIOMESIP 2021, LNCS 12940, pp. 361–370, 2021.
https://doi.org/10.1007/978-3-030-88163-4_31

PEAK includes a scalable, parallelized engine to easily add new features and specific modules to simplify and automate data analysis. This manuscript demonstrated PEAK usability and efficiency by performing a particular case study using the dataset of the 10000 samples (digital twins) obtained from the Universal Immune System Simulator for SARS-CoV-2 (UISS-SARS-CoV-2) [4]. UISS is a computational platform based on an agent-based model that reproduces the entities of the immune system (and consequently its dynamics), along with the significant immune responses induced by a specific pathogen or stimulus. This platform can be extended to reproduce different diseases and related treatments [5–12]. UISS-SARS-CoV-2 is an extension of UISS capable to reflects the dynamics of COVID-19.

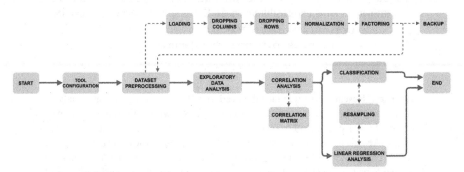

Fig. 1. PEAK functional scheme. The tool consists of different steps: dataset import, data processing, data exploration, correlation analysis, regression analysis, and/or classification.

2 Materials and Methods

PEAK workflow is straightforward to carry out different analyses, as depicted in Fig. 1. First, it consists of the input dataset processing followed by the regression or classification analysis according to the question of interest. Specifically, PEAK requires four parameters section to get started: i) settings, ii) dataset, iii) regression, and iv) classification. Each section requires additional sub-parameters. The advantage of using this tool lies in getting the results automatically and quickly, saving time, and decreasing complexity. This process would have taken much longer if conducted manually.

As case study, the tool was used on a well-defined dataset retrieved from UISS-SARS-CoV-2 [4]. Specifically, a cohort of 10000 digital twins with different immunological characteristics was generated. For each dataset entry, the mean was calculated over columns of our interest (Fig. 2), which concern:

- Cytotoxic T cell (TC)
- IgG antibodies (IgG)
- Interferon gamma (IFNG)
- Lung epithelial cells (LEP)
- Interleukin 6 (IL-6)
- Interleukin 12 (IL-12)

The dataset will be available on the GitHub repository in anonymized form.

2.1 Import Parameters

The configuration file is imported through the 'read_args()' method, a structure similar to the one found in Microsoft Windows INI files containing a set of parameters, divided by section, needed to start the analysis:

- Settings: this section contains the general settings of the tool, such as the seed, the number of CPUs, and the clearing of the previous results.
- Dataset: this section contains parameters related to the dataset, such as file name, separator, and the number of rows to skip.
- Regression: it contains all the settings needed to start a regression analysis, such as the dependent variable name and the parameters useful for the resampling phase.
- Classification: it contains all the settings required for categorization, such as the variable to be classified, the targets and the parameters needed for the resampling phase.

2.2 Dataset Preprocessing

Here, several operations are performed on the dataset. First, it is loaded into the memory using the data structure type of "Dataframe" provided by the Pandas library. After that, columns that are entirely or at least 50% equal to "Not a Number" (NaN) are removed, and rows with at least one NaN element are removed. After that, columns of numeric type (int64 or float64) are normalized between 0 and 1 using the MinMaxScaler function, while columns of "object" type are factored in and added to the initial dataset. Finally, the new dataset obtained is exported in CSV inside the "results" folder (Figs. 2 and 3).

TC_mean	TH1_mean	IL6_mean	IL12_mean	IFNG_mean	Ag_mean	IGG_mean	LEP_mean
582,507937	4397,69048	137,968379	90729,9644	549162,802	98,9126984	0	287,825397
561,75	656,353175	348,509881	14703,0949	73865,1225	33,2142857	518,865079	289,130952
587,210317	4318,63095	261,403162	101914,336	487980,545	30,1706349	3826,0754	288,924603
567,599206	1207,54762	73,1343874	20722,7273	123959,838	8,13888889	1800,45635	300,146825
654,563492	3525,43651	873,818182	64900,3004	361557,652	35,3849206	1521,91667	271,912698
567,718254	1816,79762	29,8774704	29363,9328	188223,542	35,7222222	691,892857	289,527778
575,936508	418,031746	370,869565	26763,2134	48433,332	17,3095238	1462,42857	289,25
566,507937	8,55952381	69,0118577	7589,83399	424,351779	3,76984127	2807,28571	293,65873
695,853175	1954,09921	1883,30435	28437,5613	180901,885	78,6865079	34,8928571	251,428571
568,376984	78,4761905	1102,61265	10367,4269	10977,2292	36,6269841	527,81746	262,257937
594,337302	6018,21032	793,071146	152180,893	730728,419	52	2218,65873	272,865079
611,337302	3184,36111	443,743083	55782,664	322177,925	32,3015873	1456,11508	285,246032
562,083333	7,72619048	0	2646,57312	101,482213	1,99603175	253,027778	296,083333
607,615079	4381,9246	937,905138	97114,1581	506006,071	36,0277778	6990,11508	270,107143
619,22619	4631,19444	787,648221	71914,7273	482038,008	72,6388889	620,365079	271,738095
569,075397	14,0119048	0	8138,05138	4630,86561	110,996032	3604,33333	290,365079
600,686508	2054,32143	302,754941	36198,2609	216702,949	25,7857143	3669,98413	289,904762
663	1359,62698	853,798419	24615,8814	123013,229	32,6150794	4030,99603	271,857143
691,670635	988,785714	1627,11067	15105,8379	84814,498	29,1190476	1775,88095	252,833333
566,551587	1952,89683	24,9525692	77075,0474	271839,17	70,1587302	1450,54762	295,055556
563,912698	1600,18254	0	80769,166	296306,652	50,6190476	2084,99603	300,825397
625,650794	516,019841	548,869565	9546,21739	52572,1028	32,0912698	1224,1627	284,940476
559,480159	6,09126984	0	16112,6996	125,27668	2325,19444	514,888889	275,484127
566,444444	2241,96825	34,5928854	59890,3992	307129,075	50,0555556	1477,37698	293,678571
565,97619	5464,0754	93,9288538	128979,194	665022,229	24,2857143	5928,6746	293,876984
704,035714	2614,62698	1296,4585	36855,6838	246776,66	49,1428571	2805,16667	256,519841
577,293651	1259,53968	87,8063241	27325,1265	123834,609	43,8650794	0	292,174603
608,357143	1995,64683	817,098814	28959,3557	186518,032	6,71428571	709,365079	277,960317
658,361111	478,857143	666,952569	15029,249	54343,4387	30,9007937	3588,17857	278,785714
606,761905	2498,45238	339,774704	33383,2292	254838,142	10,3888889	4383,46429	281,833333
558,884921	6,8452381	8,55731225	10663,3281	300,881423	60,4047619	0	297,345238
580,93254	41,9285714	962,146245	31835,0198	4637,5336	34,5634921	662,412698	263,484127
626,646825	199,47619	1306,11858	16473,9684	31820,3794	22,4087302	5554,59921	259,666667
643,519841	1459,32143	1140,083	37115,6561	173138,411	25,1349206	1422,9246	270,468254
580,876984	822,861111	233,644269	41048,6206	97307,9881	63,3769841	415,984127	287,876984

Fig. 2. UISS-SARS-CoV-2 dataset. The figure shows the dataset provided as input to PEAK.

TC_mean	TH1_mean	IL6_mean	IL12_mean	IFNG_mean	Ag_mean	IGG_mean	LEP_mean
0,096888154	0,667482184	0,052036917	0,485383547	0,604440175	0,017690942	0	0,735935759
0,031356484	0,099621393	0,131445916	0,078152298	0,081300204	0,005801227	0,025075488	0,751206833
0,111733313	0,655482516	0,098592263	0,545291651	0,537099463	0,005250405	0,184904922	0,748793167
0,049822109	0,183281776	0,02758377	0,11039593	0,136437329	0,001263228	0,087011678	0,880059413
0,3243636	0,535091333	0,329574101	0,347029221	0,397951153	0,006194056	0,073550533	0,54980505
0,050197935	0,275753841	0,011268752	0,156681789	0,207169659	0,006255099	0,0334375	0,755848496
0,076142514	0,063448927	0,139879218	0,142751264	0,053308512	0,002922876	0,070675617	0,752599332
0,046377029	0,001299166	0,026028894	0,040050741	0,000467066	0,000472544	0,135669294	0,804168214
0,454712868	0,296593499	0,71031749	0,151719761	0,199111023	0,014030524	0,001686287	0,310202377
0,052277511	0,011911129	0,415867488	0,054928673	0,01208217	0,006418837	0,025508135	0,436873375
0,134232812	0,913444952	0,299119102	0,814540051	0,804281739	0,009200956	0,107222383	0,560945043
0,187900882	0,483322853	0,167364597	0,298191402	0,35460756	0,005636052	0,070370502	0,705764946
0,032408799	0,001172682	0	0,013572598	0,000111697	0,00015153	0,012228217	0,832528778
0,17615003	0,665089237	0,353745492	0,51957992	0,556939394	0,006310397	0,337815268	0,528685481
0,212805672	0,702923455	0,297073762	0,384601382	0,530558765	0,012936062	0,029980736	0,547762718
0,054482361	0,002126729	0	0,042987219	0,005096997	0,019877713	0,174188667	0,765642406
0,154276909	0,311805244	0,114188729	0,193289267	0,238515733	0,004456848	0,177361411	0,760258076
0,350997194	0,206364407	0,322023337	0,131249268	0,135395437	0,005692786	0,194808238	0,549155217
0,441508819	0,150078058	0,613690065	0,080309556	0,093351716	0,005060095	0,085824009	0,326633866
0,046514833	0,296411001	0,009411249	0,412242184	0,29920183	0,012487217	0,07010144	0,82050687
0,038184005	0,242875969	0	0,432029405	0,326132149	0,008951039	0,100762789	0,887996658
0,233087793	0,078321576	0,207014683	0,050529937	0,057863881	0,00559799	0,059160807	0,702190865
0,02419072	0,000924534	0	0,085702722	0,000137887	0,420590407	0,024883328	0,591580022
0,046176588	0,34028631	0,013047244	0,320194125	0,33804393	0,008849062	0,071398038	0,804400297
0,044698336	0,829338263	0,035426726	0,695082955	0,731961726	0,004185386	0,28651843	0,806721129
0,480544698	0,396848514	0,488979462	0,196810695	0,27161659	0,008683887	0,135566885	0,36975492
0,080426939	0,19117314	0,033117519	0,145761102	0,136299495	0,007728746	0	0,786808392
0,178492684	0,302899603	0,308181511	0,154514707	0,205292477	0,001005412	0,03428189	0,620544003
0,336352475	0,072681016	0,251551522	0,079899314	0,059813515	0,005382545	0,173407947	0,630198663
0,173456605	0,379215513	0,128151307	0,178210797	0,280489521	0,00167042	0,211842172	0,665846639
0,022311585	0,001038971	0,003227523	0,056513642	0,000931167	0,010722001	0	0,847289268
0,091914712	0,006363925	0,362888402	0,169917949	0,005104336	0,006045399	0,032012795	0,451216116

Fig. 3. Dataset processed. A processed dataset is shown. Specifically, the columns were normalized across 0 and 1, and no columns were factored because there is no column of categorical type.

2.3 Exploratory Data Analysis

Exploratory data analysis (EDA) investigates the datasets and summarizes their key features using statistical plots and other visualization methods. Initially developed by the American mathematician John Tukey in the 1970s, EDA techniques continue to be a widely used method in the data discovery process. In particular, it helps determine how to manipulate data sources to get the best answers, making it easier to discover patterns, detect anomalies, and test or verify hypotheses. EDA also helps find whether the statistical techniques that are going to be considered for data analysis are appropriate. Next, PEAK retrieves all those object-type columns by plotting their frequency using a barplot. In our case study, we do not have any column of type object, and therefore the creation of the specific plot is skipped.

2.4 Correlation Analysis

In this step, columns of numerical type are considered, and all pairwise combinations of two are defined. The correlation coefficient is calculated for each of these pairs using Pearson [13], Spearman [14], and Kendall [15] correlation indices. After obtaining the three correlations of each pair at the end of the process, the indices are graphed with a barplot (Fig. 4). According to the COVID19 dataset, in panel A, negative correlations equal to −0.73 (calculated through Pearson index) and −0.77 (calculated through Spearman index) between TC and LEP are depicted. Also, Kendal index shows a negative correlation (−0.58). This reflects the immunological behavior generally observed when TC become active, migrating into the site of infection, recognizing and killing infected LEP to attempt the eradication of the reservoir of infection.

In panel B, strong negative correlations equal to −0.96 (calculated through Pearson index) and -0.94 (calculated through Spearman index) between IL-6 and LEP are depicted. Also, Kendal index shows a strong negative correlation (−0.82). This reflects the well observed scenario in which IL-6 is correlated with fatal prognosis. In panel C, strong positive correlations equal to 0.97 (calculated through Pearson index) and 0.98 (calculated through Spearman index) between TH1 and IFN-G are depicted. Also, Kendal index shows a strong positive correlation (0.89). This reflects the well-known behavior that links TH1 with the IFN-G secretion. In panel D, positive correlations equal to 0.77 (calculated through Pearson index) and 0.83 (calculated through Spearman index) between TC and IL-6 are depicted. Also, Kendal index shows a positive correlation (0.65). This reflects the inflammatory response that, in effective immune response, is able to contribute the eradication of any infection reservoir.

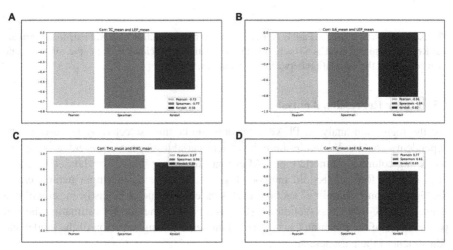

Fig. 4. Panels A–D show the correlation among immune system entities reported in the generated synthetic dataset. Pearson, Spearman and Kendall indices are considered.

Correlation matrices (Fig. 5) are then generated using the same indices abovementioned. Observed correlations are not related by a cause-and-effect relationship but represent the capability of one variable to change as a function of the other considered variable.

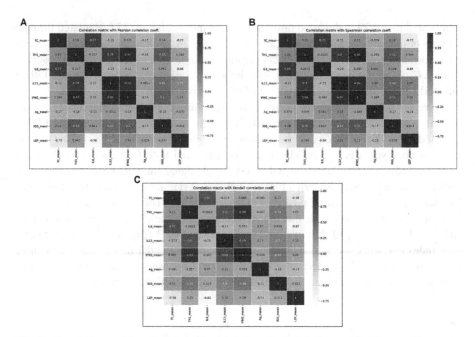

Fig. 5. Correlation matrices. Panels A, B, and C show the correlation matrix, Pearson, Spearman, and Kendall, respectively. Each row shows the correlation coefficients between the variables, and each cell shows the correlation between two variables.

2.5 Linear Regression Analysis

For the regression analysis, PEAK considers the column selected by the user as the dependent variables Y_i, while the independent variables X_i are represented by all the remaining columns (numeric type). After that, the resampling of the dataset is carried out using the RepeteadK-fold method (Figs. 6 and 7) using the input parameters of the "Regression-resampling" section. In this case, the value of K has been set within a range [2–5]. K-fold Cross-Validation (CV) is a popular method for estimating the real performance of the machine learning (ML) model, allowing selection of the model and adjustment of the parameters.

However, the CV process itself requires random partitioning of the data. K-fold CV consists of averaging the prediction estimates of K-train-test splits, specifically chosen to be sure that each data is used only in a single set [16]. The data are randomly divided into approximately equal sizes of K-folds. Increasing K improves the mean in training but may worsen the standard deviation in testing. PEAK is based on RepeteadK-Fold working in the same way as K-fold. Comparing the two methods, users can define the number of iterations. After completing the resampling phase, two CSV files are saved: the first contains all the tested data divisions, and the second contains the best results. Finally, regression analysis is performed on the best results obtained from resampling and calculating r-squared and Adjusted-R-squared (Fig. 8) (Table 1).

	model	cv	n_splits	n_repeats	random_state	Y	n_features_Y	n_features_X	scoring	mean_test_score	std_test_score
2	RFE(estimator=LinearRegression(positive=True))	RepeatedKFold	2	4	2021	LEP_mean,IGG_mean	2	1	r2	0,115304275	0,011599574
3	RFE(estimator=LinearRegression(positive=True))	RepeatedKFold	2	4	2021	LEP_mean,IGG_mean	2	2	r2	0,165670575	0,006344752
4	RFE(estimator=LinearRegression(positive=True))	RepeatedKFold	2	4	2021	LEP_mean,IGG_mean	2	3	r2	0,168031227	0,006164015
5	RFE(estimator=LinearRegression(positive=True))	RepeatedKFold	2	4	2021	LEP_mean,IGG_mean	2	4	r2	0,16805639	0,006155922
6	RFE(estimator=LinearRegression(positive=True))	RepeatedKFold	2	4	2021	LEP_mean,IGG_mean	2	5	r2	0,16805639	0,006155922
7	RFE(estimator=LinearRegression(positive=True))	RepeatedKFold	2	4	2021	LEP_mean,IGG_mean	2	6	r2	0,16805639	0,006155922
8	RFE(estimator=LinearRegression(positive=True))	RepeatedKFold	3	4	2021	LEP_mean,IGG_mean	2	1	r2	0,111017917	0,011773657
9	RFE(estimator=LinearRegression(positive=True))	RepeatedKFold	3	4	2021	LEP_mean,IGG_mean	2	2	r2	0,165679449	0,007833551
10	RFE(estimator=LinearRegression(positive=True))	RepeatedKFold	3	4	2021	LEP_mean,IGG_mean	2	3	r2	0,167911905	0,007634827
11	RFE(estimator=LinearRegression(positive=True))	RepeatedKFold	3	4	2021	LEP_mean,IGG_mean	2	4	r2	0,167921979	0,007620921
12	RFE(estimator=LinearRegression(positive=True))	RepeatedKFold	3	4	2021	LEP_mean,IGG_mean	2	5	r2	0,167921979	0,007620921
13	RFE(estimator=LinearRegression(positive=True))	RepeatedKFold	3	4	2021	LEP_mean,IGG_mean	2	6	r2	0,167921979	0,007620921
14	RFE(estimator=LinearRegression(positive=True))	RepeatedKFold	4	4	2021	LEP_mean,IGG_mean	2	1	r2	0,111579399	0,010268996
15	RFE(estimator=LinearRegression(positive=True))	RepeatedKFold	4	4	2021	LEP_mean,IGG_mean	2	2	r2	0,165692479	0,00800361
16	RFE(estimator=LinearRegression(positive=True))	RepeatedKFold	4	4	2021	LEP_mean,IGG_mean	2	3	r2	0,168027191	0,007736965
17	RFE(estimator=LinearRegression(positive=True))	RepeatedKFold	4	4	2021	LEP_mean,IGG_mean	2	4	r2	0,168050079	0,007744174
18	RFE(estimator=LinearRegression(positive=True))	RepeatedKFold	4	4	2021	LEP_mean,IGG_mean	2	5	r2	0,168050079	0,007744174
19	RFE(estimator=LinearRegression(positive=True))	RepeatedKFold	4	4	2021	LEP_mean,IGG_mean	2	6	r2	0,168050079	0,007744174
20	RFE(estimator=LinearRegression(positive=True))	RepeatedKFold	5	4	2021	LEP_mean,IGG_mean	2	1	r2	0,109751197	0,012683687
21	RFE(estimator=LinearRegression(positive=True))	RepeatedKFold	5	4	2021	LEP_mean,IGG_mean	2	2	r2	0,165581138	0,010719111
22	RFE(estimator=LinearRegression(positive=True))	RepeatedKFold	5	4	2021	LEP_mean,IGG_mean	2	3	r2	0,16797845	0,010703383
23	RFE(estimator=LinearRegression(positive=True))	RepeatedKFold	5	4	2021	LEP_mean,IGG_mean	2	4	r2	0,167989326	0,010706967
24	RFE(estimator=LinearRegression(positive=True))	RepeatedKFold	5	4	2021	LEP_mean,IGG_mean	2	5	r2	0,167989326	0,010706967
25	RFE(estimator=LinearRegression(positive=True))	RepeatedKFold	5	4	2021	LEP_mean,IGG_mean	2	6	r2	0,167989326	0,010706967

Fig. 6. Regression Resampling. The figure describes all the combinations obtained by varying n_splits and the number of features. For each combination, the mean and deviation are calculated during the testing phase of the model.

	model	cv	n_splits	n_repeats	random_state	Y	n_features_Y	n_features_X	scoring	mean_test_score	std_test_score
2	RFE(estimator=LinearRegression(positive=True))	RepeatedKFold	2	4	2021	LEP_mean,IGG_mean	2	4	r2	0,16805639	0,006155922
3	RFE(estimator=LinearRegression(positive=True))	RepeatedKFold	3	4	2021	LEP_mean,IGG_mean	2	5	r2	0,167921979	0,007620921
4	RFE(estimator=LinearRegression(positive=True))	RepeatedKFold	4	4	2021	LEP_mean,IGG_mean	2	4	r2	0,168050079	0,007744174
5	RFE(estimator=LinearRegression(positive=True))	RepeatedKFold	5	4	2021	LEP_mean,IGG_mean	2	4	r2	0,167989326	0,010706967

Fig. 7. Regression Resampling (best rows). Here, one can observe the best rows obtained from resampling (Fig. 8) grouped by n_splits.

method	Y	X	train_size	test_size	random_state	r2_score_test	adj_r2_score_test	mean_absolute_error	mean_squared_error	median_absolute_error	explain_variance_score

Fig. 8. Regression results. Regression results calculated through R-squared applied to data coming from Fig. 7 are shown for each combination.

Table 1. A sketch of the best results obtained from the MLR analysis.

Method	Y_i	X_i	Training set size	Test set size	R^2 score	Adjusted R^2 score
MLR[a]	LEP_mea IGG_mean	Ag_mean IFNG_mean IL12_mean TC_mean TH1_mean	6666	3334	0,1738	0,1733
MLR	LEP_mean IL6_mean	IL12_mean TC_mean	8000	2000	0,3237	0,3235
MLR	TH1_mea IFNG_mean	Ag_mean IGG_mean IL12_mean LEP_mean TC_mean	5000	5000	0,7723	0,7722
MLR	TC_mean LEP_mean	IL12_mean IL6_mea TH1_mean	7500	2500	0,3331	0,3329
MLR	Ag_mean TC_mean	IL6_mea TH1_mean	7500	2500	0,3038	0,3036

[a]MLR = Multivariate Linear Regression.

2.6 Classification

Classification consists of categorizing a given set of data into classes, and it can be performed on both structured or unstructured data. The process starts with the prediction of the class of given data points. The classes are often referred to as specific targets, labels, or categories. The main goal is to identify the specific class into which the new data fall into. Since classification is a type of supervised learning, the targets are also provided with the input data. A bunch of algorithms exists for classification in machine learning [17]. Seven classifiers have been implemented in PEAK:

1. Logistic Regression;
2. K-Nearest Neighbor (K-NN);
3. Support Vector Machine (SVM);
4. Random Forest;
5. Naive Bayes;
6. Decision Tree;
7. Multilayer Perceptron (MLP).

A technique called "Hyper-parameters" [18] is applied to find the best combination of parameters for each of them. Finally, the best combination of each classifier in which the accuracy is maximum is returned. In summary, a figure containing three plots is generated presenting: i) the confusion matrix, ii) the performance metrics (Accuracy,

F1-score, Precision, and Recall) [19], and iii) the ROC curve. Within the above-described working example no classification was performed as it is simply not applicable.

3   Conclusions

PEAK is an open-source tool that offers a wide range of features for data analysis through regression or classification of the provided dataset in a fully automated way. Users can find the source code freely available on the GitHub repository. An intuitive graphical interface will be added to PEAK to allow the user to perform analysis. New analyses (e.g., Bag-of-word) will be added and existing analyses improved in due course.

References

1. Li, Z., Yang, S., Wu, J.: The prediction of the spread of COVID-19 using regression models. In: 2020 International Conference on Public Health and Data Science (ICPHDS), pp. 247–252 (2020). https://doi.org/10.1109/ICPHDS51617.2020.00055
2. Syeda, H.B., et al.: Role of machine learning techniques to tackle the COVID-19 crisis: systematic review. JMIR Med. Inform. **9** (2021). https://doi.org/10.2196/23811
3. Lindstrom, G.: Programming with Python. IT Prof. **7**, 10–16 (2005). https://doi.org/10.1109/MITP.2005.120
4. Russo, G., et al.: In silico trial to test COVID-19 candidate vaccines: a case study with UISS platform. BMC Bioinform. **21**, 527 (2020). https://doi.org/10.1186/s12859-020-03872-0
5. Russo, G., et al.: Moving forward through the in silico modeling of tuberculosis: a further step with UISS-TB. BMC Bioinform. **21**, 458 (2020). https://doi.org/10.1186/s12859-020-03762-5
6. Pennisi, M., Russo, G., Sgroi, G., Palumbo, G.A.P., Pappalardo, F.: In silico evaluation of daclizumab and vitamin D effects in multiple sclerosis using agent based models. In: Cazzaniga, P., Besozzi, D., Merelli, I., Manzoni, L. (eds.) CIBB 2019. LNCS, vol. 12313, pp. 285–298. Springer, Cham (2020). https://doi.org/10.1007/978-3-030-63061-4_25
7. Pappalardo, F., et al.: A computational model to predict the immune system activation by citrus-derived vaccine adjuvants. Bioinformatics **32**, 2672–2680 (2016). https://doi.org/10.1093/bioinformatics/btw293
8. Pappalardo, F., Flower, D., Russo, G., Pennisi, M., Motta, S.: Computational modelling approaches to vaccinology. Pharmacol. Res. **92**, 40–45 (2015). https://doi.org/10.1016/j.phrs.2014.08.006
9. Pappalardo, F., Motta, S., Lollini, P.-L., Mastriani, E.: Analysis of vaccine's schedules using models. Cell. Immunol. **244**, 137–140 (2006). https://doi.org/10.1016/j.cellimm.2007.03.002
10. Viceconti, M., Juarez, M.A., Curreli, C., Pennisi, M., Russo, G., Pappalardo, F.: Credibility of in silico trial technologies—a theoretical framing. IEEE J. Biomed. Heal. Inform. **24**, 4–13 (2020). https://doi.org/10.1109/JBHI.2019.2949888
11. Pennisi, M., et al.: Predicting the artificial immunity induced by RUTI® vaccine against tuberculosis using universal immune system simulator (UISS). BMC Bioinform. **20**, 504 (2019). https://doi.org/10.1186/s12859-019-3045-5
12. Pennisi, M., Russo, G., Ravalli, S., Pappalardo, F.: Combining agent based-models and virtual screening techniques to predict the best citrus-derived vaccine adjuvants against human papilloma virus. BMC Bioinform. **18**, 544 (2017). https://doi.org/10.1186/s12859-017-1961-9

13. Pearson's correlation coefficient. In: Kirch, W. (ed.) Encyclopedia of Public Health, pp. 1090–1091. Springer Netherlands, Dordrecht (2008). https://doi.org/10.1007/978-1-4020-5614-7_2569
14. Spearman Rank Correlation Coefficient. In: The Concise Encyclopedia of Statistics, pp. 502–505. Springer New York, New York, NY (2008). https://doi.org/10.1007/978-0-387-32833-1_379
15. Kendall, A.M.G.: Biometrika Trust: A New Measure of Rank Correlation, vol. 30, pp. 81–93. Oxford University Press on behalf of Biometrika Trust Stable. https://www.jstor.org/stable/2332226 (1938).
16. Kohavi, R.: A study of cross-validation and bootstrap for accuracy estimation and model selection. In: Proceedings of the 14th International Joint Conference on Artificial Intelligence, vol. 2, pp. 1137–1143. Morgan Kaufmann Publishers Inc., San Francisco, CA, USA (1995)
17. Muhamedyev, R., Yakunin, K., Iskakov, S., Sainova, S., Abdilmanova, A., Kuchin, Y.: Comparative analysis of classification algorithms. In: 2015 9th International Conference on Application of Information and Communication Technologies (AICT), pp. 96–101 (2015). https://doi.org/10.1109/ICAICT.2015.7338525
18. Joy, T.T., Rana, S., Gupta, S., Venkatesh, S.: Hyperparameter tuning for big data using Bayesian optimisation. In: 2016 23rd International Conference on Pattern Recognition (ICPR), pp. 2574–2579 (2016). https://doi.org/10.1109/ICPR.2016.7900023
19. Seliya, N., Khoshgoftaar, T.M., Van Hulse, J.: A study on the relationships of classifier performance metrics. In: 2009 21st IEEE International Conference on Tools with Artificial Intelligence, pp. 59–66 (2009). https://doi.org/10.1109/ICTAI.2009.25

Prevalence of COVID-19 Amongst Arizona First Responders

Vershalee Shukla[1]([✉]), Jared Johns[1], Christine S. M. Lau[1], Sharon Kanya[1], Jennifer Mayer[1], Kara Kalkbrenner[2], Felicia Washington[2], and Pablo Prichard[1]

[1] Vincere Cancer Center, Scottsdale, Arizona, USA
drshukla@vincerecancer.com
[2] City of Phoenix, Phoenix, Arizona, USA

Abstract. COVID-19 continues to be a major public health crisis in the United States and around the world. In the state of Arizona alone there have been over 887,000 cases, and 17,779 deaths reported since the pandemic first began. First responders, including firefighters, law enforcement officers, and emergency medical services personnel, are in continuous contact with the public and are therefore believed to be at high risk for COVID-19. A retrospective study analyzing COVID-19 antigen positivity rates among first responders in the Phoenix metropolitan area between December 27, 2020 and February 6, 2021 was conducted. A total of 201 first responders received COVID-19 antigen testing and a total of 45 tested positive yielding a 22.4% positivity rate. Positivity rates among firefighters were equivalent to, or above, the rate of the general public in both Phoenix and Arizona. Continued vigilance is required to ensure the safety of first responders during this continued pandemic.

Keywords: COVID-19 · SARS-CoV-2 · First responder · Phoenix · Antigen · Firefighter · Arizona

1 Introduction

SARS-CoV-2 is a major public health concern in the United States (US) and around the world, with 33.4 million cases reported in the US alone by June 10, 2021 [1]. The first case of Coronavirus (COVID-19) in the State of Arizona was confirmed on January 22, 2020, and there have been over 887,000 new cases since that time [1]. This disease is highly contagious and quickly spread through the community via close contact.

COVID-19 has been shown to be transmitted primarily through aerosolized particles; however, respiratory droplets, oro-fecal transmission, surface-human transmission, and indirect routes have also been suggested [2, 3]. Close contact with infected individuals is primarily responsible for the spread of infection. Most individuals experience mild to moderate respiratory symptoms and recover without requiring hospitalization and medical intervention. Symptoms begin to develop 2–14 days following exposure, during which time the individual can spread the virus to others. As such, the spread of COVID-19 among healthcare workers and in both community and inter-family settings have been well documented [4, 5].

© Springer Nature Switzerland AG 2021
I. Rojas et al. (Eds.): BIOMESIP 2021, LNCS 12940, pp. 371–379, 2021.
https://doi.org/10.1007/978-3-030-88163-4_32

In Arizona, numerous measures have been implemented to prevent the spread of the virus, namely social distancing and the use of personal protective equipment (PPE) such as face masks. On March 11, 2020 a state of emergency was declared, which attempted to limit social interaction by closing many businesses and enforcing social distancing guidelines and mask use [6]. These measures were effective at decreasing case counts during the initial surge, and in May 2020, executive orders were signed that allowed many businesses to reopen [7]. During June 2020, schools were also allowed to reopen via executive order [8, 9]. As a result, infection rates began to increase in the final months of 2020, with a significant surge in cases that peaked during December 2020 and January 2021, during which time there were over 10,000 new cases per day [1]. Positivity rates have steadily declined since February and are now as low as 500 new cases per day [10]. This has been attributed in part to the emergence of COVID-19 vaccinations in December 2020 [11].

First responders, including firefighters, law enforcement officers, and emergency medical services (EMS) personnel, are believed to be at high risk of exposure to SARS-CoV-2 due to frequent in-person contact inherent in their work environment. A previous study by Murphy et al. reported 988 total EMS provider encounters during the treatment of 220 COVID-19 positive patients during a 6-week timeframe in Washington, US [12]. First responders are often in close proximity to the individuals they are assessing and treating, putting them at higher risk of exposure. Furthermore, they work closely with one another, which further increases the risk of rapid transmission between first responders.

Current Centers for Disease Control and Prevention (CDC) guidelines for first responders encourage the use of PPE and physical distancing in the workplace to minimize the risk of exposure and call for symptomatic individuals to self-quarantine [13]. Despite the use of PPE, studies show that first responders have higher rates of COVID-19. During the initial outbreak first responders were shown to experience a higher prevalence of COVID-19. For example, a study by McGuire et al. documented a 1.2% IgG antibody positivity rate among first responders, which represented a three-fold increase compared to the general population at the time [14]. Given the elevated risk of infection, it is necessary to continue tracking positivity rates of first responders to determine the effectiveness of evolving health and safety practices. This current study utilizes COVID-19 antigen testing performed between December 2020 and February 2021 to observe trends in the prevalence of COVID-19 among Phoenix first responders and aims to compare this data to positivity rates among the general population in Phoenix and throughout Arizona.

2   Methods

A retrospective study was conducted collecting data from Vincere's COVID-19 testing. In a partnership with the City of Phoenix, Vincere provided COVID-19 testing to first responders and the general public. Testing was performed at the fire stations at zero-cost to the firefighter or department. A mobile COVID-19 testing center in the Phoenix area offered COVID-19 antigen testing at zero-cost to all individuals 12 years and older regardless of insurance status. Both individual appointments and walk-ups were accepted, and both evening and weekend appointments were available.

2.1 COVID-19 Antigen Test

The Quidel SOFIA SARS antigen fluorescent immunoassay test was utilized. This antigen test received Food and Drug Administration (FDA) Emergency Use Authorization (EUA), and has a sensitivity of 100%, specificity of 98.8%, positive predictive accuracy of 96.7%, and negative predictive accuracy of 100% [15]. This qualitative test detects the nucleocapsid protein from SARS-CoV-2 from nasal or nasopharyngeal specimens. Samples were processed on-site and results were given to patients within 15–20 min. Machines were calibrated prior to each testing day and produced a digital read-out indicating positive or negative for SARS-CoV-2. Invalid results were repeated. All tests were performed and interpreted by trained individuals, including certified emergency medical technicians/paramedics, medical assistants, registered nurses, and medical doctors.

2.2 Outcomes

The primary outcome was COVID-19 antigen positivity rate.

2.3 Statistical Analysis

COVID-19 antigen testing results from December 27, 2020 to February 6, 2021 were extracted. Subject data was grouped into weekly case counts and positivity rates were calculated. Trends were analyzed and compared to data from the Vincere Phoenix mobile test site, as well as Arizona case counts and positivity rates. All statistical analysis was performed using Microsoft Excel and IBM SPSS®v25 and statistical significance was accepted at $p < 0.05$.

3 Results

A total of 201 first responders received COVID-19 testing and a total of 45 were positive (22.4% positivity) (Table 1). Positivity rates were highest in the beginning weeks (late

Table 1. Covid 19 antigen positivity rates in first responders compared to Phoenix and Arizona

Week [Ending]	First responders	Phoenix	Arizona
Overall	22.39%*	12.91%	14.82%
Jan 2, 2021	31.58%*	13.96%	14.94%
Jan 9, 2021	13.46%	13.74%	20.14%
Jan 16, 2021	30.36%*	12.18%	14.47%
Jan 23, 2021	18.52%	12.65%	13.63%
Jan 30, 2021	17.65%	11.74%	11.90%
Feb 6, 2021	9.09%	10.54%	9.24%

Note: * indicates statistical significance at $p < 0.05$ compared to both Phoenix mobile and Arizona state

December 2020 and early January 2021) (Fig. 1) and steadily declined throughout the rest of January into February.

Positivity rates in the first few weeks were significantly higher among first responders than the general public, when compared to Phoenix and Arizona case data ($p < 0.05$). The remaining weeks were also elevated, but not significantly so.

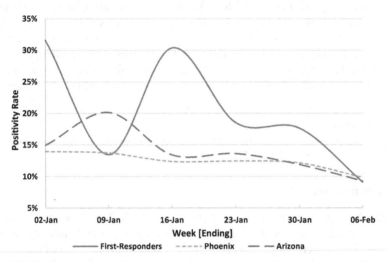

Fig. 1. COVID-19 antigen positivity rates in first responders when compared to Phoenix and Arizona.

4   Discussion

This study focused on COVID-19 antigen positivity rates among first responders compared to the general population in Phoenix and Arizona. COVID-19 remains a major public health concern, and observing trends in disease prevalence is an important step in guiding future health policy.

The results of this study, taken during the second surge of cases in Arizona, demonstrated a 22.4% positivity rate, with 45 of the 201 first responders testing positive for COVID-19. This was significantly higher than Phoenix and Arizona state data from the comparable timeframe, where Phoenix exhibited an overall positivity rate of 12.9%, and Arizona exhibited a 14.8% positivity rate [10]. When looking at overall test results, positivity rates were significantly elevated in first responders ($p < 0.05$) when compared to the positivity rates in both the Phoenix and Arizona populations. There are undoubtedly many factors which contributed to these elevated test results, though numerous workplace exposures to COVID-19 are likely to significantly contribute to these findings.

Test results may also be analyzed on a weekly basis to assess for trends in first responder incidence over time. Positivity rates during the weeks ending on January 2, 2021 and January 16, 2021 were significantly elevated ($p < 0.05$) when compared to Phoenix and Arizona general populations. Conversely, weeks 2, 4, 5, and 6 did not display statistically significant elevations from average positivity rates in the Phoenix and Arizona populations. This indicates that Phoenix first responders were experiencing COVID-19 infections at a rate equivalent to, or greater than the general population. The significantly elevated positivity rates seen in the initial weeks of January may be attributable to increased exposures during the holidays. Large gatherings, especially those occurring indoors, are known to significantly elevate the risk of COVID-19 infection [16, 17]. Furthermore, holidays have been shown to result in far more travel via airports, with Transportation Security Administration (TSA) estimates exceeding 7.1 million passengers transiting through airports across the country in the week preceding December 25, 2020 [18]. As seen in Fig. 1 positivity rates throughout Arizona also peaked in the first 2 weeks of January before declining, further supporting this argument.

As the case counts and positivity rates among the general population decrease, similar declines were seen among first responders. The decline in cases since February is likely attributable to the increase in COVID-19 vaccinations. COVID-19 vaccines were first introduced in December 2020, with the Pfizer vaccine being granted emergency use authorization on December 11, 2020 [11]. Vaccinations peaked during March and April of 2021, and the Arizona Department of Health Services estimates that 48% of all individuals in Arizona have received at least their first dose of a COVID-19 vaccine, while 38% have been fully vaccinated against COVID-19 as of June 14, 2021 [1].

Heightened positivity rates for COVID-19 among first responders may also be attributable to the overall surge in COVID-19 cases observed among the general public in December 2020 and January 2021 [19]. Cases in Phoenix peaked during these months with positivity rates consistently greater than 12% before steadily declining throughout February, March, and April [20]. It seems likely that during this dramatic surge in COVID-19 cases throughout Phoenix, first responders would come into contact with many more individuals with COVID-19 in need of medical services. This effect may compound the risk first responders experience during periods of time when COVID-19 is more prevalent in the population and represents a possible explanation for increased positivity in early January. Continuing to monitor positivity rates among first responders and the general population is necessary to confirm any trends in first responder positivity over time.

The results from this study which demonstrate higher rates of COVID-19 among first responders are similar to other published results. Numerous other studies evaluating rates of COVID-19 among first responders utilizing polymerase chain reaction (PCR) nasopharyngeal tests have reported similar results, with either equivalent or significantly elevated positivity rates in first responders compared to the general population [21, 22]. These tests were performed between March 2020 and April 2020 during a time when the COVID-19 pandemic was far less widespread, which may explain why positivity rates varied greatly between locations. Rates of infection varied widely between studies, depending on location and time of the study [21, 22].

Similar studies have previously demonstrated elevated rates of IgG antibody prevalence in first responders when compared to the general population, indicating higher COVID-19 exposure among first responders [23–26]. In one study by Sami et al., the seroprevalence of IgG antibodies among 22,647 tested first responders in New York

City from May 2020 – July 2020 was demonstrated to be 22.5%, showing that a significant number of first responders had experienced previous exposures to COVID-19 [27]. Another study by Matthias et al., reported IgG antibody positivity rates averaging 4.1% among first responders tested during the months of May 2020 and June 2020 in Miami, Florida [28]. Both of these studies were also performed when the COVID-19 pandemic was less widespread, and first responder safety procedures have continued to be updated over time as more information regarding COVID-19 transmission was reported.

The initial outbreak of COVID-19 resulted in a significant shortage in PPE across the country for several months, leading to reusing PPE and improvising when required [29]. Availability of PCR testing was also limited at the time, with significant wait times for results, which allowed for continued community transmission and spread of the virus. Although testing has improved with rapid antigen tests and more tests gaining FDA EUA, insufficient PPE for healthcare workers and first responders have continued to be a barrier to effective safety measures in some places throughout the course of the pandemic [30]. Although Phoenix had improved safety policies and sufficient PPE available, our current study indicates that a year following the first documented case of COVID-19 in Arizona, first responders continue to experience heightened risk for infection.

It is important to note that first responders may be at increased risk of exposure from asymptomatic COVID-19 transmission. Asymptomatic and pre-symptomatic transmission of COVID-19 has been well documented, and viral load has been shown to be comparable to symptomatic transmissions [31, 32]. Asymptomatic cases are also more difficult to safeguard against, and while social distancing has been an effective method of preventing spread, it is unfeasible for many first responders. For instance, EMS providers often meet in close working conditions, and the living quarters in fire stations facilitate close contact between firefighters. Some studies have also found significant asymptomatic cases among first responders. A study by Akinbami et al. found that 28.9% of all COVID-19 positive first responders were asymptomatic, and half of all positive first responders in Tarabichi et al. were asymptomatic [33, 34]. As part of their workplace environment, first responders often need to be in close contact with patient's inside of closed, indoor environments such as homes, ambulances, and hospitals. Furthermore, first responders will often need to transport individuals who have tested positive for COVID-19 or are experiencing similar symptoms. A study by Nishiura et al. has previously demonstrated that the risk of COVID-19 infection may be as high as 18.7 times greater in these closed off environments than the risk of working in an open-air environment [35]. This shows that not only do first responders experience a large volume of COVID-19 exposures, but each exposure represents a higher risk due to the circumstances behind the exposure. First responders had higher positivity rates in this study, indicating higher risks for infection. They are known to be exposed to COVID more often, and this data may indicate the need for continued or additional safety precautions.

Given the heightened occupational risk first responder's experience, frequent COVID-19 testing and effective safety practices are necessary to prevent infection.

Despite the findings of this study there are numerous limitations. This study was only able to evaluate antigen positivity rates among the Phoenix metropolitan area, which is the fourth largest city in the US. As a result of sampling in a large metropolitan area, the data collected here may differ from other areas, especially places with lower population density, such as rural areas. Furthermore, this study evaluated test results taken only between December 2020 and February 2021 when PPE was more readily available and numerous safety protocols had already been implemented to safeguard against infection. The effect of vaccinations on positivity rate also cannot be fully observed during this timeframe, as the first vaccines were given in December 2020, and it takes five to six weeks for individuals to be fully vaccinated. This study also only analyzed data over a 6-week period, which is insufficient for showing temporal trends. The subjects included in this study were also limited, as only firefighters were tested. COVID-19 positivity rates may differ among other first responders.

Future studies involving police officers and EMS workers are necessary to determine if similar trends are present among all categories of first responders. Testing first responders in rural areas may also yield different results. Furthermore, as vaccinations continue to roll-out, exposure and positivity rates may vary.

5 Conclusions

COVID-19 positivity rates among firefighters were at or above the rate of the general public. Continued vigilance is required to ensure the safety of firefighters during this and future pandemics.

Acknowledgements. The authors would like to thank the first responders, including firefighters, law enforcement officers, and emergency medical services personnel, in both Phoenix and across the state of Arizona for working the frontlines and serving the communities during this pandemic. The authors would also like to thank the City of Phoenix for the partnership in the COVID-19 testing. Lastly, we would like to acknowledge the staff and individuals who helped operate the sites each day and perform the testing.

References

1. Arizona Department of Health Services COVID Database. https://www.azdhs.gov/covid19/data/index.php. Accessed 16 June 2021
2. Vella, F., et al.: Transmission mode associated with coronavirus disease 2019: a review. Eur. Rev. Med. Pharmacol. Sci. **24**(14), 7889–7904 (2020). https://doi.org/10.26355/eurrev_202007_22296
3. Ge, Z.Y., Yang, L.M., Xia, J.J., Fu, X.H., Zhang, Y.Z.: Possible aerosol transmission of COVID-19 and special precautions in dentistry. J. Zhejiang Univ. Sci. B **21**, 361–368 (2020). https://doi.org/10.1631/jzus.B2010010
4. Liu, J., et al.: Community transmission of severe acute respiratory syndrome coronavirus 2, Shenzhen, China, 2020. Emerg. Infect. Dis. **26**(6), 1320–1323 (2020). https://doi.org/10.3201/eid2606.200239
5. Yang, C., Ma, Q.Y., Zheng, Y.H., Yang, Y.X.: Transmission routes of 2019-novel coronavirus (2019-nCoV). Zhonghua yu Fang yi xue za zhi [Chin. J. Prev. Med.] **54**(4), 374–377 (2020). https://doi.org/10.3760/cma.j.cn112150-20200216-0016
6. Office of the Arizona Governor. https://azgovernor.gov/executive-orders. Accessed 14 June 2021

7. Office of the Governor, Executive Orders. https://azgovernor.gov/executive-orders. Accessed 14 June 2021
8. Arizona Open for Learning. https://azgovernor.gov/executive-orders. Accessed 14 June 2021
9. Arizona Department of Health Services. Safely Returning to In-Person Instruction. https://www.azdhs.gov/documents/preparedness/epidemiology-disease-control/infectious-disease-epidemiology/novel-coronavirus/covid-19-safely-return-to-in-person-instruction. pdf. Accessed 14 June 2021
10. John Hopkins Coronavirus Resource Center. https://coronavirus.jhu.edu/region/us/arizona. Accessed 16 June 2021
11. US Food and Drug Administration. https://www.fda.gov/emergency-preparedness-and-res ponse/coronavirus-disease-2019-covid-19/pfizer-biontech-covid-19-vaccine. Accessed 16 June 2021
12. Murphy, D.L., et al.: Occupational exposures and programmatic response to COVID-19 pandemic: an emergency medical services experience. Emerg. Med. J. **37**(11), 707–713 (2020). https://doi.org/10.1136/emermed-2020-210095
13. Centers for Disease Control and Prevention – COVID-19. https://www.cdc.gov/coronavirus/ 2019-ncov/community/organizations/firefighter-EMS.html. Accessed 16 June 2021
14. McGuire, S.S., Klassen, A.B., Heywood, J., Sztajnkrycer, M.D.: Prevalence of COVID-19 IgG antibodies in a cohort of municipal first responders. Prehosp. Disast. Med. **36**(2), 131–134 (2021). https://doi.org/10.1017/S1049023X2000151X
15. Quidel Sofia SARS Antigen FIA. Product specifications. https://www.quidel.com/immuno assays/rapid-sars-tests/sofia-sars-antigen-fia. Accessed 04 May 2021
16. Bae, S., Lim, J.S., Kim, J.Y., Jung, J., Kim, S.H.: Transmission characteristics of SARS-CoV-2 that hinder effective control. Immune Netw. **21**(1), e9 (2021). https://doi.org/10.4110/in. 2021.21.e9
17. Bulfone, C.B., Malekinejad, M., Rutherford, G.W., Nooshin, R.: Outdoor transmission of SARS-CoV-2 and other respiratory viruses: a systematic review. J. Infect. Dis. **223**(4), 550–561 (2021). https://doi.org/10.1093/infdis/jiaa742
18. TSA Checkpoint Travel Numbers. https://www.tsa.gov/coronavirus/passenger-throughput. Accessed 16 June 2021
19. Lau, C.S.M., et al.: COVID-19 trends in the phoenix metropolitan area from a mobile testing program: last quarter of 2020. J. Community Health. 1–5 (2021). https://doi.org/10.1007/s10 900-021-00991-4
20. Lau, C.S.M., et al.: Trends in COVID-19 testing and positivity rates from a mobile testing program in the phoenix metropolitan area. J. Commun. Health. 1–5 (2021). https://doi.org/ 10.1007/s10900-021-01011-1
21. Tang, O., Bigelow, B.F., Katz, M.: Earlier and widespread screening for SARS-CoV-2 is needed for first responders. Am. J. Emerg. Med. **40**, 215–216 (2021). https://doi.org/10.1016/ j.ajem.2020.05.070
22. Niu, J., Rodriguez, J.A., Sareli, C., Goldman, J., Puga, M., Eckardt, P.A.: COVID-19 infection among first responders in Broward County, Florida, March-April 2020. J. Public Health (Oxford, England). fdaa231 (2020) https://doi.org/10.1093/pubmed/fdaa231
23. Newberry, J.A., Gautreau, M., Staats, K., Carrillo, E., Mulkerin, W., et al.: SARS-CoV-2 IgG seropositivity and acute asymptomatic infection rate among firefighter first responders in an early outbreak county in California. Prehosp. Emerg. Care. 1–10 (2021). https://doi.org/10. 1080/10903127.2021.1912227. Epub ahead of print. PMID: 33819128
24. Caban-Martinez, A.J., et al.: Epidemiology of SARS-CoV-2 antibodies among firefighters/paramedics of a US fire department: a cross-sectional study. Occup Environ Med. **772**, 857–861 (2020). https://doi.org/10.1136/oemed-2020-106676
25. Shukla, V., et al.: COVID-19 exposure among first responders in Arizona. J. Occup. Environ. Med. **62**(12), 981–985 (2020). https://doi.org/10.1097/JOM.0000000000002027

26. Iwuji, K., Islam, E., Berdine, G., Nugent, K., Test V., Tijerina, A.: Prevalence of coronavirus antibody among first responders in Lubbock, Texas. J. Prim. Care Community Health **11** (2020)
27. Sami, S., et al.: Prevalence of SARS-CoV-2 antibodies in first responders and public safety personnel, New York City, New York, USA, May–July 2020. Emerg. Infect. Dis. **27**(3), 796–804 (2021)
28. Matthias, J., et al.: SARS-COV-2 antibody prevalence among healthcare workers and first responders, Florida, May–June 2020. Florida Public Health Rev. **18**(1), 1–10 (2021)
29. Burris, S., de Guia, S., Gable, L., Levin, D.E., Parmet, W.E., Terry, N.P.: COVID-19: State and local responses to PPE shortages. Northeastern University School of Law Research Paper No. 394-2020
30. Department of Homeland Security. https://www.dhs.gov/science-and-technology/first-responder-protective-equipment-challenges-during-covid-19. Accessed 16 June 2021
31. Alexander, M., Unruh, L., Koval, A., Belanger, W.: United States response to the COVID-19 pandemic, January-November 2020. Health Econ. Policy Law. 1–14 (2021)
32. Huff, H.V., Avantika, S.: Asymptomatic transmission during the coronavirus disease 2019 pandemic and implications for public health strategies. Clin. Infect. Dis. **71**(10), 2752–2756 (2020)
33. Tarabichi, Y., et al.: SARS-CoV-2 infection among serially tested emergency medical services workers. Prehosp. Emerg. Care **25**(1), 39–45 (2021)
34. Akinbami, L.J., et al.: COVID-19 symptoms and SARS-CoV-2 antibody positivity in a large survey of first responders and healthcare personnel, May–July 2020. Clin. Infect. Dis. ciab080 (2021)
35. Nishiura, H., et al.: Closed environments facilitate secondary transmission of coronavirus disease 2019 (COVID-19). medRxiv (2020)

Interpretable COVID-19 Classification Leveraging Ensemble Neural Network and XAI

Shakib Mahmud Dipto⑩, Irfana Afifa⑩, Mostofa Kamal Sagor⑩,
Md. Tanzim Reza$^{(\boxtimes)}$⑩, and Md. Ashraful Alam⑩

BRAC University, 66 Mohakhali, Dhaka, Bangladesh
ashraful.alam@bracu.ac.bd
http://www.bracu.ac.bd

Abstract. COVID-19, also known as Corona Virus Disease, was first discovered in a city of China named Wuhan in December 2019 and it has been announced as a global pandemic in the middle of 2020. According to experts, this virus may also infect the upper respiratory system, which includes the sinuses, nose, and throat, and the lower respiratory system, which includes the windpipe and lungs. The disease can infect other people via respiratory droplets and come near to the COVID-19 infected people and a low rate of contamination is stated through surfaces and objects touch. Nowadays, millions of people across the globe are suffering from this disease, causing a huge death rate. Even after taking serious precaution measures, the number of patients dealing with this disease and the death toll are still rising at a drastic rate. In this paper, we approach a fast and effective measure to detect COVID-19 using CT scan images. First, we collected data and classified using VGG16, VGG19, EfficientNetB0, ResNet50, and ResNet101. From our result; we got an accuracy rate of 85.33% from VGG16, 87.86% from VGG19, and 82.35% from ResNet101. Then we formed an ensemble model with these best three classifiers and achieved a best overall accuracy rate of 90.89% from COV19EXAI V1 and 91.82% from COV19EXAI V2. Finally, we integrated XAI in our model to achieve a better understanding of our classification.

Keywords: COVID-19 · Corona Virus · Deep neural network · VGG · Inception V3 · ResNet · XAI · Ensemble modeling · Explainable AI · VGG16 · VGG19 · ResNet50 · ResNet101 · EfficientNet · COV19EXAI

1 Introduction

More than 153 million individuals have been diagnosed with COVID-19 since early December 2019 [1], with more than 3.5 million people dying as a result of the virus. The rate at which the virus is spreading and killing people, on the other hand, is increasing day by day, breaking all previous records. As the consequence, all radiologists throughout the world have had a difficult problem

© Springer Nature Switzerland AG 2021
I. Rojas et al. (Eds.): BIOMESIP 2021, LNCS 12940, pp. 380–391, 2021.
https://doi.org/10.1007/978-3-030-88163-4_33

testing so many patients and delivering test results on time. After a day or two, many people receive their test results. As a result, their health is deteriorating at this time, as the virus is wreaking havoc on their lungs. CT scan pictures of the lungs, on the other hand, reveal the abnormalities caused by COVID-19 infection. Therefore, CT scan data are conveyed sooner than COVID-19 PCR test results. Therefore, to achieve the quickest binary classification of COVID-19, we're attempting to develop a system that will identify COVID-19 from infected patients' lungs CT scan pictures by comparing them to CT scan pictures of normal lungs.

2   Background Study

2.1   Literature Review

Most of the COVID-19 patients suffer from lung complications that include pneumonia or acute respiratory distress syndrome (ARDS). Therefore, one of the easiest and fastest ways to identify the COVID-19 patients from other people is the CT scan images as well as x-ray images of their lungs. Meanwhile, the most common indications and patterns of lung variation from the normal one are on CXR in COVID-19 and to prepare the clinical network. CXR is a less delicate methodology in the discovery of COVID-19 lung disease contrasted with CT, with an announced baseline CXR affectability of 69% [2]. In another study [3], many researchers have created a new model to detect COVID-19 automatically using raw images of chest x-ray in which both advanced artificial intelligence techniques and radiological images is applied in a combined manner for the accurate detection of the virus as well as for resolving the problem due to the lack of well-specialized physicians in remote areas. In paper [4], they developed a COVID-19 diagnostic model utilizing Bayes-SqueezeNet for COVID-19 identification utilizing x-ray pictures.

In addition, the deep learning-based strategy is also successful for the detection of coronavirus contaminated patients utilizing X-ray images [5]. In paper [6], to detect the presence of CoronaVirus, a three-dimensional deep learning method is presented by using the images of chest CT scan images because CT may share certain comparable imaging highlights between COVID-19 and other sorts of pneumonia, hence, making it troublesome to differentiate. In contrast, computed tomography images are utilized to pre-train the deep learning system as well as to train and assess the deep learning system's performance [7]. This approach is capable of distinguishing high-risk individuals from low-risk individuals and also provides a handy tool for quickly screening COVID-19 infection.

On the other hand, pre-trained deep learning models ResNet and Inception are used for the automatic classification of white blood cell [8]. Initially, they proposed three consecutive pre-processing calculations named color distortion, bounding box distortion, and image flipping mirroring. After that, Inception and ResNet architectures are used in recognizing white blood cells with hierarchy topological feature extraction. In [9], researchers used VGG architecture for the successful identification and prediction of lung cancer. Their research shows that VGG is the most efficient architecture in finding the most accurate result compared to the others.

Besides this, the paper [10] is based on the use of EfficientNet with differential privacy practice in the diagnosis of Corona Virus utilizing radiological images. They described their system using the Grad-Cam method, in which the areas of the pictures EfficientNet-B0 model leverages the characteristics in CXR pictures for the diagnosis of COVID-19. In the article [11], the researchers proposed a model which is based on the EfficientNet CNN named "Efficient-CovidNet" which is also an approach based on deep learning for detecting COVID-19 from the chest x-ray images. Again, a transfer learning–BiLSTM network architecture based on Convolutional Neural Network has been an approach for detecting COVID-19 infection [12]. Here, the researchers have proposed mainly two deep learning architectures for detecting COVID-19 infected patients automatically using chest CT scan images. The first one is lung segmentation also known as the processing of the CT scan images and this thing is automatically performed with ANN (Artificial Neural Networks). Again, the second architecture which is proposed is one kind of hybrid layer that includes a Bidirectional Long Short-Term Memories layer and the job of this layer is to consider temporal properties.

In the article, [13] a prospective framework is used for the COVID-19 risk prediction depending on XAI (Explainable Artificial Intelligence). The researchers used one kind of two-step procedure for the non-clinical prediction of the infection risk of COVID-19. At first, the primary risk of COVID-19 is detected carefully by considering selected parameters that are associated with COVID-19 infection symptoms. After the result of the first step is generated, an optional prediction system is also provided by analyzing the chest x-ray images. In addition, in the study [14], the researchers proposed and developed XAI techniques for COVID-19 classification models, and also compared them. The findings show that quantitative and qualitative visualizations can help clinicians understand and make better decisions by providing more granular information from the learned XAI models' outcomes. Furthermore, in the paper [15], the researchers presented an explainable DNN-based methodology for automated identification of COVID-19 symptoms from chest x-ray images. They have proposed 'Deep-COVIDExplainer,' a novel diagnosis methodology based on neural ensemble technique, as the first step toward an AI-based clinical aid tool for COVID-19 diagnosis. The 'DeepCOVIDExplainer' pipeline begins with histogram equalization, filtering, and not so sharp masking of CXR pictures, then trains DenseNet, ResNet, and VGGNet architectures in a transfer learning (TL) environment, resulting in model samples.

2.2 Algorithms and Architectures

Visual Geometry Group (VGG): VGG consists of different layers, such as convolutional layers with ReLU activation function, pooling layers, fully connected layers, and Softmax activation function in the final output. The network input is fixed to $224 \times 224 \times 3$ RGB images which are s transferred with kernels of dimension 3×3 across multiple convolutional layers. The pooling filter layers are of dimension 2 × 2 and applied with a stride of 2. Two mostly used VGG architectures are VGG16 which consists of 16 layers and VGG19 which consists of 19 layers.

ResNet: ResNet is built on the idea of skip connection which allows training extremely deep neural networks of more than 150 layers. In our methodology, we used ResNet50 and ResNet101. In ResNet50, there are 5 stages, each stage consisting of different convolution layer combinations. On the other hand, ResNet101 is a CNN model which is 101 layers deep.

EfficientNet: EfficientNet is a newly introduced scaling architecture that uses a compound coefficient to uniformly scale network width, depth, and resolution. The compound scaling method allows EfficientNet models to be scaled in such a way that it achieves state-of-the-art accuracy with an order of magnitude fewer parameters and FLOPS, on ImageNet and other commonly used transfer learning datasets.

Ensemble Model: An ensemble model is the fusion of multiple architectures in which the input layer contains the dimension equivalent to the symmetric output dimension of the combined architectures. Here, the individual architectures will provide the probability for all the labels and these individual label-wise probabilities will get averaged to classify the image at the output layer of the ensemble model. So, the dimension for both input and output of an ensemble model will be the same and it will give better results by minimizing the errors and maximizing the accuracy.

Explainable Artificial Intelligence (XAI): XAI provides a deep explanation by modifying deep learning techniques to learn explainable features and also provides interpretable models including different techniques to learn more structured, interpretable, and causal models and model induction.

3   Research Methodology

An overview of every step that we have taken to train and validate our models is shown through the workflow diagram in Fig. 1. Firstly, we gathered our data and performed data preprocessing that includes data scaling and augmentation. Then, we trained our dataset via several deep learning models such as VGG16, VGG19, EfficientNetB0, ResNet50, and ResNet101. After this, the dataset was tested and validated. In the next step, we used the models that we have created, COV19EXAI V1 (Ensemble of VGG16 and VGG19 architecture) and COV19EXAI V2 (Ensemble of VGG16, VGG19, and ResNet101 architecture), to train the data set and then tested and validated the data to find accuracy.

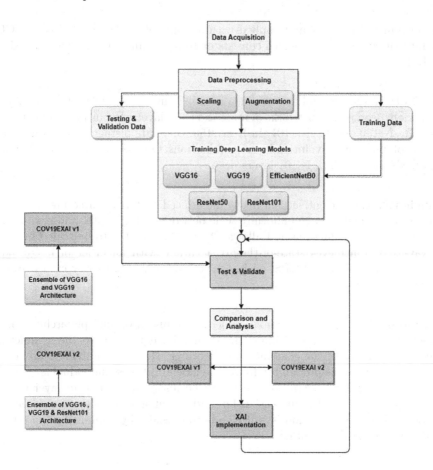

Fig. 1. Research methodology

4   Dataset Details and Processing

We created our dataset CT-scan pictures of COVID-19 patients using datasets provided in [16] and [17].

4.1   Data Sample

In Fig. 2, we can see some data samples of the CT-scan images of lungs.

4.2   Data Classification

We divided the dataset into 7:2:1 in our study, where 70% of the data was used to train the model, 20% was used as a test set and the remainder of the 10% was used to validate our models.

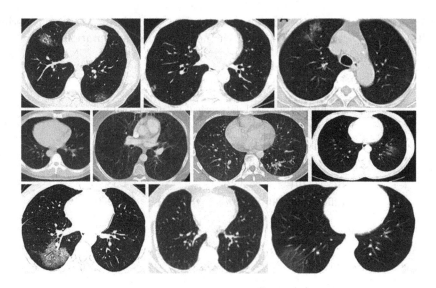

Fig. 2. Sample data of the dataset

4.3   Data Pre-processing

Resize Images: Since we used pre-trained convolutional neural network models while training the network, each image was re-sized into a fixed size of 224 × 224. For this purpose, we used scikit-image, TensorFlow, and Caffe frameworks.

Scaling Images: We used the ImageDataGenerator class of Keras for scaling our images. We scaled the pixel values (originally between 0 and 255) to the range of 0 to 1.

Data Augmentation: We augmented our data by applying a set of random transformations to the images for increasing our model performance. We applied rotation (90°, 180°and 270°) and translation to the images and also horizontally and vertically flipped the images. For this purpose, the ImageDataGenerator class of Keras was used.

5   Implementation and Result Analysis

5.1   Individual Models

From the validation accuracy provided in Table 1 and Fig. 3, we can determine that VGG19, VGG16, and ResNet101 show us 87.86%, 85.33% and 82.35%. So, these are the best three performing architecture. Therefore, we are considering VGG19, VGG16, and ResNet101 for the next level implementation.

Table 1. Comparison of models

Architecture	val_categorical_accuracy	val_loss
VGG16	85.33%	0.7079
VGG19	87.86%	0.6309
ResNet50	79.44%	1.6673
ResNet101	82.35%	1.3806
EfficientNetB0	80.75%	0.5900

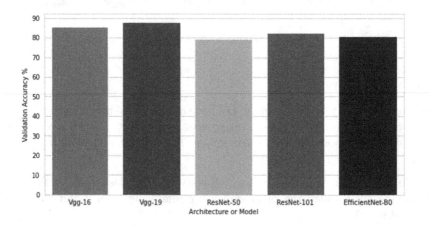

Fig. 3. Comparison between our used models using a bar chart

5.2 COVID-19 Analysis by Ensemble Modelling and Explainable AI Version 1 (COV19EXAI V1)

In our "COV19EXAI v1" model, we have combined our two best performing architectures which are VGG19 and VGG16 for ensemble modeling and achieved 90.89% validation accuracy from this model.

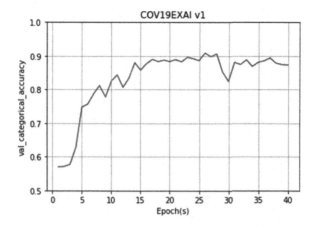

Fig. 4. Validation accuracy curve of COV19EXAI v1

From Fig. 4, we can see that the validation accuracy increases up to 25 epochs. After that, the accuracy level stabilizes within 25 to 40 epochs and, it reaches the peak at 0.9089 after 25 epochs.

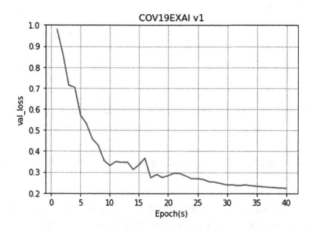

Fig. 5. Validation loss curve of COV19EXAI v1

In Fig. 5, we can see a gradual loss reduction all the way up to 40 epochs. However, it does not improve the validation accuracy rate after 28 epochs.

5.3 COVID-19 Analysis by Ensemble Modelling and Explainable AI Version 2 (COV19EXAI V2)

In our "COV19EXAI v2" model, we have combined our three best performing architecture which are VGG19, VGG16, and ResNet101 for ensemble modeling and achieved 91.82% validation accuracy from this model.

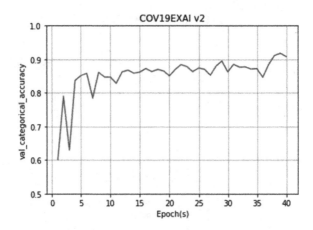

Fig. 6. Validation accuracy curve of COV19EXAI v2

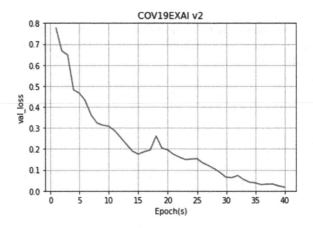

Fig. 7. Validation loss curve of COV19EXAI v2

From Fig. 6, we can see that the validation accuracy increases up to 15 epochs. After that, the accuracy level stabilizes within 15 to 40 epochs, and it reaches the peak at 0.9182 after 36 epochs. Meanwhile, in Fig. 7, the loss gradually reduces all the way up to 40 epochs.

5.4   COV19EXI-v1 Vs COV19EXI-v2

From the validation accuracy provided in Table 2, we can determine that "COV19EXAI v2" shows us 91.82% validation accuracy. So, among our two models, "COV19EXAI v2" is the best performing model. Therefore, we have considered "COV19EXAI v2" for the next level implementation.

Table 2. Comparison between our proposed models

Model	val_categorical_accuracy	val_loss
COV19EXAI v1	90.89%	0.2652
COV19EXAI v2	91.82%	0.2358

5.5   Explainable Artificial Intelligence (XAI)

After implementing Explainable AI on "COV19EXAI v2", we have noticed that there are 3 types of masks which is represent by 3 different colors such as Yellow, Red and Green. Here, Yellow borders represent the interpretable regions, the Green mask represents the COVID positive responding regions and Red mask represents the COVID negative responding regions.

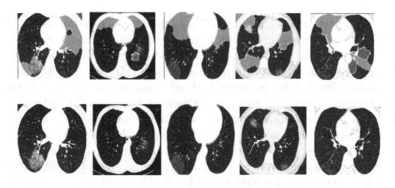

Fig. 8. Output of XAI for COVID positive cases

We can see from Fig. 8 and Fig. 9 that the COVID positive region responded mostly mid to the higher portion of the lungs. However, we can also see that there are some wrong classification have occurred.

Additionally, in the figures, we can see that there are several CT-scan images have masked incorrectly at the very bottom part of the images. From our research, we figured out that, positive level images and negative level images have some distinct differences at the bottom portion of the images. Therefore, the neural network is interpreting it as a feature for distinguishing COVID and Non-COVID.

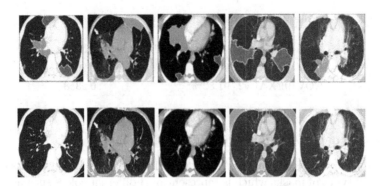

Fig. 9. Output of XAI for COVID negative cases

6   Conclusion

The entire world is suffering beyond our imagination as a result of the COVID-19 pandemic, and the situation is deteriorating day by the. The number of COVID19 patients, as well as the number of deaths, is rapidly rising. Every day, millions of people visit hospitals to get tested, yet the findings take 10 to 15 h to arrive. Due to the lengthy time it takes to obtain findings, some patients in critical condition are not receiving correct treatment in a timely manner, and this delay is costing them their lives. Therefore, to improve this condition a little bit, our model will be able to detect the Corona Virus by analyzing the CT-scan images of the patients in the fastest way and also be able to classify the intensity of COVID-19 based on the image data. In this research work, we implemented VGG16, VGG19, EfficientNetB0, ResNet50, and ResNet152 architecture on the dataset to train the data and compared the result with our architecture COV19EXAI V1 (Ensemble of VGG16 and VGG19 architecture), COV19EXAI V2 (Ensemble of VGG16, VGG19, and ResNet101 architecture) and XAI implantation. In the future, we will try to gather more data to improve our model and resolve the wrong classifications which are visible in the XAI implementation. Thus, we will be able to build a process that will generate an efficient way to contribute to the COVID-19 crisis.

References

1. World Health Organization, et al.: Coronavirus disease (COVID-19) (2020)
2. Jacobi, A., Chung, M., Bernheim, A., Eber, C.: Portable chest x-ray in coronavirus disease-19 (COVID-19): a pictorial review. Clin. Imaging **64**, 35–42 (2020)
3. Ozturk, T., Talo, M., Yildirim, E.A., Baloglu, U.B., Yildirim, O., Acharya, U.R.: Automated detection of COVID-19 cases using deep neural networks with x-ray images. Comput. Biol. Med. **121**, 103792 (2020)
4. Ucar, F., Korkmaz, D.: COVIDiagnosis-Net: Deep Bayes-SqueezeNet based diagnostic of the coronavirus disease: (COVID-19) from x-ray images. Med. Hypotheses **140**, 109761 (2020)

5. Sethy, P.K., Behera, S.K.: Detection of coronavirus disease (COVID-19) based on deep features. Preprints 2020030300 (2020)
6. Li, L., et al. Artificial intelligence distinguishes COVID-19 from community acquired pneumonia on chest CT. Radiology **296** (2020)
7. Wang, S., et al.: A fully automatic deep learning system for COVID-19 diagnostic and prognostic analysis. Eur. Respir. J. **56** (2020)
8. Habibzadeh, M., Jannesari, M., Rezaei, Z., Baharvand, H., Totonchi, M.: Automatic white blood cell classification using pre-trained deep learning models: ResNet and inception. In: Tenth International Conference on Machine Vision (ICMV 2017), vol. 10696, p. 1069612. International Society for Optics and Photonics (2018)
9. Amma, T.A., Sunny, A.R., Biji, K.P., Mohanan, M.: Lung cancer identification and prediction based on VGG architecture. In. J. Res. Eng. Sci. Manage. **3**(7), 88–92 (2020)
10. Müftüoğlu, Z., Kizrak, M.A., Yildlnm, T.: Differential privacy practice on diagnosis of COVID-19 radiology imaging using EfficientNet. In: 2020 International Conference on INnovations in Intelligent SysTems and Applications (INISTA), pp. 1–6. IEEE (2020)
11. Chaudhary, Y., Mehta, M., Sharma, R., Gupta, D., Khanna, A., Rodrigues, J.J.: Efficient-CovidNet: deep learning based COVID-19 detection from chest x-ray images. In: 2020 IEEE International Conference on E-health Networking, Application & Services (HEALTHCOM), pp. 1–6. IEEE (2021)
12. Aslan, M.F., Unlersen, M.F., Sabanci, K., Durdu, A.: CNN-based transfer learning-BiLSTM network: a novel approach for COVID-19 infection detection. Appl. Soft Comput. **98**, 106912 (2021)
13. Sharma, V., Chhatwal, S., Singh, B., et al.: An explainable artificial intelligence based prospective framework for COVID-19 risk prediction. medRxiv (2021)
14. Ye, Q., Xia, J., Yang, G.: Explainable AI for COVID-19 CT classifiers: an initial comparison study. arXiv preprint arXiv:2104.14506 (2021)
15. Karim, M.R., Döhmen, T., Rebholz-Schuhmann, D., Decker, S., Cochez, M., Beyan, O.: DeepCOVIDExplainer: explainable COVID-19 diagnosis based on chest x-ray images. arXiv e-prints arXiv-2004 (2020)
16. Zhao, J., Zhang, Y., He, X., Xie, P.: COVID-CT-dataset: a CT scan dataset about COVID-19. arXiv preprint arXiv:2003.13865 (2020)
17. Cohen, J.P., Morrison, P., Dao, L., Roth, K., Duong, T.Q., Ghassemi, M.: COVID-19 image data collection: prospective predictions are the future. arXiv:2006.11988 (2020)

CoroPy: A Deep Learning Based Comparison Between X-Ray and CT Scan Images in Covid-19 Detection and Classification

Md. Jamilur Rahman[1(✉)], Ahashan Habib Niloy[1], Shammi Akhter Shiba[1],
S. M. Farah Al Fahim[1], Faizun Nahar Faria[1], Emtiaz Hussain[1],
and Mohammad Zavid Parvez[2]

[1] BRAC University, Dhaka, Bangladesh
md.jamilur.rahman@g.bracu.ac.bd
[2] Engineering Institute of Technology, Melbourne, Australia

Abstract. Coronavirus 2019 (in short, Covid-19), was first found in the Wuhan province of China in December 2019 and has been declared a global pandemic by WHO in March 2020. Since its inception, its rapid spread among nations had initially collapsed the world economy and the increasing death-pool created a strong fear among people as the virus spread through human contact. Initially doctors struggled to diagnose the increasing number of patients as there was less availability of testing kits and failed to treat people efficiently which ultimately led to the collapse of the health sector of several countries. To help doctors primarily diagnose the virus, researchers around the world have come up with some radiology imaging techniques using the Convolutional Neural Network (CNN). While some of them worked on X-ray images and some others on CT scan images, very few of them worked on both the image types where their works are limited to detecting only covid and normal cases and none of them performed any comparative analysis between the performance of these two image types as far as our knowledge goes. This, therefore, has insisted us to perform a comparative analysis between X-ray and CT scan images. Thus we came up with a novel CNN model named CoroPy which works for both the image types and can detect normal, Covid-19 and viral pneumonia with great accuracy and shows that X-ray images have overall better performance.

Keywords: Covid-19 · Machine learning · Deep learning · Convolutional neural network · X-ray · CT scan · CoroPy

1 Introduction

Covid-19 was first reported in the Wuhan city of China [1] back in December 2019 and started spreading rapidly across different nations and was declared a global pandemic by WHO in March 2020 [2]. Since its inception, it has completely changed the way our life used to be. As this virus spread through human contact,

© Springer Nature Switzerland AG 2021
I. Rojas et al. (Eds.): BIOMESIP 2021, LNCS 12940, pp. 392–404, 2021.
https://doi.org/10.1007/978-3-030-88163-4_34

the world faced several lockdowns which created drastic effects on the world economy [3]. Within a short span of only one and half years, it has affected 170 million people and taken the life of 3.54 million people [4] (as of 29th May 2021). From the beginning of this pandemic, testing has been considered as one of the major issues. Several problems related to detection of Covid-19 such as less availability of testing kits, less testing centers, more detection time, less number of tests compared to the total population primarily worsened the situation. With the passage of time, though the availability of testing kits has increased and the test duration got reduced, the availability of test centers and the number of test cases is still not enough. This low number of testing is, in fact, hiding the actual number of patients and thus facilitating the rapid spread of Covid-19 [5].

Pereira et al. [6] presented a categorization technique based solely on X-ray images to differentiate pneumonia caused by Covid-19 in other species from healthy lungs. Narin et al. [7] offered three distinct models for coronavirus pneumonia diagnosis using X-ray images. They have analyzed their models and found 98% accuracy for the ResNet50 model. However, X-ray images are not considered as gold standard like that of CT scan images. Therefore, it would be really great work if they could tell something about CT scan image related detection systems. Zheng et al. [8] created a software method for detecting COVID-related disorders that is based on weakly supervised deep learning and employs 3D CT volumes. The model used in this case, DeCoVNet, consisted of three stages. Panwar et al. [25] proposed a deep learning model for detecting covid-19 from images in another study. They used both X-ray and CT scan images in this study. Their experiment includes 3 binary classifications: covid vs normal for X-ray images, covid vs normal for CT scan images, and covid vs pneumonia for X-ray images.

2 Methodology

Before building our proposed model, we have created a workflow to perform our research efficiently. Figure 1 shows workflow of our proposed model, CoroPy, to demonstrate the step by step process from dataset generation to the performance evaluation.

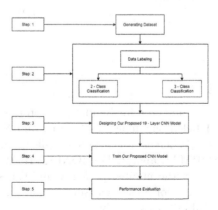

Fig. 1. Workflow for our proposed 19-layer CNN model (CoroPy).

We have worked on each step for several times and then have constructed our proposed model. And the details of these steps of our proposed model, CoroPy, has been described below.

2.1   Generating the Dataset (CovRecker)

Generating our dataset was the first step to build our proposed model. And, we have generated one of the largest datasets having both X-ray and CT scan images called CovRecker. It consists of 3841 X-ray images and 560 CT scan images. So, the total dataset comprises 4401 images. However, our CovRecker is generated from six different data sources. Which are: COVID-chestxray-dataset [9], COVID-CT [10], SARS-COV-2 Ct-Scan Dataset [11], COVID-19 Xray Dataset (Train & Test Sets) [12], COVID-19 Radiography Database [13] and COVID-19 and common pneumonia chest CT dataset [14]. The number of images contained in these datasets have been illustrated in Table 1. However, from this table we can see that the total number of X-ray and CT scan images are more than our created dataset, CovRecker. Because, some of those images are for 4 class classifier. But in our case, we do not need those images. Thus, we collected only those images which are related to our research. In Fig. 2 we can see some sample X-Ray and CT scan images of our CovRecker Dataset.

Table 1. Number of images contained in the mentioned publicly available data sources.

Name of datasets	Number of X-ray images	Number of CT scan images
COVID-chestxray-dataset [9]	468	0
COVID-CT [10]	0	1250
SARS-COV-2 Ct-Scan Dataset [11]	0	1250
COVID-19 Xray Dataset (Train & Test Sets) [12]	5451	0
COVID-19 Radiography Database [13]	3616	0
COVID-19 and common pneumonia chest CT dataset [14]	0	828
Total	9535	3328

2.2   Data Labeling

Data Labeling was the second step for building our proposed model. For 2 class classification we have labeled our images as COVID and NORMAL for both X-ray and CT scan images. Whereas, for 3 class classification, we have labeled our images as COVID, NORMAL and PNEUMONIA_VIRAL for both X-ray and CT scan images. However, the number of X-ray and CT scan images we used from our CovRecker dataset for 3 class classification and 2 class classification is shown in Table 2 and Table 3 respectively.

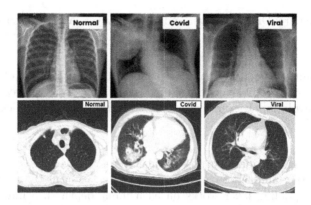

Fig. 2. Some sample X-ray and CT scan images of our CovRecker dataset.

Table 2. The number of X-ray and CT scan images to train our proposed model for 3 class classification.

Labels	Number of X-ray images	Number of CT scan images
COVID	1185	200
NORMAL	1326	160
PNEUMONIA_VIRAL	1330	200
Total	3841	560

Table 3. The number of X-ray and CT scan images to train our proposed model for 2 class classification.

Labels	Number of X-ray images	Number of CT scan images
COVID	1200	160
NORMAL	1341	200
Total	2541	360

2.3 Our Proposed 19-Layer CNN Model (CoroPy) for Detecting Covid-19

In this section we discuss our 19-layer proposed CNN model called CoroPy for detecting Covid-19 from X-ray and CT scan images. For building our proposed model, at first, we have converted our image to an array so that the layers can easily read them. To convert the images to TensorFlow data types we used a method provided by Tensorflow called "flow_from_dataframe". We also introduced image augmentation to generate some random data and make sure the model is introduced to all possible variations of images. CNN model is one of the best ways to detect any features from different images. The CNN consists of three base layers: Convolution Layer, Pooling Layer and Fully Connected Layer [26]. However, we have used another two types of layers in our proposed model,

CoroPy, which are: Dropout Layer and Flatten Layer. A brief discussion of these layers is given below.

Convolutional Layer: Our proposed model CoroPy consists of 10 convolutional layers or Conv2D layers named by TensorFlow. We kept kernel size to (3 × 3). All convolutional layers require an activation function which is ReLU in our case.

Pooling Layer: The main purpose of this layer is to lower the size of the curved map so that the number of parameters and calculation in the network can be reduced. The pooling layer works on each input depth slice individually and spatially resizes it [26]. We have used 3 MaxPooling and 2 AvgPooling layer in our proposed 19 layer CNN model.

Fully Connected Layer: The Dense Layer or Fully Connected Layer works with features with a specific weight which can help to determine the end class. That is why a dense layer is the end process of a CNN or DNN model. Our model contains 2 Dense layers. The activation function we have used is Sigmoid.

Dropout Layer: CNN models can overfit if there is less data available for training. In order to fix this problem, we use the dropout layer. In our case we have used 1 Dropout Layer.

Flatten Layer: Our 19 layer CNN model or CoroPy model consists of one Flatten layer. The job of the flatten layer is to convert the 2 dimensional matrix into a single dimension and pass it down for further processing.

There are many architectures for creating a CNN model. Our proposed 19-layer CNN model, CoroPy is a sequential model. This means that the input data is passed from the top to bottom pattern. The first layer takes the input data, after processing it passes it to the next layer and so on. Architecture of our model can be seen in the Fig. 3.

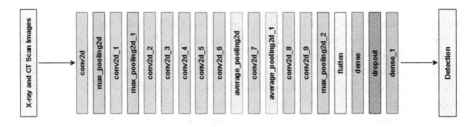

Fig. 3. Architecture of our 19-layer proposed model CoroPy.

We can see that the model starts with a conv2D layer which has an input shape of (348, 348, 32). As our first layer is conv2D and we have used no padding, as a result our input size of the image has reduced from 350 * 350 to 348 * 348 as our filter size is 3 * 3. And we have used 48 images to create a batch and we have 32 such batches. This layer then passes its output to the max-pooling layer. In this layer, our image size become half of its previous value and become a new size of 174 * 174. Then there are some more conv2d layer and pooling layer. There is also a flatten layer after max_pooling2d_2. The flatten layer takes the output of max_pooling2d_2 layer which is (8 * 8 * 256) in shape and converts it to a single column of 16384 rows. Then the dropout layer drops some neurons and their connections randomly. And when it finally reaches the last dense or fully-connected layer the input data is converted into an array with a possible probability value for each class. However, the model we have proposed consists of 1,571,900 params where there are 1,571,900 trainable params and 0 non-trainable params. Table 4 shows the details of each layer of our proposed model, CoroPy.

Table 4. Summary of our proposed model CoroPy.

Layer	Output shape	Param #
conv2d_coro_py	(348, 348, 32)	896
activation_coro_py	(348, 348, 32)	0
max_pooling2d_coro_py	(174, 174, 32)	0
conv2d_1_coro_py	(172, 172, 32)	9248
activation_1_coro_py	(172, 172, 32)	0
max_pooling2d_1_coro_py	(86, 86, 32)	0
conv2d_2_coro_py	(84, 84, 64)	18496
activation_2_coro_py	(84, 84, 64)	0
conv2d_3_coro_py	(82, 82, 64)	36928
activation_3_coro_py	(82, 82, 64)	0
conv2d_4_coro_py	(80, 80, 250)	144250
activation_4_coro_py	(80, 80, 250)	0
conv2d_5_coro_py	(78, 78, 128)	288128
activation_5_coro_py	(78, 78, 128)	0
conv2d_6_coro_py	(76, 76, 128)	147584
activation_6_coro_py	(76, 76, 128)	0
average_pooling2d_coro_py	(38, 38, 128)	0
conv2d_7_coro_py	(36, 36, 64)	73792
activation_7_coro_py	(36, 36, 64)	0
average_pooling2d_1_coro_py	(18, 18, 64)	0
conv2d_8_coro_py	(17, 17, 256)	65792
activation_8_coro_py	(17, 17, 256)	0
conv2d_9_coro_py	(16, 16, 256)	262400
activation_9_coro_py	(16, 16, 256)	0
max_pooling2d_2_coro_py	(8, 8, 256)	0
flatten_coro_py	16384	0
dense_coro_py	32	524320
dropout_coro_py	32	0
dense_1_coro_py	2	66
activation_10_coro_py	2	0

2.4   Training Our Proposed Model

We have used 3841 X-ray images and 560 CT scan images to train our model. Out of which 45 (15 from each class) of X-ray images and 30 (10 from each class) of CT scan images have been reserved for testing the CoroPy model. The data generation library splits the data into test and train sets which were 80% for training and 20% for testing for our proposed model. Then we have used Keras and Tensorflow to implement our proposed model. Our model was trained using our prepared data and Adam optimizer. We have implemented the EarlyStopping (only for X-ray images) which will stop training that particular training set when there are no fluctuations in consecutive 7 epochs. We have also implemented the ReduceLROnPlateau method which decreases the learning rate if there are no changes detected for 3 epochs. We have set the value of the learning rate as 0.001. Batch size is 32 and each epoch has the value of 250. While training the dataset, we have shuffled the data before each epoch. We have used a 5-fold cross-validation approach for 2 class and 3 class classification. We have divided the training set into 5 parts on a random basis and each of these subsets has the same number of values. Among the 5 parts, 4 subsets were considered for training CoroPy whereas the other one was used for validation.

3   Experimental Results and Discussion

Our results of detecting Covid-19 using both X-ray images and CT scan images are shown here. The performance evaluation between these images are also displayed here so that we can get a clear idea based on our result analysis.

3.1   Evaluation Metrics

We have calculated Specificity, Sensitivity, Precision, F1 score, Accuracy and Confusion Matrix to analyze the performance of our proposed model. Confusion matrix is one of the best processes for understanding the results of a classifier [15]. It shows the short review of classifiers [16]. There are some terms associated with this confusion matrix. These are: TN (True Negative), TP (True Positive), FN (False Negative) and FP (False Positive). Specificity is one of the ways to find out the values of TN for every category [17]. Sensitivity is one of the ways to find out the values of TP for every category [17]. It is one of the ways of understanding the model's performance [18]. It is the ratio between the correct assumptions and all the inputs. In the whole predicted positive result, how many results were actually positives are known as precision. It is the ratio of the true positives to all positives [19]. F1 Score is the harmonic mean of precision and recall [20]. Cross validation is a statistical method to understand the performance of various models and also to test the performance of those models. It is used to reduce the problem of overfitting issues when there is a limited number of data [21]. The equations to determine these metrics are shown below.

$$Specificity = TN/(TN + FP) \tag{1}$$

$$Sensitivity = TP/(TP + FN) \tag{2}$$

$$Accuracy = TP + TN/(TP + FP + TN + FN) \tag{3}$$

$$Precision := TP/(TP + FP) \tag{4}$$

$$F1\_score = 2 * (Precision * Recall)/(Precision + Recall) \tag{5}$$

3.2 Performance of Our Proposed Model

We have evaluated our proposed model based on the previously discussed evaluation metrics. The performance of our proposed model is discussed below.

Performances on the X-Ray Images: At first, we measured the performance of our model for a 2-class classifier on X-ray images.

Table 5. Performance measurement of X-ray images for 2-class and 3-class.

Class	Specificity	Sensitivity	Accuracy	Precision	F1 Score
2-class	0.8	1.0	0.897	0.823	0.903
3-class	0.857	1.0	0.89	0.778	0.875

From Table 5, we can conclude that our proposed model performs better in case of 2 class classification for X-ray images. This incident occurs as for 2 class classification we only have images of normal patients and Covid patients. These two types of images vary a lot which helps our proposed model to distinguish more effectively. Moreover, we have performed 5-fold cross-validation for X-ray images for our proposed model.

Table 6. Evaluation based on 2 class classification for 5-fold X-ray images.

Folds	Specificity	Sensitivity	Precision	Accuracy	F1 score
Fold 1	0.8	1.0	0.824	0.897	0.903
Fold 2	0.67	1.0	0.737	0.828	0.848
Fold 3	0.67	1.0	0.737	0.828	0.848
Fold 4	0.67	0.929	0.722	0.793	0.813
Fold 5	0.67	1.0	0.737	0.828	0.848
Average	0.696	0.9858	0.7514	0.8348	0.852

Table 7. Evaluation based on 3 class classification for 5-fold X-ray images.

Folds	Specificity	Sensitivity	Precision	Accuracy	F1 score
Fold 1	0.923	0.992	0.822	0.8	1.0
Fold 2	0.857	0.987	0.82	0.8	0.92
Fold 3	0.8	1.0	0.877	0.8	0.89
Fold 4	0.8	1.0	0.85	0.813	0.862
Fold 5	0.8	1.0	0.822	0.8	0.912
Average	0.836	0.9958	0.8382	0.8026	0.9168

Same conclusions can be drawn from the Table 6 and Table 7 for 5-fold cross validation in case of 2 class and 3 class classification for X-ray images. When we run 5-fold cross validation on our model, we can see that our proposed model performs better in case of 2 class classification and the results are quite similar to the results when we ran the model without 5-fold cross validation.

Performances on the CT Scan Images: To compare the results of X-ray images with the result of CT scan images, we have measured the performance of CT scan images like X-ray images.

Table 8. Performance measurement of CT scan images for 2-class and 3-class.

Class	Specificity	Sensitivity	Accuracy	Precision	F1 Score
2-class	1	0.9	0.957	1.0	0.947
3-class	0.857	0.6	0.3	0.2	0.433

From the Table 8 we can see that our proposed model performs better for the CT scan images compared to the X-ray images in case of 2 class classification but decreases the accuracy in case of 3 class classification. This phenomenon occurs due to the lack of images for CT scan for 3 class classification. We have also performed 5-fold cross-validation for CT scan images for our proposed model.

Table 9. Evaluation based on 2 class classification for 5-fold of CT scan images.

Folds	Specificity	Sensitivity	Precision	Accuracy	F1 score
Fold 1	1.0	1.0	1.0	1.0	1.0
Fold 2	1.0	0.6	1.0	0.8	1.0
Fold 3	1.0	1.0	1.0	1.0	1.0
Fold 4	1.0	0.6	1.0	0.8	1.0
Fold 5	1.0	1.0	1.0	1.0	1.0
Average	1.0	0.84	1.0	0.92	1.0

Table 10. Evaluation based on 3 class classification for 5-fold of CT scan images.

Folds	Specificity	Sensitivity	Precision	Accuracy	F1 score
Fold 1	0.32	0.56	0.34	0.67	0.68
Fold 2	0.35	0.43	0.311	0.69	0.61
Fold 3	0.31	0.52	0.337	0.63	0.628
Fold 4	0.32	0.56	0.34	0.67	0.68
Fold 5	0.33	0.57	0.38	0.58	0.58
Average	0.326	0.528	0.3416	0.648	0.6356

Same conclusion can be drawn from the Table 9 and Table 10 for 5-fold cross validation in case of 2 class and 3 class classification for CT scan images. Though our proposed model shines in case of 2 class classification but performance drops significantly in case of 3 class classification for CT scan images.

From the result analysis, we have found that our proposed 19 layer CNN model, CoroPy performs better on the X-ray dataset. For X-ray 2 class classification, our proposed model achieves 95.75% accuracy and for 3 class classification, our proposed model achieves 92.45% accuracy. On the other hand our proposed model achieves 99.17% accuracy on CT scan 2 class classification but falls behind on 3 class classification. CoroPy only manages to achieve 68.81% accuracy on CT scan 3 class classification. This phenomenon can be explained by the fact that the difference on chest CT scan images varies very little in case of Covid and pneumonia patients. This makes the model harder to differentiate the images, although it is able to distinguish the difference in X-ray images. For this reason, our model was able to achieve higher accuracy on x-ray images.

3.3 Comparative Analysis with the Previous Models

We are not the only ones who have made a unique model in this regard. So, after evaluating our proposed model, CoroPy, we have compared the accuracy of our model in Table 11 with the existing models.

Table 11. Comparison of our proposed Covid-19 diagnostic method, CoroPy,with the other existing deep learning methods.

Study	Type of image	Architecture	Accuracy for 2 class (X-ray image)	Accuracy for 2 class (CT scan image)	Accuracy for 3 class (X-ray image)	Accuracy for 3 class (CT scan image)
Ioannis et al. [27]	X-ray	VGG-19	98.75%	–	93.48%	–
Sethy and Behra [24]	X-ray	ResNet-50	95.38%	–	–	–
Maghdid et al. [22]	X-ray and CT scan	Modified CNN	94%	94.1%	–	–
Panwar et al. [25]	X-ray and CT scan	Modified VGG-19	89.47%	95%	–	–
Shah et al. [23]	CT scan	CTnet-10	–	82.1%	–	–
Zheng et al. [8]	CT scan	UNet+3D	–	90.8%	–	–
Proposed Study	X-ray and CT scan	CoroPy	95.73%	99.17%	92.45%	68.81%

There are some models which focused only on X-ray images and there are some other models which focused only on CT scan images. From this Table 11, we can see that Ioannis et al. [27] and Sethy and Behra [24] used only X-ray images for detecting the Covid-19. Whereas, Shah et al. [23] and Zheng et al. [8] only used CT scan images for detecting Covid-19. To our knowledge, most of the models that exist currently depend either on X-ray images or CT scan images for detecting Covid-19. However, there are a few models with both X-ray and CT scan images for detecting Covid-19. Among those few researches, Maghdid et al. [22] and Panwar et al. [25] used both X-ray images and CT scan images for detecting Covid-19. But they were only confined within 2 class classification. Moreover, in different models, different types of dataset were used. And we have gathered six different datasets used in these papers to build our own model. However, to our knowledge, our proposed model is the first one which uses both X-ray images and CT scan images for both 2-class and 3-class classification for detecting Covid-19, normal and viral pneumonia patients. And X-ray images perform better in our proposed model compared to CT scan images.

4   Conclusion

Covid-19 has caused a devastating effect in our daily life and global economy and also has a dreadful impact in the world health sector. In this research, we have done a comparative study of X-ray images and CT scan images in detecting Covid-19. In order to do that, we have proposed a novel CNN model named CoroPy which works well for both X-ray and CT scan images and provides results for both 2 class classification (normal and covid) and 3 class classification (normal, covid and viral pneumonia) for both the image types. By analyzing the obtained results, we have seen that in the case of 2 class classification, CT scan images work better for our proposed model where it has an accuracy of 99.17% for CT scan images and 95.73% for X-ray images. And, in case of 3 class classification, the images of X-ray work better for our model where it has an accuracy of 92.45% for X-ray images and 68.81% for CT scan images. However, our proposed model shows an overall better performance on X-ray image dataset. Our proposed model CoroPy thus provides a unique contribution by attaining great accuracy for both 2 class and 3 class classification for both the image types to the best of our knowledge. Another major contribution of our research is the preparation of the largest dataset on X-ray and CT scan images as far as our knowledge goes. In this research, we couldn't work for 4 classes (normal, covid, viral pneumonia, and bacterial pneumonia) due to less availability of the dataset. Therefore, our future plan is to work on 4 class classification. We are also planning to create an app with our proposed model where people will be able to upload X-ray images or CT scan images and get results within seconds.

References

1. Hussain, E., Hasan, M., Rahman, M.A., Lee, I., Tamanna, T., Parvez, M.Z.: CoroDet: a deep learning based classification for COVID-19 detection using chest X-ray images. Chaos, Solitons Fractals **142**, 110495 (2021)
2. Cucinotta, D., Vanelli, M.: WHO declares COVID-19 a pandemic. Acta Bio Medica: Atenei Parmensis **91**(1), 157 (2020)
3. Shrestha, N., et al.: The impact of COVID-19 on globalization. One Health **11**, 100180 (2020)
4. Worldometer: COVID-19 coronavirus pandemic (n.d.). COVID Live Update. https://www.worldometers.info/coronavirus/
5. Li, R., et al.: Substantial undocumented infection facilitates the rapid dissemination of novel coronavirus (SARS-CoV-2). Science **368**(6490), 489–493 (2020)
6. Pereira, R.M., Bertolini, D., Teixeira, L.O., Silla, C.N., Jr., Costa, Y.M.: COVID-19 identification in chest X-ray images on flat and hierarchical classification scenarios. Comput. Meth. Prog. Biomed. **194**, 105532 (2020)
7. Narin, A., Kaya, C., Pamuk, Z.: Automatic detection of coronavirus disease (COVID-19) using x-ray images and deep convolutional neural networks. arXiv preprint arXiv:2003.10849 (2020)
8. Zheng, C., et al.: Deep learning-based detection for COVID-19 from chest CT using weak label. medRxiv (2020)
9. Cohen, J.P.: COVID-chestxray-dataset (2020). https://github.com/ieee8023/covid-chestxray-dataset
10. UCSD-AI4H: COVID-CT (2020). https://github.com/UCSD-AI4H/COVID-CT
11. Eduardo, P.: SARS-CoV-2 CT-scan dataset: a large dataset of real patients CT scans for SARS-CoV-2 identification (2020). https://www.kaggle.com/plameneduardo/sarscov2-ctscan-dataset
12. Khoong, W.H.: COVID-19 Xray Dataset (Train & Test Sets) with COVID-19 CNN pneumonia detector (2020). https://www.kaggle.com/khoongweihao/covid19-xray-dataset-train-test-sets
13. Rahman, T.: COVID-19 radiography database COVID-19 chest X-ray database (2020). https://www.kaggle.com/tawsifurrahman/covid19-radiography-database
14. Yan, T.: COVID-19 and common pneumonia chest CT dataset (416 COVID-19 positive CT scans) (2020). https://data.mendeley.com/datasets/3y55vgckg6/2
15. Nitin1901: Confusion matrix in machine learning (2020). https://www.geeksforgeeks.org/confusion-matrix-machine-learning/
16. Brownlee, J.: What is a confusion matrix in machine learning (2020). https://machinelearningmastery.com/confusion-matrix-machine-learning/
17. Mitrani, A.: Evaluating categorical models II: sensitivity and specificity (2019). https://towardsdatascience.com/evaluating-categorical-models-ii-sensitivity-and-specificity-e181e573cff8
18. Gad, A.F.: Evaluating deep learning models: the confusion matrix, accuracy, precision, and recall (2020). https://blog.paperspace.com/deep-learning-metrics-precision-recall-accuracy/
19. Huilgol, P.: Precision vs. recall – an intuitive guide for every machine learning person (2020). https://www.analyticsvidhya.com/blog/2020/09/precision-recall-machine-learning/
20. Mishra, A.: Metrics to evaluate your machine learning algorithm (2018). https://towardsdatascience.com/metrics-to-evaluate-your-machine-learning-algorithm-f10ba6e38234

21. Mujtaba, H.: What is cross validation in machine learning? Types of cross validation (2020). https://www.mygreatlearning.com/blog/cross-validation/

22. Maghdid, H.S., Asaad, A.T., Ghafoor, K.Z., Sadiq, A.S., Mirjalili, S., Khan, M.K.: Diagnosing COVID-19 pneumonia from X-ray and CT images using deep learning and transfer learning algorithms. In: Multimodal Image Exploitation and Learning 2021, vol. 11734, p. 117340E. International Society for Optics and Photonics, April 2021

23. Shah, V., Keniya, R., Shridharani, A., Punjabi, M., Shah, J., Mehendale, N.: Diagnosis of COVID-19 using CT scan images and deep learning techniques. Emerg. Radiol. 28(3), 497–505 (2021). https://doi.org/10.1007/s10140-020-01886-y

24. Sethy, P.K., Behera, S.K.: Detection of coronavirus disease (COVID-19) based on deep features. Preprints 2020030300 (2020)

25. Panwar, H., Gupta, P.K., Siddiqui, M.K., Morales-Menendez, R., Bhardwaj, P., Singh, V.: A deep learning and grad-CAM based color visualization approach for fast detection of COVID-19 cases using chest X-ray and CT-scan images. Chaos, Solitons Fractals 140, 110190 (2020)

26. Stanford University: CS231n: convolutional neural networks for visual recognition (n.d.). https://cs231n.github.io/convolutional-networks/

27. Apostolopoulos, I.D., Mpesiana, T.A.: COVID-19: automatic detection from x-ray images utilizing transfer learning with convolutional neural networks. Phys. Eng. Sci. Med. 43(2), 635–640 (2020)

Tomographic Identification and Evaluation of Pulmonary Involvement Due to SARS-CoV-2 Infection Using Artificial Intelligence and Image Segmentation Technique

Ariela Marçal Stefanini[✉][ID], Taylor Oliveira Fidelis[✉][ID],
Gustavo Moreira Penna[✉][ID], Gabriel Rodrigo Gomes Pessanha[✉][ID],
Reinaldo Antônio Gomes Marques[✉][ID], and Deive Ciro de Oliveira[✉][ID]

Federal University of Alfenas-, Varginha, MG, Brazil
{ariela.stefanini,gustavo.penna}@sou.unifal-mg.edu.br
http://cia-research.com.br/

Abstract. In 2019 coronavirus pandemic was required to find ways to further early diagnosis of COVID-19. This research aims to implement deep neural networks. Thus, we sought work to present analyses about the Deep Learning model, CNN, COVID-19 detection, and segmentation image. The training dataset to train the model we used exams the computerized tomography (CT scan) with dataset the Harvard Dataverse, available since May 2020, was used. The data were collected from the Public Hospital of the Government of the Employees of São Paulo (HSPM) and the Hospital Metropolitano da Lapa - São Paulo - Brazil. We applied it to four different architectures like VGG 19, Resnet 50, Inception, Xception. Each architecture has its advantages and disadvantages, and to supply the needs that each architecture presents, we generated ensembles among them. In general, the segmentation has shown that it is possible to capture regions with COVID-19 and differentiate them from other diseases. This study has pointed out the accuracy of 95.05% with a low false-positive rate for detection using computed tomography imaging. Thus, for automatic image renewal to show lung involvement, preliminary results translate into the lung and area affected by SARS-CoV-2. Future works can be done to improve our results, in particular, more databases may include detection of multiple disease cases such as pneumonia, bronchitis. Thus, it may be indicated more information to the classification result.

Keywords: CNN · Image segmentation techniques · SARS-CoV-2 · Health

1 Introduction

The COVID-19 pandemic is an ongoing global coronavirus 2019 pandemic, and researchers are working to find several practical solutions for healthcare

---

Federal University of Alfenas-Minas Gerais-Brazil.

© Springer Nature Switzerland AG 2021
I. Rojas et al. (Eds.): BIOMESIP 2021, LNCS 12940, pp. 405–416, 2021.
https://doi.org/10.1007/978-3-030-88163-4_35

professionals to diagnose patients with COVID-19. In 2019, the COVID-19 pandemic began, and according to the World Health Organization, by 02/08/2021, more than 105.5 million cases and 2.3 million deaths were confirmed [22]. Patients with this clinical lung disease can be detected using computed tomography (CT) examinations of the chest, and exams enable early detection and assessment of the course of the disease [7].

The tomographic characteristics of COVID-19 are related to the duration of the infection: initial stage (0 to 4 days), progressive stage (5–8 days), peak stage (10 to 13 days), and absorption stage (after 14 days) [4]. Besides, we still cannot consider the chest CT pattern as an accurate diagnosis because there are non-specific characteristics of COVID-19. The COVID-19 does not differentiate among other viral pneumonia such as H1N1 and pneumonia. However, a chest CT is one of the main tools used to diagnostic in symptomatic COVID-19 infection along with RRT-PCR and clinical symptoms.

In Brazil, the Brazilian College of Radiology and Diagnostic Imaging (CBR) indicates Computed tomography (CT) for specific cases and medical recommendations to diagnose COVID-19. Since then, we have been working with images of CT of COVID-19 patients. Thus, the aims at providing the deep neural networks (CNN) to classify COVID-19 through chest CT scan, to facilitate early diagnosis of the disease, as well as treatment and possible isolation measures.

In this project, we go beyond statistics and reporting, providing a more accurate assessment. Thus, it will enable new insights that lead to more effective decision-making [17]. The convolutional neural network is demonstrating high performance in extracting features from an image. CNN can classify it from a difference between images [21].

For this project, we collected CT-scan images in the Public Hospital of the Government Employees of Sao Paulo (HSPM) and the Metropolitan Hospital of Lapa. Then, this project aims to contribute to academia about how we can use CNN deep neural networks to classify chest CT-scan images between COVID and Non-COVID.

2   Literature Revision

2.1   AI and Medicine

To start understanding artificial intelligence and its application in medicine. In many works such as [12,13,16,20] present a simple answer that artificial intelligence is the ability of computers to perform activities that require human intelligence.

The doctors and health specialists are taught during years of medical schooling, doing tasks and practical exams, taking grades, and learning from mistakes Artificial Intelligence algorithms also follow the same line of learning. Besides, the AI algorithms require human intelligence to complete, such as pattern and voice recognition, image analysis, and decision making. However, humans need to explicitly tell the computer what they looked for in the image that they provide to the algorithm. However, while some algorithms can compete and sometimes outperform physicians on tasks, they still need to be fully integrated into every-day medical practice. Since these algorithms can significantly impact medicine and enhance the power of medical interventions, numerous regulatory issues need to cite first [2].

2.2   Convolutional Neural Network

Technically, for the deep learning, CNN models train and test, each input image will be passed through a series of convolution layers with filters (Kernels), Pooling, fully connected layers (FC), and the appliance of the Softmax function to classify an object with probabilistic values between 0 and 1.

Convolution is the first layer to extract features from an input image; it preserves the relationship between pixels by learning image features using small squares of input data. The CNN's architecture simulates clusters of neurons to detect attributes of what has been seen, arranged hierarchically and abstractly enough to generalize independently of size, position, and rotation [11]. Some examples of architectures are VGG-19, ResNet-50, Efficient Net, MobileXpert, AlexNet, MobileNet, Inception-v3, Xception, Inception-ResNets, and others. The applications areas of these networks range from disease detection through CT and X-ray images to weather forecast through satellite images.

As for the importance of these architectures, it's the search for automating perceptual, cognitive, and manipulative activities through the computer, bringing greater security in decision-making in jobs that require higher levels of security and processing than the human brain [12]. To understand the differences between the main architectures highlighted, see Table 1.

Performing the analysis of Table 1, it is possible to conclude that there are architectures with less use of memory space and others with better performance. Another point is that the maximum precision achieved in a CNN architecture can influence the classification. Thus, when comparing the models, it is visible that the Mobile Net and EfficientNet architectures stood out in terms of accuracy. Given this study, the VGG-19, Resnet 50, Inception, and Xception architectures have high performance in image feature extraction, especially in the field of medical images, and are easy to apply, allowing for more specific modeling for the problem. As for the results evaluation methods architectures, we analyze learning curves with the accuracy metrics are used to verify the performance and the loss to verify if the validation set is adequate for the problem. For the metric of the algorithm test, precision and F1 scores are used, which identify false-positive predictions.

2.3   Characterization of COVID-19 in the Lung by Chest CT

Thus, to understand how diagnostic COVID-19. The literature search appointed up patterns to classify COVID-19 in CT. Besides, differences among pulmonary infection on CT scan, and evolutionary of the disease and its severity as raised by most of the studies analyzed. For purposes of understanding what each pattern is, through Fig. 1, the patterns perceived by specialists in CT.

Table 1. Main differences between VGG-19, ResNet-50, Efficient Net and MobileNet architectures.

Architectures	Strengths	Negative points	Maximum accuracy achieved	Size of training base used	memory demanded	Parameters
VGG19	The successive smaller convolution nuclei	Accumulation of layers	94,60%	1583-1865	549 MB	143.667.240
ResNet 50	Add layer jumps to eliminate errors	Layer stacking causes network performance degradation	92%	1583-1865	98 MB	23.534.592
Efficient Net	Small and fast architecture	Limitation with new data	96,70%	2482	29 MB	5.330.571
MobileNet	Small architecture, ideal for applications	Difficulty extracting some features such as temperature	97,40%	179	16 MB	4.253.864

Source: Own Elaboration

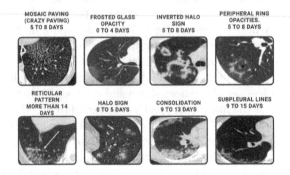

Fig. 1. Covid-19 patterns on chest CT scans. Source: Own authorship based on all works analyzed

2.4 Characterization of COVID-19 Severity in the Lung by Chest CT

When entering works such as Yang [23], Lee [9], Chung [5] and Araújo [1], it appointed that the tomographic findings of pneumonia caused by the coronavirus of severe acute respiratory syndrome 2 (SARS-CoV-2) present reasonably typical patterns of impairment on computed tomography images. These studies also make an association of the degrees of pulmonary involvement of the disease presented by CT images with the clinical picture of patients. See Table 2.

Table 2. Visual characterization of the severity degree by specialists in CT images

TC-chest	Sex	Age	Specialist Diagnosis	Figure
	M	36	COVID-19 in early stage	axial (A) and coronal (B) section
	M	43	COVID-19 in early stage, had a peripheral lesion unilateral in the posterobasal segment of the left lower lobe (yellow rectangles)	axial (A) and coronal (B) section
	M		COVID-19 in progressive stage, smooth thickening of the interlobular and intralobular septum (red arrows) are seen in the posterobasal segment of the lower left lobe	axial (A) and coronal (B) section
	M	35	COVID-19 in critical condition, giving the appearance of a white lung as indicated by the red arrows.	axial (A) and coronal (B) section

Source: Own Elaboration

By associating Fig. 1 with Table 2, it is possible to understand the degree of disease severity according to the symptoms that a given person may present, as well as the degree of pulmonary impairment. Regarding the understanding of how the disease can behave about evolution to a critical condition, as was presented by the Pan American Health Organization-PAHO, the following report:

"Most people (about 80%) recover from the disease without needing hospital treatment. One in six people infected with COVID-19 becomes seriously ill and develops difficulty breathing. Elderly, and those with other health conditions such as high blood pressure, heart, lung problems, diabetes, or cancer are at greater risk of becoming seriously ill. However, anyone can take COVID-19 and become seriously ill" [14, p. 1]

Thus, it was possible to identify a consistent pattern of tomographic findings in the study participants. Besides, these findings allow the distinction between different stages of disease evolution through pulmonary involvement.

3 Methodology

The Fig. 2, it is possible to see the simplified general structure of the application of this project, in which we have the input of CT scans of a new patient, which in turn an artificial neural network already trained to detect COVID-19. If you present any characteristic of the disease, this image flows automatic segmentation image. Then, the segmentation of the compromised area of the lung. Then returns the degree of pulmonary compromise of the patient.

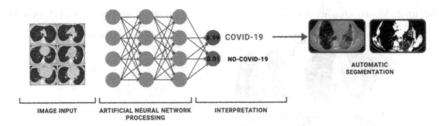

Fig. 2. Project overview. Source: Own Elaboration

3.1 Data Base

For this project, we used the chest computed tomography database collected in the Harvard Dataverse, available since May 2020. This dataset were collected in the Public Hospital of the Government Employees of Sao Paulo (HSPM) and the Metropolitan Hospital of Lapa, both in Sao Paulo - Brazil.

Which currently contains 4,173 CT scans of 210 different patients, out of which 2,168 correspond to 80 patients infected with SARS-CoV-2 and confirmed by RT-PCR. The dataset is composed of CT scans in png format, which has 758 correspond to 50 healthy patients, 2,168 CT scans for patients infected by SARS-CoV-2, and 1,247 correspond to 80 patients with other pulmonary directions. 20 CT scans per patient on average. See Fig. 3.

3.2 Machine Learning

CNN is composed of several layers that use the convolution operation to perform such feature extraction [18]. From a filter, through the entire network input and operates in an analogous way to the superposition of receptive fields.

A Convolutional Neural Network (CNN) is one of the main categories of neural networks for classifying images. Among the CNNs, we selected the VGG-19 network for the extraction of characteristics from COVID-19 positive cases.

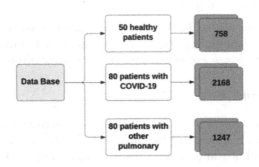

Fig. 3. Data base. Source: Own Elaboration

Each image enters through a series of layers of convolutions with filters, pooling, connection, and applying the softmax function to classify the object with probabilistic values between 0 and 1 [19].

The first layer has the function of extracting image features, and in this way, the model learns the patterns that differentiate lung CT images through a combination of information sources, and that we are trying to learn to identify patterns in the exams with the features that differentiate between a lung with COVID-19.

3.3   Learning Training

Then, all CNNs were parameterizing as the basic structures used were added to the Dense network with 128 neurons after adding the Pooling layer, which will reduce the resolution of each image by average and added to Flatten so that it can better understand the exams.

To reduce overfitting, a Dropout method was used, which will turn off 5 neurons and try to train with these 5 neurons, and thus manage to regularize the neural network. The Batch Normalization technique was also used, which during training is done with normalization at each pass by neurons and this will increase the stability of the neural network. And for a compilation of the model a binary cross-entropy is used, which has the role of assigning values between 0 or 1, and the Adam optimizer, which makes a stochastic gradient descent, maintains a single learning rate each time it updates the weights of the neural network. For training, the cross-validation technique was also used [3].

The metric used for optimization and selection of the best models during learning was the Adam Optimizer to evaluate the prediction hit performance in a stochastic way. Computer simulations were performed to assess the accuracy of the deep learning method.

Another method that we applied was Ensemble. Where each model is used to make a prediction from calculated as the weighted average of the predictions. Therefore expect to reduce the error still further if we give greater weight to some members than to others. Thus, we consider a generalization. The architectures included in the ensemble were VGG-19, RestNet 50, Inception and Xception.

3.4   Metrics

For the analysis of results, we apply Accuracy. Accuracy is the most direct way to evaluate a neural network model: we make a prediction, look at the predicted label, and then compare it to the training or test. If the values agree, the model is correct. Then, we can do this for all the data we have and see the proportion of the examples correctly predicted [15]. Equation 1 Follows the calculation of the Accuracy.

$$accuracy = \frac{TP + TN}{TP + FP + TN + FN} \tag{1}$$

3.5   Automatic Segmentation

Automatic segmentation is one of the last steps in the COVID-19 identification process. After the execution in the neural network, it is possible to segment the COVID-19 and the lung and thus calculate the pulmonary impairment by calculating the volume. For this project, the segmentation of the area affected by COVID-19 was performed, applying image processing algorithms and use information from medical images in DICOM format.

After loading the image, the histogram of the HU (Hounsfield Units) values. Each pixel of the image has an assigned HU value, and this value is available due to the DICOM format of the image; the HU represents a value on the radiodensity scale, allowing us to identify materials in the exams according to their density value.

During the experiment, we observe that COVID-19 has a HU value in the range $[-150, -300]$, but it is found more specifically in the range $[-200, -300]$. As for the calculation of pulmonary impairment. See Fig. 4.

3.6   Application

Before the segmentation, it is necessary to format and clean the image. Thus, the first step is to transform through the Curvature Flow Image Filter, when we add a filter to smooth the image but keeping its border and contour properties. Then, the Label Statistics Image Filter is executed, which calculates image values such as maximum, minimum, variance, mean, and intensity. These values will use in other functions.

Through the Signed Maurer Distance Map and Threshold Segmentation Image Filter, we have calculated the pixels segmentation, given the differences of HU for the COVID-19, in the interval $[-300, -200]$. With the segmentation pixels defined, it is possible to display them over the original image, providing an easy view of the affected areas, as shown in Fig. 5.

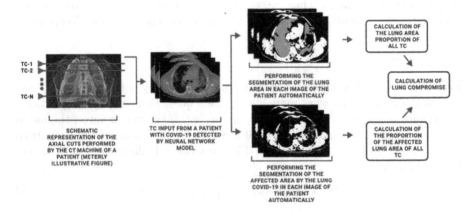

Fig. 4. Steps for calculating lung involvement from a CT image. Source: Own Elaboration

4   Results

We design and conduct comprehensive experiments to assess the performance of models in classifying and locating the area affected by COVID-19. To obtain a holistic view of the model's behavior, we investigate the performance from loss functions and adjustment parameter values for image classification. The parameters used are undefined in Table 3.

In evaluating the model, we first report the classification accuracy to select the best models under different hyper-parameter values Table 3, followed by the systematic assessment of the discriminant power of the differentiation between the COVID-19 and Healthy classes. With the transfer learning of the pre-trained networks, VGG-19, Resnet 50, Inception V3 and Xception with the set of cases of lung diseases, when performed weighted average between the predictions of the neural networks demonstrates remarkably high accuracy of 0.9505 in the classification of CT-scan images.

From this table, we can see that the CNN that stood out was VGG-19 and that the detection of COVID-19 for COVID images versus other diseases still needs to be improved. We apply the ensemble with a weight of 0.5 for VGG, 0.1 for ResNet, 0.3 for Inception, and 0.1 for Xception. We have an improvement in inaccuracy. The final result was 95.05% of accuracy. See Table 4.

Table 3. Hyperparameters for the construction of the classifying neural network.

PAR METERS	VALUE
IMAGE_SIZE	224x224
batch_size	32
epochs	120
learning_rate	0,001
loss	binary_crossentropy|
optimize	adam

Source: Own Elaboration

Table 4. Accuracy of each model.

	VGG-19	Resnet 50	Inception V3	Xception
Accuracy	97.73%	83.41%	85,74%	89,59%
Weight	0.5	0.1	0.3	0.1

Source: Own Elaboration

The results Hounsfield (HU) scale proved to be efficient in capturing the following patterns: Consolidation, Inverted Halo Sign, subpleural lines, reticular pattern, and mosaic paving since these patterns showed HU values within the range of $[-200, -300]$ and did not show confusion with other parts of the lung. Features with less sharpness, such as ground-glass opacity and Halo signal, did not classify by this automatic method because the range of values for its detection ends up being confused with air, which in turn ends up catching the lung as a whole.

It is noteworthy that to capture these features the best path is semi-automatic segmentation methods based on the expert's inference in the location of the patterns and application of their search in a clustering algorithm based on statistical models. In this sense, it is possible to see some segmentation's performed through Fig. 5.

As can be seen in Fig. 5, the segmentation based on the Hounsfield scale (HU) accurately captures the dense consolidations in the lung instead of captures the ground-glass opacity.

Regarding the calculation of pulmonary impairment, this reflects the amount of segmented pixels, which is shown as a reflection of the applied segmentation, which in turn, is only useful for the specialist to have an estimate closer to the patient's reality in a more precise way than the visual assessment.

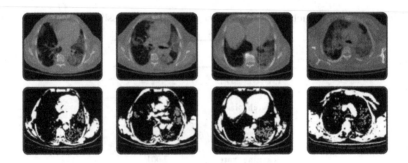

Fig. 5. Segmentation of the affected area of a patient with COVID-19. Source: Own Elaboration

5 Conclusion

To conclude, we observe that, in general, the performance is considered regular, and an increase in the database is suggested. In this way, we can conclude that. The construction of a single image per patient and the use of the ensemble technique with four CNN's offers satisfactory results for the detection of COVID-19 from chest CT images.

Although classifying CT scan appears to be successful. The CNN has some problems during classify cases between COVID-19 and Other Diseases generate ambiguity because both have similarities from the hazy opacity that is not obscure. And also, the small number of images available in the database found further aggravates the situation.

And so, the application of trained models for classification and medical images can help hospital triage at points of care for other human diseases, such as pulmonary abnormalities. For future work, we would like to test with other different dataset and study the possibility of detecting other diseases, such as pneumonia and tuberculosis.

References

1. Araujo, J.D.A.B., Sawamura, M.V.Y., Teixeira, F.B., Apanavicius, A., Costa, A.N.: Temporal evolution of tomographic findings of pulmonary infection in COVID-19. Einstein (São Paulo) **18** (2020)
2. Barreto, J.: Inteligência artificial no limiar do século XXI. Florianópolis: PPP edições **97** (1999)
3. Bock, S., Goppold, J., Weib, M.: An improvement of the convergence proof of the ADAM-optimizer. arXiv preprint arXiv:1804.10587 (2018)
4. Chate, R.: Apresentação tomográfica da infecção pulmonar na COVID-19: experiência brasileira inicial. Jornal Brasileiro de Pneumologia **46**(2) (2020)
5. Chung, M., et al.: CT imaging features of 2019 novel coronavirus (2019-nCoV). Radiology **295**(1), 202–207 (2020)
6. Clinical management of COVID-19. Interim guidance. Geneva: World Health Organization, 27 May 2020. Homepage, https://www.who.int/publications-detail/clinical-management-of-covid-19. Accessed 28 May 2020
7. Fan, B.: Hematologic parameters in patients with COVID-19 infection: a reply. Am. J. Hematol. **95**(6), E131–E134 (2020)
8. KERAS: Aplicativos Keras. Homepage https://keras.io/api/applications/
9. Lee, E.Y.: Practical pediatric imaging. Issue Radiol. Clin. North Am. E-Book **55**(4), 609–904 (2017). Elsevier Health Sciences. Homepage, https://neupsykey.com/lung/
10. Li, X., Li, C., Zhu, D.: COVID-MobileXpert: on-device COVID-19 patient triage and follow-up using chest X-rays. In: 2020 IEEE International Conference on Bioinformatics and Biomedicine (BIBM), pp. 1063–1067. IEEE (2020)
11. Lecun, Y.: Reconhecimento de objetos com aprendizagem baseada em gradientes. In: Forma, contorno e agrupamento em visão computacional, pp. 319–345. Springer, Heidelberg (1999)
12. Lobo, L.: Inteligência artificial e medicina. Revista Brasileira de Educação Médica **41**(2), 185–193 (2017)
13. Moldoveanu, M.: Intelligent Artificiality (2013)
14. Organização Pan-Americana da Sáude-OPAS, (2021). Folha informativa sobre COVID-19, Homepage. https://www.paho.org/pt/covid19
15. Orwant, J.: Algoritmos de masterização com Perl. O'Reilly Media, Inc., Sebastopol (1999)
16. Rouhiainen, L.: Inteligencia Artificial. Alienta Editorial, Madrid (2018)
17. Santos, H.: Machine learning para análises preditivas em saúde: exemplo de aplicação para predizer óbito em idosos de São Paulo, Brasil. Cad. Saúde Pública, **35**(7), e00050818 (2019)
18. Simonyan, K., Zisserman, A.: Very deep convolutional networks for large-scale image recognition. arXiv preprint arXiv:1409.1556 (2014)

19. Szegedy, C.: Inception-v4, inception-resnet and the impact of residual connections on learning. In: Proceedings of the AAAI Conference on Artificial Intelligence (2017)
20. Veen, M.: Intelligent Artificiality (2005)
21. Wang, S.: Um algoritmo de aprendizado profundo que usa imagens de TC para detectar a doença do vírus Corona (COVID-19). MedRxiv (2020)
22. WHO, Dados Covid-19, Homepage. https://covid19.who.int/
23. Yang, Q., Liu, Q., Xu, H., Lu, H., Liu, S., Li, H.: Imaging of coronavirus disease 2019: a Chinese expert consensus statement. Eur. J. Radiol. **120**, 109008 (2020)

COVID-19. General

Risk Group Determination in Case of COVID-19 Infection

Borys Biletskyy$^{(\boxtimes)}$ and Anatoliy Gupal

V. M. Glushkov Institute of Cybernetics, Kyiv 03187, Ukraine
borys.biletskyy@incyb.kiev.ua

Abstract. The possibility of quick decoding of individual human genome has allowed us to amass vast data arrays of diseases, as well as associated human DNA mutations. It is well-known that DNA mutations cause genetic diseases and disorders. Among the risk group of severe coronavirus disease cases are patients with preexisting cardiovascular or respiratory diseases, oncologic pathologies, hypertension, and other disorders. Coronavirus disease severity can be predicted using machine learning methods trained on features corresponding to single nucleotide polymorphisms in gene coding sequences of patient genomes.

Keywords: Coronavirus disease severity prediction · Single nucleotide polymorphism · Naïve Bayes classifier

1 Introduction

Coronavirus Disease. Coronavirus disease is a contagious disease caused by SARS-CoV-2 virus. The virus was identified in China, in Winter 2019 and it quickly reached the level of pandemic. As of Summer 2021, there are more than 190 million confirmed cases, and more than 4.14 million confirmed deaths related to the virus.

The global impact of COVID-19 is hard to estimate. There are various dimensions of this problem including impact on world economy, healthcare, media, society, culture, entertainment, political and other aspects.

Symptoms of coronavirus disease can greatly vary. They may include fever, cough, headache, fatigue, breathing difficulties, loss of smell and taste. Coronavirus disease case severity can be very different:

- In 1/3 of cases the symptoms are not noticeable enough to consider their carriers as patients [1]
- 2/3 of cases develop noticeable enough symptoms [2]:

  o 80% have mild or moderate symptoms up to pneumonia
  o 15% have severe symptoms like dyspnea, hypoxia, or massive lung damage
  o 5% have critical symptoms like respiratory failure, shock, multiorgan dysfunction

© Springer Nature Switzerland AG 2021
I. Rojas et al. (Eds.): BIOMESIP 2021, LNCS 12940, pp. 419–430, 2021.
https://doi.org/10.1007/978-3-030-88163-4_36

There are ongoing multi-year studies to investigate the long-term effects of the coronavirus disease [3]. Long term effects include respiratory system disorders, nervous system and neurocognitive disorders, mental health disorders, metabolic disorders, cardiovascular disorders, gastrointestinal disorders, malaise, fatigue, musculoskeletal pain, and anemia according to [4].

Ability to predict accurately the severity of each coronavirus disease case could greatly improve the efficiency of our preventing measures, treating severe cases patients, managing healthcare resources, and dealing with post coronavirus disease disorders.

Coronavirus Disease Risk Factors. Multiple studies identify various factors that can relate to the severity of the coronavirus disease. The most studied factors are the following:

- SARS-CoV-2 variants. Different virus variants appear due to mutations which accumulate in virus genomes. There are around 300000 genomic sequences associated with SARS-CoV-2 collected worldwide [5]. Those sequences are grouped into variants, clades and lineages. The most concerning mutations are labelled, for instance Alpha, Beta, Gamma, Delta, etc. There are on-going investigations of risks related to different SARS-CoV-2 variants [6].
- Age. It is well known that the coronavirus disease case severity depends greatly on the age of the patient. While children are less exposed to the severe forms of the disease, 85+ years old patients have 28.3% infection fatality rate [7].
- Gender. In most countries coronavirus disease fatality rates are higher among men than women, but there are exceptions [8].
- Pre-existing conditions. Most of fatal case patients were suffering from pre-existing diseases and disorders [9]. Such conditions often play an important role in coronavirus disease severity prediction. Among the most concerning pre-existing conditions are the following: hypertension, diabetes mellitus, cardiovascular disease, asthma, and tuberculosis.
- Other. Other patient's conditions that associated with high coronavirus disease case severity, for instance ethnic differences, smoking habits or pregnancy. Local factors such as the level of healthcare system and its availability, the access to the clean water, working conditions and others can play an important role in coronavirus disease associated risk evaluation.

Machine Learning for Coronavirus Disease Severity Prediction. There are around 200 million COVID-19 cases reported worldwide. Large volumes of clinical and laboratory data were collected about the coronavirus disease. The publicly available data sources are discussed in [10]. The availability of data makes machine learning widely used for learning to make predictions about the severity of coronavirus disease. Various machine learning techniques are investigated such as LSTM, XGBoost, Naïve Bayes, SVM, etc. and there are various approaches to using those methods for predicting the severity of coronavirus disease [11]. Among the broad variety of approaches there are two extents based on training datasets.

One extent contains methods based on complex multi-domain datasets. Most effective machine learning algorithms make advantage of using complex data structures for training and making predictions. Therefore, the most complete and enriched data sources are always preferable because they provide predictions based on different aspects of patient information. An example of such approach is the method discussed in [12] where researchers predict mortality in next 7 and 28 days based on various clinical and laboratory data. Initial dataset contained 2370 patient records. Each record contained 63 attributes, describing different aspects of patient condition, among them:

- basic: age, gender, exposure history, travel history, the number of days of symptoms before admission
- vitals: temperature, oxygen saturation, rate of respiration, pulse rate
- symptoms: fever, cough, shortness of breath
- history of associated chronic diseases: diabetes, hypertension, heart and kidney disease, cancer
- laboratory: complete hemogram, kidney and liver profile tests, coagulation profile

Out of 63 only 23 attributes were selected as significant. XGBoost algorithm was used and reached the performance: AUC of 97%, sensitivity of 81.9%, and specificity of 97.9%

The use of complex patient data which includes clinical and laboratory data provides most reliable results as it benefits from various aspects of patient information. Collecting such data is quite complex and expensive procedure which is based on well-defined standards and require planning, special equipment, and trained stuff with multidomain experience. The necessary setup might be unavailable in the areas with poor healthcare, then the collection of complete and enriched data sources can be a challenge. It might be problematic to collect the necessary data due to lack of technology, expertise or funding. Even for countries with developed health care systems the lack of standardization of data collection and data exchange protocols can complicate the process of merging datasets collected in different facilities by following different protocols. Moreover, the required clinical and laboratory data are often obtained only after patient's hospitalization when the case is severe already. It is problematic to apply such methods for preventing measures.

Another extent is represented by methods based on simple datasets. Such datasets normally contain one or few aspects of patient information. They are easy to collect and to process, which makes such approach more practical in the circumstances of training data shortage. One example is discussed in [13] where COVID-19 diagnosis was predicted based on routine blood tests, age and gender. The dataset of 52306 patients (with only 160 positive cases in it) was used for training 2 models (a positive and negative one). 33 most significant blood test features were selected out of 117. Method demonstrated performance: AUC of 0.97, sensitivity of 81.9% and a specificity of 97.9%.

The use of less complete (but easier to collect) patient data, like blood samples in the example above, can be beneficial and more practical in some areas with poor healthcare and lack of equipment and expertise. A single aspect of patient information often can be collected and processed at the same facility without external dependencies. In some cases self-tests are possible when patients can collect their analysis at home and send biomaterial samples to the testing facility for further analysis. Another benefit of such approach is higher chance of using it in preventive measures. The easier the medical testing procedure is the more willingly people undergo the test.

2 Prediction of Coronavirus Disease Severity Based on Genetic Mutations

Current research extends the previous work by one of co-authors [14] and proposes a method in between the described above approaches. New method should benefit from using different aspects of patient data, like methods of the first group. In the same very time, new method should be based on easy to collect and process datasets making such methods available, like the methods of the second group.

Those criteria can be satisfied by using the specific type of mutations in patient genomes that are associated with disorders and diseases identified as preexisting conditions of sever coronavirus disease cases. Such training features provide information about different aspects of patient organism.

In case of using SNP mutations as prediction features patient data collection can be quite affordable as the full genome sequencing is not necessary. Information about SNP mutations in the patient genome are extracted from patient's saliva sample. The biomaterial collection procedure is simple and can be executed be patients at home. All SNP features are collected in one saliva test which costs around 200 Euro per patient.

There are numerous mutations identified in human genes associated with wide variety of disorders and diseases. The simplest type of mutations is SPN which occurs when a single nucleotide is substituted by another nucleotide. Depending on their locations SNP mutations can have different effects on the organism.

Mutations are quite rare events; their rate is estimated as 10^{-8} mutations per genome per generation, which means around 30 mutations in human genome, containing $3 * 10^9$ base pairs in total. We can assume that mutations are independent for all classes of severity cases. Based on conditional independence assumption Naïve Bayes methods can be applied for prediction of case severity based on SNP data. Naïve Bayes approach is known to be optimal for classification of data structures with independent features. Due to the factorization Naïve Bayes methods are effective under the circumstances of limited train data availability. There are several variations of Naïve Bayes method applicable depending on the interpretation of patient data. Bernoulli and Categorical variations of Naïve Bayes are the most applicable for severity classification based on patient SNP data.

Diseases and Disorders Associated with Gene Mutations. Nowadays decoding (sequencing) of patient genomes for medical purposes can be afforded in many countries as the cost of "reading genomes" is constantly dropping. The obtained genetic information is used for the early diagnosis of different diseases. The main task of this area is to determine genetic predisposition to complex diseases such as cardiovascular diseases, cancer, diabetes, and schizophrenia. For each disease, there exists a certain gene set, mutations in which raise the risk of disease development.

The most common mutations type causing diseases is point mutations or Single Nucleotide Polymorphisms (SNP). SNP occurs when a single nucleotide in some gene

Table 1. Examples of disease or disorder associated SNP mutations

Disease/Disorder	SNP ID	GENE ID	Original Triplet	utated Triplet	Original AA	utated AA
High blood pressure	rs17376328	CLCN6	-	-	-	-
High blood pressure	rs198358	NPPA-AS1	-	-	-	-
High blood pressure	rs3754777	STK39	-	-	-	-
High blood pressure	rs6749447	STK39	-	-	-	-
High blood pressure	rs5370	EDN1	AAG	AAT	Lys	Asn
Cardiovascular disease	rs1799983	NOS3	GAT	GAG	Asp	Glu
Cardiovascular disease	rs9536314	KL	TTT	GTT	Phe	Val
Cardiovascular disease	rs9527025	KL	TGC	TCC	Cys	Ser
Cardiovascular disease	rs4970834	CELSR2	-	-	-	-
Cardiovascular disease	rs2774279	ARHGAP30	AGG	AGA	Arg	Arg
Cardiovascular disease	rs2943634	-	-	-	-	-
Cardiovascular disease	rs5370	EDN1	AAG	AAT	Lys	Asn
Cardiovascular disease	rs326	LPL	-	-	-	-
Cardiovascular disease	rs1800588	LIPC	-	-	-	-
Cardiovascular disease	rs183130	-	-	-	-	-
Cardiovascular disease	rs2229616	MC4R	GTC	ATC	Val	Ile
Cardiovascular disease	rs3843763	-	-	-	-	-

is replaced by another nucleotide. SNP mutations can arise spontaneously due to DNA replication errors, they can be a result of mutagen influence, such as high temperatures, chemical substances, impacts of ultraviolet light or X-ray radiation.

Effects of SNP mutations greatly vary. Some SNP mutations are silent, when such mutations occur the nucleotide substitution does not change the product amino acid due to the redundancy of the genetic code. In some other cases SNP mutations can result in the amino acid substitutions in product proteins. Such mutations can cause protein spatial structure corruption followed by the loss of the protein function, which is usually very harmful for the organism. There are cases when SNP mutations cause amino acid substitutions with preservation of the polarity of amino acids. Such cases are less severe as the function of the product protein is often preserved but with some loss of efficiency. SNP mutations can cause errors of alternative splicing which also results in the loss of protein function.

Workflow. The complete workflow of the proposed method of coronavirus disease severity prediction based on SNP features consists of multiple steps, see Fig. 1. The process is meant to be available and affordable with automated execution and minimum human factor involved. But there are some workflow steps that are more expensive and more time consuming due to the involvement of equipment and skilled personnel. Therefore, coordination and planning of workflow activities is very important.

The workflow consists of 4 main steps:

1. Preparation. The goal of this step is to prepare all the necessary infrastructure for the next step (Data Collection). This step is quite time consuming and expensive as it is poorly automated and involves skilled personnel and equipment. Preparation step is executed only once at the beginning of the whole process.

   a) Identification of diseases and disorders. Domain experts must identify locally specific disorders and diseases associated with severe coronavirus disease cases. Such disorders can include the ones identified as preconditions of severe coronavirus disease cases: hypertension or cardiovascular disease.

   b) Identification of SNP mutations. Once the diseases and disorders are identified the next step is to identify the associated SNP mutations. Such information can be collected from online data sources, like NCBI in our case.

   c) SNP details collection. Once the SNP mutations are identified we need to enrich them with genomic details. Each SNP record must be enriched with gene identifier where the mutation occurred, the reference sequence and the mutated sequence.

   d) Patient data collection setup. The goal of this step is to prepare infrastructure for smooth patient data collection. Information about SNP mutations retrieved on the previous step is used to prepare the process of detecting mutations from patient's saliva sample. Preselecting SNP mutations in advance at the previous steps allows to omit the expensive process of complete genome sequencing and reduce procedure cost from ~ \$10000 to ~ \$200.

2. Data collection. The goal of this step is to collect patient SNP data and to extract prediction features.

    a. Biomaterial collection. The goal of this stage is to collect patient saliva samples. If the process was set up properly this manipulation should be possible to execute by patients at home.

    b. SNP mutations detection. During this stage the saliva samples are process using prepared special equipment and the information about SNP mutations is extracted. This stage is semi-automatic, it requires expensive equipment and trained staff.

    c. Patient data pre-processing. Extracted SNP data must be pre-processed. The corrupt data records and outliers are removed. Data are normalized.

    d. Feature engineering. The considered SNP mutations used as ML features were pre-selected by domain experts. This choose should be tested with data. During feature selection the most significant SNP features are extracted for further training and prediction.

3. Training. During this stage training data are transformed into trained models ready to make predictions.

    a. Data labeling. Before data can be used for training, they must be labeled with target values which is coronavirus disease case severity.

    b. Model training. During this stage labeled training data are transformed into a trained model ready to make prediction. This stage is executed automatically, but it can be time consuming depending and on the size of training dataset and on the specific ML method used.

    c. Model Evaluation. During its lifecycle model get trained and evaluated multiple times. This process is automatic due to predefined evaluation metrics. Commonly used ML model evaluation metrics for classification problems are Accuracy, Precision and Recall.

    d. Hyper parameter tuning. Some model parameters con not be estimated from training datasets during ML Model training, for example the number of training features used in the model or feature significance threshold. The process of finding such parameter values uses cross validation together with some strategy of hyper parameter space discovery. The best hyper parameter values are obtained as the result of multiple rounds of data splitting into training and testing subsets, model training and evaluation. The best model is deployed for serving predictions. This step can be time consuming depending on the size of train data and on ML methods used.

4. Prediction. At this stage the trained model is used for making case severity predictions by patient SNP data. Only the meaningful SNP mutation features are extracted and used for prediction. Once the model is trained it can make prediction very fast.

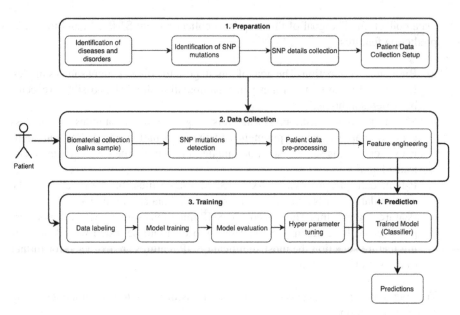

Fig. 1. Workflow of the coronavirus disease severity prediction system

Data. Preparation for patient data collection requires information about SNP mutations enriched by genomic and protein data. Such details include the location of SNP mutation, original and mutated nucleotides, clinical significance, original amino acid, mutated amino acid. Selected SNPs are used to prepare the process of patient data collection from patient saliva samples.

ML Models training requires patient SNP data merged with coronavirus disease case severity. There are no publicly available data sources containing such information. Training datasets are proposed to be collected from the patients' salvia samples using semi-automated procedure. One saliva test allows to identify all SNP features $x_1, \ldots, x_n$, where each feature $x_i \in \{0, 1\}$ is a Boolean identifiers of specific SNP mutations in patient's genome, $x_i = 1$ if the i-th SNP is detected in patient's DNA and $x_i = 0$ otherwise.

Methods. Naïve Bayes methods are proposed for coronavirus disease severity classification based on patient SNP mutations data. The Naïve version of Bayes method was selected due to the assumption of conditional independence of SNP mutations in patient genomes in each severity class of cases. Bayes classifier maximizes the probability of patient record $x \in X$ in the severity class $y \in X$

$$y = argmax_{y \in Y} P(x_1, \ldots, x_n | y) P(y) \tag{1}$$

The conditional independence of features assumption allows to factorize of the classifier (1) as follows

$$y = argmax_{y \in Y} \prod_{i=1}^{n} P_i(x_i | y) P(y) \tag{2}$$

In such representation the classifier can be efficiently used on small training datasets.

Different variations of Naive Bayes are applicable depending on the interpretation of features $x_1, \ldots, x_n$ and the assumptions on conditional probability in (2). In the basic setup features $x_1, \ldots, x_n$ correspond to n pre-selected SNP mutations, where each feature $x_i \in \{0, 1\}$ is a binary value indicating if the corresponding SNP is present in the patient's genome. In such case features $x_1, \ldots, x_n$ can be interpreted as independent Bernoulli variables and Bernoulli version of Naïve Byes classifier is applicable.

$$y = argmax_{y \in Y} \prod_{i=1}^{n} [p_{iy}x_i + (1 - p_{iy})(1 - x_i)]P(y) \qquad (3)$$

Bernoulli Naïve Bayes classifier represents the conditional probability $P(x_1, \ldots, x_n|y)$ as the product of probabilities $p_{iy}x_i + (1 - p_{iy})(1 - x_i)$, where p_{iy} is the probability of SNP i occurring among patient records with case severity y, and $P(y)$ is the probability of occurrence of case with severity y.

SNP mutations indicators are not actually independent because some of them can be mutually exclusive, for instance different substitutions of the same nucleole. Taking that into account we can group SNP data by genes and interpret features $x_1, \ldots, x_n$ as n categorical variables, representing n genes shich the selected SNP mutations are associated with. Each patient feature $x_i \in X_i$ is a categorical variable representing different possible variants of the i-th gene. Different gene variants are results of applying a single SNP mutation. This approach assumes that multiple mutations in one gene are rare and all available gene variants are results of a single SNP mutation. Cases violating this assumption can be filtered out during data pre-processing. The Categorical version of Naïve Bayes classifier has the following view

$$y = argmax_{y \in Y} \prod_{i=1}^{n} p_i(x_i|y)P(y) \qquad (4)$$

where $p_i(x_i|y)$ is probability of x_i variant of the i-th gene occurring in the severity class y. According to the study on upper and lower complexity bounds for Machine Learning algorithms [15] Categorical Naïve Bayes is optimal (hard to significantly improve) for conditionally independent categorical features.

3 Preliminary Results

Inflammation Processes Prediction Using Categorical Naïve Bayes. The proposed approach was tested in similar clinical environment with training data shortage. Categorical Naïve Bayes classifier was previously used to predict inflammation processes in brain gliomas by the research team members [16]. This method was selected due shortage of training data. Training data had to be extracted from patient's blood samples using semi-automatic procedure.

Distributed Declarative Machine Learning Pipelines. Solving ML problem is more than training ML models and using them to make predictions. ML Pipeline consists of different stages, like data collection, preprocessing, cleaning, feature extraction, prediction evaluation, hyper-parameter tuning (Fig. 2). Defining and maintaining complex ML

Pipelines can be a challenging task. Their execution on large datasets and optimization can be non-trivial.

The challenges above can be addressed by the open-source project [17] designed by one of co-authors. This framework simplifies the process of distributed ML Pipelines definition and execution. The framework allows to define ML Pipelines declaratively. Managed ML Pipelines are horizontally scalable, the framework supports distributed execution out of the box.

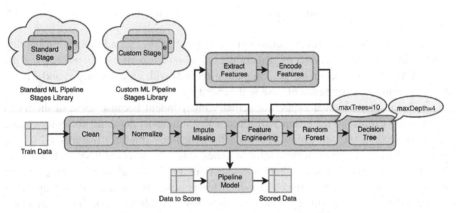

Fig. 2. Example of machine learning pipeline

The proposed framework is based on Spark – distributed computation framework for in-memory computing with APIs available in different programming languages including Scala, Java, Python and R. The proposed extension of Spark ML Pipelines API provides additional means for efficient organization, maintenance and reuse of data transformations within ML Pipelines.

ML Pipelines model is based on several basic assumptions (see Fig. 3):

- ML Pipelines consist of sequential stages. The stages are chained in such a way that stage outputs are forwarded to inputs of the next stage.
- ML Pipeline stages can be of 2 types:

  o Transformers ($T : Data \rightarrow Data$) transform the input dataset and return the results to output. Transformers are the most used type of ML Pipeline stage. Trained ML models are transformers: they transform the input datasets with encoded features by adding the predictions column.
  o Estimators ($E : Data \rightarrow T$) transforms the input dataset and returns a transformer. Estimators are stages responsible for ML models training. Estimators perform features dataset processing to calculate model parameters and return the trained model represented by a Transformer.

- ML Pipelines are stages too. ML Pipelines can be nested inside other ML Pipelines as stages. This property allows to reuse definitions. New ML Pipeline stages can be defined using the existing stages. Stage definitions can be grouped by the level of abstraction of their functions in the ML Pipeline.

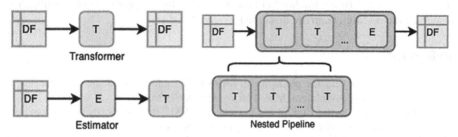

Fig. 3. Two types of ML pipeline stages: transformer and estimator and ML pipeline nesting

Scalability by default together with declarative definitions of ML Pipelines allows Spark to optimize the process of the ML Pipelines execution. Scalable data transformations are interpreted by Spark as sequences of primitive operations (map, reduce) satisfying some algebraic properties which make them easy to scale horizontally. Such low-level representations of ML pipelines allow Spark to guarantee horizontal scalability of ML Pipelines. Low-level representations based on primitives allow to use algebraic properties of primitives for optimization of ML Pipeline execution.

Distributed Categorical Naïve Bayes Method. Spark ML provides built in implementations of Bernoulli and Multivariate Naïve Byes methods. Categorical version of Naïve Bayes is not available among standard Spark ML classification methods. Therefore, Categorical Naïve Bayes was implemented as a pair of custom Estimator and Transformer. Estimator's role is to process training data and to constructs a transformer. The resulting transformer represents the trained model, its role is making predictions based on new patient data. The method is implemented in Scala and available as on open-source project by one of co-authors [18].

Disease Associated SNPs Retrieval and Analysis. Disease associated SNP data ingestion pipelines were built using R programming language. The pipelines are available as open-source project [19] by one of co-authors. The developed pipeline merges data from several online NCBI data sources. The resulting dataset contains SNP data, such as location, original nucleotide, mutated nucleotide, original amino acid and mutated amino acid, as shown in Table 1.

4 Summary

A method for prediction coronavirus disease cases severity is proposed. The proposed method uses SNP mutations associated with diseases and disorders identified as preconditions of severe coronavirus disease cases. Patient data for ML models training is obtained from patients' saliva samples. Collected biomaterial is processed to identify the presence of selected SNPs in patient genomes. Collected datasets are labeled by coronavirus disease severity levels and used for training of ML models. Due to the shortage of training data and some specifics of features selected for model training Categorical or Bernoulli Naïve Bayes methods are recommended to be applied. Some preliminary results by the research team are discussed.

References

1. Oran, D.P., Topol, E.J.: The proportion of SARS-CoV-2 infections that are asymptomatic: a systematic review. Ann. Intern. Med. **174**(5), 5655–5662 (2021)
2. U.S. Centers for Disease Control and Prevention (CDS). https://www.cdc.gov/coronavirus/2019-ncov/hcp/clinical-guidance-management-patients.html
3. U.S. Centers for Disease Control and Prevention (CDS). https://www.cdc.gov/coronavirus/2019-ncov/long-term-effects.html
4. Al-Aly, Z., Xie, Y., Bowe, B.: High-dimensional characterization of post-acute sequelae of COVID-19. Nature **594**(7862), 259–264 (2021)
5. Thomson, E.C., et al.: Circulating SARS-CoV-2 spike N439K variants maintain fitness while evading antibody-mediated immunity. Cell **184**(5), 1171–1187 (2021)
6. World Health Organization. https://www.who.int/en/activities/tracking-SARS-CoV-2-variants/
7. Levin, A.T., Hanage, W.P., Owusu-Boaitey, N., Cochran, K.B., Walsh, S.P., Meyerowitz-Katz, G.: Assessing the age specificity of infection fatality rates for COVID-19: systematic review, meta-analysis, and public policy implications. Eur. J. Epidemiol. **35**(12), 1123–1138 (2020). https://doi.org/10.1007/s10654-020-00698-1
8. Dehingia, N., Raj, A.: Sex differences in COVID-19 case fatality: do we know enough? Lancet Glob. Health **9**(1), 14–15 (2021)
9. WHO Director-General's Statement on the Advice of the IHR Emergency Committee on Novel Coronavirus. https://www.who.int/director-general/speeches/detail/who-director-general-s-statement-on-the-advice-of-the-ihr-emergency-committee-on-novel-coronavirus
10. Tayarani, N.M.-H.: Applications of artificial intelligence in battling against covid-19: a literature review. Chaos Solitons Fractals **142**, 110338 (2020)
11. Alballa, N., Al-Turaiki, I.: Machine learning approaches in COVID-19 diagnosis, mortality, and severity risk prediction: a review. Inform. Med. Unlocked **24**, 100564 (2021)
12. Kar, S., Chawla, R., Haranath, S.P., et al.: Multivariable mortality risk prediction using machine learning for COVID-19 patients at admission (AICOVID). Sci Rep **11**, 12801 (2021)
13. Kukar, M., et al.: COVID-19 diagnosis by routine blood tests using machine learning. Sci. Rep. **11**(1), 10738 (2021)
14. Vagis, A.A., Gupal, A.M., Sergienko, I.V.: Determination of risk groups for the Covid-19 underlying diseases. Cybern. Syst. Anal. **57**(2), 223–227 (2021). https://doi.org/10.1007/s10559-021-00347-9
15. Gupal, A.M., Pashko, S.V., Sergienko, I.V.: Efficiency of Bayesian classification procedure. Cybern. Syst. Anal. **31**(4), 543–554 (1995). https://doi.org/10.1007/BF02366409
16. Gridina, N.J., Gupal, A.M., Tarasov, A.L.: Bayesian recognition of inflammatory processes in brain gliomas. Cybern. Syst. Anal. **53**(3), 366–372 (2017). https://doi.org/10.1007/s10559-017-9936-4
17. Pipeline-oriented Analytics on GitHub. https://github.com/bbiletskyy/pipeline-oriented-analytics
18. Categorical Bayes Method on GitHub. https://github.com/bbiletskyy/categorical-bayes
19. SNP Retrieval on GitHub. https://github.com/bbiletskyy/snp-retrieval

COVID-19 Biomarkers Detection Using 'KnowSeq' R Package

Javier Bajo-Morales$^{(\boxtimes)}$ ⓘ, Daniel Castillo-Secilla ⓘ, Luis Javier Herrera,
and Ignacio Rojas ⓘ

Department of Computer Architecture and Technology, University of Granada
C.I.T.I.C., Periodista Rafael Gomez Montero, 2, 18014 Granada, Spain
jbajo@ugr.es

Abstract. *'KnowSeq'* R Package includes all the essential tools to carry out transcriptomic analysis, providing intuitive functions to build efficient and robust pipelines. In this paper, its capacities are demonstrated in a practical COVID-19 biomarkers detection problem using RNA-Sequencing data. Through Machine Learning techniques such as feature selection and supervised classification models, a clinical decision system for COVID-19 was developed using four genes proposed as COVID-19 signature: *OAS3, CXCL9, IFITM1* and *IFIT3*. These four genes are highly related to different processes that affect the immune system behaviour and its response when facing viruses such as SARS-CoV-2. The final model reaches an accuracy over 97% when predicting over unseen samples.

Keywords: COVID-19 · KnowSeq · Biomarker · RNA-Seq · Machine learning

1 Introduction

Since the 2000s, the available transcriptomic data has increased enormously [1], largely due to the reduction in the cost of sequencing the human genome [2] and the new possibilities opened up by bioinformatics. This new medical paradigm brings to the table a much more personalized medicine, in which each individual can be treated in a more precise and targeted manner [3–6]. Using biological data such as genomic data [7], medical imaging [8] or electric signal [9] among others, as input data for Machine Learning and Deep Learning models [10–13], it is possible to get closer to that personalized medicine.

As aforementioned, previous studies have implemented several Machine Learning and Deep Learning techniques to develop recognition and clinical decision support systems (CDSS) for many diseases using different biological data. This includes the novel coronavirus 19 disease (COVID-19) caused by a severe coronavirus acute respiratory syndrome coronavirus 2 (SARS-CoV-2) [14–17].

Large scale RNA-Sequencing (RNA-Seq) is a transcriptomic technology, framed within Next Generation Sequencing (NGS) [18], which allows for determining the presence and quantity of RNA in a biological sample at a given moment

© Springer Nature Switzerland AG 2021
I. Rojas et al. (Eds.): BIOMESIP 2021, LNCS 12940, pp. 431–443, 2021.
https://doi.org/10.1007/978-3-030-88163-4_37

in a precise manner [19]. RNA-Seq has been established as the predominant transcriptomic technology due to its precision and noise reduction compared to other
well-known technologies such as Microarray [20]. RNA-Seq has been widely used
to obtain gene signatures for different diseases such as cancer, [21,22] or viruses
such as influenza [23,24]. These gene signatures are usually obtained through a
Differentially Expressed Genes (DEGs) [25] analysis between disease status. By
implementing Machine Learning techniques, CDSS are built using gene signatures
as features to predict samples status. Through this pipeline, it is possible to better
understand the genetic influence on the development of a given disease, selecting
better treatments and knowing possibles outcomes beforehand. Among the most
relevant Machine Learning techniques used in this field, the following stand out:

- Feature selection algorithm: The human genome is composed of 30.000 genes
  approximately. In order to extract a reduced gene signature of 2–10 genes,
  it is necessary to select the most relevant features (genes). For this purpose,
  several feature selection algorithms have been implemented in previous studies
  [26–28].
- Supervised classification models: Classification models are usually built to
  assess the performance of the genes selected as a predictive and clinical decision tool [29]. Support Vector Machines (SVM) [30], Random Forest (RF) [31]
  or k-Nearest Neighbors (k-NN) [32] are some of the most known supervised
  model used for this task.

KnowSeq. R package developed by D. Castillo-Secilla et al. [33] encom-
passes different feature selection algorithms and supervised classification models,
together with other interesting tools such as outliers detection system, plotting
tools and other functionalities that help researchers to carry out their transcriptomic analysis and build their diagnosis systems. In this work, in order to
demonstrate the performance and capabilities of *KnowSeq*, SARS-CoV-2 complete transcriptomic analysis was carried out. Developing an intelligent, efficient
and robust *KnowSeq* pipeline. The main objectives were to obtain a small number of genes that could work as a SARS-CoV-2 gene signature, developing also
a COVID-19 CDSS.

2   Methods

This section shows all the steps followed to carry out the study. A theoretical explanation of each stage is presented together with the *KnowSeq* functions
to perform each one. *KnowSeq* can be downloaded from Bioconductor repository [34]. All scripts and documentation can be found at https://github.com/
CasedUgr/KnowSeq. Figure 1 shows the flowchart of the followed pipeline, in
which, for each step, the respective *KnowSeq* function is detailed.

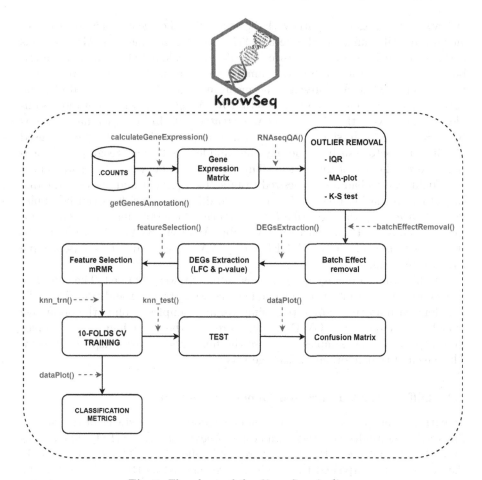

Fig. 1. Flowchart of the *KnowSeq* pipeline.

2.1   Preprocessing

Following a robust preprocessing step is crucial to ensure quality results. RNA-Seq data for this experiment was obtained from the public repository NCBI/GEO [35]. Although more detailed information on the raw data will be provided later in the text, it should be noted that counts files are available. Thus, the first step consisted of getting gene expression data from the counts files that contain the reads for each gene. To complete this task, it was necessary to normalize the reads for each gene in the counts files using gene lengths and Guanine-Cytosine (GC) content. Through *getGenesAnnotation()* and *calculate-GeneExpressionValues()* gene expression values were obtained.

Afterward, two quality processes to remove unwanted data and reduce dispersion were carried out. Firstly, an outliers detection step was done. This process consisted of a majority voting system between three different tests. The first one was a Kolmogorov Smirnov (K-S) test [36]. The second one consisted of an interquartile range (IQR) method [37]. For the last method, MA-plot was performed and Hoeffding's statistic (Da) [38] was calculated on the joint distribution of A and M for each of the samples to try to find outliers. M represents the log ratio, while A represents the mean average [39]. The removal of these outliers, *KnowSeq* integrates the function *RNASeqQA()*. Once, unwanted samples were removed, the Batch effect was treated [40]. In biological data such as RNA-Seq gene expression, it exists an intrinsic deviation in the data, caused by different factors such as the day the sample was taking, geographical location or even the age of the patient. This deviation is known as the Batch effect and could lead to bad and undesired results. To remove it and preserve the disease status deviation presented in the data, different algorithms can be implemented. *KnowSeq*, through *batchEffectRemoval()* function, integrates two algorithms, Combat [41] and Surrogate Variable Analysis (SVA) [42]. Attending to the characteristic of the NCBI/GEO data, SVA was carried out because sample batches were unknown.

At this point, a quality gene expression matrix was obtained. The complete matrix was divided into two independent datasets, training and test. The split was done with an 80%–20% ratio, using training samples to build the predictive model and extract the COVID-19 signature. On the other hand, test samples were kept as unseen samples to assess the final model over independent data. This ensured that information leakage was nil.

2.2   Differentially Expressed Genes Extraction

To extract genes whose expression differs according to the status of the sample (infected or non-infected), two parameters, $Log_2FoldChange$ (LFC) [43] and p-value, had to be tuned. By setting threshold values for LFC and p-value, only the genes which surpassed these value, were selected as DEGs. To ensure the robustness in DEGs extraction, 5 folds Cross-Validation (CV) strategy was followed. Only the genes that was selected in all folds, were labelled as DEGs. Thus, the relation and dependency between DEGs and the samples was reduced, and robustness of the DEGs selected increased. It is important to note that the 5-folds CV made this filter more restrictive, decreasing the number of genes selected compared to the number of genes we would get if we did this process with all the training samples together without CV. Therefore, LFC and p-value could not be set too restrictive in order to get some genes out of this filter. Different combinations of LFC and p-value were tested trying to extract the optimal number of the most differentially expressed genes. If the number of extracted DEGs is too low, the feature selection algorithm becomes meaningless. Otherwise, a large number of DEGs would imply that genes not too differentially expressed between disease states would be selected. This CV strategy was carried out using only the 80% training samples, test samples was not used to extract these DEGs. To carried out this 5-folds CV DEGs extraction process, the *DEGsExtraction()* function was used, tuning CV parameter to *TRUE* and numFolds parameter to 5.

2.3   Feature Selection

The aim of this step was to get a ranking of the DEGs selected in the previous step, reducing, even more, the dimensionality of the problem. This ranking was obtained by applying a feature selection algorithm, concretely, *minimum Redundancy Maximum Relevance* (mRMR). It is based on the mutual information (MI) concept, providing a ranking of genes that calculates, for each gene, the maximum information while ensuring the minimum redundancy with the already selected genes in the ranking [44]. *KnowSeq* provides a function, *featureSelection()*, which implements different feature selection algorithms such as Random Forest (RF) or mRMR.

2.4   Classification Model

Once mRMR was applied, the features (genes) that would be used to build the predictive model were known. Not only that, mRMR provides an order/sequencing of the most important genes. Still using the 80% training dataset, the first step was training the supervised model. For this purpose, a 10-folds CV training process was carried out. Attending to CV results, the hyperparameter of the model and the exact number of genes used to predict were selected. Here, the COVID-19 gene signature was defined. Next, the 20% test dataset was used to assess the model. *KnowSeq* implements three supervised classification models, k-NN, SVM and RF. Even though all of them performed greatly with our data, k-NN was selected due to its less computational cost, as our dataset was not too large, but especially for its interpretability. As shown in Fig. 1, *KnowSeq* function to train the model is *knn_trn()*, specifying with CV and numFolds parameters the characteristics named before. To carry out the prediction over test samples, *knn_test()* function is integrated in *KnowSeq*.

2.5   Graphical Plots

It is crucial to visualize the results through different plots that capture the model performance, as well as how great the genes selected distinguish between samples labelled differently. *KnowSeq* integrates several plotting tools that allow the researcher to get clean and visuals plots of their transcriptomic analysis. Through *dataPlot()* function it is possible to obtain graphics such as confusion matrixes, gene expression boxplots or gene expression heatmaps. To select which one to plot, the parameter *mode* must be defined.

The only plot that was not obtained with *KnowSeq* was T-Distributed Stochastic Neighbour Embedding (T-SNE) plot. Usually, the number of genes selected as gene signature is bigger than 2. Therefore, in order to obtain a 2-Dimensional scatter plot, it is necessary to apply a feature reduction algorithm such as Principal Component Analysis (PCA) or T-SNE. T-SNE is a non-linear technique used for dimensionality reduction [45]. Plot was built using *tsne()* function from *M3C* R package [46].

3   Results and Discussions

Transcriptomic RNA-Seq data were obtained from NCBI/GEO repository under GSE152075 ID. The data contain information about 484 nasopharyngeal swabs divided into SARS-CoV-2 positive samples and negative samples. The data were unbalanced, 430 out of 484 samples were positive and the rest were negative. Once, outliers detection was carried out, the number of samples was reduced to 454, being 28 of the outliers positive samples and 2 negative. At this point, training and test splits were created and DEGs extraction process started (Table 1).

Table 1. Data description.

GSE152075	Nᵒ Samples	Nᵒ Outliers	Total samples
Positive	430	28	402
Negative	54	2	52
Total	484	30	**454**

LFC threshold value was tuned to 2 and p-value to 0.05. Using these parameter values, only 7 genes were common DEGs across all folds. Thus, after carrying out the CV DEGs extraction process *CXCL10, CXCL9, IFI44L, IFIT1, IFIT3, IFITM1* and *OAS3* were selected at first instance as possible COVID-19 biomarkers. Comprehensive functional analysis and literature review of these genes revealed that they are highly related to different important cellular responses and regulation processes in virus infections. Concretely, *IFIT1, IFI44L, OAS3, IFIT3* and *IFITM1* [47–50] play a key role in interferon (IFN)-mediated activation of the immune response. On the other hand, *CXCL10* and *CXCL9* play a key role in the cytokine storm produced in COVID-19 infected patients [51,52]. In Fig. 2, gene expression boxplots of these 7 genes were plotted, comparing positive and negatives distributions. It can be seen that all DEGs were overexpressed in SARS-CoV-2 samples over the healthy samples. Several previous studies in the literature highlight the importance of up-regulation of these genes in COVID-19 infection, modulating the immune response to the virus. [53–58].

Next, mRMR was applied and a ranking of these 7 genes was obtained. Through this feature selection algorithm the respective genes order achieved was:

1. *OAS3*
2. *CXCL9*
3. *IFITM1*
4. *IFIT3*
5. *CXCL10*
6. *IFIT1*
7. *IFI44L*

Therefore, they were used sequentially to train the predictive model and select the most efficient COVID-19 gene signature.

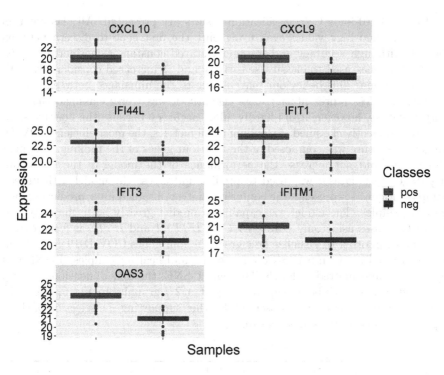

Fig. 2. Gene expression boxplots of the 7 genes extracted as COVID-19 DEGs through 5-folds CV LFC analysis.

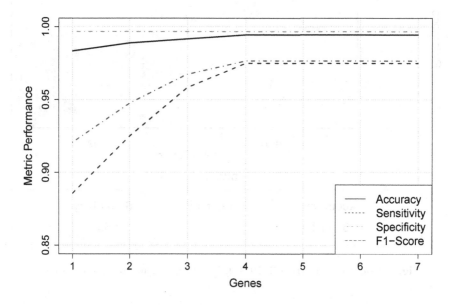

Fig. 3. 10-folds CV results using mRMR + k-NN.

In Fig. 3, 10-folds CV classification results are presented. All classification metrics reached high values even using only the first gene to discern between classes. Although accuracy and specificity stayed constant when increasing the number of genes used to classify, sensitivity and f1 increased considerably until the fourth gene. This behaviour may be due to the unbalance between classes. Initially, the less representative class (negative), was worse classified than the majority class, however, it did hardly affect accuracy because the positive samples were correctly classified. Attending to all metrics, the most efficient COVID-19 gene signature was composed of the first four genes of the ranking. The next three genes did not increase the performance of the model in the CV training stage. Test dataset was used to predict and assess the model with unseen samples. Figure 4 represents the confusion matrix obtained after predicting over 90 test samples. The model was capable to predict greatly both, majority and minority classes using only *OAS3*, *CXCL9*, *IFITM1* and *IFIT3* as features.

Finally, in order to visualize how great the four genes COVID-19 gene signature discerned between SARS-CoV-2 samples and healthy samples, T-SNE was carried out and plotted in Fig. 5. Through T-SNE, the four dimensions (genes) were reduced to two, being capable to plot a 2D graphic. In Fig. 5, two well-differentiated clusters can be observed. Further supporting the selection of these 4 genes as COVID-19 gene signature.

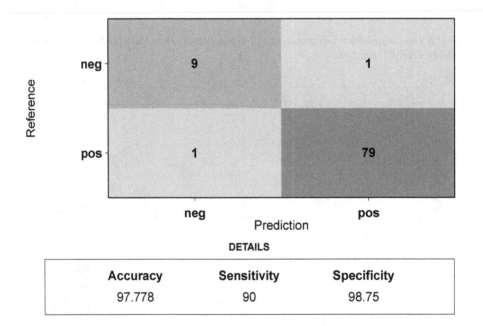

Fig. 4. Confusion matrix mRMR + k-NN using 4 genes to predict in test.

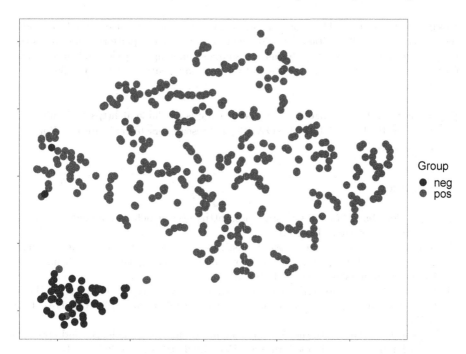

Fig. 5. Scatter plot of all samples by applying T-SNE to the four genes selected as COVID-19 gene signature.

4   Conclusions

Throughout this research, *KnowSeq* R package capabilities and functionalities were presented by targeting host transcriptomic response to SARS-CoV-2 problem. Data was acquired through NCBI/GEO repository under GSE152075 ID, being counts files for each sample available. Exploiting *KnowSeq* tools we were able to extract four genes, *OAS3*, *CXCL9*, *IFITM1* and *IFIT3*, as our COVID-19 gene signature. After a detailed literature review of these four genes, we concluded that they are closely related to host defence pathways against viruses such as interferon type I response and chemokine receptors and are up-regulated in infected SARS-CoV-2 samples compared to healthy samples.

Using these genes as features, a k-NN classification model was built, reaching an accuracy over 97% in test, after a 5-folds CV training stage. Therefore, an effective COVID-19 CDSS capable of discerning with high accuracy an infected sample from a healthy sample was developed. Due to the novelty of SARS-CoV-2, there is still a scarcity of COVID-19 transcriptomic data. Therefore, future lines of work could be oriented towards the integration of heterogeneous data sources and batches to increase the number of samples, providing greater robustness and significance to the results obtained.

Acknowledgements. This work was funded by the Government of Andalusia under the Project CV20-64934 titled "Development of an intelligent platform that allows the integration of heterogeneous information sources (imaging, genetics and proteomics) for the characterization and prediction of virulence and pathogenicity in patients with COVID-19".

Supplemetary Information. Open source code is available at https://github.com/jbajo09/BIOMESIP-COVID19-KNOWSEQ for researchers to replicate the *KnowSeq* pipeline proposed.

References

1. NCBI. Genbank and WGS statistics. https://www.ncbi.nlm.nih.gov/genbank/statistics/. Accessed May 2021
2. National human genome research institute. the cost of sequencing a human genome. https://www.genome.gov/about-genomics/fact-sheets/Sequencing-Human-Genome-cost. Accessed May 2021
3. Fernald, G.H., Capriotti, E., Daneshjou, R., Karczewski, K.J., Altman, R.B.: Bioinformatics challenges for personalized medicine. Bioinformatics **27**(13), 1741–1748 (2011)
4. Overby, C.L., Tarczy-Hornoch, P.: Personalized medicine: challenges and opportunities for translational bioinformatics. Pers. Med. **10**(5), 453–462 (2013)
5. Suwinski, P., Ong, C., Ling, M.H., Poh, Y.M., Khan, A.M., Ong, H.S.: Advancing personalized medicine through the application of whole exome sequencing and big data analytics. Front. Genet. **10**, 49 (2019)
6. Lightbody, G., et al.: Review of applications of high-throughput sequencing in personalized medicine: barriers and facilitators of future progress in research and clinical application. Briefings Bioinform. **20**(5), 1795–1811 (2019)
7. Castillo, D., et al.: Leukemia multiclass assessment and classification from microarray and rna-seq technologies integration at gene expression level. PloS One **14**(2), e0212127 (2019)
8. Fan, Z., Jamil, M., Sadiq, M.T., Huang, X., Yu, X.: Exploiting multiple optimizers with transfer learning techniques for the identification of COVID-19 patients. J. Healthcare Eng. **2020**, 8889412 (2020)
9. Akbari, H., et al.: Depression recognition based on the reconstruction of phase space of eeg signals and geometrical features. Appl. Acoust. **179**, 108078 (2021)
10. Sadiq, M.T., Yu, X., Yuan, Z.: Exploiting dimensionality reduction and neural network techniques for the development of expert brain–computer interfaces. Expert Syst. Appl. **164**, 114031 (2021)
11. Hassantabar, S., Wang, Z., Jha, N.K.: SCANN: synthesis of compact and accurate neural networks. arXiv preprint arXiv:1904.09090 (2019)
12. Hassantabar, S., Dai, X., Jha, N.K.: Steerage: synthesis of neural networks using architecture search and grow-and-prune methods. arXiv preprint arXiv:1912.05831 (2019)
13. Hassantabar, S., Terway, P., Jha, N.K.: Tutor: training neural networks using decision rules as model priors. arXiv preprint arXiv:2010.05429 (2020)
14. Hassantabar, S., et al.: COVIDDEEP: SARS-COV-2/COVID-19 test based on wearable medical sensors and efficient neural networks. arXiv preprint arXiv:2007.10497 (2020)

15. Imran, A., et al.: AI4COVID-19: AI enabled preliminary diagnosis for COVID-19 from cough samples via an app. Inform. Med. Unlocked **20**, 100378 (2020)
16. Farooq, M., Hafeez, A.: COVID-ResNet: a deep learning framework for screening of covid19 from radiographs. arXiv preprint arXiv:2003.14395 (2020)
17. Hassantabar, S., Ahmadi, M., Sharifi, A.: Diagnosis and detection of infected tissue of COVID-19 patients based on lung x-ray image using convolutional neural network approaches. Chaos Solitons Fractals **140**, 110170 (2020)
18. Besser, J., Carleton, H.A., Gerner-Smidt, P., Lindsey, R.L., Trees, E.: Next-generation sequencing technologies and their application to the study and control of bacterial infections. Clin. Microbiol. Infection **24**(4), 335–341 (2018)
19. Ozsolak, F., Milos, P.M.: RNA sequencing: advances, challenges and opportunities. Nat. Rev. Genet. **12**(2), 87–98 (2011)
20. Technology networks. RNA-Seq: Basics, applications and protocol. https://www.technologynetworks.com/genomics/articles/rna-seq-basics-applications-and-protocol-299461. Accessed May 2021
21. Wang, C., et al.: RNA-Seq profiling of circular RNA in human lung adenocarcinoma and squamous cell carcinoma. Mol. Cancer **18**(1), 1–6 (2019)
22. Wang, J., Dean, D.C., Hornicek, F.J., Shi, H., Duan, Z.: RNA sequencing (RNA-Seq) and its application in ovarian cancer. Gynecol. Oncol. **152**(1), 194–201 (2019)
23. Andres-Terre, M., et al.: Integrated, multi-cohort analysis identifies conserved transcriptional signatures across multiple respiratory viruses. Immunity **43**(6), 1199–1211 (2015)
24. Woods, C.W., et al.: A host transcriptional signature for presymptomatic detection of infection in humans exposed to influenza H1N1 or H3N2. PloS One **8**(1), e52198 (2013)
25. Wang, D., Li, J.R., Zhang, Y.H., Chen, L., Huang, T., Cai, Y.D.: Identification of differentially expressed genes between original breast cancer and xenograft using machine learning algorithms. Genes **9**(3), 155 (2018)
26. Townes, F.W., Hicks, S.C., Aryee, M.J., Irizarry, R.A.: Feature selection and dimension reduction for single-cell RNA-Seq based on a multinomial model. Genome Biol. **20**(1), 1–16 (2019)
27. Saeys, Y., Inza, I., Larranaga, P.: A review of feature selection techniques in bioinformatics. Bioinformatics **23**(19), 2507–2517 (2007)
28. Lee, C.P., Leu, Y.: A novel hybrid feature selection method for microarray data analysis. Appl. Soft Comput. **11**(1), 208–213 (2011)
29. Ayyad, S.M., Saleh, A.I., Labib, L.M.: Gene expression cancer classification using modified k-nearest neighbors technique. Biosystems **176**, 41–51 (2019)
30. Cristianini, N., Shawe-Taylor, J., et al.: An Introduction to Support Vector Machines and Other Kernel-Based Learning Methods. Cambridge University Press, Cambridge (2000)
31. Breiman, L.: Random forests. Mach. Learn. **45**(1), 5–32 (2001)
32. Cover, T., Hart, P.: Nearest neighbor pattern classification. IEEE Trans. Inf. Theory **13**(1), 21–27 (1967)
33. Castillo-Secilla, D., et al.: KnowSeq R-Bioc package: the automatic smart gene expression tool for retrieving relevant biological knowledge. Comput. Biol. Med. **133**, 104387 (2021)
34. Gentleman, R.C., et al.: Bioconductor: open software development for computational biology and bioinformatics. Genome Biol. **5**(10), 1–16 (2004)
35. Barrett, T., et al.: NCBI geo: archive for functional genomics data sets—update. Nucl. Acids Res. **41**(D1), D991–D995 (2012)

36. Massey, F.J., Jr.: The Kolmogorov-Smirnov test for goodness of fit. J. Am. Stat. Assoc. **46**(253), 68–78 (1951)
37. Walfish, S.: A review of statistical outlier methods. Pharm. Technol. **30**(11), 82 (2006)
38. Fujita, A., Sato, J.R., Demasi, M.A.A., Sogayar, M.C., Ferreira, C.E., Miyano, S.: Comparing Pearson, Spearman and Hoeffding's d measure for gene expression association analysis. J. Bioinform. Comput. Biol. **7**(04), 663–684 (2009)
39. Dudoit, S., Fridlyand, J., Speed, T.P.: Comparison of discrimination methods for the classification of tumors using gene expression data. J. Am. Stat. Assoc. **97**(457), 77–87 (2002)
40. Lazar, C., et al.: Batch effect removal methods for microarray gene expression data integration: a survey. Briefings Bioinform. **14**(4), 469–490 (2013)
41. Zhang, Y., Parmigiani, G., Johnson, W.E.: Combat-seq: batch effect adjustment for RNA-Seq count data. NAR Genom. Bioinform. **2**(3), lqaa078 (2020)
42. Leek, J.T., Storey, J.D.: Capturing heterogeneity in gene expression studies by surrogate variable analysis. PLoS Genet. **3**(9), e161 (2007)
43. Love, M.I., Huber, W., Anders, S.: Moderated estimation of fold change and dispersion for RNA-Seq data with DESeq2. Genome Biol. **15**(12), 1–21 (2014)
44. Peng, H., Long, F., Ding, C.: Feature selection based on mutual information criteria of max-dependency, max-relevance, and min-redundancy. IEEE Trans. Pattern Anal. Mach. Intell. **27**(8), 1226–1238 (2005)
45. Van der Maaten, L., Hinton, G.: Visualizing data using t-SNE. J. Mach. Learn. Res. **9**(11), 2579–2605 (2008)
46. John, C.R., et al.: M3c: Monte Carlo reference-based consensus clustering. Sci. Rep. **10**(1), 1–14 (2020)
47. DeDiego, M.L., Martinez-Sobrido, L., Topham, D.J.: Novel functions of IFI44l as a feedback regulator of host antiviral responses. J. Virol. **93**(21), e01159-19 (2019)
48. Fensterl, V., Sen, G.C.: The ISG56/IFIT1 gene family. J. Interferon Cytokine Res. **31**(1), 71–78 (2011)
49. Yang, G., Xu, Y., Chen, X., Hu, G.: IFITM1 plays an essential role in the antiproliferative action of interferon-γ. Oncogene **26**(4), 594–603 (2007)
50. Rebouillat, D., Hovanessian, A.G.: The human 2', 5'-oligoadenylate synthetase family: interferon-induced proteins with unique enzymatic properties. J. Interferon Cytokine Res. **19**(4), 295–308 (1999)
51. Coperchini, F., Chiovato, L., Ricci, G., Croce, L., Magri, F., Rotondi, M.: The cytokine storm in COVID-19: further advances in our understanding the role of specific chemokines involved. Cytokine Growth Factor Rev. **58**, 82–91 (2021)
52. Coperchini, F., Chiovato, L., Rotondi, M.: Interleukin-6, CXCL10 and infiltrating macrophages in COVID-19-related cytokine storm: not one for all but all for one! Front. Immunol. **12**, 668507 (2021)
53. Shaath, H., Vishnubalaji, R., Elkord, E., Alajez, N.M.: Single-cell transcriptome analysis highlights a role for neutrophils and inflammatory macrophages in the pathogenesis of severe COVID-19. Cells **9**(11), 2374 (2020)
54. Jain, R., et al.: Host transcriptomic profiling of COVID-19 patients with mild, moderate, and severe clinical outcomes. Comput. Struct. Biotechnol. J. **19**, 153–160 (2021)
55. Blot, M., et al.: CXCL10 could drive longer duration of mechanical ventilation during COVID-19 ARDS. Critical Care **24**(1), 1–15 (2020)
56. Callahan, V., et al.: The pro-inflammatory chemokines CXCL9, CXCL10 and CXCL11 are upregulated following SARS-COV-2 infection in an AKT-dependent manner. Viruses **13**(6), 1062 (2021)

57. Zhou, S., et al.: A neanderthal OAS1 isoform protects individuals of European ancestry against COVID-19 susceptibility and severity. Nat. Med. **27**(4), 659–667 (2021)
58. Wu, M., et al.: Profiling Covid-19 genetic research: a data-driven study utilizing intelligent bibliometrics. Front. Res. Metrics Analytics **6**, 30 (2021)

Exit Strategy from COVID-19: Vaccination and Alternate Solution

Indrani Roy[(✉)] [ID]

IRDR, University College London (UCL), London, UK
indrani.roy@ucl.ac.uk, indrani_r@hotmail.com

Abstract. Vaccination groups all over the globe made a strong coordinated effort to put an end to the current COVID-19 crisis. Since vaccination started first in the UK on 8th December 2020, we have sufficient data to analyze and derive useful results. It addressed issues viz. seasonality, indirect consequences of mass vaccination and fast mutation of the virus after mass vaccination. To develop useful timely insights, some similarities between COVID-19 and Flu received attention. Critical and open analyses, balanced discussion in the current crucial stage are desperately needed. Questioning, debating and criticism are always the basis of good science and the main pillars to its advancement. With that objective in mind, it is an effort to explore areas relating to the effectiveness of COVID-19 vaccines with a pragmatic viewpoint. Policymakers will be greatly benefitted from such analyses. An alternative optimistic pathway is also mentioned which was proposed as early as 17th March 2020 and is practically without side effects and no vested interest involved.

Keywords: COVID-19 · Temperature · Exit strategy · Solution · Seasonality · Mass vaccination

This analysis explores few important aspects of current COVID-19 situations from pragmatic viewpoints. In this context, an alternate optimistic pathway is also discussed.

1 Effects of Lockdown vs. Vaccination vs. Seasonality

In winter, many countries showed a sudden surge. After the imposition of strict lockdown, surges are likely to be reduced. Moreover, different countries started vaccination at different time of the winter; some started early winter e.g. the UK (8th December 2020 [1]) whereas, some started late e.g. South Africa (17th February 2021 [2]). It is beneficial to study the effects of Lockdown vs. Vaccination vs. Seasonality in various countries.

For UK and Israel, the 2nd peak was much stronger than the first one (Fig. 1). For both countries, the second peak occurred after vaccination started. South Africa did not start vaccination till 17th February, but the 2nd wave peaked same time with the UK and Israel (around mid-January). Not only that but also the 2nd wave was **falling**

Electronic supplementary material The online version of this chapter (https://doi.org/10.1007/978-3-030-88163-4_38) contains supplementary material, which is available to authorized users.

I. Rojas et al. (Eds.): BIOMESIP 2021, LNCS 12940, pp. 444–459, 2021.
https://doi.org/10.1007/978-3-030-88163-4_38

much faster than UK and Israel upto 17th February [2] (Fig. 1). Even for the UK and Israel, where massive vaccination took place, the total deaths in the three months after vaccination (also had strict lockdown), reached the overall death of the past 10 months before vaccination [2].

The UK had much higher vaccination than any other EU country. Also, the UK showed the highest daily Deaths than any other EU country [3, see 7-day average till 28th February]. The UK had a strict lockdown and as expected Death is decreasing in late winter (Fig. 2).

A success story on vaccination in Israel attracted global attention [4]. However, a study [5] authored by Dr Hervé Seligmann, a scientist from the Faculty of Medicine, Aix-Marseille University, France who is of Israeli-Luxembourg nationality rejected the success story that claimed Israel could be a role model. That study raised issues towards unsubstantiated claims and biased analyses and suggested a mismatch between data published by authorities with the observed reality. It explored how after vaccination started, the overall outcome of the health situation in Israel deteriorated in various respects.

UAE had much high vaccination and it started on 14th Dec, 2020 [6]. Some days after the start of vaccination, there is a very steep rise in Cases and thereafter a steep rise in Deaths (Fig. 3). Similar surges are noticed for India, Brazil, Bangladesh and Pakistan among others [3]. Globally, Cases and Deaths started increasing after 5 weeks of a steady decline [3] and coincidentally, the period of recent rise matches when major

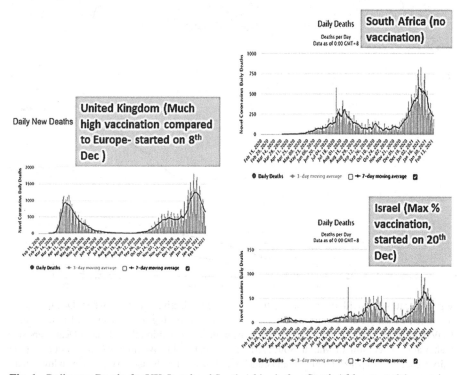

Fig. 1. Daily new Deaths for UK, Israel and South Africa before South Africa started the vaccination programme (on 17/02/21). The seven-day moving average is marked by a thick line. (https://www.worldometers.info/coronavirus/country/, accessed on 17/02/2021)

vaccinations programme was initiated worldwide. A highly populated country India was having a steady decrease for five months. India did not have any lockdown. Though neighbouring countries Pakistan and Bangladesh experienced the 2nd wave this winter but India did not. India passed major festive seasons where social distancing was very difficult to be maintained, still cases and deaths continued to decline. There is a sudden reversal in the trend of cases and deaths in India, from declining to rising, within a month after the start of vaccination.

a)

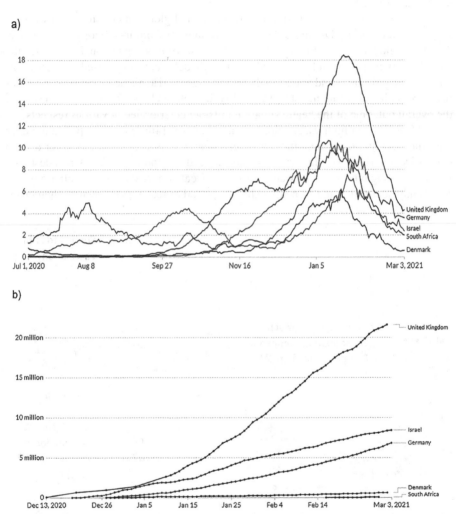

b)

Fig. 2. Deaths of Covid-19 and Vaccination data of few selective countries, where Deaths peaked in winter. a) daily new confirmed Deaths per million in rolling 7-day average, b) cumulative COVID vaccination dose. Israel and UK had the highest vaccination though daily Deaths are still higher at the beginning of March. South Africa practically did have nominal vaccination, but the daily Death though peaked higher than Israel but falling at a much faster pace and even lower than Israel. Source: [https://ourworldindata.org/coronavirus-data-explorer].

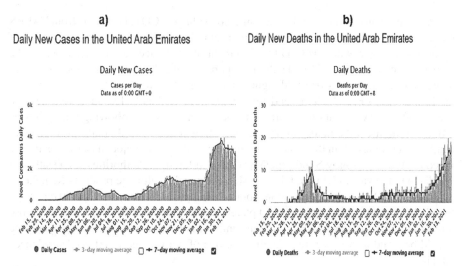

Fig. 3. Daily new Cases (a) and Deaths (b) for the United Arab Emirates (UAE). Seven-day moving averages are marked by coloured thick lines. Vaccination programme started on 14th December [6]. Source: (https://www.worldometers.info/coronavirus/country/united-arab-emirates/)

Thus, it could be of interest to check which country showed a decrease after the vaccination started, eliminating the effect of lockdown and seasonality.

2   Reporting of Short-Term Adverse Effects After Vaccination

In the short time frame of clinical trials, there are hardly any possibilities to test the medium and long-term adverse effects. Even for the short term, only few thousand people took part in trials among which half were given Placebo. Many complicated interactions among various underlying health issues are likely to be missed and could not be tested due to the small sample size.

For short term adverse effects, recent data also raised questions [7]. In the United States, a total of 1136 individuals have died till 26th February after receiving mRNA vaccines for COVID-19. A total of 587 (51.7 percent) died within a week; among those who died, 94 (8.3 percent) died on the same day, 150 (13.2 percent) died the day after, 105 died 2 days after, and 68 within 3 days [7, 8]. More recent record upto April 5, 2021 shows VAERS received 2,794 reports of death among vaccinated people [9]. Cardiac arrest was one of the main causes of death; whereas, blood clots, anaphylaxis, temporary facial paralysis and Bell's palsy were reported among the majority of other critical patients. It would be advisable to track all these vaccinated people afterwards and to note if they were affected by any of **those particular diseases** in later stages or not. Also, a monitoring system could be proposed to check if deaths caused due to some of those specific symptoms/diseases exceeds normal count or not in the coming months. Such anomaly counts of death or symptom could give some ideas of medium and long-term side effects, if any, due to vaccination.

A comparison between deaths after Influenza (Flu) and COVID vaccine from VAERS reports gives useful information. For Flu vaccine in 2019 influenza season, a total of 45 deaths occurred which is 0.0000265 percent of total vaccination. Whereas, for the COVID vaccine, a total of 1136 deaths are reported as of Feb. 26, which is approximately a rate of .0024 percent, a 100-fold higher than reported deaths after the Flu vaccine [8].

In India as of March 29, around 180 people have died and 617 had serious adverse events following vaccination, according to the Adverse Events Following Immunisation (AEFI) committee, the main government reporting centre [10]. A major proportion of deaths occurred less than three days after the vaccination and major causes of deaths are noted as Acute Coronary Syndrome/Myocardial Infarction. Authorities say Deaths are unrelated to the vaccine. In the UK, the Medicines and Healthcare products Regulatory Agency (MHRA), a govt organisation reported that upto March 31, there are 79 reports of blood clots accompanied by low blood platelet count. A total of 19 people died, of those three were under the age of 30 [11]. Currently, it is concluded that clotting syndrome should be listed as a very rare side-effect of one of the vaccines, Oxford/AstraZeneca jab [11].

3 Importance of Healthy Peer-review and Service to Humanity

Constructive criticism, healthy peer review are always the pillars of good science, which became more important when the lives of billions of people are involved. Healthy open peer-review from qualified scientists and experts from various disciplines are likely to dismantle many unsorted puzzles and now urgently required. It is such an important step and enough scrutiny in every step is indeed expected.

Experts, scientists raised various sensible questions on several platforms e.g., questions on mRNA technique, the trial process for understanding medium and long-term effects etc. among others. Those are very important steps and need to have complied with when millions of people are vaccinated on a regular basis. It is pointed out that COVID-19 vaccine trials and 'studies seem designed to answer the easiest question in the least amount of time, not the most clinically relevant questions' [12, 13]. Studies also discussed that current trials aren't designed to tell whether covid-19 vaccines can save lives [13, Table 1]. The frail elderly are disproportionately contributing to the serious cases of the disease, yet in the randomized trials, they were insufficiently recruited [14]. In the end, it should not be the media that will control and lead science. Prof Fiona Godlee, editor in chief, BMJ made a very valuable comment in this regard, "Science by press release" is just one of many flaws in the way new treatments are evaluated, brought into stark relief by the pandemic' [15]. Fabricated analyses and biased results should not be on the headline in everyday news; whereas, many important research/analyses will be suppressed. Those areas need to be addressed/monitored and brought to the knowledge of respective authorities in various steps of decision making. We need to analyse the whole situation to take a timely intervention, we need to ask whether the intervention with vaccines is making situations better or worse, whether we have more and more liberty to accept excuses when the solution does not work. With fixed world resources, the proposition of vaccinating billions and billions of people every six months times raises a very obvious question, whether such an effort is worth it and essential. The direct and indirect cost of that strategy needs attention so as the effectiveness of such a strategy.

As there are huge vested interests involved for vaccine and allied businesses, long chains of beneficiaries are linked, additional precautions should be in place. Ethics and integrity should not be compromised in that novel goal of saving humanity. One proposition in that direction could be producing and distributing vaccines on a **not-for-profit basis**.

It could be very welcoming coordinated initiatives from all vaccine groups and will be highly appreciated and valued.

Table 1. Characteristics of ongoing phase III covid-19 vaccine trials.

	Moderna	Pfizer	AstraZeneca (US)	AstraZeneca (UK)	Janssen	Sinopharm *	Sinovac
Vaccine name	mRNA-1273	BNT162	AZD1222	AZD1222	Ad26.COV2.S	Sinopharm vaccine	Sinovac CoronaVac
Registration No	NCT04470427	NCT04368728	NCT04516746	NCT04400838 (UK), NCT04536051 (Brazil), NCT04444674 (South Africa)	NCT04505722	NCT04510207	NCT04456595
Target enrolment	30 000	43 998	30 000	19 330	60 000	45 000	8870
Ages eligible	18+	12+	18+	5-12, 18+	18+	18+	18+
Protocol publicly available	Y	Y	Y	N†	Y	N	N
Notable excluded populations:							
Children and adolescents	Excluded	Many excluded	Excluded	13-17 excluded	Excluded	Excluded	Excluded
Immunocompromised patients	Excluded	Excluded	Excluded	Excluded	Excluded	Excluded	Excluded
Pregnant or breastfeeding women	Excluded	Excluded	Excluded	Excluded	Excluded	Excluded	Excluded
Endpoints undergoing formal study‡:							
Prevention of symptomatic disease in vaccine recipient	Y	Y	Y	Y	Y	Presumably§	Y
Reduction in severe covid-19 (hospital admission, ICU, or death)	N	N	N	N¶	N	N	N
Interruption of transmission (person to person spread)	N	N	N	N	N	N	N

[after Doshi P, 2020 [13], see, details there, used with copyright permission]

4 Similarities Between Influenza and COVID-19

There are still not any vaccines for many diseases, e.g. AIDS etc. Hence a balanced media coverage, focus on varied medical research or remedy on COVID-19 other than the vaccine is equally important.

Every winter, tens of thousands of people die in the UK, Europe and northern America from Influenza (Flu), a virus-borne respiratory disease. Centers for Disease Control and Prevention (CDC) estimated 61,000 deaths in the United States during 2017–2018 from influenza, which was higher than any season since 2009 [16]. At the beginning of every winter, people mainly from old and vulnerable groups are vaccinated against Flu virus; but still, it is not yet been possible to eradicate Flu. On the contrary, it became more powerful and destructive in later years. The main reason is that the virus is mutating over time and space. Hence the question arises could it be similar for COVID-19? There are many similarities between these two virus-borne respiratory diseases COVID-19 and Flu.

Few resemblances were noted from the web [17]: 'flu season occurs in the fall and winter. In the U.S., that means October-March, and in the southern hemisphere, June-September. Although the reason for this seasonality is not entirely understood, influenza virus has been shown to survive longer at low temperatures and low humidity. Other suggested explanations include weakened host immunity due to decreased sunlight and vitamin D and increased exposure to the virus due to indoor cohabitation in the winter.'

Other relevant facts and observations:

- Both the viruses are mutating over time and space. Many new strains of COVID-19 are emerging over time [18]. Since the first vaccine came up only in December 2020, many new variants are already detected in the next three months which are ineffective to the vaccine [19, 20]. One comment from journal the Lancet, 'rapid regulatory approval and roll-out of several vaccines have ignited much optimism. However, this optimism has been dampened by the emergence of several new virus variants that are more transmissible and less sensitive to vaccine-induced antibodies [20].
- There are many dissimilarities between COVID-19 with other vaccines (polio, small-pox etc.) too; e.g., unlike other vaccines, if people are vaccinated for COVID-19, they still can get the disease, can transmit it and even die from it [10, 21]. Even after 15 days of the second dose, people can be a carrier of the disease [10]. In Michigan, 246 breakthrough Covid-19 cases have occurred after the 2nd dose, which resulted in 11 hospitalizations and even **three deaths** [21]. 'Breakthrough cases,' happen when at least 14 days after receiving the final dose of the vaccine people test positive.
- Like Flu, during summer the situation improved in Europe and North America. Last summer, in Europe, deaths from COVID-19 were practically nil without any vaccine. People vaccinated in March 2021 for COVID-19, will require to be vaccinated again after six months i.e., before the next winter. This is because the immunity to the disease is expected to reduce after six months [22]. Whether the same vaccine will work or not that time will be another issue. Following our past experience with the Flu vaccine, it can be speculated beforehand.

There could be relevance to this discussion to **Flu vaccine ineffectiveness in excess of 50,100 deaths in the UK and EU in 2017–18** [23]. Deaths were highest in more than 40 years, though many vaccines were evolved and modified during that last 40 years. 'The Office for National Statistics said **flu and the ineffectiveness of the flu vaccine were key reasons for the rise of excess winter deaths in 2017–18**' [23]. Even for 2016, the rise in deaths in England and Wales for the previous 12 years, was attributed to the failure to provide an effective Flu vaccine, government's public health agency had admitted [24]. Those records indicated how poorly Flu vaccines performed in recent periods compared to the past.

5   New Variants and Fast Mutation

An inspiring initiative was taken to develop a COVID-19 virus mutation tracker, which is immensely beneficial to monitor the progression of mutated variants [18, 25]. It gives an idea of how rapidly it can mutate over temporal and spatial scales [Fig. 4]. The fingerprints reveal the route of virus transmission so as timelines of different mutations. For the UK, till 03/03/21 the number of unique variants identified as 11,098, of which local variants 10,7038 and foreign variants 3,066 [18]. Interestingly, the timeline of new variants suggests a sudden increase in mutation since December 2020 [18] (Fig. 4b), the time when major vaccination programme was initiated. Prior to that in the last 11 months, upto November 2020, the progression was really slow in comparison (see the numbers in Fig. 4b).

Vaccines themselves can drive viral mutations and hence COVID-19 vaccines can add fuel to the evolution of mutation of Coronavirus as suggested by Professor Paul Bieniasz from Rockefeller University, USA [26]. Those may explain why there is a surge in the number of mutated variants, so as cases globally after the mass vaccination started.

6   Mass Vaccination and Transmission - Trial Experiments

Trial experiments and protocols set for COVID-19 vaccination did not take into consideration of many direct and indirect consequences of mass vaccination.

Apart from looking into details of direct side effects after vaccination, the secondary effect that might be caused after mass vaccination needs attention too. Here is a trial experiment that showed vaccinated people can spread the disease and they can be carrier even after 15 days of 2nd dose.

Asymptomatic cases also have role in the transmission and spread of SARS-CoV2 infections [27]. Some clinical trial experiments are conducted among vaccinated health-care workers in the US, that also allowed for increased detection of asymptomatic infections [28]. Among vaccinated people, 14,604 were monitored in trials and out of which 379 tested positive at least 1 day after vaccination. The majority (71%) were tested positive within the first 2 weeks after the first vaccination. Whereas, 37 health care workers were tested positive after receiving both doses and 22 had positive test results 1 to 7 days after the second dose. Only 7 tested positive 15 or more days after the second dose [Table 2, 28]. This study indicated that after vaccination, the absolute risks of testing positive for SARS-CoV-2 are higher than the risks noted in original phase III trial experiments. **Vaccinated, over-confident people, if asymptomatic or develop mild symptoms, can act as super-spreaders.**

Such analyses may raise major worries for developing countries like India and most countries of African continents where deaths per million were practically very less in comparison to developed countries prior to mass vaccination. It may explain why highly

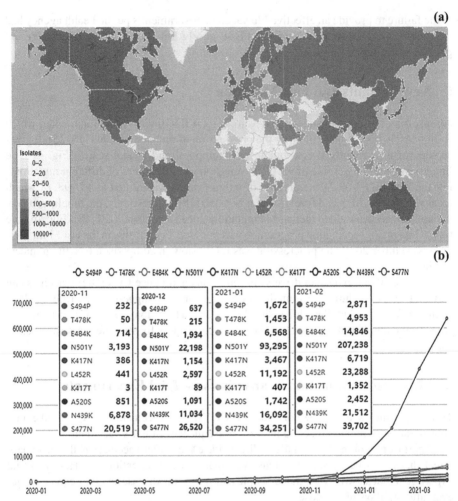

Fig. 4. COVID-19 virus genome isolates from patients are being regularly sequenced worldwide and continuously updated; for each sample, there is an accession number. The spatial distribution patterns (a) and temporal patterns (b) are presented. b) shows the top 10 major virus mutations timelines which are progressing at a very rapid scale since December, 2020. Numbers in each month from November to February are shown in the top left box and shows how slow was the pace, in comparison, upto November, 2020. [https://www.cbrc.kaust.edu.sa/covmt/, Accessed on 03/03/2021 (a) and 1/04/2021(b) respectively].

populated countries like Brazil and India are worst affected as very high number of people are vaccinated in a short space of time. Brazil started vaccination at around mid-February and just after a month a very steep rise in deaths is noticed [2]. A highly populated country India was about to control the disease without any vaccine or lockdown, but since the middle of February (vaccination started on 16th January, [2]) was showing a sudden surge in transmission, raising major concerns. Such a steep rise in deaths and cases for Brazil and India never happened in the entire period of the pandemic [3].

Such analyses raise few questions that need in-depth investigation and could have been attended before any rapid **mass vaccination** drive: i) is vaccine causing more mutation of virus? ii) if true, can more different vaccines can create more forms of mutations? iii) if vaccines have roles on viral mutation, is it dependent on climate, various genetic groups of people and ethnic groups, past health conditions of individuals etc.? iv) in some countries reduction of vaccination doses and imposition of lockdown, could abate the uncontrolled rate of transmission (e.g., India in May 2021, [3]). Such timely intervention indicated do the government and policy makers have the control on transmission rate of the virus by varying the number of vaccine doses, temporally as well as spatially? Can the timing and severity of global third/forth and other waves in future be controlled by regulating vaccine doses? v) Professor Paul Bieniasz mentioned, the time between initial vaccination and the time of second shot to maximize the immune response might serve as a sort of breeding ground for the virus to acquire new mutations

Table 2. New SARS-CoV-2 infections among vaccinated health care workers from December 16, 2020, through February 9, 2021.

Days after Vaccination	Vaccinated Persons		
	With New Infection (N=379)	Tested (N=14,604)*	Eligible for Testing (N=36,659)+
	Number		number (percent)
Dose 1			
Days 1-7	145	5794	35,673 (97.3)
Days 8-14	125	7844	34,404 (93.8)
Days 15-21	57	7958	32,667 (89.1)
Day 22 or later, Before dose 2	15	4286	32,327 (88.2)
Dose 2			
Days 1-7	22	5546	23,100 (63.0)
Days 8-14	8	4909	16,082 (43.9)
Days 15 or later	7	4167	14,990 (40.9)

[after, Keehner et al., 2021 [28], see details there]

[26]. vi) if vaccine can cause mutation, it is not only traveling that can spread the mutated virus from country to country or regionally; it can equally happen within any community sooner or later, even if, there is a strict travel ban or lockdown. vii) At the beginning of winter 2021, like Flu, there is another surge likely to happen in Europe and the northern US. It is very likely that we are going to blame new mutant variants and another lockdown will be impending. Thus, we need not be optimistic or pessimistic but **Pragmatic.** We need to explore alternate pathways side by side and be well-prepared with substitute solutions beforehand (to mention a few [29–31]).

Furthermore, it is worth mentioning that without proper checking of all direct and indirect effects of mass vaccination, any hasty steps **can cause more harm than good.** It can lead to severe consequences to highly populated countries that we eye witnessed recently. Those areas need thorough investigation and urgent attention on time to stop further escalation of a worsening situation.

7   Seasonality and COVID-19

Seasonal effects should be considered very important for the transmission of COVID-19. By around mid-April last winter, almost all European countries and countries from the northern USA showed a decline in transmission without any intervention of vaccines. Like Flu, transmission in fact was nominal during mid-June to September 2020, compared to the severity of other months. It would have been also expected **likewise from mid-April this year,** if vaccines were not in place. After major vaccination started there were surges in transmission in almost all countries and most countries had to impose strict lockdown conditions. It would be of interest to monitor how the effect of vaccine, (including the proportion of vaccinated percentage, time of major vaccination programme) override the effect of seasonality in various European countries and countries of northern US.

A recent systematic review work of several papers found almost all studies detected that temperature played a huge role in the transmission of the virus [32]. However, authors finally concluded that certainty of the evidence was graded as low, which is based on their (Table 3 [32]). A careful observation suggests that 'low' grading was not supported by their Table. On the contrary, it is completely the other way round. The area of seasonality, the dependence of seasonal temperature, though was very evident throughout, till vaccination started [29–31, 33], but surprisingly undermined by the scientific community and in many important publications.

Then the question is why? Could it be due to the previous experience with the Seasonal Flu Vaccine?

8   Optimism with Alternative Pathways

Studies explored whether the global temperature had any role in the spread and vulnerability to COVID-19 [29–31] and highlighted that global temperature played an important role in transmitting the virus. The risk from the virus was reduced significantly for warm places and countries; whereas, a moderately cool environment was the most favourable state. Various degrees of vulnerability were identified based on the temperature of March and April and countries were specified. It was shown countries can even switch from one state of vulnerability to another following the variability of temperature and that knowledge can be used for planning country-wise mitigation strategies [29–31]. Interestingly, the dependency of temperature on the global spread of the disease was consistent throughout before the vaccination drive, though deviated after initiation of mass vaccination programme on a global scale [2].

The dependency of temperature is true for similar generic category Coronavirus SARS (Severe Acute Respiratory Syndrome) and MERS (Middle East Respiratory Syndrome) ([34, 35]) and also true for other similar seasonal air-borne Flu viruses [36]. The virus remains active for a long time in low temperatures [34] and low temperature significantly contributes to its survival and transmission ([35, 37, 38]). A study using seasonally dependent endemic virus [36] showed when the temperature is 5 °C and relative humidity between (35 to 50)%, the infection rate was very high (75–100%); whereas, when relative humidity was still kept at 35%, but *only the temperature was increased to 30 °C, the infection rate was surprisingly reduced to zero.*

Solutions : General Measures

- **Using Sauna facilities:** Usually hotels, gyms, leisure centres contain existing Sauna facilities. Also, mobile and Caravan Sauna facilities can be thought of in future. After Sauna, if surfaces in public places are touched, hand washing is advisable.

- **Portable Convector Room Heater:** Stay close to a convector room heater and inhale hot air at least two times a day for around half an hour each time (keeping comfort level). It would be very useful at the initial stages of the disease.

- **Disinfect any place using High Temperature:** Before start of office, school or business, temperature of premises may be kept very high, (say, 60°C) for half an hour. For airports, train and bus, the same method of disinfecting could be thought of. *Optimum temperature and duration can be tested easily.* For any external object or material, disinfecting using high temperature could be a useful solution.

- **Using Blow Dryer/ Hair Dryer:** For minor symptoms, inhaling hot air intermittently through the nose (keeping comfort level) even for five minutes, say two/three times a day, will also be useful to kill virus in the nasal cavity.

- **Hot Drinks:** For very mild symptoms, take hot drinks (could be tea, coffee, warm milk, hot water with lemon etc.) few times a day to destroy virus in the mouth and throat. Gargle with warm salt water at least three/four times a day will be very beneficial. Hot soup will also be useful.

> **Why:** The virus is very sensitive to Temperature. It mainly enters through the Nose (WHO). Testing is done with swabs from the nasal cavity and the back of the Mouth.
> **Important:** Only even Convector Room Heater and Hot Salt Water gargle, Hot Drinks can serve the main purpose.

Indrani Roy

Fig. 5. Heat-based general measures at initial stages of the disease. (Roy, 2020, [29–31])

A laboratory experiment with similar generic Coronavirus (viz. SARS-CoV) using a variable temperature [37] showed inactivation of the virus was faster at all humidity

456   I. Roy

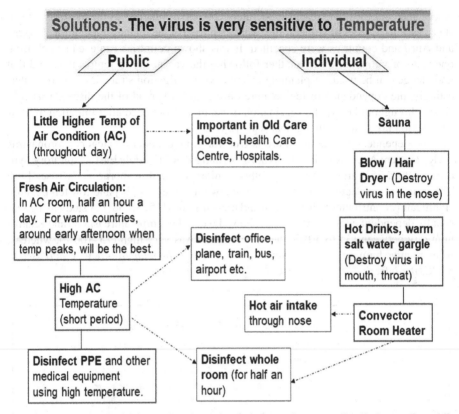

Fig. 6. An overview in the form of a schematic, depicting actions towards solutions at the public level (left) and individual level (right). (Roy, 2020, [29–31]).

levels if the temperature was simply raised to 20 °C from 4 °C; which is more rapid if the temperature was further increased to 40 °C from 20 °C. However, contact transmission is still possible at high temperatures and lab experiments with guinea pigs showed contact transmission takes place even at 30 °C temperature [36]. In typical Air-Conditioning (AC) environments, which has room temperature 22–25 °C and relative humidity (40–50)%, SARS can be active for at least five days [35].

The influence of temperature on the COVID-19 virus at global scale [29–33] and results of previous clinical trials with similar viruses that showed the strong dependency on temperature [34–38] provided a useful insight that regulating the level of temperature can offer remarkable results to stop and arrest the outbreak. Based on that knowledge, some urgent and simple heat-based solutions were proposed as early as 17th March 2020 [39, 40], which are practically without side effects, no vested interest involved and very cost-effective too [Fig. 5, Fig. 6]. These measures at the initial stages of the disease are proposed because the virus, which is very sensitive to temperature, mainly accumulates at high volume in the nose and back of the mouth. Testing is done with swabs from backs of the mouth and nasal cavity. High temperature can reduce viral loads in those places and thus, the body will have strengths and time to defend against the disease easily.

Successful clinical trial experiments following heat-based solutions to reduce transmission of COVID-19 were conducted and published [41] after receiving approval from the ethical committee. A thorough literature review in support of heat-based solutions to fight COVID-19 was also published in a peer-reviewed journal [42]. Being a medical doctor, the author discussed various mechanisms involved in the biological processes [42].

If these simple heat-based solutions at the initial stages of the disease [Fig. 5] become popular then people and government do not need to worry about mutated variants, long COVID, losing immunity after six months and further lockdown etc.

Competing Interest Statement.   This study did not receive any funding and there is no financial interest. The first version was submitted to journal on 11th March 2021, and preprint is [43] https://doi.org/10.22541/au.161642232.28976638/v1 and [44] https://doi.org/10.22541/au.162584191.11801390/v1.

References

1. Website: BBC. https://www.bbc.co.uk/news/uk-55227325. Accessed 6 Mar 2021
2. Website: Ourworldindata. https://ourworldindata.org/coronavirus-data-explorer. Accessed 9 Mar 2021
3. Website: Worldometers. https://www.worldometers.info/coronavirus/country/
4. Mallapaty, S.: Vaccines are curbing COVID: data from Israel show drop in infections. Nature **590**, 197 (2021). https://doi.org/10.1038/d41586-021-00316-4
5. Website: Israelnationalnews, 18 February 2021. https://www.israelnationalnews.com/News/News.aspx/297051
6. Website: Medicalxpress. https://medicalxpress.com/news/2020-12-uae-covid-vaccinations-capital.html. Accessed 8 Mar 2021
7. Website: Vaccine Adverse Event Reporting System (VAERS), Government website. https://vaers.hhs.gov/resources/govtsites.html
8. Website: The Epoch Times. https://www.theepochtimes.com/adverse-incident-reports-show-966-deaths-following-vaccination-for-covid-19_3723384.html. Published 6 Mar 2021, Updated 10 Mar 2021, Accessed 14 Mar 2021
9. Website CDC. https://www.cdc.gov/coronavirus/2019-ncov/vaccines/safety/adverse-events.html
10. Website: Indian Express. https://indianexpress.com/article/explained/explained-post-vaccination-effects-deaths-reading-the-data-available-so-far-7266875/. Accessed 13 Apr 2021
11. Website: The Guardian. https://www.theguardian.com/world/2021/apr/07/what-do-i-need-to-know-about-the-oxfordastrazeneca-vaccine. Accessed 12 Apr 2021
12. Doshi, P.: Covid-19 vaccine trial protocols released a rare opportunity for public scrutiny of these key trials. BMJ **371**, m4058 (2020). https://doi.org/10.1136/bmj.m4058
13. Doshi, P.: Will covid-19 vaccines save lives? Current trials aren't designed to tell us. BMJ 371, m4037 (2020). https://doi.org/10.1136/bmj.m4037. https://www.bmj.com/content/371/bmj.m4037. https://www.bmj.com/company/newsroom/covid-19-vaccine-trials-cannot-tell-us-if-they-will-save-lives/
14. Doshi, P.: BMJ, Rapid Response (2021). https://www.bmj.com/content/371/bmj.m4037/rr-23
15. Godlee, F.: Covid-19: we need new thinking and new leadership BMJ (2020). https://www.bmj.com/content/371/bmj.m4358

16. Website: CDC. https://www.cdc.gov/flu/about/burden-averted/2017-2018.htm. Accessed 6 Mar 2021
17. Website: American Society for Microbiology. https://asm.org/Articles/2020/July/COVID-19-and-the-Flu. Accessed 6 Mar 2021
18. Website: King Abdullah University of Science and Technology. https://www.cbrc.kaust.edu.sa/covmt/. Accessed 6 Mar 2021
19. Website: The Guardian, Published 8 February 2021. https://www.theguardian.com/world/2021/feb/08/oxford-covid-vaccine-10-effective-south-african-variant-study
20. Sanders, R.W.: Pandemic moves and countermoves: vaccines and viral variants. Lancet 397(10282), 1326–1327 (2021). https://doi.org/10.1016/S0140-6736(21)00730-3
21. Dailymail.   https://www.dailymail.co.uk/health/article-9441695/Three-people-Michigan-DIED-contracting-COVID-19-despite-fully-vaccinated.html. Accessed 13 Apr 2021
22. Website: BBC, 20 November 2020. https://www.bbc.co.uk/news/health-55022287
23. Website: The Guardian, Published 30 November 2018. https://www.theguardian.com/society/2018/nov/30/excess-winter-deaths-in-england-and-wales-highest-since-1976
24. Website: The Guardian, Published 7 April 2016. https://www.theguardian.com/uk-news/2016/apr/07/number-deaths-england-wales-12-year-high-life-expectancy
25. Alam, I., et al.: CovMT: an interactive SARS-CoV-2 mutation tracker, with a focus on critical variants. Lancet Infect. Dis. 2021. https://doi.org/10.1016/S1473-3099(21)00078-5. ISSN 1473-3099. https://www.sciencedirect.com/science/article/pii/S1473309921000785
26. Website: npj. 2021, Vaccines Could Add Fuel To Evolution Of Coronavirus Mutations, Published 10 February 2021. https://www.npr.org/sections/health-shots/2021/02/10/965940914/covid-19-vaccines-could-add-fuel-to-evolution-of-more-coronavirus-mutation
27. Muller, C.P.:Do asymptomatic carriers of SARS-COV-2 transmit the virus? Lancet Regional Health - Europe, 2021, 4, May, 2021, 100082, ISSN 2666-7762, doi.org/https://doi.org/10.1016/j.lanepe. 2021.100082.
28. Keehner, et al.: SARS-CoV-2 infection after vaccination in health care workers in California. N. Engl. J. Med. (2021). https://doi.org/10.1056/NEJMc2101927
29. Roy, I.: The role temperature on the global spread of COVID-19 and urgent solutions. Int. J. Environ. Sci. Technol. 18(9), 2903 (2020). https://doi.org/10.1007/s13762-020-02991-8
30. Website AGU: Roy, I. Influence of Temperature on the global spread of COVID-19 invited presentation, August 2020. https://agu2020fallmeeting-agu.ipostersessions.com/Default.aspx?s=4F-D9-45-B2-4C-B0-2A-F4-10-B5-71-05-DA-1D-45-4D. Accessed 27 July 2021
31. Roy, I.: Influence of temperature on the global spread of COVID-19 (2020). https://doi.org/10.22541/au.159301639.90704061/v2
32. Paulo, M., Travassos, d.R.M.B.R., Carlos, R.V.A., David, N.: Effects of temperature and humidity on the spread of COVID-19: a systematic review. Plos One. (2020). https://doi.org/10.1371/journal.pone.0238339
33. Scafetta, N.: Distribution of the SARS-CoV-2 pandemic and its monthly forecast based on seasonal climate patterns. Int. J. Environ. Res. Public Health 17(10), 3493 (2020). https://doi.org/10.3390/ijerph17103493
34. Van Doremalen, N., et al.: Stability of Middle East respiratory syndrome coronavirus (MERS-CoV) under different environmental conditions. Euro Surveill. 18(38), 20590 (2013). https://doi.org/10.2807/1560-7917.ES2013.18.38.20590
35. Chan, K.H., Malik Peiris, J.S., Lam, S.Y., Poon, L.L.M., Yuen, K.Y., Seto, W.H.: The effects of temperature and relative humidity on the viability of the SARS coronavirus. Adv. Virol. 2011, Article ID 734690, 7 p. (2011). https://doi.org/10.1155/2011/734690
36. Lowen, A.C., et al.: Influenza virus transmission is dependent on relative humidity and temperature. PLoS Pathog. 3(10), 1470–1476 (2007). https://doi.org/10.1371/journal.ppat.0030151

37. Casanova, L., et al.: Effects of air temperature and relative humidity on coronavirus survival on surfaces. Appl Environ Microbiol. **76**(9), 2712–2717 (2010)
38. Kim, S.W., Ramakrishnan, M.A., Raynor, P.C., Goyal, S.M.: Effects of humidity and other factors on the generation and sampling of a coronavirus aerosol. Aerobiologia **23**(4), 239–248 (2007). https://doi.org/10.1007/s10453-007-9068-9
39. Roy, I.: Combating recent pandemic of COVID-19 - an urgent solution. (2020). https://doi.org/10.13140/RG.2.2.22632.83208. 17 March 2020
40. Roy, I.:Atmospheric variables and additional urgent solutions for combating COVID-19 (2020). https://www.preprints.org/manuscript/202003.0366/v2. https://www.researchgate.net/publication/340552840_Atmospheric_Variables_and_Additional_Urgent_Solutions_for_Combating_COVID-19. 9 April 2020
41. Marca, G.L., et al.: Thermal inactivation of SARS COVID-2 virus: are steam inhalations a potential treatment? Life Sci. 265, 118801 (2021) https://doi.org/10.1016/j.lfs.2020.118801. ISSN 0024-3205
42. Cohen, M.: Turning up the heat on COVID-19: heat as a therapeutic intervention, F1000Research (2020). pubmed.ncbi.nlm.nih.gov/32742639/
43. Roy, I.: 2021 COVID-19 crisis -exit strategy: part 1-exploring pathways of vaccination (2021). https://doi.org/10.22541/au.161642232.28976638/v1
44. Roy, I.: 2021 Exit strategy from COVID-19: vaccination and an alternative solution (2021). https://doi.org/10.22541/au.162584191.11801390/v1

COVID-19. Health

Effect of COVID-19 Lockdown on Adherence to the Mediterranean Diet Among Participants in a Health-Promotion Program

Evelia Franco[1]([✉]) and Rubén Barakat[2]

[1] Universidad Pontificia Comillas, Madrid, Spain
efalvarez@comillas.edu
[2] Universidad Politécnica de Madrid, Madrid, Spain
rubenomar.barakat@upm.es

Abstract. Mediterranean diet, characterized by being abundant in plant-based foods, rich in olive oil, and lower in saturated fat, meats, and dairy products has been associated with several health benefits such as reduced mortality and incidence of cardiovascular disease. Despite this evidence, adult population does not seem to display a high adherence to the dietary patterns proposed by this diet. On the other hand, the COVID-19 pandemic has forced most of the population to shift to working from home when possible and this might have well affected their dietary patterns. The aim of the present work is to analyze how adherence to the Mediterranean diet among employees participating in a health-promotion program have been affected during lockdown due to the COVID-19 pandemic. Around 300 adults fulfilled validated questionnaires to measure their adherence to Mediterranean Diet both in October 2019 and May 2020. A series of $\chi 2$ tests were performed to test for any potential effects of the pandemic on Mediterranean diet-related variables. Results showed that working from home might have had a positive effect on Spanish employees' adherence to the Mediterranean Diet. More specifically, it seems that adults have been likely to increase their vegetables, fruit and legumes intake. Results are discussed in terms of working-from-home effects on healthy habits. The relevance of implementing programs to promote healthy behaviours is also discussed.

Keywords: Dietary patterns · Healthy habits · Working from home

1 Introduction

Diet habits have increasingly gained attention from the scientific community because of their potential consequences for health [1]. In this line, the Mediterranean diet has been linked to a number of health benefits, including reduced mortality and incidence of cardiovascular disease [2] as well as a relatively high level of self-rated health [3]. This diet is abundant in minimally processed plant-based foods, is rich in monounsaturated fat from olive oil, and is lower in saturated fat, meats, and dairy products. With the literature addressing the assessment of adherence to Mediterranean diet among office workers

© Springer Nature Switzerland AG 2021
I. Rojas et al. (Eds.): BIOMESIP 2021, LNCS 12940, pp. 463–471, 2021.
https://doi.org/10.1007/978-3-030-88163-4_39

being scarce, it has been suggested that workers of large companies show moderate adherence to this dietary pattern [4]. In 2020, the world experienced such exceptional circumstances that the usual health determinants were affected at all levels. The spread of the SARS-CoV2 (severe acute respiratory syndrome coronavirus 2), which gave rise to the disease known as COVID-19, led the WHO to declare a global pandemic inMarch 2020 [5]. Spain has been one of the hardest hit and earliest inflicted countries. In an attempt to fight the spread of the virus, the Spanish government approved a period of strict home confinement from 15 March to 2 May 2020. The confinement measures were then gradually relaxed working up until the summer months, but many companies maintained working-from-home (WFH) measures. Some of the immediate consequences of the confinement period were that people had to stay at home more than usual, interrupting their usual activities, and had to change their lifestyle habits [6].

Prolonged quarantine measures have forced businesses to adapt to their workforces being confined at home and no longer able to come into the office. Since the start of mandatory quarantine measures, there has been a significant rise in both public and private sector WFH participation, as well as WFH employee production and working hours [7].

A comparison between Spanish data in 2019 and 2020 revealed that remote work rose from less than 5% to 34% during the quarantine [8]. This shift from office to home working may well have affected healthy habits among workers. Thus, assessing how health risks and benefits of WFH are affected by its sudden, large-scale uptake in the context of COVID-19 is key to best preserving occupational health. This explains the emergence of studies aiming to understand health-related behavioral changes during quarantine [9, 10].

There is existing evidence of the benefits of health promotion by companies among their employees [e.g., 11]. This fact explains the interest of companies to introduce corporate health programs. To the best of our knowledge, no previous studies have analyzed how dietary patterns reported before and during confinement have changed among workers from companies participating in a health promotion program. Given the possibility of new virus outbreaks and thus the continuation of WFH for many people, the spread of WFH to new people seems to be a more than likely future situation. Considering this possibility, it might be of great value to companies to understand the health-related impacts of WFH. This knowledge might be helpful to design their own programs to proactively address the occupational health of their staff in these types of situations in the future.

The main aim of the present work is to analyze how adherence to the Mediterranean diet among workers participating in the Healthy Cities program have been affected during confinement, i.e., WFH due to the COVID-19 pandemic.

2 Methods

2.1 Participants

The sample was composed of Spanish office employees participating in the Healthy Cities scheme developed by Sanitas (https://corporativo.sanitas.es/sobre-nosotros/sos tenibilidad/healthy-cities/ accessed on 3 March 2021). There were 2491 employees who completed an online survey containing the questionnaires used in the present study before the pandemic. These participants were contacted via e-mail again in May 2020. This time, the questionnaires were answered by 297 subjects, who, therefore, constitute the research sample (148 women and 149 men). The average age of the participants was 42.76 years (SD = 7.79) ranging from 24 to 63.

2.2 Instruments

Information about the participants' demographic variables, such as gender, age, and the company they belonged to, was gathered in the first data collection. For the second data collection, the participants were also asked whether they had suffered from COVID- 19. On the other hand, the PREDIMED (Prevención con dieta mediterránea) questionnaire was used [12] to measure the adherence to a Mediterranean diet (Table 1). This instrument consists of 14 items in which participants are asked about their diet habits (e.g., "Do you mainly use olive oil to cook?"). Depending on their answers, participants could score 0 or 1 points for each question. Those who reached nine points in the questionnaire were deemed as Mediterranean diet followers.

Table 1. PREDIMED items and analysis criteria

Questions	Criteria for 1 point
1. Do you use olive oil as main culinary fat?	Yes
2. How much olive oil do you consume in a given day (including oil used for frying, salads, out-of-house meals, etc.)?	≥ 4 table spoons
3. How many vegetable servings do you consume per day? (1 serving: 200 g [consider side dishes as half a serving])	≥ 2 (≥ 1 portion raw or as a salad)
4. How many fruit units (including natural fruit juices) do you consume per day?	≥ 3
5. How many servings of red meat, hamburger, or meat products (ham, sausage, etc.) do you consume per day? (1 serving: 100–150 g)	< 1
6. How many servings of butter, margarine, or cream do you consume per day? (1 serving: 12 g)	< 1
7. How many sweet or carbonated beverages do you drink per day?	< 1
8. How much wine do you drink per week?	≥ 7 glasses
9. How many servings of legumes do you consume per week? (1 serving: 150 g)	≥ 3

(continued)

Table 1. (*continued*)

Questions	Criteria for 1 point
10. How many servings of fish or shellfish do you consume per week? (1 serving 100–150 g of fish or 4–5 units or 200 g of shellfish)	≥ 3
11. How many times per week do you consume commercial sweets or pastries (not homemade), such as cakes, cookies, biscuits, or custard?	< 3
12. How many servings of nuts (including peanuts) do you consume per week? (1 serving 30 g)	≥ 3
13. Do you preferentially consume chicken, turkey, or rabbit meat instead of veal, pork, hamburger, or sausage?	Yes
14. How many times per week do you consume vegetables, pasta, rice, or other dishes seasoned with sofrito (sauce made with tomato and onion, leek, or garlic and simmered with olive oil)?	≥ 2

2.3 Procedure

Sanitas, a leading Spanish health company, developed the Healthy Cities Challenge which was carried out from September 2019 to September 2020 aiming (1) to promote healthy lifestyle habits among the employees belonging to the big Spanish companies who participated in the programme and (2) to generate a financial donation by Sanitas to an urban regeneration project, in a Spanish city, as a vehicle to develop more areas where people can go to carry out PA. As for the first aim, workers belonging to the participant companies were invited to participate in some health-related offline events and online workshops.

An online platform was used to create and distribute the questionnaire. The initial questionnaire was administered in October 2019 and the second questionnaire was administered in May 2020. In both cases, the questionnaire was disseminated through platforms available for the staff of companies participating in the Healthy Cities Project.

The time required to answer the questionnaire was approximately 10 min. The participants were able to answer the questionnaire at different times. The responses to the questionnaires were stored in an online database to which the authors had access. All of the participants were treated in agreement with the ethical guidelines of the American Psychological Association [13].

2.4 Data Analysis

A series of $\chi 2$ tests were performed to test for any potential effects of the pandemic on Mediterranean diet-related variables.

3   Results

Table 2 shows the distribution of participants in terms of every item in the PREDIMED questionnaire both before and during the pandemic. Pearson $\chi 2$ tests, together with the analysis of the adjusted residuals, revealed that in all of the items the participants displayed a pattern closer to the Mediterranean diet features during pandemic than before. More specifically, there was an increase in the number of participants reporting that the olive oil was the main culinary lipid used, as well as an increase in the intake of olive oil, vegetables, fruit, red meat, wine, legumes, fish and seafood, tree nuts and sofrito sauce. On the other hand, participants intake of butter, cream and margarine, or commercial sweets decreased during the pandemic. Overall, the adherence to the Mediterranean diet was higher during the pandemic than before.

Table 2. Distribution of the participants in the different items of PREDIMED before and during the Pandemic

	Before Pandemic	During Pandemic	(d.f.) Pearson $\chi 2$
Use of olive oil as main culinary lipid			
No	7	3	(1) 9.03 ***
Yes	290	294	
Olive oil			
0–3 tablespoons	59	36	(3) 65.03 **
More than 3 tablespoons	238	261	
Vegetables			
1–2 servings	107	190	(3) 37.07 ***
More than 2 servings	98	199	
Fruits			
0–3 servings	204	197	(3) 39.68***
More than 3 servings	93	100	
Red/processed meats			
None	106	97	(1) 27.71***
At least one	191	200	
Butter, cream, margarine			
None	250	225	(1)29.36***
At least one	47	72	
Soda drinks			
None	225	204	69.02***

(continued)

Table 2. (*continued*)

	Before Pandemic	During Pandemic	(d.f.) Pearson χ2
At least one	72	93	
Wine glasses			
None	251	233	61.69***
One or more	46	64	
Legumes			
None	226	203	30.88***
At least one	71	94	
Fish/seafood			
0- 2 servings per week	186	180	41.43***
At least 3 servings per week	111	117	
Commercial sweets and confectionary			
Less than 2 servings per week	68	86	(4)46.54***
At least 2 servings per week	229	211	
Tree nuts			
Less than 3 servings per week	40	33	(4)18.61**
At least 3 servings per week	257	264	
Poultry more than red meats			
No	20	18	(4)43.62***
Yes	277	279	
Use of sofrito sauce			
Less than twice per week	93	77	(3)13.82**
At least twice per week	204	220	
Adherence to the Mediterranean Diet			
No	135	70	(1)22.26***
Yes	162	227	

Note. When it is not specified, the table indicates the number of servings per day *0.05, **0.01; ***0.001

4   Discussion

The main aim of the present work is to analyze how adherence to the Mediterranean diet among workers participating in the Healthy Cities program have beenaffected during confinement, i.e., WFH due to the COVID-19 pandemic. As has been previously pointed out, it could have been expected that during the pandemic, our diet would have taken a step back from being a healthy diet rich in fresh food to one containing foods with a long shelf life [14]. The reasons supporting this belief are both the threat of a potential food shortage and that a typical response to chronic stressful situations is the consumption of energy-dense foods [15]. However, our results show that the adherence to a Mediterranean diet was higher during the pandemic than before. This fact is not surprising in light of recent studies addressing both dietary and cooking habits. In this vein, Rodríguez-Pérez et al. [16] suggested that COVID-19 confinement in Spain has led to the adoption of healthier dietary habits reflected in a higher adherence to a Mediterranean diet. As was pointed out, devoting more time to both cooking and eating when WFH compared to when working at the office might explain why people have been more likely to engage in healthier diet behaviors [17].

The analysis of benefits and disadvantages of WFH has gained much attention during the pandemic we are going through. Recent research has pointed out that WFH might lead to positive outcomes such an improvement in work-life balance, work efficiency, and work control [18]. However, there are several aspects of WFH which could negatively affect to the employees wellbeing such as the existence of home office constraints, work uncertainties and inadequate tools [18]. A study carried out among researchers found that the effect of WFH did improve the efficiency for some people, while acted as a barrier for eficiency in others [19]. This fact makes us think that there must be personal and/or contextual factors affecting WFH experiences. However, it seems that workers might be unaware about what WFH entails and lack resources required for this change, like software, access to official documents and proper working space [20]. This all sugests that, while companies trends in terms of WFH are likely to change once the pandemic is over, proper training will be required if this practice is to be a feasible option or the new normal. Possibly the working balance will be visible post-pandemic when WFH is not a forced mandate, rather a flexible option.

The findings of the present study, suggesting that employees are more likely to follow a healthy diet (Mediterranean one) when working from home, could be taking into consideration for companies when it comes to make a decision about the future scenario. The practical implications of the present findings are twofold. On the one hand, companies could facilitate WFH on the basis that it might positively affect their employees' health. On the other hand, it would be interesting to explore which barriers employees find to follow a healthy dietary pattern when working from the office and tackle them accordingly. Health-promotion programs could thus implement training about dietary patterns and specially, encouraging actions such the provision of comfortable spaces for employees to have their home-made lunch, the provision of fruits during the breaks, or the existence of an affordable and healthy offer for lunch.

The main strength of the present study is having data gathering just before the pandemic, when it was not possible to foresee that situation. This allowed us to compare the study variables before and after the pandemic. Furthermore, it is focused on a specific population (Spanish employees attending a health promotion program) which contributes to the sample homogeneity, As stated below, this could be both a strength and a limitation. This study has some limitations that must be mentioned. While this is one of the very few studies assessing the impact of the pandemic with data gathered both before and during the pandemic, only 297 participants out of the initial 2491 completed the second wave of questionnaires. Second, our sample represents a specific population group, i.e., employees participating in a health promotion program, and the findings cannot be extended to the whole population. The health promotion program that the participants were taking part of could have partially explained the changes observed. It would be interesting for future studies to explore the effects of such programs when under different sanitary conditions.

References

1. Kandel, S.: An evidence-based look at the effects of diet on health. Cureus **11**, e4715 (2019)
2. Martínez-González, M.A., Gea, A., Ruiz-Canela, M.: The Mediterranean diet and cardiovascular health. Circ. Res. **124**, 779–798 (2019)
3. Novak, D., et al.: Mediterranean diet and its correlates among adolescents in non-Mediterranean European countries: a population-based study. **9**, 177 (2017)
4. Papadaki, A., Wood, L., Sebire, S.J., Jago, R.: Adherence to the Mediterranean diet among employees in South West England: formative research to inform a web-based, work-place nutrition intervention. Prev. Med. Rep. **2**, 223–228 (2015)
5. World Health Organization: Coronavirus disease 2019 (COVID-19). Situation Report - 51. (2020)
6. España: Real Decreto, 463/2020, de 14 de marzo, por el que se declara el estado de alarma para la gestón de la situación de crisis sanitaria ocasionada por el COVID-19., pp. 25390–25400, Boletín Oficial del Estado, 14 de marzo, núm. 67 (2020)
7. Kniffin, K.M., et al.: COVID-19 and the workplace: implications, issues, and insights for future research and action. Am. Psychol. **76**, 63–77 (2021)
8. Peiró, J.M., Soler, A.: El impulso al teletrabajo durante el Covid-19 y los retos que plantea Laboratorio de Análisis y Evaluación de Políticas Públicas. Comunidad Valenciana. (2020)
9. Ueda, M., Stickley, A., Sueki, H., Matsubayashi, T.: Mental health status of the general population in Japan during the COVID-19 pandemic. Psychiatry Clin. Neurosci. **74**, 505–506 (2020)
10. López-Bueno, R., et al.: Association between current physical activity and current perceived anxiety and mood in the initial phase of COVID-19 confinement. Front. Psychiatry **11**, 729 (2020)
11. Chapman, L.S.: Meta-evaluation of worksite health promotion economic return studies: 2012 update. Am. J. Health Promot. **26**, 1–12 (2012)
12. Martínez-González, M.A., et al.: A 14-item Mediterranean diet assessment tool and obesity indexes among high-risk subjects: the PREDIMED trial. PLoS ONE **7**, e43134 (2012)
13. American Psychological Association: Ethical principles of psychologists and code of conduct (Amended August 3, 2016). American Psychological Association (2002)
14. Mattioli, A.V., Sciomer, S., Cocchi, C., Maffei, S., Gallina, S.: Quarantine during COVID-19 outbreak: changes in diet and physical activity increase the risk of cardiovascular disease. Nutr. Metab. Cardiovasc. Dis. **30**, 1409–1417 (2020)
15. Bracale, R., Vaccaro, C.M.: Changes in food choice following restrictive measures due to Covid-19. Nutr Metab Cardiovasc Dis **30**, 1423–1426 (2020)
16. Rodríguez-Pérez, C., et al.: Changes in dietary behaviours during the COVID-19 outbreak confinement in the Spanish COVIDiet study. Nutrients **12**, article no. 1730 (2020)
17. Restrepo, B.J., Zeballos, E.: The effect of working from home on major time allocations with a focus on food-related activities. Rev. Econ. Household **18**(4), 1165–1187 (2020). https://doi.org/10.1007/s11150-020-09497-9
18. Ipsen, C., van Veldhoven, M., Kirchner, K., Hansen, J.P.: Six key advantages and disadvantages of working from home in Europe during COVID-19. Int. J. Environ. Res. Public Health **18**, 1826 (2021)

19. Aczel, B., Kovacs, M., van der Lippe, T., Szaszi, B.: Researchers working from home: Benefits and challenges. PLoS ONE **16**, e0249127 (2021)
20. Vyas, L., Butakhieo, N.: The impact of working from home during COVID-19 on work and life domains: an exploratory study on Hong Kong. Policy Des. Pract. **4**, 59–76 (2021)

Memory Chains for Optimizing the Table Disposition During the COVID-19 Pandemic

Rubén Ferrero-Guillén[(✉)] ⓘ, Javier Díez-González ⓘ, Paula Verde ⓘ,
Alberto Martínez-Gutiérrez ⓘ, José-Manuel Alija-Pérez ⓘ, and Hilde Perez ⓘ

Department of Mechanical, Computer, and Aerospace Engineering, Universidad de León,
24071 León, Spain
{rferrg00,amartg22}@estudiantes.unileon.es, {jdieg,pverg,jmalip,
hilde.perez}@unileon.es

Abstract. The coronavirus disease 2019 (COVID-19) pandemic has supposed a challenge for some economic sectors that have suffered preventive lockdowns during the last year for mitigating the virus propagation. Among them, hostelry is one of the most affected sectors, especially indoor establishments in which the contagion probability significantly increases. In this context, preserving the interpersonal distance while wearing facemasks in these establishments has been demonstrated as a key factor to control the virus propagation in hostelry environments. The achievement of this objective entails the addressing of the Table Location Problem (TLP) which allows the maximization of the distance among the tables of a particular establishment. The TLP is considered as NP-Hard suggesting the application of metaheuristics to achieve competitive results in acceptable times. In this paper we propose a novel algorithm for the TLP (MA-GB-Chains) based on memory chains to select the more promising individuals for applying a local search procedure to introduce knowledge during the optimization process. This algorithm has been proved in a real hostelry environment reaching improved results to previous approaches to the TLP thus fulfilling the main objectives of this paper.

Keywords: Table distribution optimization · COVID-19 · Memetic algorithm

1 Introduction

COVID-19 pandemic has supposed a challenge for our normal coexistence over the last year. This pandemic has been caused by the virus known as the severe acute respiratory syndrome coronavirus 2 (SARS-CoV-2) [1, 2]. In particular, SARS-CoV-2 is closely related to two bat-derived SARS-like coronaviruses first found in China in 2018 although further research to conclude the origins of this virus is still needed to trace its path to human hosts [3].

Although other previous coronaviruses with superior fatality rates have appeared in the last decades (e.g., MERS-CoV and SARS-CoV), the SARS-CoV-2 has shown a rapid worldwide spread due to its capacity to survive and be transmitted to novel human hosts [4].

© Springer Nature Switzerland AG 2021
I. Rojas et al. (Eds.): BIOMESIP 2021, LNCS 12940, pp. 472–483, 2021.
https://doi.org/10.1007/978-3-030-88163-4_40

In addition, SARS-CoV-2 is well-known for its initial asymptomatic stage which causes a blind propagation complicating the isolation of positive cases and the contact tracing efforts to contain the virus [5]. However, recent investigations have proposed the implementation of neural networks for daily monitoring and disease diagnosis based on the physiological signals received from smartwatches and smartphones [6].

Nevertheless, the virus ability to propagate through airborne transmission has threatened the control of the virus spread [7] specially affecting the indoor environments where the infection rates significantly increase [8].

Therefore, many different protective measurements have been taken to reduce the contagion probability in these spaces such as wearing facemasks [9], preserving the social distance [10], ventilation [11] or hydroalcoholic gels [12]. In this sense, scientific evidence has proven that preserving the social distance in indoor spaces while wearing facemasks is a key factor for reducing the COVID-19 spread [13].

However, keeping the interpersonal distance in dynamic dense environments has been demonstrated as a difficult task [14] due to the unpredictable paths followed for the rest of the people in the indoor rooms. Thus, reducing the contagion probability in these scenarios can only be attained through occupancy restrictions [15]. Nevertheless, other different places where people stay seated (e.g., schools, cinema, or hostelry) suppose an interesting scenario for maximizing the social distance through the optimal separation of the chairs occupied by the people, thus reducing the probability of contagion of the COVID-19. For this purpose, governments suggested the implementation of regular patterns for the table dispositions which allows to attain acceptable results to maximize the social distance but supposes a suboptimal solution especially in irregular scenarios with obstacles.

Thus, the optimal address of this problem requires the solution of the combinatorial Table Location Problem (TLP) which has been defined as NP-Hard [16] due to its similarity to the Node Location Problem (NLP) which is also known to be NP-Hard [17]. The TLP entails the definition of the optimal Cartesian coordinates in space of each of the tables used in a defined environment thus reaching the maximal table distancing to maximize the interpersonal distance.

The high number of potential combinatorial solutions to the TLP and the impossibility to define continuous optimization functions due to the changes in the contiguous tables analyzed during the optimization suggest the employment of metaheuristic techniques to obtain valuable results in acceptable computation times.

In this sense, we first applied Genetic Algorithms (GA) [16] to address the TLP in school contexts where each of the students were associated to a particular table. This methodology reached promising solutions in these situations. However, the designed algorithm suffered for finding the scenario limits during the optimization process. In addition, no knowledge was introduced during the optimization process thus trusting in the evolution to achieve valid results which supposed an imbalanced quality in the solutions reached among different algorithm runs.

For these reasons, we later developed a Memetic Algorithm (MA) [18] for solving the TLP in hostelry environments. We first defined the particularities of the TLP in restaurants (e.g. including the necessary distance for the waiter optimal service around the tables or the free disposition of the clients around the tables) for later introducing knowledge during the optimization process looking for better optimization results. The introduction of knowledge was achieved through the application of a Gradient-Based local search procedure (GB) due to the local derivability of a table which defines the gradient direction as the direction of the maximal improvement in the distance reached among the tables.

In this paper, we improve our previous MA through the consideration of memory chains for optimally select the individuals to apply the local search procedure and the adequate tables to perform the GB calculations to improve the fitness results, and for preserving the diversity of the evolutionary population. This entails the definition of a novel algorithm for the TLP (MA-GB-Chains) which is proved in a novel hostelry scenario obtaining improved results.

The remainder of the paper is organized as follows: we introduce the mathematical model for the TLP in hostelry applications and the fitness function for the optimization in Sect. 2; the MA-GB-Chains algorithm is proposed in Sect. 3; the results are shown in Sect. 4 and the conclusions are presented in Sect. 5.

2 Mathematical Model for the Table Location Problem

The TLP looks for finding the optimal table disposition for maximizing the distance among the tables for reducing the contagion probability during the COVID-19 pandemic. This entails the definition of the Cartesian coordinates of each of the tables considered during the optimization process ($\langle t_i \rangle = \langle x_i, y_i \rangle$) which constitute the decision variables of the optimization.

All these tables are combined in a subset (T_i) which is contained in the global set (T) which is composed of all the possible combinations of table dispositions in the application scenario considered during the optimization process.

The number of potential combinations is factorial and can be obtained through the following equation:

$$P = \prod_{j=0}^{n_t-1} (n_{TLE} - j) \tag{1}$$

where P represents the number of potential combinations of tables; n_t is the number of tables considered during the optimization process and n_{TLE} is the number of potential points in space in which a table can be located.

These considerations are used to design computational optimizations obtaining representativeness of all the space of solutions with time-competitive results. Thus, the definition of the n_{TLE} is based on a pre-optimization in which the definition of deeper grids only supposes slight changes in the fitness function proposed.

Therefore, the mathematical model for the TLP can be defined as follows [18]:

$$Maximize\ Z = ff\left(ff_d(T_i), ff_{pen}(T_i)\right) \tag{2}$$

Subject to:

$$x_{lim_1} \leq x_i \leq x_{lim_2} \quad \forall x_i \in t_i;\ t_i \in T_i;\ t_i \notin U \tag{3}$$

$$y_{lim_1} \leq y_i \leq y_{lim_2} \quad \forall y_i \in t_i; t_i \in T_i; t_i \notin U \tag{4}$$

$$d_{CLE_{ij}} \geq d_{sd} \quad \forall i, j \in 1, \ldots, n_t; i \neq j \tag{5}$$

$$d_{io} \geq d_w \quad \forall i \in 1, \ldots, n_t; \forall o \in 1, \ldots, n_{obs} \tag{6}$$

where ff_d and ff_{pen} represent the fitness functions for characterizing the distances among the closest tables and for defining the penalizations for guiding the optimization process in cases where the restrictions are not completely fulfilled respectively; x_{lim_1}, x_{lim_2}, y_{lim_1} and y_{lim_2} are the lower and upper bounds for the location of the tables in the scenario; U is the subset that contains each of the forbidden regions in the scenario for the location of any table (e.g., inside an obstacle); $d_{CLE_{ij}}$ is the distance between the Chair Location Environment (CLE) of the tables i and j as defined in Fig. 1; d_{sd} represents the safe interpersonal distance for reducing the contagion probability of the COVID-19 which is fixed in 1.5 m in Spain; d_{io} is the distance from table i to the obstacle o which must exceed for each table and obstacle the distance for guaranteeing an optimal service in the entire table for the waiter (d_w).

Figure 1 shows the effective distance between two different tables to preserve the social distancing among clients ($d_{CLE_{ij}}$) which must consider the distance measured from the chair potential locations around the table.

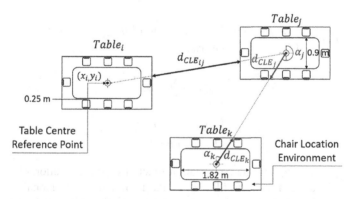

Fig. 1. Representation of the effective distance to preserve the social distancing in a hostelry application.

This distance is calculated through a method introduced in [18] in which a predefinition of the distance from the center of the table to the potential space to locate chairs around it is stored in a memory before the optimization. This memory is accessed through the angles formed by the intersection of the line joining the center of two different tables with the vertical as shown in Fig. 1.

Therefore, this distance is used for measuring the quality of a table disposition in the application environment during the optimization process. Particularly, the fitness function is calculated through the mean value of the effective distance of each table to the closest one (i.e., the more restrictive value for the safety achieved by the table disposition). In addition, since we are not only looking for a high mean in the table distances, we consider the standard deviation for guiding the optimization process to reach a well-distributed table distances for achieving equilibrized table dispositions:

$$ff_d = \frac{1}{n_t} \sum_{i=1}^{n_t} \min(d_{CLE_{ij}}) - \lambda \sqrt{\frac{1}{n_t} \sum_{i=1}^{n_t} (\min(d_{CLE_{ij}}) - \mu_{closest})^2} \tag{7}$$

where $\mu_{closest}$ is the mean distance between the closest tables of the hostelry distribution and λ is a weight hyperparameter.

The fulfillment of the restrictions is considered through a negative fitness function which analyzes the locations of the tables in obstacles, the minimum interpersonal distance for reducing the contagion probability and the necessary distance for the waiter around the table for providing an optimal service to the clients:

$$ff_{pen} = -(ff_{obs} + ff_{sd} + ff_w) \tag{8}$$

$$ff_{obs} = Jk \tag{9}$$

$$ff_{sd} = \sum_{i=1}^{n_t} ff_{sd_i} \tag{10}$$

$$ff_{sd_i} = \begin{cases} (d_{sd} - \min(d_{CLE_{ij}}))^2 & if \ \min(d_{CLE_{ij}}) \le d_{sd} \ (i \ne j) \\ 0 & otherwise \end{cases} \tag{11}$$

$$ff_w = \sum_{i=1}^{n_t} ff_{w_i} \tag{12}$$

$$ff_{w_i} = \begin{cases} (d_w - d_{io})^2 & if \ d_{io} \le d_w \\ 0 & otherwise \end{cases} \tag{13}$$

where ff_{obs}, ff_{sd} and ff_w are the penalization functions for the location of some tables in scenario obstacles, for the fulfillment of the minimum interpersonal distance and the optimal service of the waiter respectively; J the number of tables located inside an obstacle and k a weighted hyperparameter for the optimization.

3 MA for the TLP

The origin of the first MAs is dated in the decade of 1980 and arose due to the need by researchers to solve or reduce some of the limitations and restrictions of the metaheuristic techniques discovered up to that moment. Evolutionary Algorithms (EA) were one of the most favored branches due to the fact that MA allows the combination of EA with other techniques such as Simulated Annealing (SA) which compensates its limitations through its success in reaching a global optimal approximation.

Moscato and Norman formalized the term MA defined as a cultural evolution for introducing specific knowledge on a concrete problem. A meme is a "unit of culture" (i.e. minimal entity of information, idea or belief) with the capacity to integrate or influence an individual or its traits. This learning acquired by the individual is transmissible and reproducible by other individuals, establishing this cultural inheritance among individuals of a given collective.

Genetic Algorithms (GA) are a field of EAs that encode individuals applying Darwinian theory where evolution follows the rules of natural selection and the survival of the strongest. This type of algorithms allows a large exploration of the study scenario due to the diversification provided by the operators. The great effectiveness of GAs in solving various problems such as multimodal problems (i.e. with several valid solutions) [19], with not detailed search space, if it is necessary to calculate non-derivable functions or if it is not possible to apply techniques such as the spanning tree due to its complexity (i.e. polynomial time is not achievable) [20], makes them suitable for its application in multiple fields. GA optimizations have been performed for many applications including architecture search and design of cyber-physical systems [21], wing design [22], and node location optimization [23–25].

The analysis of an environment or scenario such as the one proposed in this paper reaches NP-Hard complexity, due to the large number of possible combinations needed to solve it. However, the GA have limitations when performing an intensified search in each sector of the scenario, so it is necessary to enhance the evolutionary process with other metaheuristics or reinforcement learning to improve its results [26, 27].

Our previous research determined the suitability of GA binding with the Local Search (LS) in the resolution of the TLP [16]. The intensification provided by the LS allows for more thorough searches in the neighborhoods of the tables comprising the individuals. However, these displacements are to adjacent locations, which implies that sometimes several LS are necessary to attain the optimal individual. In addition, each of the LS executions selects a random set of individuals, in addition to the elites, with the goal that no individual lacks the chance of being enhanced. In this way we ensured that we kept diversity in the exploration of potential regions of the space of solutions. Nevertheless, as the algorithm progresses, the possibility of selecting individuals that have been executed several times in the LS and thus have reached their optimal fitness increases. This implies that the computational resources of the LS are not exploited to the fullest and that the number of individuals improved by the MA decreases as convergence advances. Therefore, in this paper, we propose the improvement of the MA introduced in [18] through the MA-Gradient Based-Chains (MA-GB-Chains) algorithm.

The MA-Chains metaheuristic was first proposed in 2010 with the goal of performing an intensive local search that would decrease the computational cost employed in LS for high-dimensional continuous optimization problems through the MA-Solis Wets-Chains (MA-SW-Chains) algorithm [28]. Subsequently, it was adapted to obtain solutions in discrete problems through a novel MA-Variable Neighborhood Descent-Chains (MA-VND-Chains) algorithm, where its efficiency against the traditional MA procedure was demonstrated in discrete optimization problems obtaining better final results due to the improvement of a larger number of individuals [29]. The structure of this technique presents a memory that is preserved during the whole process, called MA-Chains where some parameters about the individuals of the population are stored. In the MA-GB-Chains algorithm we store the improvement step used in the LS for each table, the improvement margin obtained from the individual after being executed by the LS and the number of times that the individual has not improved in thereof. Therefore, the algorithm can quantify the suitability of each individual to be improved by the LS and facilitates the selection of the more promising individuals to continue enhancing their fitness properties. Figure 2 discusses the modifications made with respect to our previous developed MA for the TLP [18].

Algorithm 1: Changes for the MA-GB-Chains in TLP (*LS Criteria, LS Depth*)

```
 1 if  LS Criteria is fulfilled then
 2 |    for each Individual in Memory do
 3 |    |   Intensity of the Individual ← analyze the upgrade step from the previous LS from Tables
   |    |   (ρ), the range of Improvement of the previous executions in the LS (δ) and the number of
   |    |   times the Individual has failed to improve (η);
 4 |    |   Update List of intensities with new Intensity from Individual;
 5 |    end
 6 |    LS Individuals ← List of elitist and random individuals from Population;
 7 |    for each Individual in LS Individuals do
 8 |    |   if Intensity from Individual is less than κ then
 9 |    |   |   Update LS Individuals with new Individual;
10 |    |   end
11 |    end
12 |    for LS Individual in LS Individuals do
13 |    |   for each iteration in LS Depth do
14 |    |   |   Upload the ρ of Memory
15 |    |   |   New Individual ← Gradient Based Local Search algorithm by ρ of LS Individual;
16 |    |   |   Update ρ if has achieved a great improvement;
17 |    |   end
18 |    |   ffFinal ← Fitness evaluation of the intensified individual (New Individual);
19 |    |   if ffFinal ≥ ffInitial then
20 |    |   |   Update δ with the improvement;
21 |    |   |   Substitute New Individual for LS Candidate in Population;
22 |    |   end
23 |    |   else
24 |    |   |   Reset δ and ρ to initial values;
25 |    |   |   Increase η;
26 |    |   end
27 |    end
28 end
29 for each Individual in  Crossover and Mutation do
30 |    if Modified then
31 |    |   Reset ρ, δ and η to initial values;
32 |    end
33 end
```

Fig. 2. Pseudocode for the introduction of the memory chains into the MA.

This algorithm introduces the novelty of memory chains into the MA optimization developed in previous works [18]. This memory chains are initialized in default values for all individuals equally. When the LS execution criterion is met, the selection of individuals is performed. The Intensity is the parameter in charge of quantifying the suitability of each individual:

$$I_i = C1 \cdot \delta + C2 \cdot \mu + C3 \cdot \frac{1}{n} \tag{14}$$

where $C1$, $C2$ and $C3$ are co-factors experimentally squeezed, following the methodology stated in [29, 30]. δ is the fitness value improvement, n the number of times the individual has been selected for the local search and μ is defined as the need of this individual to be improved, obtained from:

$$\mu = \frac{\rho}{n} \sum N_i \tag{15}$$

where ρ is the step used to move a table, n is the number of tables and N_i is the number of table movements underwent by the studied individual.

At each in-depth execution of the LS, the ρ is updated based on the improvement obtained in the previous one. Once the LS of the individual is completed, the degree of improvement is verified, and all the values of the memory are updated. This memory is updated each time an individual is modified.

4 Results

In order to evaluate the MA-GB-Chains performance, a real hostelry application has been selected. The Torio Salon is a multipurpose area in the Conde Luna Hotel, in the city of León, Spain. The expected resiliency of this establishment requires a restructuration of the table arrangement for each celebration.

The presence of obstacles such as columns and furniture represent an adversity when trying to allocate the maximum number of tables inside the salon, being these obstacles shown as a prohibited region in Fig. 3. The additional complexity introduced by the current pandemic restrictions results in a highly restrictive problem, where the implementation of the analyzed metaheuristics is required.

In order to test the performance of the MA-GB-Chains and previously analyzed methodologies (i.e., GA and MA), a comparative analysis of these algorithms is proposed. All simulations were coded and executed in the Python software environment, being performed with an Intel® i7 2.4 GHz of CPU and 16 GB of RAM.

The selected simulation hyperparameters are shown in Table 1, following the methodology introduced in [30].

The resulting metrics for the best simulation of each configuration is represented on Table 2.

Obtained results show an increase in mean distance and minimum distance along a decrease of standard deviation for the MA-GB-Chains. Due to the obstacle density of the proposed scenario, no GA optimization achieved a valid solution, being the minimum distance achieved under the 1.5 m restriction.

On the other hand, the MA configuration, performed better than its predecessor. The introduction of a LS into the GA optimization introduces a more focused intensification into the optimization, resulting in an overall greater performance, especially for adverse scenarios.

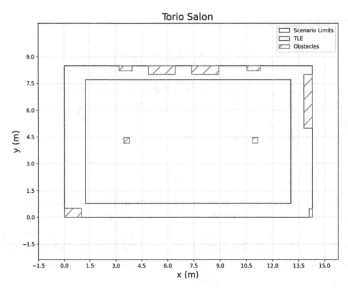

Fig. 3. Representation of the dimensions and shape of the Salon modeled for the TLP. The Table Location Environment (TLE) is a discretized space composed of 263169 points which gives rise to 4.18×10^{59} number of possible solutions for 11 tables.

Table 1. Values of the hyperparameters of the MA-GB-Chains algorithm. The MA and GA parameter adjustment is based on [16, 18, 30].

	Parameter	Value
GA Hyperparameters	Number of individuals	150
	Selection methodology	Tournament 3
	Crossover methodology	Multipoint – 3 Crossover points
	Elitism percentage	15%
	Mutation percentage	10%/10%
	Stop criteria	150 generations or 90% population equal
MA-GB-Chains	C_1	1.0
	C_2	0.5
	C_3	1.5

Furthermore, the introduction of memory chains into the optimization through the MA-GB-Chains achieves an overall better solution than previous methodologies. The resulting efficiency of conserving the performance of each individual in a memory chain along a more complete definition of the most suited individuals for the LS proves essential for achieving the desired solution. Moreover, the MA-GB-Chains is also the only methodology that achieved a valid distribution for the 11 tables distribution, shown in Fig. 4.

Table 2. Comparison of the obtained distribution metrics for the GA, MA and MA-GB-Chains algorithms in the Torio Salon.

Optimization	Mean distance	Standard deviation	Min distance
GA – 10 Tables	2.73 m	1.11 m	0.87 m
MA – 10 Tables	2.80 m	1.08 m	1.66 m
MA-GB-Chains – 10 Tables	2.83 m	0.57 m	1.85 m
MA-GB-Chains – 11 Tables	2.87 m	0.97 m	1.84 m

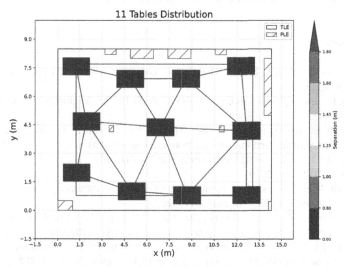

Fig. 4. Obtained table distribution from the MA-GB-Chains for 11 tables. No other analyzed methodology achieved a valid solution for this number of tables.

5   Conclusions

COVID-19 pandemic has supposed a considerable challenge to our society. The reduction of the probability of contagion in normal activities of our daily lives has attracted the research interest to mitigate the effects of this virus preserving the economic activities.

Hostelry is one of the most affected sectors, suffering preventive lockdowns during the last year to reduce the virus spread. Specially, indoor canteens have been systematically controlled due to the easy propagation of the virus in indoor environments. For this reason, technological solutions to guarantee the safe opening of indoor hostelry establishments are being promoted such as wearing facemasks or keeping safety distances among the clients.

This situation has promoted the research conducted in this paper that allows addressing the optimal location of the tables in defined irregular environments for maximizing the distances among the clients. This entails the solution of the Table Location Problem

(TLP) which is considered as NP-Hard suggesting the employment of metaheuristics to attain competitive results.

In this paper, we propose a novel algorithm MA-GB-Chains based on the hybridization of an evolutionary algorithm with a local search procedure using memory chains to enhance the search properties of the algorithm for finding optimal table dispositions. This algorithm has supposed a novelty for the TLP achieving improved results to the previous literature of the TLP, thus fulfilling the main objectives of this paper and solving this problem surged during the current pandemic.

Funding. The research conducted in this paper has been funded by the Spanish Ministry of Science and Innovation grant number PID2019-108277GB-C21.

References

1. Lim, Y., Ng, Y., Tam, J., Liu, D.: Human coronaviruses: a review of virus-host interactions. Diseases. **4**, 26 (2016)
2. Dhama, K., et al.: Coronavirus disease 2019-COVID-19. Clin Microbiol Rev. **33**(4), e00028–e120 (2020)
3. Alanagreh, L., Alzoughool, F., Atoum, M.: The human coronavirus disease covid-19: Its origin, characteristics, and insights into potential drugs and its mechanisms (2020)
4. Guarner, J.: Three Emerging Coronaviruses in Two Decades: The Story of SARS, MERS, and Now COVID-19 (2020)
5. Hellewell, J., et al.: Feasibility of controlling COVID-19 outbreaks by isolation of cases and contacts. Lancet Glob. Heal. **8**, e488–e496 (2020)
6. Hassantabar, S., Zhang, J., Yin, H., Jha, N.K.: Mhdeep: Mental health disorderdetection system based on body-area and deep neural networks. arXiv:2102.10435 (2021)
7. Polianski, I.J.: Airborne infection with Covid-19? A historical look at a current controversy. Microbes Infect. 104851 (2021). https://doi.org/10.1016/j.micinf.2021.104851
8. Noorimotlagh, Z., Jaafarzadeh, N., Martínez, S.S., Mirzaee, S.A.: A systematic review of possible airborne transmission of the COVID-19 virus (SARS-CoV-2) in the indoor air environment. Environ. Res. **193**, 110612 (2021)
9. Eikenberry, S.E., et al.: To mask or not to mask: Modeling the potential for face mask use by the general public to curtail the COVID-19 pandemic. Infect. Dis. Model. **5**, 293–308 (2020)
10. Sun, C., Zhai, Z.: The efficacy of social distance and ventilation effectiveness in preventing COVID-19 transmission. Sustain. Cities Soc. **62**, 102390 (2020)
11. Bhagat, R.K., Davies Wykes, M.S., Dalziel, S.B., Linden, P.F.: Effects of ventilation on the indoor spread of COVID-19. J. Fluid Mech. **903**,(2020). https://doi.org/10.1017/jfm.2020.720
12. Berardi, A., et al.: Hand sanitisers amid CoViD-19: a critical review of alcohol-based products on the market and formulation approaches to respond to increasing demand. Int. J. Pharm. **584**, 119431 (2020). https://doi.org/10.1016/j.ijpharm.2020.119431
13. Lelieveld, J., et al.: Model calculations of aerosol transmission and infection risk of covid-19 in indoor environments. Int. J. Environ. Res. Public Health. **17**, 1–18 (2020)
14. Echeverría-Huarte, I., Garcimartín, A., Hidalgo, R.C., Martín-Gómez, C., Zuriguel, I.: Estimating density limits for walking pedestrians keeping a safe interpersonal distancing. Sci. Rep. **11**, (2021). https://doi.org/10.1038/s41598-020-79454-0
15. Jens, K., Gregg, J.S.: The impact on human behaviour in shared building spaces as a result of COVID-19 restrictions. Build. Res. Inf. 1–15 (2021). https://doi.org/10.1080/09613218.2021.1926217

16. Ferrero-Guillén, R., Díez-González, J., Verde, P., Álvarez, R., Perez, H.: Table organization optimization in schools for preserving the social distance during the covid-19 pandemic. Appl. Sci. **10**, 1–17 (2020)
17. Nguyen, N.T., Liu, B.H.: The mobile sensor deployment problem and the target coverage problem in mobile wireless sensor networks are NP-Hard. IEEE Syst. J. **13**, 1312–1315 (2019)
18. Ferrero-Guillén, R., Díez-González, J., Martínez-Guitiérrez, A., Álvarez, R.: Optimal COVID-19 adapted table disposition in hostelry for guaranteeing the social distance through memetic algorithms. Appl. Sci. **11**, 4957 (2021)
19. Li, Y., Chwee, K.N.G., Murray-Smith, D.J., Gay, G. J., Sharman, K.C.: Genetic algorithm automated approach to the design of sliding mode control systems, Int. J. Control **63**, 4, 721–739 (1996)
20. Díez-González, J., Álvarez, R., González-Bárcena, D., Sánchez-González, L., Castejón-Limas, M., Perez, H.: Genetic algorithm approach to the 3D Node Localization in TDOA systems. Sensors **19**, 3880 (2019)
21. Hassantabar, S., Dai, X., Jha, N.K.: Steerage: Synthesis of neural networks using architecture search and grow-and-prune methods. arXiv:1912.05831. (2019)
22. Ferrero-Guillén, R., Álvarez, R., Díez-González, J., Sánchez-Fernández, Á., Pérez, H.: Genetic algorithm optimization of lift distribution in subsonic low-range designs. In: Herrero, Á., Cambra, C., Urda, D., Sedano, J., Quintián, H., Corchado, E. (eds.) SOCO 2020. AISC, vol. 1268, pp. 520–529. Springer, Cham (2021). https://doi.org/10.1007/978-3-030-57802-2_50
23. Domingo-Perez, F., Lazaro-Galilea, J.L., Bravo, I., Gardel, A., Rodriguez, D.: Optimization of the coverage and accuracy of an indoor positioning system with a variable number of sensors. Sensors **16**(6), 934 (2016)
24. Díez-González, J., Álvarez, R., Perez, H.: Optimized cost-effective node deployments in asynchronous time local positioning systems. IEEE Access **8**, 154671–154682 (2020)
25. Yoon, Y., Kim, Y.-H.: An efficient genetic algorithm for maximum coverage deployment in wireless sensor networks. IEEE Trans. Cybern. **43**(5), 1473–1483 (2013). https://doi.org/10.1109/TCYB.2013.2250955
26. Díez-González, J., Verde, P., Ferrero-Guillén, R., Álvarez, R., Pérez, H.: Hybrid Memetic algorithm for the node location problem in local positioning systems. Sensors **20**, 5475 (2020)
27. Rashtian, H., Gopalakrishnan, S.: Using deep reinforcement learning to improve sensor selection in the internet of things. IEEE Access **8**, 95208–95222 (2020)
28. D. Molina, M. Lozano, F. Herrera.: MA-SW-Chains: memetic algorithm based on local search chains for large scale continuous global optimization. IEEE Congress on Evolutionary Computation, pp. 1–8 (2010)
29. Verde, P., Díez-González, J., Ferrero-Guillén, R., Martínez-Gutiérrez, A., Perez, H.: Memetic chains for improving the local wireless sensor networks localization in urban scenarios. Sensors **21**, 2458 (2021)
30. Ferrero-Guillén, R., Díez-González, J., Álvarez, R., Pérez, H.: Analysis of the Genetic Algorithm Operators for the Node Location Problem in Local Positioning Systems. In: Antonio, E., de la Cal, J., Flecha, R. V., Quintián, H., Corchado, E. (eds.) HAIS 2020. LNCS (LNAI), vol. 12344, pp. 273–283. Springer, Cham (2020). https://doi.org/10.1007/978-3-030-61705-9_23

Protected Discharge Model for Mild to Moderate Covid Patients in a North-East Italian Hospital

Emanuela Zilli[1]([✉]), Antonio Madia[1], Paola Giuriato[1], Davide Bonaldo[1], Sofia Barbar[2], Francesca Cassutti[3], Eleonora Bertoli[3], Guido Di Gregorio[4], Luca Cancian[5], Claudio Bozzoli[6], and Maria Rita Marchi[3]

[1] Hospital Direction, ULSS 6 Euganea, Hospital of Cittadella (Padua), Cittadella, Italy
[2] Department of Medicine, Hospital of Cittadella (Padua), Cittadella, Italy
[3] Division of Pulmonary Medicine, Hospital of Cittadella (Padua), Cittadella, Italy
[4] Department of Anaesthesiology, Hospital of Cittadella (Padua), Cittadella, Italy
[5] Department of Radiology, Hospital of Cittadella (Padua), Cittadella, Italy
[6] Emergency Department, Hospital of Cittadella (Padua), Cittadella, Italy

Abstract. The Covid-19 emergency has determined an unpredictable increase in the number of patients with Covid-like symptoms in the Emergency Department (ED) of Italian hospitals.

A continuity of care pathway between hospital and territorial services that defines the possibility of activating a protected discharge model has been implemented in the ULSS 6 Euganea – Health Trust (District of Padua) for patients with a mild-moderate degree of respiratory insufficiency (phenotyped according to clinical-functional and radiological criteria).

The protected discharge model integrates territorialservices (active surveillance of General Practitioners and Covid Special Units) and hospital services (provided by Pulmonology and Emergency Department) and aims to guarantee a coordinated healthcare pathway for Covid patients (daily interaction, early identification of risk factors and constant monitoring of the respiratory function), in order to efficiently use the human and technological resources available and reduce inappropriate hospitalizations.

The prescription and monitoring of oxygen home therapy (with an oxygen concentrator) is part of the therapeutic process for the home management of this patients.

Between November 2020 and April 2021 at the Hospital of Cittadella (ULSS 6 Euganea) the above mentioned discharge model was activated for 205 patients with a mild-moderate degree of respiratory insufficiency (average age 66.5).

The average duration of hospital telemonitoring was 8.2 days.

Up to April 30, in 86/205 patients (42.0%) no access to the ED nor hospitalization were reported; for 69/205 patients (33.7%) one or more accesses to the ED and no hospitalization were reported; 38/205 patients were later hospitalized (18.5%), 3/205 patients (1.5%) died.

Preliminary analysis of our data suggests that the protected discharge model implemented is proving to be efficient in the management of mild-moderate Covid patients.

Keywords: Protected discharge model · Mild-moderate Covid · Oxygen concentrator

© Springer Nature Switzerland AG 2021
I. Rojas et al. (Eds.): BIOMESIP 2021, LNCS 12940, pp. 484–490, 2021.
https://doi.org/10.1007/978-3-030-88163-4_41

1 Introduction

During Covid-19 emergency, Health Trusts have faced enormous organizational challenges in order to provide an effective, efficient and sustainable management of the pandemic, both for hospital services and territorial services.

Padua (in Veneto Region) represents one of the first areas in Italy where the Coronavirus emergency started on February 21, 2020.

Cittadella Hospital (in the Province of Padua) has 380 beds, including 12 beds of Pulmonary Medicine and 6 beds of Respiratory Semi-Intensive Care Unit, serving a population of approximately 260.000 habitants.

During the Covid-19 emergency Cittadella Hospital assisted both Covid patients and non-Covid patients.

In particular, the Covid-19 emergency has determined an unpredicted increase in the number of patients with Covid and Covid-like symptoms accessing the Emergency Department of Cittadella hospital; this increase has been observed between February 2020 and May 2020 (first wave), between October 2020 and February 2021 (second wave) and between March 2021 and May 2021 (third wave), reaching its peak especially between November 2020 and January 2021.

Covid wards (Medicine, Pulmonary Medicine, Respiratory Semi-Intensive Care Unit, Intensive Care Unit, ext.) were characterized by a massive inflow of patients (more than 700 patients assisted, 650 during second and third wave) with almost 100% occupation rate and the possibility of moving between different settings of intensity of care depending on improvement or worsening of clinical conditions.

In this complicated scenario, the implementation of innovative solutions to minimize the impact of the pandemic and guarantee at the same time the quality of the health services provided and the safety of patients and healthcare workers has been essential [1].

According to clinical, functional and radiological criteria, different phenotypes of Covid disease (related to different levels of risk) were defined, taking into account the presence of comorbidities (ex. adults ≥ 65 years with respiratory diseases, presence of diabetes mellitus, hypertension, obesity, etc.) and the social issues.

An algorithm for risk stratification in the diagnosis of the Covid disease was defined, according to literature [4, 5].

2 Methods

A continuity of care pathway between hospital and territorial services that defines the possibility of activating a protected discharge model has been implemented in the ULSS 6 Euganea – Health Trust (District of Padua).

The model can be applied to patients with a mild-moderate degree of respiratory insufficiency (phenotyped according to clinical-functional and radiologicalcriteria) [2–4].

The protected discharge model integrates territorial services (active surveillance on the part of General Practitioners and Special Covid Units) together with hospital services (provided by the Pulmonary Medicine and Emergency Department) and aims to guarantee a coordinated healthcare pathway for Covid patients (daily interaction, early identification of risk factors and constant monitoring of the respiratory function), in order to make use of the human and technological resources available efficiently and reduce inappropriate hospitalizations.

The prescription and monitoring of oxygen home therapy (with an oxygen concentrator) is part of the therapeutic process for the home management of these patients.

In details, the Emergency Ward delivers an oxygen concentrator (which stores oxygen), to patients with mild or moderate Covid symptoms and a pulse oximeter.

The Emergency Ward then communicates to the Covid Special Unit the name and details of the patient and his or her clinical notes and medical history filling in the details using the shared IT support programme.

The Pulmonary Ward or Acute Respiratory Care Unit (ARCU) of the hospital, by means of a programme of telemedicine, verifies the health condition of the patient twice a day.

If necessary, the ARCU sends the patient to the Special Covid Unit, which includes a nursing unit, in which the "haemogas treatment" will be carried out at the patient's home with a portable appliance.

If necessary the nurse from the Special Covid Unit contacts the patient's General Practitioner to organize home check-ups for the patient.

At the end of the management of the patient, the Pneumologist will prepare a letter via internet to the patient's Doctor with all the information necessary including dates for the following check-ups that will be necessary.

The Special Covid Unit will pick up the Oxygen Concentrator from the patient's home as well as the pulse oximeter and will organize their sanitization.

The Special Covid Unit Manager shall check the stores of oxygen available in theEmergency Ward daily and make sure that they are ready for use after sanitization and technical control.

3 Technology Assessment

The solution adopted for patients undergoing an integrated hospital-territory management program consists in a protected discharge model defining the telemedicine home management of mild-moderate Covid positive patients discharged from the Emergency Department and in remote follow-up.

The telemedicine kit is composed by:

- Telemonitoring and Teleassistance Software Platform: it allows the management of the patient, the management of instrumental examinations, analysis and visualization of monitored data, reporting of examinations, administration and evaluation of questionnaires;
- Medical devices for monitoring health parameters: according to the different needs, the patient at home could acquire and send data (SpO_2: range 35–100%, accuracy ±2% from 75% to 100% or ±3% from 50% to 74%; Cardiac Frequency: range 30–240 bpm, accuracy ±2 bpm or ±2%; systolic pressure: range 30–270 mmHg, accuracy ±3 mmHg; dyastolic pressure: range 20–235 mmHg, accuracy ±3 mmHg; temperature: range 32–43,9 °C, accuracy ±0,2 °C between 36 °C to 39 °C, ±0,3 °C for other values.
- Tablet: HUB system for data acquisition via dedicated App from connected medical devices and sending via integrated SIM card.

From the software point of view, the user interface has been made accessible from a common browser of the latest generation through which, according to specific permissions, users can interact with thesystem.

In particular:

- Data from medical device to platform is encrypted and travels over a private network
- The medical devices are protected from attacks because they are connected to a private network and unreachable in the public internet.
- The data and platform are hosted in tier 4 cloud data centers that offer the highest protection, redundancy and reliability features.
- Data is processed in accordance with ISO27001 quality processes, and our data center infrastructure is also ISO 27001, HIPAA, FedRAMP, SOC 1, and SOC 2 compliant.
- Privacy is extremely important for the telemedicine service offered. Ensuring the security, confidentiality of data and the correct treatment is a top priority. The data are in accordance with the provisions of the GDPR - Regulation (EU) 2016/679 and the Code for the Protection of Personal Data (d.lgs. 196/2003 as amended).

4   Flow-Chart

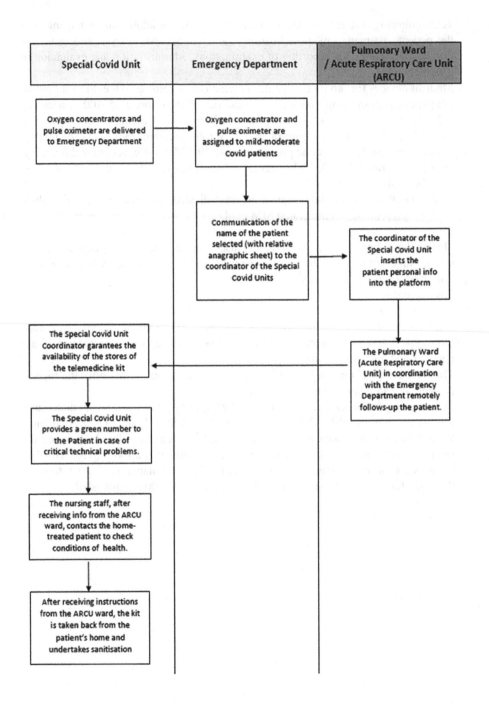

5   Preliminary Results

Between November 2020 and April 2021 at Cittadella Hospital the above descrive protected discharge model was implemented for patients with a mild-moderate degree of respiratory insufficiency (phenotyped according to clinical-functional and radiological criteria).

A total of 205 patients with a mild to moderate degree of respiratory insufficiency (average age 66.5) living in the area of Cittadella (province of Padua, north-east of Italy) were treated according to this model.

The average duration of tele-monitoring performed by the Division of Pulmonary Medicine (in strong and constant collaboration with Emergency Department, General Practitioners and Covid Special Units) was 8.2 days.

Up until 30th April:

- in 86 out of 205 patients (42.0%) no access to the Emergency Department nor hospitalization were reported after the application of the protected discharge model;
- for 69 out of the 205 patients (33.7%) one or more needed access to the Emergency Department and no hospitalization was reported;
- 38 out of the 205 patients were later hospitalized (18.5%),
- 3 out of the 205 patients (1.5%) died.

According to literature [6], the most common cause for return to the Emergency Department (and for some patients the cause of the hospitalization) was respiratory distress.

A complete and extensive analysis of the results of our project will be implemented in the next months, with data regarding the outcome of patients followed by telemedicine.

6   Conclusions

A preliminary analysis of our data suggests that the protected discharge model implemented is proving to be efficient in the management of mild - moderate Covid patients.

The remote management tools adopted, exploiting a synergic and integrated approach between hospital services and territorial services, and the use of up-to-date telemedicine devices has given the possibility to cure at home a significant amount of Covid patients.

The first results collected and analyzed highlight that the safety of patients treated has been guaranteed; at the same time, hospital wards (in particular Medicine, Pulmonary Medicine, Respiratory Semi-Intensive Care Unit) have been able to accept patients with worse clinical conditions.

Innovative solutions to minimize the impact of the pandemic need to be studied, implemented and constantly monitored in order to increase the preparedness of the public health system to provide a sustainable response to new pandemic threats that may arise in the future.

Financial Support and Sponsorship.   Nil.

Conflict of Interest. The authors declare that the research was conducted in the absence of any commercial or financialrelationships that could be construed as a potentialconflict of interest.

References

1. International Labor Organization. In the face of a pandemic: Ensuring Safety and Health at Work. Geneva: ILO 2020. https://www.hsdl.org
2. Mansab, F., Donnelly, H., Kussner, A., Neil, J., Bhatti, S., Goyal, D.K.: Oxygen and mortality in COVID-19 pneumonia: a comparative analysis of supplemental oxygen policies and health outcomes across 26 countries. Front. Public Health **9** (2021). https://doi.org/10.3389/fpubh.2021.580585
3. Nacoti, M.: A community-based approach in response to the COVID-19 humanitariancrisis in Bergamo province. Bergamo, 6 March 2020. https://www.unicef-irc.org
4. Sardesai, I., et al.: Short term home oxygen therapy COVID-19 patients: The COVID-HOT algorithm. J. Family Med. Primary Care **9**(7), 3209 (2020). https://doi.org/10.4103/jfmpc.jfmpc_1044_20
5. Banerjee, J.: With COVID-19 After discharge from acute care setting with supplemental oxygen. JAMA Netw. Open. **4**(4), e213990 (2021). https://doi.org/10.1001/jamanetworkopen.2021.3990
6. Somani, S.S., et al.: Characterization of patients who return to hospital following discharge from hospitalization for COVID-19. J. Gen. Intern. Med. **35**(10), 2838–2844 (2020). https://doi.org/10.1007/s11606-020-06120-6

Exploring the Effects of Loneliness and Internet Addiction on Adults' Well-Being During COVID-19 Quarantine

Loulwah AlSumait[1]([✉]), Hasah AlHeneidi[2], and Andrew P. Smith[3]

[1] Department of Information Science, Kuwait University, 5969 Safat, Kuwait City, Kuwait
Loulwah.alsumait@ku.edu.kw
[2] The Social Development Office, Ministry of Social Affairs and Labor,
13150 Kuwait City, Kuwait
[3] School of Psychology, Cardiff University, Cardiff C10 3AS, UK

Abstract. As the COVID-19 pandemic continues to hit in repeated spreading waves, the population worldwide continues to be under stressful lockdowns and quarantine and getting more dependent on Information and Communication Technology (ICT). Evidence is needed to identify the mental health impact of quarantine on loneliness and Problematic Internet Use (PIU) and find the significant risk factors. This study explores the association of loneliness, internet addiction and related factors such as the number of hours spent online, and the quality of the relationship of people spending the quarantine with on well-being using the Internet addiction scale, UCL loneliness short scale, and WHO-5 measure. The data from a sample of 613 adults from the Middle East were analyzed through SPSS using correlation and regression. The results showed an association between loneliness, internet addiction and low well-being; the number of hours spent online was negatively correlated with well-being, and the quality of the relationship with people spending the quarantine was positively associated with well-being. The results confirm the negative consequences of internet addiction, loneliness and spending long hours online on well-being during quarantine, and the importance of the quality of the relationship with whom one is spending quarantine in supporting well-being.

Keywords: Internet addiction · PIU · COVID-19 · Loneliness · Mental health · Quarantine · Well-being

1 Introduction

The "Severe Acute Respiratory Syndrome Coronavirus" (SARS-COV-2), which causes COVID-19, remains a significant threat to public health and medical service providers. Lockdown measures and quarantine are still being enforced by governments worldwide. Evidence of the psychological harm of lockdown, social isolation, and quarantine on the well-being of people are emerging, allowing policymakers to identify the vulnerable.

Given the buffering role of Information and Communication Technology (ICT) on the effect of social isolation on mental health, and as an immediate mitigation measure,

© Springer Nature Switzerland AG 2021
I. Rojas et al. (Eds.): BIOMESIP 2021, LNCS 12940, pp. 491–501, 2021.
https://doi.org/10.1007/978-3-030-88163-4_42

mental health advisors recommended (increasing) the use of the ICT to reduce anxiety and feelings of social isolation [1, 2]. However, this can lead to excessive internet use, leading to social/occupational dysfunctionalities. Other mental health concerns include the feeling of loneliness and internet addiction, which can include social media addiction, gaming addiction, problematic pornography use, and Problematic Internet Use (PIU).

This paper extends our previous work [3]. The first purpose of the current study was to determine the risk factors for mental disorders during the lockdown periods of COVID-19. The second aim was to identify mental health, loneliness, and PIU levels during the same period. The study provided insight for ICT policymakers to set appropriate policies to mitigate and/or prevent ICT-related mental health disorders.

The current study investigated risk factors for mental health, loneliness, PIU, and their association, utilizing the WHO-5 well-being scale (WHO-5), the Revised UCLA Loneliness Scale (ULS-6), and PIU scores based on the Internet Addiction Test (IAT). The study investigated the association of loneliness, internet addiction and WHO-5 scores under the regulated quarantine during the peak periods of COVID-19. Data were collected from adults from the Middle East region. In addition, analyses were used to study other contributing factors such as the number of hours spent online and the quality of the relationships with those they were spending lockdown with.

The paper is organized as follows. The literature review in Sect. 2 lists recent work on the prevalence and predictors of mental health disorders related to COVID-19 lockdowns and quarantine. The section also includes the available work explicitly focusing on loneliness and/or PIU disorders during the pandemic. The methodology and results are described in Sect. 3. The paper is closed with discussions and conclusions in Sects. 4 and 5.

2 Literature Review

2.1 Mental Health Under COVID-19 Quarantine

Early calls to study and mitigate the effect of the COVID-19 pandemic on mental health were made [1]. Alongside this, a body of research has emerged that has evaluated the well-being of people during COVID-19 and analyzed risk factors. The research [4, 5] has provided evidence from previous pandemics on the psychological impact of quarantine and suggested a set of urgent intervention measures to reduce it. Many studies have reported adverse effects of COVID-19 lockdowns on the mental health of people in China [6–10], Italy [11, 12], the Middle East [13–15], and globally [16–18].

The earliest studies appeared from China, where the first wave of the virus happened. This research [8, 9] analyzed the prevalence and predictors of post-traumatic stress symptoms and other mental health outcomes during the COVID-19 outbreak. They identified the presence of home quarantine as a significant risk factor and other factors such as female gender, health status, and poor sleep quality. Other research [14] showed the differences in the predictors of distress during the COVID-19 pandemic across Iran and China, emphasizing the importance of culture, health system, employment conditions, and other factors that vary between countries. Furthermore, Reagu et al. [15] conducted a similar analysis within Qatar's institutional quarantine and isolation centers, focusing on immigrants rather than native populations. In their study, higher distress and anxiety levels were strongly related to individuals who experienced a lack of contact with family or were poor socio-economic groups. Parcani et al. [11] found that long periods of isolation, limited physical space, and local contagion rates were critical moderating factors between Italians mental health and social isolation. On the other hand, another study [12] found an association between discontinued working activity and the mental health outcomes of the survey, including post-traumatic stress symptoms, depression, and anxiety. Special consideration of children's mental health under COVID-19 quarantine has been the focus of many papers, e.g. [19–22].

2.2 Loneliness and PIU Under COVID-19 Quarantine

The strict lockdown measures being placed worldwide have accompanied an unpresented demand for online connection communication for all aspects of life. It has even been suggested to use ICT and the internet as a buffering tool during lockdowns and quarantine. However, the psychological impact of social isolation and abnormal levels of internet usage on the feelings of loneliness and internet addiction is under-represented. Several studies have recently focused on the effect of isolation and quarantine on internet misuse and the feeling of loneliness in people during the COVID-19 pandemic [3, 23–25]. AlHenaidi et al. [3] showed the association between loneliness and PIU and other factors such as the number of hours spent online and the quality of relationship with the person(s) one is spending lockdown with. Boursier et al. [23] also report that the feelings of loneliness reinforced by the isolation predicted social media addiction and anxiety.

While both studies [24, 25] analyzed the links between isolation, loneliness and the PIU of adolescents, only the results of [24] confirmed the association. On the other hand, Sista et al. [25] found that the prevalence of internet addiction among adolescents was higher than that of adults during COVID-19. However, they discovered that quarantine did not elevate the risk of internet addiction due to other psychological factors such as internalization, externalization, and prosocial effects.

As the pandemic continues to hit in repeated waves, the population worldwide will continue to be under stressful lockdowns and quarantine and will be more dependent on ICT. Evidence is needed to identify the mental health impact of quarantine and the compulsive use of the internet and find significant risk factors. This paper provides new evidence on the prevalence of well-being and its correlation to loneliness and PIU under quarantine measures in the Middle East region.

3 Methodology

The study was conducted online using Qualtrics on a sample of Arab adults; most of the participants were from Kuwait and Saudi Arabia. The questionnaire link was distributed online through social media platforms (WhatsApp and Twitter); the participants volunteered to answer the questionnaires. The study investigated the cross-sectional association of loneliness, internet addiction and well-being during the restricted lockdown related to the COVID-19 pandemic.

3.1 Measures

Internet Addiction Test. The questionnaire was displayed bilingually in both English and Arabic to reach the most significant number of participants. The questionnaire contained the IAT, consisting of 20 items that examined the participant's internet use in the previous month for non-academic and non-job-related use, by evaluating addiction based on DSM-IV pathological gambling criteria [26]. The individual answered the questions using Likert scales ranging from 0 = not applicable to 5 = always. The results identify three categories of internet users based on their online dependency: regulated internet users, problematic internet users, and internet addicts. The scale's Arabic version was adapted from [27]. The IAT items in Arabic are given in Table 4 in the Appendix.

UCLA Loneliness Scale. In this study, the Revised UCLA Loneliness Scale (UCLA-R) was used in its shortened form. The scale assesses loneliness as well as social isolation [28]. It is one of the most extensively used loneliness scales. The original scale included 20 statements, but the abridged variant ULS-6 had six UCLA-R items. Five questions were written negatively, and one in a positive way [29]. The items were answered on a 4-point Likert scale ranging from 1 = never to 4 = often. A high score suggests a greater sense of loneliness. The ULS-6 was translated into Arabic and tested for validity on 19 persons in a pilot study. The Cronbach's alpha reliability of the translated scale was .76. The Arabic translation of ULS-6 is given in Table 5 in the Appendix.

World Health Organization Well-Being Index (WHO-5). In 1982, the WHO European Regional Office developed a 28-item questionnaire to measure positive and negative well-being. Further analysis identified ten items of the 28-item WHO as the key indicators of positive and negative well-being in a single uni-dimensional scale. [30] This has subsequently been shortened to a five-item scale. The WHO Regional Office in Europe initially presented the WHO-5 at a WHO meeting in Stockholm in 1998 as part of the DEPCARE initiative on well-being measures in primary health care [31].

The WHO-5 is a widely used tool in clinical and research studies for assessing subjective well-being. The questionnaire consists of 5 positively phrased items, and the participants consider their feelings in the last five weeks on a Likert scale (0 = never, 5 = always). 'I have felt cheerful and in good spirits, and 'I woke up feeling fresh and rested'. The scale has adequate validity as a screening tool for depression and an outcome measure in clinical studies, and it has been successfully used in various research disciplines. The WHO-5 scale in Arabic is given in Table 6 in the Appendix.

Demographic data were collected on age, gender, nationality, marital status, number of children, number of hours spent online and self-rating the quality of the relationship with the person(s) they were spending the lockdown with.

3.2 Participants

The study involved 618 volunteers from Kuwait (N = 459), Saudi Arabia (N = 99), and other Arab nations (N = 60). 68.9% of the participants were female, and 53% were between 19 and 35 years. 55.2% of the participants were single, 39.6% were married, and 4.9% were divorced.

3.3 Analysis Strategy

The analyses conducted here aimed to use standard univariate and multivariate tests to determine predictors of the WHO score. This approach was intended to identify robust effects which would provide the basis of future more detailed modelling. All statistical analyses were conducted through SPSS 25. Data met the assumption of normality. Pearson univariate correlations were conducted to assess the strength of the associations of UCLA-R loneliness score (dependent variable), internet addiction IAT score (dependent variable), the number of hours spent online (dependent variable), quality of the relationship with whom the participants spending the lockdown with (dependent variable), and the sum score of WHO (dependent variable) using Cohen standards [32]. Following the correlation, regression was conducted to assess the influence of the variables on the sum of the WHO score. This used the ENTER method of regression analysis. Holm-Bonferroni corrections were applied to adjust for multiple comparisons.

3.4 Results

Prevalence of Well-Being. Well-Being scores were classified based on the WHO scale. Scores below 13 were classified as poor well-being and is an indication for testing for depression.

- 10.1% of the participants were in the poor well-being or depressed category.
- 89.9% of the participants reported good or average well-being.

Prevalence of Loneliness. Loneliness scores were divided using the median (*median* = 13). Scores above 13 were classified as high loneliness scores, scores below 13 were classified as low loneliness scores.

Prevalence of Internet Addiction. Internet Addiction scores were classified based on the IAD test classifications [33]; scores 0–49 indicate controlled internet use, scores 50–79 indicate problematic internet use and scores 80–100 indicates internet addiction.

- 89.1% of the participants controlled their internet use.
- 9.9% of the participants were problematic internet users.
- 1% of the participants are internet addicts.

Correlation. Initial analyses examined the correlations between the individual variables. These are shown in Table 1.

The WHO well-being measure was significantly correlated with the IAT score, loneliness and hours on the internet. IAT scores, loneliness and hours on the internet were all positively correlated. Having a good relationship with those in isolation was positively correlated with the WHO score and negatively correlated with IAT, loneliness and hours on the internet.

Table 1. Correlations between the key variables.

	WHO total	IAT	Loneliness	Hours online
WHO total	1.000			
IAT	−.362**	1.000		
Loneliness	−.404**	.417**	1.000	
Hours online	−.266**	.489**	.249**	1.000
Quality of relationship	.346**	−.266**	−.280**	−.166**

** p < 0/001

Regression. The subsequent analysis involved a regression to determine what remained significant when the other variables were included in the model. The model summary of this regression is shown in Table 2.

Table 2. Regression model summary.

R	R square	Adjusted R square	Std. error of the estimate
.508	.258	.254	4.37348

The analysis (see Table 3) showed that all variables remained significant even when they were included in the same analysis. In summary, high IAT scores, high loneliness and a high number of hours spent on the internet were associated with lower WHO well-being scores. In contrast, a good relationship with those sharing isolation was associated with a higher WHO well-being score. A Holm-Bonferroni correction for multiple comparisons showed that all the effects remained significant.

Table 3. Regression examined predictors of the WHO well-being score.

	B	SE	Beta	t	Sig
(Constant)	33.524	2.055		16.310	.000
IAT	−.050	.013	−.152	−3.836	.000
Loneliness	−.370	.052	−.257	−7.157	.000
Hours online	−.228	.091	−.092	−2.505	.012
Quality of relationship	.055	.009	.218	6.458	.000

4 Discussion

Loneliness was found to be associated with a low well-being score. The number of hours spent online was significantly associated with the loneliness score, confirming the hypothesis [34] that internet use may be high due to feelings of loneliness and inadequate social support. However, the findings oppose those of Girdhar et al. [35], who found that greater internet use predicts less loneliness under lockdown due to online social platforms. Loneliness was negatively associated with the quality of the relationship with the people spending quarantine with, the results suggesting that the quality of face-to-face relationships predicts psychological well-being and low loneliness.

Internet addiction was significantly correlated with the quality of the relationship with whom the person is spending lockdown. This finding supports previous studies that internet addicts and problematic internet users have low social skills and social support. However, the preference of problematic internet users to virtual relationships could be related to lack of social skills, self-esteem, and isolation [36, 37]. Internet addiction was negatively associated with well-being, confirming the findings from previous studies on the negative associations and consequences of internet addiction. The results indicate that the quality of the relationship with whom a person spent lockdown predicts internet addiction, supporting the findings [26] that show that internet addicts prefer using the internet rather than spending time with their family members or spouses.

5 Conclusion and Future Work

The present study has provided a firm basis for future analysis of this topic. New research should extend the range of variables present to include established predictors of well-being, including demands, resources and individual differences. Negative outcomes (e.g. perceived stress, anxiety and depression) should also be included. Other methods of analysis will also shed more light on underlying mechanisms. These should examine moderation and mediation, as well as including structural equation modelling. Qualitative information could also provide more detail about the reason why certain factors predict well-being.

Overall, the results reveal that during quarantine, the primary well-being support comes from the quality of the relationship with the people one is spending quarantine. The internet plays a primary buffering role in connecting people, especially under restricted circumstances during the lockdown. However, the overuse of the internet predicts negative well-being. Further studies are needed, preferably with a longitudinal design, to investigate the casualty of internet addiction and loneliness on well-being during the quarantine.

Appendix

Table 4. The IAT items in Arabic.

5 = دائما	4 = غالبا	3 = كثيرا	2 = بين حين وأخر	1 = نادرا	0 = لا ينطبق	العبارة
						1- غالبا ما تقضي وقت في الانترنت أكثر مما نويت؟
						2- كثيرا ما تهمل الاعمال المنزلية لتقضي وقت أكثر على الانترنت
						3- تفضل الاستمتاع بالإنترنت على علاقتك مع شريك حياتك؟
						4- غالبا ما تنشئ علاقات جديدة مع أعضاء من مستخدمي الانترنت
						5- كثيرا ما يشتكي الاخرون من كمية الوقت الذي تقضية على الانترنت؟
						6- يتأثر معدلك الدراسي ودرجاتك بسبب الساعات التي تقضيها على الانترنت.
						7- كثيرا ما تتصفح رسائلك (الايميل، رسائل نصية، الرسائل الفورية) قبل البدء بعمل شيء آخؤ
						8- أحيانا يتأثر ادائك أو انتاجك سلبيا بسبب الانترنت
						9- غالبا ما تصبح متحفظا او دفاعي في حال سألك شخص ماذا تفعل على الانترنت
						10- كثيرا ما تحاول تجاهل الافكار المزعجة والهروب لما يريحك على الانترنت
						11- تجد نفسك تنتظر الفرصة للعودة للإنترنت مرة اخرى؟
						12- غالبا ما تفكر أن الحياة بدون الانترنت ستكون مملة وبدون بهجة؟
						13- أحيانا ترد بعنف أو تصرخ أو تبدو منزعجا عندما يقاطعك أحد خلال استخدامك للإنترنت
						14- غالبا ما تصحو طوال الليل بسبب استخدام الانترنت
						15- غالبا ما تتخيل الرجوع للإنترنت عندما تكون بعيدا عنه ؟
						16- غالبا ما تجد نفسك تردد عبارة "بعد عدة دقائق سأوقف اتصالي بالإنترنت"
						17- كثيرا ما تحاول تقليل الوقت الذي تقضيه على الانترنت وتفشل.
						18- كثيرا ما تحاول اخفاء حقيقة الوقت الذي تمضية على الانترنت.
						19- غالبا ما تفضل امضاء الوقت على الانترنت بدل الخروج والاستمتاع مع الاخرين.
						20- غالبا ما تشعر انك مكتئب، ومتوتر، ومزاجي وانت غير متصل على الانترنت، وتختفي هذه المشاعر فور العودة الى الانترنت

ببساطة اجب عن العبارات التالية عن طريق اختيار الاجابة المقاربة لك. فقط اجب عن الوقت الذي تمضيه على الانترنت لأسباب غير اكاديمية او تتعلق بالعمل

Table 5. ULS-6 short loneliness scale in Arabic.

غالباً	أحياناً	نادراً	أبداً	
				إلى أي مدى تشعر بأنك تفتقد الصحبة؟ .1
				إلى أي مدى تشعر بأنك وحيد ؟ .2
				إلى أي مدى تشعر بأنك عضو في صحبة أو جماعة ؟ .3
				إلى أي مدى تشعر بأنك في عزلة عن الآخرين؟ .4
				إلى أي مدى تشعر بأن الناس من حولك ولكنهم ليسوا معك؟ .5
				إلى أي مدى تشعر بأنك غير سعيد لأنك منعزل عن الاخرين؟ .6

Table 6. The WHO-5 scale in Arabic.

(6) بتاتاً	قليل من (5) الوقت/نادراً-	أقل بقليل (4) من نصف الوقت	أكثر بقليل (3) من نصف الوقت	أكثر(2) الاحيان	(1) دائماً	في الأسبوعين الماضيين
						1- كنت سعيداً وبمزاج جيد
						2- كنت أشعر بالهدوء أو الاسترخاء
						3- كنت أشعر بالحيوية والنشاط
						4- كنت أستيقظ نشطاً ومرتاحاً
						5- كانت أيامي مليئة بأمور محببة إلى قلبي

References

1. Holmes, E.A., et al.: Multidisciplinary research priorities for the COVID-19 pandemic: a call for action for mental health science. Lancet Psychiatry 7(6), 547–560 (2020)
2. Mucci, F., Mucci, N., Diolaiuti, F.: Lockdown and isolation: psychological aspects of COVID-19 pandemic in the general population. Clin. Neuropsychiatry 17(2), 63–64 (2020)
3. Alheneidi, H., AlSumait, L., AlSumait, D., Smith, A.P.: Loneliness and problematic internet use during COVID-19 lock-down. Behav. Sci. 11(1), 5 (2021)
4. Brooks, S.K., et al.: The psychological impact of quarantine and how to reduce it: rapid review of the evidence. Lancet 395, 912–920 (2020)
5. Hossain, M.M., Sultana, A., Purohit, N.: Mental health outcomes of quarantine and isolation for infection prevention: a systematic umbrella review of the global evidence. Epidemiol. Health 42, e2020038 (2020). https://doi.org/10.4178/epih.e2020038
6. Cao, W., et al.: The psychological impact of the COVID-19 epidemic on college students in China. Psychiatry Res. 287, 112934 (2020)
7. Dong, L., Bouey, J.: Public mental health crisis during COVID-19 pandemic. China. Emerging Infect. Dis. 26(7), 1616 (2020)
8. Liu, N., et al.: Prevalence and predictors of PTSS during COVID-19 outbreak in China hardest-hit areas: gender differences matter. Psychiatry Res. 287, 112921 (2020). https://doi.org/10.1016/j.psychres.2020.112921
9. Wang, C., et al.: A longitudinal study on the mental health of general population during the COVID-19 epidemic in China. Brain Behav. Immun. 87, 40–48 (2020)

10. Zhang, S.X., Wang, Y., Rauch, A., Wei, F.: Unprecedented disruption of lives and work: health, distress and life satisfaction of working adults in China one month into the COVID-19 outbreak. Psychiatry Res. **288**, 112958 (2020)

11. Pancani, L., Marinucci, M., Aureli, N., Riva, P.: Forced social isolation and mental health: a study on 1,006 Italians under COVID-19 lockdown. Front. Psychol. **12**, 663799 (2021). https://doi.org/10.3389/fpsyg.2021.663799

12. Rossi, R., et al.: COVID-19 pandemic and lockdown measures impact on mental health among the general population in Italy. Front. Psych. **11**, 790 (2020). https://doi.org/10.3389/fpsyt.2020.00790

13. Fawaz, M., Samaha, A.: COVID-19 quarantine: post-traumatic stress symptomatology among Lebanese citizens. Int. J. Soc. Psychiatry **66**(7), 666–674 (2020)

14. Jahanshahi, A.A., Dinani, M.M., Madavani, A.N., Li, J., Zhang, S.X.: The distress of Iranian adults during the Covid-19 pandemic - more distressed than the Chinese and with different predictors. Brain Behav. Immun. **87**, 124–125 (2020). https://doi.org/10.1016/j.bbi.2020.04.081

15. Reagu, S., et al.: Psychological impact of the COVID-19 pandemic within institutional quarantine and isolation centres and its sociodemographic correlates in Qatar: a cross-sectional study. BMJ Open **11**(1), e045794 (2021)

16. Brodeur, A., Clark, A.E., Fleche, S., Powdthavee, N.: COVID-19, lockdowns and well-being: evidence from Google Trends. J. Public Econ. **193**, 104346 (2021). https://doi.org/10.1016/j.jpubeco.2020.104346

17. Gobbi, S., et al.: Worsening of preexisting psychiatric conditions during the COVID-19 pandemic. Front. Psychiatry **11**, 1407 (2020)

18. Mukhtar, S.: Mental health and psychosocial aspects of coronavirus outbreak in Pakistan: psychological intervention for public mental health crisis. Asian J. Psychiatr. **51**, 102069 (2020). https://doi.org/10.1016/j.ajp.2020.102069

19. Fegert, J.M., Vitiello, B., Plener, P.L., Clemens, V.: Challenges and burden of the Coronavirus 2019 (COVID-19) pandemic for child and adolescent mental health: a narrative review to highlight clinical and research needs in the acute phase and the long return to normality. Child Adolesc. Psychiatry Ment. Health **14**, 1–11 (2020)

20. Liu, J.J., Bao, Y., Huang, X., Shi, J., Lu, L.: Mental health considerations for children quarantined because of COVID-19. Lancet Child Adolesc. Health **4**(5), 347–349 (2020)

21. Saurabh, K., Ranjan, S.: Compliance and psychological impact of quarantine in children and adolescents due to COVID-19 pandemic. Indian J. Pediatr. **87**, 532–536 (2020)

22. Thakur, K., Kumar, N., Sharma, N.: Effect of the pandemic and lockdown on mental health of children. Indian J. Pediatr. **87**(7), 552 (2020). https://doi.org/10.1007/s12098-020-03308-w

23. Boursier, V., Gioia, F., Musetti, A., Schimmenti, A.: Facing loneliness and anxiety during the COVID-19 isolation: the role of excessive social media use in a sample of Italian adults. Front. Psychiatry **11**, 586222 (2020). https://doi.org/10.3389/fpsyt.2020.586222

24. Li, J., Zhan, D., Zhou, Y., Gao, X.: Loneliness and problematic mobile phone use among adolescents during the COVID-19 pandemic: the roles of escape motivation and self-control. Addict. Behav. **118**, 106857 (2021)

25. Siste, K., et al.: Implications of COVID-19 and lockdown on internet addiction among adolescents: data from a developing country. Front. Psychiatry **12**, 665675 (2021). https://doi.org/10.3389/fpsyt.2021.665675

26. Young, K.S.: Internet addiction: the emergence of a new clinical disorder. Cyberpsychol. Behav. **1**, 237–244 (1998)

27. Alheneidi, H.: The influence of information overload and problematic Internet use on adults well-being. Ph.D. thesis, Cardiff University, United Kingdom (2019)

28. Russell, D., Peplau, L.A., Ferguson, M.L.: Developing a measure of loneliness. J. Pers. Assess. **42**, 290–294 (1978)

29. Neto, F.: Loneliness among Portuguese adolescents. Soc. Behav. Personal. Int. J. **20**, 15–21 (1992)
30. Bech, P., Gudex, C., Johansen, S.: The WHO (Ten) well-being index: validation in diabetes. Psychother. Psychosom. **65**(4), 183–190 (1996)
31. Staehr, J.K.: The use of well-being measures in primary health care – the DepCare project; in World Health Organization, Regional Office for Europe: Well-Being Measures in Primary Health Care – the DepCare Project. World Health Organization, Geneva. Target, vol. 12, p. E60246 (1998)
32. Cohen, J.: Statistical Power Analysis for the Behavior Sciences, 2nd edn. West Publishing Company, St. Paul (1988)
33. Young, K.: Internet Addiction Test (IAT). http://netaddiction.com/internet-addiction-test/. Accessed 1 Apr 2020
34. Caplan, S.E.: Problematic internet use and psychosocial well-being: development of a theory-based cognitive–behavioral measurement instrument. Comput. Hum. Behav. **18**, 553–575 (2002)
35. Girdhar, R., Srivastava, V., Sethi, S.: Managing mental health issues among elderly during COVID-19 pandemic. J. Geriatr. Care Res. **7**, 32–35 (2020)
36. Davis, R.: A cognitive-behavioral model of pathological Internet use. Comput. Hum. Behav. **17**(2), 187–195 (2001). https://doi.org/10.1016/s0747-5632(00)00041-8
37. Davis, R.: Psychological implications of technology in the workplace. Cyberpsychol. Behav. **5**(4), 277–278 (2002). https://doi.org/10.1089/109493102760275545

Short Papers

Short Papers

Application of Neurometrics to the Assessment of Attention Regulation Skills for Peak Performance in Sports: A Multi-method Neuroassessment Protocol

Davide Crivelli[1,2](✉) ⓘ and Michela Balconi[1,2] ⓘ

[1] International Research Center for Cognitive Applied Neuroscience (IrcCAN),
Catholic University of the Sacred Heart, Milan, Italy
davide.crivelli@unicatt.it
[2] Research Unit in Affective and Social Neuroscience, Department of
Psychology, Catholic University of the Sacred Heart, Milan, Italy

Abstract. When focusing on peak performance and highly specialized activities, such as in sport practice, the accurate assessment of physiological events that mark cognitive-motor learning, attention focusing, and re-enacting of athletic gestures, as well as their behavioral and psychological correlates provides new opportunities to profile athletes on their primary attention regulation and control skills and to identify factors promoting optimal performance. Wearable and lab-based neuroscientific devices (e.g. EEG, autonomic indices) may help in shedding light on peculiar aspects of sport activity and its neurofunctional characteristics. In order to try and overcome potential methodological biases induced by grounding such assessment only on psychometric testing, we propose and discuss a novel multi-method neuroassessment protocol where self-report evaluation of the ability to regulate attention in sport/competitive contexts (self-awareness level), neuropsychological testing of the efficiency of attention regulation (behavioral performance level), as well as autonomic (EDA, HR, HRV) and electrophysiological (EEG, ERPs) markers of neurocognitive efficiency contribute to outline the attentional profile of the athlete. Preliminary validation data highlighted internally consistent profiles across the multi-dimensional metrics of attention regulation and executive control performance, hinting at the potential of the protocol for in-depth assessment of athletes main characteristics.

Keywords: Neuroassessment · Attention styles · Sport · EEG · Peak performance

1 Sport Neuroscience and Neuroscientific Devices for Athletes' Assessment

Our brains show, together with our bodies, the remarkable ability to learn and capitalize from experience to reach mastery and excellence in specialized skills. That is particularly important when focusing on peak performance and highly specialized activities,

© Springer Nature Switzerland AG 2021
I. Rojas et al. (Eds.): BIOMESIP 2021, LNCS 12940, pp. 505–507, 2021.
https://doi.org/10.1007/978-3-030-88163-4

such as in sport practice. By accurately measuring the cascade of physiological events that mark cognitive-motor learning, attention focusing, and re-enacting of athletic gestures and by linking them to behavior and psychological processes it is possible to open a window on how our brain functions during different tasks and contexts so to identify factors promoting optimal performance.

Specifically, as underlined by Nakata and colleagues [1], to perform skilled movements in sport real-life situations, an athlete needs to be able to flexibly and efficiently adapt movements constituting the athletic gesture based on the perception of environmental information, discrimination of relevant stimuli, rapid decision-making processes, integration of afferent signals, and anticipatory action preparation. Set-shifting, behavioral inhibition, focusing and attention regulation mechanisms are all the same crucial to maintain high-performance levels.

Basic neuroscience research, therefore, focused on understanding how our brain support us during sport and exercise activity and also when, where and to what extent an athlete brain is different from the one of a common person. Yet, integrating psychometric, behavioral, and observational assessment tools with neuroscientific devices able to capture covert biomarkers of the efficiency of processes supporting executive control and attention regulation also represents a valuable advantage in the quest for novel, objective, and actually predictive tools for assessment of performance in sport contexts, as is beginning to happen even in other applied contexts [2]. By helping us in getting a better look on sensory, motor, and cognitive processes contributing to the preparation, execution and imagination of complex behaviors, as well as to the orientation of attention resources on the athletic gesture and on competition, both wearable and lab-based neuroscientific devices (among which, in particular, electroencephalography - EEG, autonomic indices, and – more recently – functional Near Infrared Spectroscopy - fNIRS) also help in shedding light on peculiar aspects of sport activity and its neurofunctional characteristics [3, 4].

2 Assessment of Attention Traits in Sports: A Neurometric Approach

The ability to focus attention only to stimuli that are relevant to current goals while minimizing the processing of interfering or irrelevant information notwithstanding their perceptual or affective salience is considered a key aspect of optimal performance and a valuable trans-disciplinary trait in athletes. Yet, notwithstanding the established relevance of those abilities, profiling athletes on their primary attention regulation and control skills is still commonly based on psychometric testing based on the traditional theory of attentional styles by Nideffer [5]. In order to try and overcome potential methodological biases induced by grounding the assessment only on psychometric testing (e.g. desirability biases, limited self-awareness and self-reflection abilities), we propose and discuss a multi-method neuroassessment protocol where psychometric, neuropsychological, neural, and psychophysiological measures contribute to outline the attentional profile of the examinee.

The protocol, in particular, integrates: self-report evaluation of the ability to regulate attention in sport/competitive contexts (self-awareness level), computerized and neuropsychological testing of the efficiency of attention regulation (behavioral performance level), as well as autonomic (EDA, HR, HRV) and electrophysiological (EEG, ERPs) markers of neurocognitive efficiency during challenging ecological tasks implementing salient stimuli evoking sport-specific contexts (psychophysiological and neurofunctional level).

Preliminary validation data highlighted internally consistent profiles across the multi-dimensional metrics of attention regulation and executive control performance, hinting at the potential of the protocol for in-depth assessment of athletes main characteristics.

References

1. Nakata, H., Yoshie, M., Miura, A., Kudo, K.: Characteristics of the athletes' brain: evidence from neurophysiology and neuroimaging. Brain Res. Rev. **62**, 197–211 (2010). https://doi.org/10.1016/j.brainresrev.2009.11.006
2. Balconi, M., Angioletti, L., Crivelli, D.: Neuro-empowerment of executive functions in the workplace: the reason why. Front. Psychol. **11**, 1519 (2020). https://doi.org/10.3389/fpsyg.2020.01519
3. Balconi, M., Crivelli, D.: Fundamentals of electroencephalography and optical imaging for sport and exercise science. From the laboratory to on-the-playing-field acquired evidence. In: Carlstedt, R.A., Balconi, M. (eds.) Handbook of Sport Neuroscience and Psychophysiology, pp. 40–69. Routledge, New York (2019)
4. Crivelli, D., Balconi, M.: Event-Related Electromagnetic Responses (2017). https://doi.org/10.1016/B978-0-12-809324-5.03053-4.
5. Nideffer, R.M.: Test of attentional and interpersonal style J. Pers. Soc. Psychol. **34**, 394–404 (1976). https://doi.org/10.1037/0022-3514.34.3.394

Electrophysiological Markers of Excessive Internet Use: Evidence from an ERP Study

Laura Angioletti[1,2(✉)] and Michela Balconi[1,2]

[1] International Research Center for Cognitive Applied Neuroscience, Faculty of Psychology, Catholic University of the Sacred Heart, Largo Gemelli, 1, 20123 Milan, Italy
laura.angioletti1@unicatt.it
[2] Research Unit in Affective and Social Neuroscience, Department of Psychology, Catholic University of the Sacred Heart, Largo Gemelli, 1, 20123 Milan, Italy

Abstract. This research investigated electrophysiological correlates of early selective attention, reward process, and vulnerability to excessive internet use in a non-clinical population. The degree of internet use, evaluated through Internet Addiction Test (IAT), was assessed in 24 young healthy adults. Event Related-Potential (ERPs) components were monitored during a Go/NoGo Task performance with different addiction-related background pictures (videogames, online gambling, and neutral stimuli). Results indicated that IAT scores were positively correlated with trait anxiety, depression levels, Go N1 amplitude in Pz, and Go P2 amplitude in Cz for videogames stimuli, and Go N2pc in Pz for gambling stimuli. In contrast, a negative correlation was found between IAT and No-Go P2 amplitude in Cz for videogames stimuli. Findings suggested an early attentional facilitation effect for specific addiction-related stimuli, online gambling-related and videogames stimuli, suggesting a selective attention bias for salient stimuli in individuals with high IAT scores. In line with this evidence, to identify neurophysiological markers linked to excessive internet use can help researchers to deepen the pathophysiology of Internet Gaming Disorder and its potential development.

Keywords: Excessive internet use · ERP · Go/No-Go task

1 Introduction

Excessive use of internet applications, particularly online gaming, has become even more important in the wake of the current Covid-19 epidemic, since social isolation has raised the risk of behavioral addiction [1, 2]. Thus, identifying the neurophysiological markers associated to excessive internet usage and Internet Gaming Disorder might aid researchers in better understanding the disease's pathophysiology and possible progression. To the best of our knowledge, no prior research has explored the link between Internet Addiction Test [3] scores, and N1, N2, P2 Event Related Potentials (ERPs) components, which are utilized as markers of selective attention and reward sensitivity toward rewarding stimuli, and behavioral addiction vulnerability.

© Springer Nature Switzerland AG 2021
I. Rojas et al. (Eds.): BIOMESIP 2021, LNCS 12940, pp. 508–510, 2021.
https://doi.org/10.1007/978-3-030-88163-4

2   Method and Materials

2.1   Sample

24 healthy volunteers (M (Mean) = 24.54, SD (Standard Deviation) = 0.80; age between 20 and 26 years old; 13 females), university students, right-handed, with a normal or corrected-to-normal vision. The Internet Addiction Test (IAT (Young, 1998) was used to assess the presence and severity of internet use.

2.2   Experimental Procedure

During electroencephalographic (EEG) recording, participants were instructed to perform the Go/No-Go task for internet addiction, composed of 4 sessions and a black screen appeared at the beginning of each session with instructions indicating which letter (M or W) represented the Go signal (press the button) and which letter was the No-Go signal (do not press the button). The Go/No-Go trials were superimposed to three different categories of backgrounds: online-gambling-related stimuli, videogames stimuli and neutral (see Balconi and Finocchiaro [4] for the full task description).

2.3   EEG Acquisition and Analysis

EEG activity [SynAmps system (DC amplifier) and Scan4.2 acquisition software (Compumedics Neuroscan Inc., Charlotte, NC)] was collected from the following positions: F3, Fz, F4, C3, Cz, C4, P3, Pz, P4, T7, T8, O1, Oz, and O2, referenced to the earlobes and placed according to the 10–20 International system [5]. A sampling rate of 500 Hz was used; the input filter was set as a 0.01–50 Hz bandpass with a 50 Hz notch filter. Blinks were monitored with two EOG electrodes on the outer canthi and data segments containing artifacts were deleted to maximize accuracy. We have then computed averaged waveforms for each experimental condition.

In relation to the appearance of the letter on the PC display (corresponding to Go/No-Go trials), the peak amplitude was quantified relative to the 100 ms pre-stimulus baseline and N1, N2 and P2 deflection were identified, specific peak profiles were computed for the Go/No-Go condition and each category of the stimuli. Separate analyses were applied to each of the average profiles for the EEG electrodes. The time range for the three components were: 100 ms to 180 ms for the N1 deflection, 210 ms for the N2, and 150 to 250 ms for the P2 component.

3   Results: Correlational Analysis Between IAT and ERP

A set of Pearson's correlation analyses was applied to IAT scores and ERP (N1, N2, and P2) measures collected during the Go/No-Go task. A significant positive correlation was found between IAT levels and N1 amplitude in Pz for Go trials in response to videogames stimuli ($r = 499$; $p \leq .01$), between IAT scores and N2 amplitude in Pz for Go trials in response to gambling stimuli ($r = .567$; $p \leq .001$) Moreover, a significant positive correlation was found between IAT levels and P2 amplitude in Cz for

Go trials in response to videogames stimuli ($r = 543$; $p \leq .01$) Finally, a significant negative correlation was found between IAT levels and P2 amplitude in Cz for NoGo trials in response to videogames stimuli ($r = -589$; $p \leq .01$). No other significant effects were found (all $p > .05$).

4 Discussion

In conclusion, even healthy participants with high IAT scores could display an early selective attention bias and reward sensitivity for addiction-related stimuli, particularly for videogames and online gambling stimuli, implying a possible perceptual and cognitive facilitation effect for salient stimuli in this population. Indeed, high IAT values appear to be linked to the requirement for more top-down inhibitory control for video games and online-gambling stimuli during the early cognitive processes anticipating behavioral inhibition, as suggested by the increase in electrophysiological markers supporting these processes. Nevertheless, more research is still needed to determine the potential impairment of inhibitory control mechanisms and the precursors of IGD in this healthy population.

Moreover, to better outline the neurophysiological profile of the vulnerability to IGD, future research should also focus on the hemodynamic and peripheral correlates of excessive internet use or IGD in order to better understand neurocognitive markers and affective reactions to rewarding stimuli and planning targeted and personalized preventive or clinical interventions for these populations.

References

1. Paschke, K., Austermann, M.I., Kathrin Simon-Kutscher, R.T.: Adolescent gaming and social media usage before and during the COVID-19 pandemic. Sucht **67**(1), 13–22 (2021)
2. Sun, Y., Li, Y., Bao, Y., et al.: Brief report: increased addictive internet and substance use behavior during the COVID-19 pandemic in China. Am. J. Addict. **29**(4) 268–270 (2020)
3. Young, K.S.: Internet addiction: the emergence of a new clinical disorder. CyberPsychol. Behav. **1**(3), 237–244 (1998)
4. Balconi, M., Finocchiaro, R.: Deficit in rewarding mechanisms and prefrontal left/right cortical effect in vulnerability for internet addiction. Acta Neuropsychiatr. **28**(5), 272–285 (2016)
5. Jasper, H.H.: The ten-twenty electrode system of international federation EEG. Electroencephalogr. Clin. Neurophysiol. **10**, 371–375 (1958)

A Computational Pipeline to Identify Potential SARS-CoV-2 Vaccine Targets

Giulia Russo[1]([⊠]), Valentina Di Salvatore[1], Giuseppe Sgroi[2],
Giuseppe Alessandro Para-siliti Palumbo[2],
and Francesco Pappalardo[1]([⊠])

[1] Department of Drug and Health Sciences, University of Catania, Catania, Italy
{giulia.russo, valentina.disalvatore,
francesco.pappalardo}@unict.it
[2] Department of Mathematics and Computer Science, University of Catania,
Catania, Italy
giuseppe.sgroi@unict.it,
giuseppe.parasilitipalumbo@phd.unict.it

Keywords: COVID-19 · SARS-CoV-2 · In silico trials · Vaccine

1 Extended Abstract

COVID-19 devastating pandemic is still ongoing since the end of 2019, when it made its first appearance in China before spreading worldwide within months. Due to its high rate of transmission between humans and the fact that it was relatively un-known, SARS-CoV-2 caused more than 83 million known cases of coronavirus dis-ease and more than 2.5 million victims in just over a year and a half from the first known infections. After the initial phase of bewilderment, in which medical doctors and researchers groped literally in the dark, trying the most disparate strategies to stem infections and prevent the number of deaths grew disproportionately, from laboratories all around the world several different vaccines, developed incredibly quickly and with different technologies, have started to come out.

Today about 90 vaccines are being currently testing in clinical trials on humans, and 27 of them have reached the final stages of testing [1].

But the scenario has further complicated due to the insurgence of a large number of variants that have continued to claim victims despite massive vaccination campaigns launched around the world.

In response to this new wave of outbreaks caused by variants, many alternatives have been proposed in an attempt to bring the situation under control: one of these is the study of potential cross-reactive immunity obtained from common pediatric vaccinations or other types of pre-existing vaccines as general protection from COVID-19 infections. Cross-reactivity is a widely documented phenomenon of the immune system whose importance is still under investigation, and it is strictly related to the concept of immunological memory [2].

In light of this important phenomenon, and of the impact it could have in facilitating the resolution of this and any other future pandemics, we present a complete

I. Rojas et al. (Eds.): BIOMESIP 2021, LNCS 12940, pp. 511–512, 2021.
https://doi.org/10.1007/978-3-030-88163-4

multi-step and multi-scale bioinformatic procedure for the analysis of cross-reactivity induced by pre-existing vaccination and the resulting potential immunity to infection from SARS-Cov-2.

The complete workflow consists of 4 distinct steps:

1. In the first pre-processing phase, a search for similarity between the amino acidic sequences generated by the genome of SARS-COV-2 and the antigens of our interest was performed, through a series of queries on BLASTp database (https://blast.ncbi.nlm.nih.gov/Blast.cgi). Only matching sequences showing a significant identity level with SARS-CoV-2 peptides were selected in this phase.
2. In the second phase, T cell reactivity of hit sequences identified through BLASTP queries was tested, by predicting their binding to class I and II human leukocyte antigen (HLA I and HLA II) molecules. Peptide binding was predicted to the most well-known alleles using IEDB MHC I binding tool (http://tools.iedb.org/mhci/) with default recommended method through the RESTful interface. To assert that the binding had happened a percentile rank of 2% cut-off was used. Regarding HLA II, peptide binding was estimated using the IEDB MHC II binding tool (http://tools.iedb.org/mhcii/) with default recommended method through the RESTful interface. To assert that the binding had happened a percentile rank of 10% cut-off was used.
3. In the third phase, we tested B cell reactivity by using BediPred software at the IEDB Analysis Resource (http://http://tools.iedb.org/bcell/). BediPred calculates an antigenicity value for each residue and then, a global value of antigenicity for the entire peptide, B, is calculated. Peptides showing $B \geq 0.4$ were considered as antigenic.
4. To evaluate the immune system response at cellular and organ levels, we run Universal Immune System Simulator (UISS) [3–5] by using the scores obtained from previous steps as input.

This procedure, aimed at investigating cross reactive immunity induced by existing vaccinations, not only could make easier and faster the vaccine development process, but it could also be useful from the perspective of drug repurposing strategies.

References

1. Forni, G., Mantovani, A.: COVID-19 vaccines: where we stand and challenges ahead. Cell Death Differ. **28**, 626–639 (2021). https://doi.org/10.1038/s41418-020-00720-9
2. Petrova, G., Ferrante, A., Gorski, J.: Cross-reactivity of T cells and its role in the immune system. Crit. Rev. Immunol. **32**, 349–372 (2012). https://doi.org/10.1615/CritRevImmunol.v32.i4.50
3. Russo, G., et al.: In silico trial to test COVID-19 candidate vaccines: a case study with UISS platform. BMC Bioinform. **21**, 527 (2020). https://doi.org/10.1186/s12859-020-03872-0
4. Viceconti, M., Juarez, M.A., Curreli, C., Pennisi, M., Russo, G., Pappalardo, F.: Credibility of in silico trial technologies—a theoretical framing. IEEE J. Biomed. Heal. Inform. **24**, 4–13 (2020). https://doi.org/10.1109/JBHI.2019.2949888
5. Pappalardo, F., et al.: A computational model to predict the immune system activation by citrus-derived vaccine adjuvants. Bioinformatics **32**, 2672–2680 (2016). https://doi.org/10.1093/bioinformatics/btw293

Neuroscientific Hyperscanning and Digital-Caregiving System for Monitoring and Prevention of Relational Deprivation in Dyad Frail People-Caregiver

Davide Crivelli[1,2(✉)] ⓘ and Michela Balconi[1,2] ⓘ

[1] International Research Center for Cognitive Applied Neuroscience (IrcCAN), Catholic University of the Sacred Heart, Milan, Italy
davide.crivelli@unicatt.it
[2] Research Unit in Affective and Social Neuroscience, Department of Psychology, Catholic University of the Sacred Heart, Milan, Italy

Abstract. Frailty is characterized by the progressive increase of vulnerability to adverse clinical events. It is to date recognized that such vulnerability can be exacerbated by acquired conditions of personal and social disadvantage, as dramatically highlighted by the impact of COVID-19 pandemic on frail people and their caregivers. Positive caregiving relations and adaptive social networks may mitigate those adverse effects by limiting relational deprivation and reducing the risk of social disadvantage. In this scenario, being able to remotely assess, to monitor and to foster the integrity of communication and interpersonal skills, as well as the quality of social relations between frail people and caregivers (both formal and informal ones), via efficient and objective tools represent a current challenge for psychosocial assistance and healthcare. The opportunities provided by recent developments in wearable neurotechnologies, automated biosignal processing, and digital tools for neurocognitive assessment and empowerment allow for devising accessible system for digital-caregiving, understood as solutions for remote evaluation and improvement of emotional regulation, inter-personal syntonization skills, and social resilience of frail people and caregivers. Though it has to be acknowledged that computational, miniaturization, and user optimization issues may represent a challenge for developing similar embedded systems, available technology and theoretical/methodological knowledge already provides a flourishing background for further developments. Novel solutions for digital caregiving based on embedded hyperscanning systems could provide valuable support to formal and informal caregivers in monitoring their relations with frail people and, in turn, improve frail people's quality of life by fostering positive and efficient interpersonal dynamics.

Keywords: Frailty · Caregiver · Social deprivation · Remote monitoring · Wearable neurotechnologies · Hyperscanning · Digital caregiving

© Springer Nature Switzerland AG 2021
I. Rojas et al. (Eds.): BIOMESIP 2021, LNCS 12940, pp. 513–515, 2021.
https://doi.org/10.1007/978-3-030-88163-4

1 Frailty and Relational Deprivation: The Challenge of Remote Assessment and Monitoring

The condition of frailty is typically defined in healthcare as a multifaceted syndrome, determined by a reduction in the physiological functional reserve and of the ability to cope with environmental stressors, and characterized by a progressive increase of vulnerability to adverse clinical events and of the risk of functional decline, hospitalization and mortality [1, 2]. Many factors can exacerbate pre-existing conditions of frailty, including individual and social factors. The COVID-19 pandemic has shown how frail people have suffered more than the general population, with significant consequences in the medium to long term.

Caregivers and adaptive social networks may mitigate those adverse effects by limiting relational deprivation and reducing the risk of social disadvantage. The distress deriving from social impairments, indeed, represents a primary risk factor for both frail people and their caregivers, affecting their quality of life, autonomy, and subjective/social wellbeing. In this scenario, being able to remotely assess, to monitor, and to foster the integrity of communication and interpersonal skills, as well as the quality of social relations between frail people and caregivers (both formal and informal ones), via efficient and objective tools represent a current challenge for psychosocial assistance and healthcare.

2 Evaluating the Quality of Relations in the Patient-Caregiver Dyad: The Hyperscanning Paradigm

The opportunities provided by recent developments in wearable neurotechnologies, automated biosignal processing, and digital tools for neurocognitive assessment and empowerment [3–5] allow for devising accessible solutions for remote evaluation and improvement of emotional regulation, inter-personal syntonization skills, and social resilience of frail people and caregivers across the life-span – namely, systems for digital-caregiving. In particular, an approach known as hyperscanning allows real-time monitoring of physiological and behavioral correlates of social dynamics involving two or more inter-agents [6]. Those parameters are known to be a specific and unique marker of mental and relational integrity, signaling possible cognitive impairment or emotional disease during the inter-personal interactions. The dense set of data produced via hyperscanning recordings can then be integrated and analyzed to qualify and quantify the degree of inter-brain coupling as objective marker of the efficiency of inter-personal syntonization.

Building on the well-established literature on the value and potential of the hyperscanning approach for the investigation of complex social dynamics [7, 8], it seems now possible to bring those empirical evidence and expertise to the real world, thus promoting technology transfer projects. By integrating efficient machine learning algorithms devised to process biosignals and compute inter-brain coupling metrics, wearable brain-sensing devices as data collection units, and non-invasive biometric sensors, embedded system for hyperscanning might be able to collect, integrate, and analyze physiological responses of two inter-agents during real-life social exchanges even in ecological contexts, as well as to provide a feedback on the development of social dynamics and on the quality of their relation for neuroscientific assessment/empowerment purposes.

Though it has to be acknowledged that computational, miniaturization, and user optimization issues may represent a challenge for developing a similar embedded system, available technology and theoretical/methodological knowledge already provides a flourishing background for further developments [5]. Novel solutions for digital caregiving based on embedded hyperscanning systems could provide valuable support to formal and informal caregivers in monitoring their relations with frail people and, in turn, improve frail people's quality of life by fostering positive and efficient interpersonal dynamics.

References

1. Fried, L.P., et al.: Frailty in older adults: evidence for a phenotype. J. Gerontol. Ser. A Biol. Sci. Med. Sci. **56**, M146–M157 (2001). https://doi.org/10.1093/gerona/56.3.M146.
2. Lang, P.-O., Michel, J.-P., Zekry, D.: Frailty syndrome: a transitional state in a dynamic process. Gerontology **55**, 539–549 (2009). https://doi.org/10.1159/000211949
3. Balconi, M., Fronda, G., Venturella, I., Crivelli, D.: Conscious, pre-conscious and unconscious mechanisms in emotional behaviour. Some applications to the mindfulness approach with wearable devices. Appl. Sci. **7**, 1280 (2017). https://doi.org/10.3390/app7121280.
4. Balconi, M., Crivelli, D.: Wearable devices for self-enhancement and improvement of plasticity: effects on neurocognitive efficiency. In: Esposito, A., Faundez-Zanuy, M., Morabito, F.C., Pasero, E. (eds.) WIRN 2017 2017. SIST, vol. 103, pp. 11–22. Springer, Cham (2019). https://doi.org/10.1007/978-3-319-95095-2_2
5. Schmidt, P., Reiss, A., Dürichen, R., Laerhoven, K.V.: Wearable-based affect recognition—a review. Sensors. **19**, 4079 (2019). https://doi.org/10.3390/s19194079
6. Crivelli, D., Balconi, M.: Near-infrared spectroscopy applied to complex systems and human hyperscanning networking. Appl. Sci. **7**, 922 (2017). https://doi.org/10.3390/app7090922
7. Babiloni, F., Astolfi, L.: Social neuroscience and hyperscanning techniques: past, present and future. Neurosci. Biobehav. Rev. **44**, 76–93 (2014). https://doi.org/10.1016/j.neubiorev.2012.07.006
8. Balconi, M., Vanutelli, M.E.: Cooperation and competition with hyperscanning methods: review and future application to emotion domain. Front. Comput. Neurosci. **11**, 86 (2017). https://doi.org/10.3389/fncom.2017.00086

Author Index

Printed in the United States
by Baker & Taylor Publisher Services